Counseling the
Culturally Diverse

Theory and Practice

Fifth Edition

Derald Wing Sue
David Sue

WILEY

JOHN WILEY & SONS, INC.

This publication is designed to provide accurate and authoritative information in regard to the
subject matter covered. It is sold with the understanding that the publisher is not engaged in
rendering professional services. If legal, accounting, medical, psychological or any other expert
assistance is required, the services of a competent professional person should be sought.

Designations used by companies to distinguish their products are often claimed as trademarks.
In all instances where John Wiley & Sons, Inc. is aware of a claim, the product names appear in
initial capital or all capital letters. Readers, however, should contact the appropriate companies
for more complete information regarding trademarks and registration.

For general information on our other products and services please contact our Customer Care
Department within the United States at (800) 762-2974, outside the United States at
(317) 572-3993 or fax (317) 572-4002.

Wiley also publishes its books in a variety of electronic formats. Some content that appears in
print may not be available in electronic books. For more information about Wiley products,
visit our Web site at www.wiley.com.

Library of Congress Cataloging-in-Publication Data

Sue, Derald Wing.
    Counseling the culturally diverse : theory and practice / Derald Wing Sue, David Sue. —
5th ed.
        p. cm.
    Includes index.
    ISBN 978-0-470-08632-2 (cloth)
    1. Cross-cultural counseling. I. Sue, David. II. Title.
BF637.C6S85 2007
158'.3—dc22

                                                                        2007002547

Printed in the United States of America.

10 9 8 7 6

Chapter 4

Chapter 5

Part III

Chapter 6

Chapter 7 _____

Culturally Appropriate Intervention Strategies   157

Chapter 8 _____

Multicultural Family Counseling and Therapy   183

Chapter 9 _____

**Non-Western Indigenous Methods of Healing:
Implications for Counseling and Therapy   209**

Part IV

**Racial/Cultural Identity Development in Multicultural
Counseling and Therapy   231**

Chapter 10 _____

**Racial/Cultural Identity Development in People of Color:
Therapeutic Implications   233**

Chapter 11
White Racial Identity Development: Therapeutic Implications

Part V
Social Justice Dimensions in Counseling/Therapy

Chapter 12
Social Justice Counseling/Therapy

Section II
Multicultural Counseling and Specific Populations

Chapter 16 _____

Chapter 17 _____

Since its publication in 1981, *Counseling the Culturally Diverse: Theory and Practice* (*CCD*) has become a classic in its field, used in nearly 50 percent of graduate training programs in counseling, and now forms part of the multicultural knowledge base of licensing and certification exams. It continues to lead the field in the theory, research, and practice of multicultural counseling/therapy, and upholds the highest standards of scholarship; it is the most frequently cited text in multicultural psychology and ethnic minority mental health. We believe that the success of *CCD* is related to its (1) integrated conceptual framework, (2) up-to-date coverage of research in the field, (3) ability to actively address clinical applications through translating research and concepts to practice, (4) use of numerous examples, vignettes, and case studies that add life and meaning to the material, (5) engaging writing style, and (6) passionate style of communication—hard hitting, intense, and challenging. The 14 specific population chapters, including several new ones, continue to be hailed as among the best thumbnail sketches of how multicultural counseling relates to the various marginalized populations in our society.

The fifth edition of *CCD* does not change its basic formula, which continues to make it a success in the academic and clinical markets. There are significant revisions, however, that reflect changes in the field and new frontiers of importance to the mental health professions. Major updating of references, introduction of new research and concepts, and future directions in counseling, therapy, and mental health are reflected in the fifth edition.

Section 1—"The Multiple Dimensions of Multicultural Counseling and Therapy" is divided into five parts that discuss broad theoretical, conceptual, research, and practice issues related to multicultural counseling/therapy, cultural competence, and sociopolitical influences that cut across specific populations.

- Part I—"The Affective and Conceptual Dimensions of Multicultural Counseling/Therapy" includes Chapter 1: "The Multicultural Journey to Cultural Competence: Personal Narratives" and Chapter 2: "The Superordinate Nature of Multicultural Counseling and Therapy."

- Part II—"The Political Dimensions of Mental Health Practice" includes Chapter 3: "The Politics of Counseling and Psychotherapy," Chapter 4: "Sociopolitical Considerations of Oppression: Trust and Mistrust in Counseling/Therapy" and Chapter 5: "Racial, Gender, and Sexual Orientation Microaggressions: Implications for Counseling and Psychotherapy."

- Part III—"The Practice Dimensions of Multicultural Counseling/Therapy" includes Chapter 6: "Barriers to Multicultural Counseling/Therapy," Chapter 7: "Culturally Appropriate Intervention Strategies," Chapter 8: "Multicultural Family Counseling and Therapy," and Chapter 9: "Non-Western and Indigenous Methods of Healing."
- Part IV—"Worldview Dimensions in Multicultural Counseling and Therapy" includes Chapter 10: "Racial/Cultural Identity Development in People of Color" and Chapter 11: "White Racial Identity Development."
- Part V—"Social Justice Dimensions in Counseling/Therapy" includes Chapter 12: "Social Justice Counseling/Therapy."

Section 2—"Multicultural Counseling and Specific Populations" is divided into three parts that cover unique and culture-specific chapters on special populations. The extensive coverage allows instructors freedom to use all of the chapters in this section or to selectively choose those that fit their course requirements.

- Part VI—"Counseling and Therapy Involving Minority Group Counselors/Therapists" includes Chapter 13: "Minority Group Therapists: Working with Majority and Other Minority Clients."
- Part VII—"Counseling and Therapy with Racial/Ethnic Minority Populations" includes Chapter 14: "Counseling African Americans," Chapter 15: "Counseling American Indians and Alaskan Natives," Chapter 16: "Counseling Asian Americans and Pacific Islanders," Chapter 17: "Counseling Hispanic/Latino Americans," and Chapter 18: "Counseling Individuals of Multiracial Descent."
- Part VIII—"Counseling and Special Circumstances Involving Racial/Ethnic Populations" includes Chapter 19: "Counseling Arab Americans," Chapter 20: "Counseling Jewish Americans," Chapter 21: "Counseling Immigrants," and Chapter 22: "Counseling Refugees."
- Part IX—"Counseling and Therapy with Other Multicultural Populations" includes Chapter 23: "Counseling Sexual Minorities," Chapter 24: "Counseling Older Adult Clients," Chapter 25: "Counseling Women," and Chapter 26: "Counseling Individuals with Disabilities."

Many of the additions and revisions incorporated into the fifth edition arose from instructor and student feedback. While the emotive and passionate nature of the text has proven to be a strength in generating difficult dialogues on race, gender, sexual orientation, and other sociodemographic differences, it has also posed unique challenges to instructors. For some students, the strong passions and feelings aroused by these topics occasionally lead to defensiveness and require a skilled instructor to help them through the learning process. To aid the instructor in helping students process the meaning of their emotional reactions, Chapter 1 presents two personal narratives by Drs. Mark Kiselica and Derald Wing Sue that speak to their racial/cultural awakening to reading *CCD* and to personal reflections of how it came to be written.

Dr. Mark Kiselica, a White counseling psychologist, has written in several professional publications of how influential the book was for his personal awakening to multicultural issues as a graduate student at Penn State University. A well-respected scholar and researcher in counseling psychology, Dr. Kiselica describes his initial reactions of anger and disgust with the contents of the book and his eventual understanding of his strong emotional reactions. The inclusion of two brief personal narratives, back to back in the same chapter, illustrate lessons related to topical areas of the text. It is hoped that students will be able to obtain insights into how *CCD* was developed, from the senior author's perspective, and also understand Kiselica's initial defensiveness and anger toward the contents of the book and how he realized that his strong feelings were defenses against self-exploration. We are hopeful that many White students will be able (a) to see themselves in Kiselica's account, making the material more meaningful, and (b) to understand the passionate and emotive meaning of the text.

Several new and important chapters are included in the fifth edition. First, new chapters on "Racial, Gender, and Sexual Orientation Microaggressions: Implications for Counseling and Therapy" (Chapter 5), "Social Justice Counseling/Therapy" (Chapter 12), and one on "Minority Group Therapists: Working with Majority and Other Minority Clients" (Chapter 13) have been added.

Chapter 5, on microaggressions, discusses a cutting-edge area of research that has important implications for our society and for the mental health of its marginalized groups. Microaggressions deal with the unconscious and subtle manifestations of bias and discrimination that many well-intentioned individuals are unaware they possess. How microaggressions affect the mental health status of marginalized populations, how well-intentioned mental health professionals are unaware that they may be guilty of bias and discrimination, and how they infect the process of counseling/therapy are discussed in detail. More importantly, we spend considerable time illustrating how microaggressions may lead to a breakdown in the therapeutic alliance, and we indicate the importance of research in this area. We are especially grateful for the help of Christina M. Capodilupo in the writing of this chapter.

Chapter 12, on social justice counseling/therapy, continues the direction taken toward addressing issues across all marginalized groups in our society and broadening the umbrella of multiculturalism. Social justice counseling is increasingly becoming an area counseling psychology views as central to the helping professions. Social justice counseling/therapy is an active philosophy and approach aimed at producing conditions that allow for equal access and opportunity, reducing or eliminating disparities in education, health care, employment, and other areas that lower the quality of life for affected populations, encouraging mental health professionals to consider micro, meso, and macro levels in the assessment, diagnosis, and treatment of client and client systems, and broadening the role of the helping professional to include not only counselor/therapist but advocate, consultant, psychoeducator, change agent, community worker, and so on.

Chapter 13 addresses issues related to interethnic relationships, where the counselor is a member of a marginalized group and the client is of another minority or majority group. This issue has been relatively unexplored and is likely to be controversial. But we believe that such a first step in addressing these relationships in general and to counseling/therapy dyads is much needed. In this chapter, we hope to make the point that multicultural counseling is more than White–People of Color, but White–Black, Black–Asian, Asian–Latino, Latino–Native American and numerous combinations. To cover this matter, we briefly review the findings on relationships between various racial/ethnic minorities. Matters related to counselors of color working with White clients, and different racial/ethnic counselor combinations (African American–Asian American, Latino(a)-Hispanic American–Native American, Native American–Asian American, etc.) are described. This chapter also discusses other counseling combinations that involve members of traditional marginalized groups as therapists and a dominant member as client.

We are also adding four brief chapters covering specific populations because of the unique circumstances they face: "Counseling Arab Americans" (Chapter 19), "Counseling Jewish Americans" (Chapter 20), "Counseling Immigrants" (Chapter 21), and "Counseling Refugees" (Chapter 22). In light of the current "hot buttons" associated with worldwide events like the conflicts in the Middle East, the terrorist attacks on the World Trade Center, and the strongly divisive issue of immigration, much misunderstanding surrounding Middle Eastern and immigrant/refugee groups have led to their being demonized. These new chapters present information and issues that we hope will allow mental health professionals to liberate themselves from such stereotypes, to more fully understand their life circumstance, and to provide helpful and culturally relevant services to them.

All chapters have undergone changes, some more than others. We have tried to integrate greater coverage of social class issues throughout the text. The aim of such changes and/or additions is to make sure the topical chapters continue to both reflect and lead the field. Due to positive reactions to the clinical implications section at the end of each chapter, we have decided to retain that feature.

For instructors using the text, new auxiliary materials have been developed to aid in teaching the concepts to students. We are grateful to Gina Torino, who has developed materials (overheads, tests, resources, learning activities, role-plays, etc.) that correlate with specific chapters of *CCD*. Professors will find the instructor's manual a valuable tool in teaching the concepts of multicultural counseling and therapy.

To further aid instructors using the text are a series of videotapes/DVDs in lecture format produced and developed independently by Microtraining Associates to accompany specific chapters of the book. These tapes were developed to be stand-alone lectures of multicultural counseling to be used in courses on multicultural counseling and therapy, minority mental health issues, broader multicultural/diversity topics, or can be used with *CCD*. With respect to the latter, such usage allows instructors to assign specific chapters of the text and show the tapes associated with the content. We are hopeful that such an approach will allow instructors greater freedom in developing their own class activities (see instructor's manual) to supplement both chapter readings and taped lectures. Approximately a dozen tapes can be used throughout the duration of the course. Please see the Instructor's Manual for information on how to order the tapes from Microtraining Associates.

There is an African American proverb that states, "We stand on the head and shoulders of many who have gone on before us." Certainly, this book would not have been possible without the wisdom, commitment, and sacrifice of others. We thank them for their inspiration, courage, and dedication, and hope that they will look down on us and be pleased with our work. We would like to acknowledge all the dedicated multicultural pioneers in the field who have journeyed with us along the path of multiculturalism before it became fashionable. They are too numerous to name, but their knowledge and wisdom have guided the production of *CCD*. Special thanks go to Lisa Gebo, our editor, who supported the revision efforts and constantly encouraged the many new directions exemplified in this fifth edition.

Working on this fifth edition continues to be a labor of love. It would not have been possible, however, without the love and support of our families, who provided the patience and nourishment that sustained us throughout our work on the text. Derald Wing Sue wishes to express his love for his wife, Paulina, his son, Derald Paul, and his daughter, Marissa Catherine. David Sue wishes to express his love to his wife, Diane, and his daughters, Jenni and Cristi.

We hope that *Counseling the Culturally Diverse: Theory and Practice*, fifth edition, will stand on "the truth" and continue to be the standard bearer of multicultural counseling and therapy texts in the field.

DERALD WING SUE
DAVID SUE

THE MULTIPLE DIMENSIONS OF MULTICULTURAL COUNSELING AND THERAPY

The Affective and Conceptual Dimensions of Multicultural Counseling/Therapy

The Multicultural Journey to Cultural Competence: Personal Narratives

1

Reading *Counseling the Culturally Diverse: Theory and Practice (CCD)* is very likely to elicit strong emotions among readers. Not only may the content of the book challenge your racial reality, but it is passionate, direct, and likely to arouse deep feelings of guilt, defensiveness, anger, sadness, hopelessness, and anxiety in some of you. Becoming culturally competent in mental health practice, however, demands that nested or embedded emotions associated with race, culture, gender, and other sociodemographic differences be openly experienced and discussed. It is these intense feelings that often block our ability to hear the voices of those most oppressed and disempowered. How we, as helping professionals, deal with these strong feelings can either enhance or negate a deeper understanding of ourselves as racial/cultural beings and our understanding of the worldviews of culturally diverse clients. Sara Winter (1977, p. 24), a White female psychologist, powerfully enumerates the reactions that many Whites experience when topics of race or racism are openly discussed. These disturbing feelings, she contends, serve to protect us from having to examine our own prejudices and biases.

> When someone pushes racism into my awareness, I feel guilty (that I could be doing so much more); angry (I don't like to feel like I'm wrong); defensive (I already have two Black friends . . . I worry more about racism than most whites do—isn't that enough); turned off (I have other priorities in my life with guilt about that thought); helpless (the problem is so big— what can I do?). I HATE TO FEEL THIS WAY. That is why I minimize race issues and let them fade from my awareness whenever possible.

On the other hand, many marginalized groups react equally strongly when issues of oppression are raised, especially when their stories of discrimination and pain are minimized or neglected. Their reality of racism, sexism, and homophobia, they contend, is relatively unknown or ignored by those in power because of the discomfort that

5

pervades such topics. Vernon E. Jordan, Jr., an African American attorney and former confidant of President Bill Clinton, made this point about racism in startling terms. In making an analogy between the terrorist attacks of September 11 (known by an overwhelming majority in our nation) and those suffered by Blacks (seemingly minimized by the public), Jordan stated:

> *None of this is new to Black people. War, hunger, disease, unemployment, deprivation, dehumanization, and terrorism define our existence. They are not new to us. Slavery was terrorism, segregation was terrorism, and the bombing of the four little girls in Sunday school in Birmingham was terrorism. The violent deaths of Medgar, Martin, Malcolm, Vernon Dahmer, Chaney, Shwerner, and Goodman were terrorism. And the difference between September 11 and the terror visited upon Black people is that on September 11, the terrorists were foreigners. When we were terrorized, it was by our neighbors. The terrorists were American citizens.*

Our opening chapter is meant to be a reflective and emotional one. While the entire volume is filled with the knowledge base of multicultural counseling and therapy derived from research findings, it is important to realize that cognitive understanding and intellectual competence are not enough. Concepts of multiculturalism, diversity, race, culture, ethnicity, and so forth are more than intellectual concepts. Multiculturalism deals with real human experiences, and as a result, understanding your emotional reactions is equally important in the journey to cultural competence. To aid you in your journey, we present two personal narratives concerning the text you are about to read. We hope that you will carefully monitor your own emotional reactions, not allow them to interfere with your journey to cultural competence, and try to understand them as they relate to your own racial/cultural awakening and identity.

My Personal and Professional Journey as a White Person: Reactions to "Counseling the Culturally Diverse: Theory and Practice"

by Mark S. Kiselica

I was shaken to my core the first time I read *Counseling the Culturally Different* (now *Counseling the Culturally Diverse*) by Derald Wing Sue (1981). I can remember the moment vividly. I was a doctoral candidate at Penn State University's counseling psychology program, and I had been reading Sue's book in preparation for my comprehensive examinations, which I was scheduled to take toward the end of the spring semester of 1985.

I wish I could tell you that I had acquired Sue's book because I was gen-

Figure 1.1

Mark S. Kiselica

uincly interested in learning about multicultural counseling, or, as it was labeled back then, "cross-cultural counseling." I am embarrassed to say, however, that that was not the case. I had purchased Sue's book purely out of necessity, figuring that I had better read the book because I was likely to be asked a major question about cross-cultural counseling on the comps. During the early and middle 1980s, taking a course in multicultural counseling was not a requirement in many graduate counseling programs, including mine, and I had decided not to take my department's pertinent course as an elective. I saw myself as a culturally sensitive person, and I concluded that the course wouldn't have much to offer me. Nevertheless, I understood that Dr. Harold Cheatham, the professor who taught the course, would likely submit a question to the pool of material being used to construct the comps. So, I prudently went to the university bookstore and purchased a copy of *Counseling the Culturally Different (CCD)* because that was the text Dr. Cheatham used for his course. I had decided that reading and studying the book would prepare me for whatever question Dr. Cheatham might devise, so I read it carefully, making sure to take detailed notes on everything Sue had to say.

I didn't get very far with my highlighting and note taking before I started to react to Sue's book with great anger and disgust. Early on in the text, Sue blasted the mental health system for its historical mistreatment of people who were considered to be ethnic minorities in the United States. He especially took on White mental health professionals, charging them with a legacy of ethnocentric and racist beliefs and practices that had harmed people of color and made them leery of counselors, psychologists, and psychiatrists. It seemed that Sue didn't have a single good thing to say about White America, and I was ticked off at him! I resented that I had to read his book, and couldn't wait for the task to be over. I wished that there were some other way than reading Sue's book to get through the comps, but I knew I had better complete his text and know the subject matter covered in it if I wanted to succeed on the examinations. So, out of necessity, I read on, and struggled with the feelings that Sue's words stirred in me.

I was very upset as I read and reread Sue's book. I felt that Sue had an axe to grind with White America and that he was using his book to do so. I believed his accusations were grossly exaggerated and, at least to some extent, unfair. And I felt defensive because I am White and my ancestors had not perpetrated any of the offenses against ethnic minorities that Sue had charged. I was so angry at Sue that I vowed I would toss his book away once I passed the comps. I looked forward to the day when I would be relieved of him and his writings.

Yet, for reasons I didn't fully understand at the time, my anger, defensiveness, and resentment began to fade, and rather than dumping Sue's book, I found myself reading it again and again. Something was happening to me, and I couldn't put my finger on it. Surprisingly, once I had reached the point where I understood the content and theory provided in Sue's book, and hence, had achieved my purposes for reading the text, I kept opening it up again. And strangely, with each fresh reading, I experienced new waves of emotions. Instead of reacting with bitterness, I was now feeling sadness—mild sadness at first, but later, a profound sense of sadness, and even grief. At times, my eyes filled with tears, and I found myself now wanting to absorb the message that Sue was trying to convey. *What was happening to me?*

I tried to make sense of my emotions—to ascertain why I was drawn back to Sue's book again and again in spite of my initial rejection of it. I know it may sound crazy, but I read certain sections of Sue's book repeatedly, and then reflected on what was happening inside of me. I spent quite a bit of time alone with Sue's book, sometimes in my office. A couple of other times, I went for long walks in the woods, trying to understand why this book was becoming so important to me. *My life was changing and I needed to know why.*

The tears kept coming. I began to discover important lessons about me, significant insights, prompted by reading Sue's book, that would shape the direction of my future. I gradually realized that over my entire life I had identified with oppressed peoples because my ancestors and my immediate family had encountered so many hardships throughout our history. My mother's family was from Ireland, and throughout the ages, they had suffered severe poverty and political and cultural domination by the British. Their language, Gaelic, had been taken from them. They were forced to change the spelling of their last name. They left Ireland for a better life in America, realizing that they would never be able to return to their homeland, and their hearts were ripped apart by such a heart-wrenching departure. Yet, they arrived in America with the hope of providing something better for their children, and they stood up to the terrible stereotypes about and maltreatment of the Irish by the American establishment. My maternal grandfather worked as a railroad laborer until it killed him, and my grandmother cleaned the homes of wealthy Americans until she could work no longer, still poor and living in a ghetto at the time of her death. All of these images came back to me as I read Sue's book, and with their arrival, the tears began to fall.

More images entered my mind, this time regarding my father's family, who were from Slovakia. They, too, had been poor. They, too, suffered through years of external domination and persecution, including the destruction of their homes and villages by invading armies and the desecration of their churches and political institutions. My paternal grandparents fled to the United States, and my father was raised in a poor, immigrant neighborhood where English was his second language. My father was learning disabled and lame from a horrific leg injury for which he received inadequate medical care. For decades, he labored in factories under deplorable conditions that would eventually disable him. Yet, all he ever dreamed about was giving my brothers and sisters and me a better life. Sue's book reminded me of my father and all that he and his family went through, and their suffering surged through me, leaving me teary-eyed.

These memories helped me to look at Sue's book from a different point of view. They caused me to realize more fully that the historical experiences of other racial and ethnic groups were similar in some respects to those of my family. And with that particular realization, more tears swelled in my eyes—tears of empathy, and tears of shame. I began to feel—*really feel*—for what people of color had experienced in this country, and I was ashamed of the fact that it had taken me so long to develop that level of empathic understanding. "How could I have been so clueless?" I wondered to myself at the time.

My head began to spin as a vortex of thoughts swirled in my mind. I now realized that Sue was right! The system *had* been destructive toward people of color, and although my ancestors and I had not directly been a part of that oppressive system, I had unknowingly contributed to it. I began to think about how I had viewed people of color throughout my life, and I had to admit to myself that I had unconsciously bought into the racist stereotypes about African Americans and Latinos. Yes, I had laughed at and told racist jokes. Yes, I had used the "N" word when referring to African Americans. *Yes, I had been a racist.*

Admitting that I have been racist is not an easy thing for me to do. It isn't easy now, and it certainly wasn't easy in 1985, when I naively thought I was such a culturally sensitive person. I had good reasons to conclude, albeit erroneously, that I was *not* a racist. I had never been a member of the Ku Klux Klan. When I was a boy, I had had a handful of Cuban American and African American friends. My family and I had always supported the Democratic Party and liberal legislative initiatives. Yes, I was one of the good guys, so the word "racist" couldn't apply to me. But I was wrong, blinded by the insular world in which I had been raised, a world of well-meaning Whites in an era of racial segregation that dictated little substantive contact with people who were different from me: a world that socialized American Whites, including me, to become racist.

Sue's book forced me to remove my blinders. He helped me to see that I was both a product and an architect of a racist culture. Initially, I didn't want to admit this to myself. That is part of the reason I got so angry at Sue for his book. "His accusations don't apply to *me*!" was the predominant, initial thought that went through my mind. But Sue's words were too powerful to let me escape my denial of my racism. It was as though I was in a deep sleep and someone had dumped a bucket of ice-cold water on me, shocking me into a state of sudden wakefulness: The sleep was the denial of my racism; the water was Sue's provocative words, and the wakefulness was the painful recognition that I was a racist.

It was very unsettling to achieve this recognition, and I faced a tough dilemma afterward: Should I continue to confront my ethnocentrism and racism and experience all of the discomfort that goes with that process, or should I retreat from that process and go on living my life of comfort in my White-dominated world? What else would I discover about myself if I continued with the process of exploring my cultural biases? Where would it take me?

As I wrestled with this dilemma, two considerations helped me to move beyond my anxiety about fully committing myself to becoming a more culturally sensitive person. I realized I had an obligation to my ancestors to confront my fears and cultural biases, for without further growth on my part, I would continue to do to others what had been done to my ancestors. I also was deeply moved by the historical experiences of people of color in the United States. Sue and the contributing authors who wrote some of the chapters in the first edition of his book did a nice job of summarizing these experiences. Their work inspired me to learn more about the history and experiences of people who were culturally different from me.

As I look back on this period of soul-searching, I now realize that the reading of *CCD* sparked a period of important White racial identity development for me. Prior to reading Sue's book, I had not thought of myself as a racial being nor considered my role as a White person in a racist society. Reading *CCD* pushed me to have a greater awareness of racial issues. My decision to explore racial matters further led me to make an important professional decision that would have a lasting impact on me and move me to yet deeper levels of understanding about my Whiteness: I decided to apply for and accept a predoctoral internship in clinical child and adolescent psychology in the outpatient unit of the Community Mental Health Center of the University of Medicine and Dentistry of New Jersey (UMDNJ), which was located in the heart of Newark, New Jersey. Because the center at UMDNJ served primarily African American and Latino families, the internship provided me with extensive contact with people who are culturally different from me. So, when I left Penn State in the summer of 1986 to begin my internship in Newark, I was about to immerse myself in a cross-cultural experience.

The year I spent in Newark changed me forever. Developing everyday relationships with African American and Latino colleagues at UMDNJ, studying about the history and traditions of African Americans and Latinos, and counseling children, adolescents, and families from these two racial/ethnic groups gave me a real-world feel for the material I had first read about in *CCD*. By immersing myself in the cultures of these two populations, I acquired an affective understanding about racism and oppression, which is a form of understanding that Sue said is necessary for true multicultural growth. I also became acutely aware of my Whiteness. Being one of the few White, non-Latino people at UMDNJ, I was now the minority, and I stood out as a White person. I enjoyed many conversations with my colleagues and clients about our respective roots. I learned that we shared distinct, yet overlapping, historical experiences. I understood for the first time the advantages I had enjoyed by being White in America, of how the system is open to people who look like me but is often closed and dangerous for people of color. To put it in a different way, I recognized that my White skin and blond hair and blue eyes afforded me "White privilege" in a racist society. Best of all, I experienced the joy that comes with crossing cultural boundaries and discovering the beauty of different cultures and people.

When my year in Newark was over, I felt compelled to write an account of these experiences, which had been prompted by reading *CCD*. I had a week off between the completion of my internship and the start of a new job at the Piscataway campus of UMDNJ. Rather than go on vacation, I sequestered myself in the bedroom of our apartment in Bordentown, New Jersey, where my wife and I lived at the time, pouring my heart into writing about my cross-cultural experiences. When that week was over, I had completed the first draft of a manuscript titled *Reflections of a Multicultural Internship Experience*. I sent the manuscript to Dr. Cheatham, who was still a professor at Penn State, and asked him to critique my paper, even though I had never enrolled in his course. In a gesture of kindness and generosity I will always appreciate, Harold not only reviewed the manuscript, but he encouraged me to try to publish it. Shortly afterward, I noticed a call for manuscripts for a special issue of the *Journal of Counseling and Development* (*JCD*) on multiculturalism as a fourth force in counseling, which was to be edited by Paul Pedersen, a well-known multicultural scholar who was a professor of counseling at Syracuse University at the time. I considered sending my manuscript to Dr. Pedersen but hesitated due to several doubts I had about the paper. I had little experience as a writer and feared that my paper was too personal and heartfelt for a professional journal. I also felt vulnerable knowing that I was about to allow others to read my intensely personal experiences. I nevertheless submitted the manuscript to Dr. Pedersen. Much to my surprise, the manuscript was accepted for publication after the reviewers who read it commented that it was a very special article representing a unique voice in the field.

I was now on my way to complementing my clinical experiences of counseling the culturally different with extensive scholarship on the subject. In the fall of 1990, I took a position as an assistant professor of counseling psychology at Ball State University in Muncie, Indiana, and my article about my multicultural internship appeared in *JCD* during the following year. Over the course of the next 15 years, I would focus many of my 100-plus publications on the subjects of multicultural counseling and education, and the process of confronting prejudice and racism. I owe much of my productivity in multicultural counseling to Dr. Derald Wing Sue, not only for the influence *Counseling the Culturally Diverse* had on me, but also for the personal manner in which Dr. Sue has mentored me. That he and I would become friends is yet another reason why I am grateful that I read his book.

On January 30, 1995, approximately 10 years after I had read *CCD* for the first time, I decided to write a letter to Dr. Sue. By this point in my career, I was an assistant professor of counselor education at Trenton State College (now The College of New Jersey). I had just published my first book, *Multicultural Counseling with Teenage Fathers*, the seventh volume in the Sage Series on Multicultural Aspects of Counseling. I wanted to mark the publication of my book by expressing my gratitude to Dr. Sue for the profound impact he had on me. So, once again, I poured my heart into words, composing a three-page letter to Dr. Sue. In my letter, I told him the entire story about my comprehensive exams, my initial and later reactions to his book, and the racial identity development his words had prompted in me. I also described the impact of some of his subsequent publications on me, and I thanked him for the role he had played in my life.

A few weeks later, the phone in my office rang, and Dr. Sue was on the other end of the line. He introduced himself to me and then reported that, although he had received many letters from people about his book over the years, he had never read any commentary about his book that was as moving and honest as mine. So, he was calling to thank me for my thoughtfulness.

I will cherish that phone call for the rest of my life. It was a fantasy come true to talk with a man who had become one of my idols. We talked for a while about our lives and our interests. When I hung up the phone at the conclusion of our conversation, I was in a state of disbelief. Derald Wing Sue had just taken the time to call and thank *me*.

This thoughtful gesture was just one of many acts of kindness by people like Derald, who understand the importance of affirming multicultural allies. People like Harold Cheatham, Cheryl Thompson, Joe Ponterotto, Paul Pedersen, Don Locke, MaryLou Ramsey, Roger Herring, Allen Ivey, Michael D'Andrea, Judy Daniels, Larry Gerstein, Leo Hendricks, Sharon Bowman, Kelley Kenney, Mark Kenney, Nancy Boyd-Franklin, Courtland Lee, Bea Wehrly, John McFadden, Fred Bemak, Rita Chung, Charles Ridley, Chalmer Thompson, Sandra Tomlinson-Clarke, Vivian Ota Wang, Mary Swigonski, and Amy Reynolds—all accomplished, respected scholars who have supported and affirmed my efforts to be a positive contributor to the multicultural movement. This support was crucial to me because the emotionally laden process of developing multicultural sensitivity did not stop with the completion of my internship in 1986. On the contrary, my cultural immersion experience in Newark was only one phase of my White racial identity development, and I would need the understanding and counsel of these and other friends as I struggled with the ups and downs of my never-ending multicultural journey.

What were these struggles? For one, I went through a period of over-identifying with people of color, which is a common reaction of Whites who experience guilt after they have an awakening about themselves as racial beings. For a while, I acted as though I were one of the saved, a former racist who was now on a mission to save other, fellow Whites from their racism. At times, I became a judgmental nuisance to my White friends. I also became overbearing with friends who were people of color, seeking their approval for my conversion and annoying them in the process. I got slammed a few times for this behavior, and at other times, as I continued to cross cultural boundaries, I encountered the stinging resentment of me by people of color who drew conclusions about my character based simply on that fact that I am White. As I became more involved in intercultural forums and organizations, I grew weary of the tensions that had to be negotiated about racial matters. These were painful times, so I retreated from substantive interracial contact for about a year, feeling that the price I had to pay for my cross-cultural involvement just wasn't worth it. During this hiatus I did a lot of soul-searching, and I confided in people I trusted about the feelings I was having, emerging with some new perspectives about racial matters and relations. I realized that we will never make progress with the racial problems that have plagued our country unless Whites like me are willing to accept and manage the pain and discomfort associated with negotiating racial issues. I recognized more fully the complicated nature of racial issues and was less prone to judge others for their racism, even though I stood ready to confront racism whenever it reared its ugly head. I gradually re-engaged myself in the work to promote cultural harmony, joining national organizations, such as the Southern Poverty Law Center, and local movements, such as the Newtown Township No Place for Hate Campaign, to combat prejudice in all its forms. Through my work with these organizations and my continued interchange with students, colleagues, and friends about racial issues, I have realized that a variety of different tactics are necessary in the battle to eliminate hate. Virulent racism must be confronted with strong systemic policies and community-wide stands communicating that hatred will not be tolerated. More subtle forms of racism can be addressed by taking a less ardent approach, one that involves the tricky challenge of balancing discomforting confrontation with empathic understanding. I have learned that the language we use to promote multiculturalism can be problematic, and that we must replace certain terminology, such as "teaching tolerance," with the words, "fostering appreciation." People who sense that they are being "tolerated" don't feel welcome, but people who know that they are being "appreciated" feel that they have an honored place at the table.

As I have made these discoveries and moved toward higher stages of White racial identity development, Derald Wing Sue has repeatedly influenced me along the way, affirming me and promoting my growth through his continued writings and encouragement. For example, in one especially cogent article, Derald criticized the professions of counseling and psychology for sometimes lacking a soul (Sue, 1993), thereby affirming that there must be a place in the professional literature for publications like mine, which tend to be written both from the head *and* the heart. Bolstered by his words, I have published several influential manuscripts in which I have merged material from counseling theory and research with narratives about my own highly personal reflections regarding racism, anti-Semitism, and multicultural education (Kiselica, 1991, 1998, 1999a, 1999b, 2003). Derald has also reinforced my belief that people from different backgrounds must work together in order to address interracial difficulties when he wrote, "If we are to move forward, both minority and majority researchers must make a genuine effort to reach out to one another for mutual understanding and respect" (Sue, 1993, p. 245). In addition, Derald has welcomed Whites like me to the multicultural movement by expressing his belief, "We should view them [White multicultural scholars] as allies because the future of multiculturalism depends on the positive alliances we form with our White brothers and sisters" (p. 248). Finally, like me, Derald emphasized the importance of empathic understanding regarding racial matters when he offered this compassionate statement regarding White racism:

I do not believe that any of us were born wanting to be biased, prejudiced, racist, or sexist. These statements are not meant to absolve White people from the guilt of bias and discrimination (although guilt is counterproductive), but to indicate that some White researchers are engaged in a different battle: overcoming negative aspects of their cultural conditioning. (Sue, 1993, pp. 247–248)

Derald's influence on me has not been limited to these writings or that one unforgettable phone call he made to me in 1995. On two occasions, he and I served on the same panels at conference symposia pertaining to multicultural counseling and education (Iwamasa, 1995; McCree & Bromley, 2002). A few years ago, I played a key role in convincing the administration of The College of New Jersey to bring Derald to our campus to give an address for our Multicultural Lecture Series, during which he shared his keen observations about the status of racial relations in our country. Every time we see each other at conferences of the American Psychological Association, the American Counseling Association, and other professional organizations, we enjoy a warm exchange, updating each other about our families and our work. From time to time, we talk via the phone or e-mail, discussing both professional issues and personal matters that are important to us.

Throughout all of these contacts, Derald Wing Sue has welcomed me to the multicultural movement and made me feel that I am his respected colleague. To think that he and I have reached this stage in our relationship in spite of my initial, unfair reactions to the first edition of *CCD* is a remarkable accomplishment, for which we both deserve credit and about which I am once again moved to tears. As for me, I feel proud of the fact that I worked through my strong, harsh reactions to Derald's book and saw the truth and wisdom in his observations. I am grateful to Derald for writing that book because it was the catalyst for so much growth in me. I know that his words will echo in my mind for years to come as I continue on my multicultural journey. I also have no doubt that this, the fifth edition of *Counseling the Culturally Diverse*, will have a positive influence on a new generation of counseling students, just as it did with me over 20 years ago. To those students, I send my warmest regards and my wish that you will embrace this book and the soul-searching that it will stimulate in you. And if you struggle with unsettling feelings as you read Dr. Sue's latest edition, please know that I will be there to help you during your multicultural journey, just as Derald Wing Sue was there to support me with mine.

In closing, to Derald Wing Sue, I say this: Thank you for being my brother!

My Personal and Professional Journey as a Person of Color: The Heart and Soul of "Counseling the Culturally Diverse"

by Derald Wing Sue*

I am grateful to Mark Kiselica for his willingness to share such deep personal reflections with all of us. Mark's honesty in confronting his own racism is refreshing, and his insights invaluable to those who wish to become allies in the struggle for equal rights. He is a rarity in academic circles, even rarer because he was willing to put his words on paper for the whole world to read as a means to help others understand the meaning of racism on a human level. Mark Kiselica's courageous and open exploration of his initial reactions to *CCD* indicates what I have come to learn is a common, intensely emotional experience from many readers. Because *CCD* deals openly, honestly, and passionately with issues of racism, sexism, and homophobia, and challenges our belief that we are free of biases, it is likely to evoke defensiveness, resentment, and anger in readers. In Mark's case, he did not allow these reactions to sabotage his own self-exploration and journey to cultural competence.

Counseling the Culturally Diverse: Theory and Practice represents a labor of love, and is written from my heart and soul. It is filled with all the passion, frustration, and anger concerning the detrimental nature and harm our society and its helping professions have wrought on many marginalized groups, albeit unintentionally. Its goals are to enlighten you about how counseling and psychotherapy may represent cultural oppression, and to provide a vision of change that is rooted in social justice. Let me say at the onset that my anger is not directed at White Americans nor our country. The anger *is* directed, however, at White supremacy, sexism, heterosexism, and the many manifestations of bigotry and discrimination that accompany it. As someone once said about racism, "White people are not the enemies, but White supremacy is!"

When first written in 1981, I knew my words and assertions would come across as provocative and accusatory and would make many in the field defensive and angry, despite the fact that it was based heavily on research findings. Upon publication, that was what happened. I received calls from colleagues who criticized the book and claimed that it was a prime example of White bashing. Strangely enough, while many colleagues and students found the book distressful and disturbing, it became a success that surprised

---

*Adapted from Sue, D. W. (2005). The Continuing Journey to Multicultural Competence. In R. K. Conyne and F. Bemak (eds.), *Journeys to Professional Excellence: Lessons from Leading Counselor Educators and Practitioners* (pp. 73–84). Alexandria, VA: American Counseling Association. Reprinted with permission

Figure 1.2

Derald Wing Sue

even my publisher. Much of this was fueled by scholars and students of color who embraced it and claimed it was one of the few texts that spoke to their experiential reality. Since its publication, *Counseling the Culturally Diverse* has gone through four revisions, and I am proud to say it is now the most frequently used text on multicultural counseling; further, it forms the knowledge base of many items on counseling and psychology licensing exams. Many have credited the text as the forerunner of the cultural competence movement, but in actuality the product was the result of many pioneers of color whose important contributions have been overlooked, ignored, or neglected.

Many professors and students have written to me about their reactions to *CCD*. Some assert that it is too political and too emotional. I have also discovered that my writings are often seen by people in the profession as too filled with emotions, and not consistent with the objective style so prevalent in academia. That has been one of my pet peeves regarding so-called "scholarly writings" in the field. Many of my colleagues operate from a mistaken notion that rational thought can only come from objective discourse, devoid of emotions. To me, speaking from the heart and with passion is not antagonistic to reason. Further, speaking the truth, especially pointing out how counseling and therapy have oppressed, harmed, and damaged marginalized groups (often unintentionally) is difficult for many of my White colleagues and students to hear. They are likely to react negatively, making it difficult for them to accept challenges to their concept of mental health practice, and perhaps their own complicity in perpetuating unjust treatment of clients of color. I suppose they view my writings as accusatory and off-setting. Yet, how does one "nicely" and objectively speak about stereotyping, prejudice, and discrimination in the helping professions and the helping professional? Should I soften the message and not speak about the unspeakable?

Being Chinese American in a Monocultural Society

To understand the passion of *CCD*, it may be helpful to share some of my life experiences as a minority in this society. The lessons I have learned as a Chinese American, born and raised in a predominantly White western society, have played a central role in the content and context of this text. I was born and raised in Portland, Oregon, to proud parents who believed strongly in the primacy of the family and extolled the virtues of hard work and achievement. My father emigrated from China; indeed, he stowed away on a ship to the United States at the age of 14. Not knowing how to speak English and unfamiliar with this country, my father survived. And that has been the story of our family, surviving in the face of great odds. My brothers and sister have learned that lesson well, and *it has been watching my mother and father deal with our early experiences of poverty and discrimination that has taught us to struggle and fight against social injustice. I attribute my work on social justice, multiculturalism, and diversity to these early experiences.*

As a family, we have always been in awe at the courage it must have taken for our father to journey to a strange country without family, friends, formal education, or employable skills. Yet, my father married, raised five sons and one daughter, and was able to provide for the family. He met my mother and married her when she was 16, both never attaining an education beyond the third grade. My mother taught herself to read and write English, but my father refused to part with the old ways; his pride in being Chinese was immense, and he eventually made his mark in Portland's Chinatown, where he became a respected elder in the community. Prior to that, he found work in the shipyards and as a gambler, and provided as best he could for the family. Despite the limited schooling of my parents, they always stressed the importance of an education. They instilled within us the value and importance it had for our future. It always amazes my colleagues when I tell them that I have three brothers with doctorates, all in the field of psychology. My sister, unlike her brothers, became a computer programmer.

The earliest memories of my childhood are filled primarily with images of a close-knit family who struggled economically to make ends meet. For the brief period we were on welfare, I could sense the shame and humiliation my parents felt. Everyone in the family worked to contribute until we could again stand with our heads held high. *People who have never seriously lacked the necessities of life will never truly understand the experience of being poor, constantly worrying about how to pay even the most inexpensive bills, what a catastrophic event a broken appliance represents, not being able to pay for school field trips, walking miles every day to save bus fare, working after school till midnight to help the family financially, purchasing soda or candy as holiday gifts for one another, having to completely support ourselves through college and graduate school, and knowing that others seemed to shun us because we were poor.* To deal with our isolation, we kept to ourselves as a family, and learned to depend only on ourselves or one another.

In graduate school I recall how my classmates in counseling psychology often spoke about the desire to help those less fortunate than them, actively spoke against inequality in our society, and spoke of their desire to work on behalf of social justice. I never doubted their sincerity, but I often doubted their ability to understand what they spoke so passionately about. To me, the many social injustices they talked about were purely an intellectual exercise. While well intentioned, they seemed much more interested in private practice, opening an office, and hanging out their shingles. Perhaps I am being harsh on them, but that was how it struck me then. *These experiences led me to conclude that helping others required understanding worldviews influenced by socioeconomic status and race on both cognitive and emotional levels.*

When I was in fourth grade, my father wanted better housing for his family, and moved us outside of Chinatown. The new neighborhood, which was primarily White, was not receptive to a family of color, and we were not only objects of curiosity, but of ridicule and scorn as well. *As I reflect upon it now, this was the beginning of my racial/cultural awakening and my experience with racial prejudice and discrimination. And, while I did not know it then, it was the beginning of my journey to understanding the meaning of racism, and the many social injustices that infect our society.* But in those early days, I allowed the reactions of my classmates to make me feel ashamed of being Chinese.

My older brother David and my younger brother Stan entered Abernathy grade school with me, where we immediately became objects of hostility and constant teasing. We were called "ching-chong chinaman," made fun of because of our "slanty eyes" and strange language. In Chinatown, we lived among other Chinese Americans, accepted by the community and protected and buffered from the larger society. In the southeast district of Portland, we were no longer in the majority, and were considered undesirable by many. As I recall, this was the most unpleasant and painful part of my early childhood. We were the victims of stereotyping, considered to be nerds—passive, weak, inhibited, and subhuman aliens. Because my brother Dave was the oldest, he was often forced to fight White classmates on behalf of his younger brothers.

I vividly recall one incident that was to forever change my perception of being Chinese American. A large group of White students, who had been antagonistic to us for the better part of our early school years, chased the three of us to our front yard. There they circled us, chanting unmentionable names, and told us to leave the neighborhood. I was truly frightened, but stood shoulder to shoulder with Dave and Stan to confront the large group. All three of us were much smaller than our White peers and I kept glancing to our house porch, trying to get my brothers to break for it. Dave, however, kept inching toward the group, and I could see he had somehow turned his fear to anger. I realized later that for us to start running would reinforce the stereotype that Asians were weaklings and were afraid to fight.

Just as it appeared a fight was imminent, my mother opened the door of the house, strode to the edge of the porch, and in a voice filled with anger, asked what was going on. When no one responded, she said if a fight was to happen, it should be fair. She identified one of the ringleaders, probably the biggest of the boys in the group. Then she asked my brother Dave to fight him. This not only shocked us, but the entire group of boys. To make a long story short, Dave gave the other boy a bloody nose due to a series of lucky blows. The fight ended as fast as it had begun. At times, I have often wondered what would have happened if he had lost. It was a gamble that my mother was willing to take, because she believed that despite the outcome, pride and integrity could not be lost.

I will never forget that incident. *It taught me several important lessons in life that have remained with me to this day and form the basis of much of my professional work. First, we live in a society that has low tolerance for racial/cultural differences. Our unconscious social conditioning makes it easy for us to associate differences with deviance, pathology, and lesser value in society. Second, stereotypes held by society can also do great harm to racial/ethnic minorities. Not only are they held by the majority culture, but they can become deeply ingrained in minorities as well. When facing the wrath of the band of boys, I never imagined Dave would stand his ground and fight as he did. More astonishing, however, was to witness a tiny Asian woman—my mother— take charge of the situation and encourage a fight. Any thought on my part that Asians were weak and unable to fight back disappeared that day. Third, I felt a sense of pride in being a member of the Sue family and of being Chinese; something my Dad had always stressed. No group, I realized, should be made to feel ashamed of themselves.*

The College and Graduate School Years

In my college and graduate school years, I continued to feel like an outsider. Perhaps that was the reason I chose to go into the field of psychology. Not only was I always trying to understand people as an observer, but I became attuned to myself as a racial/cultural being. While my classmates were friendly and accepting, I felt that the curriculum often lacked validity and did not seem to match my experiential reality. *I found psychology fascinating, but the theories of human behavior seemed culture bound and limited in their ability to explain my own personal journey as an Asian American.* This was especially true when I entered the counseling psychology program at the University of Oregon.

Despite being enthused and motivated by graduate work, my education continued to be monocultural. Indeed, while the terms *multicultural, diversity, cultural competence,* and *racial identity* are common in psychology curricula today, they were nonexistent during my graduate school years. While issues relating to minority groups were occasionally raised in my courses, the focus was always on the uniqueness of the individual or the universal aspects of the human condition. My professors operated with the certainty that similarities could bridge all differences, that stressing differences was potentially divisive, and that we were all the same under the skin. *It was only later that I realized why I was so alienated from these concepts, although they had a degree of legitimacy. First, as an Asian American, the avoidance of discussing racial differences negated an important aspect of my racial identity. Second, I realized that my professors knew little about racial groups and felt uncomfortable with talking about group differences.*

During my undergraduate and graduate years, I became very involved with the Vietnam antiwar movement, participated in teach-ins, demonstrations, and other educational forums, trying to get others to see the moral injustice of the United States' actions. For the first time in my life, I no longer felt like an outsider. *I felt a powerful kinship and camaraderie that made me realize the power of the collective and group action. At times it was almost spiritual.* I also became involved intellectually with the Free Speech movement and the Third World Strike. I longed to be at Berkeley or San Francisco State University, where all the demonstrations and outpouring of intellectual thought emerged. I could relate well to the denunciations of oppression and injustice, and they stirred up feelings from my childhood. The Black Power movement, rise of the Black Panthers, the words of Malcolm X, Huey Newton, H. Rap Brown, and other activists seemed to resonate with my experiential reality. They spoke about oppression, injustice, prejudice, and discrimination in a way that made more sense to me than much of my graduate school education.

First Job—A Counseling Psychologist

I guess you would say that it was no coincidence that my first job was as a counseling psychologist at the University of California, Berkeley, Counseling Center. Throughout my doctoral studies, I always believed that I wanted to practice and work with clients. While I interviewed at places that offered me a larger salary, the allure of Berkeley and its social activism was too much to resist. *As it was at the end of the Third World Strike, my Berkeley years represented a racial and cultural awakening for me unsurpassed in any other period of my life.* In Oregon, there were few Asian Americans, but at Berkeley, the student body was greatly represented by Asian Pacific Islanders.

While I was working at Berkeley, I had the good fortune to meet my future wife, Paulina. She was in her last year of obtaining a teaching credential, and was a resident assistant at one of the dormitories on campus. I must confess that I was originally attracted to her because of her startling beauty. But, it did not take me long to realize that she was exceptionally intelligent and firm in her beliefs and values, and I marveled at her racial/ethnic pride. Contrary to my early feelings of inferiority associated with being Asian, she had never experienced such feelings; another important seed was planted in my journey to cultural awareness and pride. We eventually married and raised two children, a son and a daughter, whom I hope will always feel pride in their ethnic heritage.

At the counseling center, I saw many Asian American clients, many of them expressing personal and social problems that were similar to mine. *It was not the cultural differences, and the invalidation of being a racial minority in this country, that seemed to affect their lives, but the sociopolitical pressures placed upon them.* Like me, they were made to believe that being different was the problem. *It was at that period in my life that I came to the realization that being different was* not *the problem. It was society's perception of being different that lay at the basis of the problems encountered by many racial/ethnic minorities.* While I like to think that I helped them in their adjustment to societal intolerance, I confess that they helped me more. They validated my thinking, made me see how counseling/therapy attempted to adjust them to an intolerant system, and demonstrated how the practices of clinical work were antagonistic to their cultural and life experiences, and the importance of realizing that much of the problems encountered by minorities lay in the social system.

Going into Academia

While I enjoyed working with clients, I was not satisfied with the slow pace of therapy and the knowledge that the problems encountered by many clients were due to external circumstances. *I discovered that many of the problems encountered, for example, by Asian Americans and other people of color were due to systemic forces such as discrimination, prejudice, and injustice.* Having access to data at the Berkeley Counseling Center on Asian American students led me to conduct a series of studies on Chinese and Japanese students. The results reaffirmed my belief that sociopolitical forces were important considerations in the lives of people of color. The results of my early research instilled a hunger in me to contribute to the knowledge base of psychology. At that time, getting research published in top-notch psychology journals was difficult. Editors and editorial boards did not consider ethnic research of importance or of major relevance to the profession. It was a difficult time to get multicultural research published.

My early work on Asian American psychology and my eventual move into academia, however, eventually brought me to the attention of the American Personnel and Guidance Association (now the American Counseling Association), and I was appointed editor of their flagship journal. As the youngest editor ever appointed (at the age of 31), I was still quite naive about the internal organizational politics of the association. I radically altered the appearance of the journal, appointed many racial/ethnic minority members to the editorial board, and changed the philosophy of the journal to be more inclusive. The journal published major articles on racial/ethnic minority mental health, work with minorities, systems intervention, and psychoeducational approaches. Many of our special issues pushed the envelope on social justice; one of them, on human sexuality, caused quite a stir in the profession. There was a move to remove me as editor because of the controversial nature of the topics and my stand on social justice issues. While it was one of the most painful periods of my professional life, fortunately many colleagues rallied to my defense. Nevertheless, the toll from those who called for my resignation or removal made me decide not to continue in my second term. *The lesson, however, that I learned from this experience was that swimming upstream, or going against the prevailing beliefs/practices of the times, can lead to great stress and pain.*

Work on Multicultural Counseling and Therapy

Throughout the 70s, my clinical experience and research on minority mental health led me to conclude that traditional counseling and psychotherapy were Western European constructions that were oftentimes inappropriately applied to racial/ethnic minorities. Indeed, I began to realize that while mental health providers could be well intentioned in their desire to help clients of color, the goals and process of counseling and psychotherapy were often antagonistic to the life experiences and cultural values of their clients. *Without awareness and knowledge of race, culture, and ethnicity, counselors and other helping professionals could unwittingly engage in cultural oppression.* Studying the culture-bound nature of counseling led me to study other racial groups as well. What I found were similar concerns among African American, Latino/Hispanic American, and Native American colleagues. All felt that traditional mental health concepts and practices were inappropriate and sometimes detrimental to the life experiences of the very clients they hoped to help.

My work led to several publications that attacked the culture-bound nature of mental health practice and suggested radical changes in the delivery of services to a diverse population. Because I took great pains to document my work, it was well received on an academic level, but failed to have a major impact on mental health delivery systems. Psychologists continued to believe that traditional forms of counseling and psychotherapy could be universally applied to all populations and situations.

In the early 1980s, things began to change. Increasingly, ethnic minority psychologists voiced concerns with the need for counselors to own up to their biases, stereotypes, and inaccurate assumptions of people of color. I credit two major events that radically altered my work and influence on the field. First, Leo Goldman, a valued colleague and elder in the field of counseling psychology, asked me to write a book for his series on counseling and human services. He was one of the few White psychologists who seemed genuinely to understand my research and ideas. More importantly, being a critic himself of traditional counseling, he encouraged me to put what I had to say in a book that would be unconstrained by reviewers. Concurrently, Allen Ivey, then president of the division of counseling psychology, asked me to chair the education and training committee and to develop standards or competencies for multicultural counseling. These publications became two of the most frequently cited in the field (Ponterotto & Sabnani, 1989).

Expanding Social Justice Horizons

In 1997 I was invited to address President Clinton's Race Advisory Board on what the average American could do to help eradicate racism. As some of you may recall, the National Dialogue on Race was one of President Clinton's attempts to address what many of us consider to be one of the great social ills of our society, that of racism. *The preparation that went into the national address, which was shown on C-Span, CNN, and many major outlets, combined with my increasing awareness of racism and the hate mail that I received as a result of my testimony, made me realize several things. First, honest discussions of racism are difficult for our society, and hot buttons are pushed in people when this is brought to their attention. Second, negative reactions are often the result of defensiveness brought forth by their denial of personal responsibility for racial inequities in our society. Third, it made me realize the reason why many have difficulty in the battle to eliminate racism. It is because they are unaware of their own personal and professional complicity in perpetuating racism.*

That experience had a major impact on my current work and my burgeoning belief that social therapy or work toward social justice is also a part of what helping professionals should be doing. I do not mean to minimize the importance of counseling and therapy (it will always be needed), but such an approach tends toward remediation rather than prevention. *If injustice in the form of racism, sexism, homophobia, and other forms of social oppression form the basis of the many individual and social ills of society, do not we as helping professionals also have a moral and ethical responsibility to address those systemic forces responsible for psychological problems?* R. D. Laing, an existential psychotherapist, once made a statement that went something like this: Is schizophrenia always a sick response to a healthy society? Or, can schizophrenia be seen as a healthy response to a sick society? Changing the individual to adjust or conform to a sick system or unhealthy situation may (unwittingly) be the goal of unenlightened therapy. If depression, anxiety, and feelings of low self-esteem are the result of unhealthy societal forces (stereotyping, limited opportunities, prejudice, and discrimination), shouldn't our efforts be directed at eradicating societal policies, practices, and structures that oppress, rather than simply changing the individual?

While all of us must make choices about where to place our efforts, it is now clear to me that multiculturalism and the eradication of racism are about social justice. And this current edition of *CCD* is filled with this belief. Social justice is about equal access and opportunity and about building a healthy, validating society for all groups. That is why it is so important that psychology, and especially counseling, move toward cultural competence and multiculturalism. In this edition, I make several important points that have since guided my understanding of prejudice and discrimination. First, the goal of our society—and by association, of the helping professions—should be to make the invisible, visible. What I call ethnocentric monoculturalism and *whiteness* represent invisible veils that define the reality of most White Americans. Second, power resides in the group that is able to define reality (in this case, White America). Last, the group that owns history possesses the power to impose their worldview or reality upon less powerful groups. As such, if one's reality or truth does not correspond with those in power, unintentional oppression may be the result. From viewing the importance of changing individuals so they can function better in our society, to work with organizations and systems, I have become increasingly involved in social policy.

In closing, please note that understanding the worldview of diverse populations means not only acquiring knowledge of cultural values and differences, but being aware of the sociopolitical experiences of culturally diverse groups in a monocultural society. This perspective means the ability to empathize with the pain, anguish, mistrust, and sense of betrayal suffered by persons of color, women, gays, and other marginalized groups. *Sad to say, this empathic ability is blocked when readers react with defensiveness and anger upon hearing the life stories of those most disempowered in our society.* I implore you not to allow your initial negative feelings to interfere with your ultimate aim of learning from this text as you journey toward cultural competence. I have always believed that our worth as human beings is derived from the collective relationships we hold with all people; that we are people of emotions, intuitions, and spirituality, and that the lifeworld of people can only be understood through lived realities. While I believe strongly in the value of science and the importance psychology places on empiricism, *Counseling the Culturally Diverse* is based on the premise that a profession that fails to recognize the heart and soul of the human condition is a discipline that is spiritually and emotionally bankrupt. *In many respects,* CCD *is the story of my life journey as a person of color.* As such, the book not only touches on the theory and practice of multicultural counseling and psychotherapy, but also reveals the hearts and souls of our diverse clienteles.

Implications for Clinical Practice

1. Listen and be open to the stories of those most disempowered in this society. Counseling has always been about listening to our clients. Don't allow your emotional reactions to negate their voices because you become defensive. Know that while you were not born wanting to be racist or sexist, your cultural conditioning has imbued certain biases and prejudices in you. No person or group is free from inheriting the biases of this society. It does not matter whether you are gay or straight, White or person of color, or male or female. All of us have inherited biases. Rather than deny them and allow them to unintentionally control our lives and actions, openly acknowledge them so that their detrimental effects can be minimized. As a helping professional, the ability to understand the worldview of clients means listening in an open and nondefensive way.

2. Understanding groups different from you requires more than book learning. While helpful in your journey to cultural competence, it is also necessary to supplement your intellectual development with experiential reality. Socialize, work with, and get to know culturally diverse groups by interacting with them on personal and intimate levels. You must actively reach out to understand their worldviews. After all, if you want to learn about sexism, do you ask men or women? If you want to learn about racism, do you ask Whites or persons of color? If you want to understand homophobia, do you ask straights or gays?

3. Don't be afraid to explore yourself as a racial/cultural being. An overwhelming number of mental health practitioners believe they are decent, good, and moral people. They believe strongly in the basic tenets of the Declaration of Independence, the U.S. Constitution, and the Bill of Rights. Concepts of democracy and fairness are present throughout these important and historic documents. Because most of us would not intentionally discriminate, we often find great difficulty in realizing that our belief systems and actions may have oppressed others. As long as we deny these aspects of our upbringing and heritage, we will continue to be oblivious to our roles in perpetuating injustice to others. As mentioned in this chapter, multiculturalism is about social justice.

4. When you experience intense emotions, acknowledge them and try to understand what they mean for you. For example, *CCD* speaks about unfairness, racism, sexism, and prejudice, making some feel accused and blamed. The "isms" of our society are not pleasant topics, and we often feel unfairly blamed. However, blame is not the intent of multicultural training, but accepting responsibility for rectifying past injustices and creating a community that is more inclusive and equitable in its treatment of racial/ethnic minorities are central to its mission. We realize that it is unfair and counterproductive to attribute blame to counselors for past injustices. However, it is important that helping professionals realize how they may still benefit from the past actions of their predecessors and continue to reap the benefits of the present social/educational arrangements. When these arrangements are unfair to some and benefit others, we must all accept the responsibility for making changes that will allow for equal access and opportunity. Further, our concerns are directed at the present and the future, not the past. While history is important in many ways, there are certainly enough issues in the here and now that require our attention. Prejudice and discrimination in society are not just things of the past.

5. Don't be afraid or squelch dissent and disagreements. Open dialogue—to discuss and work through differences in thoughts, beliefs, and values—is crucial to becoming culturally competent. It is healthy when we are allowed to freely dialogue with one another. Many people of color believe that dialogues on race, gender, and sexual orientation turn into monologues in order to prevent dissenting voices. The intense expressions of affect often produce discomfort in all of us. It is always easier to avoid talking or thinking about race and racism, for example, than entering into a searching dialogue about the topics. The academic protocol, and to some extent the politeness protocol, serve as barriers to open and honest dialogue about the pain of discrimination, and how each and every one of us perpetuate bias through our silence or obliviousness.

6. Last, continue to use these suggestions in reading throughout the text. While every chapter ends with a section titled "Implications for Clinical Practice," we encourage you to apply these five suggestions at the end of every reading. What emotions or feelings are you experiencing? Where are they coming from? Are they blocking your understanding of the material? What do they mean for you personally and as a helping professional? Take an active role in exploring yourself as a racial cultural being, as Mark Kiselica did.

The Superordinate Nature of Multicultural Counseling and Therapy

What is multicultural counseling/therapy? Isn't "good counseling," good counseling? How applicable are our standards of clinical practice for racial/ethnic minority populations? Is there any difference between counseling a White client and counseling a Black client? What do we mean by multiculturalism and diversity? Do other special populations such as women, gays and lesbians, the elderly, and those with disabilities constitute a distinct cultural group? What do we mean by the phrase *cultural competence*?

Chapter 2

Professor Jonathon Murphy felt annoyed at one of his Latina social work graduate students. Partway through a lecture on family systems theory, the student had interrupted him with a question. Dr. Murphy had just finished an analysis of a case study on a Latino family in which the 32-year-old daughter was still living at home and could not obtain her father's approval for her upcoming marriage. The caseworker's report suggested excessive dependency as well as "pathological enmeshment" on the part of the daughter. As more and more minority students entered the program and took Dr. Murphy's classes on social work and family therapy, this sort of question began to be asked more frequently, and usually in a challenging manner.

STUDENT: *Aren't these theories culture-bound? It seems to me that counseling strategies aimed at helping family members to individuate or become autonomous units would not be received favorably by many Latino families. I've been told that Asian Americans would also find great discomfort in the value orientation of the White social worker.*

PROFESSOR: *Of course we need to consider the race and cultural background of our clients and their families. But it's clear that healthy development of family members must move toward the goal of maturity, and that means being able to make decisions on their own without being dependent or enmeshed in the family network.*

STUDENT: *But isn't that a value judgment based on seeing a group's value system as pathological? I'm just wondering whether the social worker might be culturally insensitive to the Latino family. She doesn't appear culturally competent. To describe a Latino family member as "excessively dependent" fails to note the value placed on the importance of the family. The social worker seems to have hidden racial biases, as well as difficulty relating to cultural differences.*

PROFESSOR: *I think you need to be careful about calling someone incompetent and "racist." You don't need to be a member of a racial minority group to understand the experience of discrimination. All counseling and therapy is to some extent multicultural. What we need to realize is that race and ethnicity are only one set of differences. For example, class, gender, and sexual orientation are all legitimate group markers.*

STUDENT: *I wasn't calling the social worker a racist. I was reading a study that indicated the need for social workers to become culturally competent and move toward the development of culture-specific strategies in working with racial minorities. Being a White person, she seems out of touch with the family's experience of discrimination and prejudice. I was only trying to point out that racial issues appear more salient and problematic in our society and that. . . .*

PROFESSOR [INTERRUPTING AND RAISING HIS VOICE]: *I want all of you [class members] to understand what I'm about to say. First, our standards of practice and codes of ethics have been developed over time to apply equally to all groups. Race is important, but our similarities far exceed differences. After all, there is only one race, the human race! Second, just because a group might value one way of doing things does not make it healthy or right. Culture does not always justify a practice! Third, I don't care whether the family is red, black, brown, yellow, or even white: Good counseling is good counseling! Further, it's important for us not to become myopic in our understanding of cultural differences. To deny the importance of other human dimensions such as sexual orientation, gender, disability, religious orientation, and so forth is not to see the whole person. Finally, everyone has experienced bias, discrimination, and stereotyping. You don't have to be a racial minority to understand the detrimental consequences of oppression. As an Irish descendant, I've heard many demeaning Irish jokes, and my ancestors certainly encountered severe discrimination when they first immigrated to this country. Part of our task, as therapists, is to help all our clients deal with their experiences of being different.*

In one form or another, difficult dialogues such as these are occurring throughout our training institutions, halls of ivy, governmental agencies, corporate boardrooms, and community meeting places. Participants in such dialogues come with different perspectives and strong convictions that operate from culturally conditioned assumptions outside their levels of awareness. These assumptions are important to clarify because they define different realities and determine our actions. In the helping professions, insensitive counseling and therapy can result in cultural oppression rather than liberation (Constantine, 2007). Let us explore more thoroughly the dialogue between professor and student to understand the important multicultural themes being raised.

Theme One: Cultural Universality versus Cultural Relativism

One of the primary issues raised by the student and professor relates to the *etic* (culturally universal) versus *emic* (culturally specific) perspectives. The professor operates from the etic position. He believes, for example, that good counseling is good counseling; that disorders such as depression, schizophrenia, and sociopathic behaviors appear in all cultures and societies; that minimal modification in their diagnosis and treatment is required; and that Western concepts of normality and abnormality can be considered universal and equally applicable across cultures (Howard, 1992; Suzuki, Kugler, & Aquiar, 2005).

The student, however, operates from an emic position and challenges these assumptions. She tries to make the point that lifestyles, cultural values, and worldviews affect the expression and determination of deviant behavior. She argues that all theories of human development arise from a cultural context and that using the Euro-American value of "independence" as healthy development—especially on collectivistic cultures such as Latinos or Asian Americans—may constitute bias (Ivey, Ivey, Myers, & Sweeney, 2005; D. Sue, D. W. Sue, & S. Sue, 2006).

This is one of the most important issues currently confronting the helping professions. There is little doubt that to a large degree the code of ethics and standards of practice in counseling, psychotherapy, social work, and other mental health specialties assume universality. Thus, if the assumption that the origin, process, and manifestation of disorders are similar across cultures were correct, then guidelines and strategies for treatment would appear to be appropriate in application to all groups.

In the other camp, however, are mental health professionals who give great weight to how culture and life experiences affect the expression of deviant behavior and who propose the use of culture-specific strategies in counseling and therapy (Moodley & West, 2005; Parham, White, & Ajamu, 1999; D. W. Sue & Constantine 2005). Such professionals point out that current guidelines and standards of clinical practice are culture-bound and often inappropriate for racial/ethnic minority groups.

Which view is correct? Should treatment be based on cultural universality or cultural relativism? Few mental health professionals today embrace the extremes of either position, although most gravitate toward one or the other. Proponents of cultural universality focus on disorders and their consequent treatments and minimize cultural factors, whereas proponents of cultural relativism focus on the culture and on how the disorder is manifested and treated within it. Both views have validity. It is naive to believe that no disorders cut across different cultures/societies or share universal characteristics. In addition, one could make the case that even though hallucinating may be viewed as normal in some cultures (cultural relativism), proponents of cultural universality argue that it still represents a breakdown in "normal" biological-cognitive processes. Likewise, it is equally naive to believe that the relative frequencies and manners of symptom formation for various disorders do not reflect the dominant cultural values and lifestyles of a society. Nor would it be beyond our scope to entertain the notion that various diverse groups may respond better to culture-specific therapeutic strategies. A more fruitful approach to these opposing views might be to address the following two questions: "What is universal in human behavior that is also relevant to counseling and therapy?" and "What is the relationship between cultural norms, values, and attitudes, on the one hand, and the manifestation of behavior disorders and their treatments, on the other?"

Theme Two: The Emotional Consequences of "Race"

A tug-of-war appears to be occurring between the professor and the student concerning the importance of "race" in the therapeutic process. Disagreements of this type are usually related not only to differences in definitions, but also to hot buttons being pushed in the participants. We address the former shortly but concentrate on the latter because the interaction between the professor and the student appears to be related more to the emotive qualities of the topic, as discussed in Chapter 1. What motivates the professor, for example, to make the unwarranted assumption that the Latina was accusing the social worker of being a racist? What leads the professor, whether consciously or unconsciously, to minimize or avoid considering race as a powerful variable in the therapeutic process? He seemingly does this by two means: (1) diluting the importance of race by using an abstract and universal statement ("There is only one race, the human race") and (2) shifting the dialogue to discussions of other group differences (gender, sexual orientation, disability, and class) and equating race as only one of these many variables.

We are not dismissing the importance of other group differences in affecting human behavior, nor the fact that we share many commonalities regardless of our race or gender. These are very legitimate points. We submit, however, that like many others the professor is uncomfortable with open discussions of race because of the embedded or nested emotions that he has been culturally conditioned to hold. For example, discussions of race often evoke strong passions associated with racism, discrimination, prejudice, personal blame, political correctness, anti-White attitudes, quotas, and many other emotion-arousing concepts. At times, the deep reactions that many people have about discussions on race interfere with their ability to communicate freely and honestly and to listen to others. Feelings of guilt, blame, anger, and defensiveness (as in the case of the professor) are unpleasant. No wonder it is easier to avoid dealing with such a hot potato. Yet it is precisely these emotionally laden feelings that must be expressed and explored before productive change will occur. In Chapter 11 we devote considerable space to this issue. Until mental health providers work through these intense feelings, which are often associated with their own biases and preconceived notions, they will continue to be ineffective in working with a culturally diverse population.

Theme Three: The Inclusive or Exclusive Nature of Multiculturalism

While the professor may be avoiding the topic of race by using other group differences to shift the dialogue, he raises a very legitimate content issue about the inclusiveness or exclusiveness of multicultural dialogues. Are definitions of multiculturalism based only on race, or does multiculturalism encompass gender, sexual orientation, disability, and other significant reference groups? Isn't the professor correct in observing that almost all counseling is multicultural? We believe that resistance to including other groups in the multicultural dialogue is related to three factors: (1) Many racial minorities believe that including other groups (as in the previous example) in the multicultural dialogue will enable people who are uncomfortable with confronting their own biases to avoid dealing with the hard issues related to race and racism; (2) taken to the extreme, saying that all counseling is multicultural makes the concept meaningless because the ultimate extension equates all differences with individual differences; and (3) there are philosophical disagreements among professionals over whether gender and sexual orientation, for example, constitute distinct overall cultures.

We believe that each of us is born into a cultural context of existing beliefs, values, rules, and practices. Individuals who share the same cultural matrix with us exhibit similar values and belief systems. The process of socialization is generally the function of the family and occurs through participation in many cultural groups. Reference groups related to race, ethnicity, sexual orientation, gender, age, and socioeconomic status exert a powerful influence over us and influence our worldviews.

Whether you are a man or a woman, Black or White, gay or straight, disabled or able-bodied, married or single, and whether you live in Appalachia or

New York all result in sharing similar experiences and characteristics. While this text is focused more on racial/ethnic minorities, we also believe in the inclusive definition of multiculturalism.

Theme Four: The Sociopolitical Nature of Counseling/Therapy

The dialogue between professor and student illustrates nicely the symbolic meanings of power imbalance and power oppression. Undeniably, the relationship between the professor and student is not an equal one. The professor occupies a higher-status role and is clearly in a position of authority and control. He determines the content of the course, the textbooks to read, right or wrong answers on an exam, and he evaluates the learning progress of students. Not only is he in a position to define reality (standards of helping can be universally applied; normality is equated with individualism; and one form of discrimination is similar to another), but he can enforce it through grading students as well. As we usually accept the fact that educators have knowledge, wisdom, and experience beyond that of their students, this differential power relationship does not evoke surprise or great concern, especially if we hold values and beliefs similar to those of our teachers. However, what if the upbringing, beliefs, and assumptions of minority students render the curriculum less relevant to their experiential reality? More important, what if the students' worldviews are a more accurate reflection of reality than are those of the professors?

Many racial/ethnic minorities, gays and lesbians, and women have accused those who hold power and influence of imposing their views of reality upon them. The professor, for example, equates maturity with autonomy and independence. The Latina student points out that among Hispanics collectivism and group identity may be more desirable than individualism. Unfortunately, Dr. Murphy fails to consider this legitimate point and dismisses the observation by simply stating, "Culture does not always justify a practice." In the mental health fields, the standards used to judge normality and abnormality come from a predominantly Euro-American perspective. As such, they are culture-bound and may be inappropriate in application to culturally diverse groups. When mental health practitioners unwittingly impose these standards without regard for differences in race, culture, gender, and sexual orientation, they may be engaging in cultural oppression (Neville, Worthington, & Spanierman, 2001). As a result, counseling and psychotherapy become a sociopolitical act. Indeed, a major thesis of this book is that counseling and psychotherapy have done great harm to culturally diverse groups by invalidating their life experiences, by defining their cultural values or differences as deviant and pathological, by denying them culturally appropriate care, and by imposing the values of a dominant culture upon them.

Theme Five: The Nature of Multicultural Counseling Competence

The Latina student seems to question the social worker's clinical or cultural competence in treating a family of color. In light of the professor's response to his student, one might question his cultural sensitivity as a teacher as well. If counseling, psychotherapy, and education can be viewed as sociopolitical acts, and if we accept the fact that our theories of counseling are culture-bound, then is it possible that mental health providers trained in traditional Euro-American programs may be guilty of cultural oppression in working with clients of color? The question our profession must ask is this: Is counseling/clinical competence the same as multicultural counseling competence? Dr. Murphy seems to believe that "good counseling" subsumes cultural competence, or that it is a subset of good clinical skills. Our contention, however, is that cultural competence is superordinate to counseling competence. Let us briefly explore the rationale for our position.

While there are disagreements over the definition of cultural competence, many of us know clinical incompetence when we see it; we recognize it by its horrendous outcomes, or by the human toll it takes on our minority clients. For example, for some time the profession and mental health professionals themselves have been described in very unflattering terms by multicultural specialists: (1) they are insensitive to the needs of their culturally diverse clients, do not accept, respect, and understand cultural differences, are arrogant and contemptuous, and have little understanding of their prejudices (Ridley, 2005; Thomas & Sillen, 1972); (2) clients of color, women, and gays and lesbians frequently complain that they feel abused, intimidated, and harassed by nonminority personnel (Atkinson, Morten, & Sue, 1998; President's Commission on Mental Health, 1978); (3) discriminatory practices in mental health delivery systems are deeply embedded in the ways in which the services are organized and in how they are delivered to minority populations, and are reflected in biased diagnosis and treatment, in indicators of "dangerousness," and in the type of personnel occupying decision-making roles (T. L. Cross, Bazron, Dennis, & Isaacs, 1989); and (4) mental health professionals continue to be trained in programs in which the issues of ethnicity, gender, and sexual orientation are ignored, regarded as deficiencies, portrayed in stereotypic ways, or included as an afterthought (Laird & Green, 1996; Ponterotto, Utsey & Pedersen, 2006; U.S. Public Health Service, 2001).

From our perspective, mental health professionals have seldom functioned in a culturally competent manner. Rather, they have functioned in a monoculturally competent manner with only a limited segment of the population (White Euro-Americans), but even that is debatable. We submit that much of the current therapeutic practice taught in graduate programs derives mainly from clinical experience and research with middle- to upper-class Whites (Constantine, 2007). Even though our profession has advocated moving into the realm of empirically supported treatments (EST), little evidence exists that they are applicable to racial/ethnic minorities (Atkinson, Bui, & Mori, 2001). A review of studies on EST reveals few, if any, on racial minority populations, which renders assumptions of external validity questionable when applied to people of color (Atkinson et al.; Hall, 2001; S. Sue, 1999). If we are honest with ourselves, we can only conclude that many of our standards of professional competence (Eurocentric) are derived primarily from the values, belief systems, cultural assumptions, and traditions of the larger society.

Thus, values of individualism and psychological mindedness and using "rational approaches" to problem solve have much to do with how competence is defined. Yet many of our colleagues continue to hold firmly to the belief that good counseling is good counseling, thereby dismissing the centrality of culture in their definitions. The problem with traditional definitions of counseling, therapy, and mental health practice is that they arose from monocultural and ethnocentric norms that excluded other cultural groups. Mental health professionals must realize that "good counseling" uses White Euro-American norms that exclude three quarters of the world's population. Thus, it is clear to us that the more superordinate and inclusive concept is that of multicultural counseling competence, not clinical/counseling competence. Standards of helping derived from such a philosophy and framework are inclusive and offer the broadest and most accurate view of cultural competence.

A Tripartite Framework for Understanding the Multiple Dimensions of Identity

All too often, counseling and psychotherapy seem to ignore the group dimension of human existence. For example, a White counselor who works with an African American client might intentionally or unintentionally avoid acknowledging the racial or cultural background of the person by stating, "We are all the same under the skin" or "Apart from your racial background, we are all unique." We have already indicated possible reasons why this happens, but such avoidance tends to negate an intimate aspect of the client's group identity. These forms of microinvalidations will be discussed more fully in Chapter 5. As a result, the African American client might feel misunderstood and resentful toward the helping professional, hindering the effectiveness of multicultural counseling. Besides unresolved personal issues arising from the counselor, the assumptions embedded in Western forms of therapy exaggerate the chasm between therapist and minority client.

First, the concepts of counseling and psychotherapy are uniquely Euro-American in origin, as they are based on certain philosophical assumptions and values that are strongly endorsed by Western civilizations. On the one side are beliefs that people are unique and that the psychosocial unit of operation is the individual; on the other side are beliefs that clients are the same and that the goals and techniques of counseling and therapy are equally applicable across all groups. Taken to its extreme, this latter approach nearly assumes that persons of color, for example, are White and that race and culture are insignificant variables in counseling and psychotherapy. Statements like "There is only one race, the human race" and "Apart from your racial/cultural background, you are no different from me" are indicative of the tendency to avoid acknowledging how race, culture, and other group dimensions may influence identity, values, beliefs, behaviors, and the perception of reality (Carter, 2005; Helms, 1990; D. W. Sue, 2001).

Related to the negation of race, we have indicated that a most problematic issue deals with the inclusive or exclusive nature of multiculturalism. A number of psychologists have indicated that an inclusive definition of multiculturalism (gender, ability/disability, sexual orientation, etc.) can obscure the understanding and study of race as a powerful dimension of human existence (Carter, 2005; Helms & Richardson, 1997). This stance is not intended to minimize the importance of the many cultural dimensions of human identity but rather emphasizes the greater discomfort that many psychologists experience in dealing with issues of race rather than with other sociodemographic differences. As a result, race becomes less salient and allows us to avoid addressing problems of racial prejudice, racial discrimination, and systemic racial oppression. This concern appears to have great legitimacy. We have noted, for example, that when issues of race are discussed in the classroom, a mental health agency, or some other public forum, it is not uncommon for participants to refocus the dialogue on differences related to gender, socioeconomic status, or religious orientation (à la Dr. Murphy).

On the other hand, many groups often rightly feel excluded from the multicultural debate and find themselves in opposition to one another. Thus, enhancing multicultural understanding and sensitivity means balancing our understanding of the sociopolitical forces that dilute the importance of race, on the one hand, and our need to acknowledge the existence of other group identities related to social class, gender, ability/disability, age, religious affiliation, and sexual orientation, on the other (D. W. Sue, Bingham, Porche-Burke, & Vasquez, 1999).

There is an old Asian saying that goes something like this: "All individuals, in many respects, are (a) like no other individuals, (b) like some individuals, and (c) like all other individuals." While this statement might sound confusing and contradictory, Asians believe these words to have great wisdom and to be entirely true with respect to human development and identity. We have found the tripartite framework shown in Figure 2.1 (D. W. Sue, 2001) to be useful in exploring and understanding the formation of personal

Figure 2.1

Tripartite Development of Personal Identity

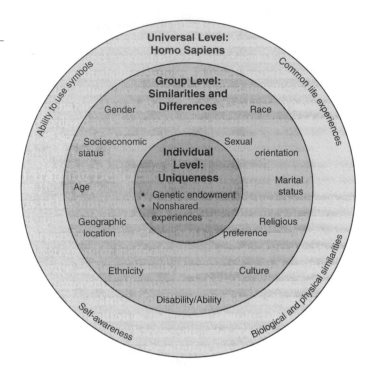

Figure 2.1

Tripartite Development of Personal Identity

identity. The three concentric circles illustrated in Figure 2.1 denote individual, group, and universal levels of personal identity.

Individual level: "All individuals are, in some respects, like no other individuals." There is much truth in the saying that no two individuals are identical. We are all unique biologically, and recent breakthroughs in mapping the human genome have provided some startling findings. Biologists, anthropologists, and evolutionary psychologists had looked to the Human Genome Project as potentially providing answers to comparative and evolutionary biology, to find the secrets to life. Although the project has provided valuable answers to many questions, scientists have discovered even more complex questions. For example, they had expected to find 100,000 genes in the human genome, but approximately 20,000 were initially found, with the possible existence of another 5,000—only two or three times more than are found in a fruit fly or a nematode worm. Of those 25,000 genes, only 300 unique genes distinguish us from the mouse. In other words, human and mouse genomes are about 85 percent identical! While it may be a blow to human dignity, the more important question is how so relatively few genes can account for our humanness.

Likewise, if so few genes can determine such great differences between species, what about within the species? Human inheritance almost guarantees differences because no two individuals ever share the same genetic endowment. Further, no two of us share the exact same experiences in our society. Even identical twins, who theoretically share the same gene pool and are raised in the same family are exposed to both shared and nonshared experiences. Different experiences in school and with peers, as well as qualitative differences in how parents treat them, will contribute to individual uniqueness. Research indicates that psychological characteristics and behavior are more affected by experiences specific to a child than are shared experiences (Plomin, 1989; Rutter, 1991).

Group level: "All individuals are, in some respects, like some other individuals." As mentioned earlier, each of us is born into a cultural matrix of beliefs, values, rules, and social practices (D. W. Sue, Ivey, & Pedersen, 1996). By virtue of social, cultural, and political distinctions made in our society, perceived group membership exerts a powerful influence over how society views sociodemographic groups and over how its members view themselves and others (Atkinson et al., 1998). Group markers such as race and gender are relatively stable and less subject to change. Some markers, such as education, socioeconomic status, marital status, and geographic location, are more fluid and changeable. While ethnicity is fairly stable, some argue that it can also be fluid. Likewise, debate and controversy surround the discussions about whether sexual orientation is determined at birth and whether we should be speaking of sexuality or sexualities. Nevertheless, membership in these groups may result in shared experiences and characteristics. They may serve as powerful reference groups in the formation of worldviews. On the group level of identity, Figure 2.1 reveals that people may belong to more than one cultural group (i.e., an Asian American female with a disability), that some group identities may be more salient than others (race over religious orientation), and that the salience of cultural group identity may shift from one to the other depending on the situation. For example, a gay man with a disability may find that his disability identity is more salient among the able-bodied but that his sexual orientation is more salient among those with disabilities.

Universal level: "All individuals are, in some respects, like all other individuals." Because we are members of the human race and belong to the species *Homo sapiens,* we share many similarities. Universal to our commonalties are (a) biological and physical similarities, (b) common life experiences (birth, death, love, sadness, etc.), (c) self-awareness, and (d) the ability to use symbols such as language. In Shakespeare's *Merchant of Venice,* Shylock attempts to acknowledge the universal nature of the human condition by asking, "When you prick us, do we not bleed?" Again, while the Human Genome Project indicates that a few genes may cause major differences between and within species, it is startling how similar the genetic material within our chromosomes is and how much we share in common.

Individual and Universal Biases in Psychology and Mental Health

Unfortunately, psychology—and mental health professionals in particular—have generally focused on either the individual or universal levels of identity, placing less importance on the group level. There are several reasons for this orientation. First, our society arose from the concept of rugged individualism, and we have traditionally valued autonomy, independence, and uniqueness. Our culture assumes that individuals are the basic building blocks of our society. Sayings such as "be your own person," "stand on your own two feet," and "don't depend on anyone but yourself" reflect this value. Psychology and education represent the carriers of this value, and the study of individual differences is most exemplified in the individual intelligence testing movement that pays homage to individual uniqueness (Suzuki, Kugler, & Aquiar, 2005).

Second, the universal level is consistent with the tradition and history of psychology, which has historically sought universal facts, principles, and laws in explaining human behavior. Although an important quest, the nature of scientific inquiry has often meant studying phenomena independently of the context in which human behavior originates. Thus, therapeutic interventions from which research findings are derived may lack external validity (Chang & S. Sue, 2005).

Third, we have historically neglected the study of identity at the group level for sociopolitical and normative reasons. As we have seen, issues of race, gender, sexual orientation, and disability seem to touch hot buttons in all of us because they bring to light issues of oppression and the unpleasantness of personal biases (Helms & Richardson, 1997; D. W. Sue et al., 1998). In addition, racial/ethnic differences have frequently been interpreted from a deficit perspective and have been equated with being abnormal or pathological (Guthrie, 1997; Lee, 1993; White & Parham, 1990). We have more to say about this in the next chapter.

Nevertheless, disciplines that hope to understand the human condition cannot neglect any level of our identity. For example, psychological explanations that acknowledge the importance of group influences such as gender, race, culture, sexual orientation, socioeconomic class, and religious affiliation lead to more accurate understanding of human psychology. Failure to acknowledge these influences may skew research findings and lead to biased conclusions about human behavior that are culture-bound, class-bound, and gender-bound.

Thus, it is possible to conclude that all people possess individual, group, and universal levels of identity. A holistic approach to understanding personal identity demands that we recognize all three levels: individual (uniqueness), group (shared cultural values and beliefs), and universal (common features of being human). Because of the historical scientific neglect of the group level of identity, this text focuses primarily on this category.

Before closing this portion of our discussion, however, we would like to add a caution. While the concentric circles in Figure 2.1 might unintentionally suggest a clear boundary, each level of identity must be viewed as permeable and ever-changing in salience. In counseling and psychotherapy, for example, a client might view his or her uniqueness as important at one point in the session and stress commonalities of the human condition at another. Even within the group level of identity, multiple forces may be operative. As mentioned earlier, the group level of identity reveals many reference groups, both fixed and nonfixed, that might impact our lives. Being an elderly, gay, Latino male, for example, represents four potential reference groups operating on the person. The culturally competent helping professional must be willing and able to touch all dimensions of human existence without negating any of the others.

The Impact of Group Identities on Counseling and Psychotherapy

Accepting the premise that race, ethnicity, and culture are powerful variables in influencing how people think, make decisions, behave, and define events, it is not far-fetched to conclude that such forces may also affect how different groups define a helping relationship (Fraga, Atkinson, & Wampold, 2002; D. W. Sue, 2001). Multicultural psychologists have noted, for example, that theories of counseling and psychotherapy represent different worldviews, each with its own values, biases, and assumptions about human behavior (Katz, 1985). Given that schools of counseling and psychotherapy arise from Western European contexts, the worldview that they espouse as reality may not be that shared by racial/ethnic minority groups in the United States, nor by those who reside in different countries (Parham, White, & Ajamu, 1999). Each cultural/racial group may have its own distinct interpretation of reality and offer a different perspective on the nature of people, the origin of disorders, standards for judging normality and abnormality, and therapeutic approaches.

Among many Asian Americans, for example, a "self orientation" is considered undesirable while a "group orientation" is highly valued. The Japanese have a saying that goes like this: "The nail that stands up should be pounded back down." The meaning seems clear: Healthy development is considering the needs of the entire group, while unhealthy development is thinking only of oneself. Likewise, relative to their Euro-American counterparts, many African Americans value the emotive and affective quality of interpersonal interactions as qualities of sincerity and authenticity (Parham, 1997; Parham et al., 1999). Euro-Americans often view the passionate expression of affect as irrational, lacking objectivity, impulsive, and immature on the part of the communicator. Thus, the autonomy-oriented goal of counseling and psychotherapy and the objective focus of the therapeutic process might prove antagonistic to the worldviews of Asian Americans and African Americans, respectively.

It is therefore highly probable that different racial/ethnic minority groups perceive the competence of the helping professional differently than do mainstream client groups. Further, if race/ethnicity affects perception, what about other group differences, such as gender and sexual orientation? If that is the case, minority clients may see a clinician who exhibits therapeutic skills that are associated primarily with mainstream therapies as having lower credibility. The important question to ask is, "Do groups such as racial/ethnic minorities define cultural competence differently than do their Euro-American counterparts?" Anecdotal observations, clinical case studies, conceptual analytical writings, and some empirical studies seem to suggest an affirmative response to the question (Constantine, 2007; Fraga et al., 2002; McGoldrick, Giordano, & Garcia-Preto, 2005; Nwachuku & Ivey, 1991; D. W. Sue & Sue, 1999; Wehrly, 1995).

What Is Multicultural Counseling/Therapy?

In light of the previous analysis, let us define *multicultural counseling/therapy* (*MCT*) as it relates to the therapy process and the roles of the mental health practitioner:

> *Multicultural counseling and therapy can be defined as both a helping role and process that uses modalities and defines goals consistent with the life experiences and cultural values of clients, recognizes client identities to include individual, group, and universal dimensions, advocates the use of universal and culture-specific strategies and roles in the healing process, and balances the importance of individualism and collectivism in the assessment, diagnosis, and treatment of client and client systems. (D. W. Sue & Torino, 2005)*

This definition often contrasts markedly with traditional definitions of counseling and psychotherapy. A more thorough analysis of these characteristics is described in Chapter 4. For now, let us extract implications for counseling practice from the definition just given.

1. *Helping role and process.* MCT involves broadening the roles that counselors play and expands the repertoire of therapy skills considered helpful and appropriate in counseling. The more passive and objective stance taken by therapists in clinical work is seen as only one method of helping. Likewise, teaching, consulting, and advocacy can supplement the conventional counselor or therapist role.

2. *Consistent with life experiences and cultural values.* Effective MCT means using modalities and defining goals for culturally diverse clients that are consistent with their racial, cultural, ethnic, gender, and sexual orientation backgrounds. Advice and suggestions, for example, may be effectively used for some client populations.

3. *Individual, group, and universal dimensions of existence.* As we have already seen, MCT acknowledges that our existence and identity are composed of individual (uniqueness), group, and universal dimensions. Any form of helping that fails to recognize the totality of these dimensions negates important aspects of a person's identity.

4. *Universal and culturespecific strategies.* Related to the second point, MCT believes that different racial/ethnic minority groups might respond best to culture-specific strategies of helping. For example, research seems to support the belief that Asian Americans are more responsive to directive/active approaches and that African Americans appreciate helpers who are authentic in their self-disclosures. Likewise, it is clear that common features in helping relationships cut across cultures and societies as well.

5. *Individualism and collectivism.* MCT broadens the perspective of the helping relationship by balancing the individualistic approach with a collectivistic reality that acknowledges our embeddedness in families, significant others, communities, and cultures. A client is perceived not just as an individual, but as an individual who is a product of his or her social and cultural context.

6. *Client and client systems.* MCT assumes a dual role in helping clients. In many cases, for example, it is important to focus on the individual clients and encourage them to achieve insights and learn new behaviors. However, when problems of clients of color reside in prejudice, discrimination, and racism of employers, educators, and neighbors, or in organizational policies or practices in schools, mental health agencies, government, business, and society, the traditional therapeutic role appears ineffective and inappropriate. The focus for change must shift to altering client systems rather than individual clients.

What Is Cultural Competence?

Consistent with this definition of MCT, it becomes clear that a culturally competent healer is working toward several primary goals (D. W. Sue et al., 1982; D. W. Sue, Arredondo, & McDavis, 1992; D. W. Sue et al., 1998). First, a culturally competent helping professional is one who is actively in the process of becoming aware of his or her own assumptions about human behavior, values, biases, preconceived notions, personal limitations, and so forth. Second, a culturally competent helping professional is one who actively attempts to understand the worldview of his or her culturally different client. In other words, what are the client's values and assumptions about human behavior, biases, and so on? Third, a culturally competent helping professional is one who is in the process of actively developing and practicing appropriate, relevant, and sensitive intervention strategies and skills in working with his or her culturally different client. These three goals make it clear that cultural competence is an active, developmental, and ongoing process and that it is aspirational rather than achieved. Let us more carefully explore these attributes of cultural competence.

Competency One: Therapist Awareness of One's Own Assumptions, Values, and Biases

In almost all human service programs, counselors, therapists, and social workers are familiar with the phrase, "Counselor, know thyself." Programs stress the importance of not allowing our own biases, values, or hang-ups to interfere with our ability to work with clients. In most cases, such a warning stays primarily on an intellectual level, and very little training is directed at having trainees get in touch with their own values and biases about human behavior. In other words, it appears to be easier to deal with trainees' cognitive understanding about their own cultural heritage, the values they hold about human behavior, their standards for judging normality and abnormality, and the culture-bound goals toward which they strive.

What makes examination of the self difficult is the emotional impact of attitudes, beliefs, and feelings associated with cultural differences such as racism, sexism, heterosexism, able-body-ism, and ageism. For example, as a member of a White Euro-American group, what responsibility do you hold for the racist, oppressive, and discriminating manner by which you personally and professionally deal with persons of color? This is a threatening question for many White people. However, to be effective in MCT means that one has adequately dealt with this question and worked through the biases, feelings, fears, and guilt associated with it.

Competency Two: Understanding the Worldview of Culturally Diverse Clients

It is crucial that counselors and therapists understand and can share the worldview of their culturally diverse clients. This statement does not mean that providers must hold these worldviews as their own, but rather that they can see and accept other worldviews in a nonjudgmental manner. Some have referred to the process as cultural role taking: The therapist acknowledges that he or she has not lived a lifetime as an Asian American, African American, American Indian, or Hispanic American person. It is almost impossible for the therapist to think, feel, and react as a racial minority individual. Nonetheless, cognitive empathy, as distinct from affective empathy, may be possible. In cultural role taking the therapist acquires practical knowledge concerning the scope and nature of the client's cultural background, daily living experience, hopes, fears, and aspirations. Inherent in cognitive empathy is the understanding of how therapy relates to the wider sociopolitical system with which minorities contend every day of their lives.

Competency Three: Developing Appropriate Intervention Strategies and Techniques

Effectiveness is most likely enhanced when the therapist uses therapeutic modalities and defines goals that are consistent with the life experiences and cultural values of the client. This basic premise will be emphasized throughout future chapters. Studies have consistently revealed that (1) economically and educationally marginalized clients may not be oriented toward "talk therapy"; (2) self-disclosure may be incompatible with the cultural values of Asian Americans, Hispanic Americans, and American Indians; (3) the sociopolitical atmosphere may dictate against self-disclosure from racial minorities and gays and lesbians; (4) the ambiguous nature of counseling may be antagonistic to life values of certain diverse groups; and (5) many minority clients prefer an active/directive approach to an inactive/nondirective one in treatment. Therapy has too long assumed that clients share a similar background and cultural heritage and that the same approaches are equally effective with all clients. This erroneous assumption needs to be buried.

Because groups and individuals differ from one another, the blind application of techniques to all situations and all populations seems ludicrous. The interpersonal transactions between the counselor and client require differential approaches that are consistent with the person's life experiences (Sue et al., 1996). In this particular case, and as mentioned earlier, it is ironic that equal treatment in therapy may be discriminatory treatment! Therapists need to understand this. As a means to prove discriminatory mental health practices, racial/ethnic minority groups have in the past pointed to studies revealing that minority clients are given less preferential forms of treatment (medication, electroconvulsive therapy, etc.). Somewhere, confusion has occurred, and it was believed that to be treated differently is akin to discrimination. The confusion centered on the distinction between equal access and opportunities versus equal treatment. Racial/ethnic minority groups may not be asking for equal treatment so much as they are asking for equal access and opportunities. This dictates a differential approach that is truly nondiscriminatory. Thus, to be an effective multicultural helper requires cultural competence. In light of the previous analysis, we define it in the following manner:

> *Cultural competence is the ability to engage in actions or create conditions that maximize the optimal development of client and client systems. Multicultural counseling competence is defined as the counselor's acquisition of awareness, knowledge, and skills needed to function effectively in a pluralistic democratic society (ability to communicate, interact, negotiate, and intervene on behalf of clients from diverse backgrounds), and on a organizational/societal level, advocating effectively to develop new theories, practices, policies, and organizational structures that are more responsive to all groups. (D. W. Sue & Torino, 2005)*

This definition of cultural competence in the helping professions makes it clear that the conventional one-to-one, in-the-office, objective form of treatment aimed at remediation of existing problems may be at odds with the sociopolitical and cultural experiences of their clients. Like the complementary definition of MCT, it addresses not only clients (individuals, families, and groups) but also client systems (institutions, policies, and practices that may be unhealthy or problematic for healthy development). This is especially true if problems reside outside rather than inside the client. For example, prejudice and discrimination such as racism, sexism, and homophobia may impede the healthy functioning of individuals and groups in our society.

Second, cultural competence can be seen as residing in three major domains: (a) attitudes/beliefs component—an understanding of one's own cultural conditioning that affects the personal beliefs, values, and attitudes of a culturally diverse population; (b) knowledge component—understanding and knowledge of the worldviews of culturally diverse individuals and groups; and (c) skills component—an ability to determine and use culturally appropriate intervention strategies when working with different groups in our society. Table 2.1 provides an outline of cultural competencies related to these three domains.

Third, in a broad sense, this definition is directed toward two levels of cultural competence: the person/individual and the organizational/system levels. The work on cultural competence has generally focused on the micro level, the individual. In the education and training of psychologists, for example, the goals have been to increase the level of self-awareness of trainees (potential biases, values, and assumptions about human behavior); to acquire knowledge of the history, culture, and life experiences of various minority groups; and to aid in developing culturally appropriate and adaptive interpersonal skills (clinical work, management, conflict resolution, etc.). Less emphasis is placed on the macro level: the profession of psychology, organizations, and the society in general (Lewis, Lewis, Daniels, & D'Andrea, 1998; D. W. Sue, 2001). We suggest that it does little good to train culturally com-

Table 2.1   **Multicultural Counseling Competencies**

I. Cultural Competence: Awareness
 1. Moved from being culturally unaware to being aware and sensitive to own cultural heritage and to valuing and respecting differences.
 2. Aware of own values and biases and of how they may affect diverse clients.
 3. Comfortable with differences that exist between themselves and their clients in terms of race, gender, sexual orientation, and other sociodemographic variables. Differences are not seen as deviant.
 4. Sensitive to circumstances (personal biases; stage of racial, gender, and sexual orientation identity; sociopolitical influences, etc.) that may dictate referral of clients to members of their own sociodemographic group or to different therapists in general.
 5. Aware of their own racist, sexist, heterosexist, or other detrimental attitudes, beliefs, and feelings.

II. Cultural Competence: Knowledge
 1. Knowledgeable and informed on a number of culturally diverse groups, especially groups therapists work with.
 2. Knowledgeable about the sociopolitical system's operation in the United States with respect to its treatment of marginalized groups in society.
 3. Possess specific knowledge and understanding of the generic characteristics of counseling and therapy.
 4. Knowledgeable of institutional barriers that prevent some diverse clients from using mental health services.

III. Cultural Competence: Skills
 1. Able to generate a wide variety of verbal and nonverbal helping responses.
 2. Able to communicate (send and receive both verbal and nonverbal messages) accurately and appropriately.
 3. Able to exercise institutional intervention skills on behalf of their client when appropriate.
 4. Able to anticipate impact of their helping styles, and limitations they possess on culturally diverse clients.
 5. Able to play helping roles characterized by an active systemic focus, which leads to environmental interventions. Not restricted by the conventional counselor/therapist mode of operation.

Source: D.W. Sue et al. (1992) and D. W. Sue et al. (1998). Readers are encouraged to review the original 34 multicultural competencies, which are fully elaborated in both publications.

petent helping professionals when the very organizations that employ them are monocultural and discourage or even punish psychologists for using their culturally competent knowledge and skills. If our profession is interested in the development of cultural competence, then it must become involved in impacting systemic and societal levels as well.

Last, our definition of cultural competence speaks strongly to the development of alternative helping roles. Much of this comes from recasting healing as involving more than one-to-one therapy. If part of cultural competence involves systemic intervention, then roles such as a consultant, change agent, teacher, and advocate supplement the conventional role of therapy. In contrast to this role, alternatives are characterized by the following:

- Having a more active helping style
- Working outside the office (home, institution, or community)
- Being focused on changing environmental conditions as opposed to changing the client
- Viewing the client as encountering problems rather than having a problem
- Being oriented toward prevention rather than remediation
- Shouldering increased responsibility for determining the course and outcome of the helping process

It is clear that these alternative roles and their underlying assumptions and practices have not been perceived as activities consistent with counseling and psychotherapy.

Multidimensional Model of Cultural Competence in Counseling

Elsewhere, one of the authors (D. W. Sue, 2001) has proposed a *multidimensional model of cultural competence (MDCC)* in counseling/therapy. This was an attempt to integrate three important features associated with effective multicultural counseling: (1) the need to consider specific cultural group worldviews associated with race, gender, sexual orientation, and so on; (2) components of cultural competence (awareness, knowledge, and skills); and (3) foci of cultural competence. These dimensions are illustrated in Figure 2.2. This model is used throughout the text to guide our discussion because it allows for the systematic identification of where interventions should potentially be directed.

Dimension I: Group-Specific Worldviews
In keeping with our all-encompassing definition of multiculturalism, we include the human differences associated with race, gender, sexual orientation, physical ability, age, and other significant reference groups. Figure 2.2 originally identified only five major groups organized around racial/ethnic categories. This dimension can be broadened to include multiracial groups and other culturally diverse groups such as sexual minorities, the elderly, women, and those with disabilities. In turn, these group identities can be further broken down into specific categories along the lines of race/ethnicity (African Americans, American Indians, Asian Americans, and Euro-Americans), sexual orientation (straights, gays, lesbians, and bisexuals), gender (men and women), and so forth. We are aware that a strong case can be made for including socioeconomic status, religious preference, and other group differences as well. Unfortunately, space limitations force us to make hard choices about which groups to cover.

Figure 2.2

A Multidimensional Model for Developing Cultural Competence

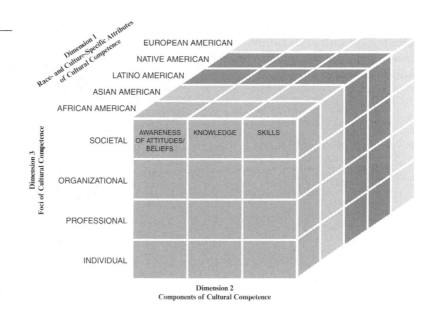

Dimension 1
Race- and Culture-Specific Attributes of Cultural Competence

EUROPEAN AMERICAN
NATIVE AMERICAN
LATINO AMERICAN
ASIAN AMERICAN
AFRICAN AMERICAN

Dimension 3
Foci of Cultural Competence

SOCIETAL

ORGANIZATIONAL

PROFESSIONAL

INDIVIDUAL

AWARENESS OF ATTITUDES/ BELIEFS   KNOWLEDGE   SKILLS

Dimension 2
Components of Cultural Competence

Dimension II: Components of Cultural Competence

As we have already stated, most multicultural specialists have used the divisions of awareness, knowledge, and skills to define cultural competence. To be effective multicultural therapists, specialists must be aware of their own biases and assumptions about human behavior, must acquire and have knowledge of the particular groups they are working with, and must be able to use culturally appropriate intervention strategies in working with different groups.

Dimension III: Foci of Therapeutic Interventions

A basic premise of MCT is that culturally competent helping professionals must not confine their perspectives to just individual treatment, but must be able to intervene effectively at the professional, organizational, and societal levels as well. Figure 2.3 reveals the four foci of intervention and development.

Focus 1: Individual. To provide culturally effective and sensitive mental health services, helping professionals must deal with their own biases, prejudices, and misinformation/lack of information regarding culturally diverse groups in our society. In this case, positive changes must occur in their attitudes, beliefs, emotions, and behaviors regarding multicultural populations.

Focus 2: Professional. It is clear that our profession has developed from a Western European perspective. As a result, how we define psychology (the study

Figure 2.3

The Foci of Cultural Competence: Individual, Professional, Organizational, and Societal

of mind and behavior) may be biased and at odds with different cultural groups. Further, if the professional standards and codes of ethics in mental health practice are culture bound, then they must be changed to reflect a multicultural worldview.

Focus 3: Organizational. Since we all work for or are influenced by organizations, it is important to realize that institutional practices, policies, programs, and structures may be oppressive to certain groups, especially if they are monocultural. If organizational policies and practices deny equal access and opportunity for different groups or oppress them (redlining in home mortgages, laws against domestic partners, inequitable mental health care, etc.), then they should become the targets for change.

Focus 4: Societal. If social policies (racial profiling, misinformation in educational materials, inequities in health care, etc.) are detrimental to the mental and physical health of minority groups, for example, does not the mental health professional have a responsibility to advocate for change? Our answer, of course, is affirmative.

   Often, psychologists treat individuals who are the victims of failed systemic processes. Intervention at the individual level is primarily remedial when a strong need exists for preventive measures. Because psychology concentrates primarily on the individual, it has been deficient in developing more systemic and large-scale change strategies.

Implications for Clinical Practice

Using our tripartite levels of identity model (Figure 2.1), the multidimensional model of cultural competence (Figure 2.2), and the foci of cultural competence (Figure 2.3), we can discern several guiding principles for effective MCT.

1. Understand the terms "sociodemographic" and "diverse backgrounds" in the MCT definition to be inclusive and encompass race, culture, gender, religious affiliation, sexual orientation, elderly, women, disability, and so on.

2. Realize that you are a product of cultural conditioning and that you are not immune from inheriting biases associated with culturally diverse groups in our society. As such, you must be vigilant of emotional reactions that may lead to a negation of other group values and lifestyles.

3. When working with different cultural groups, attempt to identify culture-specific and culture-universal domains of helping. Do not neglect the ways in which American Indians, Latinos/Hispanics, and African Americans, for example, may define normality-abnormality, the nature of helping, and what constitutes a helping relationship.

4. Be aware that persons of color, gays/lesbians, women, and other groups may perceive mental illness/health and the healing process differently than do Euro-Americans. To disregard differences and impose the conventional helping role and process on culturally diverse groups may constitute cultural oppression.

5. Be aware that Euro-American healing standards originate from a cultural context and represent only one form of helping that exists on an equal plane with others. As a helping professional, you must begin the task of recognizing the invisible veil of Euro-American cultural standards that influence your definitions of a helping relationship. As long as counselors and therapists continue to view Euro-American standards as normative, they will unwittingly set up a hierarchy among the groups.

6. Realize that the concept of cultural competence is more inclusive and superordinate than is the traditional definition of *clinical competence*. Do not fall into the trap of "good counseling is good counseling." Know that cultural competence must replace clinical competence. The latter is cul-

ture bound, ethnocentric, and exclusive. It does not acknowledge racial, cultural, and gender differences sufficiently to be helpful. To assume universality of application to all groups is to make an unwarranted inferential leap.

7. If you are planning to work with the diversity of clients in our world, you must play roles other than that of the conventional counselor. Simply concentrating on the traditional clinical role ignores the importance of interventions at other levels. New helping roles such as consultant, advisor, change agent, facilitator of indigenous healing systems, and so on have been suggested as equally valuable.

8. Realize that organizational/societal policies, practices, and structures may represent oppressive obstacles that prevent equal access and opportunity. If that is the case, systems intervention is most appropriate.

9. Use modalities that are consistent with the lifestyles and cultural systems of clients. In many cases, psychoeducational approaches, working outside of the office, and engaging in practices that violate traditional Euro-American standards (advice giving and self-disclosure) may be dictated.

10. Finally, but most important, realize that MCT (and cultural competence) is inclusive because it includes all groups (including Whites, males, and heterosexuals). Conventional counseling and therapy are exclusive and narrow and are based on Euro-American norms. As such, cultural competence is superordinate to clinical competence.

The Political Dimensions of Mental Health Practice

The Politics of Counseling and Psychotherapy

3

Chapter

On August 29, 2005, Hurricane Katrina struck the Gulf Coast with destructive winds of 175 mph to occasional gusts of 215 mph. It caused extensive damage to the coasts of Louisiana, Mississippi, and Alabama, and is acknowledged as the most destructive tropical cyclone on record to strike the United States. In New Orleans it caused sections of the levee system to collapse and flooded 80 percent of the city, much of which is below sea level. Widespread property damage resulted, as well as over one thousand deaths and over one million displaced people, leading to the greatest humanitarian crisis since the Great Depression (Gheytanchi et al., 2007).

An unprecedented mandatory evacuation of the city was issued; major transportation systems such as airlines, buses, and trains were suspended or developed alternative routes. Residents took whatever belongings they could carry and left the city in droves, usually by automobile; they clogged major roads and highways in their desire to flee the hurricane; tourists also sought alternative transportation (rental cars) as many airlines and trains were completely booked. It is estimated that 80 to 85 percent of the population left New Orleans.

Approximately 150,000 people did not leave the city. It is difficult to determine the percentage that was either unwilling or unable to obey the evacuation order. Nevertheless, both the Louisiana Superdome and the New Orleans Convention Center were designated "refuges of last resort" for citizens who did not leave. Tens of thousands of people overwhelmed the capacity and resources of the Superdome. Air conditioning, electricity, and plumbing failed, food and water were scarce, conditions were uncomfortable and unsanitary, and rumors of rape, suicide, and drug dealing floated about.

It took an agonizing 9 days to rescue the citizens; long before then, the flood damage and human waste in the Superdome were declared potential biohazards. In light of all the resources available to U.S. governmental agencies, the general consensus is that rescue efforts in the gulf states were examples of ineptitude and neglect. Many openly wonder why

the most powerful nation in the world moved so slowly and with apparent dis-
regard for the human suffering of its own citizens. In general, people of color be-
lieve that the failure to help was intimately linked to race and class bias (Bourne,
Watts, Gordon, & Figueroa-Garcia, 2006).

It may seem surprising and unusual for us to open a chapter on *Counseling the Culturally Diverse* with a description of Hurricane Katrina. While the event is certainly ingrained in the consciousness of everyone, just how does it relate to the topic of multicultural counseling and therapy? Why should we give it such broad prominence? After all, as mental health practitioners, we are here to help people, especially our clients, whether they are Black or White, rich or poor. While this statement is true, it fails to recognize how sociopolitical forces play an intimate part in determining how people view the world, especially as it relates to issues of racism and classism. Katrina is a prime example of the clash of racial realities and the multitude of political issues that are likely to arise in clinical sessions between counselors and culturally diverse clients. Let us pose some major questions related to Katrina and tease out their political and mental health implications.

1.   How much of the inadequate and inept response on the part of government officials and other key individuals had to do with race and class? A disproportionate number of Blacks and the poor bore the brunt of the suffering and loss. Horrifying images of mainly African American citizens who could not leave and who were confined for days in the Superdome or convention center without food or water made it clear that it was marginalized groups in our society who suffered most (American Psychological Association [APA], 2006). In what ways does this tragedy reveal how social and economic stratifications exist within our society? *How might such stratifications affect the quality of life of minorities and the delivery of mental health services to those most disempowered in our society (see Chapter 12)?*

2.   Did the 150,000 who stayed do so voluntarily? In the mass media, commentators often decried the fact that citizens who chose to stay had only themselves to blame. However, the 2000 U.S. Census revealed that 27 percent of New Orleans households were without privately owned transportation, primarily due to poverty. While more affluent citizens could hop into their cars or pay for transportation to leave, how could they expect the homeless, the poor, the elderly, and the disabled to leave without transportation? Are we blaming the victims? Some have argued that the blame rightly lies with a society that foresaw what could happen, but failed to act because of classism and racism (Gheytanchi et al., 2007). *When clients of color come to us for help, how might "blaming the victim" operate in our assessment, diagnosis, and treatment of them (see Chapter 4)?*

3. Why do so many people of color object to the use of the term "refugees" to refer to the displaced citizens of the gulf states? The Reverend Jesse Jackson vehemently denounced the term and even President George Bush openly discouraged its use. In what ways might the use of the term reflect potential racial bias? Does the term itself reveal society's mind-set—that large groups of people are not "Americans," are lesser beings, and are dispensable (DeVos & Banaji, 2005)? *In counseling and psychotherapy, how do our unconscious, biased perceptions of clients of color, women, and gays influence the clinical process (see Chapter 5)?*

4. In a televised fundraiser for the victims of Hurricane Katrina, rapper Kanye West departed from his script and claimed that "George Bush doesn't care about Black people." He went on to say: "I hate the way they portray us in the media. You see a Black family, it says, 'They're looting.' You see a White family, it says, 'They're looking for food.'" West's comments were prompted by photos, one from the Associated Press and the other from Getty Images, that juxtaposed a young Black man wading in water up to his chest, carrying a case of soda and a floating bag, with a White couple wading in the same murky water, holding bags of food. The first image had a caption stating that the Black man had been "looting a grocery store," while the second caption read "after finding bread and soda from a local grocery store." "Looting" and "finding" have two completely different meanings. *In what ways are clients and counselors influenced by a biased racial curriculum in their socialization processes (via media, education, and social groups), and what are the implications for clinical practice (Sue, 2003; Chapters 3, 10, and 11)?*

5. Why do people of color perceive racism operating before, during, and after Katrina? Why do many Whites tend to claim that race had nothing to do with the responses? Why is the worldview of persons of color so different from that of their White counterparts? In an ABC poll reported 9/11/05, Whites and Blacks responded quite differently to a question asking whether the response would have been quicker if the citizens were White instead of Black. Only 17 percent of Whites said "yes," while 66 percent of Blacks said "yes." What do you think accounts for this major difference in perception? Further, which perspective is the correct one? *When counseling culturally diverse clients, how does one reconcile such major differences in worldviews (see Chapters 6 and 7)?*

6. While many Whites deny that race played a role, media commentators and Bush administration officials seemed willing to entertain the notion that poverty and class did play a part in who was affected. Indeed, First Lady Laura Bush came to her husband's defense by claiming that the president cares deeply about "all Americans" and stated that it was clear that poor people were more vulnerable and that's what we saw on TV, not race. Does she have a point here? Or, if not, why is it easier for many

to acknowledge class issues (poverty) as opposed to race issues (Helms, 1994)? *As a helping professional, what emotional reactions around "race" do you possess that may act as a barrier to effective multicultural counseling (Chapters 1, 2, and 6)?*

7. During initial search-and-rescue efforts, authorities who were attempting to reach citizens trapped in attics and rooftops reported gunfire and suspended searches, for fear of their lives. Members of the Association of Black Psychologists have expressed outrage at the suspension of rescue efforts by authorities. After all, they reasoned, when people's lives are at stake all efforts should be made, regardless of the danger. Why did they not call in troops or police to help safeguard them? If in Iraq we are willing to endure enemy fire to police citizens of another country, why not in our own? Did the fact that those who needed rescuing were Black have anything to do with suspending rescue efforts? Social psychological findings on the "failure to help" indicate that in emergency situations, Blacks are significantly less likely to receive help than if the victims are White (Dovidio, Gaetner, Kawakami, & Hodson, 2002). *How might the unconscious biases of helping professionals affect their ability to deliver culturally appropriate mental health services to marginalized groups (Chapters 7 and 11)?*

While Katrina is a relatively recent event, the differing perspectives of persons of color and other marginalized groups reveal how race, class, and other sociodemographic categories may ultimately be linked to the historical and current experiences of oppression in the United States (Ponterotto, Utsey, & Pedersen, 2006). As such, helping professionals must understand the worldview of culturally diverse clients from both a cultural and a political perspective (Ridley, 2005). Clients of color, for example, are likely to approach counseling and therapy with a great deal of healthy skepticism regarding the institutions from which therapists work, and even the conscious and unconscious motives of the helping professional. The main thesis of *CCD* is that counseling and psychotherapy do not take place in a vacuum isolated from the larger social-political influences of our societal climate (Constantine, 2006; Katz, 1985; Liu, Hernandez, Mahmood, & Stinson, 2006). Counseling people of color, for example, often mirrors the nature of race relations in the wider society as well as the dominant-subordinate relationships of other marginalized groups (gay/lesbian, women, and the physically challenged). It serves as a microcosm, reflecting Black-White, Asian-White, Hispanic-White, American Indian-White, interethnic, and minority-majority relations.

We will explore the many ways in which counseling and psychotherapy have failed with respect to providing culturally appropriate mental health services to disempowered groups in our society. We do this by using racial minorities as an example of the damaging majority-minority relationships that historically characterize many other marginalized groups. Many readers may have a very powerful negative reaction to the following material. However, only by honestly confronting these unpleasant social realities and accepting responsibility for changing them will our profession be able to advance and grow (Strickland, 2000). For racial/ethnic minorities, these failures can be seen in three primary areas: (1) the education and training of mental health professionals, (2) biased and inaccurate therapeutic and mental health literature, and (3) the inappropriate process and practice of counseling and psychotherapy. We deal with only the first two areas in this chapter. Therapeutic process and practice is discussed in chapters 6 and 7. Prior to our journey, however, it is important to present some important demographic data regarding the diversification of the United States, and its implications for our society and the mental health profession.

The Diversification of the United States

The United States is the most diverse nation in the world. Nowhere is the diversification of society more evident than in the workplace, where three major trends can be observed: (1) the graying of the workforce (Burris, 2005), (2) the feminization of the workforce (Taylor & Kennedy, 2003), and (3) the changing complexion of the workforce (Sue, Parham, & Santiago, 1998).

The Graying of the Workforce and Society

As the baby boomers head into old age (those born between 1946 and 1961), the elderly population of those 65 and older will surge to 53.3 million by 2020, an increase of 63 percent from 1996 (Study: 2020 Begins, 1996). In 1950, the elderly population stood at 8 percent; in the year 2000 it was 13 percent, and by 2050 it will be 20 percent. The dramatic increase in the elderly population can be attributed to the aging baby boomer generation, declining fertility rates, and increased longevity (Huuhtanen, 1994; Keita & Hurrell, 1994; Sue, Parham, & Santiago, 1998). The median age of people in the workforce has risen from 36.6 years in 1990 to 40.6 in 2005. In 2005, 70 percent of workers were in the 25 to 54 age group, and the number of workers 55 and older rose 15 percent. The implications are many.

- There is a serious lack of knowledge concerning issues of the elderly and the implications of an aging population on mental health needs, occupational health, quality-of-life issues, economic impact, and social service needs.

- In American society, the elderly suffer from the beliefs and attitudes of society (stereotypes) that diminish their social status; they have declining physical and mental capabilities, have grown rigid and inflexible, are incapable of learning new skills, are crotchety and irritable, and should step aside for the benefit of the young (Brammer, 2004; Zastrow, 2004). More importantly is the belief that their lives are worth less than their younger counterparts.

- The elderly are increasingly at the mercy of governmental policies and company changes in social security and pension funds that reduce their benefits and protection as they begin their retirement years.

- Social service agencies are ill prepared to deal with the social and mental health needs of the elderly. Many of these disparities are due to ageism.

The Feminization of the Workforce and Society

Women are increasingly playing a larger and more significant role in society. Over a fifteen-year period from 1990 to 2005 women accounted for 62 percent of the net increase in the civilian labor force. The upward trend is dramatic: 38 percent in 1970, 42 percent in 1980, and 45 percent in 1990 (U.S. Department of Labor, Women's Bureau, 1992). The trend is not confined to single women alone, but also to married women. For example, in 1950, married women accounted for less that 25 percent of the labor force; only 12 percent of women with preschool children worked, and only 28 percent with school-age children worked. Now, however, 58 percent of married women are in the labor force, 60 percent with preschoolers work, and 75 percent with school-age children work. The problem, however, is that women continue to occupy the lower rungs of the occupational ladder but are still responsible for most domestic responsibilities. The implications of these changes and facts are many.

- Common sense would indicate that women are subjected to a greater number of stressors than their male counterparts. This is due to issues related to family life and role strain. Studies continue to indicate that working women carry more of the domestic burden, more responsibility for child care arrangements, and more responsibility for social and interpersonal activities outside of the home than do married or partnered men (Morales & Sheafor, 2004).

- Family relationships and structures have progressively changed as we have moved from a traditional single-earner, two-parent family to two wage earners. The increasing number of women in the workforce cannot be seen in isolation from the wider social, political, and economic context (Farley, Smith, & Boyle, 2003). For example, one quarter of the nation's families are poor, one sixth have no health insurance, one in six small children live in a family where neither parent has a job, women continue to be paid less than men, and 25 percent of children will be on welfare at some point before reaching adulthood. Social workers must be cognizant of these changes and the implications for their work.

- These disparities are systemic in nature. If counselors are concerned with the welfare of women, then it is imperative that meaningful policies and practices be enacted to deal with gender disparities.

The Changing Complexion of the Workforce and Society

People of color have reached a critical mass in the United States, and their numbers are expected to continue increasing (Lum, 2004). The rapid increase in racial/ethnic minorities in the United States has been referred to as the "diversification of the United States" or, literally, the "changing complexion of society." From 1990 to 2000, the U.S. population increased 13 percent, to over 281 million (U.S. Census Bureau, 2001). Most of the population increase consisted of visible racial/ethnic minority groups (VREG): The Asian American/Pacific Islander population increased by almost 50 percent, the Latino/Hispanic population by over 58 percent, African Americans by 16 percent, and American Indians/Alaska Natives by 15.5 percent, in marked contrast to the 7.3 percent increase of Whites. Currently, people of color constitute over 30 percent of the U.S. population, approximately 45 percent of whom are in the public schools (D. W. Sue et al., 1998; U.S. Bureau of the Census, 2000). Projections indicate that persons of color will constitute a numerical majority sometime between 2030 and 2050 (D. W. Sue et al.).

The rapid demographic shift stems from two major trends: immigration rates and differential birth rates. The current immigration rates (documented immigrants, undocumented immigrants, and refugees) are the largest in U.S. history. Unlike the earlier immigrants, who were primarily White Europeans oriented toward assimilation, the current wave consists primarily of Asian (34 percent), Latin American (34 percent), and other VREGs who may not be readily assimilated (Atkinson et al., 1998). In addition, the birth rates of White Americans have continued to decline (Euro-American = 1.7 per mother) in comparison to other racial/ethnic minorities (e.g., African American = 2.4, Mexican American = 2.9, Vietnamese = 3.4, Laotians = 4.6, Cambodians = 7.4, and Hmong = 11.9). Societal implications of the changing complexion are many:

- Approximately 75 percent of those now entering the labor force are visible racial/ethnic minorities and women. The changing complexion and feminization of the workforce have become a reality.

■ By the time the so-called baby boomers retire, the majority of people contributing to social security and pension plans will be racial/ethnic minorities. In other words, those planning to retire (primarily White workers) must depend on their coworkers of color. If racial/ethnic minorities continue to encounter the glass ceiling and to be the most undereducated, underemployed, underpaid, and unemployed, the economic security of retiring White workers looks grim.

■ Businesses are aware that their workforces must be drawn increasingly from a diverse labor pool and that the current U.S. minority marketplace equals the entire gross domestic product of Canada; projections are that it will become immense as the shift in demographics continues. The economic viability of businesses will depend on their ability to effectively manage a diverse workforce, allow for equal access and opportunity, and appeal to consumers of color. On a much larger scale, however, a nation that denies equal access and opportunity to these groups bodes poorly for our future viability.

■ Students of color now constitute 45 percent of the population in our public schools. Some school systems, such as California's, reached a ratio of 50 percent students of color as early as the late 1980s. Thus, it appears that our educational institutions must wrestle with issues of multicultural education and the development of bilingual programs.

■ The diversity index of the United States stands at 49, indicating that there is approximately one in two chances that two people selected at random are racially or ethnically different.

These three pressing trends are only the tip of the iceberg in considering the importance of diversity: the demographic growth of the elderly, of women, and people of color in mental health practice. For the profession to respond adequately, it must also address issues of sexual orientation, ability/disability, religion, socioeconomic status, and so forth (Guadalupe & Lum, 2005).

In recognition of the changing composition of the nation, there has recently been a movement by business and industry toward diversity training, the infusion of multicultural concepts into school curricula, as well as attempts to fight bigotry, bias, and discrimination in our social, economic, and political systems. Yet, the changing demographics have also caused alarm in many of our White citizens, and have often resulted in conflicts and major clashes. Perhaps this is to be expected, as different worldviews, lifestyles and value systems challenge the myth of the melting pot concept and as we move from a monocultural to a multicultural society.

Mental Health Implications
Like they are for the rest of society, the implications for the mental health professions are many.

1. First, the clash of worldviews, values, and lifestyles is inescapable, not only for the therapist's personal life, but for the professional one as well. It is impossible for any of us not to encounter client groups who differ from us in terms of race, culture, and ethnicity. Increasingly, therapists will come into contact with diverse clients who may not share their worldview of what constitutes normality-abnormality; who define helping in a manner that contrasts sharply with our codes of ethics and standards of practice; that require culture-specific strategies and approaches in counseling and psychotherapy; and who may correctly or incorrectly perceive the profession as a sociopolitical tool.

2. If counselors and therapists are to provide meaningful help to a culturally diverse population, we must reach out and acquire not only new understandings, but develop new, culturally effective helping approaches. To prepare counselors with multicultural expertise means (a) revamping our training programs to include accurate and realistic multicultural content and experiences, (b) developing multicultural competencies as core standards for our profession, and (c) providing continuing education for our current service providers (Sue, Bingham, Porche-Burke, & Vasquez, 1999).

3. Because therapeutic and ethical practice may be culture bound, therapists who work with diverse clients may be engaging in cultural oppression, using unethical and harmful practices for that particular population. Our professional organizations need to adopt ethical guidelines, codes of ethics, standards of practice, and bylaws that are multicultural in scope (APA, 2004; Sue, 2001). Omission of such standards and failed translation into actual practice are inexcusable, and represent a powerful indictment of our low priority and lack of commitment to cultural diversity. If we are indeed committed to multiculturalism, then each and every one of us must become advocates in demanding that our professional associations seriously undertake a major revision of standards used to ascertain counseling competence. Furthermore, these multicultural criteria must be incorporated into licensing and credentialing standards as well.

4. The education and training of psychologists have, at times, created the impression that its theories and practices are apolitical and value free. Yet, we are often impressed by the fact that the actual practice of therapy can result in cultural oppression; that what happens in the therapist's office may represent a microcosm of race relations in the larger society; that the so-called psychological problems of minority groups may reside not within, but outside of our clients; and that no matter how well intentioned the helping professional, he or she is not immune from inheriting the racial biases of his or her forebears.

5. Since none of us is immune from inheriting the images/stereotypes of the larger society, we can assume that most therapists are prisoners of

their own cultural conditioning. As a result, they possess stereotypes and preconceived notions that may be unwittingly imposed upon their culturally different clients. It may affect how they define problems, the goals they develop, and the standards that they use to judge normal and abnormal behavior. If their biases and prejudices influence their work with culturally diverse clients they may potentially oppress and harm them. Thus it is imperative that all therapists explore their own stereotypes and images of various minority groups. Since many of our stereotypes are unconscious, we need to work tirelessly in uncovering them, with as much nondefensiveness as possible. One of the greatest obstacles to this process is our fear that others will see our racism, sexism, heterosexism, and biases. Thus, we try to deny the existence of these stereotypes or to hide them from public view. This works against our ability to uncover them.

The Education and Training of Mental Health Professionals

While national interest in the mental health needs of ethnic minorities has increased, the human service professions have historically neglected this population (U.S. Public Health Service, 2001). Evidence reveals that the populations of color, in addition to the common stresses experienced by everyone else, are more likely to encounter problems such as immigrant status, poverty, cultural racism, prejudice, and discrimination. Yet studies continue to reveal that American Indians, Asian Americans, African Americans, and Latino/Hispanic Americans tend to underutilize traditional mental health services, in a variety of contexts (Cheung & Snowden, 1990; Kearney, Draper, & Baron, 2005). Some years back, S. Sue and associates found that clients tended to terminate counseling/therapy at a rate of more than 50 percent after only one contact with the therapist. This was in marked contrast to the less than 30 percent termination rate among White clients (S. Sue, Allen, & Conaway, 1975; S. Sue & McKinney, 1974; S. Sue, McKinney, Allen, & Hall, 1974; S. Sue, Fujino, Hu, Takeuchi, & Zane, 1991). While utilization data for groups of color are changing, these early findings led many to search for enlightened explanations.

For example, some researchers hypothesized that minority-group individuals underutilize and prematurely terminate counseling/therapy because of the biased nature of the services themselves (Kearney, Draper, & Baron, 2005). The services offered are frequently antagonistic or inappropriate to the life experiences of the culturally different client; they lack sensitivity and understanding, and they are oppressive and discriminating toward minority clients (Cokley, 2005). Many believed that the presence of ill-prepared mental health professionals was the direct result of a culture-bound and biased training system (Mio, 2005; Utsey, Grange, & Allyne, 2006). While directors of training programs report that multicultural coursework has increased significantly in mental health education (Bernal & Castro, 1994; Hills & Strozier, 1992), it is interesting to note that graduate students in mental health programs have a different view. They report few courses offered in multicultural psychology, and inadequate coverage of work with diverse populations within required core courses (Allison, Crawford, Echemendia, Robinson, & Knepp, 1994; Mintz, Bartels, & Rideout, 1995).

It is our contention that reports of increased multicultural coverage (while gaining a degree of prominence) are inflated and/or are superficially developed. Most graduate programs continue to give inadequate treatment to the mental health issues of ethnic minorities. Cultural influences affecting personality formation, career choice, educational development, and the manifestation of behavior disorders are infrequently part of mental health training or they are treated in a tangential manner (Parham, White, & Ajamu, 1997; Vazquez & Gargia-Vazquez, 2003). When minority-group experiences are discussed, they are generally seen and analyzed from the White, Euro-American, middle-class perspective. In programs where minority experiences have been discussed, the focus tends to be on their pathological lifestyles and/or maintenance of false stereotypes. The result is twofold: (1) professionals who deal with mental health problems of ethnic minorities lack understanding and knowledge about ethnic values and their consequent interaction with a racist society, and (2) mental health practitioners are graduated from our programs believing minorities are inherently pathological and that therapy involves a simple modification of traditional White models.

This ethnocentric bias has been highly destructive to the natural help-giving networks of minority communities (Duran, 2006). Oftentimes mental health professionals operate with the assumption that racial and ethnic minorities never had such a thing as "counseling" and "psychotherapy" until it was "invented" and institutionalized in Western cultures. For the benefit of those people, the mental health movement has delegitimized natural help-giving networks that have operated for thousands of years by labeling them as unscientific, supernatural, mystical, and not consistent with "professional standards of practice." Mental health professionals are then surprised to find that there is a high incidence of psychological distress in the minority community, that their treatment techniques do not work, and that some culturally diverse groups do not utilize their services.

Contrary to this ethnocentric orientation, we need to expand our perception of what constitutes valid mental health practices. Equally legitimate methods of treatment are nonformal or natural support systems, so powerful in many minority groups (family, friends, community self-help programs, and occupational networks), folk-healing methods, and indigenous formal systems of therapy (Lee, 1996; Moodley & West, 2005). Instead of attempting to destroy these practices, we should be actively trying to find out why they may work better than Western forms of counseling and therapy.

Definitions of Mental Health

Counseling and psychotherapy tend to assume universal (*etic*) applications of their concepts and goals to the exclusion of culture-specific (*emic*) views (Draguns, 2002). Likewise, graduate programs have often been accused of fostering *cultural encapsulation,* a term first coined by Wrenn (1962). The term refers specifically to (a) the substitution of modal stereotypes for the real world, (b) the disregarding of cultural variations in a dogmatic adherence to some universal notion of truth, and (c) the use of a technique-oriented definition of the counseling process. The results are that counselor roles are rigidly defined, implanting an implicit belief in a universal concept of "healthy" and "normal."

If we look at criteria used by the mental health profession to judge normality and abnormality, this ethnocentricity becomes glaring. Several fundamental approaches that have particular relevance to our discussion have been identified (D. Sue, D. W. Sue, & S. Sue, 2006): (a) normality as a statistical concept, (b) normality as ideal mental health, and (c) abnormality as the presence of certain behaviors (research criteria).

First, statistical criteria equate normality with those behaviors that occur most frequently in the population. Abnormality is defined in terms of those behaviors that occur least frequently. In spite of the word *statistical,* however, these criteria need not be quantitative in nature: Individuals who talk to themselves, disrobe in public, or laugh uncontrollably for no apparent reason are considered abnormal according to these criteria simply because most people do not behave in that way. Statistical criteria undergirds our notion of a normal probability curve, so often used in IQ tests, achievement tests, and personality inventories. Statistical criteria may seem adequate in specific instances, but they are fraught with hazards and problems. For one thing, they fail to take into account differences in time, community standards, and cultural values. If deviations from the majority are considered abnormal, then many ethnic and racial minorities that exhibit strong cultural differences from the majority have to be so classified. When we resort to a statistical definition, it is generally the group in power that determines what constitutes normality and abnormality. For example, if a group of African Americans were to be administered a personality test and it was found that they were more suspicious than their White counterparts, what would this mean?

Some psychologists and educators have used such findings to label African Americans as paranoid. Statements by Blacks that "The Man" is out to get them may be perceived as supporting a paranoid delusion. This interprctation, however, has been challenged by many Black psychologists as being inaccurate (Grier & Cobbs, 1968, 1971; Guthrie, 1997; Parham, White, & Ajamu, 1999). In response to their heritage of slavery and a history of White discrimination against them, African Americans have adopted various behaviors (in particular, behaviors toward Whites) that have proven important for survival in a racist society. "Playing it cool" has been identified as one means by which Blacks, as well as members of other minority groups, may conceal their true thoughts and feelings. A Black person who is experiencing conflict, anger, or even rage may be skillful at appearing serene and composed. This tactic is a survival mechanism aimed at reducing one's vulnerability to harm and to exploitation in a hostile environment.

The personality test that reveals Blacks as being suspicious, mistrustful, and paranoid needs to be understood from a larger social-political perspective. Minority groups who have consistently been victims of discrimination and oppression in a culture that is full of racism have good reason to be suspicious and mistrustful of White society. In their classic book *Black Rage,* Grier and Cobbs (1968) point out how Blacks, in order to survive in a White racist society, have developed a highly functional survival mechanism to protect them against possible physical and psychological harm. The authors perceive this "cultural paranoia" as adaptive and healthy rather than dysfunctional and pathological. Indeed, some psychologists of color have indicated that the absence of a *paranorm* among minorities may be more indicative of pathology than of its presence. The absence of a paranorm may indicate either poor reality testing (denial of oppression/racism in our society) and/or naiveté in understanding the operation of racism.

Second, humanistic psychologists have proposed the concept of ideal mental health as a criteria of normality. Such criteria stress the importance of attaining some positive goal. For example, the consciousness-balance of psychic forces (Freud, 1960; Jung, 1960), self-actualization/creativity (Maslow, 1968; Rogers, 1961), competence, autonomy, and resistance to stress (Allport, 1961; White, 1963), or self-disclosure (Jourard, 1964) have all been historically proposed. The discriminatory nature of such approaches is grounded in the belief of a universal application (all populations in all situations) and reveals a failure to recognize the value base from which the criteria are derived. The particular goal or ideal used is intimately linked with the theoretical frame of reference and values held by the practitioner. For example, the psychoanalytic emphasis on *insight* as a determinant of mental health is a value in itself (London, 1988). It is important for the mental health professional to be aware, however, that certain socioeconomic groups and ethnic minorities do not particularly value insight. Furthermore, the use of self-disclosure as a measure of mental health tends to neglect the earlier discussion presented on the paranorm. One characteristic often linked to the healthy personality is the ability to talk about the deepest and most intimate aspects of one's life; to self-disclose. This orientation is very characteristic of our counseling and therapy process, in which clients are expected to talk about themselves in a very personal manner. The fact that many minorities are initially reluctant to self-disclose can place them in a situation where they are judged to be mentally unhealthy, and in this case, paranoid (Parham, 2002).

Definitions of mental health such as competence, autonomy, and resistance to stress are related to White middle-class notions of individual maturity (Ahuvia, 2001; Triandis, 2000). The mental health professions originated from the ideological milieu of individualism (Ivey, D'Andrea, Ivey, & Simek-Morgan, 2007). Individuals make their lot in life. Those who succeed in society do so because of their *own* efforts and abilities. Successful people are seen as mature, independent, and possessing great ego strength. Apart from the potential bias in defining what constitutes competence, autonomy, and resistance to stress, the use of such a person-focused definition of maturity places the responsibility on the individual. When a person fails in life, it is because of his or her own lack of ability, interest, maturity, or some inherent weakness of the ego. If, on the other hand, we see minorities as being subjected to higher stress factors in society and placed in a one-down position by virtue of racism, then it becomes quite clear that the definition will tend to portray the lifestyle of minorities as inferior, underdeveloped, and deficient. Ryan (1971) was the first to coin the phrase "blaming the victim" to refer to this process. Yet a broader system analysis would show that the economic, social, and psychological conditions of minorities are related to their oppressed status in America, as illustrated in our Katrina example.

Third, an alternative to the previous two definitions of abnormality is a research one. For example, in determining rates of mental illness in different ethnic groups, "psychiatric diagnosis," "presence in mental hospitals," and scores on "objective psychological inventories" are frequently used (Samuda, 1998). Diagnosis and hospitalization present a circular problem. The definition of normality-abnormality depends on what mental health practitioners say it is! In this case, the race or ethnicity of mental health professionals is likely to be different from that of minority clients. Bias on the part of the practitioner with respect to diagnosis and treatment is likely to occur (Constantine, Myers, Kindaichi, & Moore, 2004). The inescapable conclusion is that minority clients tend to be diagnosed differently and to receive less preferred modes of treatment (Paniagua, 2001).

Furthermore, the political and societal implications of psychiatric diagnosis and hospitalization were forcefully pointed out nearly 40 years ago by Laing (1967, 1969) and Szasz (1970, 1971). While it appears that minorities underutilize outpatient services, they appear to face greater levels of involuntary hospital commitments (Snowden & Cheung, 1990). Laing believes that individual madness is but a reflection of the madness of society. He describes schizophrenic breakdowns as desperate strategies by people to liberate themselves from a "false self" used to maintain behavioral normality in our society. Attempts to adjust the person back to the original normality (sick society) are unethical. Szasz states this opinion even more strongly:

> *In my opinion, mental illness is a myth. People we label "mentally ill" are not sick, and involuntary mental hospitalization is not treatment. It is punishment. . . . The fact that mental illness designates a deviation from an ethnical rule of conduct, and that such rules vary widely, explains why upper-middle-class psychiatrists can so easily find evidence of "mental illness" in lower-class individuals; and why so many prominent persons in the past fifty years or so have been diagnosed by their enemies as suffering from some types of insanity. Barry Goldwater was called a paranoid schizophrenic. . . . Woodrow Wilson, a neurotic. . . . Jesus Christ, according to two psychiatrists . . . was a born degenerate with a fixed delusion system. (Szasz, 1970, pp. 167–168)*

Szasz (1987, 1999) sees the mental health professional as an inquisitor, an agent of society exerting social control over those individuals who deviate in thought and behavior from the accepted norms of society. Psychiatric hospitalization is believed to be a form of social control for persons who annoy or disturb us. The label *mental illness* may be seen as a political ploy used to control those who are different, and therapy is used to control, brainwash, or reorient the identified victims to fit into society. It is exactly this concept that many people of color find frightening. For example, many Asian Americans, American Indians, African Americans, and Hispanic/Latino Americans are increasingly challenging the concepts of normality and abnormality. They believe that their values and lifestyles are often seen by society as pathological and thus are unfairly discriminated against by the mental health professions (Constantine, 2006).

In addition, the use of "objective" psychological inventories as indicators of maladjustment may also place people of color at a disadvantage. Many are aware that the test instruments used on them have been constructed and standardized according to White middle-class norms. The lack of culturally unbiased instruments makes many feel that the results obtained are invalid. Indeed, in a landmark decision in the State of California (*Larry P. v. California*, 1986), a judge ruled in favor of the Association of Black Psychologists' claim that individual intelligence tests such as the WISC-R, WAIS-R, and Stanford Binet could not be used in the public schools on Black students. The improper use of such instruments can lead to an exclusion of minorities in jobs and promotion, to discriminatory educational decisions, and to biased determination of what constitutes pathology and cure in counseling/therapy (Samuda, 1998). Further, when a diagnosis becomes a label, it can have serious consequences. First, a label can cause people to interpret all activities of the affected individual as pathological. No matter what a Black person may do or say that breaks a stereotype, his or her behavior will seem to reflect the fact that he or she is less intelligent than others around him or her. Second, the label may cause others to treat an individual differently even when he or she is perfectly normal. Third, a label may cause those who are labeled to believe that they do indeed possess such characteristics (Rosenthal & Jacobson, 1968) or that the threats of being perceived as less capable can seriously impair their performance (Steele, 1997; Steele & Aronson, 1995).

Curriculum and Training Deficiencies

It appears that many of the universal definitions of mental health that have pervaded the profession have primarily been due to severe deficiencies in training programs. Various specialists (Chen, 2001; Mio & Morris, 1990) have asserted that the major reason for ineffectiveness in working with culturally different populations is the lack of culturally sensitive material taught in the curricula. It has been ethnocentrically assumed that the material taught in traditional mental health programs is equally applicable to all groups. Even now, when there is high recognition of the need for multicultural curricula, it has become a battle to infuse such concepts into course content (Vera, Buhin, & Shin, 2006). As a result, course offerings continue to lack a non-White perspective, to treat cultural issues as an adjunct or add-on, to continue portraying cultural groups in stereotypic ways, and to create an academic environment that does not support minority concerns, needs, and issues (Grieger & Toliver, 2001). Further, a major criticism has been that training programs purposely leave out antiracism, antisexism and antihomophobia curricula for fear they require students to explore their own biases and prejudices (Carter, 2005; Vera, Buhin, & Shin, 2006). Because multicultural competence cannot occur without students or trainees confronting these harmful and detrimental attitudes about race, gender, and sexual orientation, the education and training of psychologists remain at the cognitive and objective domain, preventing self-exploration. It allows students to study the material from their positions of safety. The curriculum must also enable students to understand feelings of helplessness and powerlessness, low self-esteem, poor self-concept, and how they contribute to low motivation, frustration, hate, ambivalence, and apathy. Each course should contain (1) a *consciousness-raising* component, (2) an *affective/experiential* component, (3) a *knowledge* component, and (4) a *skills* component. Importantly, it was recommended by the American Psychological Association (2004) that psychology training programs at all levels provide information on the political nature of the practice of psychology, and that professionals need to "own" their value positions.

Counseling and Mental Health Literature

Many writers have noted how the social science literature, and specifically research, has failed to create a realistic understanding of various ethnic groups in America (Guthrie, 1997; Samuda, 1998; Thomas & Sillen, 1972). In fact, certain practices are felt to have done great harm to minorities, by ignoring them, maintaining false stereotypes, and/or distorting their lifestyles. Mental health practice may be viewed as encompassing the use of social power and functioning as a handmaiden of the status quo (Halleck, 1971; Katz, 1985). Social sciences are part of a culture-bound social system, from which researchers are usually drawn; moreover, organized social science is often dependent upon it for financial support. Ethnic minorities frequently see the mental health profession in a similar way—as a discipline concerned with maintaining the status quo (Highlen, 1996). As a result, the person collecting and reporting data is often perceived as possessing the social bias of his or her society.

Social sciences, for example, have historically ignored the study of Asians in America (Hong & Domokos-Cheng Ham, 2001). This deficit has contributed to the perpetuation of false stereotypes, which has angered many younger Asians concerned with raising consciousness and group esteem. When studies have been conducted on minorities, research has been appallingly unbalanced. Many social scientists (Jones, 1997; Wilson & Stith, 1991) have pointed out how "White social science" has tended to reinforce a negative view of African Americans among the public by concentrating on unstable Black families instead of on the many stable ones. Such unfair treatment has also been the case in studies on Latinos that have focused on the psychopathological problems encountered by Mexican Americans (Falicov, 2005). Other ethnic groups, such as Native Americans (Sutton & Broken Nose, 2005) and Puerto Ricans (Garcia-Preto, 2005) have fared no better. Even more disturbing is the assumption that the problems encountered by minorities are due to intrinsic factors (racial inferiority, incompatible value systems, etc.) rather than to the failure of society (Katz, 1985; Samuda, 1998). While there are many aspects of how minorities are portrayed in social science literature, two seem crucial for us to explore: (1) minorities and pathology, and (2) the role of scientific racism in research.

Minorities and Pathology

When we seriously study the "scientific" literature of the past relating to people of color, we are immediately impressed with how an implicit equation of minorities and pathology is a common theme. The historical use of science in the investigation of racial differences seems to be linked with White supremacist notions (Jones, 1997; Samuda, 1998). The classic work of Thomas and Sillen (1972) refer to this as *scientific racism* and cite several historical examples to support their contention: (1) 1840 census figures (fabricated) were used to support the notion that Blacks living under unnatural conditions of freedom were prone to anxiety, (2) mental health for Blacks was contentment with subservience, (3) psychologically normal Blacks were faithful and happy-go-lucky, (4) influential medical journals presented fantasies as facts, supporting the belief that anatomical, neurological, or endocrinological aspects of Blacks were always inferior to those of Whites, (5) the Black person's brain is smaller and less developed, (6) Blacks were less prone to mental illness because their minds were so simple, and (7) the dreams of Blacks are juvenile in character and not as complex as Whites. More frightening, perhaps, is a survey that found that many of these stereotypes continue to be accepted by White Americans: 20 percent publicly expressed a belief that African Americans are innately inferior in thinking ability, 19 percent believe that Blacks have thicker craniums, and 23.5 percent believe they have longer arms than Whites (Plous & Williams, 1995). One wonders how many White Americans hold similar beliefs privately, but because of social pressures do not publicly voice them.

Furthermore, the belief that various human groups exist at different stages of biological evolution was accepted by G. Stanley Hall. He stated explicitly in 1904 that Africans, Indians, and Chinese were members of adolescent races and in a stage of incomplete development. In most cases, the evidence used to support these conclusions was either fabricated, extremely flimsy, or distorted to fit the belief in non-White inferiority (Thomas & Sillen, 1972). For example, Gossett (1963) reports that when one particular study in 1895 revealed that the sensory perception of Native Americans was superior to that of Blacks, and that of Blacks was superior to that of Whites, the results were used to support a belief in the mental superiority of Whites. "Their reactions were slower because they belonged to a more deliberate and reflective race than did the members of the other two groups" (p. 364). The belief that Blacks were "born athletes," as opposed to scientists or statesmen, derives from this tradition. The fact that Hall was a well-respected psychologist, often referred to as "the father of child study," and first president of the American Psychological Association, did not prevent him from inheriting the racial biases of the times.

The Genetically Deficient Model

The portrayal of people of color in literature has generally taken the form of stereotyping them as deficient in certain desirable attributes. For example, de Gobineau's (1915) *Essay on the Inequality of the Human Races* and Darwin's (1859) *The Origin of Species by Means of Natural Selection* were used to support the genetic intellectual superiority of Whites and the genetic inferiority of the "lower races." Galton (1869) wrote explicitly that African "Negroes" were "half-witted men" who made "childish, stupid and simpleton like mistakes," while Jews were inferior physically and mentally and only designed for a parasitical existence on other nations of people. Terman (1916), using the Binet scales in testing Black, Mexican American, and Spanish Indian families, concluded that they were uneducable.

The genetically deficient model is present in the writings of educational psychologists and academicians. In 1989, Professor Rushton of the University of Western Ontario claimed that human intelligence and behavior were largely determined by race, that Whites have bigger brains than Blacks, and that Blacks are more aggressive (Samuda, 1998). Shockley (1972) has expressed fears that the accumulation of weak or low intelligence genes in the Black population will seriously affect overall intelligence. Thus, he advocates that people with low IQs should not be allowed to bear children; they should be sterilized. Allegations of scientific racism can also be seen in the work of the late Cyril Burt, eminent British psychologist, who fabricated data to support his contention that intelligence is inherited and that Blacks have inherited inferior brains. Such an accusation is immensely important when one considers that Burt is a major influence in American and British psychology, is considered by many to be the father of educational psychology, was the first psychologist to be knighted, was awarded the APA's Thorndike Prize, and that his research findings form the foundation for the belief that intelligence is inherited.

The publication of *The Bell Curve* (Herrnstein & Murray, 1994) continues to echo the controversy in both the public and academic domains. The two authors assert that intelligence is inherited to a large degree, race is correlated with intellect, and programs such as Head Start and Affirmative Action should be banished because they do no good. Instead, resources and funding should be reallocated to those who can profit from it (meaning White Americans). Samuda (1998) concludes about the authors: "Simply stated, they essentially recommend that those of lower intelligence should serve those of higher intelligence" (p. 175). He further concludes: "*The Bell Curve* remains astonishingly antiquated and immune to evidence from the physiological and neurobiological sciences, quantitative genetics, and statistical theory, and it overlooks the significance of environmental factors that research has uncovered" (p. 176).

The questions about whether there are differences in intelligence between races are both complex and emotional. The difficulty in clarifying this question is compounded by many factors. Besides the difficulty in defining "race," there exist questionable assumptions regarding whether research on the intelligence of Whites can be generalized to other groups, whether middle-class and lower-class ethnic minorities grow up in similar environments to middle- and lower-class Whites, and whether test instruments are valid for both minority and White subjects. More important, we should recognize that the average values of different populations tells us nothing about any one individual. Heritability is a function of the population, *not* a trait. Ethnic groups all have individuals in the full range of intelligence, and to think of any racial group in terms of a single stereotype goes against all we know about the mechanics of heredity. Yet, much of social science literature continues to portray ethnic minorities as being genetically deficient in one sense or another. Those interested in both the issues and consequences in the testing of American minorities and the technical and sociopolitical analyses of *The Bell Curve* are directed to the excellent rebuttal by Samuda (1998).

The Culturally Deficient Model.
Well-meaning social scientists who challenged the genetic deficit model by placing heavy reliance on environmental factors nevertheless tended to perpetuate a view that saw minorities as culturally disadvantaged, deficient, or deprived. Instead of a biological condition that caused differences, the blame now shifted to the lifestyles or values of various ethnic groups (Dana, 1993; Sumada, 1998). The term *cultural deprivation* was first popularized by Riessman's widely read book, *The Culturally Deprived Child* (1962). It was used to indicate that many groups perform poorly on tests or exhibit deviant characteristics because they lack many of the advantages of middle-class culture (education, books, toys, formal language, etc.). In essence, these groups were culturally impoverished!

While Riessman introduced such a concept so as to add balance to working with minorities and ultimately to improve their condition in America, some educators strenuously objected to the term. First, the term *culturally deprived* means to lack a cultural background (enslaved Blacks arrived in America culturally naked), which is contradictory, because everyone inherits a culture. Second, such terms cause conceptual and theoretical confusions that may adversely affect social planning, educational policy, and research. For example, the oft-quoted Moynihan Report (Moynihan, 1965) asserts that "at the heart of deterioration of the Negro society is the deterioration of the Black family. It is the fundamental source of the weakness in the Negro community" (p. 5). Action was thus directed toward infusing White concepts of the family into those of Blacks. Third, cultural deprivation is used synonymously with deviation from and superiority of White middle-class values. Fourth, these deviations in values become equated with pathology, in which a group's cultural values, families, or lifestyles transmit the pathology. Thus it provides a convenient rationalization and alibi for the perpetuation of racism and the inequities of the socioeconomic system.

The Culturally Diverse Model.
There are many who now maintain that the culturally deficient model only serves to perpetuate the myth of minority inferiority. The focus tends to be a

person-blame one, an emphasis on minority pathology, and a use of White middle-class definitions of desirable and undesirable behavior. The social science use of a common, standard assumption implies that to be different is to be deviant, pathological, or sick. Is it possible that intelligence and personality scores for minority group children really measure how Anglicized a person has become? Therefore, minorities should no longer be viewed as deficient, but rather as *culturally diverse*. The goal of society should be to recognize the legitimacy of alternative lifestyles, the advantages of being bicultural (capable of functioning in two different cultural environments), and the value of differences.

Relevance of Research

So far, our discussion of minority portrayal in the professional literature has been a general one. We have made minimal reference to research as it relates to minorities in particular. Research findings are supposed to form the basis of any profession that purports to be a science. The data generated from research should be objective and free of bias. As we have seen in the last section, what a researcher proposes to study and how he or she interprets such findings are intimately linked to a personal, professional, and societal value system. Cheek (1987) goes so far as to assert that "social science is a vehicle of White supremacy."

It is an inescapable conclusion that personal and societal values often affect the interpretation of data as it relates to minorities (Atkinson, Bui, & Mori, 2001). A very similar analogy can be drawn with respect to the mental health profession. For example, the profession's preoccupation with pathology tends to encourage the study of personality deficits and weaknesses rather than strengths or assets. Racist attitudes may intensify this narrow view, as minorities may be portrayed in professional journals as a neurotic, psychotic, psychopath, parolee, and so on, instead of as a well-rounded person.

It is not surprising that minority groups are often suspicious of the motives of the researcher. The researcher of ethnic matters may find his or her attitudes and values toward minority groups being challenged. No longer can the researcher claim that research is solely in the interest of science and is morally neutral. The late Carl Rogers, a well-known humanistic psychologist, stated, "If behavioral scientists are concerned solely with advancing their science, it seems most probable that they will serve the purpose of whatever group has the power" (quoted in Brecher & Brecher, 1961, p. 20). C. W. Thomas (1970) has even voiced this thought in stronger form:

White psychologists have raped Black communities all over the country. Yes raped. They have used Black people as the human equivalent of rats run through

Ph.D. experiments and as helpless clients for programs that serve middle-class White administrators better than they do the poor. They have used research on Black people as green stamps to trade for research grants. They have been vultures. (p. 52)

Blacks point to what is known as the "Tuskegee experiment" as a prime example of this allegation. The Tuskegee experiment was carried out from 1932 to 1972 by the U.S. Public Health Service, in which over 600 Alabama Black men were used as guinea pigs in the study of what damage would occur to the body if syphilis were left untreated. Approximately 399 were allowed to go untreated, even when medication was available. Records indicate that seven died as a result of syphilis, and an additional 154 died of heart disease that may have been caused by the untreated syphilis! In a moving ceremony in 1997, President Clinton officially expressed regret for the experiment to the few survivors and apologized to Black America. Experiments of this type are ghastly, and give rise to suspicions that people of color are being used as guinea pigs in other experiments of this sort. It is this type of study and others that portray people of color as deviants that makes minorities extremely distrustful about the motives of the White researcher. Whereas social scientists in the past have been able to enter ethnic communities and conduct their studies with only minimal justification to those studied, researchers are now being received with suspicion and overt hostility. Minorities are actively raising questions and issues regarding the values system of researchers and the outcome of their research. The question increasingly asked relates to the motives of the researcher. Is research conducted for some definable good, or is it opportunistic, exploitative, and potentially damaging to the target populations?

Implications for Clinical Practice

If the mental health profession and its practitioners are to receive acceptance from marginalized groups in our society, they must demonstrate, in no uncertain terms, their good faith and their ability to contribute to the betterment of a group's quality of life. This demonstration can take several directions.

1. The mental health profession must take the initiative in confronting the potential political nature of mental health practice. For too long we have deceived ourselves into believing that the practice of counseling/therapy and the database that underlie the profession are morally, ethically, and politically neutral. The results have been (a) subjugation of minority groups, (b) perpetuation of the view that they are inherently pathological, (c) perpetuation of racist practices in treatment, and

(d) provision of an excuse to the profession for not taking social action to rectify inequities in the system.

2. Mental health professionals must move quickly to challenge certain assumptions that permeate our training programs. We must critically re-examine our concepts of what constitutes normality and abnormality, begin mandatory training programs that deal with these issues, critically examine and reinterpret past and continuing literature dealing with the culturally different, and use research in such a manner as to improve the life conditions of the researched populations.

3. We must make sure that educational programs can no longer present a predominantly White Anglo-Saxon Protestant (WASP) orientation. The study of minority group cultures must receive equal treatment and fair portrayal on all levels of education. Courses dealing with minority group experiences and internship practices must become a required part of the training programs.

4. Research can be a powerful means of combating stereotypes and of correcting biased studies. The fact that previous studies have been used to perpetuate stereotypes does not preclude the usefulness of research. If social scientists believe that research has been poorly conducted or misinterpreted to the detriment of minority groups, they should feel some moral commitment to investigate their beliefs. Researchers cannot escape the moral and ethical implications of their research and must take responsibility for the outcome of their studies. They must guard against misinterpretations and take into account cultural factors and limitations of their instruments.

5. Social scientists must realize that many so-called pathological socio-emotional characteristics of ethnic minorities can be directly attributed to unfair practices in society. There must be a shift in research, from focusing on the poor and culturally diverse to focusing on the groups and institutions that have perpetuated racism and obstructed needed changes.

6. We need to balance our study by also focusing on the positive attributes and characteristics of ethnic minorities. Social scientists have had a tendency to look for pathology and problems among minorities. Too much research has concentrated on the mental health problems and cultural conflict of minorities, while little has been done to determine the advantages of being bicultural. Hopefully, such an orientation will do much to present a more balanced picture of different minority groups.

Sociopolitical Implications of Oppression: Trust and Mistrust in Counseling/Therapy

4

Chapter

I have worked with very few African American clients during my internship at the clinic, but one particular incident left me with very negative feelings. A Black client named Malachi was given an appointment with me. Even though I'm White, I tried not to let his being Black get in the way of our sessions. I treated him like everyone else, a human being who needed help.

At the onset, Malachi was obviously guarded, mistrustful, and frustrated when talking about his reasons for coming. While his intake form listed depression as the problem, he seemed more concerned about nonclinical matters. He spoke about his inability to find a job, about the need to obtain help with job-hunting skills, and about advice in how best to write his résumé. He was quite demanding in asking for advice and information. It was almost as if Malachi wanted everything handed to him on a silver platter without putting any work into our sessions. Not only did he appear reluctant to take responsibility to change his own life, but I felt he needed to go elsewhere for help. After all, this was a mental health clinic, not an employment agency. Confronting him about his avoidance of responsibility would probably prove counterproductive, so I chose to focus on his feelings. Using a humanistic-existential approach, I reflected his feelings, paraphrased his thoughts, and summarized his dilemmas. This did not seem to help immediately, as I sensed an increase in the tension level, and he seemed antagonistic toward me.

After several attempts by Malachi to obtain direct advice from me, I stated, "You're getting frustrated at me because I'm not giving you the answers you want." It was clear that this angered Malachi. Getting up in a very menacing manner, he stood over me and angrily shouted, "Forget it, man! I don't have time to play your silly games." For one brief moment, I felt in danger of being physically assaulted before he stormed out of the office.

This incident occurred several years ago, and I must admit that I was left with a very unfavorable impression of Blacks. I see myself as basically a good person who truly wants to help others less fortunate than myself. I know it sounds racist, but Malachi's behavior only reinforces my belief that Blacks have trouble controlling their anger, like to take the easy way out, and find it difficult to be open and trusting of others. If I am wrong in this belief, I hope this workshop [multicultural counseling/therapy] will help me better understand the Black personality.

A variation of the above incident was supplied at an in-service training workshop by a White male therapist, and is used here to illustrate some of the major issues addressed in this chapter. In Chapter 3 we asserted that mental health practice is strongly influenced by historical and current sociopolitical forces that impinge on issues of race, culture, and ethnicity. Specifically, we made a point that (a) the therapeutic session is often a microcosm of race relations in our larger society, (b) the therapist often inherits the biases of his or her forebears, and (c) therapy represents a primarily Euro-American activity that may clash with the worldviews of culturally diverse clients. In this case, we question neither the sincerity of the White therapist nor his desire to help the African American client. However, it is obvious to us that the therapist is part of the problem and not the solution. The male therapist's preconceived notions and stereotypes about African Americans appear to have affected his definition of the problem, assessment of the situation, and therapeutic intervention. Let us analyze this case in greater detail to illustrate our contention.

First, statements about Malachi's wanting things handed to him on a "silver platter," his "avoidance of responsibility," and his "wanting to take the easy way out" are symbolic of social stereotypes that Blacks are lazy and unmotivated. The therapist's statements that African Americans have difficulty "controlling their anger," that Malachi was "menacing," and that the therapist was in fear of being assaulted seem to paint the picture of the hostile, angry, and violent Black male—again an image of African Americans to which many in this society consciously and unconsciously subscribe. While it is always possible that the client was unmotivated and prone to violence, studies suggest that White Americans continue to cling to the image of the dangerous, violence-prone, and antisocial image of Black men (J. M. Jones, 1997). Is it possible, however, that Malachi has a legitimate reason for being angry? Is it possible that the therapist and the therapeutic process are contributing to Malachi's frustration and anger? Is it possible that the therapist was never in physical danger, but that his own affectively based stereotype of the dangerous Black male caused his unreasonable fear? Might not this potential misinterpretation be a clash of different communications styles that triggers unrealistic racial fears and apprehensions? We strongly encourage you to explore these questions with colleagues and students.

Second, mental health practice has been characterized as primarily a

White middle-class activity that values rugged individualism, individual responsibility, and autonomy. Because people are seen as being responsible for their own actions and predicaments, clients are expected to "make decisions on their own" and to "be primarily responsible for their fate in life." The traditional therapist's role should be to encourage self-exploration so that the client can act on his or her own behalf. The individual-centered approach tends to view the problem as residing within the person. If something goes wrong, it is the client's fault. In the last chapter we pointed out how many problems encountered by minority clients reside externally to them (bias, discrimination, prejudice, etc.) and that they should not be faulted for the obstacles they encounter. To do so is to engage in victim blaming (Ridley, 2005; W. Ryan, 1971).

Third, therapists are expected to avoid giving advice or suggestions and disclosing their thoughts and feelings—not only because they may unduly influence their clients and arrest their individual development, but also because they may become emotionally involved, lose their objectivity, and blur the boundaries of the helping relationship (Pack-Brown & Williams, 2003). Parham (1997) states, however, that a fundamental African principle is that human beings realize themselves only in moral relations to others (collectivity, not individuality): "Consequently, application of an African centered worldview will cause one to question the need for objectivity absent emotions, the need for distance rather than connectedness, and the need for dichotomous relationships rather than multiple roles" (p. 110). In other words, from an African American perspective, the helper and helpee are not separated from one another but are bound together both emotionally and spiritually. The Euro-American style of objectivity encourages separation that may be interpreted by Malachi as uninvolved, uncaring, insincere, and dishonest—that is, "playing silly games."

Fourth, the more active and involved role demanded by Malachi goes against what the helping profession considers "therapy." Studies seem to indicate that clients of color prefer a therapeutic relationship in which the helper is more active, self-disclosing, and not adverse to giving advice and suggestions when appropriate (D. W. Sue, Ivey, & Pedersen, 1996). The therapist in this scenario fails to entertain the possibility that requests for advice, information, and suggestions may be legitimate and not indicative of pathological responding. The therapist has been trained to believe that his role as a therapist is to be primarily nondirective; therapists do "therapy," not provide job-hunting information. This has always been the conventional counseling and psychotherapy role, one whose emphasis is a one-to-one, in-the-office, and remedial relationship aimed at self-exploration and the achievement of insight (Atkinson, Thompson, & Grant, 1993). We will have more to say about how these generic characteristics of counseling and psychotherapy may act as barriers to effective multicultural counseling/therapy in the next chapter.

Many of the previous conflicts lead us to our fifth point. If the male therapist is truly operating from unconscious biases, stereotypes, and preconceived notions with his culturally different client, then much of the problem seems to reside within him and not with Malachi. In almost every introductory text on counseling and psychotherapy, lip service is paid to the axiom, "Counselor, know thyself." In other words, therapeutic wisdom endorses the notion that we become better therapists the more we understand our own motives, biases, values, and assumptions about human behavior. Unfortunately, as indicated in the last chapter, most training programs are weak in having their students explore their values, biases, and preconceived notions in the area of racist/sexist/homophobic attitudes, beliefs, and behaviors. We are taught to look at our clients, to analyze them, and to note their weaknesses, limitations, and pathological trends; less often do we either look for positive healthy characteristics in our clients or question our conclusions. Questioning our own values and assumptions, the standards that we use to judge normality and abnormality, and our therapeutic approach is infrequently done. As mental health professionals, we may find it difficult and unpleasant to explore our racism, sexism, and homophobia, and our training often allows us the means to avoid it.

When the therapist ends his story by stating that he hopes the workshop will "help me better understand the Black personality," his worldview is clearly evident. There is an assumption that multicultural counseling/therapy simply requires the acquisition of knowledge, and that good intentions are all that is needed. This statement represents one of the major obstacles to self-awareness and dealing with one's own biases and prejudices. While we tend to view prejudice, discrimination, racism, and sexism as overt and intentional acts of unfairness and violence, unintentional and covert forms of bias may be the greater enemy because they are unseen and more pervasive. Like this therapist, well-intentioned individuals experience themselves as moral, just, fair-minded, and decent. Thus, it is difficult for many mental health professionals to realize that what they do or say may cause harm to their minority clients:

> *Unintentional behavior is perhaps the most insidious form of racism. Unintentional racists are unaware of the harmful consequences of their behavior. They may be well-intentioned, and on the surface, their behavior may appear to be responsible. Because individuals, groups, or institutions that engage in unintentional racism do not wish to do harm, it is difficult to get them to see themselves as racists. They are more likely to deny their racism. . . . The major challenge facing counselors is to overcome unintentional racism and provide more equitable service delivery. (Ridley, 1995, p. 38)*

Sixth, the therapist states that he tried to not let Malachi's "being Black get in the way" of the session and that he treated him like any other "human being." This is a very typical statement made by Whites who unconsciously subscribe to the belief that being Black, Asian American, Latino American, or a person of color is the problem. In reality, color is not the problem. It is society's perception of color that is the problem! In other words, the locus of the problem (racism, sexism, and homophobia) resides not in marginalized groups, but in the society at large. Often this view of race is manifested in the myth of color blindness: If color is the problem, let's pretend not to see it. Our contention, however, is that it is nearly impossible to overlook the fact that a client is Black, Asian American, Hispanic, and so forth. When operating in this manner, color-blind therapists may actually be obscuring their understandings of who their clients really are. To overlook one's racial group membership is to deny an intimate and important aspect of one's identity. Those who advocate a color-blind approach seem to operate under the assumption that Black is bad and that to be different is to be deviant.

Last, and central to the thesis of this chapter, is the statement by the counselor that Malachi appears guarded and mistrustful and has difficulty being open (self-disclosing). We have mentioned several times that a counselor's inability to establish rapport and a relationship of trust with culturally diverse clients is a major therapeutic barrier. When the emotional climate is negative, and when little trust or understanding exists between the therapist and the client, therapy can be both ineffective and destructive. Yet if the emotional climate is realistically positive and if trust and understanding exist between the parties, the two-way communication of thoughts and feelings can proceed with optimism. This latter condition is often referred to as *rapport*, and sets the stage in which other essential conditions can become effective. One of these, self-disclosure, is particularly crucial to the process and goals of counseling because it is the most direct means by which an individual makes him- or herself known to another.

This chapter attempts to discuss the issue of trust as it relates to minority clients. Our discussion does not deal with cultural variables among certain groups (Asian Americans, American Indians, etc.) that dictate against self-disclosure to strangers. This topic is presented in Chapter 6. We first present a brief discussion of the sociopolitical situation as it affects the trust-mistrust dimension of certain culturally diverse populations. Second, we look at factors that enhance or negate the therapist's cultural effectiveness as it relates to the theory of social influence. Third, we systematically examine how therapist credibility and similarity affect a client's willingness to work with a therapist from another race/culture.

Effects of Historical and Current Oppression

Mental health practitioners must realize that racial/ethnic minorities and other marginalized groups (women, gays/lesbians, and the disabled) in our society live under an umbrella of individual, institutional, and cultural forces that often demean them, disadvantage them, and deny them equal access and opportunity (Croteau, Lark, Lidderdale & Chung, 2005; Ponterotto, Utsey, & Pedersen, 2006; Ridley, 2005). Experiences of prejudice and discrimination are a social reality for many marginalized groups and affect their worldview of the helping professional who attempts to work in the multicultural arena. Thus, mental health practitioners must become aware of the sociopolitical dynamics that form not only their clients' worldviews, but their own as well. As in the clinical case presented earlier, racial/cultural dynamics may intrude into the helping process and cause misdiagnosis, confusion, pain, and a rein- forcement of the biases and stereotypes that both groups have of one another. It is important for the therapist to realize that the history of race relations in the United States has influenced us to the point that we are extremely cau- tious about revealing to strangers our feelings and attitudes about race. In an interracial encounter with a stranger (i.e., therapy), each party will attempt to discern gross or subtle racial attitudes of the other while minimizing vul- nerability. For minorities in the United States, this lesson has been learned well. While White Americans may also exhibit caution similar to that of their minority counterparts, the structure of society places more power to injure and damage in the hands of the majority culture. In most self-disclosing situ- ations, White Americans are less vulnerable than their minority counter- parts.

As the individual chapters on American Indians, Asian Americans, Blacks, Hispanics, and other culturally diverse groups (gays/lesbians, women, persons with disabilities, and the elderly) will reveal, the histories and expe- riences of these groups have been fraught with oppression, discrimination, and racism. Institutional racism has created psychological barriers among mi- norities and White Americans that are likely to interfere with the therapy process. Understanding how the invisibility of ethnocentric monoculturalism has affected race, gender, and sexual orientation relationships is vital to suc- cessful multicultural competence.

Ethnocentric Monoculturalism

It is becoming increasingly clear that the values, assumptions, beliefs, and practices of our society are structured in such a manner as to serve only one narrow segment of the population (D. W. Sue, 2001). Most mental health professionals, for example, have not been trained to work with anyone other than mainstream individuals or groups. This is understandable in light of the historical origins of education, counseling/guidance, and our mental health systems, which have their roots in Euro-American or Western cultures (Highlen, 1994; Wehrly, 1995). As a result, American (U.S.) psychology has been severely criticized as being ethnocentric, monocultural, and inherently biased against racial/ethnic minorities, women, gays/lesbians, and other culturally diverse groups (Constantine & Sue, 2006; Laird & Green, 1996; Ridley, 2005). As voiced by many multicultural specialists, our educational system and counseling/psychotherapy have often done great harm to our minority citizens. Rather than educate or heal, rather than offer enlightenment and freedom, and rather than allow for equal access and opportunities, historical and current practices have restricted, stereotyped, damaged, and oppressed the culturally different in our society.

In light of the increasing diversity of our society, mental health professionals will inevitably encounter client populations that differ from themselves in terms of race, culture, and ethnicity. Such changes, however, are believed to pose no problems as long as psychologists adhere to the notion of an unyielding, universal psychology that is applicable across all populations. While few mental health professionals would voice such a belief, in reality the very policies and practices of mental health delivery systems do reflect such an ethnocentric orientation. The theories of counseling and psychotherapy, the standards used to judge normality-abnormality, and the actual process of mental health practice are culture-bound and reflect a monocultural perspective of the helping professions (Highlen, 1994; Katz, 1985; D. Sue, 1990). As such, they are often culturally inappropriate and antagonistic to the lifestyles and values of minority groups in our society. Indeed, some mental health professionals assert that counseling and psychotherapy may be handmaidens of the status quo, instruments of oppression, and transmitters of society's values (Halleck, 1971; D. W. Sue & Sue, 1990; A. Thomas & Sillen, 1972).

We believe that ethnocentric monoculturalism is dysfunctional in a pluralistic society such as the United States. It is a powerful force, however, in forming, influencing, and determining the goals and processes of mental health delivery systems. As such, it is very important for mental health professionals to unmask or deconstruct the values, biases, and assumptions that reside in it. Ethnocentric monoculturalism combines what Wrenn (1962, 1985) calls *cultural encapsulation* and what J. M. Jones (1972, 1997) refers to as *cultural racism*. Five components of ethnocentric monoculturalism have been identified (D. W. Sue, 2004; D. W. Sue et al., 1998).

Belief in Superiority
First, there is a strong belief in the superiority of one group's cultural heritage (history, values, language, traditions, arts/crafts, etc.). The group norms and values are seen positively, and descriptors may include such phrases as "more

advanced" and "more civilized." Members of the society may possess conscious and unconscious feelings of superiority and feel that their way of doing things is the best way. In our society, White Euro-American cultures are seen as not only desirable, but normative as well. Physical characteristics such as light complexion, blond hair, and blue eyes; cultural characteristics such as a belief in Christianity (or monotheism), individualism, Protestant work ethic, and capitalism; and linguistic characteristics such as standard English, control of emotions, and the written tradition are highly valued components of Euro-American culture (Katz, 1985). People possessing these traits are perceived more favorably and often are allowed easier access to the privileges and rewards of the larger society. McIntosh (1989), a White woman, refers to this condition as *White privilege:* an invisible knapsack of unearned assets that can be used to cash in each day for advantages not given to those who do not fit this mold. Among some of the advantages that she enumerates are the following (paraphrased):

- I can if I wish arrange to be in the company of people of my race most of the time.
- I can turn on the television or open to the front page of the newspaper and see people of my race widely represented.
- When I am told about our national heritage or about "civilization," I am shown that people of my color made it what it is.
- I can be sure that my children will be given curricular materials that testify to the existence of their race.

Belief in the Inferiority of Others
Second, there is a belief in the inferiority of racial/ethnic minorities' entire cultural heritage, which extends to their customs, values, traditions, and language. Other societies or groups may be perceived as less developed, uncivilized, primitive, or even pathological. The group's lifestyles or ways of doing things are considered inferior. Physical characteristics such as dark complexion, black hair, and brown eyes; cultural characteristics such as belief in non-Christian religions (Islam, Confucianism, polytheism, etc.), collectivism, present time orientation, and the importance of shared wealth; and linguistic characteristics such as bilingualism, non-standard English, speaking with an accent, use of nonverbal and contextual communication, and reliance on the oral tradition are usually seen as less desirable by the society. Studies consistently reveal that individuals who are physically different, who speak with an accent, and who adhere to different cultural beliefs and practices are more likely to be evaluated more negatively in our schools and workplaces. Culturally diverse groups may be seen as less intelligent, less qualified, and more unpopular, and as possessing more undesirable traits.

Power to Impose Standards

Third, the dominant group possesses the power to impose their standards and beliefs on the less powerful group. This third component of ethnocentric monoculturalism is very important. All groups are to some extent ethnocentric; that is, they feel positively about their cultural heritage and way of life. Minorities can be biased, can hold stereotypes, and can strongly believe that their way is the best way. Yet if they do not possess the power to impose their values on others, then hypothetically they cannot oppress. It is power or the unequal status relationship between groups that defines ethnocentric monoculturalism. The issue here is not to place blame but to speak realistically about how our society operates. Ethnocentric monoculturalism is the individual, institutional, and cultural expression of the superiority of one group's cultural heritage over another combined with the possession of power to impose those standards broadly on the less powerful group. Since minorities generally do not possess a share of economic, social, and political power equal to that of Whites in our society, they are generally unable to discriminate on a large-scale basis. The damage and harm of oppression is likely to be one-sided, from majority to minority group.

Manifestation in Institutions

Fourth, the ethnocentric values and beliefs are manifested in the programs, policies, practices, structures, and institutions of the society. For example, chain-of-command systems, training and educational systems, communications systems, management systems, and performance appraisal systems often dictate and control our lives. Ethnocentric values attain "untouchable and godfather-like" status in an organization. Because most systems are monocultural in nature and demand compliance, racial/ethnic minorities and women may be oppressed. J. M. Jones (1997) labels institutional racism as a set of policies, priorities, and accepted normative patterns designed to subjugate, oppress, and force dependence of individuals and groups on a larger society. It does this by sanctioning unequal goals, unequal status, and unequal access to goods and services. Institutional racism has fostered the enactment of discriminatory statutes, the selective enforcement of laws, the blocking of economic opportunities and outcomes, and the imposition of forced assimilation/acculturation on the culturally different. The sociopolitical system thus attempts to define the prescribed role occupied by minorities. Feelings of powerlessness, inferiority, subordination, deprivation, anger and rage, and overt/covert resistance to factors in interracial relationships are likely to result.

The Invisible Veil

Fifth, since people are all products of cultural conditioning, their values and beliefs (worldviews) represent an *invisible veil* that operates outside the level of conscious awareness. As a result, people assume universality: that regardless of race, culture, ethnicity, or gender, everyone shares the nature of reality and truth. This assumption is erroneous but is seldom questioned because it is firmly ingrained in our worldview. Racism, sexism, and homophobia may be both conscious (intentional) and unconscious (unintentional). Neo-Nazis, skinheads, and the Ku Klux Klan would definitely fall into the first category. While conscious and intentional racism as exemplified by these individuals, for example, may cause great harm to culturally different groups, it is the latter form that may ultimately be the most insidious and dangerous. As mentioned earlier, it is the well-intentioned individuals who consider themselves moral, decent, and fair-minded who may have the greatest difficulty in understanding how their belief systems and actions may be biased and prejudiced. It is clear that no one is born wanting to be racist, sexist, or homophobic. Misinformation related to culturally diverse groups is not acquired by our free choice, but rather is imposed through a painful process of social conditioning; all of us were taught to hate and fear others who are different in some way (D. W. Sue, 2003). Likewise, because all of us live, play, and work within organizations, those policies, practices, and structures that may be less than fair to minority groups are invisible in controlling our lives. Perhaps the greatest obstacle to a meaningful movement toward a multicultural society is our failure to understand our unconscious and unintentional complicity in perpetuating bias and discrimination via our personal values/beliefs and our institutions. The power of racism, sexism, and homophobia is related to the invisibility of the powerful forces that control and dictate our lives. In a strange sort of way, we are all victims. Minority groups are victims of oppression. Majority group members are victims who are unwittingly socialized into the role of oppressor.

Historical Manifestations of Ethnocentric Monoculturalism

The European-American worldview can be described as possessing the following values and beliefs: rugged individualism, competition, mastery and control over nature, a unitary and static conception of time, religion based on Christianity, separation of science and religion, and competition (Katz, 1985). It is important to note that worldviews are neither right or wrong, nor good or bad. They become problematic, however, when they are expressed through the process of ethnocentric monoculturalism. In the United States, the historical manifestations of this process are quite clear. First, the European colonization efforts toward the Americas operated from the assumption that the enculturation of indigenous peoples was justified because European culture was superior. Forcing the colonized to adopt European beliefs and customs was seen as civilizing them. In the United States, this practice was clearly evident in the treatment of Native Americans, whose lifestyles, customs, and practices were seen as backward and uncivilized, and attempts were made to make over the "heathens." Such a belief is also reflected in Euro-American culture and has been manifested also in attitudes toward other racial/ethnic minority groups in the United States. A common belief is that racial/ethnic minorities would not encounter problems if they assimilate and acculturate.

Monocultural ethnocentric bias has a long history in the United States and is even reflected as early as the uneven application of the "Bill of Rights," which favored White immigrants/descendants over "minority" populations (Barongan et al., 1997). Over some 200 years ago, Britain's King George III accepted a "Declaration of Independence" from former subjects who moved to this country. This proclamation was destined to shape and reshape the geopolitical and sociocultural landscape of the world many times over. The lofty language penned by its principal architect, Thomas Jefferson, and signed by those present was indeed inspiring: "We hold these truths to be self-evident, that all men are created equal."

Yet as we now view the historic actions of that time, we cannot help but be struck by the paradox inherent in those events. First, all 56 of the signatories were White males of European descent, hardly a representation of the current racial and gender composition of the population. Second, the language of the declaration suggests that only men were created equal; what about women? Third, many of the founding fathers were slave owners who seemed not to recognize the hypocritical personal standards that they used because they considered Blacks to be subhuman. Fourth, the history of this land did not start with the Declaration of Independence or the formation of the United States of America. Nevertheless, our textbooks continue to teach us an ethnocentric perspective ("Western Civilization") that ignores over two thirds of the world's population. Last, it is important to note that those early Europeans who came to this country were immigrants attempting to escape persecution (oppression), who in the process did not recognize their own role in the oppression of indigenous peoples (American Indians) who had already resided in this country for centuries. As Barongan et al. (1997, p. 654) described,

> *the natural and inalienable rights of individuals valued by European and European American societies generally appear to have been intended for European Americans only. How else can European colonization and exploitation of Third World countries be explained? How else can the forced removal of Native Americans from their lands, centuries of enslavement and segregation of African Americans, immigration restrictions on persons of color through history, incarceration of Japanese Americans during World War II, and current English-only language requirements in the United States be explained? These acts have not been perpetrated by a few racist individuals, but by no less than the governments of the North Atlantic cultures. . . . If Euro-American ideals include a philosophi-*

cal or moral opposition to racism, this has often not been reflected in policies and behaviors.

We do not take issue with the good intentions of the early founders. Nor do we infer in them evil and conscious motivations to oppress and dominate others. Yet the history of the United States has been the history of oppression and discrimination against racial/ethnic minorities and women. The Western European cultures that formed the fabric of the United States of America are relatively homogeneous compared not only to the rest of the world, but also to the increasing diversity in this country. This Euro-American worldview continues to form the foundations of our educational, social, economic, cultural, and political systems.

As more and more White immigrants came to the North American continent, the guiding principle of blending the many cultures became codified into such concepts as the "melting pot" and "assimilation/acculturation." The most desirable outcome of this process was a uniform and homogeneous consolidation of cultures—in essence, to become monocultural. Many psychologists of color, however, have referred to this process as *cultural genocide,* an outcome of colonial thought (Guthrie, 1997; Parham et al., 1999; Samuda, 1998; A. Thomas & Sillen, 1972). Wehrly (1995, p. 24) states, "Cultural assimilation, as practiced in the United States, is the expectation by the people in power that all immigrants and people outside the dominant group will give up their ethnic and cultural values and will adopt the values and norms of the dominant society—the White, male Euro-Americans."

While ethnocentric monoculturalism is much broader than the concept of race, it is race and color that have been used to determine the social order (Carter, 1995). The "White race" has been seen as being superior and White culture as normative. Thus, a study of U.S. history must include a study of racism and racist practices directed at people of color. The oppression of the indigenous people of this country (Native Americans), enslavement of African Americans, widespread segregation of Hispanic Americans, passage of exclusionary laws against the Chinese, and the forced internment of Japanese Americans are social realities. Thus it should be of no surprise that our racial/ethnic minority citizens may view Euro-Americans and our very institutions with considerable mistrust and suspicion. In health care delivery systems and especially in counseling and psychotherapy, which demand a certain degree of trust among therapist and client groups, an interracial encounter may be fraught with historical and current psychological baggage related to issues of discrimination, prejudice, and oppression. Carter (1995, p. 27) draws the following conclusion related to mental health delivery systems: "Because any institution in a society is shaped by social and cultural forces, it is reasonable to assume that racist notions have been incorporated into the mental health systems."

Therapeutic Impact of Ethnocentric Monoculturalism

Many multicultural specialists (Kochman, 1981; Locke, 1998; Parham, 2002; Ponterotto, Utsey, & Pedersen, 2006) have pointed out how African Americans, in responding to their forced enslavement, history of discrimination, and America's reaction to their skin color, have adopted toward Whites behavior patterns that are important for survival in a racist society. These behavior patterns may include indirect expressions of hostility, aggression, and fear. During slavery, to rear children who would fit into a segregated system and who could physically survive, African American mothers were forced to teach them (a) to express aggression indirectly, (b) to read the thoughts of others while hiding their own, and (c) to engage in ritualized accommodating-subordinating behaviors designed to create as few waves as possible. This process involves a "mild dissociation" whereby African Americans may separate their true selves from their roles as "Negroes" (Boyd-Franklin, 2003; C. A. Pinderhughes, 1973). In this dual identity the true self is revealed to fellow Blacks, while the dissociated self is revealed to meet the expectations of prejudiced Whites. From the analysis of African American history, the dissociative process may be manifested in two major ways.

First, "playing it cool" has been identified as one means by which African Americans or other minorities may conceal their true feelings (Boyd-Franklin, 2003; Cross, Smith, & Payne, 2002; Grier & Cobbs, 1971; A. C. Jones, 1985). This behavior is intended to prevent Whites from knowing what the minority person is thinking or feeling and to express feelings and behaviors in such a way as to prevent offending or threatening Whites (Jones & Shorter-Gooden, 2003; Ridley, 2005). Thus, a person of color who is experiencing conflict, explosive anger, and suppressed feelings may appear serene and composed on the surface. This is a defense mechanism aimed at protecting minorities from harm and exploitation. Second, the *Uncle Tom syndrome* may be used by minorities to appear docile, nonassertive, and happy-go-lucky. Especially during slavery, Blacks learned that passivity is a necessary survival technique. To retain the most menial jobs, to minimize retaliation, and to maximize survival of the self and loved ones, many minorities have learned to deny their aggressive feelings toward their oppressors.

The overall result of the experiences of minorities in the United States has been to increase their vigilance and sensitivity to the thoughts and behaviors of Whites in society. We mentioned earlier that African Americans have been forced to read the thoughts of others accurately in order to survive (Cross, Smith, & Payne, 2002). It has been found that certain minority groups, such as African Americans, are better readers of nonverbal communication that their White counterparts (Kochman, 1981; D. W. Sue, 1990). This will be discussed in greater detail in Chapter 7. Many African Americans have often stated that Whites say one thing but mean another. This better understanding and sensitivity to nonverbal communication has enhanced Black people's survival in a highly dangerous society. As we see later, it is important for the minority individual to read nonverbal messages accurately—not only for physical survival, but for psychological reasons as well.

In summary, it becomes all too clear that past and present discrimination against certain culturally diverse groups is a tangible basis for minority distrust of the majority society (Ponterotto, Utsey, & Pedersen, 2006). White people are perceived as potential oppressors unless proved otherwise. Under such a sociopolitical atmosphere, minorities may use several adaptive devices to prevent Whites from knowing their true feelings. Because multicultural counseling may mirror the sentiments of the larger society, these modes of behavior and their detrimental effects may be reenacted in the sessions. The fact that many minority clients are suspicious, mistrustful, and guarded in their interactions with White therapists is certainly understandable in light of the foregoing analysis. Despite their conscious desires to help, White therapists are not immune from inheriting racist attitudes, beliefs, myths, and stereotypes about Asian American, African American, Latino/Hispanic American, and American Indian clients (D. W. Sue, 2005). For example, White counselors often believe that Blacks are nonverbal, paranoid, and angry, and that they are most likely to have character disorders (Carter, 1995; A. C. Jones, 1985) or to be schizophrenic (Pavkov, Lewis, & Lyons, 1989). As a result, they view African Americans as unsuitable for counseling and psychotherapy. Mental health practitioners and social scientists who hold to this belief fail to understand the following facts:

1. As a group, African Americans tend to communicate nonverbally more than their White counterparts and to assume that nonverbal communication is a more accurate barometer of one's true feelings and beliefs. E. T. Hall (1976) observed that African Americans are better able to read nonverbal messages (high context) than are their White counterparts and that they rely less on verbalizations than on nonverbal communication to make a point. Whites, on the other hand, tune in more to verbal messages than to nonverbal messages (low context). Because they rely less on nonverbal cues, Whites need greater verbal elaborations to get a point across (D. W. Sue et al., 1996). Being unaware of and insensitive to these differences, White therapists are prone to feel that African Americans are unable to communicate in "complex" ways. This judgment is based on the high value that therapy places on intellectual/verbal activity.

2. Rightfully or not, White therapists are often perceived as symbols of the Establishment who have inherited the racial biases of their forebears. Thus, the culturally diverse client is likely to impute all the negative experiences of oppression to them. This may prevent the minority client

from responding to the helping professional as an individual. While the therapist may be possessed of the most admirable motives, the client may reject the helping professional simply because he or she is White. Thus, communication may be directly or indirectly shut off.

3. Some culturally diverse clients may lack confidence in the counseling and therapy process because the White counselor often proposes White solutions to their concerns (Atkinson et al., 1998). Many pressures are placed on minority clients to accept an alien value system and reject their own. We have already indicated how counseling and psychotherapy may be perceived as instruments of oppression whose function is to force assimilation and acculturation. As some racial/ethnic minority clients have asked, "Why do I have to become White in order to be considered healthy?"

The "playing it cool" and "Uncle Tom" responses of many minorities are present also in the therapy sessions. As pointed out earlier, these mechanisms are attempts to conceal true feelings, to hinder self-disclosure, and to prevent the therapist from getting to know the client. These adaptive survival mechanisms have been acquired through generations of experience with a hostile and invalidating society. The therapeutic dilemma encountered by the helping professional in working with a client of color is how to gain trust and break through this maze. What the therapist ultimately does in the sessions will determine his or her trustworthiness.

To summarize, culturally diverse clients entering counseling or therapy are likely to experience considerable anxiety about ethnic/racial/cultural differences. Suspicion, apprehension, verbal constriction, unnatural reactions, open resentment and hostility, and passive or cool behavior may all be expressed. Self-disclosure and the possible establishment of a working relationship can be seriously delayed or prevented from occurring. In all cases, the therapist's trustworthiness may be put to severe tests. A culturally effective therapist is one who (a) can view these behaviors in a nonjudgmental manner (i.e., they are not necessarily indicative of pathology but are a manifestation of adaptive survival mechanisms), (b) can avoid personalizing any potential hostility expressed toward him or her, and (c) can adequately resolve challenges to his or her credibility. Thus, it becomes important for us to understand those dimensions that may enhance or diminish the culturally different client's receptivity to self-disclosure.

Credibility and Attractiveness in Multicultural Counseling

Theories of counseling and psychotherapy attempt to outline an approach designed to make them effective. It is our contention that multicultural helping cannot be approached through any one theory of counseling (D. W. Sue et al., 1996). There are several reasons for such a statement. First, theories of counseling are composed of philosophical assumptions regarding the nature of "man" and a theory of personality. As pointed out earlier, these characteristics are highly culture-bound (Katz, 1985; D. W. Sue, 1995a). The "true" nature of people is a philosophical question. What constitutes the healthy and unhealthy personality is also debatable and varies from culture to culture and from class to class.

Second, theories of counseling and psychotherapy are composed also of a body of therapeutic techniques and strategies. These techniques are applied to clients with the hope of effecting change in behaviors, perceptions, or attitudes. A theory dictates what techniques are to be used and, implicitly, in what proportions (Corey, 2005; D. W. Sue et al., 1996). For example, it is clear that humanistic-existential therapists behave differently than do rational-emotive ones. The fact that one school of counseling/therapy can be distinguished from another has implications: It suggests a certain degree of rigidity in working with culturally different clients who might find such techniques offensive or inappropriate. The implicit assumption is that these techniques are imposed according to the theory and not based on client needs and values.

Third, theories of counseling and psychotherapy have often failed to agree among themselves about what constitutes desirable outcomes. This makes it extremely difficult to determine the effectiveness of counseling and therapy. For example, the psychoanalytically oriented therapist uses "insight"; the behaviorist uses "behavior change"; the client-centered person uses "self-actualization"; and the rational-emotive person uses "rational cognitive content/processes." The potential for disagreement over appropriate outcome variables is increased even further when the therapist and client come from different cultures.

Counseling as Interpersonal Influence

Therapy may be conceptualized as an interpersonal-influence process in which the counselor uses social power to influence the client's attitudes and behaviors. Strong (1969) is probably the person most credited with providing a conceptual framework for understanding parallels between the role of the therapist, the process of therapy, and the outcome of therapy with those of the persuasive communicator, the influencing process, and opinion/behavior change, respectively. Specifically, counselors who are perceived by their clients as credible (expert and trustworthy) and attractive are able to exert greater influence than are those perceived as lacking in credibility and attractiveness (Heesacker & Carroll, 1997). Regardless of the counseling orientation (person-centered, psychoanalytic, behavioral, transactional analysis, etc.), the therapist's effectiveness tends to depend on the client's perception of his or her expertness, trustworthiness, and attractiveness.

Most of the studies on social influence and counseling have dealt exclusively with a White population (Heesacker, Conner, & Pritchard, 1995). Thus, findings that certain attributes contribute to a counselor's credibility and attractiveness may not be so perceived by culturally diverse clients. It is entirely possible that credibility, as defined by credentials indicating specialized training (e.g., MFCC, MSW, PsyD, PhD, MD), might only indicate to a Latino client that the White therapist has no knowledge or expertise in working with Latinos. This assumption is based on the fact that most training programs are geared for White middle-class clients and are culturally exclusive. It seems important, therefore, for helping professionals to understand what factors/conditions may enhance or negate counselor credibility and attractiveness when working with clients of color.

Psychological Sets of Clients

The therapist's credibility and attractiveness depend very much on the mindset or frame of reference for culturally diverse clients. We all know individuals who tend to value rational approaches to solving problems and others who value a more affective (attractiveness) approach. It would seem reasonable that a client who values rationality might be more receptive to a rational counseling approach as a means to enhance counselor credibility. Understanding a client's psychological mindset may facilitate the therapist's ability to exert social influence in counseling. In a very useful model, Collins (1970) proposed a set of conceptual categories that can be used to understand people's perception of communicator (counselor) credibility and receptiveness to influence. We apply those categories here with respect to the therapy situation. Note that race, ethnicity, and the experience of discrimination often affect the type of set that will be operative in a minority client.

1. The problem-solving set: Information orientation. In the problem-solving set, the client is concerned about obtaining correct information (solutions, outlooks, and skills) that has adaptive value in the real world. The client accepts or rejects information from the therapist on the basis of its perceived truth or falsity: Is it an accurate representation of reality? The processes that are used tend to be rational and logical in analyzing and attacking the problem. First, the client may apply a consistency test and compare the new facts with earlier information. For example, a White male therapist might try to reassure an African American client that he is not against interracial marriage, but hesitate in speech and tense up whenever the topic is broached (Utsey, Gernat, & Hammer, 2005). In this case, the verbal or content message is inconsistent with nonverbal cues, and the credibility and social influence of the therapist are likely to decline. Second, the Black client may apply a corroboration test by actively seeking information from others for comparison purposes. If he or she hears from a friend that the therapist has racial hang-ups, then again the therapist's effectiveness is likely to be severely diminished. The former test makes use of information that the individual already has (understanding of nonverbal meanings), while the latter requires him or her to seek out new information (asking a trusted African American friend). Through their experiences, clients of color may have learned that many Whites have little expertise when it comes to their lifestyles and that the information or suggestions that they give are White solutions or labels. Likewise, many Puerto Ricans who come for counseling and therapy expect information, advice, and direct suggestions. Therapists who do not value the problem-solving set and who may be affectively oriented may actually have great difficulties in relating to the client.

2. The consistency set. People are operating under the consistency set whenever they change an opinion, belief, or behavior in such a way as to make it consistent with other opinions, beliefs, or behaviors. This principle is best illustrated in Festinger's classic book *A Theory of Cognitive Dissonance* (1957). Stated simply, the theory says that when a person's attitudes, opinions, or beliefs are met with disagreement (inconsistencies), cognitive imbalance or dissonance will be created. The dissonance is psychologically uncomfortable and produces tension with drive characteristics. The result is an attempt to reduce the dissonance. For example, since therapists are supposed to help, we naturally believe that they would not do something to hurt us. The rules of the consistency set specify that "good people do good things" and "bad people do bad things." It is important to note that the consistency set states that people are not necessarily *rational* beings but *rationalizing* ones. A therapist who is not in touch with personal prejudices or biases may send out conflicting messages to a minority client. The counselor may verbally state, "I am here to help you," but at the same time indicate racist attitudes and feelings nonverbally. This can destroy the counselor's credibility very quickly, for example, in the case of a minority client who accurately applies a consistency set such as, "White people say one thing, but do another. You can't believe what they tell you." A culturally different client will actively seek out disclosures on the part of the therapist to compare them with the information he or she has about the world. Should the therapist pass the test, new information may be more readily accepted and assimilated.

3. The identity set. An individual who strongly identifies with a particular group is likely to accept the group's beliefs and conform to behaviors dictated by the group. If race or ethnicity constitute a strong reference group for a client, then a counselor of the same race/ethnicity is likely to be more influential than is one who is not. A number of studies (see reviews by Atkinson, 1983, 1985; Atkinson & Schein, 1986) indicate that certain similarities between the counselor and client may actually enhance therapeutic longevity and therapist preference. For example, racial similarity between therapist and client may actually increase willingness to return for therapy and facilitate effectiveness. The studies on this are quite mixed, as there is considerable evidence that membership group similarity may not be as effective as belief or attitude similarity. It has also been found that the stage of cultural or racial identity affects which dimensions of similarities will be preferred by the racial/ethnic minority client (Cross, Smith, & Payne, 2002; Helms, 1995; Parham, 1989). We have much more to say about cultural identity development later. It is obvious, however, that racial differences between counselor and client makes bridging this gap a major challenge.

4. The economic set. In the economic set, the person is influenced because of the perceived rewards and punishments that the source is able to deliver. In this set, a person performs a behavior or states a belief in order to gain rewards and avoid punishments. In the counseling setting, this means that the therapist controls important resources that may affect the client. For example, a therapist may decide to recommend the expulsion of a student from the school or deny a positive parole recommendation to a client who is in prison. In less subtle ways, the therapist may ridicule or praise a client during a group counseling session. In these cases, the client may decide to alter his or her behavior because the therapist holds greater power. The major problem with the use of rewards and punishments to induce change is that while it may assure *behavioral compliance,* it does not guarantee *private acceptance.* As noted, racial/ethnic minorities are well versed in recognizing power differentials and behaving accordingly (i.e., playing it cool or using the Uncle Tom approach; Cross et al., 2002). Furthermore, for rewards and coercive power to be effective, the therapist must maintain constant surveillance. Once the surveillance is removed, the client is likely to revert back to previous modes of behavior. For culturally diverse clients, therapy that operates primarily on the economic set is more likely to prevent the development of trust, rapport, and self-disclosure.

5. The authority set. Under this set, some individuals are thought to have a particular position that gives them a legitimate right to prescribe attitudes or behaviors. In our society, we have been conditioned to believe that certain authorities (police officers, chairpersons, designated leaders, etc.) have the right to demand compliance. This occurs via training in role behavior and group norms. Mental health professionals, like counselors, are thought to have a legitimate right to recommend and provide psychological treatment to disturbed or troubled clients. It is this psychological set that legitimizes the counselor's role as a helping professional. Yet for many minorities, it is exactly these roles in society that are perceived as instruments of institutional oppression and racism. The 1996 O. J. Simpson trial and verdict brought out major differences in how African Americans and White Americans perceived the police. African Americans were more likely, as a group, to entertain the notion that police officers deliberately tampered with evidence because Simpson was a Black man; White Americans, however, were much less inclined to believe the police could act in such a manner.

It should be clear at this point that characteristics of the influencing source (therapist) are of the utmost importance in eliciting types of changes. In addition, the type of mental or psychological set placed in operation often dictates the permanency and degree of attitude/belief change. While these sets operate similarly for both majority and minority clients, their manifestations may be quite different. Obviously, a minority client may have great difficulty identifying (identification set) with a counselor from another race or culture. Also, what constitutes credibility to minority clients may be far different from what constitutes credibility to a majority client.

Therapist Credibility

Credibility (which elicits the problem-solving, consistency, and identification sets) may be defined as the constellation of characteristics that makes certain individuals appear worthy of belief, capable, entitled to confidence, reliable, and trustworthy. Expertness is an "ability" variable, while trustworthiness is a "motivation" variable. Expertness depends on how well informed, capable, or intelligent others perceive the communicator (counselor). Trustworthiness is dependent on the degree to which people perceive the communicator (therapist) as motivated to make invalid assertions. The weight of evidence supports our commonsense beliefs that the helping professional who is perceived as expert and trustworthy can influence clients more than can one who is perceived to be lower on these traits.

Expertness. Clients often go to a therapist not only because they are in distress and in need of relief, but also because they believe the counselor is an expert, that is, that he or she has the necessary knowledge, skills, experience, training, and tools to help (problem-solving set). Perceived expertness is typically a function of (a) reputation, (b) evidence of specialized training, and (c) behavioral evidence of proficiency/competency. For culturally diverse clients, the issue of therapist expertness seems to be raised more often than when clients go to a therapist of their own culture and race. As mentioned previously, the fact that therapists have degrees and certificates from prestigious institutions (authority set) may not enhance perceived expertness. This is especially true of clients who are culturally different and are aware that institutional bias exists in training programs. Indeed, it may have the opposite effect, by reducing credibility! Additionally, reputation-expertness (authority set) is unlikely to impress a minority client unless the favorable testimony comes from someone of his or her own group.

Thus behavior-expertness, or demonstrating the ability to help a client, becomes the critical form of expertness in effective multicultural counseling (problem-solving set). It appears that using counseling skills and strategies appropriate to the life values of the culturally diverse client is crucial. We have already mentioned evidence that certain minority groups prefer a much more active approach to counseling. A counselor playing a relatively inactive role may be perceived as being incompetent and unhelpful. The following example shows how the therapist's approach lowers perceived expertness.

> *ASIAN AMERICAN MALE CLIENT: It's hard for me to talk about these issues. My parents and friends . . . they wouldn't understand . . . if they ever found out I was coming here for help. . . .*
> *WHITE MALE THERAPIST: I sense it's difficult to talk about personal things. How are you feeling right now?*
> *ASIAN AMERICAN CLIENT: Oh, all right.*
> *WHITE THERAPIST: That's not a feeling. Sit back and get in touch with your feelings. [pause] Now tell me, how are you feeling right now?*
> *ASIAN AMERICAN CLIENT: Somewhat nervous.*
> *WHITE THERAPIST: When you talked about your parents' and friends' not understanding and the way you said it made me think you felt ashamed and disgraced at having to come. Was that what you felt?*

While this exchange appears to indicate that the therapist could (1) see the client's discomfort and (2) interpret his feelings correctly, it also points out the therapist's lack of understanding and knowledge of Asian cultural values. While we do not want to be guilty of stereotyping Asian Americans, many do have difficulty, at times, openly expressing feelings publicly to a stranger. The therapist's persistent attempts to focus on feelings and his direct and blunt interpretation of them may indicate to the Asian American client that the therapist lacks the more subtle skills of dealing with a sensitive topic or that the therapist is shaming the client (see Chapter 15).

Furthermore, it is possible that the Asian American client in this case is much more used to discussing feelings in an indirect or subtle manner. A direct response from the therapist addressed to a feeling may not be as effective as one that deals with it indirectly. In many traditional Asian groups, subtlety is a highly prized art, and the traditional Asian client may feel much more comfortable when dealing with feelings in an indirect manner.

In many ways, behavioral manifestations of therapist expertness override other considerations. For example, many educators claim that specific therapy skills are not as important as the attitude one brings into the therapeutic situation. Behind this statement is the belief that universal attributes of genuineness, love, unconditional acceptance, and positive regard are the only things needed. Yet the question remains: How does a therapist communicate these things to culturally diverse clients? While a therapist might have the best of intentions, it is possible that his or her intentions might be misunderstood. Let us use another example with the same Asian American client.

> ASIAN AMERICAN CLIENT: *I'm even nervous about others seeing me come in here. It's so difficult for me to talk about this.*
> WHITE THERAPIST: *We all find some things difficult to talk about. It's important that you do.*
> ASIAN AMERICAN CLIENT: *It's easy to say that. But do you really understand how awful I feel, talking about my parents?*
> WHITE THERAPIST: *I've worked with many Asian Americans and many have similar problems.*

In this sample dialogue we find a distinction between the therapist's intentions and the effects of his comments. The therapist's intentions were to reassure the client that he understood his feelings, to imply that he had worked with similar cases, and to make the client feel less isolated (i.e., that others have the same problems). The effects, however, were to dilute and dismiss the client's feelings and concerns and to take the uniqueness out of the situation.

Trustworthiness. Perceived trustworthiness encompasses such factors as sincerity, openness, honesty, or perceived lack of motivation for personal gain. A therapist who is perceived as trustworthy is likely to exert more influence over a client than is one who is not. In our society, many people assume that certain roles such as ministers, doctors, psychiatrists, and counselors exist to help people. With respect to minorities, self-disclosure is very much dependent on this attribute of perceived trustworthiness. Because mental health professionals are often perceived by minorities to be "agents of the Establishment," trust is something that does not come with the role (authority set). Indeed, many minorities may perceive that therapists cannot be trusted unless otherwise demonstrated. Again, the role and reputation you have as being trustworthy must be evidenced in behavioral terms. More than anything, challenges to the therapist's trustworthiness will be a frequent theme blocking further exploration and movement until it is resolved to the satisfaction of the client. These verbatim transcripts illustrate the trust issue.

> WHITE MALE THERAPIST: *I sense some major hesitations. . . . It's difficult for you to discuss your concerns with me.*

> BLACK MALE CLIENT: *You're damn right! If I really told you how I felt about my [White] coach, what's to prevent you from telling him? You Whities are all of the same mind.*
>
> WHITE THERAPIST [ANGRY]: *Look, it would be a lie for me to say I don't know your coach. He's an acquaintance, but not a personal friend. Don't put me in the same bag with all Whites! Anyway, even if he were a close friend, I hold our discussion in strictest confidence. Let me ask you this question: What would I need to do that would make it easier for you to trust me?*
>
> BLACK CLIENT: *You're on your way, man!*

This verbal exchange illustrates several issues related to trustworthiness. First, the minority client is likely to test the therapist constantly regarding issues of confidentiality. Second, the onus of responsibility for proving trustworthiness falls on the therapist. Third, to prove that one is trustworthy requires, at times, self-disclosure on the part of the mental health professional. That the therapist did not hide the fact that he knew the coach (openness), became angry about being lumped with all Whites (sincerity), assured the client that he would not tell the coach or anyone else about their sessions (confidentiality), and asked the client how he could work to prove he was trustworthy (genuineness) were all elements that enhanced his trustworthiness.

Handling the "prove to me that you can be trusted" ploy is very difficult for many therapists. It is difficult because it demands self-disclosure on the part of the helping professional, something that graduate training programs have taught us to avoid. It places the focus on the therapist rather than on the client and makes many uncomfortable. In addition, it is likely to evoke defensiveness on the part of many mental health practitioners. Here is another verbatim exchange in which defensiveness is evoked, destroying the helping professional's trustworthiness:

> BLACK FEMALE CLIENT: *Students in my drama class expect me to laugh when they do "steppin' fetchin'" routines and tell Black jokes.... I'm wondering whether you've ever laughed at any of those jokes.*
>
> WHITE MALE THERAPIST: *[long pause] Yes, I'm sure I have. Have you ever laughed at any White jokes?*
>
> BLACK CLIENT: *What's a White joke?*
>
> WHITE MALE THERAPIST: *I don't know [nervous laughter]; I suppose one making fun of Whites. Look, I'm Irish. Have you ever laughed at Irish jokes?*
>
> BLACK CLIENT: *People tell me many jokes, but I don't laugh at racial jokes. I feel we're all minorities and should respect each other.*

Again, the client tested the therapist indirectly by asking him if he ever laughed at racial jokes. Since most of us probably have, to say "no" would be a blatant lie. The client's motivation for asking this question was to find out (1) how sincere and open the therapist was and (2) whether the therapist could recognize his racist attitudes without letting it interfere with therapy. While the therapist admitted to having laughed at such jokes, he proceeded to destroy his trustworthiness by becoming defensive. Rather than simply stopping with his statement of "Yes, I'm sure I have," or making some other similar remark, he defends himself by trying to get the client to admit to similar actions. Thus the therapist's trustworthiness is seriously impaired. He is perceived as motivated to defend himself rather than help the client.

The therapist's obvious defensiveness in this case has prevented him from understanding the intent and motive of the question. Is the African American female client really asking the therapist whether he has actually laughed at Black jokes before? Or is the client asking the therapist if he is a racist? Both of these speculations have a certain amount of validity, but it is our belief that the Black female client is actually asking the following important question of the therapist: "How open and honest are you about your own racism, and will it interfere with our session here?" Again, the test is one of trustworthiness, a motivational variable that the White male therapist has obviously failed.

To summarize, expertness and trustworthiness are important components of any therapeutic relationship. In multicultural counseling/therapy, however, the counselor or therapist may not be presumed to possess either. The therapist working with a minority client is likely to experience severe tests of his or her expertness and trustworthiness before serious therapy can proceed. The responsibility for proving to the client that you are a credible therapist is likely to be greater when working with a minority client than with a majority client. How you meet the challenge is important in determining your effectiveness as a multicultural helping professional.

Implications for Clinical Practice

It is clear that counseling and psychotherapy, in both process and goals, contain a powerful sociopolitical dimension. How minority clients relate to therapists different from themselves often mirrors the state of interracial relationships in the wider society. Several guidelines suggested from this chapter can aid us in our journey toward cultural competence.

1. In working with diverse clients, it is important to distinguish between behaviors indicative of a true mental disorder and those that result from oppression and survival. A client of color may not readily self-disclose to you and may engage in specific behaviors for self-protection. These represent functional survival skills rather than pathology.

2. Do not personalize the suspicions a client may have of your motives. If you become defensive, insulted, or angry with the client, your effectiveness will be seriously diminished.

3. Monitor your own reactions and question your beliefs. All of us are victims of our social conditioning and have unintentionally inherited the racial biases of our forebears. Be willing to understand and overcome your stereotypes, biases, and assumptions about other cultural groups.

4. Be aware that clients of color or other marginalized groups may consider your professional credentials insufficient. Know that your credibility and trustworthiness will be tested. Evidence of specialized training is less impressive than factors such as authenticity, sincerity, and openness. Tests of credibility may occur frequently in the therapy session, and the onus of responsibility for proving expertness and trustworthiness lies with the therapist.

5. In multicultural counseling/therapy you may be unable to use the client's identification set (membership group similarity) to induce change. At times, racial dissimilarity may prove to be so much of a hindrance as to render therapy ineffective. In this situation, referring out should not be viewed negatively or as a defeat. One could argue that a counselor or therapist who is aware of limitations and is nondefensive enough to refer out is evidencing cultural competence.

6. Be aware that difficulties in multicultural counseling may not stem from race factors per se, but from the implications of being a minority in the United States and thus having secondary status. In any case, a broad statement on this matter is overly simplistic. By virtue of its definition, multicultural therapy implies major differences between the client and the helper. How these differences can be bridged and under what conditions a therapist is able to work effectively with culturally diverse clients are key questions.

Racial, Gender, and Sexual Orientation Microaggressions: Implications for Counseling and Psychotherapy

Derald Wing Sue & Christina M. Capodilupo

Tiffany is a 25-year-old Haitian American bisexual female who self-identifies as Black. She was born and raised in a large metropolitan city in the northeast. Both of Tiffany's parents emigrated from Haiti when they were children. Tiffany attended a prestigious university to obtain her graduate degree and currently teaches French at a private secondary school. Recently, Tiffany has been feeling hopeless about various aspects of her life, including her career and future. She feels "beaten down" and "emotionally exhausted" and has visited a community mental health counseling center to address these concerns. She was assigned to work with Kate, a 28-year-old White therapist.

In the first therapy session, Tiffany described her experiences interviewing for teaching positions. She had been thrilled at the response her resume had generated—she received an interview at nearly every school! However, Tiffany felt that there were similar responses to her when she was greeted by interviewers. She described "a look of shock or surprise on their faces" when they met her in the waiting room, and on more than one occasion, interviewers even repeated her first and last name to make sure she was the applicant. Tiffany tried to "shake the experience off" and wondered if their reactions were related to her race. When exploring the topic in counseling, Kate suggested that Tiffany may have been nervous and reading too much into the interviewers' reactions. She also implied that Tiffany's sensitivity may have been a defense against fears of rejection. Even if there might have been racial overtones, it was such a small matter that she should just shrug it off. Tiffany agreed with the therapist that she might have overreacted, but tried to impress upon Kate that the experience had really stayed with her over the last year. She now felt reluctant to enter the job market, even though she was not happy with her current position.

Tiffany also relayed to Kate that she did not "feel free to be myself" at school. She mentioned several "incidents" that depressed and frustrated her. When asked to explain, she described how students frequently referred to things as gay when they meant stupid or undesirable. She also relayed a story about comments and "looks" she received from several of the teach-

ers when she came to school with her hair short and braided (as opposed to long and straight, which is how she wore it when she was originally hired). She had not given much thought to her change in hairstyle, but noticed immediately that it was a "conversation piece" in the teacher's lounge. She got asked questions such as, "Wow, what caused this change?" A male teacher even remarked to her that she had "looked like a model with her hair straight but now looked more butch." The therapist was able to empathize with Tiffany, and shared a similar feeling that "as a woman, people always seem to think it is their right" to make comments about physical appearance. Even though Tiffany appreciated Kate's comments about being a woman, she had a nagging feeling that Kate was uncomfortable discussing race issues. She felt that Kate didn't seem to "get it."

Tiffany also wanted to talk about similar experiences with other teachers at her school, but she now felt reluctant to share other incidents with the therapist. She had noticed Kate's facial features express surprise when she mentioned in their first session that she was bilingual in French and English, and that she had obtained a master's degree. The look was similar to what Tiffany had observed in her interviews, and she began to feel uncomfortable with Kate. When she shared this impression, Kate denied that race had anything to do with her reactions. She suggested that Tiffany was projecting her own fears and doubts about her competence onto Kate to make the fears more manageable. Tiffany felt discouraged and invalidated from their discussions and failed to return for another session.

There is clearly misunderstanding and miscommunication between Tiffany and her therapist. This anecdote illustrates how racial, gender, and sexual orientation microaggressions can have a detrimental impact on marginalized groups and also undermine the therapeutic process. First, Tiffany has a nagging suspicion that the White job interviewers were surprised or taken off guard to find a Black woman with such sterling credentials on her resume and application. Yet, she is placed in an unenviable position of not being absolutely certain that interviewers were reacting to her race. Second, being bisexual and hearing students use "gay" in a negative fashion made her feel uncomfortable because it assailed her sexual identity. Third, her change in hairstyle was obviously disturbing to fellow teachers because her appearance did not conform to their standards. Fourth, Kate's attempt to connect with her by stressing their similar experiences as women seemed to have a negative rather than a positive impact on the therapeutic relationship. Finally, the therapist seems unaware that she has invalidated Tiffany's experiential reality by suggesting that race did not play a role in her reaction or the reactions of the interviewers, and that the locus of the problem resided with the client's own fears and doubts.

The incidents experienced by Tiffany are examples of *microaggressions.* Microaggressions are "brief, everyday exchanges that send denigrating messages" to a target group such as people of color, women, and gays (Sue et al., 2007). These microaggressions are often subtle in nature and can be manifested in the verbal, nonverbal, visual, or behavioral realm. They are often enacted automatically and unconsciously (Solorzano, Ceja, & Yosso, 2000), although the person who delivers the microaggression can do so intentionally or unintentionally (Sue et al., 2007). The interviewers who were surprised to see Tiffany reacted nonverbally (facial expression) and verbally (repeating her name to make sure it was her). While seemingly innocuous, the hidden message communicated by the interviewers was that Black people are less qualified, competent, and educated. This proved to be very distressful for Tiffany. As we shall see, microaggressions may seem innocent and innocuous, but their cumulative nature can be extremely harmful to the victim's physical and mental health. In addition, they create inequities such as not being offered a job because of unconscious biases and beliefs held by the interviewers.

To help understand the effects of microaggressions on people of color, women, and gays/lesbians, it would be important to ask the following questions: What do microaggressions look like? How can people who commit microaggressions be so unaware of their actions? If they represent unintentional slights and insults, have I been guilty of committing microaggressive acts? What types of psychological impact do they have on marginalized groups? What lessons can we learn from a better understanding of the psychological dynamics of racial, gender, and sexual orientation microaggressions? In what ways do microaggressions cause problems in the therapeutic process and relationship? These questions will be addressed by (1) reviewing literature on racism, sexism, and heterosexism; (2) presenting a framework for classifying and understanding the hidden and damaging messages of microaggressions; and (3) presenting findings from studies that have explored the experiences of people exposed to microaggressions.

Racism, Sexism, and Heterosexism

Most people associate racism with blatant and overt acts of discrimination that are epitomized by White supremacy and hate crimes. Studies suggest, however, that what has been called "old-fashioned racism" has seemingly declined (Dovidio & Gaertner, 2000). However, the nature and expression of racism (see Chapter 3) has evolved into a more subtle and ambiguous form, perhaps reflecting people's belief that overt and blatant acts of racism are unjust and "politically incorrect" (Dovidio, Gaertner, Kawakami, & Hodson, 2002). In a sense, racism has gone underground, become better disguised, and is more likely to be covert. A similar process seems to have occurred with sexism as well. Three types of sexism have been identified: overt, covert, and subtle (Swim & Cohen, 1997). Overt sexism is blatant unequal and unfair treatment of women. Covert sexism refers to unequal and harmful treatment of women that is conducted in a hidden manner (Swim & Cohen, 1997). For example, a person may endorse a belief in gender equality but engage in hiring practices that are gender biased. The third type, subtle sexism, represents "unequal and unfair treatment of women that is not recognized by many people because it is perceived to be normative, and therefore does not appear unusual" (Swim, Mallett, & Stangor, 2004, p. 117). Whereas overt and covert sexism are intentional, subtle sexism is not deliberate or conscious. An example of subtle sexism is sexist language, such as the use of the pronoun "he" to convey universal human experience.

In many ways, subtle sexism contains many of the features that define aversive racism, a form of subtle and unintentional racism (Dovidio & Gaertner, 2000). Aversive racism is manifested in individuals who consciously assert egalitarian values, but unconsciously hold anti-minority feelings; therefore, aversive racists consciously sympathize with victims of past injustice, support the principles of racial equality, and regard themselves as nonprejudiced. At the same time, however, they possess negative feelings and beliefs about historically disadvantaged groups that may be unconscious (Gaertner & Dovidio, 2006). Inheriting such negative feelings and beliefs about members of marginalized groups (i.e., people of color, women, and lesbians/gays) is unavoidable and inevitable due to the socialization process in the United States (Sue, 2004), where biased attitudes and stereotypes reinforce group hierarchy (Gaertner & Dovidio, 2006). Subtle sexism is very similar to aversive racism in that individuals support and actively condone gender equality, yet unknowingly engage in behaviors that contribute to the unequal treatment of women (Swim & Cohen, 1997). For example, it has been found that people who endorsed egalitarian beliefs rated male and female leaders equally, but their nonverbal behaviors reflected greater negativity toward female leaders (Butler & Geis, 1990). In one study, participants were asked to pronounce 72 familiar and 72 unfamiliar famous and unfamous names of men and women. Participants assigned fame to more male names and used a lower criterion to judge the fame of familiar male names than female names. However, these same participants did not explicitly endorse stereotypes or sexism (Banaji & Greenwald, 1995). Much like aversive racism, subtle sexism devalues women, dismisses their accomplishments, and limits their effectiveness in a variety of social and professional settings (Benokraitis, 1997).

Researchers have used the templates of modern forms of racism and sexism to better understand the various forms of heterosexism, though research in this area is relatively new (Morrison & Morrison, 2002). Heterosexism and antigay harassment has a long history and is currently prevalent in the United States, with as many as 94 percent of lesbian, gay, and bisexual (LGB) adults reporting hate crime victimization (Herek, Cogan, & Gillis, 2002). Antigay harassment can be defined as "verbal or physical behavior that injures, interferes with, or intimidates lesbian women, gay men, and bisexual individuals" (Burn, Kadlec, & Rexler, 2005, p. 24). Although antigay harassment includes comments and jokes that convey the idea that LGB individuals are pathological, abnormal, or unwelcome, authors identify subtle heterosexism by the indirect nature of such remarks (Burn et al.). For example, blatant heterosexism would be calling a lesbian a "dyke," whereas subtle heterosexism would be referring to something as "gay" to convey that it is stupid. As in the case of Tiffany, hearing this remark may result in a vicarious experience of insult and invalidation (Burn et al.). Subtle heterosexism is related both to aversive racism and subtle sexism in that those who engage in it may not intend to display prejudice toward LGB individuals, particularly in the case of comments or jokes related to LGB persons (Plummer, 2001). There is evidence to suggest that heterosexuals do not associate homophobic language with sexual orientation (Thurlow, 2001). Further, studies that have measured the use of heterosexist language and antigay and homophobic attitudes have found that participants who use this language were not strongly antigay or biased against LGB individuals (Burn, 2000; Plummer, 2001).

Researchers have also used the templates of modern racism and sexism to understand modern homonegativity (Morrison & Morrison, 2002). As opposed to old-fashioned homonegativity, which refers to an antigay sentiment that is based on religious or moral condemnation (i.e., "Male homosexuality is a sin"), modern homonegativity reflects the belief that prejudice against LGB persons no longer exists, and that this group contributes to its own marginalization by overemphasizing sexual orientation (Morrison, Kenny, & Harrington, 2005). There is considerable evidence to support the notion that old-fashioned and modern homonegativity are distinct concepts (Morrison & Morrison, 2002). Researchers simulated a movie theater situation and created two conditions: covert and overt. In both conditions, there was a confederate wearing a t-shirt that implied a gay sexual orientation. In the covert condition, there were two movies playing to choose from, enabling participants who chose not to sit next to the confederate to do so on grounds of movie preference. In the overt condition, this justification of movie choice was removed and participants were told that due to a technical glitch, the same movie would be shown in both theaters. The researchers found that those who scored highest on modern homonegativity were more likely to avoid sitting next to the confederate, but only in the covert condition. Those who scored high on old-fashioned homonegativity elected not to sit next to the confederate regardless of condition (Morrison & Morrison, 2002). This research is very similar to the foundational research of aversive racism, which found that well-intentioned White liberals who endorsed racial equality were less likely to help a Black confederate with a simulated car breakdown when the situation was ambiguous and they were not sure their help was needed

(Gaertner, 1973). In other words, when the situation is ambiguous and the individual is able to justify his or her actions based on some criteria other than the target's identity, he or she will act in a discriminatory and biased manner. What makes this phenomenon particularly complex is that such ambiguity and alternative explanations obscure the true meaning of the event, not only for the person who engages in this behavior, but also for the person on the receiving end of the action. This is the central dilemma created by microaggressions, which are manifestations of these subtle forms of racism, sexism, and heterosexism.

The Evolution of Racism, Sexism, and Heterosexism: Microaggressions

As mentioned previously, microaggressions are "brief and commonplace daily verbal or behavioral indignities, whether intentional or unintentional, that communicate hostile, derogatory, or negative racial slights and insults that potentially have a harmful or unpleasant psychological impact on the target person or group" (Sue et al., 2007). Microaggressions can also be delivered environmentally through the physical surroundings of target groups where they are made to feel unwelcome, isolated, unsafe, and alienated. For example, a prestigious eastern university conducts new faculty orientations in their main conference room, which displays portraits of all past presidents of the university. One new female faculty member of color mentioned that during the orientation she noticed that every single portrait was that of a White male. She described feelings of unease, alienation, and a strong desire to quickly leave the room. To her, the all-White males' portraits sent a power message: "Your kind does not belong here." "You will not be comfortable here." "If you stay, there is only so far you can rise at this University!" Environmental microaggressions can occur when there is absence of students of color on college campuses, or few women in the upper echelons of the workplace.

Research suggests that the socialization process culturally conditions racist, sexist, and heterosexist attitudes and behaviors in well intentioned individuals, and these biases are often automatically enacted without conscious awareness, particularly for those who endorse egalitarian values (Dovidio & Gaertner, 2002). Based on literature covering subtle forms of racism, sexism, and heterosexism, one might conclude the following about microaggressions: They (1) tend to be subtle, unintentional, and indirect, (2) often occur in situations where there are alternative explanations, (3) represent unconscious and ingrained biased beliefs and attitudes, and (4) are more likely to occur when people pretend not to notice differences, thereby denying that race, gender, or sexual orientation had anything to do with their actions (Sue et al.,

2007). Three types of microaggressions have been identified: microassault, microinsult, and microinvalidation.

Microassault

The term *microassault* refers to a blatant verbal, nonverbal, or environmental attack intended to convey discriminatory and biased sentiments. This notion is related to overt racism, sexism, and heterosexism in which individuals deliberately convey derogatory messages to target groups. Using epithets like spic or faggot, hiring only men for managerial positions, and deliberately serving Black patrons last are examples. Unless we are talking about White supremacists, most perpetrators with conscious biases will engage in overt racism, sexism, and heterosexism only under three conditions: (1) when some degree of anonymity can be ensured, (2) when they are in the presence of others who share or tolerate their biased beliefs and actions, or (3) when they lose control of their feelings and actions. Two recent high-profile examples exemplify the latter: (1) Actor Mel Gibson made highly inflammatory anti-semitic public statements to police officers when he was arrested for driving while intoxicated, and (2) comedian Michael Richards, who played Kramer on the television show *Seinfeld*, went on an out-of-control rant at a comedy club when he publicly insulted African American audience members by hurling racial epithets at them and demeaning their race. Gibson and Richards disclaimed being anti-semitic or racist and issued immediate apologies, but it was obvious both had lost control. Because microassaults are most similar to old-fashioned racism, no guessing game is likely to occur as to their intent—to hurt or injure the recipient. Both the perpetrator and recipient are clear about what has transpired. We submit that microassaults are, in many respects, easier to deal with than behavior that is unintentional and outside the perpetrator's level of awareness (microinsults and microinvalidations).

Microinsult

Microinsults are unintentional behaviors or verbal comments that convey rudeness or insensitivity or demean a person's racial heritage identity, gender identity, or sexual orientation identity. Despite being outside the level of conscious awareness, these subtle snubs are characterized by an insulting hidden message. When the interviewers expressed surprise (nonverbally and verbally) that a Black female (Tiffany) could possess such outstanding credentials on her resume, they were conveying a hidden message—Blacks are less capable intellectually. African Americans consistently report that intellectual inferiority is a common communication they receive from Whites in their everyday experiences (Sue et al., in press). Similarly, when teachers in a classroom consistently call on male students rather than females to answer questions, the hidden message is that men are brighter and more capable than women. When California Governor Arnold Schwarzenegger referred to

Democrats as "girly men," he meant to ridicule his political opponents, but what he insinuated was that women and men who possess feminine traits are weak and ineffective.

Microinvalidation

Microinvalidations are verbal comments or behaviors that exclude, negate, or dismiss the psychological thoughts, feelings, or experiential reality of the target group. Like microinsults, they are unintentional and usually outside the perpetrator's awareness. When Kate dismissed Tiffany's belief that race played a role in her interviews and suggested that her interpretation was due to personal insecurities, she negated the client's thoughts and feelings. The hidden message delivered to Tiffany is that she is overly sensitive and paranoid. Because Kate is in a position of power as a White therapist, she is able to define Tiffany's experiential reality, thereby engaging in microinvalidation. When a male interviewer informs a female applicant that "I believe the most qualified person should get the job," he is potentially conveying a message that "women are not qualified and his decision will have nothing to do with the applicant's gender." When gay students are always selected last by fellow classmates for sports teams, and share their feelings of discrimination with gym teachers, they are likely to be told that they are misreading the situation (invalidating their experiences of discrimination).

To further illustrate the concepts of microinsults and microinvalidations, Table 5.1 provides examples of comments, actions, and situations, as well as their accompanying hidden message and/or assumption. There are 12 distinct categories represented in this table: alien in one's own land, ascription of intelligence, assumption of abnormality, color blindness, criminality/ assumption of criminal status, denial of individual racism/sexism/heterosexism, myth of meritocracy, pathologizing cultural values/communication styles, second-class status, sexual objectification, use of sexist/heterosexist language, and traditional gender role prejudice and stereotyping. Some of these categories may be more applicable to certain forms of microaggressions (racial, gender, or sexual orientation), but they all seem to share commonalities.

The Dynamics and Dilemmas of Microaggressions

Let us use the case of Tiffany to illustrate some of the dynamics and dilemmas presented by microaggressions. Research on subtle forms of racism (Dovidio et al., 2002; Ridley, 2005), sexism (Swim et al., 2004), and heterosexism (Morrison & Morrison, 2002) provide evidence that they operate in individuals who endorse egalitarian beliefs, adamantly deny that they are biased, and consider themselves to be moral, just, and fair. What people consciously believe or say (e.g., "I have no gay bias"), however, is oftentimes at odds with what they actually do (e.g., avoiding sitting next to an ostensibly gay man). Proving that one's actions or comments stem from an unconsciously held set of negative beliefs toward the target group is virtually impossible when alternative explanations exist. Because Whites who engage in microaggressions truly believe they act without racial bias toward persons of color, for example, they will disclaim any racist meaning. The subtle and insidious nature of racial microaggressions is not only outside the level of awareness of perpetrators, but recipients also find their ambiguity difficult to handle. Victims are placed in an unenviable position of not only questioning perpetrators, but themselves as well ("Did I misread what happened?") In the face of microaggressions, many members of historically marginalized groups describe feeling a vague unease that something is not right, and that they were insulted or disrespected. In this respect, overt acts of racism, sexism, or heterosexism may be easier to handle than microaggressions because the intent and meaning of the event is clear and indisputable (Solorzano et al., 2000; Sue, 2004). Microaggressions toward marginalized groups, however, pose special problems. Four psychological dilemmas have been identified when microaggressions occur (Sue et al., 2007).

Dilemma One: Clash of Racial Realities

For Tiffany, one major question was, "were interviewers reacting to her race, or did she misinterpret their verbal and nonverbal behavior?" Although personal experience tells her that many Whites believe Blacks to be less capable and competent, chances are the White interviewers would be offended at such a suggestion. They would likely deny they possessed any stereotypes and even point to the number of people of color they have hired. In other words, they would emphasize that they and their organizations do not discriminate on the basis of color, gender, sexual orientation, or creed. The question becomes, "whose reality is the true reality?" Oftentimes the perceptions held by the dominant group differ significantly from those of marginalized groups in our society. For example, studies show that many Whites believe racism is no longer prevalent in our society nor important in the lives of people of color (Sue, 2004); heterosexuals believe that homophobia is a "thing of the past" and that gay harassment is on the decline (Morrison & Morrison, 2002); and men (and women) assert that women have achieved equal status and are no longer discriminated against (Swim & Cohen, 1997). Most importantly, individuals in power positions do not consider themselves capable of discrimination based on race, gender, or sexual orientation because they believe themselves free of bias. On the other hand, people of color perceive Whites to be racially insensitive, that they enjoy holding power over others, and that they think they are superior (Sue et al., in press). LGB individuals consider homonegativity and gay harassment to be a crucial aspect of their everyday existence (Burn et al., 2005), and women contend that sexism

Table 5.1   **Examples of Racial, Gender, and Sexual Orientation Microaggressions**

Themes	Microaggression	Message
Alien in Their Own Land		
When Asian Americans and Latino Americans are assumed to be foreign-born.	"Where are you from?" "Where were you born?" "You speak good English."	You are not American.
	A person asking an Asian American to teach them words in their native language.	You are a foreigner.
Ascription of Intelligence		
Assigning intelligence to a person of color or a woman based on their race/gender.	"You are a credit to your race."	People of color are generally not as intelligent as Whites.
	"Wow! How did you become so good in math?"	It is unusual for a woman to be smart in math.
	Asking an Asian person to help with a math or science problem.	All Asians are intelligent and good in math/sciences.
Color Blindness		
Statements that indicate a White person does not want to acknowledge race.	"When I look at you, I don't see color."	Denying a person of color's racial/ethnic experiences.
	"America is a Melting Pot."	Assimilate/acculturate to dominant culture.
	"There is only one race, the human race."	The individual is denied as a racial/cultural being.
Criminality/Assumption of Criminal status		
A person of color is presumed to be dangerous, a criminal, or a deviant based on their race.	A White man or woman clutches their purse or checks their wallet as a Black or Latino approaches or passes.	You are a criminal.
	A store owner follows a customer of color around the store.	You are going to steal. You are poor. You do not belong.

Table 5.1   **continued**

Themes	Microaggression	Message
	A White person waits to ride the next elevator when a person of color is on it.	You are dangerous.

Use of Sexist/Heterosexist Language

Themes	Microaggression	Message
Terms that exclude or degrade women and LGB persons.	Using the pronoun "he" to refer to all people.	Male experience is universal. Female experience is meaningless.
	Assuming only two options for Relationship Status: Married or Single	LGB partnerships do not matter or are meaningless.
	An assertive woman is labeled a "bitch."	Women should be passive.
	A heterosexual man who hangs out with his female friends more than his male friends is labeled a "faggot."	Men who act like women are inferior (women are inferior)/gay men are inferior.

Denial of Individual Racism/Sexism/Heterosexism

Themes	Microaggression	Message
A statement made when bias is denied.	"I'm not racist. I have several Black friends."	I am immune to racism because I have friends of color.
	"As an employer, I always treat men and women equally."	I am incapable of sexism.

Myth of Meritocracy

Themes	Microaggression	Message
Statements which assert that race or gender does not play a role in life successes.	"I believe the most qualified person should get the job."	People of color are given extra, unfair benefits because of their race.
	"Men and women have equal opportunities for achievement."	The playing field is even, so if women cannot make it, the problem is with them.

(*continued*)

Table 5.1   continued

Themes	Microaggression	Message
Pathologizing Cultural Values/Communication Styles		
The notion that the values and communication styles of the dominant/White culture are ideal.	Asking a Black person: "Why do you have to be so loud/animated? Just calm down."	Assimilate to dominant culture.
	To an Asian or Latino person: "Why are you so quiet? We want to know what you think. Be more verbal. Speak up more."	
	An individual who brings up race/culture in work/school setting is dismissed.	Leave your cultural baggage outside.
Second Class Citizen		
Occurs when a target group member receives differential treatment from the power group.	A person of color mistaken for a service worker.	People of color are servants to Whites. They couldn't possibly occupy high status positions.
	A female doctor is mistaken for a nurse.	Women occupy nurturing roles.
	A taxi cab passes a person of color and to pick up a White passenger.	You are likely to cause trouble and/or travel to a dangerous neighborhood.
	A person of color is ignored at a store counter as attention is given to a White customer behind them.	Whites are more valued customers than people of color.
	A lesbian woman is not invited out with a group of girlfriends because they think she would be bored if they talk to men.	You don't belong.

Table 5.1   **continued**

Themes	Microaggression	Message
Traditional Gender Role Prejudicing and Stereotyping		
Occurs when expectations of traditional roles or stereotypes are conveyed.	A female student asks a male professor for extra help on a chemistry assignment, and he asks, "What do you need to work on this for anyway?"	Women are less capable in math and science.
	A person asks a woman her age and upon hearing she is 31, looks quickly at her ring finger.	Women should be married during child bearing ages because that is their primary purpose.
	A woman is assumed to be a lesbian because she does not put a lot of effort into her appearance.	Lesbians do not care about being attractive to others.
Sexual Objectification		
Occurs when women are treated like objects at men's disposal.	A male stranger puts his hands on a woman's hips or on the small of her back to pass by her.	Your body is not yours.
	Men whistle and catcall as a woman walks down the street.	Your body/appearance is for men's enjoyment and pleasure.
Assumption of Abnormality		
Occurs when it is implied that there is something wrong with being LGB.	Two men holding hands in public receive stares from strangers.	You should keep your displays of affection private because they are offensive.
	Students use the term "gay" to describe a fellow student who is socially ostracized at school.	People who are weird and different are "gay."

Adapted from Sue et al., 2007.

is alive and well in social and professional settings (Burn, 2000). While research supports the fact that those most disempowered are more likely to have a more accurate perception of reality, it is groups in power that have the ability to define reality. Thus, people of color, women, and LGB individuals are likely to experience their perceptions and interpretations being negated or dismissed.

Dilemma Two: The Invisibility of Unintentional Expressions of Bias

Although Tiffany did not ask her fellow teachers in the student lounge the meaning behind their comments about her hair, one can imagine that they might feel stunned and surprised to learn that Tiffany felt offended. They would likely explain that they were only remarking about the drastic change in her hairstyle and that race had nothing to do with it. They might even state they would have responded the same way to any woman who changed her hair so dramatically. To Tiffany, however, it was less about the content of what they said than the tone of voice (fear, apprehension, and defiance of expectations), which indicated they were reacting to her race and gender. The message being conveyed to Tiffany was that she was violating White standards of appearance and that her braided hair, a natural Black hairstyle, was threatening. How could Tiffany *prove* that the teachers sounded scared when they made comments to her? She cannot replay a tape of their voices or show a video of their facial expressions—her only evidence is her felt experience and interpretation, which are easily explained away and disregarded by teachers with alternative explanations. That the microaggression is essentially invisible to the perpetrator creates a psychological dilemma for victims that can leave them frustrated, feeling powerless, and even questioning their own sanity (Sue et al., in press).

Dilemma Three: Perceived Minimal Harm of Microaggressions

Oftentimes, when perpetrators are confronted about microaggressions, they accuse the victim of overreacting or being hypersensitive, or touchy. Because the microaggression is often invisible to the perpetrator, they cannot understand how the event could cause any significant harm to the victim. They see the event as innocent, innocuous, and often tell victims to "just let it go." Visible and overt forms of discrimination, however, are more readily acknowledged as being dangerous and harmful (Sue, 2004). It has been found that chronic experiences of discrimination and exclusion create levels of stress that are traumatic for target groups (Bloom, 1997; Pierce, 1995). Racism and racial/ethnic discrimination cause significant psychological distress (Fang & Meyers, 2001; Krieger & Sidney, 1996), depression (Comas-Diaz & Greene, 1994; Kim, 2002), and negative health outcomes (Harrell, Hall, & Taliaferro, 2003). Researchers have even coined the term *racism-related stress* (Harrell, 2000). With regard to sexism, studies have found that 94 percent of women queried reported experiencing sexual harassment, 92 percent reported disrespect because of their gender, and 87 percent reported experiencing sexism from strangers (Berg, 2006). Researchers have long contended that the sociopolitical climate of the United States serves to subjugate, degrade, and objectify women (Root, 1992). Similarly, research has found a host of negative effects related to stigmatization based on sexual orientation (APA Division 44, 2000). This stress has been linked to depression (D'Augelli, 1989), substance abuse, running away, and prostitution (APA Division 44, 2000).

Despite the perpetrator's perception that microaggressions result in minimal harm, more recent research has suggested that subtle forms of racism, sexism, and heterosexism cause significant distress and negatively impact well-being. One study that looked at racial microaggressions in the lived experience of African Americans found that the cumulative effect of these events was feelings of self-doubt, frustration, and isolation (Solorzano et al., 2000). Another study found that consequences of microaggressions for African Americans included feelings of powerlessness, invisibility, and loss of integrity (Sue et al., in press). In a similar study, Asian Americans reported feeling belittled, angry, invalidated, invisible, and trapped by their experiences of racial microaggressions (Sue, Bucceri, Lin, Nadal, & Torino, 2007).

With regard to subtle sexism, researchers have discovered that everyday sexist events, such as sexist language, gender role stereotyping, and objectifying commentaries lead to feelings of anger, anxiety, and depression in women (Swim, Hyers, Cohen, & Ferguson, 2001). In this same study, female participants who recorded daily incidents in diaries reported an average of one to two experiences of subtle sexism a week (in the study, they were to record daily hassles and then judge how prejudicial they felt they were). A recent study found that "the impact of daily, personal sexist interaction has an incremental effect that may result in the disturbing [Posttraumatic Stress Disorder] PTSD symptomology" (Berg, 2006, p. 984).

There is very little research on the effects of subtle heterosexism on LGB persons. One study provided LGB participants with subtle heterosexism scenarios (e.g., a heterosexual assumes two unmarried men who spend a lot of time together are gay) to first assess if the participants found such scenarios to be offensive and prejudicial (due to the indirect nature of the scenario). Not only were participants offended by the scenarios and felt they were prejudicial against LGB persons, but they were also less likely to come out as a consequence of feeling offended (Burn, Kadlec, & Rexer, 2005). When one assumes that people of color, women, and LGB individuals are constantly exposed to multiple microaggressions, it becomes clear that their cumulative nature takes a huge psychological toll on their lives. Thus, microaggressions cause significant harm and psychological distress to victims. That perpetrators tend to deny the existence of the microaggressions (because they are invisible) only serves to compound the detrimental effects.

Dilemma Four: The Catch-22 of Responding to Microaggressions

When a microaggression occurs, the recipient is often placed in an unenviable position of having to decide what to do. This is compounded by the numerous questions likely to go through the mind of the recipient. Did what I think happened really happen? If it did, how can I possibly prove it? How should I respond? Will it do any good if I bring it to the attention of the perpetrator? If I do, will it affect my relationship with coworkers, friends, or acquaintances? In Tiffany's case, will it jeopardize her chances of being hired if she confronts the interviewers? Many well-intentioned perpetrators are unaware of the exhausting nature of these internal questions, and how they sap the spiritual and psychic energy of victims. Tiffany was obviously caught in a conflict: Should I respond by asking what interviewers, teachers, or her students meant by their comments, or should I bother to respond at all? As a Black female, Tiffany has probably experienced many microaggressions throughout her lifetime, and so microaggressive comments from coworkers do not feel random (Ridley, 2005). On the other hand, White teachers who have not faced similar experiences are unable to see a pattern running throughout incidents encountered by people of color—hidden bias associated with race. People of color, for example, use context and experiential reality to interpret the meaning of microaggressions. The common thread operating in multiple situations is that of race. Whites, however, see such situations as isolated incidents, so the pattern of racism experienced by persons of color is invisible to them.

The fundamental issue is that responding to a microaggression can have detrimental consequences for the victim. If Tiffany responds to the teachers and shares her feelings, they might invalidate her racial reality by claiming that the incident had absolutely nothing to do with race; an extremely common stance taken by well-intentioned Whites. They might attribute Tiffany's reactions to some internal attribute (being touchy or insecure). If she chooses to pursue the matter she could be accused of being a troublemaker reinforcing a commonly held stereotype of the angry Black woman. Tiffany might feel compelled to avoid this label and to simply forgo the hassles. Unfortunately, it has been found that such a reaction takes a psychological toll on the recipient because it requires Tiffany to suppress and obscure her authentic thoughts and feelings in order to avoid further discrimination (Franklin, 2004).

Confronting sexual orientation microaggressions is further complicated by LGB individuals who may not necessarily be out of the closet. In one study, half of lesbian and gay participants were uncomfortable disclosing their sexual orientation, and two-thirds occasionally feared for their public safety (D'Augelli, 1989). The reality of looming gay harassment and differential (unequal) treatment may prevent LGB persons from coming out in a variety of settings, especially when there is evidence to suggest that the environment is heterosexist. For example, Tiffany hears students at schools using the term "gay" in a derogatory fashion in public areas and observes that teachers never object or take issue with its use. The message she receives from colleagues is that they are complicit through their silence. Telling others she is offended by the word butch may out her, or will cause the other teachers to wonder about her sexual orientation. She might also fear that the teachers will tell her she is hypersensitive and overly emotional—both microaggressions themselves!

Let us look at the meaning of these two terms. The first, *hypersensitive*, conveys that Tiffany is sensitive about her sexual orientation—as if there is no valid reason she should be—therefore, her experiential reality of being a bisexual person who always feels marginalized is invalidated. The second, *overly emotional*, is a gender role stereotype about women. Women are supposed to be nurturing and caring, and so therefore emotional (and by association, irrational) when it comes to making sense of real issues. Tiffany runs the risk of hearing any one of these things if she confronts the microaggressions she experiences. On the flip side, by not confronting these experiences, she is forced to shoulder the burden herself with detrimental mental health consequences. In one study, African American participants revealed some strategies for dealing with this catch-22: empowering and validating the self and the sanity check. Empowering and validating the self refers to a process of interrupting the racism by "calling it what it is" and staying true to one's thoughts and feelings—that the incident is related to their race. Sanity check refers to a process of checking in with like-minded and same-race people about microaggressive incidents. Talking about the incident with someone who has faced similar discrimination helped participants to feel validated in their experience that the incident is racially motivated (Sue et al., in press).

Therapeutic Implications

We have repeatedly emphasized that clients of color tend to prematurely terminate counseling and therapy at a 50 percent rate after only initial contact with a mental health provider (à la Tiffany). We submit that racial microaggressions may lie at the core of the problem. Likewise, if gender and sexual orientation microaggressions operate through therapists, they may also affect the therapeutic alliance for these groups as well. The result is that clients of color, women, and gays may not receive the help they need. In counseling and psychotherapy, the credibility of the therapist is paramount in determining whether clients stay or leave sessions (Strong, 1969). Credibility is composed of two dimensions: expertness and trustworthiness. Expertness is a function of how much knowledge, training, experience, and skills clinicians possess with respect to the population being treated. It is an *ability component*.

Trustworthiness, however, is a *motivational component* that encompasses trust, honesty, and genuineness. While expertness is always important, trustworthiness becomes central in multicultural counseling and therapy.

Effective counseling is likely to occur when both therapists and clients are able to form a working relationship, therapeutic alliance, or some form of positive coalition. In mental health practice there is a near universal belief that effective and beneficial counseling requires that clients trust their counselors (Corey, 2005; Day, 2004). Essentially the therapist works to build rapport and establish a connection with the client through verbal and nonverbal interventions. Research supports the idea that the therapeutic alliance is a key component in therapy work and is correlated with successful outcomes (Lui & Pope-Davis, 2005). When clients do not feel heard or understood, or when they are not sure they can trust the therapist, they often fail to return. A comprehensive report on the role of culture, race, and ethnicity in mental health care suggests that racism plays a major role in creating inequities that result in inferior and biased treatments for diverse clients (Surgeon General, 2000).

Because all people inherit bias about various identity groups through cultural conditioning in the United States, no one, including helping professionals, is free from these biases (Ridley, 2005). Therefore, racial, gender, and sexual orientation dynamics that exist in society are often recreated and re-enacted between the therapist and client in the therapy room. This fact poses a unique dilemma in therapy, for several reasons. Helping professionals are supposed to work for the welfare of all groups, are trained to be "objective," are inclined to see problems as internally situated, and are usually in a position of power over the client. Mental health professionals who enter the field usually have a strong desire to help clients regardless of race, creed, gender, and so on. They operate under the dictum of "liberating clients from their distress and doing no harm" whenever possible. Because helping professionals view themselves as just, fair, and nondiscriminating, they find it difficult to believe that they commit microaggressions and may be unhelpful and even oppressive. The fact that therapists possess unconscious biases and prejudices is problematic, especially when they sincerely believe they are capable of preventing these attitudes from entering sessions. Rather than heal or help, however, well-intentioned therapists may contribute to the oppressive experiences of culturally diverse clients. Although there have certainly been movements to understand the sociopolitical context of clients, less attention is given to the social context of the therapeutic relationship, which may reflect a microcosm of negative race relations in the larger society. Lastly, counselors often find themselves in positions of power through their ability to define their client's experiential reality (i.e., interpretation), which may prove harmful, especially if counselors adamantly deny the presence of microaggressions both inside and outside of the therapy situation. There is recent research to suggest that prejudice and bias continue to be manifested in the therapeutic process, despite the good intentions of mental health professionals (Utsey, Gernat, & Hammar, 2005).

Manifestations of Microaggressions in Counseling/Therapy
The importance of understanding how microaggressions manifest in the therapeutic relationship cannot be understated, especially as this phenomenon may underlie the high prevalence of dropout rates among people of color. Let us use the case of Tiffany to illustrate how microaggressions may operate in the counseling process.

1. Tiffany revealed to Kate her experiences of racial, gender, and sexual orientation microaggressions, using therapy as a space for deeper exploration of a meaningful issue. Because Kate and Tiffany are not the same race, they do not share similar racial realities (Dilemma One: Clash of Racial Realities) or worldviews. The therapist has minimal understanding of what constitutes racial microaggressions, how they make their appearance during everyday interactions, how she herself may be guilty of microaggressive behaviors, the psychological toll it takes on persons of color, and the negative effects they have on the therapeutic relationship. We have emphasized earlier that cultural competence requires helping professionals to understand the worldviews of their culturally diverse clients.

2. The therapist tends to minimize the importance of the shocked reactions of interviewers to Tiffany's resume, believes the event is trivial, and cannot relate to the negative impact these microaggressions have on her client. Even if the reactions do have some racial overtones, the therapist concludes they are insignificant ("a small matter") and Tiffany should simply ignore them or "shrug it off" (Dilemma Three: Minimal Harm). For Tiffany, on the other hand, the looks of surprise represent one of many cumulative messages of intellectual inferiority about her race. She is placed in a constant state of vigilance by maintaining her sense of integrity in the face of constant invalidations and insults. Racial, gender, and sexual microaggressions are a constant reality for people of color as they assail group identities and experiences. White people seldom understand how much time, energy and effort are expended to retain some semblance of worth and self-esteem. No wonder Tiffany is emotionally exhausted, frustrated, and occasionally doubts her own interpretations.

3. Another major detrimental event in the first session is that the therapist locates the source of problems within Tiffany: insecurities about her own abilities. While there may be some legitimacy to this interpreta-

tion, Kate is unaware that she has engaged in person-blame and that she has invalidated Tiffany's experiential reality by dismissing race as an important factor. When Tiffany observes that Kate might not understand her experiences as a Black woman, Kate was shocked and hurt. As a mental health professional, Kate probably considers herself unbiased and objective. She attempts to relate to Tiffany as a woman first, with an attempt to empathize and connect with Tiffany over the subtle sexist comments Tiffany describes at work. This reaction, however, represents a colorblind reaction and only reinforces Tiffany's feelings of invalidation by removing the salience of her race from the conversation (Dilemma Two: Invisibility).

4. As a client, Tiffany is caught in a "damned if you do, and damned if you don't" conflict (Dilemma Four: Catch-22). Both inside and outside of therapy, Tiffany is probably internally wrestling with a series of questions: "Did what I think happen, really happen? Was this a deliberate act or an unintentional slight? How should I respond? Sit and stew on it, or confront the person? What are the consequences if I do? If I bring the topic up, how do I prove it? Is it really worth the effort? Should I just drop the matter?" These questions take a tremendous psychological toll on many people of color. If Tiffany chooses to do nothing, she may suffer emotionally by having to deny her own experiential reality, or allow her sense of integrity to be assailed. Feelings of powerlessness, alienation, and frustration may not only take a psychological but physical toll on her. If she chooses to raise issues with the interviewers, students, or fellow teachers, she risks being isolated by others, seen as a troublemaker, oversensitive, and even paranoid. Worse yet, if she raises these issues in therapy, her reality is invalidated and her reactions are pathologized by the therapist.

Table 5.2 provides several more therapy-specific examples of microaggressions, using the same organizing themes presented in Table 5.1. We ask that you study these themes and ask yourself if you have ever engaged in these or similar actions. If so, how can you prevent your own personal microaggressions from impairing the therapy process?

Implications for Clinical Practice

Clients trust mental health professionals to take an intimate and deeply personal journey of self-exploration with them through the process of therapy. They grant these professionals the opportunity to look into their inner world and also invite them to walk where they live in their everyday lives. Therapists

Table 5.2   **Examples of Racial, Gender, and Sexual Orientation Microaggressions in Therapeutic Practice**

Themes	Microaggression	Message
Alien in Their Own Land		
When Asian Americans and Latino Americans are assumed to be foreign-born.	A White client does not want to work with an Asian American therapist because she "will not understand my problem."	You are not American.
	A White therapist tells an American-born Latino client that he/she should seek a Spanish-speaking therapist.	
Ascription of Intelligence		
Assigning a degree of intelligence to a person of color or woman based on their race or gender.	A school counselor reacts with surprise when an Asian American student had trouble on the math portion of a standardized test.	All Asians are smart and good at math.
	A career counselor asking a Black or Latino student "Do you think you're ready for college?"	It is unusual for people of color to succeed.
	A school counselor reacts with surprise that a female student scored high on a math portion of a standardized test.	It is unusual for women to be smart and good in math.
Color Blindness		
Statements which indicate that a White person does not want to acknowledge race.	A therapist says "I think you are being too paranoid. We should emphasize similarities not people's differences" when a client of color attempts to discuss her feelings about being the only person of color at her job and feeling alienated and dismissed by her coworkers.	Race and culture are not important variables that affect people's lives.

(continued)

Table 5.2   **continued**

Themes	Microaggression	Message
	A client of color expresses concern in discussing racial issues with her therapist. Her therapist replies with, "When I see you, I don't see color."	Your racial experiences are not valid.
Criminality/Assumption of Criminal status		
A person of color is presumed to be dangerous, criminal, or deviant based on their race.	When a Black client shares that she was accused of stealing from work, the therapist encourages the client to explore how she might have contributed to her employer's mistrust of her.	You are a criminal.
	A therapist takes great care to ask all substance abuse questions in an intake with a Native American client, and is suspicious of the client's nonexistent history with substances.	You are deviant.
Use of Sexist/Heterosexist Language		
Terms that exclude or degrade women and LGB groups.	During the intake session, a female client discloses that she has been in her current relationship for one year. The therapist asks how long the client has known her boyfriend.	Heterosexuality is the norm.
	When an adult female client explains she is feeling isolated at work, her male therapist asks, "Aren't there any girls you can gossip with there?"	Application of language that applies to adolescent females to adult females/your problems are trivial.

Table 5.2   continued

Themes	Microaggression	Message
Denial of Individual Racism/Sexism/Heterosexism		
A statement made when a member of the power group renounces their biases.	A client of color asks his/her therapist about how race affects their working relationship. The therapist replies, "Race does not affect the way I treat you."	Your racial/ethnic experience is not important.
	A client of color expresses hesitancy in discussing racial issues with his White female therapist. She replies "I understand. As a woman, I face discrimination also."	Your racial oppression is no different than my gender oppression.
	A therapist's nonverbal behavior conveys discomfort when a bisexual male client is describing a recent sexual experience with a man. When he asks her about it, she insists she has "no negative feelings toward gay people" and says it is important to keep the conversation on him.	I am incapable of homonegativity yet I am unwilling to explore this
Myth of Meritocracy		
Statements which assert that race or gender does not play a role in succeeding in career advancement or education.	A school counselor tells a Black student that "if you work hard, you can succeed like everyone else."	People of color/women are lazy and/or incompetent and need to work harder. If you don't succeed, you have only yourself to blame (blaming the victim).
	A female client visits a career counselor to share her concerns that a male coworker was chosen for a managerial position over her, despite that she was better qualified and in the job longer. The counselor responds that "he must have been better suited for some of the job requirements."	

(*continued*)

Table 5.2 **continued**

Themes	Microaggression	Message
Pathologizing Cultural Values/Communication Styles		
The notion that the values and communication styles of the dominant/White culture are ideal.	A Black client is loud, emotional, and confrontational in a counseling session. The therapist diagnoses her with borderline personality disorder.	Assimilate to dominant culture.
	A client of Asian or Native American descent has trouble maintaining eye contact with his therapist. The therapist diagnoses him with a social anxiety disorder.	
	Advising a client, "Do you really think your problem stems from racism?"	Leave your cultural baggage outside.
Second Class Citizen		
Occurs when a member of the power group is given preferential treatment over a target group member.	A male client calls and requests a session time that is currently taken by a female client. The therapist grants the male client the appointment without calling the female client to see if she can change times.	Males are more valued than women.
	Clients of color are not welcomed or acknowledged by receptionists.	White clients are more valued than clients of color.
Traditional Gender Role Prejudicing and Stereotyping		
Occurs when expectations of traditional roles or stereotypes are conveyed.	A therapist continually asks the middle age female client about dating and "putting herself out there" despite that the client has not expressed interest in exploring this area.	Women should be married, and dating should be an important topic/part of your life.

Table 5.2   **continued**

Themes	Microaggression	Message
	A gay male client has been with his partner for 5 years. His therapist continually probes his desires to meet other men and be unfaithful.	Gay men are promiscuous. Gay men cannot have monogamous relationships.
	A therapist raises her eyebrows when a female client mentions that she has had a one night stand.	Women should not be sexually adventurous.
Sexual Objectification Occurs when women are treated like objects at men's disposal.	A male therapist puts his hands on a female client's back as she walks out of the session.	Your body is not yours.
	A male therapist is looking at his female client's breasts while she is talking.	Your body/appearance is for men's enjoyment and pleasure.
Assumption of Abnormality Occurs when it is implied that there is something wrong with being LGB.	When discussing her bisexuality, the therapist continues to imply that there is a "crisis of identity."	Bisexuality represents a confusion about sexual orientation.
	The therapist of a 20-year old lesbian inadvertently refers to sexuality as a "phase."	Your sexuality is something that is not stable.

Adapted from Sue et al., 2007.

and counselors have an obligation to their clients, especially when their clients differ from them in terms of race, gender, and/or sexual orientation, to work to understand their experiential reality. There is evidence to suggest that racial, gender, and sexual orientation microaggressions are everyday experiences too innumerable to count. These experiences impact clients in ways that researchers are only beginning to understand. There is much work to be done to better understand the nuances and processes involved in this very complex phenomenon. Therapists and counselors are in a position to learn from their clients about microaggressions and their relationship to their presenting concerns and developmental issues. It is imperative to encourage clients to explore their feelings about incidents that involve their race, gender, and sexual orientation so that the status quo of silence and invisibility can be destroyed.

1. Be aware that racial, gender, and sexual orientation microaggressions are a constant reality in the lives of culturally diverse groups. They take a major psychological toll on people of color, women, and LGB individuals. The socioemotional problems brought to therapy often reside in the effects of microaggressions rather than an attribute of the individual.

2. Be aware that everyone has, and continues to engage in, unintentional microaggressions. As a helping professional these microaggressions may serve as impediments to effective multicultural counseling and therapy. All therapists have a major responsibility to make the invisible, visible. What biases, prejudices, and stereotypes do you hold that may result in microaggressions? What must you do to minimize allowing them to impact your client in the therapy sessions?

3. Do not invalidate the experiential reality of culturally diverse groups. Entertain the notion that they may have a more accurate perception of reality than you, especially when it comes to issues of racism, sexism, or heterosexism. Reach out to culturally diverse clients, try to understand their worldviews, and don't be quick to dismiss or negate racial, gender, or sexual orientation issues.

4. Don't get defensive if your culturally diverse client implies that you have engaged in a microaggressive remark or behavior. Try to clarify the situation by showing you are open and receptive to conversations on race, gender, or sexual orientation. Remember, we all commit microaggressive blunders. In some cases, a simple "I'm sorry" and encouragement to the client to feel free to raise similar issues will do wonders for the therapeutic relationship. Remember, it's how the therapist recovers, not how he or she covers up, that is important.

THE PRACTICE DIMENSIONS OF MULTICULTURAL COUNSELING/THERAPY

Barriers to Multicultural Counseling and Therapy

6

Chapter

One of the most difficult cases I have ever treated was that of a Mexican American family in southern California. Fernando M. was a 56-year-old recent immigrant to the United States. He had been married some 35 years to Refugio, his wife, and had fathered 10 children. Only four of his children, three sons and one daughter, resided with him. Fernando was born in a small village in Mexico and resided there until 3 years ago, when he moved to California. He was not unfamiliar with California, having worked as a bracero for most of his adult life. He made frequent visits to the United States during annual harvest seasons.

The M. family resided in a small, old, unpainted rental house that sat on the back of a dirt lot and was sparsely furnished with their belongings. The family did not own a car, and public transportation was not available in their neighborhood. While their standard of living was far below U.S. poverty levels, the family appeared quite pleased at their relative affluence when compared with their life in Mexico.

The presenting complaints concerned Fernando. He heard threatening voices, was often disoriented, and stated that someone was planning to kill him and that something evil was about to happen. He became afraid to leave his home, was in poor physical health, and possessed a decrepit appearance that made him essentially unemployable.

When the M. family entered the clinic I was asked to see them, because the bilingual therapist scheduled that day had called in sick. I was hoping that either Fernando or Refugio could speak enough English to understand the situation. As luck would have it, neither could understand me, nor I them. It became apparent, however, that the two older children could understand English. Since the younger one seemed more fluent, I called on him to act as a translator during our first session. I noticed that the parents seemed reluctant to participate with the younger son, and for some time the discussion between the family members was quite animated. Sensing something wrong and desiring to get the session underway, I interrupted the family and asked the son who spoke English best what was wrong. He hesitated for a second, but assured me that everything was fine.

During the course of our first session, it became obvious to me that Fernando was seriously disturbed. He appeared frightened, tense, and, if the interpretations from his son were correct, he was also hallucinating. I suggested to Refugio that she consider hospitalizing her husband, but she was adamant against this course. I could sense her nervousness and fear that I would initiate action to have her husband committed. I reassured her that no action would be taken without a follow-up evaluation and suggested that she return later in the week with Fernando. Refugio said that it would be difficult since Fernando was afraid to leave his home. She had to coerce him into coming this time and did not feel she could do it again. I looked at Fernando directly and stated, "Fernando, I know how hard it is for you to come here, but we really want to help you. Do you think you could possibly come one more time? Dr. Escobedo [the bilingual therapist] will be here with me, and he can communicate with you directly." The youngest son interpreted.

The M. family never returned for another session, and their failure to show up has greatly bothered me. Since that time I have talked with several Latino psychologists who have pointed out multicultural issues that I was not aware of then. Now I realize how uninformed and naive I was about working with Latinos, and I only hope the M. family have found the needed help elsewhere.

While Chapter 4 dealt with the sociopolitical dynamics affecting multicultural counseling/therapy, this chapter discusses the cultural barriers that may render the helping professional ineffective, thereby denying help to culturally diverse clients. The previous example illustrates important multicultural issues that are presented in the following series of questions:

1. Was it a serious blunder for the therapist to see the M. family, or to continue to see them in the session, when he could not speak Spanish and the parents could not speak English? Should he have waited until Dr. Escobedo returned?

2. While it may seem like a good idea to have one of the children interpret for the therapist and the family, what possible cultural implications might this have in a Mexican American family? Can one obtain an accurate translation through family interpreters? What are some of the pitfalls?

3. The therapist tried to be informal with the family in order to put them at ease. Yet some of his colleagues have stated that how he addresses clients (last names or first names) may be important. When the therapist used the first names of both husband and wife, what possible cultural interpretation from the family may have resulted?

4. The therapist saw Mr. M.'s symptoms as indications of serious pathology. What other explanations should he have entertained? Should he

　　　have so blatantly suggested hospitalization? How do Latinos perceive
　　　mental health issues?

　5.　Knowing that Mr. M. had difficulty leaving home, should the therapist
　　　have considered some other treatment avenues? If so, what might they
　　　have been?

　　　The clash of cultural and therapeutic barriers exemplified in these questions is both complex and difficult to resolve. They challenge mental health
professionals to (1) reach out and understand the worldviews, cultural values, and life circumstances of their culturally diverse clients; (2) free themselves from the cultural conditioning of what they believe is correct therapeutic practice; (3) develop new but culturally sensitive methods of working
with clients; and (4) play new roles in the helping process outside of conventional psychotherapy (Atkinson, Thompson, & Grant, 1993). Three major potential barriers to effective Multicultural Therapy (MCT) are illustrated in this
case: class-bound values, language bias and misunderstanding, and culture-
bound values.

　　　First, Fernando's "paranoid reactions and suspicions" and his hallucinations may have had many causes. An enlightened mental health professional
must consider whether there are sociopolitical, cultural, or biological reasons
for his symptoms. Can his fears, for example, symbolize realistic concerns
(fear of deportation, creditors, police, etc.)? How do Latino cultures view hallucinations? Some studies indicate that cultural factors make it more acceptable for some Spanish-speaking populations to admit to hearing voices or seeing visions. Indeed, Appendix I of the American Psychiatric Association's
Diagnostic and Statistical Manual of Mental Disorders (2000) now recognizes a
large group of *culture-bound syndromes*, or disorders that seem to appear only
in specific cultures and societies. Another consideration is the life circumstances of Fernando's work. Could his agricultural work and years of exposure to pesticides and other dangerous agricultural chemicals be contributing
to his mental state? Counselors and psychotherapists often focus so much on
the internal dynamics of clients that there is a failure to consider external
sources as causes. It is important for therapists to consider these explanations.

　　　In addition, mental health practice has been described as a White,
middle-class activity that often fails to recognize the economic implications in
the delivery of mental health services. Class-bound factors related to socioeconomic status may place those suffering from poverty at a disadvantage
and deny them the necessary help that they need. For example, Fernando's
family is obviously poor, they do not own an automobile, and public transportation is not available in the rural area where they reside. Poor clients
have difficulties traveling to mental health facilities for treatment. Not only is
attending sessions a great inconvenience, but it can also be costly to arrange

private transportation for the family. It seems that meeting the needs of the M. family might have entailed home visits or some other form of outreach. If the M. family was unable to travel to the therapist's office for treatment, what blocked the therapist from considering a home visit, or a meeting point between the destinations? Many therapists feel disinclined, fearful, or uncomfortable doing the former. Their training dictates that they should practice in their offices, and that clients should come to them. When mental health services are located away from the communities that they purport to serve, outreach programs are not available, and economic considerations are not addressed by mental health services, institutional bias is clearly evident.

Second, language barriers often place culturally diverse clients at a disadvantage. The primary medium by which mental health professionals do their work is through verbalization (talk therapies). Ever since Freud developed the *talking cure*, psychotherapy has meant that clients must be able to verbalize their thoughts and feelings to a practitioner in order to receive the necessary help. In addition, because of linguistic bias and monolingualism, the typical form of talk is via Standard English. Clients who do not speak Standard English, possess a pronounced accent, or have limited command of English (like the M. family) may be victimized.

The need to understand the meaning of linguistic differences and language barriers in counseling and psychotherapy has never been greater. As we mentioned previously, the result of changing demographics is that many of our clients are born outside of the United States and speak English as their second language. While the use of interpreters might seem like a solution, such a practice may suffer from certain limitations. For example, can interpreters really give an accurate translation? Cultural differences in mental health concepts are not equivalent in various cultures. In addition, many concepts in English and Spanish do not have equivalent meanings. Likewise, the good intentions of the therapist to communicate with the M. family via the son, who seemed to speak English fluently, might result in a cultural family violation. It may undermine the authority of the father by disturbing the patriarchal role relationships considered sacred in traditional Latino families. There is no doubt that the need for bilingual therapists is great. Yet the lack of bilingual mental health professionals does not bode well for linguistic minorities.

Third, a number of culture-bound issues seemed to be played out in the delivery of services to the M. family. The therapist's attempt to be informal and to put the family at ease resulted in greeting Mr. M. by using his first name (Fernando), as opposed to a more formal title (Mr. M.). In traditional Latino and Asian cultures, such informality or familiarity may be considered a lack of respect for the man's role as head of the household. Another cultural barrier might be operative in asking the son whether something was wrong. It is highly probable that the animated family discussion was based on objections to the son's interpreting because it placed the father and mother in a dependency position. Yet as you recall, the son denied that anything was wrong. Many traditional Latinos do not feel comfortable airing family issues in public and might consider it impolite to turn down the therapist's suggestion to have the younger son interpret.

Characteristics of Counseling/Therapy

Counseling and psychotherapy may be viewed legitimately as a process of interpersonal interaction, communication, and social influence (Lui & Pope-Davis, 2005). For effective therapy to occur, the therapist and client must be able to *send and receive both verbal and nonverbal messages appropriately and accurately.* While breakdowns in communication often happen between people who share the same culture, the problem becomes exacerbated between people of different racial or ethnic backgrounds. Many mental health professionals have noted that racial or ethnic factors may act as impediments to therapy by lowering social influence (Locke, 1998; Paniagua, 1998; D.W. Sue, 2001). Misunderstandings that arise from cultural variations in communication may lead to alienation or an inability to develop trust and rapport. Culture clashes can often occur between the values of counseling and psychotherapy and the values of culturally diverse groups.

Generic Characteristics of Counseling/Therapy

All theories of counseling and psychotherapy are influenced by assumptions that theorists make regarding the goals for therapy, the methodology used to invoke change, and the definition of mental health and mental illness. Counseling and psychotherapy have traditionally been conceptualized in Western individualistic terms (Ivey, Ivey, Myers, & Sweeny, 2005). Whether the particular theory is psychodynamic, existential-humanistic, or cognitive-behavioral in orientation, a number of multicultural specialists (Ponterotto, Utsey & Pedersen, 2006; Ridley, 2005) indicate that they share certain common components of White culture in their values and beliefs. Katz (1985) has described these components of White culture. These values and beliefs have influenced the actual practice of counseling and psychotherapy, as can be seen clearly in Tables 6.1 and 6.2.

In the United States and in many other countries as well, psychotherapy and counseling are used mainly with middle- and upper-class segments of the population. As a result, culturally diverse clients do not share many of the values and characteristics seen in both the goals and the processes of therapy. Schofield (1964) has noted that therapists tend to prefer clients who exhibit

Table 6.1 **Generic Characteristics of Counseling**

Culture	Middle Class	Language
Standard English	Standard English	Standard English
Verbal communication	Verbal communication	Verbal communication
Individual centered		
	Adherence to time	
Verbal/emotional/	schedules (50-minute	
behavioral expressiveness	sessions)	
Client-counselor		
communication	Long-range goals	
Openness and intimacy	Ambiguity	
Cause-effect orientation		
Clear distinction between		
physical and mental well-		
being		
Nuclear family		

the *YAVIS* syndrome: young, attractive, verbal, intelligent, and successful. This preference tends to discriminate against people from different minority groups or those from lower socioeconomic classes. This led Sundberg (1981) to sarcastically point out that therapy is not for *QUOID* people (quiet, ugly, old, indigent, and dissimilar culturally). Three major characteristics of counseling and psychotherapy may act as impediments to effective counseling.

1. Culture-bound values: individual centered, verbal/emotional/behavioral expressiveness, communication patterns from client to counselor, openness and intimacy, analytic/linear/verbal (cause-effect) approach, and clear distinctions between mental and physical well-being.

2. Class-bound values: strict adherence to time schedules (50-minute, once or twice a week meetings), ambiguous or unstructured approach to problems, and seeking long-range goals or solutions.

3. Language variables: use of Standard English and emphasis on verbal communication.

Table 6.2 summarizes these generic characteristics and compares their compatibility to those of four racial/ethnic minority groups. As mentioned earlier, such a comparison can also be done for other groups that vary in gender, age, sexual orientation, ability/disability, and so on.

While an attempt has been made to clearly delineate three major variables that influence effective therapy, these variables are often inseparable from one another. For example, use of Standard English in counseling and

Table 6.2 **Racial/Ethnic Minority Group Variables**

Culture	Lower Class	Language
	Asian Americans	
Asian language	Nonstandard English	Bilingual background
Family centered	Action oriented	
Restraint of feelings	Different time perspective	
One-way communication from authority figure to person	Immediate, short-range goals	
Silence is respect		
Advice seeking		
Well-defined patterns of interaction (concrete structured)		
Private versus public display (shame/disgrace/pride)		
Physical and mental well-being defined differently		
Extended family		
	African Americans	
Black language	Nonstandard English	Black language
Sense of "people-hood"	Action oriented	
Action oriented	Different time perspective	
Paranorm due to oppression	Immediate, short-range goals	
Importance placed on nonverbal behavior	Concrete, tangible, structured approach	
Extended family		
	Latino/Hispanic Americans	
Spanish-speaking	Nonstandard English	Bilingual background
Group centered	Action oriented	
Temporal difference	Different time perspective	
Family orientation	Extended family	
Different pattern of communication	Immediate short-range goals	
Religious distinction between mind/body	Concrete, tangible, structured approach	

(continued)

Table 6.2 **continued**

Culture	Lower Class	Language
American Indians		
Tribal dialects	Nonstandard English	Bilingual background
Cooperative, not competitive individualism	Action oriented	
	Different time perspective	
Present-time orientation	Immediate, short-range goals	
Creative/experimental/intuitive/ nonverbal	Concrete, tangible, structured approach	
Satisfy present needs		
Use of folk or supernatural explanations		
Extended family		

therapy definitely places those individuals who do not speak English fluently at a disadvantage. However, cultural and class values that govern conventions of conversation can also operate via language to cause serious misunderstandings. Furthermore, the fact that many African Americans, Latino/Hispanic Americans, and American Indians come from predominantly lower-class backgrounds often compounds class and culture variables. Thus, it is often difficult to tell which variables are the sole impediments in therapy. Nevertheless, this distinction is valuable in conceptualizing barriers to effective multicultural counseling/therapy.

Culture-Bound Values

Culture consists of all those things that people have learned to do, believe, value, and enjoy. It is the totality of the ideals, beliefs, skills, tools, customs, and institutions into which each member of society is born. While being bicultural is a source of strength, the process of negotiating dual group membership may cause problems for many minorities. The term *marginal person* was first coined by Stonequist (1937) and refers to a person's inability to form dual ethnic identification because of bicultural membership. Racial and ethnic minorities are placed under strong pressures to adopt the ways of the dominant culture. The cultural deficit models tend to view culturally diverse groups as possessing dysfunctional values and belief systems that are often handicaps to be overcome, be ashamed of, and avoid. In essence, racial and ethnic minorities may be taught that to be different is to be deviant, pathological, or sick.

Many social scientists (Boyd-Franklin, 2003; Duran, 2006; Guthrie, 1997; Halleck, 1971) believe that psychology and therapy may be viewed as encompassing the use of social power, and that therapy is a handmaiden of the status quo. The therapist may be seen as a societal agent transmitting and functioning under Western values. An early outspoken critic, Szasz (1970) believes that psychiatrists are like slave masters, using therapy as a powerful political ploy against people whose ideas, beliefs, and behaviors differ from the dominant society. Several culture-bound characteristics of therapy may be responsible for these negative beliefs.

Focus on the Individual

Most forms of counseling and psychotherapy tend to be individual centered (i.e., they emphasize the "I-thou" relationship). Pedersen (2000) notes that U.S. culture and society are based on the concept of individualism and that competition between individuals for status, recognition, achievement, and so forth, forms the basis for Western tradition. Individualism, autonomy, and the ability to become your own person are perceived as healthy and desirable goals. If we look at most Euro-American theories of human development (Piaget, Erickson, etc.), we are struck by how they emphasize individuation as normal and healthy development (Ivey, D'Andrea, Ivey, & Simek-Morgan, 2002). Pedersen notes that not all cultures view individualism as a positive orientation; rather, it may be perceived in some cultures as a handicap to attaining enlightenment, one that may divert us from important spiritual goals. In many non-Western cultures, identity is not seen apart from the group orientation (collectivism). The Japanese language does not seem to have a distinct personal pronoun *I*. The notion of *atman* in India defines itself as participating in unity with all things and not being limited by the temporal world.

Many societies do not define the psychosocial unit of operation as the individual. In many cultures and subgroups, the psychosocial unit of operation tends to be the family, group, or collective society. In traditional Asian American culture, one's identity is defined within the family constellation. The greatest punitive measure to be taken out on an individual by the family is to be disowned. What this means, in essence, is that the person no longer has an identity. While being disowned by a family in Western European culture is equally negative and punitive, it does not have the same connotations as in traditional Asian society. Although they may be disowned by a family, Westerners are always told that they have an individual identity as well. Likewise, many Hispanic individuals tend to see the unit of operation as residing within the family. African American psychologists (Parham et al., 1999) also point out how the African view of the world encompasses the concept of "groupness."

Our contention is that racial/ethnic minorities often use a different psychosocial unit of operation, in that collectivism is valued over individualism.

This worldview is reflected in all aspects of behavior. For example, many traditional Asian American and Hispanic elders tend to greet one another with the question, "How is your family today?" Contrast this with how most Americans tend to greet each other: "How are you today?" One emphasizes the family (group) perspective, while the other emphasizes the individual perspective.

Affective expressions in therapy can also be strongly influenced by the particular orientation one takes. When individuals engage in wrongful behaviors in the United States, they are most likely to experience feelings of guilt. In societies that emphasize collectivism, however, the most dominant affective element to follow a wrongful behavior is shame, not guilt. Guilt is an individual affect, while shame appears to be a group one (it reflects on the family or group).

Counselors and therapists who fail to recognize the importance of defining this difference between individualism and collectivism will create difficulties in therapy. Often we are impressed by the number of our colleagues who describe traditional Asian clients as being "dependent," "unable to make decisions on their own," and "lacking in maturity." Many of these judgments are based on the fact that many Asian clients do not see a decision-making process as an individual one. When an Asian client states to a counselor or therapist, "I can't make that decision on my own; I need to consult with my parents or family," he or she is seen as being quite immature. After all, therapy is aimed at helping individuals make decisions on their own in a "mature" and "responsible" manner.

Verbal/Emotional/Behavioral Expressiveness

Many counselors and therapists tend to emphasize the fact that verbal/emotional/behavioral expressiveness is important in individuals. For example, we like our clients to be verbal, articulate, and able to express their thoughts and feelings clearly. Indeed, therapy is often referred to as talk therapy, indicating the importance placed on Standard English as the medium of expression. Emotional expressiveness is also valued, as we like individuals to be in touch with their feelings and to be able to verbalize their emotional reactions. In some forms of counseling and psychotherapy, it is often stated that if a feeling is not verbalized and expressed by the client, it may not exist. We tend to value behavioral expressiveness and believe that it is important as well. We like individuals to be assertive, to stand up for their own rights, and to engage in activities that indicate they are not passive beings.

All these characteristics of therapy can place culturally diverse clients at a disadvantage. For example, many cultural minorities tend not to value verbalizations in the same way that Americans do. In traditional Japanese culture, children have been taught not to speak until spoken to. Patterns of communication tend to be vertical, flowing from those of higher prestige and status to those of lower prestige and status. In a therapy situation many Japanese clients, to show respect for a therapist who is older, wiser, and who occupies a position of higher status, may respond with silence. Unfortunately, an unenlightened counselor or therapist may perceive this client as being inarticulate and less intelligent.

Emotional expressiveness in counseling and psychotherapy is frequently a highly desired goal. Yet many cultural groups value restraint of strong feelings. For example, traditional Hispanic and Asian cultures emphasize that maturity and wisdom are associated with one's ability to control emotions and feelings. This applies not only to public expressions of anger and frustration, but also to public expressions of love and affection. Unfortunately, therapists unfamiliar with these cultural ramifications may perceive their clients in a very negative psychiatric light. Indeed, these clients are often described as inhibited, lacking in spontaneity, or repressed.

In therapy it has become increasingly popular to emphasize expressiveness in a behavioral sense. For example, one need only note the proliferation of cognitive-behavioral assertiveness training programs throughout the United States and the number of self-help books that are being published in the popular mental health literature. This orientation fails to realize that there are cultural groups in which subtlety is a highly prized art. Yet doing things indirectly can be perceived by the mental health professional as evidence of passivity and a need for an individual to learn assertiveness skills.

Therapists who value verbal, emotional, and behavioral expressiveness as goals in therapy may be unaware that they are transmitting their own cultural values. These generic characteristics of counseling are antagonistic not only to lower-class values, but to different cultural ones as well. In their excellent review of assertiveness training, Wood and Mallinckrodt (1990) warn that therapists need to make certain that gaining such skills is a value shared by the minority client, and not imposed by therapists. For example, statements by some mental health professionals that Asian Americans are the most repressed of all clients indicate that they expect their clients to exhibit openness, psychological-mindedness, and assertiveness. Such a statement may indicate the therapist's failure to understand the background and cultural upbringing of many Asian American clients. Traditional Chinese and Japanese cultures may value restraint of strong feelings and subtleness in approaching problems.

Insight

Another generic characteristic of counseling is the use of insight in both counseling and psychotherapy. This approach assumes that it is mentally beneficial for individuals to obtain insight or understanding into their underlying dynamics and causes. Educated in the tradition of psychoanalytic theory, many theorists tend to believe that clients who obtain better insight into themselves will be better adjusted. While many behavioral schools of thought may not subscribe to this, most therapists use insight in their individual practice, either as a process of therapy or as an end product or goal.

We need to realize that insight is not highly valued by many culturally diverse clients. There are major class differences as well. People from lower socioeconomic classes frequently do not perceive insight as appropriate to their life situations and circumstances. Their concern may revolve around questions such as "Where do I find a job?" "How do I feed my family?" and "How can I afford to take my sick daughter to a doctor?" When survival on a day-to-day basis is important, it seems inappropriate for the therapist to use insightful processes. After all, insight assumes that one has time to sit back, reflect, and contemplate motivations and behavior. For the individual who is concerned about making it through each day, this orientation proves counterproductive.

Likewise, many cultural groups do not value insight. In traditional Chinese society, psychology has little relevance. It must be noted, however, that a client who does not seem to work well in an insight approach may not be lacking in insight or psychological-mindedness. A person who does not value insight is not necessarily one who is incapable of insight. Thus, several major factors tend to affect insight.

First, many cultural groups do not value this method of self-exploration. It is interesting to note that many Asian elders believe that thinking too much about something can cause problems. In a study of the Chinese in San Francisco's Chinatown, Lum (1982) found that many believe the road to mental health was to "avoid morbid thoughts." Advice from Asian elders to their children when they encountered feelings of frustration, anger, depression, or anxiety was simply, "Don't think about it." Indeed, it is often believed that the reason one experiences anger or depression is precisely that one is thinking about it *too much!* The traditional Asian way of handling these affective elements is to "keep busy and don't think about it." Granted, it is more complex than this, because in traditional Asian families the reason self-exploration is discouraged is precisely because it is an individual approach. "Think about the family and not about yourself" is advice given to many Asians as a way of dealing with negative affective elements. This is totally contradictory to Western notions of mental health; namely, that it is best to get things out in the open in order to deal with them.

Second, many racial/ethnic minority psychologists have felt that insight is a value in itself. For example, it was generally thought that insight led to behavior change. This was the old psychoanalytic assumption that when people understood their conflicts and underlying dynamics, the symptoms or behavior would change or disappear. The behavioral schools of thought have since disproved this one-to-one connection. While insight does lead to behavior change in some situations, it does not always seem to do so. Indeed, behavioral therapies have shown that changing the behavior first may lead to insight (cognitive restructuring and understanding) instead of vice versa.

Self-Disclosure (Openness and Intimacy)

Most forms of counseling and psychotherapy tend to value one's ability to self-disclose and to talk about the most intimate aspects of one's life. Indeed, self-disclosure has often been discussed as a primary characteristic of a healthy personality. The converse of this is that people who do not self-disclose readily in counseling and psychotherapy are seen to possess negative traits such as being guarded, mistrustful, or paranoid. There are two difficulties in this orientation toward self-disclosure. One of these is cultural, and the other is sociopolitical.

First, intimate revelations of personal or social problems may not be acceptable because such difficulties reflect not only on the individual, but also on the whole family. Thus, the family may exert strong pressures on the Asian American client not to reveal personal matters to strangers or outsiders. Similar conflicts have been reported for Hispanics (Leong, Wagner, & Tata, 1995; Paniagua, 1998) and for American Indian clients (Herring, 1999; LaFromboise, 1998). A therapist who works with a client from a minority background may erroneously conclude that the person is repressed, inhibited, shy, or passive. Note that all these terms are seen as undesirable by Western standards.

Related to this example is many health practitioners' belief in the desirability of self-disclosure. Self-disclosure refers to the client's willingness to tell the therapist what he or she feels, believes, or thinks. Jourard (1964) suggests that mental health is related to one's openness in disclosing. While this may be true, the parameters need clarification. Chapter 4 uses as an example the paranorm of Grier and Cobbs (1968). People of African descent are especially reluctant to disclose to White counselors because of hardships that they have experienced via racism (Ridley, 2005). African Americans initially perceive a White therapist more often as an agent of society who may use information against them, rather than as a person of goodwill. From the African American perspective, noncritical self-disclosure to others is not healthy.

The actual structure of the therapy situation may also work against intimate revelations. Among many American Indians and Hispanics, intimate aspects of life are shared only with close friends. Relative to White middle-class standards, deep friendships are developed only after prolonged contacts. Once friendships are formed, they tend to be lifelong in nature. In contrast, White Americans form relationships quickly, but the relationships do not necessarily persist over long periods of time. Counseling and therapy also seem to reflect these values. Clients talk about the most intimate aspects of their lives with a relative stranger once every week for a 50-minute session.

To many culturally different groups who stress friendship as a precondition to self-disclosure, the counseling process seems utterly inappropriate and absurd. After all, how is it possible to develop a friendship with brief contacts once a week?

Scientific Empiricism

Counseling and psychotherapy in Western culture and society have been described as being highly linear, analytic, and verbal in their attempt to mimic the physical sciences. As indicated by Table 6.1, Western society tends to emphasize the so-called scientific method, which involves objective, rational, linear thinking. Likewise, we often see descriptions of therapists as objective, neutral, rational, and logical (Utsey, Walker & Kwate, 2005). Therapists rely heavily on the use of linear problem solving, as well as on quantitative evaluation that includes psychodiagnostic tests, intelligence tests, personality inventories, and so forth. This cause-and-effect orientation emphasizes left-brain functioning. That is, theories of counseling and therapy are distinctly analytical, rational, and verbal, and they strongly stress the discovery of cause-and-effect relationships.

The emphasis on symbolic logic contrasts markedly with the philosophies of many cultures that value a more nonlinear, holistic, and harmonious approach to the world (D. W. Sue & Constantine, 2003). For example, American Indian worldviews emphasize the harmonious aspects of the world, intuitive functioning, and a holistic approach—a world view characterized by right-brain activities (Ornstein, 1972), minimizing analytical and reductionistic inquiries. Thus, when American Indians undergo therapy, the analytic approach may violate their basic philosophy of life.

It appears that the most dominant way of asking and answering questions about the human condition in U.S. society tends to be the scientific method. The epitome of this approach is the *experiment*. In graduate schools we are often told that only through the experiment can we impute a cause-and-effect relationship. By identifying the independent and dependent variables, and controlling for extraneous variables, we are able to test a cause-and-effect hypothesis. While correlation studies, historical research, and other approaches may be of benefit, we are told that the experiment represents the epitome of our science (Seligman & Csikszentmihalyi, 2001). As indicated, other cultures may value different ways of asking and answering questions about the human condition.

Distinctions between Mental and Physical Functioning

Many American Indians, Asian Americans, Blacks, and Hispanics hold different concepts of what constitutes mental health, mental illness, and adjustment. Among the Chinese, the concept of mental health or psychological well-being is not understood in the same way as it is in the Western context. Latino/Hispanic Americans do not make the same Western distinction between mental and physical health as do their White counterparts (Rivera, 1984). Thus, nonphysical health problems are most likely to be referred to a physician, priest, or minister. Culturally diverse clients operating under this orientation may enter therapy expecting therapists to treat them in the same manner that doctors or priests do. Immediate solutions and concrete tangible forms of treatment (advice, confession, consolation, and medication) are expected.

Ambiguity

The ambiguous and unstructured aspect of the therapy situation may create discomfort in clients of color. The culturally different may not be familiar with therapy and may perceive it as an unknown and mystifying process. Some groups, such as Hispanics, may have been reared in an environment that actively structures social relationships and patterns of interaction. Anxiety and confusion may be the outcome in an unstructured counseling setting.

Patterns of Communication

The cultural upbringing of many minorities dictates different patterns of communication that may place them at a disadvantage in therapy. Counseling, for example, initially demands that communication move from client to counselor. The client is expected to take the major responsibility for initiating conversation in the session, while the counselor plays a less active role.

However, American Indians, Asian Americans, and Hispanics function under different cultural imperatives, which may make this difficult. These three groups may have been reared to respect elders and authority figures and not to speak until spoken to. Clearly defined roles of dominance and deference are established in the traditional family. Evidence indicates that Asians associate mental health with exercising will power, avoiding unpleasant thoughts, and occupying one's mind with positive thoughts. Therapy is seen as an authoritative process in which a good therapist is more direct and active, and portrays a kind of father figure (Henkin, 1985; Mau & Jepson, 1988). A racial/ethnic minority client who is asked to initiate conversation may become uncomfortable and respond with only short phrases or statements. The therapist may be prone to interpret the behavior negatively, when in actuality it may be a sign of respect. We have much more to say about these communication style differences in the next chapter.

Class-Bound Values

Social class and classism have been identified as two of the most overlooked topics in psychology and mental health practice (Liu, Ali, Soleck, Hopps, Dunston, & Pickett, 2004; L. Smith, 2005). While many believe that the gap in income is closing, statistics suggest the opposite— income inequality is increasing. Those in the top 5 percent of income have enjoyed huge increases, while those in the bottom 40 percent are stagnant (APA Task Force on Socioeconomic Status, 2006). In the United States, 32 million Americans live in poverty. Blacks are three times more likely to live in poverty than Whites; the rate of poverty for Latinos is 23 percent; for Asian/Pacific Islanders it is 11 percent; and for Whites it is 8 percent (Liu et al., 2004). These statistics clearly suggest that social class may be intimately linked to race because many racial/ethnic minority groups are disproportionately represented in the lower socioeconomic classes (Lewis et al., 1998).

Research indicates that lower socioeconomic class is related to higher incidence of depression (Lorant, Deliege, Eaton, Robert, Philippot, & Ansseau, 2003), lower sense of control (Chen, Matthews, & Boyce, 2002), and poorer physical health (Gallo & Matthews, 2003). Mental health professionals are often unaware of additional stressors likely to confront clients who lack financial resources, nor do they fully appreciate how those stressors affect their clients' daily lives. For the therapist who comes from a middle- to upper-class background, it is often difficult to relate to the circumstances and hardships affecting the client who lives in poverty. The phenomenon of poverty and its effects on individuals and institutions can be devastating (Liu, Hernandezs, Mahmood, & Stinson, 2006). The individual's life is characterized by low wages, unemployment, underemployment, little property ownership, no savings, and lack of food reserves. Meeting even the most basic needs of food and shelter is in constant jeopardy. Pawning personal possessions and borrowing money at exorbitant interest rates only leads to greater debt. Feelings of helplessness, dependence, and inferiority develop easily under these circumstances. Therapists may unwittingly attribute attitudes that result from physical and environmental adversity to the cultural or individual traits of the person. For example, note the clinical description of a 12-year-old child written by a school counselor:

> *Jimmy Jones is a 12-year-old Black male student who was referred by Mrs. Peterson because of apathy, indifference, and inattentiveness to classroom activities. Other teachers have also reported that Jimmy does not pay attention, daydreams often, and frequently falls asleep during class. There is a strong possibility that Jimmy is harboring repressed rage that needs to be ventilated and dealt with. His inability to directly express his anger had led him to adopt passive-aggressive means of expressing hostility (i.e., inattentiveness, daydreaming, falling asleep).*

It is recommended that Jimmy be seen for intensive counseling to discover the basis of the anger.

After 6 months of counseling, the counselor finally realized the basis of Jimmy's problems. He came from a home life marked by extreme poverty, where hunger, lack of sleep, and overcrowding served to severely diminish his energy level and motivation. The fatigue, passivity, and fatalism evidenced by Jimmy were more a result of poverty than of some innate group or individual trait. Likewise, poverty may cause many parents to encourage children to seek employment at an early age. Delivering groceries, shining shoes, and hustling other sources of income may sap the energy of the schoolchild, leading to truancy and poor performance. Teachers and counselors may view such students as unmotivated and potential juvenile delinquents.

Considerable bias against people who are poor has been well documented (APA Task Force on SES, 2006; L. Smith, 2005). While considerable controversy exists over whether classism is unidirectional (directed toward those in lower classes) or bidirectional (equally likely to occur between the classes; Lui, et al., 2004; Smith, 2005), it is clear to us that those who occupy the lower rungs of our society are the most likely to be oppressed and harmed. For example, lower social class clients are perceived more unfavorably than upper social class clients by clinicians (have less education, are dysfunctional, and make poor progress in therapy). Research concerning the inferior and biased quality of treatment to lower-class clients is historically legend (Atkinson, et al., 1998; Pavkov et al., 1989; Rouse, Carter, & Rodriguez-Andrew, 1995). In the area of diagnosis, it has been found that an attribution of mental illness was more likely to occur when the person's history suggested a lower rather than higher socioeconomic class origin (Liu et al., 2006). Many studies seem to demonstrate that clinicians given identical test protocols tend to make more negative prognostic statements and judgments of greater maladjustment when the individual was said to come from a lower- rather than a middle-class background.

In the area of treatment, Garfield, Weiss, and Pollock (1973) gave counselors identical descriptions (except for social class) of a 9-year-old boy who engaged in maladaptive classroom behavior. When the boy was assigned upper-class status, more counselors expressed a willingness to become ego-involved with the student than when lower-class status was assigned. Likewise, Habemann and Thiry (1970) found that doctoral candidates in counseling and guidance programmed students from low socioeconomic backgrounds into a noncollege-bound track more frequently than into a college-preparatory one.

Several conclusions can be drawn from these findings: (1) low socioeconomic class presents stressors to people, especially those in poverty, and may seriously undermine the mental and physical health of clients; (2) failure of helping professionals to understand the life circumstance of clients who lack financial resources and/or their unintentional class biases may affect their ability to delivery appropriate mental health services; and (3) classism and its discriminating nature can make its appearance in the assessment, diagnosis, and treatment of lower socioeconomic clients.

In addition, the class-bound nature of mental health practice emphasizes the importance of assisting the client in self-direction through the presentation of the results of assessment instruments and self-exploration via verbal interactions between client and therapist. However, the values underlying these activities are permeated by middle-class values that do not suffice for those living in poverty. We have already seen how this operates with respect to language. As early as the 1960s, Bernstein (1964) investigated the suitability of Standard English for the lower class in psychotherapy and has concluded that it works to the detriment of those individuals. In an extensive historic research of services delivered to minorities and low socioeconomic clients, Lorion (1973) found that psychiatrists refer to therapy those persons who are most like themselves—White rather than non-White, and from upper socioeconomic status. Lorion (1974) pointed out that the expectations of lower-class clients are often different from those of psychotherapists. For example, lower-class clients who are concerned with survival or making it through on a day-to-day basis expect advice and suggestions from the counselor. Appointments made weeks in advance with short, weekly, 50-minute contacts are not consistent with the need to seek immediate solutions. Additionally, many lower-class people, through multiple experiences with public agencies, operate under what is called *minority standard time* (Schindler-Rainman, 1967). This is the tendency of poor people to have a low regard for punctuality. Poor people have learned that endless waits are associated with medical clinics, police stations, and governmental agencies. One usually waits hours for a 10- to 15-minute appointment. Arriving promptly does little good and can be a waste of valuable time. Therapists, however, rarely understand this aspect of life and are prone to see this as a sign of indifference or hostility.

People from a lower socioeconomic status may also view insight and attempts to discover underlying intrapsychic problems as inappropriate. Many lower-class clients expect to receive advice or some form of concrete tangible treatment. When the therapist attempts to explore personality dynamics or to take a historical approach to the problem, the client often becomes confused, alienated, and frustrated. A harsh environment, where the future is uncertain and immediate needs must be met, makes long-range planning of little value. Many clients of lower socioeconomic status are unable to relate to the future orientation of therapy. To be able to sit and talk about things is perceived as a luxury of the middle and upper classes.

Because of the lower-class client's environment and past inexperience with therapy, the expectations of the minority individual may be quite different, or even negative. The client's unfamiliarity with the therapy process may hinder success and cause the therapist to blame the client for the failure. Thus, the minority client may be perceived as hostile and resistant. The results of this interaction may be a premature termination of therapy. Considerable evidence exists that clients from upper socioeconomic backgrounds have significantly more exploratory interviews with their therapists, and that middle-class patients tend to remain in treatment longer than lower-class patients (Gottesfeld, 1995; Leong, Wagner, & Kim, 1995; Neighbors, Caldwell, Thompson, & Jackson, 1994). Furthermore, the now-classic study of Hollingshead and Redlich (1968) found that lower-class patients tend to have fewer ego-involving relationships and less intensive therapeutic relationships than do members of higher socioeconomic classes.

Poverty undoubtedly contributes to the mental health problems among racial/ethnic minority groups, and social class determines the type of treatment a minority client is likely to receive. In addition, as Atkinson, Morten, et al. (1998, p. 64) conclude, "ethnic minorities are less likely to earn incomes sufficient to pay for mental health treatment, less likely to have insurance, and more likely to qualify for public assistance than European Americans. Thus, ethnic minorities often have to rely on public (government-sponsored) or nonprofit mental health services to obtain help with their psychological problems."

Working effectively with clients who are poor requires several major conditions. First, the therapist must spend time understanding his or her own biases and prejudices (Liu et al., 2004). Not confronting one's own classist attitudes can lead to a phenomenon called "White trashism." Manifestation of prejudicial or negative attitudes can be found in descriptors like "trailer parkism," "hillbillyism," "uppity," "red-neck," and so on. These attitudes can affect the diagnosis and treatment of clients. Second, it becomes essential that counselors understand how poverty affects the lives of people who lack financial resources; behaviors associated with survival should not be pathologized. Third, counselors should consider that taboos against information-giving activities and a more active approach in treatment might be more appropriate than the passive, insight-oriented and long-term models of therapy. Last, poverty and economic disparities that are root causes affecting the mental health and quality of life of people in our society demand a social justice approach (see Chapter 12).

Language Barriers

Ker Moua, a Laotian refugee, suffered from a variety of ailments but was unable to communicate with her doctor. The medical staff enlisted the aid of 12-year-old Jue as the liaison between the doctor and mother. Ker was diagnosed with a prolapsed uterus, the result of bearing 12 children. She took medication in the doses described by her son, but became severely ill after two days. Fortunately, it was discovered that she was taking an incorrect dosage that could have caused lasting harm. The hospital staff realized that Jue had mistranslated the doctor's orders. When inquiries about the translation occurred, Jue said "I don't know what a uterus is. The doctor tells me things I don't know how to say." (Burke, 2005)

Asking children to translate information concerning medical or legal problems is common in many communities with high immigrant populations, but may have devastating consequences: (1) it can create stress and hurt the traditional parent-child relationship; (2) children lack the vocabulary and emotional maturity to serve as effective interpreters; (3) children may be placed in a situation where they are privy to confidential medical or psychiatric information about their relatives; and (4) they may be unfairly burdened with emotional responsibilities that only adults should carry (Coleman, 2003). As of this writing, California Assembly Bill 775 was introduced to ban the use of children as interpreters. California will become the first state to do so, if passed. Further, the federal government has acknowledged that not providing adequate interpretation for client populations is a form of discrimination. As our opening case of the M. family suggests, the lack of bilingual therapists can result in both inferior and damaging services to linguistic minorities. Recently, the National Council on Interpreting in Health Care (2005) published national standards for interpreters of health care that address issues of cultural awareness and confidentiality.

Clearly, use of Standard English in health care delivery may unfairly discriminate against those from a bilingual or lower socioeconomic background and result in devastating consequences (Vedantam, 2005). This inequity occurs in our educational system and in the delivery of mental health services as well. The bilingual background of many Asian Americans, Latino/Hispanic Americans, and American Indians may lead to much misunderstanding. This is true even if a minority group member cannot speak his or her own native tongue. Early language studies (M. E. Smith, 1957; M. E. Smith & Kasdon, 1961) indicate that simply coming from a background where one or both of parents have spoken their native tongue can impair proper acquisition of English. Even African Americans who come from a different cultural environment may use words and phrases (Black Language, or Ebonics) not entirely understandable to the therapist. While considerable criticism was directed toward the Oakland Unified School District for their short-lived attempt to recognize Ebonics in 1996, the reality is that such a form of communication does exist in many African American communities. In therapy, however, African American clients are expected to communicate their feelings and thoughts to therapists in Standard English. For some African Americans, this is a difficult task, since the use of nonstandard English is their norm. Black language code involves a great deal of implicitness in communication, such as shorter sentences and less grammatical elaboration (but greater reliance on nonverbal cues). On the other hand, the language code of the middle and upper classes is much more elaborate, relies less on nonverbal cues, and entails greater knowledge of grammar and syntax.

Romero (1985) indicates that counseling psychologists are finding that they must interact with consumers who may have English as a second language, or who may not speak English at all. The lack of bilingual therapists and the requirement that the client communicate in English may limit the person's ability to progress in counseling and therapy. If bilingual individuals do not use their native tongue in therapy, many aspects of their emotional experience may not be available for treatment. For example, because English may not be their primary language, they may have difficulty using the wide complexity of language to describe their particular thoughts, feelings, and unique situations. Clients who are limited in English tend to feel like they are speaking as a child and choosing simple words to explain complex thoughts and feelings. If they were able to use their native tongue, they could easily explain themselves without the huge loss of emotional complexity and experience.

In therapy, heavy reliance is placed on verbal interaction to build rapport. The presupposition is that participants in a therapeutic dialogue are capable of understanding each other. Therapists often fail to understand an African American client's language and its nuances for rapport building. Furthermore, those who have not been given the same educational or economic opportunities may lack the prerequisite verbal skills to benefit from talk therapy. A client's brief, different, or poor verbal responses may lead many therapists to impute inaccurate characteristics or motives. As a result, the client may be seen as uncooperative, sullen, negative, nonverbal, or repressed on the basis of language expression alone. Since Euro-American society places such a high premium on one's use of English, it is a short step to conclude that linguistic minorities are inferior, lack awareness, or lack conceptual thinking powers. Such misinterpretation can also be seen in the use and interpretation of psychological tests. So-called IQ and achievement tests are especially notorious for their language bias.

Generalizations and Stereotypes: Some Cautions

White cultural values are reflected in the generic characteristics of counseling (Table 6.1; see also Table 12.1). These characteristics are summarized and can be compared with the values of four racial/ethnic minority groups: American Indians, Asian Americans, Blacks, and Hispanics (see Table 6.2). Although it is critical for therapists to have a basic understanding of the generic characteristics of counseling and psychotherapy and the culture-specific life values of different groups, overgeneralizing and stereotyping are ever-present dangers. For example, the listing of racial/ethnic minority group variables does not indicate that all persons coming from the same minority group will share all or even some of these traits. Furthermore, emerging trends such as short-term and crisis intervention approaches and other less verbally oriented techniques differ from the generic traits listed. Yet it is highly improbable that any of us can enter a situation or encounter people without forming impressions consistent with our own experiences and values. Whether a client is dressed neatly in a suit or wears blue jeans, is a man or a woman, or is of a different race will likely affect our assumptions.

First impressions will be formed that fit our own interpretations and generalizations of human behavior. Generalizations are necessary for us; without them, we would become inefficient creatures. However, they are guidelines for our behaviors, to be tentatively applied in new situations, and they should be open to change and challenge. It is exactly at this stage that generalizations remain generalizations or become stereotypes. *Stereotypes* may be defined as rigid preconceptions we hold about *all* people who are members of a particular group, whether it be defined along racial, religious, sexual, or other lines. The belief in a perceived characteristic of the group is applied to all members without regard for individual variations. The danger of stereotypes is that they are impervious to logic or experience. All incoming information is distorted to fit our preconceived notions. For example, people who are strongly anti-semitic will accuse Jews of being stingy and miserly and then, in the same breath, accuse them of flaunting their wealth by conspicuous spending.

The information in Tables 6.1, 6.2, and 12.1 should act as guidelines rather than absolutes. These generalizations should serve as the background from which the figure emerges. For example, belonging to a particular group may mean sharing common values and experiences. Individuals within a group, however, also differ. The background offers a contrast for us to see individual differences more clearly. It should not submerge, but rather increase the visibility of the figure. This is the figure-ground relationship that should aid us in recognizing the uniqueness of people more readily.

Implications for Clinical Practice

In general, it appears that Western forms of healing involve processes that may prove inappropriate and antagonistic to many culturally diverse groups. The mental health professional must be cognizant of the culture-bound, class-bound, and linguistic barriers that might place minority clients at a disadvantage. Some suggestions to the clinician involve the following:

1. Become cognizant of the generic characteristics of counseling and psychotherapy. It is clear that mental health services arise from a particular cultural context and are imbued with assumptions and values that may not be applicable to all groups.

2. Know that we are increasingly becoming a multilingual nation and that the linguistic demands of clinical work may place minority populations at a disadvantage. Be sensitive and ready to provide or advocate for multilingual services.

3. Consider the need to provide community counseling services that reach out to the minority population. The traditional one-to-one, in-the-office delivery of services must be supplemented by methods that are more action oriented. In other words, effective multicultural counseling must involve roles and activities in the natural environment of the clients (schools, churches, neighborhoods, playgrounds, etc.) rather than just in mental health clinics.

4. Realize that the problems and concerns of many minority groups are related to systemic and external forces rather than internal psychological problems. The effects of poverty, discrimination, prejudice, immigration stress, and so forth indicate that counselors might be most effective in aiding clients to deal with these forces rather than pursuing self-exploration and insight approaches.

5. While most theories of counseling and psychotherapy prescribe the types of actions and roles played by a therapist, these may prove minimally helpful to minority clients. The more passive approach must be expanded to include roles and behaviors that are more action oriented and educational in nature. As a helping professional, you may need to expand your repertoire of helping responses.

6. Be careful not to overgeneralize or stereotype. Knowing general group characteristics and guidelines is different from rigidly holding on to preconceived notions. In other words, knowing that certain groups such as African Americans and Asian Americans may share common values and worldviews does not mean that all Asian Americans, for example, are the same. Nor does our discussion imply that Euro-American approaches to therapy are completely inapplicable to minority groups.

7. Try not to buy into the idea that clinical work is somehow superior to other forms of helping. We are aware that many of you are attracted to the conventional psychotherapist role, that your professors may unintentionally give you the impression that it is the epitome of the therapeutic relationship, or that it represents a higher and more sophisticated form of helping. Such an attitude of arrogance not only may be detrimental to those being served, but also limits your ability to work with a culturally diverse population.

Culturally Appropriate
Intervention Strategies

7
Chapter

As an Asian American trainee, I always thought I could use my dual heritage and experience to help Chinese immigrants cope with issues they experienced in the United States. It was with that thought in mind that I entered my first counseling experience with a Chinese immigrant while serving an externship in New York's Chinatown. My client was Betty Lau, a 30-year-old woman, living with her parents, who presented with depression, somatic symptoms, and conflicts related to parental wishes versus her own desires. Betty felt guilty and at fault for her family's tension and unspoken conflicts; both parents disapproved of her new male friend, who occupied her time on the weekends. Her father was unemployed, depressed most of the time, and seemed removed from the family; her mother felt overburdened and ineffective and did little of the housework. Being the oldest sibling, Betty felt obligated to help economically and was increasingly assuming most of the household duties. She harbored strong, unexpressed resentments toward her parents and seemed to feel trapped. Betty believed that if she was a better daughter, more understanding, and worked harder, the family problems would diminish greatly. She often wondered aloud why she could not be more grateful toward her parents, as they sacrificed much to bring the family to a new country. Over the past year, her unhappiness grew so intense that she could not sleep nor eat well. She began to lose weight rapidly and sought help at the clinic.

Betty was a very difficult client to work with. She refused to involve her parents in family counseling and made me promise not to tell them about her use of our services. She was relatively quiet in the sessions, spoke in a barely audible voice, seemed unresponsive to questions, and volunteered little in the way of information. She seldom made eye contact, a sign of her shyness or depression. Her responses were polite, but very brief, and she avoided "feeling" statements. Instead, she talked about her fatigue, loss of appetite, headaches, inability to sleep, and other physical ailments. Talking with Betty was like "pulling teeth," as our sessions were punctuated by long silences. It was clear to me that Betty was too submissive and that part of her depression was putting family interests above her own. I

157

saw two therapeutic goals for her: (1) encourage Betty to think of her own needs first, leave her family, live alone, and not let her parents override her wishes, or (2) if Betty chose to stay at home, she needed to be more forceful in setting limits for her parents.

Betty was obviously dependent and enmeshed in the pathology of the family. She had to rid herself of her guilt feelings, learn to stand up for her own rights, and not be a doormat to the world. At 30 years of age she needed to make a life of her own, get married, and start her own family. My clinical goals at that time were to have Betty be more independent, assert herself appropriately (via assertiveness training), and express her feelings openly and honestly toward her parents. In the sessions, however, Betty had considerable difficulty with role-playing and talking about her feelings. While she indirectly acknowledged harboring feelings of resentment, she could never directly bring herself to verbally express them. Role-plays and behavioral rehearsal techniques failed miserably. When I tried the "Gestalt Empty Chair" technique and encouraged her to speak to her parents in the empty chair, she seemed to "freeze up" and would not cooperate. After her third appointment with me, Betty failed to return for any future sessions.

This case illustrates nicely how a Western European approach to counseling may lead to mistaken assessment, diagnosis, and treatment of culturally diverse clients. Even though the therapist is an Asian American trainee, he or she is still trained in a Western tradition that unintentionally pathologizes cultural values. The therapist seems not to consider how culture influences help-seeking behaviors, the manner of symptom formation, and what constitutes culturally relevant helping among different diverse groups. Let us briefly analyze the case to illustrate these points.

First, it is very clear that the therapist is using Western-European standards to judge normality-abnormality and desirable-undesirable goals. Part of the problem resides in the implicit assumption that individuality is healthier, that people should be their "own person" and that individuation from the family (especially at age 30) is both desirable and healthy. In an individual-centered approach, there is a tendency to locate the problem as residing in the client. Change, therefore, starts with getting the client to take responsibility for his or her own life situation. A collectivistic orientation, however, may lead to a completely different view of Betty's dilemma. This contrast in cultural values and worldviews is most explicitly stated by a Chinese counselor commenting on a very similar case.

I just cannot understand why putting the family's interest before one's own is not correct or "normal" in the dominant American culture. I believe a morally responsible son or daughter has the duty to take care of his or her parents, whether it means sacrifice on his or her own part or not.... What is wrong with this interdependence? To me, it would be extremely selfish for the client to leave her family when the family is in such need of her.... In contemporary China, submergence of self for the good of the family, community, and country is still valued, and individualism condemned. Western mental health practice could fail should we adopt American counseling theories and skills without considerable alteration.... Although I do not think the client has a significant psychological problem, I do believe that the parents have to become more sensitive to their daughter's needs. It is not very nice and considerate for the parents to think only of themselves at the cost of their daughter's well-being. If I were the counselor of this client, I would do everything in my power to try to help change the parents, rather than the client. I feel strongly that it is the selfish person who needs to change, not the selfless person." (Zhang, 1994, pp. 79–80)

Second, culture has been found to influence help-seeking behaviors and how psychological distress is expressed in counseling. It is entirely possible that Betty's reluctance to talk about her feelings toward her parents and focus on somatic complaints are manifestations of cultural dynamics. Restraint of strong feelings as a cultural dictate in Asian cultures is widely acknowledged, and an unenlightened therapist might perceive the client as repressed, inhibited, or avoiding feelings. The therapist might unwittingly not realize that asking Betty to express resentments toward her parents might violate a cultural dictate of filial piety. Further, among traditional groups, going for psychological help may bring shame and disgrace to the family, and there are strong cultural sanctions against disclosure of family problems for fear that it would bring dishonor to everyone. Studies reveal that Asians and Asian Americans tend to underutilize counseling services, especially those associated with psychiatric problems. When Chinese do seek help, they are likely to present with more severe psychological disorders and with a preponderance of somatic complaints. Some suggest that the former finding is related to a Chinese disinclination to seek psychiatric help unless it is a last resort to overwhelming problems. As a result, the disorders that are presented are more severe. These factors may account for Betty's reluctance to involve the parents in counseling, her concern that they not be told, and her use of somatic complaints as an entrée to discussing her problems. For Betty and many Asian clients, physical complaints are viewed as less stigmatic than psychological ones, and are a condition more acceptable to seek help for.

Third, the actual process of counseling and psychotherapy may be antagonistic to the values held by culturally diverse clients. Betty's perceived resistance to counseling (short but polite responses, "unresponsiveness to questions," "avoidance of feeling statements," and lack of eye contact) and the therapist's use of potentially inappropriate counseling techniques (getting client to express feelings, role-plays, and behavioral rehearsal) may prove to be an oppressive and humiliating experience for the client. The therapist seems not to be aware of differences in communication style influenced by culture. For example, Chinese culture values restraint of strong feelings, and eye contact is avoided in the presence of higher-status individuals. The therapist may be prone to interpret avoidance of eye contact and speaking in a softer voice as signs of "depression" or "unassertiveness." Further, we have stated that in many cultures similar to the Chinese, subtlety and indirectness in discussing delicate matters are highly valued attributes of communicaton. Discussion of personal and private matters is done indirectly rather than directly. In this case, Betty may be communicating her psychological and familial conflicts by talking about somatic complaints as a means to an end. Many Asian helpers are aware of this fact and would allow the client to "save face" by appearing to speak about physical/medical problems, but in actuality be discussing family matters. The relationship of communication style to helping styles is intimately bound to one another. The counselor's use of role-plays, behavioral rehearsal, and the confrontive "Gestalt Empty Chair" technique may be placing clients in an awkward position because it asks them to violate basic cultural values.

The case of Betty illustrates the major focus of this chapter: understanding the need for culturally appropriate intervention strategies. Over 30 years ago, the importance of cultural flexibility in counseling and the need to approach counseling with culture-specific techniques was voiced by Draguns (1976):

> Be prepared to adapt your techniques (e.g., general activity level, mode of verbal intervention, content of remarks, tone of voice) to the cultural background of the client; communicate acceptance of and respect for the client in terms that are intelligible and meaningful within his or her cultural frame of reference; and be open to the possibility of more direct intervention in the life of the client than the traditional ethos of the counseling profession would dictate or permit. (p. 4)

It is ironic that this statement continues to hold and that despite the large accumulation of research in support of Draguns' conclusions, the profession of counseling and psychotherapy continues to operate from a universal perspective.

Communication Styles

Effective therapy depends on the therapist and client being able to send and receive both verbal and nonverbal messages accurately and appropriately. It requires that the therapists not only *send* messages (make themselves understood) but also *receive* messages (attend to clients). The definition for effective therapy also includes *verbal* (content of what is said) and *nonverbal* (how something is said) elements. Most therapists seem more concerned with the *accuracy* of communication (getting to the heart of the matter) than with whether the communication is *appropriate*. The case of Betty illustrates how traditional Asian culture prizes a person's subtlety and indirectness in communication. The direct and confrontational techniques in therapy may be perceived by traditional Asian or Native American clients as lacking in respect for the client, a crude and rude form of communication, and a reflection of insensitivity (Duran, 2006). In most cases, therapists have been trained to tune in to the content of what is said rather than how something is said.

When we refer to communication style, we are addressing those factors that go beyond the content of what is said. Some communication specialists believe that only 30 to 40 percent of what is communicated conversationally is verbal (Condon & Yousef, 1975; Ramsey & Birk, 1983; Singelis, 1994). What people say and do is usually qualified by other things that they say and do. A gesture, tone, inflection, posture, or degree of eye contact may enhance or negate the content of a message. Communication styles have a tremendous impact on our face-to-face encounters with others. Whether our conversation proceeds with fits or starts, whether we interrupt one another continually or proceed smoothly, the topics we prefer to discuss or avoid, the depth of our involvement, the forms of interaction (ritual, repartee, argumentative, persuasive, etc.), and the channel we use to communicate (verbal-nonverbal versus nonverbal-verbal) are all aspects of communication style (Douglis, 1987; Wolfgang, 1985). Some refer to these factors as the *social rhythms* that underlie all our speech and actions. Communication styles are strongly correlated with race, culture, and ethnicity. Gender has also been found to be a powerful determinant of communication style (J. C. Pearson, 1985; Robinson & Howard-Hamilton, 2000).

Reared in a Euro-American middle-class society, mental health professionals may assume that certain behaviors or rules of speaking are universal and possess the same meaning. This may create major problems for therapists and other culturally distinct clients. Since differences in communication style are most strongly manifested in nonverbal communication, this chapter concentrates on those aspects of communication that transcend the written or spoken word. First, we explore how race/culture may influence several areas of nonverbal behavior: (a) proxemics, (b) kinesics, (c) paralanguage, and (d) high-low context communication. Second, we briefly discuss the function and importance of nonverbal behavior as it relates to stereotypes and preconceived notions that we may have of diverse groups. Last, we propose a basic thesis that various racial minorities such as Asian Americans, American Indians, African Americans, and Latino/Hispanic Americans possess unique communication styles that may have major implications for mental health practice.

Nonverbal Communication

Although language, class, and cultural factors all interact to create problems in communication between the culturally diverse client and therapist, an oft-neglected area is nonverbal behavior (Duran, 2006; Singelis, 1994). What people say can be either enhanced or negated by their nonverbals. When a man raises his voice, tightens his facial muscles, pounds the table violently, and proclaims, "Goddamn it, I'm not angry!" he is clearly contradicting the content of the communication. If we all share the same cultural and social upbringing, we may all arrive at the same conclusion. Interpreting nonverbals, however, is difficult for several reasons. First, the same nonverbal behavior on the part of an American Indian client may mean something quite different than if it were made by a White person (Duran, 2006). Second, nonverbals often occur outside our levels of awareness but influence our evaluations and behaviors. It is important to note that our discussion of nonverbal codes will not include all the possible areas, like olfaction (taste and smell), tactile cues, and artifactual communication (clothing, hairstyle, display of material things, etc.).

Proxemics

The study of *proxemics* refers to perception and use of personal and interpersonal space. Clear norms exist concerning the use of physical distance in social interactions. E. T. Hall (1969) identified four interpersonal distance zones characteristic of U.S. culture: intimate, from contact to 18 in; personal, from 1.5 ft to 4 ft; social, from 4 ft to 12 ft; and public (lectures and speeches), greater than 12 ft.

In this society, individuals seem to grow more uncomfortable when others stand too close rather than too far away. These feelings and reactions associated with a violation of personal space may range from flight, withdrawal, anger, and conflict (J. C. Pearson, 1985). On the other hand, we tend to allow closer proximity or to move closer to people whom we like or feel interpersonal attraction toward. Some evidence exists that personal space can be reframed in terms of dominance and status. Those with greater status, prestige, and power may occupy more space (larger homes, cars, or offices). However, different cultures dictate different distances in personal space. For Latin Americans, Africans, Black Americans, Indonesians, Arabs, South Americans, and French, conversing with a person dictates a much closer stance than is normally comfortable for Euro-Americans (J. V. Jensen, 1985; Nydell, 1996). A Latin American client's closeness may cause the therapist to back away. The client may interpret the therapist's behavior as indicative of aloofness, coldness, or a desire not to communicate. In some cross-cultural encounters, it may even be perceived as a sign of haughtiness and superiority. On the other hand, the therapist may misinterpret the client's behavior as an attempt to become inappropriately intimate, a sign of pushiness or aggressiveness. Both the therapist and the culturally different client may benefit from understanding that their reactions and behaviors are attempts to create the spatial dimension to which they are culturally conditioned.

Research on proxemics leads to the inevitable conclusion that conversational distances are a function of the racial and cultural background of the conversant (Mindess, 1999; Susman & Rosenfeld, 1982; Wolfgang, 1985). The factor of personal space has major implications for how furniture is arranged, where the seats are located, where you seat the client, and how far you sit from him or her. Latin Americans, for example, may not feel comfortable with a desk between them and the person they are speaking to. Euro-Americans, however, like to keep a desk between themselves and others. Some Eskimos may actually prefer to sit side by side rather than across from one another when talking about intimate aspects of their lives.

Kinesics

While proxemics refers to personal space, *kinesics* is the term used to refer to bodily movements. It includes such things as facial expression, posture, characteristics of movement, gestures, and eye contact. Again, kinesics appears to be culturally conditioned (Mindess, 1999). Much of our counseling assessments are based upon expressions on people's faces (J. C. Pearson, 1985). We assume that facial cues express emotions and demonstrate the degree of responsiveness or involvement of the individual. For example, smiling is a type of expression in our society that is believed to indicate liking or positive affect. People attribute greater positive characteristics to others who smile; they are intelligent, have a good personality, and are pleasant (Singelis, 1994). However, when Japanese smile and laugh, it does not necessarily mean happiness but may convey other meanings (embarrassment, discomfort, shyness, etc.). Such nonverbal misinterpretations also fueled many of the conflicts in Los Angeles directly after the Rodney King verdict, when many African Americans and Korean grocery store owners became at odds with one another. African Americans confronted their Korean American counterparts about exploitation of Black neighborhoods. African Americans became incensed when many Korean American store owners had a constant smile on their faces. They interpreted the facial expression as arrogance, taunting, and lack of compassion for the concerns of Blacks. Little did they realize that a smile in this situation more rightly indicated extreme embarrassment and apprehension.

On the other hand, some Asians believe that smiling may suggest weakness. Among some Japanese and Chinese, restraint of strong feelings (anger, irritation, sadness, and love or happiness) is considered to be a sign of maturity and wisdom. Children learn that outward emotional expressions (facial expressions, body movements, and verbal content) are discouraged except for extreme situations. Unenlightened therapists may assume that their Asian American client is lacking in feelings or is out of touch with them. More likely, the lack of facial expressions may be the basis of stereotypes, such as the statement that Asians are "inscrutable," "sneaky," "deceptive," and "backstabbing."

A number of gestures and bodily movements have been found to have different meanings when the cultural context is considered (LaBarre, 1985). In the Sung Dynasty in China, sticking out the tongue was a gesture of mock terror and meant as ridicule; to the Ovimbundu of Africa, it means "you're a fool" (when coupled with bending the head forward); a protruding tongue in the Mayan statues of the gods signifies wisdom; and in our own culture, it is generally considered to be a juvenile, quasi-obscene gesture of defiance, mockery, or contempt.

Head movements also have different meanings (Eakins & Eakins, 1985; Jensen, 1985). An educated Englishman may consider the lifting of the chin when conversing as a poised and polite gesture, but to Euro-Americans it may connote snobbery and arrogance ("turning up one's nose"). While we shake our head from side to side to indicate "no," Mayan tribe members say "no" by jerking the head to the right. In Sri Lanka, one signals agreement by moving the head from side to side like a metronome (Singelis, 1994).

Most Euro-Americans perceive squatting (often done by children) as improper and childish. In other parts of the world, people have learned to rest by taking a squatting position. On the other hand, when we put our feet up on a desk, it is believed to signify a relaxed and informal attitude. Yet, Latin Americans and Asians may perceive it as rudeness and arrogance, especially if the bottoms of the feet are shown to them.

Shaking hands is another gesture that varies from culture to culture and may have strong cultural/historical significance. Latin Americans tend to shake hands more vigorously, frequently, and for a longer period of time. Interestingly, most cultures use the right hand when shaking. Since most of the population of the world is right-handed, this may not be surprising. However, some researchers believe that shaking with the right hand may be a symbolic act of peace, as in older times it was the right hand that generally held the weapons. In some Moslem and Asian countries, touching anyone with the left hand may be considered an obscenity (the left hand aids in the process of elimination and is "unclean," while the right one is used for the intake of food and is "clean"). Offering something with the left hand to a Moslem may be an insult of the most serious type.

Eye contact is, perhaps, the nonverbal behavior most likely to be addressed by mental health providers. It is not unusual for us to hear someone say, "Notice that the husband avoided eye contact with the wife," or "Notice how the client averted his eyes when. . . ." Behind these observations is the belief that eye contact or lack of eye contact has diagnostic significance. We would agree with that premise, but in most cases, therapists attribute negative traits to the avoidance of eye contact: shy, unassertive, sneaky, or depressed.

This lack of understanding has been played out in many different situations when Black-White interactions have occurred. In many cases it is not necessary for Blacks to look at one another in the eye at all times to communicate (E. J. Smith, 1981). An African American may be actively involved in doing other things when engaged in a conversation. Many White therapists are prone to view the African American client as being sullen, resistant, or uncooperative. E. J. Smith (1981, p. 155) provides an excellent example of such a clash in communication styles:

> *For instance, one Black female student was sent to the office by her gymnasium teacher because the student was said to display insolent behavior. When the student was asked to give her version of the incident, she replied, "Mrs. X asked all of us to come over to the side of the pool so that she could show us how to do the backstroke. I went over with the rest of the girls. Then Mrs. X started yelling at me and said I wasn't paying attention to her because I wasn't looking directly at her. I told her I was paying attention to her (throughout the conversation, the student kept her head down, avoiding the principal's eyes), and then she said that she wanted me to face her and look her squarely in the eye like the rest of the girls [who were all White]. So I did. The next thing I knew she was telling me to get out of the pool, that she didn't like the way I was looking at her. So that's why I'm here."*

As this example illustrates, Black styles of communication may not only be different from their White counterparts, but also may lead to misinterpretations. Many Blacks do not nod their heads or say "uh-huh" to indicate they are listening (E. T. Hall, 1976; Kochman, 1981; E. J. Smith, 1981). Going through the motions of looking at the person and nodding the head is not necessary for many Blacks to indicate that they are listening (E. T. Hall, 1974, 1976).

Statistics indicate that when White U.S. Americans listen to a speaker, they make eye contact with the speaker about 80 percent of the time. When speaking to others, however, they tend to look away (avoid eye contact) about 50 percent of the time. This is in marked contrast to many Black Americans, who make greater eye contact when speaking and make infrequent eye contact when listening!

Paralanguage

The term *paralanguage* is used to refer to other vocal cues that individuals use to communicate. For example, loudness of voice, pauses, silences, hesitations, rate, inflections, and the like all fall into this category. Paralanguage is very likely to be manifested forcefully in conversation conventions such as how we greet and address others and take turns in speaking. It can communicate a variety of different features about a person, such as age, gender, and emotional responses, as well as the race and sex of the speaker (Banks & Banks, 1993; Lass, Mertz, & Kimmel, 1978; Nydell, 1996).

There are complex rules regarding when to speak or yield to another person. For example, U.S. Americans frequently feel uncomfortable with a pause or silent stretch in the conversation, feeling obligated to fill it in with more talk. Silence is not always a sign for the listener to take up the conversation. While it may be viewed negatively by many, other cultures interpret the use of silence differently. The British and Arabs use silence for privacy, while the Russians, French, and Spanish read it as agreement among the parties (Hall, 1969, 1976). In Asian culture, silence is traditionally a sign of respect for elders. Furthermore, silence by many Chinese and Japanese is not a floor-yielding signal inviting others to pick up the conversation. Rather, it may indicate a desire to continue speaking after making a particular point. Often silence is a sign of politeness and respect rather than a lack of desire to continue speaking.

The amount of verbal expressiveness in the United States, relative to other cultures, is quite high. Most Euro-Americans encourage their children to enter freely into conversations, and teachers encourage students to ask many questions and state their thoughts and opinions. This has led many from other countries to observe that Euro-American youngsters are brash, immodest, rude, and disrespectful (Irvine & York, 1995; Jensen, 1985). Likewise, teachers of minority children may see reticence in speaking out as a sign of ignorance, lack of motivation, or ineffective teaching (Banks & Banks, 1993), when in reality the students may be showing proper respect (to ask questions is disrespectful because it implies that the teacher was unclear). American Indians, for example, have been taught that to speak out, ask questions, or even raise one's hand in class is immodest.

A mental health professional who is uncomfortable with silence or who misinterprets it may fill in the conversation and prevent the client from elaborating further. An even greater danger is to impute incorrect motives to the minority client's silence. One can readily see how therapy, which emphasizes talking, may place many minorities at a disadvantage.

Volume and intensity of speech in conversation are also influenced by cultural values. The overall loudness of speech displayed by many Euro-American visitors to foreign countries has earned them the reputation of being boisterous and shameless. In Asian countries, people tend to speak more softly and would interpret the loud volume of a U.S. visitor to be aggressiveness, loss of self-control, or anger. When compared to Arabs, however, people in the United States are soft-spoken. Many Arabs like to be bathed in sound, and the volumes of their radios, phonographs, and televisions are quite loud. In some countries where such entertainment units are not plentiful, it is considered a polite and thoughtful act to allow neighbors to hear by keeping the volume high. We in the United States would view such behavior as being a thoughtless invasion of privacy.

A therapist or counselor working with clients would be well advised to be aware of possible cultural misinterpretations as a function of speech volume. Speaking loudly may not indicate anger and hostility, and speaking in a soft voice may not be a sign of weakness, shyness, or depression.

The directness of a conversation or the degree of frankness also varies considerably among various cultural groups. Observing the English in their parliamentary debates will drive this point home. The long heritage of open, direct, and frank confrontation leads to heckling of public speakers and quite blunt and sharp exchanges. Britons believe and feel that these are acceptable styles and may take no offense at being the object of such exchanges. However, U.S. citizens feel that such exchanges are impolite, abrasive, and irrational. Relative to Asians, Euro-Americans are seen as being too blunt and frank. Great care is taken by many Asians not to hurt the feelings of or embarrass the other person. As a result, use of euphemisms and ambiguity is the norm.

Since many minority groups may value indirectness, the U.S. emphasis on "getting to the point" and "not beating around the bush" may alienate others. Asian Americans, American Indians, and some Latino/Hispanic Americans may see this behavior as immature, rude, and lacking in finesse. On the other hand, clients from different cultures may be negatively labeled as evasive and afraid to confront the problem.

High-Low Context Communication

Edward T. Hall, author of such classics as *The Silent Language* (1959) and *The Hidden Dimension* (1969), is a well-known anthropologist who has proposed the concept of high-low context cultures (Hall, 1976). A high-context (HC) communication or message is one that is anchored in the physical context (situation) or internalized in the person. Less reliance is placed on the explicit code or message content. An HC communication relies heavily on nonverbals and the group identification/understanding shared by those communicating. For example, a normal-stressed "no" by a U.S. American may be interpreted by an Arab as "yes." A real negation in Arab culture would be stressed much more emphatically. A prime example of the contextual dimension in understanding communication is demonstrated in the following example:

> *I was asked to consult with a hospital that was having a great deal of difficulty with their Filipino nurses. The hospital had a number of them on its staff, and the medical director was concerned about their competence in understanding and following directions from doctors. As luck would have it, when I came to the*

hospital, I was immediately confronted with a situation that threatened to blow up. Dr. K., a Euro-American physician, had brought charges against a Filipino American nurse for incompetence. He had observed her incorrectly using and monitoring life support systems on a critically ill patient. He relates how he entered the patient's room and told the nurse that she was incorrectly using the equipment and that the patient could die if she didn't do it right. Dr. K. states that he spent some 10 minutes explaining how the equipment should be attached and used. Upon finishing his explanation, he asked the nurse if she understood. The Filipino nurse nodded her head slightly and hesitantly said, "Yes, yes, Doctor." Later that evening, Dr. K. observed the same nurse continuing to use the equipment incorrectly; he reported her to the head nurse and asked for her immediate dismissal. While it is possible that the nurse was not competent, further investigation revealed strong cultural forces affecting the hospital work situation. What the medical administration failed to understand was the cultural context of the situation. In the Philippines, it is considered impolite to say "no" in a number of situations. In this case, for the nurse to say "no" to the doctor (a respected figure of high status) when asked whether she understood would have implied that Dr. K. was a poor teacher. This would be considered insulting and impolite. Thus, the only option the Filipino nurse felt open to her was to tell the doctor "yes."

In Filipino culture, a mild, hesitant "yes" is interpreted by those who understand as a "no" or a polite refusal. In traditional Asian society, many interactions are understandable only in light of high-context cues and situations. For example, to extend an invitation only once for dinner would be considered an affront because it implies that you are not sincere. One must extend an invitation several times, encouraging the invitee to accept. Arabs may also refuse an offer of food several times before giving in. However, most Euro-Americans believe that a host's offer can be politely refused with just a "no, thank you."

If we pay attention to only the explicit coded part of the message, we are likely to misunderstand the communication. According to E. T. Hall (1976), low-context (LC) cultures place a greater reliance on the verbal part of the message. In addition, LC cultures have been associated with being more opportunistic, more individual rather than group oriented, and as emphasizing rules of law and procedure (E. J. Smith, 1981).

It appears that the United States is an LC culture (although it is still higher than the Swiss, Germans, and Scandinavians in the amount of contexting required). China, perhaps, represents the other end of the continuum; its complex culture relies heavily on context. Asian Americans, African Americans, Hispanics, American Indians, and other minority groups in the United States also emphasize HC cues.

In contrast to LC communication, HC is faster, as well as more economical, efficient, and satisfying. Because it is so bound to the culture, it is slow to change and tends to be cohesive and unifying. LC communication does not unify but changes rapidly and easily.

Twins who have grown up together can and do communicate more economically (HC) than do two lawyers during a trial (LC). B. Bernstein's (1964) work in language analysis refers to restricted codes (HC) and elaborated codes (LC). Restricted codes are observed in families where words and sentences collapse and are shortened without loss of meaning. However, elaborated codes, where many words are used to communicate the same content, are seen in classrooms, diplomacy, and law.

African American culture has been described as HC. For example, it is clear that many Blacks require fewer words than their White counterparts to communicate the same content (Irvine & York, 1995; Jenkins, 1982; Stanback & Pearce, 1985; Weber, 1985). An African American male who enters a room and spots an attractive woman may stoop slightly in her direction, smile, and tap the table twice while vocalizing a long drawn out "uh huh." What he has communicated would require many words from his White brother! The fact that African Americans may communicate more by HC cues has led many to characterize them as nonverbal, inarticulate, unintelligent, and so forth.

Sociopolitical Facets of Nonverbal Communication

There is a common saying among African Americans: "If you really want to know what White folks are thinking and feeling, don't listen to what they say, but how they say it." In most cases, such a statement refers to the biases, stereotypes, and racist attitudes that Whites are believed to possess but that they consciously or unconsciously conceal.

Rightly or wrongly, many minority individuals through years of personal experience operate from three assumptions. The first assumption is that all Whites in this society are racist. Through their own cultural conditioning, they have been socialized into a culture that espouses the superiority of White culture over all others (J. M. Jones, 1997; Parham, 1993; Ridley, 2005). The second assumption is that most Whites find such a concept disturbing and will go to great lengths to deny that they are racist or biased. Some of this is done deliberately and with awareness, but in most cases one's racism is largely unconscious. The last of these assumptions is that nonverbal behaviors are more accurate reflections of what a White person is thinking or feeling than is what they say.

There is considerable evidence to suggest that these three assumptions held by various racial/ethnic minorities are indeed accurate (McIntosh, 1989; Ridley, 2006; D. W. Sue et al., 1998). Counselors and mental health practitioners need to be very cognizant of nonverbal cues from a number of different perspectives.

In the last section we discussed how nonverbal behavior is culture bound and how the counselor or therapist cannot make universal interpretations about it. Likewise, nonverbal cues are important because they often (1) unconsciously reflect our biases and (2) trigger off stereotypes we have of other people.

Nonverbals as Reflections of Bias

Some time ago, a TV program called *Candid Camera* was the rage in the United States. It operated from a unique premise, which involved creating very unusual situations for naive subjects who were then filmed as they reacted to them. One of these experiments involved interviewing housewives about their attitudes toward African American, Latino/Hispanic, and White teenagers. The intent was to select a group of women who by all standards appeared sincere in their beliefs that Blacks and Latinos were no more prone to violence than were their White counterparts. Unknown to them, they were filmed by a hidden camera as they left their homes to go shopping at the local supermarket.

The creator of the program had secretly arranged for an African American, Latino, and White youngster (dressed casually but nearly identically) to pass these women on the street. The experiment was counterbalanced; that is, the race of the youngster was randomly assigned as to which would approach the shopper first. What occurred was a powerful statement on unconscious racist attitudes and beliefs.

All the youngsters had been instructed to pass the shopper on the purse side of the street. If the woman was holding the purse in her right hand, the youngster would approach and pass on her right. If the purse was held with the left hand, the youngster would pass on her left. Studies of the film revealed consistent outcomes. Many women, when approached by the Black or Latino youngster (approximately 15 feet away), would casually switch the purse from one arm to the other! This occurred infrequently with the White subject. Why?

The answer appears quite obvious to us. The women subjects who switched their purses were operating from biases, stereotypes, and preconceived notions about what minority youngsters are like: They are prone to crime, more likely to snatch a purse or rob, more likely to be juvenile delinquents, and more likely to engage in violence. The disturbing part of this experiment was that the selected subjects were, by all measures, sincere individuals who on a conscious level denied harboring racist attitudes or beliefs. They were not liars, nor were they deliberately deceiving the interviewer.

They were normal, everyday people. They honestly believed that they did not possess these biases, yet when tested, their nonverbal behavior (purse switching) gave them away.

The power of nonverbal communication is that it tends to be least under conscious control. Studies support the conclusion that nonverbal cues operate primarily on an unawareness level (DePaulo, 1992; Singelis, 1994), that they tend to be more spontaneous and more difficult to censor or falsify (Mehrabian, 1972), and that they are more trusted than words. In our society, we have learned to use words (spoken or written) to mask or conceal our true thoughts and feelings. Note how our politicians and lawyers are able to address an issue without revealing much of what they think or believe. This is very evident in controversial issues such as gun control, abortion, and issues of affirmative action and immigration.

Nonverbal behavior provides clues to conscious deceptions or unconscious bias (Utsey et al., 2005). There is evidence that the accuracy of nonverbal communication varies with the part of the body used: Facial expression is more controllable than the hands, followed by the legs and the rest of the body (Hansen, Stevic, & Warner, 1982). The implications for multicultural counseling are obvious. A therapist who has not adequately dealt with his or her own biases and racist attitudes may unwittingly communicate them to a culturally different client. If counselors are unaware of their own biases, their nonverbals are most likely to reveal their true feelings. Studies suggest that women and minorities are better readers of nonverbal cues than are White males (Hall, 1976; Jenkins, 1982; J. C. Pearson, 1985; Weber, 1985). Much of this may be due to their HC orientation, but another reason may be *survival*. For an African American person to survive in a predominantly White society, he or she has to rely on nonverbal cues more often than verbal ones.

One of our male African American colleagues gives the example of how he must constantly be vigilant when traveling in an unknown part of the country. Just to stop at a roadside restaurant may be dangerous to his physical well-being. As a result, when entering a diner, he is quick to observe not only the reactions of the staff (waiter/waitress, cashier, cook, etc.) to his entrance, but the reactions of the patrons as well. Do they stare at him? What type of facial expressions do they have? Do they fall silent? Does he get served immediately, or is there an inordinate delay? These nonverbal cues reveal much about the environment around him. He may choose to be himself or play the role of a "humble" Black person who leaves quickly if the situation poses danger.

Interestingly, this very same colleague talks about tuning in to nonverbal cues as a means of *psychological survival*. He believes it is important for minorities to accurately read where people are coming from in order to prevent invalidation of the self. For example, a minority person driving through an unfamiliar part of the country may find himself or herself forced to stay at a motel overnight. Seeing a vacancy light flashing, the person may stop and knock on the manager's door. Upon opening the door and seeing the Black person, the White manager may show hesitation, stumble around in his or her verbalizations, and then apologize for having forgotten to turn off the vacancy light. The Black person is faced with the dilemma of deciding whether the White manager was telling the truth or is simply not willing to rent to a Black person.

Some of you might ask, "Why is it important for you to know? Why don't you simply find someplace else? After all, would you stay at a place where you were unwelcome?" Finding another place to stay might not be as important as the psychological well-being of the minority person. Racial/ethnic minorities have encountered too many situations in which double messages are given to them. For the African American to accept the simple statement, "I forgot to turn off the vacancy light," may be to deny one's own true feelings at being the victim of discrimination. This is especially true when the nonverbals (facial expression, anxiety in voice, and stammering) may reveal other reasons.

Too often, culturally different individuals are placed in situations where they are asked to deny their true feelings in order to perpetuate *White deception*. Statements that minorities are oversensitive (paranoid?) may represent a form of denial. When a minority colleague makes a statement such as "I get a strange feeling from John; I feel some bias against minorities coming out," White colleagues, friends, and others are sometimes too quick to dismiss it with statements like, "You're being oversensitive." Perhaps a better approach would be to say, "What makes you feel that way?" rather than to negate or invalidate what might be an accurate appraisal of nonverbal communication.

Thus, it is clear that racial/ethnic minorities are very tuned in to nonverbals. For the therapist who has not adequately dealt with his or her own racism, the minority client will be quick to assess such biases. In many cases, the minority client may believe that the biases are too great to be overcome and will simply not continue in therapy. This is despite the good intentions of the White counselor/therapist who is not in touch with his or her own biases and assumptions about human behavior.

Nonverbals as Triggers to Biases and Fears

Often people assume that being an effective multicultural therapist is a straightforward process that involves the acquisition of knowledge about the various racial/ethnic groups. If we know that Asian Americans and African Americans have different patterns of eye contact and if we know that these patterns signify different things, then we should be able to eliminate biases and stereotypes that we possess. Were it so easy, we might have eradicated racism years ago. While increasing our knowledge base about the lifestyles and experiences of minority groups is important, it is not a sufficient condition in itself. Our racist attitudes, beliefs, and feelings are deeply ingrained in our total being. Through years of conditioning they have acquired a strong irrational base, replete with emotional symbolism about each particular minority. Simply opening a text and reading about African Americans and Latinos/Hispanics will not deal with our deep-seated fears and biases.

One of the major barriers to effective understanding is the common assumption that different cultural groups operate according to identical speech and communication conventions. In the United States, it is often assumed that distinctive racial, cultural, and linguistic features are deviant, inferior, or embarrassing (Kochman, 1981; Singelis, 1994; Stanback & Pearce, 1985). These value judgments then become tinged with beliefs that we hold about Black people (E. J. Smith, 1981): racial inferiority, being prone to violence and crime, quick to anger, and a threat to White folks (Irvine & York, 1995; Weber, 1985). The communication style of Black folks (manifested in nonverbals) can often trigger off these fears. We submit that the situation presented at the beginning of the chapter represents just such an example.

Black styles of communication are often high-key, animated, heated, interpersonal, and confrontational. Many emotions, affects, and feelings are generated (E. T. Hall, 1976; Shade & New, 1993; Weber, 1985). In a debate, Blacks tend to act as advocates of a position, and ideas are to be tested in the crucible of argument (Banks & Banks, 1993; Kochman, 1981). White middle-class styles, however, are characterized as being detached and objective, impersonal and nonchallenging. The person acts not as an *advocate* of the idea, but as a *spokesperson* (truth resides in the idea). A discussion of issues should be devoid of affect because emotion and reason work against one another. One should talk things out in a logical fashion without getting personally involved. African Americans characterize their own style of communication as indicating that the person is sincere and honest, while Euro-Americans consider their own style to be reasoned and objective (Irvine & York, 1995).

Many African Americans readily admit that they operate from a point of view and, as mentioned previously, are disinclined to believe that White folks do not. E. J. Smith (1981, p. 154) aptly describes the Black orientation in the following passage:

When one Black person talks privately with another, he or she might say: "Look, we don't have to jive each other or be like White folks; let's be honest with one another." These statements reflect the familiar Black saying that "talk is cheap," that actions speak louder than words, and that Whites beguile each other with words.... In contrast, the White mind symbolizes to many Black people deceit, verbal chicanery, and sterile intellectivity. For example, after long discourse with a White person, a Black individual might say: "I've heard what you've said, but what do you really mean?"

Such was the case with the African American professor who believed that his White colleagues were fronting and being insincere.

While Black Americans may misinterpret White communication styles, it is more likely that Whites will misinterpret Black styles. The direction of the misunderstanding is generally linked to the activating of unconscious triggers or buttons about racist stereotypes and fears they harbor. As we have repeatedly emphasized, one of the dominant stereotypes of African Americans in our society is that of the hostile, angry, prone-to-violence Black male. The more animated and affective communication style, closer conversing distance, prolonged eye contact when speaking, greater bodily movements, and tendency to test ideas in a confrontational/argumentative format lead many Whites to believe that their lives are in danger. It is not unusual for White mental health practitioners to describe their African Americans clients as being hostile and angry. We have also observed that some White trainees who work with Black clients respond nonverbally in such a manner as to indicate anxiety, discomfort, or fear (leaning away from their African American clients, tipping their chairs back, crossing their legs or arms, etc.). These are nonverbal distancing moves that may reflect the unconscious stereotypes that they hold of Black Americans. While we would entertain the possibility that a Black client is angry, most occasions we have observed do not justify such a descriptor.

It appears that many Euro-Americans operate from the assumption that when an argument ensues, it may lead to a ventilation of anger with the outbreak of a subsequent fight. What many Whites fail to realize is that African Americans distinguish between an argument used to debate a difference of opinion and one that ventilates anger and hostility (DePaulo, 1992; Irvine & York, 1995; Kochman, 1981; Shade & New, 1993). In the former, the affect indicates sincerity and seriousness; there is a positive attitude toward the material; and the validity of ideas is challenged. In the latter, the affect is more passionate than sincere; there is a negative attitude toward the opponent; and the opponent is abused.

To understand African American styles of communication and to relate adequately to Black communication would require much study in the origins, functions, and manifestations of Black language (Jenkins, 1982). Weber (1985) believes that the historical and philosophical foundations of Black language have led to several verbal styles among Blacks. *Rapping* (not the White usage, rap session) was originally a dialogue between a man and a woman in which the intent was to win over the admiration of the woman. Imaginary statements, rhythmic speech, and creativity are aimed at getting the woman interested in hearing more of the rap. It has been likened to a mating call, an introduction of the male to the female, and a ritual expected by some African American women.

Another style of verbal banter is called *woofing,* which is an exchange of threats and challenges to fight. It may have derived from what African Americans refer to as *playing the dozens,* which is considered by many Blacks to be the highest form of verbal warfare and impromptu speaking (Kochman, 1981; Jenkins, 1983; Weber, 1985). To the outsider, it may appear cruel, harsh, and provocative. Yet to many in the Black community, it has historical and functional meanings. The term *dozens* was used by slave owners to refer to Black persons with disabilities. Because they were considered damaged goods, disabled Black people would often be sold at a discount rate with eleven (one dozen) other damaged slaves (Weber, 1985). It was primarily a selling ploy in which "dozens" referred to the negative physical features. Often played in jest, the game requires an audience to act as judge and jury over the originality, creativity, and humor of the combatants:

> *Say man, your girlfriend so ugly, she had to sneak up on a glass to get a drink of water. . . . Man, you so ugly, yo mamma had to put a sheet over your head so sleep could sneak up on you. (Weber, 1985, p. 248)*

> *A: Eat shit.*
> *B: What should I do with your bones?*
> *A: Build a cage for your mother.*
> *B: At least I got one.*
> *A: She is the least. (Labov, 1972, p. 321)*

> *A: Got a match?*
> *B: Yeah, my ass and your face or my farts and your breath. (Kochman, 1981, p. 54)*

Woofing and playing the dozens seem to have very real functional value. First, they allow training in self-control about managing one's anger and hostility in the constant face of racism. In many situations, it would be considered dangerous by an African American to respond to taunts, threats, and insults. Second, woofing also allows a Black person to establish a hierarchy or pecking order without resorting to violence. Last, it can create an image of being fearless where one will gain respect.

This verbal and nonverbal style of communication can be a major aspect of Black interactions. Likewise, other minority groups have characteristic styles that may cause considerable difficulties for White counselors. One way of contrasting communication style differences may be in the overt activity

Table 7.1   **Communication Style Differences (Overt Activity Dimension—Nonverbal/Verbal)**

American Indians	Asian Americans and Hispanics	Whites	Blacks
1. Speak softly/slower	1. Speak softly	1. Speak loud/fast to control listener	1. Speak with affect
2. Indirect gaze when listening or speaking	2. Avoidance of eye contact when listening or speaking to high-status persons	2. Greater eye contact when listening	2. Direct eye contact (prolonged) when speaking, but less when listening
3. Interject less; seldom offer encouraging communication	3. Similar rules	3. Head nods, nonverbal markers	3. Interrupt (turn taking) when can
4. Delayed auditory (silence)	4. Mild delay	4. Quick responding	4. Quicker responding
5. Manner of expression low-keyed, indirect	5. Low-keyed, indirect	5. Objective, task oriented	5. Affective, emotional, interpersonal

dimension (the pacing/intensity) of nonverbal communication. Table 7.1 contrasts five different groups along this continuum. How these styles affect the therapist's perception and ability to work with culturally different clients is important for each and every one of us to consider.

Counseling and Therapy as Communication Style

Throughout this text we have repeatedly emphasized that *different* theories of counseling and psychotherapy represent *different* communication styles. There is considerable early research support for this statement. The film series *Three Approaches to Psychotherapy* (Shostrom, 1966), which features Carl Rogers, Fritz Perls, and Albert Ellis, and the *Three Approaches to Psychotherapy: II* (Shostrom, 1977), which features Carl Rogers, Everett Shostrom, and Arnold Lazarus, have been the subject of much analysis. Some general conclusions may be tentatively drawn from all of these studies (Dolliver, Williams, & Gold, 1980; Weinrach, 1987). Each theoretical orientation (Rogers, person-centered therapy; Perls, existential therapy; Ellis, rational-emotive therapy; Shostrom, actualizing therapy; and Lazarus, multimodal therapy) can be distinguished from one another, and the therapy styles/skills exhibited seem to be highly correlated with their theoretical orientations. For example, Rogers's style emphasizes attending skills (encouragement to talk: minimal encouragers, nonverbal markers, paraphrasing, and reflecting feelings); Shostrom relies on direct guidance, providing information, and so forth, while Lazarus takes an active, reeducative style.

Differential Skills in Multicultural Counseling/Therapy

Just as race, culture, ethnicity, and gender may affect communication styles, there is considerable evidence that theoretical orientations in counseling will influence helping styles as well. There is strong support for the belief that different cultural groups may be more receptive to certain counseling/communication styles because of cultural and sociopolitical factors (Herring, 1997; Lin, 2001; Wehrly, 1995). Indeed, the literature on multicultural counseling/therapy strongly suggests that American Indians, Asian Americans, Black Americans, and Hispanic Americans tend to prefer more active-directive forms of helping than nondirective ones (Cheatham et al., 1997; Ivey & Ivey, 2003; D. W. Sue et al., 1998). We briefly describe two of these group differences here to give the reader some idea of their implications.

Asian American clients who may value restraint of strong feelings and believe that intimate revelations are to be shared only with close friends may cause problems for the counselor who is oriented toward insight or feelings (à la the case of Betty). It is entirely possible that such techniques as reflection of feelings, asking questions of a deeply personal nature, and making depth interpretations may be perceived as lacking in respect for the client's integrity. Asian American clients may not value the process of insight into underlying processes. For example, some clients who come for vocational information may be perceived by counselors as needing help in finding out what motivates their actions and decisions. Requests for advice or information from the client are seen as indicative of deeper, more personal conflicts. Although this might be true in some cases, the blind application of techniques that clash with cultural values seriously places many Asian Americans in an uncomfortable and oppressed position. Many years ago, Atkinson, Maruyama, and Matsui (1978) tested this hypothesis with a number of Asian American students. Two tape recordings of a contrived counseling session were prepared in which the client's responses were identical but the counselor's responses differed, being directive in one and nondirective in the other. Their findings indicated that counselors who use the directive approach were rated more credible and approachable than were those using the nondirective counseling approach. Asian Americans seem to prefer a logical, rational, structured counseling approach to an affective, reflective, and ambiguous one. Other researchers have drawn similar conclusions (Atkinson & Lowe, 1995; Leong, 1986; Lin, 2001).

In a classic and groundbreaking study, Berman (1979) found similar results with a Black population. The weakness of the previous study was its failure to compare equal responses with a White population. Berman's study compared the use of counseling skills between Black and White male and female counselors. A videotape of culturally varied client vignettes was viewed by Black and White counselor trainees. They responded to the question, "What would you say to this person?" The data were scored and coded according to a microcounseling taxonomy that divided counseling skills into attending and influencing ones. The hypothesis made by the investigator was that Black and White counselors would give significantly different patterns of responses to their clients. Data supported the hypothesis. Black males and females tended to use the more active expressive skills (directions, expression of content, and interpretation) with greater frequency than did their White counterparts. White males and females tended to use a higher percentage of attending skills. Berman concluded that the person's race/culture appears to be a major factor in the counselor's choice of skills, that Black and White counselors appear to adhere to two distinctive styles of counseling. Berman also concluded that the more active styles of the Black counselor tend to include practical advice and allow for the introjection of a counselor's values and opinions.

The implications for therapy become glaringly apparent. Mental health training programs tend to emphasize the more passive attending skills. Therapists so trained may be ill equipped to work with culturally different clients who might find the active approach more relevant to their own needs and values.

Implications for Multicultural Counseling/Therapy

Ivey's continuing contributions (Ivey, 1981, 1986; Ivey & Ivey, 2003) in the field of microcounseling, multicultural counseling, and developmental counseling seem central to our understanding of counseling/communication styles. He believes that different theories are concerned with generating different sentences and constructs and that different cultures may also be expected to generate different sentences and constructs. Counseling and psychotherapy may be viewed as special types of temporary cultures. When the counseling style of the counselor does not match the communication style of his or her culturally diverse clients, many difficulties may arise: premature termination of the session, inability to establish rapport, or cultural oppression of the client. Thus, it becomes clear that effective multicultural counseling occurs when the counselor and client are able to send and receive both verbal and nonverbal messages appropriately and accurately. When the counselor is able to engage in such activities, his or her credibility and attractiveness will be increased. Communication styles manifested in the clinical context may either enhance or negate the effectiveness of MCT. Several major implications for counseling can be discerned.

Therapeutic Practice

As practicing clinicians who work with a culturally diverse population, we need to move decisively in educating ourselves about the differential meanings of nonverbal behavior and the broader implications for communication styles. We need to realize that proxemics, kinesics, paralanguage, and high-low context factors are important elements of communication, that they may be highly culture-bound, and that we should guard against possible misinterpretation in our assessment of clients. Likewise, it is important that we begin to become aware of and understand our own communication/helping style: What is my clinical/communication style? What does it say about my values, biases, and assumptions about human behavior? How do my nonverbals reflect stereotypes, fears, or preconceived notions about various racial groups? What nonverbal messages might I be communicating unknowingly to my client? In what way does my helping style hinder my ability to work effectively with a culturally different client? What culturally/racially influenced communication styles cause me the greatest difficulty or discomfort? Why?

We believe that therapists must be able to shift their therapeutic styles to meet the developmental needs of clients. We contend further that effective mental health professionals are those who can also shift their helping styles to meet the cultural dimensions of their clients. Therapists of differing theoretical orientations will tend to use different skill patterns. These skill patterns may be antagonistic or inappropriate to the communication/helping styles of clients. In research cited earlier, it was clear that White counselors (by virtue of their cultural conditioning and training) tended to use the more passive attending and listening skills in counseling/therapy, while racial/ethnic minority populations appear more oriented toward an active influencing approach. There are several reasons why this may be the case.

First, we contend that the use of more directive, active, and influencing skills is more likely to provide personal information about where the therapist is coming from (self-disclosure). Giving advice or suggestions, interpreting, and telling the client how you, the counselor or therapist, feel are really acts of counselor self-disclosure. While the use of attending or more nondirective skills may also self-disclose, it tends to be minimal relative to using influencing skills. In multicultural counseling, the culturally diverse client is likely to approach the counselor with trepidation: "What makes you any different from all the Whites out there who have oppressed me?" "What makes you immune from inheriting the racial biases of your forebears?" "Before I open up to you [self-disclose], I want to know where you are coming from." "How open and honest are you about your own racism, and will it interfere with our relationship?" "Can you really understand what it's like to be Asian, Black, Hispanic, American Indian, or the like?" In other words, a culturally

diverse client may not open up (self-disclose) until you, the helping professional, self-disclose first. Thus, to many minority clients, a therapist who expresses his or her thoughts and feelings may be better received in a counseling situation.

Second, the more positive response by people of color to the use of influencing skills appears to be related to diagnostic focus. Studies support the
thesis that White therapists are more likely to focus their problem diagnosis
in individual, rather than societal terms (Berman, 1979; Draguns, 2002;
Nwachuku & Ivey, 1991; D. W. Sue et al., 1998). In a society where individualism prevails, it is not surprising to find that Euro-American counselors
tend to view their client's problems are residing within the individual rather
than society. Thus, the role of the therapist will be person-focused because
the problem resides within the individual. Skills utilized will be individual-
centered (attending), aimed at changing the person. Many minorities accept
the importance of individual contributions to the problem, but they also give
great weight to systemic or societal factors that may adversely impact their
lives. Minorities who have been the victims of discrimination and oppression
perceive that the problem resides externally to the person (societal forces).
Active systems intervention is called for, and the most appropriate way to attack the environment (stressors) would be an active approach (Lewis et al.,
1998). If the counselor shares their perception, he or she may take a more active role in the sessions, giving advice and suggestions, as well as teaching
strategies (becoming a partner to the client).

Finally, while it would be ideal if we could effectively engage in the full
range of therapeutic responses, such a wish may prove unrealistic. We cannot be all things to everyone. That is, there are personal limits to how much
we can change our communication styles to match those of our clients. The
difficulty in shifting styles may be a function of inadequate practice, inability
to understand the other person's worldview, or personal biases or racist attitudes that have not been adequately resolved. In these cases, the counselor
might consider several alternatives: (1) seek additional training/education,
(2) seek consultation with a more experienced counselor, (3) refer the client
to another therapist, and (4) become aware of personal communication style
limitations and try to anticipate their possible impact on the culturally diverse
client. Often, a therapist who recognizes the limitations of his or her helping
style and knows how it will impact a culturally diverse client can take steps
to minimize possible conflicts.

Interestingly, one study (Yao, Sue, & Hayden, 1991) found that once
rapport and a working relationship are established with a minority client, the
counselor may have greater freedom in using a helping style quite different
from that of the client. The crucial element appears to be the counselor's ability to acknowledge limitations in his or her helping style and to anticipate the
negative impact it may have on the culturally diverse client. In this way, the

helping professional may be saying to the client, "I understand your worldview, and I know that what I do or say will appear very Western to you, but I'm limited in my communication style. I may or may not understand where you're coming from, but let's give it a try." For some minority clients, this form of communication may be enough to begin the process of bridging the communication-style gap.

Implications for Clinical Practice

This chapter has made it abundantly clear that communication styles are strongly influenced by such factors as race, culture, ethnicity, and gender. Most of the studies we have reviewed lend support to the notion that various racial groups do exhibit differences in communication styles. If counseling and therapy are seen as subsets of the communication process, then it may have significant implications for what constitutes helping. Some general suggestions gleaned from this chapter might prove helpful:

1. Recognize that no one style of counseling or therapy will be appropriate for all populations and situations. A counselor or therapist who is able to engage in a variety of helping styles and roles is most likely to be effective in working with a diverse population.

2. Become knowledgeable about how race, culture, and gender affect communication styles. It is especially important to study the literature on nonverbal communication and test it out in a real-life situation by making a concerted and conscious effort to observe the ways in which people communicate and interact. Your clinical observation skills will be greatly enhanced if you sharpen your nonverbal powers of observation of clients.

3. Become aware of your own communication and helping styles. Know your social impact on others and anticipate how it affects your clients. How we behave often unconsciously reflects our own beliefs and values. It is important for us to realize what we communicate to others. Further, knowing how we affect people allows us to modify our behaviors should our impact be negative. To do this, we need to seek feedback from friends and colleagues about how we impact them.

4. Try to obtain additional training and education on a variety of theoretical orientations and approaches. Programs that are primarily psychoanalytically oriented, cognitively oriented, existentially oriented, person-centered oriented, or behaviorally oriented may be doing a great disservice to trainees. The goals and processes espoused by the theories may not be those held by culturally different groups. These theories

tend to be not only culture-bound, but also narrow in how they conceptualize the human condition.

5. Know that each school of counseling and therapy has strengths, but they may be one-dimensional; they concentrate only on feelings, or only on cognitions, or only on behaviors. We need to realize that we are *feeling, thinking, behaving, social, cultural, spiritual,* and *political* beings. In other words, try to think holistically rather than in a reductionist manner when it comes to conceptualizing the human condition.

6. It is important for training programs to use an approach that calls for openness and flexibility both in conceptualizing the issues and in actual skill building. In many respects, it represents a metatheoretical and eclectic approach to helping. Rather than being random, haphazard, and inconsistent, the metatheoretical approach is an attempt to use helping strategies, techniques, and styles that consider not only individual characteristics, but cultural and racial factors as well.

Multicultural Family Counseling and Therapy

8

Several years ago, a female school counselor sought my advice about a Mexican American family she had recently seen. She was quite concerned about the identified client, Elena Martinez, a 13-year-old student who was referred for counseling because of alleged peddling of drugs on the school premises. The counselor had formed an impression that the parents "did not care for their daughter," "were uncooperative," and "were attempting to avoid responsibility for dealing with Elena's delinquency." When pressed for how she arrived at these impressions, the counselor provided the following information.

Elena Martinez was the second oldest of five siblings, ages 15, 12, 10, and 7. The father was an immigrant from Mexico and the mother a natural citizen. The family resided in a blue-collar Latino neighborhood in San Jose, California. Elena had been reported as having minor problems in school prior to the "drug-selling incident." For example, she had "talked back to teachers," refused to do homework assignments, and had "fought" with other students. Her involvement with a group of other Latino students (suspected of being responsible for disruptive school-yard pranks) had gotten her into trouble. Elena was well known to the counseling staff at the school. Because of the seriousness of the drug accusations, the counselor felt that something had to be done and that the parents needed to be informed immediately.

The counselor reported calling the parents to set up an interview with them. When Mrs. Martinez answered the telephone, the counselor explained that a police officer had caught Elena selling marijuana on school premises. Rather than arrest her, the officer turned the student over to the vice principal, who luckily was present at the time of the incident. After the explanation, the counselor had asked that the parents make arrangements for an appointment as soon as possible. The meeting would be aimed at informing the parents about Elena's difficulties in school and coming to some decision about what could be done.

During the phone conversation, Mrs. Martinez seemed hesitant about selecting a day and time to meet and when pressed by the counselor, excused herself from the phone. The counselor reported overhearing some whispering on the other end, and then the voice of Mr. Martinez. He immediately asked the counselor how his daughter was and expressed his consternation over the entire situation. At that point, the counselor stated that she understood his feelings, but it would be best to set up an appointment for the following day and to talk about it then. Several times the counselor asked Mr. Martinez about a convenient time for the meeting, but each time he seemed to avoid the answer and to give excuses. He had to work the rest of the day and could not make the appointment. The counselor strongly stressed how important the meeting was for the daughter's welfare, and that several hours of missed work was a small price to pay in light of the situation. The father stated that he would be able to make an evening session, but the counselor informed him that school policy prohibited evening meetings. When the counselor suggested that the mother could initially come alone, further hesitations seemed present. Finally, the father agreed to attend.

The very next day, Mr. and Mrs. Martinez and a brother-in-law (Elena's godfather) showed up in her office. The counselor reported being upset at the presence of the brother-in-law when it became obvious that he planned to sit in on the session. At that point, she explained that a third party present would only make the session more complex and the outcome counterproductive. She wanted to see only the family. The counselor reported that the session went poorly, with minimal cooperation from the parents. The father and mother volunteered little in the way of information.

The case of Elena Martinez exemplifies major misunderstandings that often occur in working with culturally diverse families. The counselor's obvious lack of understanding concerning Latino cultural values and how they traditionally affect communication patterns are present once again. This lack of knowledge and the degree of insensitivity to the Latino family's experience in the United States can lead to negative impressions such as, "They are uncooperative, avoiding responsibility and not caring for their children." The failure to understand cultural differences and the experiences of minority status in the United States compounds the problems. Consider the following points as you think about this case.

First, it is entirely possible that the incidents reported by the counselor mean something different when seen from traditional Mexican American culture. Again, like many Euro-American therapists, this counselor possesses a value system of egalitarianism in the husband-wife relationship. The helping professional may be prone to making negative judgments of patriarchal Mexican American roles. In Latino culture, division of roles (husband is protector/provider while wife cares for the home/family) allows both to exercise influence and make decisions. Breaking the role divisions (especially by the woman) is done only out of necessity. A wife would be remiss in publicly making a family decision (setting up an appointment) without consulting or obtaining agreement from the husband. Mrs. Martinez's hesitation on the phone to commit to a meeting date with the counselor may be a reflection of the husband-wife role relationship rather than a lack of concern for their daughter. The counselor's persistence in forcing Mrs. Martinez to decide may actually be asking her to violate cultural dictates about appropriate role behaviors.

Second, the counselor may have seriously undermined the Latino concept of the extended family by expressing negativism toward the godfather's attendance at the counseling session. Middle-class White Americans consider the family unit to be nuclear (husband, wife, and children related by blood), while most minorities define the family unit as an extended one. A Hispanic child can acquire a godmother (madrina) and a godfather (padrino) through a baptismal ceremony. Unlike many White Americans, the role of godparents in Latino culture is more than symbolic, as they can become coparents (compadre) and take an active part in raising the child. Indeed, the role of the godparents is usually linked to the moral, religious, and spiritual upbringing of the child. Who else would be more appropriate to attend the counseling session than the godfather? Not only is he a member of the family, but the charges against Elena deal with legal and moral/ethical implications as well.

Third, the counselor obviously did not consider the economic impact that missing a couple of hours' work might have on the family. Again, she tended to equate Mr. Martinez's reluctance to take off work for the "welfare of his daughter" as evidence of the parents' disinterest in their child. Trivializing the missing of work reveals major class/work differences that often exist between mental health professionals and their minority clients. Most professionals (mental health practitioners, educators, white collar workers) are often able to take time off for a dental appointment, teacher conference, or other personal needs without loss of income. Most of us can usually arrange for others to cover for us or make up the lost hours on some other day. If we are docked for time off, only a few hours are lost and not an entire afternoon or day's work. This, indeed, is a middle- or upper-class luxury not shared by those who face economic hardships or who work in settings that do not allow for schedule flexibility.

For the Martinez family, loss of even a few hours' wages has serious financial impact. Most blue collar workers may not have the luxury or option of making up their work. How, for example, would an assembly-line worker make up the lost time when the plant closes at the end of the day? In addition, the worker often does not miss just a few hours, but must take a half or full day off. In many work situations, getting a worker to substitute for just a few hours is not practical. To entice replacement workers, the company must offer more than a few hours (in many cases, a full day). Thus, Mr. Martinez may actually be losing an entire day's wages! His reluctance to miss work may actually represent *high concern* for the family rather than *lack of care*.

Fourth, the case of Elena and the Martinez family raises another important question: What obligation do educational and mental health services have toward offering flexible and culturally appropriate services to minority constituents? Mr. Martinez's desire for an evening or weekend meeting brings this issue into clear perspective. Does the minority individual or family always have to conform to system rules and regulations? We are not arguing with the school policy itself—in some schools, there are very legitimate reasons for not staying after school ends (high crime rate, etc.). What we are arguing for is the need to provide alternative service deliveries to minority families. For example, why not home visits or sessions off the school premises? Social workers have historically used this method with very positive results. It has aided the building of rapport (the family perceives your genuine interest), increased comfort in the family for sharing with a counselor, and allowed a more realistic appraisal of family dynamics. Counselors frequently forget how intimidating it may be for a minority family to come in for counseling. The Martinez's lack of verbal participation may be a function not only of the conflict over the absence of the godfather, but also of the impersonal and formal nature of counseling relative to the personal orientation of the Hispanic family (*personalismo*).

Let us now use another couple counseling case to illustrate other contrasting role relationship issues that arise in multicultural family counseling.

Esteban and Carmen O., a Puerto Rican couple, sought help at a community mental health clinic in the Miami area. Mr. O. had recently come to the United States with only a high school education, but had already acquired several successful printing shops. Carmen, his wife, was a third-generation Latina raised in Florida. The two had a whirlwind courtship that resulted in marriage after only a three-month acquaintance. She described her husband as handsome, outspoken, confident, and strong, a person who could be affectionate and sensitive. Carmen used the term machismo *several times to describe Esteban.*

The couple had sought marital counseling after a series of rather heated arguments over Esteban's long work hours and his tendency to "go drinking with the boys" after work. She missed his companionship, which was constantly present during their courtship but now seemed strangely absent. Carmen, who had graduated from the University of Florida with a BA in business, had been working as an administrative assistant when she met Esteban. While she enjoyed her work, Carmen reluctantly resigned the position prior to her marriage, with the urging of Esteban, who stated that it was beneath her and that he was capable of supporting them both. Carmen had convinced Esteban to seek outside help with their marital difficulties, and they had been assigned to Dr. Carla B., a White female psychologist. The initial session with the couple was characterized by Esteban's doing most of the talking. Indeed, Dr. B. was quite annoyed by Esteban's arrogant attitude. He frequently spoke for his wife and interrupted

Dr. B. often, not allowing her to finish questions or make comments. Esteban stated that he understood his wife's desire to spend more time with him but that he needed to seek financial security for "my children." While the couple did not have any children at the present time, it was obvious that Esteban expected to have many with his wife. He jokingly stated, "After three or four sons, she won't have time to miss me."

It was obvious that his remark had a strong impact on Carmen, as she appeared quite surprised. Dr. B., who during this session had been trying to give Carmen an opportunity to express her thoughts and feelings, seized the opportunity. She asked Carmen how she felt about having children. As Carmen began to answer, Esteban blurted out quickly, "Of course, she wants children. All women want children."

At this point Dr. B. (obviously angry) confronted Esteban about his tendency to answer or speak for his wife and the inconsiderate manner in which he kept interrupting everyone. "Being a 'macho man' is not what is needed here," stated Dr. B. Esteban became noticeably angry and stated, "No woman lectures Esteban. Why aren't you at home caring for your husband? What you need is a real man." Dr. B. did not fall for Esteban's baiting tactic and refused to argue with him. She was nevertheless quite angry with Esteban and disappointed in Carmen's passivity. The session was terminated shortly thereafter.

During the next few weeks Carmen came to the sessions without her husband, who refused to return. Their sessions consisted of dealing with Esteban's "sexist attitude" and the ways in which Carmen could be her "own person." Dr. B. stressed the fact that Carmen had an equal right in the decisions made at home, that she should not allow anyone to oppress her, that she did not need her husband's approval to return to her former job, and that having children was an equal and joint responsibility.

During Carmen's six months of therapy, the couple separated from one another. It was a difficult period for Carmen, who came for therapy regularly to talk about her need "to be my own person," a phrase used often by Dr. B.

Carmen and Esteban finally divorced after only a year of marriage.

As in individual therapy, family systems therapy may be equally culture-bound and, when inappropriately applied, can have disastrous consequences. Dr. B. failed to understand the gender role relationship between traditional Puerto Rican men and women, unwittingly applied a culture-bound definition of a healthy male-female relationship to Esteban and Carmen, and allowed her own (feminist) values to influence her therapeutic decisions. While we cannot blame her for the divorce of this couple, one wonders whether this would have happened if the therapist had clarified the cultural issues and conflicts occurring between the couple and realized how the values of couple counseling and those manifested in Puerto Rican culture might be at odds with one another.

For example, the egalitarian attitude held by the therapist may be in conflict with Puerto Rican values concerning male-female relationships and the division of responsibilities in the household. Traditional Puerto Rican families are patriarchal, a structure that gives men authority over women and the ability to make decisions without consulting them (Garcia-Preto, 1996; Ramos-McKay, Comas-Diaz, & Rivera, 1988). Encouraging Carmen to be her own person, having a right to make independent decisions, and sharing the decision-making process with Esteban might be violating traditional gender role relationships. These men-women relationships are reinforced by the constructs of *machismo* and *marianismo.* Machismo is a term used in many Latino cultures to indicate maleness, virility, and the man's role as provider and protector of the family. The term denotes male sexual prowess, allows males greater sexual freedom, and dictates a role that makes them responsible for protecting the honor of the women in the family. In the United States, machismo has acquired negative connotations, has been pathologized, and is often equated with sexist behavior (De La Cancela, 1991).

The construct of marianismo is the female counterpart, which is derived from the cult of the Virgin Mary; while men may be sexually superior, women are seen as morally and spiritually superior and capable of enduring greater suffering (Garcia-Preto, 1996). Women are expected to keep themselves sexually pure and to be self-sacrificing in favor of their children and especially the husband; she is the caretaker of the family and the homemaker. These gender role relationships have existed for centuries within Puerto Rican culture, although intergenerational differences have made these traditional roles an increasing source of conflict.

Dr. B. is obviously unaware that her attempts to interrupt Esteban's dialogue, to encourage Carmen to speak her mind freely, and to derogate machismo may be a violation of Puerto Rican cultural values; it may also be perceived as an insult to Esteban's maleness. The therapist is also unaware that her gender (being a woman) might also be a source of conflict for Esteban. Not only may he perceive Dr. B. as playing an inappropriate role (she should be at home taking care of her husband and children), but also it must be a great blow to his male pride to have a female therapist taking charge of the sessions.

We are not making a judgment about whether the patriarchal nature of a cultural group is good or bad. We are also not taking the position that egalitarian relationships are better than other culturally sanctioned role relationships. What is important, however, is the realization that personal values (equality in relationships), definitions of desirable male-female role relationships, and the goals of marital or family therapy (independence, or becoming one's own person) may be culture-bound and may negatively impact multicultural family counseling/therapy. Effective multicultural family therapy is very difficult not only because of these cultural clashes, but also because of the way in which they interact with class issues (the Martinez family).

Family Systems Counseling and Therapy

Family systems therapy encompasses many aspects of the family, which may include marital or couple counseling/therapy, parent-child counseling, or work with more than one member of the family (Nichols & Schwartz, 2002). Its main goal is to modify relationships within a family in order to achieve harmony (Becvar & Becvar, 2003). Family systems therapy is based on several assumptions: (1) It is logical and economical to treat together all those who exist and operate within a system of relationships (in most cases, it implies the nuclear family); (2) the problems of the "identified patient" are only symptoms, and the family itself is the client; (3) all symptoms or problematic behaviors exhibited by a member of the family serve a purpose; (4) the behaviors of family members are tied to one another in powerful reciprocal ways (circular causality emphasized over linear causality); and (5) the task of the therapist is to modify relationships or improve communications within the family system (Corey, 2005; McGoldrick, Giordano, & Garcia-Preto, 2005).

There are many family systems approaches, but two characteristics seem to be especially important. One of these, the *communications approach*, is based on the assumption that family problems are communication difficulties. Many family communication problems are both subtle and complex. Family therapists concentrate on improving not only faulty communications but also interactions and relationships among family members (Satir, 1967, 1983). The way in which rules, agreements, and perceptions are communicated among members may also be important (J. Haley, 1967). The *structural approach* also considers communication to be important, but it emphasizes the interlocking roles of family members (Minuchin, 1974). Most families are constantly in a state of change; they are in the process of structuring and restructuring themselves into systems and subsystems. The health of a family is often linked to the members' abilities to recognize boundaries of the various systems—alliances, communication patterns, and so forth. From a philosophical and theoretical perspective, both approaches appear appropriate in working with various minority groups. For example, they appear to

- Highlight the importance of the family (versus the individual) as the unit of identity
- Focus on resolving concrete issues
- Be concerned with family structure and dynamics
- Assume that these family structures and dynamics are historically passed on from one generation to another
- Attempt to understand the communication and alliances via reframing
- Place the therapist in an expert position

Many of these qualities, as we have seen, would be consistent with the worldviews of racial/ethnic minorities. Many culturally different families favorably view its emphases on the family as the unit of identity and study, understanding the cultural norms and background of the family system, and the need to balance the system.

The problem arises, however, in how these goals and strategies are translated into concepts of "the family" or what constitutes the "healthy" family. Some of the characteristics of healthy families may pose problems in therapy with various culturally different groups. They tend to be heavily loaded with value orientations that are incongruent with the value systems of many culturally different clients (McGoldrick, Giordano, & Pearce, 2005). They tend to

- Allow and encourage expressing emotions freely and openly
- View each member as having a right to be his or her own unique self (individuate from the emotional field of the family)
- Strive for an equal division of labor among members of the family
- Consider egalitarian role relationships between spouses desirable
- Hold the nuclear family as the standard

As in the cases of the Martinez family and Esteban/Carmen, these translations in family systems therapy can cause great problems in working with culturally diverse clients. It is clear that culturally effective family systems therapists must escape from their cultural encapsulation, understand the sociopolitical forces that affect minority families, become aware of major differences in the value system that they possess when contrasted with racial/cultural family values, and understand structural family relationships that are different from their own concepts of family.

Issues in Working with Ethnic Minority Families

Effective multicultural family counseling and therapy must incorporate the many racial, cultural, economic, and class issues inherent in the two clinical family examples given earlier. While not unique to families of color, there are life events that differentiate the experiences of people of color from middle-class White families. Several factors have been identified as important for culturally sensitive family therapists to take into consideration (Boyd-Franklin, 2003; Ho, 1997; McGoldrick et al., 2005).

Ethnic Minority Reality

This refers to the racism and poverty that dominate the lives of minorities. Lower family income, greater unemployment, increasing percentage falling below the poverty line, and other issues have had major negative effects not only on the individuals, but on family structures as well. The relocation of 120,000 Japanese Americans into concentration camps during World War II, for example, drastically altered the traditional Japanese family structures and relationships (D. W. Sue & Kirk, 1973). By physically uprooting these U.S. citizens, symbols of ethnic identity were destroyed, creating identity conflicts and problems. Furthermore, the camp experience disrupted the traditional lines of authority. The elderly male no longer had a functional value as head of household; family discipline and control became loosened; and women gained a degree of independence unheard of in traditional Japanese families.

Likewise, African American families have been victims of poverty and racism. Nowhere is this more evident than in statistics revealing a higher incidence of Black children living in homes without the biological father present—82 percent, as compared with 43 percent for Whites (Wilkinson, 1993). More Black families are classified as impoverished (46 percent) than are White families (10 percent). In addition, many more Black males are single, widowed, or divorced (47 percent), compared with Whites (28 percent). The high mortality rate among Black males has led some to call them an endangered species in which societal forces have even strained and affected the Black male-female relationship (Parham et al., 1999). Under slavery, class distinctions were obliterated; the slave husband was disempowered as the head of the household, and the man's inability to protect and provide for kin had a negative effect upon African American family relationships (Wilkinson, 1993).

Conflicting Value Systems

Imposed by White Euro-American society upon minority groups, conflicting value systems have also caused great harm to them. The case of Elena Martinez reveals how the White counselor's conception of the nuclear family may clash with traditional Latino/Hispanic emphasis on extended families. It appears that almost all minority groups place greater value on families, historical lineage (reverence of ancestors), interdependence among family members, and submergence of self for the good of the family (Uba, 1994). African Americans are often described as having a kinship system in which relatives of a variety of blood ties (aunts, uncles, brothers, sisters, boyfriends, preachers, etc.) may act as the extended family (Black, 1996; Hines & Boyd-Franklin, 2005). Likewise, the extended family in the Hispanic culture includes numerous relatives and friends (Falicov, 2005; Garcia-Preto, 2005), as evidenced in the case of Elena Martinez. Perhaps most difficult to grasp for many mental health professionals is the American Indian family network, which is structurally open and assumes village-like characteristics (Herring, 1999; Red Horse, 1983; Sutton & Broken Nose, 2005). This family extension may include several households. Unless therapists are aware of these value differences, they may unintentionally mislabel behaviors that they consider bizarre or make decisions that are detrimental to the family. We have more to say about this important point shortly.

Biculturalism

Biculturalism refers to the fact that minorities in the United States inherit two different cultural traditions. The therapist must understand how biculturalism influences the structures, communications, and dynamics of the family. A 22-year-old Latino male's reluctance to go against the wishes of his parents and marry a woman he loves may not be a sign of immaturity. Rather, it may reflect a conflict between duality of membership in two groups or between the positive choices of one cultural dictate over another. A culturally effective therapist is one who understands the possible conflicts that may arise as a result of biculturalism.

Related to biculturalism is the therapist's need to understand the process of acculturation and the stresses encountered by culturally diverse families. While the term was originally used to indicate the mutual influence of two different cultures on one another, biculturalism is best understood in the United States as the interaction between a dominant and nondominant culture. Some questions that need to be addressed by family systems therapists when working with culturally diverse families are: What are the psychological consequences to nondominant families as they encounter the dominant culture? What effects does the dominant culture have on minority family dynamics and structure? What types of issues or problems are likely to arise as a result of the acculturation process? For example, a recently migrated family often has parents who are allied with the culture of their country of origin while their offspring are more likely to adapt to the dominant culture more rapidly. In many cases, children may be more oriented to the culture of the larger society, resulting in intergenerational conflicts (Gushue & Sciarra, 1995). However, it is important for the therapist to understand the sociopolitical dimensions of this process. The problem may not be so much a function of intergenerational conflict as it is the dominant-subordinate clash of cultures (Gushue & Sciarra, 1995; Szapocznik & Kurtines, 1993). The multiculturally skilled family therapist would focus on the problems created by cultural oppression and reframe the goal as one of stressing the benefits of intergenerational collaboration and alliance against a common foe (Gushue & Sciarra, 1995).

Ethnic Differences in Minority Status

These differences refer to the life experiences and adjustments that occur as a result of minority status in the United States. All four racial/ethnic minority groups have been subjected to dehumanizing forces:

- The history of slavery for Black Americans has not only negatively impacted their self-esteem but has also contributed to the disruption of the Black male/female relationship and the structure of the Black family. Slavery imposed a pathological system of social organization on the African American family, resulting in disorganization and a constant fight for survival and stability. Despite the system of slavery, however, many African Americans overcame these negative forces by sheer force of will, by reasserting their ties of affection, by using extended kinship ties, by their strength of spirit and spirituality, and by their multigenerational networks (Wilkinson, 1993). It would be highly beneficial if the family systems therapist recognized these strengths in the African American family, rather than stressing its instability and problems.

- Racism and colonialism have made American Indians immigrants in their own land, and the federal government has even imposed a definition of race upon them (they must be able to prove they are at least one-quarter Indian blood). Such a legal definition of race has created problems among Native Americans by confusing the issues of identity. Like their African American brothers and sisters, Native Americans have experienced conquest, dislocation, cultural genocide, segregation, and coerced assimilation (Sutton & Broken Nose, 2005; Tafoya & Del Vecchio, 2005). American Indian family life has been strongly affected by government policies that include using missionaries, boarding schools, and the Bureau of Indian Affairs in an attempt to civilize the heathens. The results have been devastating to Native Americans: learned helplessness; gambling, alcohol, and drug abuse; suicide; and family relationship problems (Tofoya & Del Vecchio, 2005). A family systems therapist must be aware of the multigenerational disruption of the Native American family through over 500 years of historical trauma.

- Immigration status among Latino/Hispanics and Asian refugees/immigrants (legal resident to illegal alien) and the abuses, resentments, and discrimination experienced by them are constant stressful events in their lives. Anti-immigrant feelings have never been more pervasive and intense. This negativism is currently symbolized in continuing debate of the guest worker program, amnesty for illegal immigrants, and the formation of vigilante groups like the Minute Men, who patrol the border between Mexico and the United States. Mean-spirited and with potentially devastating consequences, current attempts to expel immigrant children from school who are in the United States illegally, and to deny them jobs, nonemergency health care, and other social services have increased fears of deportation and other reprisals. In addition to the hostile climate experienced by recent immigrants, the migration experience can be a source of stress and disappointment. The multicultural family systems therapist must differentiate between the reasons for migration because their impact on the family may be quite different. A family deciding to migrate in search of adventure or wealth (voluntary decision) will experience the change differently than will refugees/immigrants who must leave because of war or religious and/or political persecution. Attitudes toward assimilation and acculturation might be quite different between the two families.

Skin color and obvious physical differences are also important factors that determine the treatment of minority individuals and their families. These physical differences continue to warp the perception of White America in that persons of color are seen as aliens in their own land. Equating physical differences, and particularly skin color, with being alien, negative, pathological, or less than human has a long history. Travel logs of early European seafarers describe their encounters with Blacks and the images and judgments associated with Africans:

> And entering in [a river], we see
> A number of blacke soules,
> Whose likelinesse seem'd men to be,
> But all as blacke as coles. (Quoted in Jordan, 1969, pp. 4–5)

J. M. Jones (1997, p. 475) pointed out that the *Oxford English Dictionary* definition of the word black prior to the sixteenth century was the following:

> Deeply stained with dirt; soiled, dirty, foul. . . . Having dark or deadly purposes, malignant; pertaining to or involving death, deadly; baneful, disastrous, sinister. . . . Foul, iniquitous, atrocious, horrible, wicked. . . . Indicating disgrace, censure, liability to punishment, etc.

It is clear then, that the concept of blackness was associated with being bad, ugly, evil, and nonhuman. J. M. Jones (1997) also observes the relationship between color name and a classic clinical report of multiple personality disorder. In the *Three Faces of Eve* (Thigpen & Cleckley, 1954, p. 476), the two personalities—Eve White and Eve Black—reflect positive associations with Whiteness and negative ones with Blackness:

> Eve Black is lacking in culture but curiously likable. She is playful, childlike, entertaining. Her superego is nonfunctional, which makes her a delight, the one who has all the fun. Black is where the "fun" things go to be. Yet, just as there is a kind of nostalgia and envy directed at Eve Black, there is judgment and castigation, as well. A certain voyeurism makes Eve Black someone one would like to be around, but wouldn't want in one's family. Eve White, by contrast, has "all the right stuff." She is socialized to traditional values, properly "feminine," de-

voted, even heroic. Her saintliness is admired, but somehow she is repressed, and one's admiration for her is tinged with sadness.

The personality traits associated differentially with Eve White and Eve Black are not pulled from thin air; instead, they suggest the content of cultural beliefs about the races as well as the genders. These cultural beliefs did not, in 1954, depart substantially from the first conclusions about racial differences by Englishmen in 1550!

While skin color is probably the most powerful physical characteristic linked to racism, other physical features and differences may also determine negative treatment by the wider society. External societal definitions of race have often resulted in ideological racism that links physical characteristics of groups (usually skin color) to major psychological traits (Feagin, 1989). Beliefs that Blacks are great athletes but poor scholars are sentiments that have shaped U.S. treatment of African Americans. Likewise, other physical features, such as head form, facial features, color and texture of body hair, and so on all contrast with the ideal image of blond hair and fair skin. Not only is there an external negative evaluation of those who differ from such "desired" features, but many persons of color may form negative self-images and body images and attempt to become Westernized in their physical features. One wonders, for example, at the psychological dynamics that have motivated some Asian American women to seek cosmetic surgery to reshape their eyes in a more Westernized fashion.

Ethnicity and Language

These dimensions refer to the common sense of bonding among members of a group that contributes to a sense of belonging. The symbols of the group (ethnicity) are manifested primarily in language. Language structures meaning, determines how we see things, is the carrier of our culture, and affects our worldviews. Many minority clients do not possess vocabulary equivalents to standard English and when forced to communicate in English may appear "flat," "nonverbal," "uncommunicative," and "lacking in insight" (Romero, 1985). The problem is linguistic, not psychological. In psychotherapy, where words are the major vehicle for effective change, language has been likened to what a baton is to the conductor and what a scalpel is to the surgeon (Russell, 1988).

Studies in the field of linguistics and sociolinguistics support the fact that language conveys a wealth of information other than the primary content of the message; the cues of background, place of origin, group membership, status in the group, and the relationship to the speaker can all be determined (Kennedy, 1996; Kochman, 1981; Russell, 1988). Thus, the gender, race, and social class of the speaker can be accurately identified. More importantly, however, these studies also suggest that the listener utilizes this sociolinguistic information to formulate opinions of the speaker and in the interpretation of the message. Because our society values standard English, the use of nonstandard English, dialects, or accented speech is often associated with undesirable characteristics—being less intelligent, uncouth, lower class, unsophisticated, and uninsightful. Thus, while racial/ethnic minority groups may use their linguistic characteristics to bond with one another and to communicate more accurately, the larger society may invalidate, penalize, or directly punish individuals or groups who exhibit bilingualism or group-idiosyncratic use of language.

Ethnicity and Social Class

These refer to aspects of wealth, name, occupation, and status. Class differences between mental health professionals and their minority clients can often lead to barriers in understanding and communication. This was clearly evident in the case of Elena Martinez, in that the counselor had difficulty relating to a missed day of work. Needless to say, understanding class differences becomes even more important for therapists working with minority families, because they are disproportionately represented in the lower socioeconomic classes. Many argue that class may be a more powerful determinant of values and behavior than race or ethnicity. For example, we know that the wealthiest one million people in the United States earn more than the next 100 million combined, that the top 1 percent own over 40 percent of the nation's wealth, and that the gap between the rich and the poor is increasing (Thurow, 1995). From a political perspective, some believe that racial conflicts are promulgated by those at the very top, to detract from the real cause of inequities: a social structure that allows the dominant class to maintain power (Bell, 1993). While there is considerable truth to this view, not all differences can be ascribed to class alone. Further, while one cannot change race or ethnicity, changes in social class can occur. We contend that all three are important, and the therapist must understand their interactions with one another.

Multicultural Family Counseling/Therapy: A Conceptual Model

Effective multicultural family counseling/therapy operates under principles similar to that outlined in earlier chapters. First, counselors need to become culturally aware of their own values, biases, and assumptions about human behavior (especially as it pertains to the definition of family). Second, it is important to become aware of the worldview of the culturally different client and how that client views the definition, role, and function of the family. Last, ap-

Table 8.1 **Cultural Value Preferences of Middle-Class White Euro-Americans and Racial/Ethnic Minorities: A Comparative Summary**

Area of Relationships	Middle-Class White Americans	Asian Americans	American Indians	Black Americans	Hispanic Americans
People to nature/ environment	Mastery over	Harmony with	Harmony with	Harmony with	Harmony with
Time orientation	Future	Past-present	Present	Present	Past-present
People relations	Individual	Collateral	Collateral	Collateral	Collateral
Preferred mode of activity	Doing	Doing	Being-in-becoming	Doing	Being-in-becoming
Nature of man	Good & bad	Good	Good	Good & bad	Good

Source: From *Family Therapy with Ethnic Minorities* (p. 232) by M. K. Ho, 1987, Newbury Park, CA: Sage. Copyright 1987 by Sage Publications. Reprinted by permission.

propriate intervention strategies need to be devised to maximize success and minimize cultural oppression. While in earlier chapters the focus was on individual clients and their ethnic/racial groups, our concern in this chapter is with the family unit as defined from the group's perspective. In attempting to understand the first two goals, we are using a model first outlined by Kluckhohn and Strodtbeck (1961). This model allows us to understand the worldviews of culturally diverse families by contrasting the value orientations of the four main groups we are studying (as illustrated in Table 8.1): Asian Americans, Native Americans, African Americans, and Latino/Hispanic Americans.

People-Nature Relationship

Traditional Western thinking believes in mastery and control over nature. As a result, most therapists operate from a framework that subscribes to the belief that problems are solvable and that both therapist and client must take an active part in solving problems via manipulation and control. Active intervention is stressed in controlling or changing the environment. As seen in Table 8.1, the four other ethnic groups view people as harmonious with nature.

Confucian philosophy, for example, stresses a set of rules aimed at promoting loyalty, respect, and harmony among family members (Moodley & West, 2005). Harmony within the family and the environment leads to harmony within the self. Dependence on the family unit and acceptance of the environment seem to dictate differences in solving problems. Western culture advocates defining and attacking the problem directly. Asian cultures tend to accommodate or deal with problems through indirection. In child rearing, many Asians believe that it is better to avoid direct confrontation and to use deflection. A White family may deal with a child who has watched too many hours of TV by saying, "Why don't you turn the TV off and study?" To be more threatening, the parent might say, "You'll be grounded unless the TV goes off!" An Asian parent might respond by saying, "That looks like a boring program; I think your friend John must be doing his homework now," or, "I think father wants to watch his favorite program." Such an approach stems from the need to avoid conflict and to achieve balance and harmony among members of the family and the wider environment.

In an excellent analysis of family therapy for Asian Americans, S. C. Kim (1985) points out how current therapeutic techniques of confrontation and of having clients express thoughts and feelings directly may be inappropriate and difficult to handle. For example, one of the basic tenets of family therapy is that the identified patient (IP) typically behaves in such a way as to reflect family influences or pathology. Often, an acting-out child is symbolic of deeper family problems. Yet most Asian American families come to counseling or therapy for the benefit of the IP, not the family! Attempts to directly focus in on the family dynamics as contributing to the IP will be met with negativism and possible termination. S. C. Kim (1985, pp. 346) states,

> *A recommended approach to engage the family would be to pace the family's cultural expectations and limitations by (1) asserting that the IP's problem (therefore not the IP by implication) is indeed the problem; (2) recognizing and reinforcing the family's concerns to help the IP to change the behavior; and (3) emphasizing that each family member's contribution in resolving the problem is vitally needed, and that without it, the problem will either remain or get worse bringing on further difficulty in the family.*

Thus, it is apparent that U.S. values that call for us to dominate nature (i.e., conquer space, tame the wilderness, or harness nuclear energy) through control and manipulation of the universe are reflected in family counseling. Family systems counseling theories attempt to describe, explain, predict, and control family dynamics. The therapist actively attempts to understand what is going on in the family system (structural alliances and communication patterns), identify the problems (dysfunctional aspects of the dynamics), and attack them directly or indirectly through manipulation and control (therapeutic interventions). Ethnic minorities or subgroups that view people as harmonious with nature or believe that nature may overwhelm people ("acts of God") may find the therapist's mastery-over-nature approach inconsistent or antagonistic to their worldview. Indeed, attempts to intervene actively in changing family patterns and relationships may be perceived as the problem because it may potentially unbalance that harmony that existed.

Time Dimension

How different societies, cultures, and people view time exerts a pervasive influence on their lives. U.S. society may be characterized as preoccupied with the future (Katz, 1985; Kluckhohn & Strodtbeck, 1961). Furthermore, our society seems very compulsive about time, in that we divide it into seconds, minutes, hours, days, weeks, months, and years. Time may be viewed as a commodity ("time is money" and "stop wasting time") in fixed and static categories rather than as a dynamic and flowing process. It has been pointed out that the United States' future orientation may be linked to other values as well: (a) stress on youth and achievement, in which the children are expected to "better their parents"; (b) controlling one's own destiny by future planning and saving for a rainy day; and (c) optimism and hope for a better future. The spirit of the nation may be embodied in an old General Electric slogan, "Progress is our most important product." This is not to deny that people are concerned about the past and the present as well, but rather to suggest that culture, groups, and people may place greater emphasis on one over the other. Nor do we deny the fact that age, gender, occupation, social class, and other important demographic factors may be linked to time perspective. However, our work with various racial/ethnic minority groups and much of the research conducted support the fact that race, culture, and ethnicity are powerful determinants of whether the group emphasizes the past, present, or future.

Table 8.1 reveals that both American Indians and African Americans tend to value a present time orientation, while Asian Americans and Hispanic Americans have a combination past-present focus. Historically, Asian societies have valued the past as reflected in ancestor worship and the equating of age with wisdom and respectability. This contrasts with U.S. culture, in which youth is valued over the elderly and the belief that one's usefulness in life is over once one hits the retirement years. As the U.S. population ages, however, it will be interesting to note whether there will be a shift in the status of the elderly. As compared to Euro-American middle-class norms, Latinos also exhibit a past-present time orientation. Strong hierarchical structures in the family, respect for elders and ancestors, and the value of *personalismo* all combine in this direction. American Indians also differ from their White counterparts in that they are very grounded in the here and now rather than the future. American Indian philosophy relies heavily on the belief that time is flowing, circular, and harmonious. Artificial division of time (schedules) is disruptive to the natural pattern. African Americans also value the present because of the spiritual quality of their existence and their history of racism. Several difficulties may occur when the counselor or therapist is unaware of the differences of time perspective (Hines & Boyd-Franklin, 2005).

First, if time differences exist between the minority family and the White Euro-American therapist, it will most likely be manifested in a difference in the pace of time: Both may sense things are going too slowly or too fast. An American Indian family who values being in the present and the immediate experiential reality of being may feel that the therapist lacks respect for them and is rushing them (Herring, 1997; Sutton & Broken Nose, 2005) while ignoring the quality of the personal relationship. On the other hand, the therapist may be dismayed by the "delays," "inefficiency," and lack of "commitment to change" among the family members. After all, time is precious, and the therapist has only limited time to impact upon the family. The result is frequently dissatisfaction among the parties, no establishment of rapport, misinterpretation of the behaviors or situations, and probably discontinuation of future sessions.

Second, Inclan (1985) pointed out how confusions and misinterpretations can arise because Hispanics, particularly Puerto Ricans, mark time differently than do their U.S. White counterparts. The language of clock time in counseling (50-minute hour, rigid time schedule, once-a-week sessions) can conflict with minority perceptions of time (Garcia-Preto, 1996). The following dialogue illustrates this point clearly:

> *"Mrs. Rivera, your next appointment is at 9:30 A.M. next Wednesday."*
> *"Good, it's convenient for me to come after I drop off the children at school."*
> Or, *"Mrs. Rivera, your next appointment is for the whole family at 3:00 P.M. on Tuesday."*
> *"Very good. After the kids return from school we can come right in."* (Inclan, 1985, p. 328)

Since school starts at 8 A.M., the client is bound to show up very early, while in the second example the client will most likely be late (school ends at 3 P.M.). In both cases, the counselor is most likely to be inconvenienced, but worse yet is the negative interpretation that may be made of the client's motives (anxious, demanding, or pushy in the first case, while resistant, passive-aggressive, or irresponsible in the latter one). The counselor needs to be aware that many Hispanics may mark time by events rather than by the clock.

Third, many minorities who are present-time oriented overall would be more likely to seek immediate, concrete solutions than future-oriented, abstract goals. In earlier chapters we noted that goals or processes that are insight oriented assume that the client has time to sit back and self-explore. Career/vocational counseling, in which clients explore their interests, values, work temperaments, skills, abilities, and the world of work, may be seen as highly future oriented. While potentially beneficial to the client, these approaches may pose dilemmas for both the minority family and the counselor.

Relational Dimension

In general, the United States can be characterized as an achievement-oriented society, which is most strongly manifested in the prevailing Protestant work ethic. Basic to the ethic is the concept of *individualism:* (1) The individual is the psychosocial unit of operation; (2) the individual has primary responsibility for his or her own actions; (3) independence and autonomy are highly valued and rewarded; and (4) one should be internally directed and controlled. In many societies and groups within the United States, however, this value is not necessarily shared. Relationships in Japan and China are often described as being lineal, and identification with others is both wide and linked to the past (ancestor worship). Obeying the wishes of ancestors or deceased parents and perceiving your existence and identity as linked to the historical past are inseparable. Almost all racial/ethnic minority groups in the United States tend to be more collateral in their relationships with people. In an individualistic orientation, the definition of the family tends to be linked to a biological necessity (nuclear family), while a collateral or lineal view encompasses various concepts of the extended family. Not understanding this distinction and the values inherent in these orientations may lead the family therapist to erroneous conclusions and decisions. Following is a case illustration of a young American Indian.

> *A young probationer was under court supervision and had strict orders to remain with responsible adults. His counselor became concerned because the youth appeared to ignore this order. The client moved around frequently and, according to the counselor, stayed overnight with several different young women. The counselor presented this case at a formal staff meeting, and fellow professionals stated their suspicion that the client was either a pusher or a pimp. The frustrating element to the counselor was that the young women knew each other and appeared to enjoy each other's company. Moreover, they were not ashamed to be seen together in public with the client. This behavior prompted the counselor to initiate violation proceedings. (Red Horse, Lewis, Feit, & Decker, 1981, p. 56)*

If an American Indian professional had not accidentally come upon this case, a revocation order initiated against the youngster would surely have caused irreparable alienation between the family and the social service agency. The counselor had failed to realize that the American Indian family network is structurally open and may include several households of relatives and friends along both vertical and horizontal lines. The young women were all first cousins to the client, and each was as a sister, with all the households representing different units of the family.

Likewise, African Americans have strong kinship bonds that may encompass both blood relatives and friends. Traditional African culture values the collective orientation over individualism (J. H. Franklin, 1988; Hines & Boyd-Franklin, 2005). This group identity has also been reinforced by what many African Americans describe as the sense of "peoplehood" developed as a result of the common experience of racism and discrimination. In a society that has historically attempted to destroy the Black family, near and distant relatives, neighbors, friends, and acquaintances have arisen in an extended family support network (Black, 1996). Thus, the Black family may appear quite different from the ideal nuclear family. The danger is that certain assumptions made by a White therapist may be totally without merit or may be translated in such a way as to alienate or damage the self-esteem of African Americans.

For example, the absence of a father in the Black family does not necessarily mean that the children do not have a father figure. This function may be taken over by an uncle or male family friend. M. B. Thomas and Dansby (1985) provide an example of a group-counseling technique that was detrimental to several Black children. Clients in the group were asked to draw a picture of the family dinner table and place circles representing the mother, father, and children in their seating arrangement. They reported that even before the directions for the exercise were finished, a young Black girl ran from the room in tears. She had been raised by an aunt. Several other Black clients stated that they did not eat dinners together as a family except on special occasions or Sundays—according to Willie (1981) a typical routine in some affluent Black families.

The importance of family membership and the extended family system has already been illustrated in the case of Elena Martinez. We give one example here to illustrate that the moral evaluation of a behavior may depend on the value orientation of the subject. Because of their collective orientation, Puerto Ricans view obligations to the family as primary over all other relationships (Garcia-Preto, 2005). When a family member attains a position of power and influence, it is expected that he or she will favor the relatives over objective criteria. Businesses that are heavily weighted by family members, and appointments of family members in government positions, are not unusual in many countries. Failure to hire a family member may result in moral condemnation and family sanctions (Inclan, 1985). This is in marked contrast to what we ideally believe in the United States. Appointment of family members over objective criteria of individual achievement is condemned.

It would appear that differences in the relationship dimension between the mental health provider and the minority family receiving services can cause great conflict. While family therapy may be the treatment of choice for many minorities (over individual therapy), its values may again be antagonistic and detrimental to minorities. Family approaches that place heavy emphasis on individualism and freedom from the emotional field of the family may cause great harm. Our approach should be to identify how we might capitalize on collaterality to the benefit of minority families.

Activity Dimension

One of the primary characteristics of White U.S. cultural values and beliefs is an action (doing) orientation: (1) We must master and control nature; (2) we must always do things about a situation; and (3) we should take a pragmatic and utilitarian view of life. In counseling, we expect clients to master and control their own life and environment, to take action to resolve their own problems, and to fight against bias and inaction. The doing mode is evident everywhere and is reflected in how White Americans identify themselves by what they *do* (occupations), how children are asked what they want to do when they grow up, and how a higher value is given to inventors over poets and to doctors of medicine over doctors of philosophy. An essay topic commonly given to schoolchildren returning to school in the fall is "What I did on my summer vacation."

It appears that both American Indians and Latinos/Hispanics prefer a being or being-in-becoming mode of activity. The American Indian concepts of self-determination and noninterference are examples. Value is placed on the spiritual quality of being, as manifested in self-containment, poise, and harmony with the universe. Value is placed on the attainment of inner fulfillment and an essential serenity of one's place in the universe. Because each person is fulfilling a purpose, no one should have the power to interfere or impose values. Often, those unfamiliar with Indian values perceive the person as stoic, aloof, passive, noncompetitive, or inactive. In working with families, the counselor role of active manipulator may clash with American Indian concepts of being-in-becoming (noninterference).

Likewise, Latino/Hispanic culture may be said to have a more here-and-now or being-in-becoming orientation. Like their American Indian counterparts, Hispanics believe that people are born with *dignidad* (dignity) and must be given *respeto* (respect). They are born with innate worth and importance; the inner soul and spirit are more important than the body. People cannot be held accountable for their lot in life (status, roles, etc.) because they are born into this life state (Inclan, 1985). A certain degree of *fatalismo* (fatalism) is present, and life events may be viewed as inevitable (*Lo que Dios manda,* what God wills). Philosophically, it does not matter what people have in life or what position they occupy (farm laborer, public official, or attorney). Status is possessed by existing, and everyone is entitled to *respeto.*

Since this belief system de-emphasizes material accomplishments as a measure of success, it is clearly at odds with Euro-American middle-class society. While a doing-oriented family may define a family member's worth via achievement, a being orientation equates worth simply to belonging. Thus, when clients complain that someone is not an effective family member, what do they mean? This needs to be clarified by the therapist. Is it a complaint that the family member is not performing and achieving (doing), or does it mean that the person is not respectful and accommodating to family structures and values (being)?

Ho (1987) describes both Asian Americans and African Americans as operating from the doing orientation. However, it appears that "doing" in these two groups is manifested differently than in the White American lifestyle. The active dimension in Asians is related not to individual achievement, but to achievement via conformity to family values and demands. Controlling one's own feelings, impulses, desires, and needs to fulfill responsibility to the family is strongly ingrained in Asian children. The doing orientation tends to be more ritualized in the roles of and responsibilities toward members of the family. African Americans also exercise considerable control (endure the pain and suffering of racism) in the face of adversity to minimize discrimination and to maximize success.

Nature of People Dimension

Middle-class Euro-Americans generally perceive the nature of people as neutral. Environmental influences such as conditioning, family upbringing, and socialization are believed to be dominant forces in determining the nature of the person. People are neither good nor bad but are a product of their environment. While several minority groups may share features of this belief with Whites, there is a qualitative and quantitative difference that may affect family structure and dynamics. For example, Asian Americans and American Indians tend to emphasize the inherent goodness of people. We have already discussed the Native American concept of noninterference, which is based on the belief that people have an innate capacity to advance and grow (self-fulfillment) and that problematic behaviors are the result of environmental influences that thwart the opportunity to develop. Goodness will always triumph over evil if the person is left alone. Likewise, Asian philosophy (Buddhism and Confucianism) believes in peoples' innate goodness and prescribes role relationships that manifest the "good way of life." Central to Asian belief is the fact that the best healing source lies within the family (Daya, 2005; Wallace & Shapiro, 2006) and that seeking help from the outside (e.g., counseling and therapy) is nonproductive and against the dictates of Asian philosophy.

Latinos may be described as holding the view that human nature is both good and bad (mixed). Concepts of *dignidad* and *respecto* undergird the belief that people are born with positive qualities. Yet some Hispanics, such as Puerto Ricans, spend a great deal of time appealing to supernatural forces so that children may be blessed with a good human nature (Inclan, 1985). Thus, a child's "badness" may be accepted as destiny, so parents may be less inclined to seek help from educators or mental health professionals for such problems. The preferred mode of help may be religious consultations and ventilation to neighbors and friends who sympathize and understand the dilemmas (change means reaching the supernatural forces).

African Americans may also be characterized as having a mixed concept of people, but in general they believe, like their White counterparts, that people are basically neutral. Environmental factors have a great influence on how people develop. This orientation is consistent with African American beliefs that racism, discrimination, oppression, and other external factors create problems for the individual. Emotional disorders and antisocial acts are caused by external forces (system variables) rather than internal, intrapsychic, psychological forces. For example, high crime rates, poverty, and the current structure of the African American family are the result of historical and current oppression of Black people. White Western concepts of genetic inferiority and pathology (African American people are born that way) hold little validity for the Black person.

Implications for Clinical Practice

It is extremely difficult to speak specifically about applying multicultural strategies and techniques to minority families because of their great variations, not only among Asian Americans, African Americans, Latino/Hispanic Americans, Native Americans, and Euro-Americans, but also within the groups themselves. Worse yet, we may foster overgeneralizations that border on being stereotypes. Likewise, to attempt an extremely specific discussion would mean dealing with literally thousands of racial, ethnic, and cultural combinations, a task that is humanly impossible. What seems to be required is a balance of these two extremes: a framework that would help us both to understand differences in communication styles/structural alliances in the family and to pinpoint more specifically cultural differences that exist within a particular family.

1. Know that our increasing diversity presents us with different cultural conceptions of the family. Whether groups value a lineal, collateral, or individualistic orientation has major implications for their and our definitions of the family. One definition cannot be seen as superior to another.

2. Realize that families cannot be understood apart from the cultural, social, and political dimensions of their functioning. The traditional definition of the nuclear family as consisting of heterosexual parents in a

long-term marriage, raising their biological children, and with the father as sole wage earner is a statistical minority. Extended families, intermarriage, divorce, openly gay/lesbian relationships, commingling of races, single parent, and two parents working outside the home makes the conventional "normal family" definition an anomaly.

3. When working with a racial/ethnic group different from you, make a concerted and conscientious effort to learn as much as possible about their definition of family, the values that underlie the family unit, and your own contrasting definition.

4. Be especially attentive to traditional cultural family structure and extended family ties. As seen in the case of Elena Martinez, nonblood relatives may be considered an intimate part of the extended family system. Understanding husband-wife relationships, parent-child relationships, and sibling relationships from different cultural perspectives is crucial to effective work with minority families.

5. Do not prejudge from your own ethnocentric perspective. Be aware that many Asian Americans and Hispanics have a more patriarchal spousal relationship, while Euro-Americans and Blacks have a more egalitarian one. The concept of equal division of labor in the home between husband and wife or working toward a more equal relationship may be a violation of family norms.

6. Realize that most minority families view the *wifely* role as less important than the *motherly* role. For instance, the existence of children validates and cements the marriage; therefore, motherhood is often perceived as a more important role. Therapists should not judge the health of a family on the basis of the romantic egalitarian model characteristic of White culture.

7. Do not overlook the prospect of utilizing the natural help-giving networks and structures that already exist in the minority culture and community. It is ironic that the mental health field behaves as if minority communities never had anything like mental health treatment until it came along and invented it.

8. Recognize the fact that helping can take many forms. These forms often appear quite different from our own, but they are no less effective or legitimate. Multicultural counseling calls for us to modify our goals and techniques to fit the needs of minority populations. Granted, mental health professionals are sometimes hard pressed in challenging their own assumptions of what constitutes counseling and therapy, or they feel uncomfortable in roles to which they are not accustomed. However, the need is great to move in this most positive direction.

9. Assess the importance of ethnicity to clients and families. Be aware that acculturation is a powerful force and that this is especially important for the children, since they are most likely to be influenced by peers. Many tensions and conflicts between the younger generation and their elders are related to culture conflicts. These conflicts are not pathological, but normative responses to different cultural forces.

10. Realize that the role of the family therapist cannot be confined to culture-bound rules that dictate a narrow set of appropriate roles and behaviors. Effective multicultural family counseling may include validating and strengthening ethnic identity, increasing one's own awareness and use of client support systems (extended family, friends, and religious groups), serving as a culture broker, becoming aware of advantages and disadvantages in being of the same or different ethnic group as your client, not feeling you need to know everything about other ethnic groups, and avoiding polarization of cultural issues.

11. Accept the notion that the family therapist will need to be creative in the development of appropriate intervention techniques when working with minority populations. With traditional Asian Americans, subtlety and indirectness may be called for rather than direct confrontation and interpretation. Formality in addressing members of the family, especially the father (Mr. Lee rather than Tom), may be more appropriate. For African Americans, a much more interactional approach (as opposed to an instrumental one) in the initial approaches are often determined by cultural/racial/system factors, and the more you understand about these areas, the more effective you will become.

Non-Western Indigenous Methods of Healing: Implications for Counseling and Therapy

$$9$$

Vang Xiong is a former Hmong (Laotian) soldier who, with his wife and child, resettled in Chicago in 1980. The change from his familiar rural surroundings and farm life to an unfamiliar urban area must have produced a severe culture shock. In addition, Vang vividly remembers seeing people killed during his escape from Laos, and he expressed feelings of guilt about having to leave his brothers and sisters behind in that country. Five months after his arrival, the Xiong family moved into a conveniently located apartment, and that is when Vang's problems began:

Vang could not sleep the first night in the apartment, nor the second, nor the third. After three nights of very little sleep, Vang came to see his resettlement worker, a young bilingual Hmong man named Moua Lee. Vang told Moua that the first night he woke suddenly, short of breath, from a dream in which a cat was sitting on his chest. The second night, the room suddenly grew darker, and a figure, like a large black dog, came to his bed and sat on his chest. He could not push the dog off and he grew quickly and dangerously short of breath. The third night, a tall, white-skinned female spirit came into his bedroom from the kitchen and lay on top of him. Her weight made it increasingly difficult for him to breathe, and as he grew frantic and tried to call out he could manage nothing but a whisper. He attempted to turn onto his side, but found he was pinned down. After 15 minutes, the spirit left him, and he awoke, screaming. He was afraid to return to the apartment at night, afraid to fall asleep, and afraid he would die during the night, or that the spirit would make it so that he and his wife could never have another child. He told Moua that once, when he was 15, he had a similar attack; that several times, back in Laos, his elder brother had been visited by a similar spirit, and that his brother was subsequently unable to father children due to his wife's miscarriages and infertility. (Tobin & Friedman, 1983, p. 440)

Moua Lee and mental health workers became very concerned in light of the high incidence of *sudden death syndrome* among Southeast Asian refugees. For some reason, the incidence of unexplained deaths, primarily among Hmong men, would occur within the first 2 years of residence in the United States. Autopsies produced no identifiable cause for the deaths. All the reports were the same: A person in apparently good health went to sleep and died without waking. Often, the victim displayed labored breathing, screams, and frantic movements just before death. With this dire possibility evident for Vang, the mental health staff felt that they lacked the expertise for so complex and potentially dangerous a case. Conventional Western means of treatment for other Hmong clients had proved minimally effective. As a result, they decided to seek the services of Mrs. Thor, a 50-year-old Hmong woman who was widely respected in Chicago's Hmong community as a shaman. The description of the treatment follows.

> *That evening, Vang Xiong was visited in his apartment by Mrs. Thor, who began by asking Vang to tell her what was wrong. She listened to his story, asked a few questions, and then told him she thought she could help. She gathered the Xiong family around the dining room table, upon which she placed some candles alongside many plates of food that Vang's wife had prepared. Mrs. Thor lit the candles, and then began a chant that Vang and his wife knew was an attempt to communicate with spirits. Ten minutes or so after Mrs. Thor had begun chanting, she was so intensely involved in her work that Vang and his family felt free to talk to each other, and to walk about the room without fear of distracting her. Approximately 1 hour after she had begun, Mrs. Thor completed her chanting, announcing that she knew what was wrong. Vang said that she had learned from her spirit that the figures in Vang's dreams who lay on his chest and made it so difficult for him to breathe were the souls of the apartment's previous tenants, who had apparently moved out so abruptly they had left their souls behind. Mrs. Thor constructed a cloak out of newspaper for Vang to wear. She then cut the cloak in two and burned the pieces, sending the spirits on their way with the smoke. She also had Vang crawl through a hoop, and then between two knives, telling him that these maneuvers would make it very hard for spirits to follow. Following these brief ceremonies, the food prepared by Vang's wife was enjoyed by all. The leftover meats were given in payment to Mrs. Thor, and she left, assuring Vang Xiong that his troubles with spirits were over. (Tobin & Friedman, 1983, p. 441)*

Clinical knowledge regarding what is called the Hmong sudden death syndrome indicates that Vang was one of the lucky victims of the syndrome, in that he survived it. Indeed, since undergoing the healing ceremony that released the unhappy spirits, Vang has reported no more problems with nightmares, or with his breathing during sleep. Such a story may appear unbelievable and akin to mysticism to many people. After all, most of us have been trained in a Western ontology that does not embrace indigenous or alternative healing approaches. Indeed, if anything, it actively rejects such approaches as unscientific and supernatural. Mental health professionals are encouraged to rely on sensory information, defined by the physical plane of existence rather than the spiritual plane (Fukuyama & Sevig, 1999; Wallace & Shapiro, 2006). Such a rigid stance is unfortunate and shortsighted because there is much that Western healing can learn from these age-old forms of treatment. Let us briefly analyze the case of Vang Xiong to illustrate what these valuable lessons might be and draw parallels between non-Western and Western healing practices.

The Legitimacy of Culture-Bound Syndromes: Nightmare Deaths and the Hmong Sudden Death Phenomenon

The symptoms experienced by Vang and the frighteningly high number of early Hmong refugees who have died from these so-called nightmare deaths have baffled mental health workers for years. Indeed, researchers at the Federal Center for Disease Control and epidemiologists have studied it, but remain mystified (D. Sue, D. W. Sue, & S. Sue, 2006; Tobin & Friedman, 1983). Such tales bring to mind anthropological literature describing voodoo deaths and *bangungut*, or Oriental nightmare death. What is clear, however, is that these deaths do not appear to have a primary biological basis, and that psychological factors (primarily belief in the imminence of death—either by a curse, as in voodoo suggestion, or some form of punishment and excessive stress) appear to be causative (Moodley, 2005). Beliefs in spirits and spirit possession are not uncommon among many cultures, especially in Southeast Asia (Eliade, 1972; Faiver, Ingersoll, O'Brien, & McNally, 2001). Such worldview differences pose problems for Western-trained mental health professionals who may quickly dismiss these belief systems and impose their own explanations and treatments on culturally diverse clients. Working outside of the belief system of such clients may not have the desired therapeutic effect, and the risk of unintentional harm (in this case the potential death of Vang) is great. That the sudden death phenomenon is a culture-bound reality is being increasingly recognized by Western science (Kamarck & Jennings, 1991). Most researchers now acknowledge that attitudes, beliefs, and emotional states are intertwined and can have a powerful effect on physiological responses and physical well-being. Death from bradycardia (slowing of the heartbeat) seems correlated with feelings of helplessness, as in the case of Vang (there was nothing he could do to get the cat, dog, or white-skinned spirit off his chest).

The text revision of the fourth edition of the American Psychiatric

Table 9.1   **Culture-Bound Syndromes from the *DSM-IV***

Culture-bound syndromes are disorders specific to a cultural group or society but not easily given a DSM diagnosis. These illnesses or afflictions have local names with distinct culturally sanctioned beliefs surrounding causation and treatment. Some of these are briefly described.

Amok. This disorder was first reported in Malaysia but is found also in Laos, the Philippines, Polynesia, Papua New Guinea, and Puerto Rico, as well as among the Navajo. It is a dissociative episode preceded by introspective brooding and then an outburst of violent, aggressive, or homicidal behavior toward people and objects. Persecutory ideas, amnesia, and exhaustion signal a return to the premorbid state.

Ataque de nervios. This disorder is most clearly reported among Latinos from the Caribbean but is recognized in Latin American and Latin Mediterranean groups as well. It involves uncontrollable shouting, attacks of crying, trembling, verbal or physical aggression, and dissociative or seizure-like fainting episodes. The onset is associated with a stressful life event relating to family (e.g., death of a loved one, divorce, conflicts with children).

Brain fag. This disorder is usually experienced by high school or university students in West Africa in response to academic stress. Students state that their brains are fatigued and that they have difficulties in concentrating, remembering, and thinking.

Ghost sickness. Observed among members of American Indian tribes, this disorder is a preoccupation with death and the deceased. It is sometimes associated with witchcraft and includes bad dreams, weakness, feelings of danger, loss of appetite, fainting, dizziness, anxiety, and a sense of suffocation.

Koro. This Malaysian term describes an episode of sudden and intense anxiety that the penis of the male or the vulva and nipples of the female will recede into the body and cause death. It can occur in epidemic proportions in local areas and has been reported in China, Thailand, and other South and East Asian countries.

Mal de ojo. Found primarily in Mediterranean cultures, this term refers to a Spanish phrase that means "evil eye." Children are especially at risk, and symptoms include fitful sleep, crying without apparent cause, diarrhea, vomiting, and fever.

Nervios. This disorder includes a range of symptoms associated with distress, somatic disturbance, and inability to function. Common symptoms include headaches, brain aches, sleep difficulties, nervousness, easy tearfulness, dizziness, and tingling sensations. It is a common idiom of distress among Latinos in the United States and Latin America.

Rootwork. This refers to cultural interpretations of illness ascribed to hexing, witchcraft, sorcery, or the evil influence of another person. Symptoms include generalized anxiety, gastrointestinal complaints, and fear of being poisoned or killed (voodoo death). Roots, spells, or hexes can be placed on people. It is believed that a cure can be manifested via a root doctor who removes the root. Such a belief can be found in the southern United States among both African American and European American populations and in Caribbean societies.

Shen-k'uei (Taiwan); Shenkui (China). This is a Chinese described disorder that involves anxiety and panic symptoms with somatic complaints. There is no identifiable physical cause. Sexual dysfunctions are common (premature ejaculation and impotence). The physical symptoms are attributed to excessive semen loss from frequent intercourse, masturbation, nocturnal emission, or passing of "white turbid urine" believed to contain semen. Excessive semen loss is feared and can be life threatening because it represents one's vital essence.

Table 9.1 continued

Susto. This disorder is associated with fright or soul loss and is a prevalent folk illness among some Latinos in the United States as well as inhabitants of Mexico, Central America, and South America. Susto is attributed to a frightening event that causes the soul to leave the body. Sickness and death may result. Healing is associated with rituals that call the soul back to the body and restore spiritual balance.

Zar. This term is used to describe spirits possessing an individual. Dissociative episodes, shouting, laughing, hitting the head against a wall, weeping, and other demonstrative symptoms are associated with it. It is found in Ethiopia, Somalia, Egypt, Sudan, Iran, and other North African and Middle Eastern societies. People may develop a long-term relationship with the spirit, and their behavior is not considered pathological.

Association's *Diagnostic and Statistical Manual of Mental Disorders* (*DSM-IV-TR;* American Psychiatric Association, 2000) has made initial strides in recognizing the importance of ethnic and cultural factors related to psychiatric diagnosis. The manual warns that mental health professionals who work with immigrant and ethnic minorities must take into account (1) the predominant means of manifesting disorders (e.g., possessing spirits, nerves, fatalism, inexplicable misfortune), (2) the perceived causes or explanatory models, and (3) the preferences for professional and indigenous sources of care. Interestingly, the *DSM-IV-TR* now contains a glossary of culture-bound syndromes in Appendix I (see Table 9.1 for a listing of these disorders). They describe culture-bound syndromes as

> *recurrent, locality-specific patterns of aberrant behavior and troubling experience that may or may not be linked to a particular DSM-IV diagnostic category. Many of these patterns are indigenously considered to be "illnesses," or at least afflictions, and most have local names.... Culture-bound syndromes are generally limited to specific societies or culture areas and are localized, folk, diagnostic categories that frame coherent meanings for certain repetitive, patterned, and troubling sets of experiences and observations. (American Psychiatric Association, 2000, p. 898)*

In summary, it is very important for mental health professionals to become familiar not only with the cultural background of their clients, but to be knowledgeable about specific culture-bound syndromes. A primary danger from lack of cultural understanding is the tendency to overpathologize (overestimate the degree of pathology); the mental health professional would have been wrong in diagnosing Vang as a paranoid schizophrenic suffering from delusions and hallucinations. Most might have prescribed powerful antipsychotic medication or even institutionalization. The fact that he was cured so quickly indicates that such a diagnosis would have been erroneous. Interestingly, it is equally dangerous to underestimate the severity or complexity of a refugee's emotional condition as well.

Causation and Spirit Possession

Vang believed that his problems were related to an attack by undesirable spirits. His story in the following passage gives us some idea about beliefs associated with the fears.

> *The most recent attack in Chicago was not the first encounter my family and I have had with this type of spirit, a spirit we call* Chia. *My brother and I endured similar attacks about six years ago back in Laos. We are susceptible to such attacks because we didn't follow all of the mourning rituals we should have when our parents died. Because we didn't properly honor their memories we have lost contact with their spirits, and thus we are left with no one to protect us from evil spirits. Without our parents' spirits to aid us, we will always be susceptible to spirit attacks. I had hoped flying so far in a plane to come to America would protect me, but it turns out spirits can follow even this far. (Tobin & Friedman, 1983, p. 444)*

Western science remains skeptical of using supernatural explanations to explain phenomena and certainly does not consider the existence of spirits to be scientifically sound. Yet belief in spirits and its parallel relationship to religious, philosophic, and scientific worldviews have existed in every known culture, including the United States (e.g., the witch hunts of Salem, Massachusetts). Among many Southeast Asian groups, it is not uncommon to posit the existence of good and evil spirits, to assume that they are intelligent beings, and to believe that they are able to affect the life circumstances of the living (Fadiman, 1997; E. Lee, 1996). Vang, for example, believed strongly that his problems were due to spirits who were unhappy with him and were punishing him. Interestingly, among the Hmong, good spirits often serve a protective function against evil spirits. Because Vang's parental spirits had deserted him, he believed he was more susceptible to the workings of evil forces. Many cultures believe that a cure can come about only through the aid of a shaman or healer who can reach and communicate with the spirit world via divination skills.

While mental health professionals may not believe in spirits, therapists are similar to the Hmong in their need to explain the troubling phenomena experienced by Vang, and to construe meaning from them. Vang's sleep disturbances, nightmares, and fears can be seen as the result of emotional distress. From a Western perspective, his war experiences, flight, relocation, and survivor stress (not to mention the adjustment to a new country) may all be attributed to combat fatigue (Posttraumatic Stress Disorder, or PTSD) and survivor guilt (Mollica, Wyshak, & Lavelle, 1987; Tobin & Friedman, 1983). Studies on hundreds of thousands of refugees from Southeast Asia suggest that they were severely traumatized during their flight for freedom (Mollica et al., 1987). The most frequent diagnoses for this group were generally Major Affective Disorder and PTSD. In addition to being a combat veteran, Vang is a disaster victim, a survivor of a holocaust that has seen perhaps 200,000 of the approximately 500,000 Hmong die. Vang's sleeplessness, breathing difficulties, paranoid belief that something attacked him in bed, and symptoms of anxiety and depression are the result of extreme trauma and stress. Tobin and Friedman (1983, p. 443) believed that Vang also suffered from survivor's guilt, and concluded,

> *Applying some of the insights of the Holocaust literature to the plight of the Southeast Asian refugees, we can view Vang Xiong's emotional crisis (his breathing and sleeping disorder) as the result not so much of what he suffered as what he did not suffer, of what he was spared.... "Why should I live while others died?" so Vang Xiong, through his symptoms, seemed to be saying, "Why should I sleep comfortably here in America while the people I left behind suffer? How can I claim the right to breathe when so many of my relatives and countrymen breathe no more back in Laos?"*

Even though we might be able to recast Vang's problems in more acceptable psychological terminology, the effective multicultural helping professional requires knowledge of cultural relativism and respect for the belief system of culturally different clients. Respecting another's worldview does not mean that the helping professional needs to subscribe to it. Yet the counselor or therapist must be willing and ready to learn from indigenous models of healing and to function as a facilitator of indigenous support systems or indigenous healing systems (Atkinson, Thompson, & Grant, 1993).

The Shaman as Therapist: Commonalities

It is probably safe to conclude that every society and culture has individuals or groups designated as healers—those who comfort the ailing. Their duties involve not only physical ailments, but those related to psychological distress or behavioral deviance as well (Harner, 1990). While every culture has multiple healers, the shaman in non-Western cultures is perhaps the most powerful of all because only he or she possesses the ultimate magico-religious powers that go beyond the senses (Eliade, 1972). Mrs. Thor was a well-known and respected shaman in the Hmong community of the Chicago area. While her approach to treating Vang (incense, candle burning, newspaper, trance-like chanting, spirit diagnosis, and even her home visit) on the surface might resemble mysticism, there is much in her behavior that is similar to Western psychotherapy. First, as we saw in Chapter 4, the healer's credibility is crucial to the effectiveness of therapy. In this case, Mrs. Thor had all the cultural credentials of a shaman; she was a specialist and professional with long years of training and experience dealing with similar cases. By reputation and behavior, she acted in a manner familiar to Vang and his family. More importantly, she shared their worldview as to the definition of the problem. Second, she showed compassion while maintaining a professional detachment, did not pity or make fun of Vang, avoided premature diagnosis or judgment, and listened to his story carefully. Third, like the Western therapist, she offered herself as the chief instrument of cure. She used her expertise and ability to get in touch with the hidden world of the spirits (in Western terms we might call it the unconscious) and helped Vang to understand (become conscious of) the mysterious power of the spirits (unconscious) to effect a cure.

Because Vang believed in spirits, Mrs. Thor's interpretation that the nightmares and breathing difficulties were spiritual problems was intelligible, desired, and ultimately curative. It is important to note, however, that Vang also continued to receive treatment from the local mental health clinic in coming to grips with the deaths of others (his parents, fellow soldiers, and those of other family members).

In the case of Vang Xiong, both non-Western and Western forms of healing were combined with one another for maximum effect. The presence of a mental health treatment facility that employed bilingual/bicultural practitioners, its vast experience with Southeast Asian immigrants, and its willingness to use indigenous healers provided Vang with a culturally appropriate form of treatment that probably saved his life. Not all immigrants, however, are so fortunate. Witness the following case of the Nguyen family.

A Case of Child Abuse?

Mr. and Mrs. Nguyen and their four children left Vietnam in a boat with 36 other people. Several days later, they were set upon by Thai pirates. The occupants were all robbed of their belongings; some were killed, including two of the Nguyens' children. Nearly all the women were raped repeatedly. The trauma of the event is still very much with the Nguyen family, who now reside in St. Paul, Minnesota. The event was most disturbing to Mr. Nguyen, who had watched two of his children drown and his wife being raped. The pirates had beaten him severely and tied him to the boat railing during the rampage. As a result of his experiences, he continued to suffer feelings of guilt, suppressed rage, and nightmares.

The Nguyen family came to the attention of the school and social service agencies because of suspected child abuse. Their oldest child, 12-year-old Phuoc, came to school one day with noticeable bruises on his back and down his spinal column. In addition, obvious scars from past injuries were observed on the child's upper and lower torso. His gym teacher had seen the bruises and scars and immediately reported them to the school counselor. The school nurse was contacted about the possibility of child abuse, and a conference was held with Phuoc. He denied that he had been hit by his parents and refused to remove his garments when requested to do so. Indeed, he became quite frightened and hysterical about taking off his shirt. Since there was still considerable doubt about whether this was a case of child abuse, the counselor decided to let the matter drop for the moment. Nevertheless, school personnel were alerted to this possibility.

Several weeks later, after 4 days of absence, Phuoc returned to school. The homeroom teacher noticed bruises on Phuoc's forehead and the bridge of his nose. When the incident was reported to the school office, the counselor immediately called Child Protective Services to report a suspected case of child abuse.

Because of the heavy caseload experienced by Child Protective Services, a social worker was unable to visit the family until weeks later. The social worker, Mr. P., called the family and visited the home on a late Thursday afternoon. Mrs. Nguyen greeted Mr. P. upon his arrival. She appeared nervous, tense, and frightened. Her English was poor, and it was difficult to communicate with her. Since Mr. P. had specifically requested to see Mr. Nguyen as well, he inquired about his whereabouts. Mrs. Nguyen answered that he was not feeling well and was in the room downstairs. She said he was having "a bad day," had not been able to sleep last night, and was having flashbacks. In his present condition, he would not be helpful.

When Mr. P. asked about Phuoc's bruises, Mrs. Nguyen did not seem to understand what he was referring to. The social worker explained in detail the reason for his visit. Mrs. Nguyen explained that the scars were due to the beating given to her children by the Thai pirates. She became very emotional about the topic and broke into tears.

While this had some credibility, Mr. P. explained that there were fresh bruises on Phuoc's body as well. Mrs. Nguyen seemed confused, denied that there were new injuries, and denied that they would hurt Phuoc. The social worker pressed Mrs. Nguyen about the new injuries until she suddenly looked up and said, "Thuôc Nam." It was obvious that Mrs. Nguyen now understood what Mr. P. was referring to. When asked to clarify what she meant by the phrase, Mrs. Nguyen pointed at several thin bamboo sticks and a bag of coins wrapped tightly in a white cloth. It looked like a blackjack! She then pointed downstairs in the direction of the husband's room. It was obvious from Mrs. Nguyen's gestures that her husband had used these to beat her son.

There are many similarities between the case of the Nguyen family and that of Vang Xiong. One of the most common experiences of refugees forced to flee their country is the extreme stressors that they experience. Constantly staring into the face of death was, unfortunately, all too common an experience. Seeing loved ones killed, tortured, and raped; being helpless to change or control such situations; living in temporary refugee or resettlement camps; leaving familiar surroundings; and encountering a strange and alien culture can only be described as multiple severe traumas. It is highly likely that many

Cambodian, Hmong/Laotian, and Vietnamese refugees suffer from serious Posttraumatic Stress Disorder and other forms of major affective disorders. Mr. and Mrs. Nguyen's behaviors (flashbacks, desire to isolate the self, emotional fluctuations, anxiety and tenseness) might all be symptoms of PTSD. Accurate understanding of their life circumstances will prevent a tendency to overpathologize or underpathologize their symptoms (Mollica et al., 1987). These symptoms, along with a reluctance to disclose to strangers and discomfort with the social worker, should be placed in the context of the stressors that they experienced and their cultural background. More important, as in the case of the Nguyen family, behaviors should not be interpreted to indicate guilt or a desire not to disclose the truth about child abuse.

Second, mental health professionals must consider potential linguistic and cultural barriers when working with refugees, especially when one lacks both experience and expertise. In this case, it is clear that the teacher, school counselor, school nurse, and even the social worker did not have sufficient understanding or experience in working with Southeast Asian refugees. For example, the social worker's failure to understand Vietnamese phrases and Mrs. Nguyen's limited English proficiency placed serious limitations on their ability to communicate accurately. The social worker might have avoided much of the misunderstanding if an interpreter had been present. In addition, the school personnel may have misinterpreted many culturally sanctioned forms of behavior on the part of the Vietnamese. Phuoc's reluctance to disrobe in front of strangers (the nurse) may have been prompted by cultural taboos rather than by attempts to hide the injuries. Traditional Asian culture dictates strongly that family matters are handled within the family. Many Asians believe that family affairs should not be discussed publicly, and especially not with strangers. Disrobing publicly and telling others about the scars or the trauma of the Thai pirates would not be done readily. Yet such knowledge is required by educators and social service agencies that must make enlightened decisions.

Third, both school and social service personnel are obviously unenlightened about indigenous healing beliefs and practices. In the case of Vang Xiong, we saw how knowledge and understanding of cultural beliefs led to appropriate and helpful treatment. In the case of the Nguyen family, lack of understanding led to charges of child abuse. But is this really a case of child abuse? When Mrs. Nguyen said "Thúôc Nam," what was she referring to? What did the fresh bruises along Phuoc's spinal column, forehead, and bridge of the nose mean? And didn't Mrs. Nguyen admit that her husband used the bamboo sticks and bag of coins to beat Phuoc?

In Southeast Asia, traditional medicine derives from three sources: Western medicine (Thùôc Tay), Chinese or Northern medicine (Thúôc Bac), and Southern medicine (Thúôc Nam). Many forms of these treatments continue to exist among Asian Americans and are even more prevalent among the Vietnamese refugees, who brought the treatments to the United States (Hong & Ham, 2001). Thúôc Nam, or traditional medicine, involves using natural fruits, herbs, plants, animals, and massage to heal the body. Massage treatment is the most common cause of misdiagnosis of child abuse because it leaves bruises on the body. Three common forms of massage treatment are Băt Gió ("catching the wind"), Cao Gió ("scratching the wind," or "coin treatment"), and Giác Hoi ("pressure massage," or "dry cup massage"). The latter involves steaming bamboo tubes so that the insides are low in pressure, applying them to a portion of the skin that has been cut, and sucking out "bad air" or "hot wind." Cao Gió involves rubbing the patient with a mentholated ointment and then using coins or spoons to strike or scrape lightly along the ribs and both sides of the neck and shoulders. Băt Gió involves using both thumbs to rub the temples and massaging toward the bridge of the nose at least 20 times. Fingers are used to pinch the bridge of the nose. All three treatments leave bruises on the parts of the body treated.

If the social worker could have understood Mrs. Nguyen, he would have known that Phuoc's 4 day absence from school was due to illness, and that he was treated by his parents via traditional folk medicine. Massage treatments are a widespread custom practiced not only by Vietnamese, but also by Cambodians, Laotians, and Chinese. These treatments are aimed at curing a host of physical ailments such as colds, headaches, backaches, and fevers. In the mind of the practitioner, such treatments have nothing to do with child abuse. Yet, the question still remains: Is it considered child abuse when traditional healing practices result in bruises? This is a very difficult question to answer because it raises a larger question: Can culture justify a practice, especially when it is harmful? While unable to answer this last question directly (we encourage you to dialogue about it), we point out that many medical practitioners in California do not consider it child abuse because (1) medical literature reveals no physical complications as a result of Thúôc Nam; (2) the intent is not to hurt the child but to help him or her; and (3) it is frequently used in conjunction with Western medicine. However, we would add that health professionals and educators have a responsibility to educate parents concerning the potential pitfalls of many folk remedies and indigenous forms of treatment.

The Principles of Indigenous Healing

Ever since the beginning of human existence, all societies and cultural groups have developed not only their own explanations of abnormal behaviors, but also their culture-specific ways of dealing with human problems and distress (Harner, 1990; Solomon & Wane, 2005). Within the United States, counseling and psychotherapy are the predominant psychological healing methods. In other cultures, however, indigenous healing approaches continue to be widely used. While there are similarities between Euro-American helping systems and the indigenous practices of many cultural groups, there are major dissimilarities as well. Western forms of counseling, for example, rely on sensory information defined by the physical plane of reality (Western science), while most indigenous methods rely on the spiritual plane of existence in seeking a cure. In keeping with the cultural encapsulation of our profession, Western healing has been slow to acknowledge and learn from these age-old forms of wisdom (Constantine, Myers, Kindaichi, & Moore, 2004; C. C. Lee, 1996). In its attempt to become culturally responsive, however, the mental health field must begin to put aside the biases of Western science, to acknowledge the existence of intrinsic help-giving networks, and to incorporate the legacy of ancient wisdom that may be contained in indigenous models of healing.

The work and writings of Lee (C. C. Lee, 1996; Lee & Armstrong, 1995; Lee, Oh, & Mountcastle, 1992) are especially helpful in this regard. Lee has studied what is called the *universal shamanic tradition,* which encompasses the centuries-old recognition of healers within a community. The anthropological term *shaman* refers to people often called witches, witch doctors, wizards, medicine men or women, sorcerers, and magic men or women. These individuals are believed to possess the power to enter an altered state of consciousness and journey to other planes of existence beyond the physical world during their healing rituals (Moodley, 2005). Such was the case of Mrs. Thor, a shaman who journeyed to the spirit world in order to find a cure for Vang.

A study of indigenous healing in 16 non-Western countries found that three approaches were often used (Lee et al., 1992). First, there is heavy reliance on the use of communal, group, and family networks to shelter the disturbed individual (Saudi Arabia), to problem solve in a group context (Nigeria), and to reconnect them with family or significant others (Korea). Second, spiritual and religious beliefs and traditions of the community are used in the healing process. Examples include reading verses from the Koran and using religious houses or churches. Third, use of shamans (called *piris* and *fakirs* in Pakistan and Sudan) who are perceived to be the keepers of timeless wisdom constitutes the norm. In many cases, the person conducting a healing ceremony may be a respected elder of the community or a family member.

An excellent example that incorporates these approaches is the Native Hawaiian *ho'oponopono* healing ritual (Nishihara, 1978; Rezentes, 2006). Translated literally, the word means "a setting to right, to make right, to correct." In cultural context, *ho'oponopono* attempts to restore and maintain good relations among family members, and between the family and the supernatural powers. It is a kind of family conference (family therapy) aimed at restoring good and healthy harmony in the family. Many Native Hawaiians consider it to be one of the soundest methods of restoring and maintaining good relations that any society has ever developed. Such a ceremonial activity usually occurs among members of the immediate family, but may involve the extended family and even nonrelatives if they were involved in the *pilikia* (trouble). The process of healing includes the following:

1. The *ho'oponopono* begins with *pule weke* (opening prayer) and ends with *pule ho'opau* (closing prayer). The *pule* creates the atmosphere for the healing and involves asking the family gods for guidance. These gods are not asked to intervene, but to grant wisdom, understanding, and honesty.

2. The ritual elicits *'oia'i'o* or "truth telling," sanctioned by the gods, and makes compliance among participants a serious matter. The leader states the problem, prays for spiritual fusion among members, reaches out to resistant family members, and attempts to unify the group.

3. Once this occurs, the actual work begins through *mahiki*, a process of getting to the problems. Transgressions, obligations, righting the wrongs, and forgiveness are all aspects of *ho'oponopono*. The forgiving/releasing/severing of wrongs, the hurts, and the conflicts produces a deep sense of resolution.

4. Following the closing prayer, the family participates in *pani*, the termination ritual in which food is offered to the gods and to the participants.

In general, we can see several principles of indigenous Hawaiian healing: (1) Problems reside in relationships with people and spirits; (2) harmony and balance in the family and in nature are desirable; (3) healing must involve the entire group and not just an individual; (4) spirituality, prayer, and ritual are important aspects of healing; (5) the healing process comes from a respected elder of the family; and (6) the method of healing is indigenous to the culture (Rezentes, 2006).

Indigenous healing can be defined as helping beliefs and practices that originate within the culture or society. It is not transported from other regions, and it is designed for treating the inhabitants of the given group. Those who study indigenous psychologies do not make an a priori assumption that one particular perspective is superior to another (Mikulas, 2006). The Western ontology of healing (counseling/therapy), however, does consider its methods to be more advanced and scientifically grounded than those found in many cultures. Western healing has traditionally operated from several assumptions: (1) reality consists of distinct and separate units or objects (the therapist and client, the observer and observed); (2) reality consists of what can be observed and measured via the five senses; (3) space and time are fixed and absolute constructs of reality; and (4) science operates from universal principles and is culture-free (Highlen, 1996). While these guiding assumptions of Western science have contributed much to human knowledge and to the improvement of the human condition, most non-Western indigenous psychologies appear to operate from a different perspective. For example, many non-Western cultures do not separate the observer from the observed, and believe that all life forms are interrelated with one another, including mother nature and the cosmos; that the nature of reality transcends the senses; that space and time are not fixed; and that much of reality is culture-bound (Walsh & Shapiro, 2006). Let us briefly explore several of these parallel assumptions and see how they are manifested in indigenous healing practices.

Holistic Outlook, Interconnectedness, and Harmony

The concepts of separation, isolation, and individualism are hallmarks of the Euro-American worldview. On an individual basis, modern psychology takes a reductionist approach to describing the human condition (i.e., id, ego, and superego; belief, knowledge, and skills; cognitions, emotions, and behaviors). In Western science, the experimental design is considered the epitome of methods used to ask and answer questions about the human condition or the universe. The search for cause and effect is linear and allows us to identify the independent variables, the dependent variables, and the effects of extraneous variables that we attempt to control. It is analytical and reductionist in character. The attempt to maintain objectivity, autonomy, and independence in understanding human behavior is also stressed. Such tenets have resulted in separation of the person from the group (valuing of individualism and uniqueness), science from spirituality, and man/woman from the universe.

Most non-Western indigenous forms of healing take a holistic outlook on well-being in that they make minimal distinctions between physical and mental functioning and believe strongly in the unity of spirit, mind, and matter. The interrelatedness of life forms, the environment, and the cosmos is a given. As a result, the indigenous peoples of the world tend to conceptualize reality differently. The psychosocial unit of operation for many culturally diverse groups, for example, is not the individual, but the group (collectivism). In many cultures, acting in an autonomous and independent manner is seen as the problem because it creates disharmony within the group.

Illness, distress, or problematic behaviors are seen as an imbalance in people relationships, a disharmony between the individual and his or her group, or as a lack of synchrony with internal or external forces. Harmony and balance are the healer's goal. Among American Indians, for example, harmony with nature is symbolized by the circle, or hoop of life (McCormick, 2005; Sutton & Broken Nose, 2005). Mind, body, spirit, and nature are seen as a single unified entity with little separation between the realities of life, medicine, and religion. All forms of nature, not just the living, are to be revered because they reflect the creator or deity. Illness is seen as a break in the hoop of life, an imbalance, or a separation between the elements. Many indigenous beliefs come from a metaphysical tradition. They accept the interconnectedness of cosmic forces in the form of energy or subtle matter (less dense than the physical) that surrounds and penetrates the physical body and the world. Both the ancient Chinese practice of acupuncture and chakras in Indian yoga philosophy involve the use of subtle matter to rebalance and heal the body and mind (Highlen, 1996). Chinese medical theory is concerned with the balance of yin (cold) and yang (hot) in the body, and it is believed that strong emotional states, as well as an imbalance in the type of foods eaten, may create illness (So, 2005). As we saw in the case of Phuoc Nguyen, treatment might involve eating specific types or combinations of foods, or using massage treatment to suck out "bad" or "hot" air. Such concepts of illness and health can also be found in the Greek theory of balancing body fluids (blood, phlegm, black bile, and yellow bile; Bankart, 1997).

Likewise, the Afrocentric perspective also teaches that human beings are part of a holistic fabric—that they are interconnected and should be oriented toward collective rather than individual survival (Boyd-Franklin, 2003; Graham, 2005). The indigenous Japanese assumptions and practices of Naikan and Morita therapy attempt to move clients toward being more in tune with others and society, to move away from individualism, and to move toward interdependence, connectedness, and harmony with others (Bankart, 1997; C. P. Chen, 2005). Naikan therapy, which derives from Buddhist practice, requires the client to reflect on three aspects of human relationships: (1) what other people have done for them, (2) what they have done for others, and (3) how they cause difficulties to others (Wallace & Shapiro, 2006). The overall goal is to expand awareness of how much we receive from others, how much gratitude is due them, and how little we demonstrate such gratitude. This ultimately leads to a realization of the interdependence of the parts to the whole. Working for the good of the group ultimately benefits the individual.

Belief in Metaphysical Levels of Existence

Some time back two highly popular books—*Embraced by the Light* (Eadie, 1992) and *Saved by the Light* (Brinkley, 1994)—and several television specials described fascinating cases of near-death experiences. All had certain commonalities; the individuals who were near death felt like they were leaving their physical bodies, observed what was happening around them, saw a bright beckoning light, and journeyed to higher levels of existence. Although the popularity of such books and programs might indicate that the American public is inclined to believe in such phenomena, science has been unable to validate these personal accounts and remains skeptical of their existence. Yet many societies and non-Western cultures accept, as given, the existence of different levels or planes of consciousness, experience, or existence. They believe the means of understanding and ameliorating the causes of illness or problems of life are often found in a plane of reality separate from the physical world of existence.

Asian psychologies posit detailed descriptions of states of consciousness and outline developmental levels of enlightenment that extend beyond that of Western psychology. Asian perspectives concentrate less on psychopathology and more on enlightenment and ideal mental health (Pankhania, 2005; Walsh & Vaughan, 1993). The normal state of consciousness, in many ways, is not considered optimal and may be seen as a "psychopathology of the average" (Maslow, 1968). Moving to higher states of consciousness has the effect of enhancing perceptual sensitivity and clarity, concentration, and sense of identity, as well as emotional, cognitive, and perceptual processes. Such movement, according to Asian philosophy, frees one from the negative pathogenic forces of life. Attaining enlightenment and liberation can be achieved through the classic practices of meditation and yoga. Research findings indicate that they are the most widely used of all therapies (Walsh & Shapiro, 2006). They have been shown to reduce anxiety, specific phobias, and substance abuse (Kwee, 1990; Shapiro, 1982; West, 1987); to benefit those with medical problems by reducing blood pressure and aiding in the management of chronic pain (Kabat-Zinn, 1990); to enhance self-confidence, sense of control, marital satisfaction, and so on (Alexander, Rainforth, & Gelderloos, 1991); and to extend longevity (Alexander, Langer, Newman, Chandler, & Davies, 1989). Today, meditation and yoga in the United States have become accepted practices among millions, especially for relaxation and stress management. For practitioners of meditation and yoga, altered states of consciousness are unquestioned aspects of reality.

According to some cultures, nonordinary reality states allow some healers to access an invisible world surrounding the physical one. Puerto Ricans, for example, believe in *espiritismo* (spiritism), a world where spirits can have major impacts on the people residing in the physical world (Chavez, 2005). *Espiritistas,* or mediums, are culturally sanctioned indigenous healers who possess special faculties allowing them to intervene positively or negatively on behalf of their clients. Many cultures strongly believe that human destiny is often decided in the domain of the spirit world. Mental illness may be attributed to the activities of hostile spirits, often in reaction to transgressions of the victim or the victim's family (C. C. Lee, 1996; Mullavey-O'Byrne, 1994). As in the case of Mrs. Thor, shamans, mediums, or indigenous healers often enter these realities on behalf of their clients in order to seek answers, to enlist the help of the spirit world, or to aid in realigning the spiritual energy field that surrounds the body and extends throughout the universe. Ancient

Chinese methods of healing and Hindu chakras also acknowledge another reality that parallels the physical world. Accessing this world allows the healer to use these special energy centers to balance and heal the body and mind. Occasionally, the shaman may aid the helpee or novice to access that plane of reality so that he or she may find the solutions. The *vision quest*, in conjunction with the sweat lodge experience, is used by some American Indians as religious renewal or as a rite of passage (Heinrich, Corbin, & Thomas., 1990; D. Smith, 2005). Behind these uses, however, is the human journey to another world of reality. The ceremony of the vision quest is intended to prepare the young man for the proper frame of mind; it includes rituals and sacred symbols, prayers to the Great Spirit, isolation, fasting, and personal reflection. Whether in a dream state or in full consciousness, another world of reality is said to reveal itself. Mantras, chants, meditation, and the taking of certain drugs (peyote) all have as their purpose a journey into another world of existence (Duran, 2006).

Spirituality in Life and the Cosmos

Native American Indians look on all things as having life, spiritual energy, and importance. A fundamental belief is that all things are connected. The universe consists of a balance among all of these things and a continuous flow of cycling of this energy. Native American Indians believe that we have a sacred relationship with the universe that is to be honored. All things are connected, all things have life, and all things are worthy of respect and reverence. Spirituality focuses on the harmony that comes from our connection with all parts of the universe—in which everything has the purpose and value exemplary of personhood, including plants (e.g., "tree people"), the land ("Mother Earth"), the winds ("the Four Powers"), "Father Sky," "Grandfather Sun," "Grandmother Moon," "The Red Thunder Boys." Spiritual being essentially requires only that we seek our place in the universe; everything else will follow in good time. Because everyone and everything was created with a specific purpose to fulfill, no one should have the power to interfere or to impose on others the best path to follow (J. T. Garrett & Garrett, 1994, p. 187).

The sacred Native American beliefs concerning spirituality are a truly alien concept to modern Euro-American thinking. The United States has had a long tradition in believing that one's religious beliefs should not enter into scientific or rational decisions (Duran, 2006). Incorporating religion in the rational decision-making process or in the conduct of therapy has generally been seen as unscientific and unprofessional. The schism between religion and science occurred centuries ago and has resulted in a split between science/psychology and religion (Fukuyama & Sevig, 1999). This is reflected in the oft-quoted phrase "separation of Church and State." The separation has become a serious barrier to mainstream psychology's incorporation of indigenous forms of healing into mental health practice, especially when religion is confused with spirituality. While people may not have a formal religion, indigenous helpers believe that spirituality is an intimate aspect of the human condition. While Western psychology acknowledges the behavioral, cognitive, and affective realms, it only makes passing reference to the spiritual realm of existence. Yet indigenous helpers believe that spirituality transcends time and space, mind and body, and our behaviors, thoughts, and feelings (Lee & Armstrong, 1995; D. Smith 2005).

These contrasting worldviews are perhaps most clearly seen in definitions of "the good life," and how our values are manifested in evaluating the worth of others. In the United States, for example, the pursuit of happiness is most likely manifested in material wealth and physical well-being, while other cultures value spiritual or intellectual goals. The worth of a person is anchored in the number of separate properties he or she owns, and in their net worth and ability to acquire increasing wealth. Indeed, it is often assumed that such an accumulation of wealth is a sign of divine approval (Condon & Yousef, 1975). In cultures where spiritual goals are strong the worth of a person is unrelated to materialistic possessions, but rather resides within individuals, emanates from their spirituality, and is a function of whether they live the "right life." People from capitalistic cultures often do not understand self-immolations and other acts of suicide in countries such as India. They are likely to make statements such as "life is not valued there" or, better yet, "life is cheap." These statements indicate a lack of understanding about actions that arise from cultural forces rather than personal frustrations; they may be symbolic of a spiritual-valuing rather than a material-valuing orientation.

One does not have to look beyond the United States, however, to see such spiritual orientations; many racial/ethnic minority groups in this country are strongly spiritual. African Americans, Asian Americans, Latino/Hispanic Americans, and Native Americans all place strong emphasis on the interplay and interdependence of spiritual life and healthy functioning. Puerto Ricans, for example, may sacrifice material satisfaction in favor of values pertaining to the spirit and soul. The Lakota Sioux often say *Mitakuye Oyasin* at the end of a prayer or as a salutation. Translated, it means "to all my relations," which acknowledges the spiritual bond between the speaker and all people present, and extends to forebears, the tribe, the family of man, and mother nature. It speaks to the philosophy that all life forces, Mother Earth, and the cosmos are sacred beings, and that the spiritual is the thread that binds all together.

Likewise, a strong spiritual orientation has always been a major aspect of life in Africa, and this was also true during the slavery era in the United States.

Highly emotional religious services conducted during slavery were of great importance in dealing with oppression. Often signals as to the time and place of an escape were given then. Spirituals contained hidden messages and a language of resistance (e.g., "Wade in the Water" and "Steal Away"). Spirituals (e.g., "Nobody Knows the Trouble I've Seen") and the ecstatic celebrations of Christ's gift of salvation provided Black slaves with outlets for expressing feelings of pain, humiliation, and anger. (Hines & Boyd-Franklin, 1996, p. 74)

The African American church has a strong influence over the lives of Black people, and is often the hub of religious, social, economic, and political life. Religion is not separated from the daily functions of the church, as it acts as a complete support system for the African American family with the minister, deacons, deaconesses, and church members operating as one big family. A strong sense of peoplehood is fostered via social activities, choirs, Sunday school, health-promotion classes, day care centers, tutoring programs, and counseling. To many African Americans the road to mental health and the prevention of mental illness lie in the health potentialities of their spiritual life.

Mental health professionals are becoming increasingly open to the potential benefits of spirituality as a means for coping with hopelessness, identity issues, and feelings of powerlessness (Fukuyama & Sevig, 1999). As an example of this movement, the Association for Counselor Education and Supervision (ACES) recently adopted a set of competencies related to spirituality. They define spirituality as

the animating force in life, represented by such images as breath, wind, vigor, and courage. Spirituality is the infusion and drawing out of spirit in one's life. It is experienced as an active and passive process. Spirituality is also described as a capacity and tendency that is innate and unique to all persons. This spiritual tendency moves the individual towards knowledge, love, meaning, hope, transcendence, connectedness, and compassion. Spirituality includes one's capacity for creativity, growth, and the development of a values system. Spirituality encompasses the religious, spiritual, and transpersonal. (American Counseling Association, 1995, p. 30)

Interestingly enough, it appears that many in the United States are experiencing a "spiritual hunger," or a strong need to reintegrate spiritual or religious themes into their lives (Gallup, 1995; Hage, 2004; Thoresen, 1998). For example, it appears that there is a marked discrepancy between what patients want from their doctors and what doctors supply. Often, patients want to talk about the spiritual aspects of their illness and treatment, but doctors are either unprepared or disinclined to do so (Hage, 2006). Likewise, most mental health professionals feel equally uncomfortable, disinclined, or unprepared to speak with their clients about religious or spiritual matters.

Thoresen (1998) reported in a meta-analysis of over 200 published studies that the relationship between spirituality and health is highly positive. Those with higher levels of spirituality have lower disease risk, fewer physical health problems, and higher levels of psychosocial functioning. It appears that people require faith as well as reason to be healthy, and that psychology may profit from allowing the spirit to rejoin matters of the mind and body (Strawbridge, Cohen, Shema, & Kaplan, 1997).

In general, indigenous healing methods have much to offer to Euro-American forms of mental health practice. The contributions are valuable not only because multiple belief systems now exist in our society, but also because counseling and psychotherapy have historically neglected the spiritual dimension of human existence. Our heavy reliance on science and on the reductionist approach to treating clients has made us view human beings and human behavior as composed of separate noninteracting parts (cognitive, behavioral, and affective). There has been a failure to recognize our spiritual being and to take a holistic outlook on life. Indigenous models of healing remind us of these shortcomings and challenge us to look for answers in realms of existence beyond the physical world.

Implications for Clinical Practice

We have repeatedly stressed that the worldviews of culturally diverse clients may often be worlds apart from the dominant society. When culturally diverse clients attribute disorders to causes quite alien from Euro-American diagnosis, when their definitions of a healer are different from that of conventional therapists, and when the role behaviors (process of therapy) are not perceived as therapeutic, major difficulties are likely to occur in the provision of therapeutic services.

As a Western-trained therapist, for example, how would you treat clients who believed (1) that their mental problems were due to spirit possession, (2) that only a shaman with inherited powers could deal with the problem, and (3) that a cure could only be effected via a formal ritual (chanting, incense burning, symbolic sacrifice, etc.) and a journey into the spirit world? Most of us have had very little experience with indigenous methods of treatment and would find great difficulty in working effectively with such clients. There are, however, some useful guidelines that might help bridge the gap between contemporary forms of therapy and traditional non-Western indigenous healing.

1. Do not invalidate the indigenous belief systems of your culturally diverse client. On the surface, the assumptions of indigenous healing methods might appear radically different from our own. When we en-

counter them, we are often shocked, find such beliefs to be unscientific, and are likely to negate, invalidate, or dismiss them. Such an attitude will invalidate our clients as well. Entertaining alternative realities does not mean that the therapist must subscribe to that belief system. It does mean, however, that the helping professional must avoid being judgmental. This will encourage and allow the client to share his or her story more readily, to feel validated, and to encourage the building of mutual respect and trust. Remember that cultural storytelling and personal narratives have always been an intimate process of helping in all cultures.

2. Become knowledgeable about indigenous beliefs and healing practices. Therapists have a professional responsibility to become knowledgeable and conversant about the assumptions and practices of indigenous healing so that a process of desensitization and normalization can occur. By becoming knowledgeable and understanding of indigenous helping approaches, the therapist will avoid equating differences with deviance. Despite different explanations, many similarities exist between Western and non-Western healing practices.

3. Realize that learning about indigenous healing and beliefs entails experiential or lived realities. While reading books about non-Western forms of healing and attending seminars and lectures on the topic is valuable and helpful, understanding culturally different perspectives must be supplemented by lived experience. We suggest that you consider attending cultural events, meetings, and activities of the different cultural groups in your community. Such actions allow you to observe culturally different individuals interacting in their community, and to see how their values are expressed in relationships.

4. Avoid overpathologizing and underpathologizing a culturally diverse client's problems. A therapist or counselor who is culturally unaware and who believes primarily in a universal psychology may often be culturally insensitive and inclined to see differences as deviance. They may be guilty of overpathologizing a culturally different client's problems by seeing it as more severe and pathological than it truly may be. There is also a danger, however, of underpathologizing a culturally diverse client's symptoms. While being understanding of a client's cultural context, having knowledge of culture-bound syndromes, and being aware of cultural relativism are desirable, being oversensitive to these factors may predispose the therapist to minimize problems.

5. Be willing to consult with traditional healers or make use of their services. Mental health professionals must be willing and able to form partnerships with indigenous healers, or develop community liaisons. Such an outreach has several advantages: (1) Traditional healers may provide knowledge and insight into client populations that would prove of

value to the delivery of mental health services; (2) such an alliance will ultimately enhance the cultural credibility of therapists; and (3) it allows for referral to traditional healers (shamans, religious leaders, etc.) when treatment is rooted in cultural traditions.

6. Recognize that spirituality is an intimate aspect of the human condition and a legitimate aspect of mental health work. Spirituality is a belief in a higher power, which allows us to make meaning of life and the universe. It may or may not be linked to a formal religion, but there is little doubt that it is a powerful force in the human condition. A counselor or therapist who does not feel comfortable dealing with the spiritual needs of clients, or who believes in an artificial separation of the spirit (soul) from the everyday life of the culturally different client, may not be providing the needed help. Just as therapists might inquire about the physical health of their clients, they should feel free and comfortable to inquire about their client's values and beliefs as they relate to spirituality. We do not, however, advocate indoctrination of the client nor prescribing any particular pathway to embracing, validating, or expressing spirituality and spiritual needs.

7. Be willing to expand your definition of the helping role to community work and involvement. More than anything else, indigenous healing is community oriented and focused. Culturally competent mental health professionals must begin to expand their definition of the helping role to encompass a greater community involvement. The in-the-office setting is often nonfunctional in minority communities. Culturally sensitive helping requires making home visits, going to community centers, and visiting places of worship and other areas within the community. The type of help most likely to prevent mental health problems allow clients to build and maintain healthy connections with their family, their god(s), and their universe.

Racial/Cultural Identity Development in Multicultural Counseling and Therapy

Racial/Cultural Identity Development in People of Color: Therapeutic Implications

10

Chapter

For nearly all my life I have never seriously attempted to dissect my feelings and attitudes about being a Japanese American woman. Aborted attempts were made, but they were never brought to fruition, because it was unbearably painful. Having been born and raised in Arizona, I had no Asian friends. I suspect that given an opportunity to make some, I would have avoided them anyway. That is because I didn't want to have anything to do with being Japanese American. Most of the Japanese images I saw were negative. Japanese women were ugly; they had "cucumber legs," flat yellow faces, small slanty eyes, flat chests, and were stunted in growth. The men were short and stocky, sneaky and slimy, clumsy, inept, "wimpy looking," and sexually emasculated. I wanted to be tall, slender, large eyes, full lips, and elegant looking; I wasn't going to be typical Oriental!

At Cal [University of California, Berkeley], I've been forced to deal with my Yellow-White identity. There are so many "yellows" here that I can't believe it. I've come to realize that many White prejudices are deeply ingrained in me; so much so that they are unconscious.... To accept myself as a total person, I also have to accept my Asian identity as well. But what is it? I just don't know. Are they the images given me through the filter of White America, or are they the values and desires of my parents?...

Yesterday, I had a rude awakening. For the first time in my life I went on a date with a Filipino boy. I guess I shouldn't call him a "boy," as my ethnic studies teacher says it is derogatory toward Asians and Blacks. I only agreed to go because he seemed different from the other "Orientals" on campus. (I guess I shouldn't use that word either.) He's president of his Asian fraternity, very athletic and outgoing.... When he asked me, I figured, "Why not?" It'll be a good experience to see what its like to date an Asian boy. Will he be like White guys who will try to seduce me, or will he be too afraid to make any move when it comes to sex?... We went to San Francisco's Fisherman's Wharf for lunch. We were seated and our orders were taken before two other White women. They were, however, served first. This was painfully apparent to us, but I wanted to pretend that it was just a mixup. My friend, however, was less forgiving and made a public fuss with the waiter. Still, it took an inordinate amount of time for us to get our lunches, and the filets were overcooked (purposely?). My date made a very public scene by placing a tip on the table, and then returning to retrieve it. I was both embarrassed, but proud of his actions.

This incident and others made me realize several things. For all my life I have attempted to fit into White society. I have tried to convince myself that I was different, that I was like all my other White classmates, and that prejudice and discrimination didn't exist for me. I wonder how I could have been so oblivious to prejudice and racism. I now realize that I cannot escape from my ethnic heritage and from the way people see me. Yet I don't know how to go about resolving many of my feelings and conflicts. While I like my newly found Filipino "male" friend (he is sexy), I continue to have difficulty seeing myself married to anyone other than a White man. (Excerpts from a Nisei student journal, 1989)

This Nisei (third-generation) Japanese American female is experiencing a racial awakening that has strong implications for her racial/cultural identity development. Her previous belief systems concerning Euro-Americans and Asian Americans are being challenged by social reality and the experiences of being a visible racial/ethnic minority.

First, a major theme involving societal portrayals of Asian Americans is clearly expressed in the student's beliefs about racial/cultural characteristics: She describes the Asian American male and female in a highly negative manner. She seems to have internalized these beliefs and to be using White standards to judge Asian Americans as being either desirable or undesirable. For the student, the process of incorporating these standards has not only attitudinal but behavioral consequences as well. In Arizona, she would not have considered making Asian American friends even if the opportunity presented itself. In her mind, she was not a "typical Oriental"; she disowned or felt ashamed of her ethnic heritage; and she even concludes that she would not consider marrying anyone but a White male.

Second, her denial that she is not an Asian American is beginning to crumble. Being immersed on a campus in which many other fellow Asian Americans attend forces her to explore ethnic identity issues—a process she has been able to avoid while living in a predominantly White area. In the past, when she encountered prejudice or discrimination, she had been able to deny it or to rationalize it away. The differential treatment she received at a restaurant and her male friend's labeling it as "discrimination" makes such a conclusion inescapable. The shattering of illusions is manifest in a realization that (1) despite her efforts to "fit in," it is not enough to gain social acceptance among many White Americans; (2) she cannot escape her racial/cultural heritage; and (3) she has been brainwashed into believing that one group is superior over another.

Third, the student's internal struggle to cast off the cultural conditioning of her past and the attempts to define her ethnic identity are both painful and conflicting. When she refers to her "Yellow-White" identity, writes about the negative images of Asian American males but winds up dating one, uses the terms "Oriental" and "boy" (in reference to her Asian male friend) but acknowledges their derogatory racist nature, describes Asian men as "sexually emasculated" but sees her Filipino date as "athletic," "outgoing," and "sexy," expresses embarrassment at confronting the waiter about discrimination but feels proud of her Asian male friend for doing so, and states that she finds him attractive but could never consider marrying anyone but a White man, we have clear evidence of the internal turmoil she is undergoing. Understanding the process by which racial/cultural identity develops in persons of color is crucial for effective multicultural counseling/therapy.

Fourth, it is clear that the Japanese American female is a victim of ethnocentric monoculturalism. As we mentioned previously, the problem being experienced by the student does not reside in her, but in our society. It resides in a society that portrays racial/ethnic minority characteristics as inferior, primitive, deviant, pathological, or undesirable. The resulting damage strikes at the self-esteem and self/group identity of many culturally different individuals in our society; many, like the student, may come to believe that their racial/cultural heritage or characteristics are burdens to be changed or overcome. Understanding racial/cultural identity development and its relationship to therapeutic practice are the goals of this chapter.

Racial/Cultural Identity Development Models

One of the most promising approaches to the field of multicultural counseling/therapy has been the work on racial/cultural identity development among minority groups (Atkinson, Morten, et al., 1998; Cross, 1971, 1995, 2001; Helms, 1984, 1995; Kim, 1981; Ruiz, 1990). Most would agree that Asian Americans, African Americans, Latino/Hispanic Americans, and American Indians have a distinct cultural heritage that makes each different from the other. Yet such cultural distinctions can lead to a monolithic view of minority group attitudes and behaviors (Atkinson, Morten et al., 1998). The erroneous belief that all Asians are the same, all Blacks are the same, all Hispanics are the same, or all American Indians are the same has led to numerous therapeutic problems.

First, therapists may often respond to the culturally diverse client in a very stereotypic manner and fail to recognize within-group or individual differences. For example, research indicates that Asian American clients seem to prefer and benefit most from a highly structured and directive approach rather than an insight/feeling-oriented one (Hong & Domokos-Cheng Ham, 2001; Root, 1998; Sandhu, Leung, & Tang, 2003). While such approaches may generally be effective, they are often blindly applied without regard for possible differences in client attitudes, beliefs, and behaviors. Likewise, conflicting findings in the literature regarding whether people of color prefer therapists of their own race seem to be a function of our failure to make such distinctions. Preference for a racially or ethnically similar therapist may really be a function of the cultural/racial identity of the minority person (within-group differences) rather than of race or ethnicity per se.

Second, the strength of racial/cultural identity models lies in their potential diagnostic value (Helms, 1984; Vandiver, 2001). Premature termination rates among minority clients may be attributed to the inappropriateness of transactions that occur between the helping professional and the culturally diverse client. Research now suggests that reactions to counseling, the counseling process, and counselors are influenced by cultural/racial identity and are not simply linked to minority group membership. The high failure-to-return rate of many clients seems to be intimately connected to the mental health professional's inability to assess the cultural identity of clients accurately.

A third important contribution derived from racial identity models is their acknowledgment of sociopolitical influences in shaping minority identity (à la the Nisei student). Most therapeutic approaches often neglect their potential sociopolitical nature. The early models of racial identity development all incorporated the effects of racism and prejudice (oppression) upon the identity transformation of their victims. Vontress (1971), for instance, theorized that African Americans moved through decreasing levels of dependence on White society to emerging identification with Black culture and society (Colored, Negro, and Black). Other similar models for Blacks have been proposed (W. E. Cross, 1971; W. S. Hall, Cross, & Freedle, 1972; B. Jackson, 1975; C. W. Thomas, 1970, 1971). The fact that other minority groups such as Asian Americans (Maykovich, 1973; D. W. Sue & S. Sue, 1971a; S. Sue & D. W. Sue, 1971b), Hispanics (A. S. Ruiz, 1990; Szapocznik, Santisteban, Kurtines, Hervis, & Spencer, 1982), women (Downing & Roush, 1985; McNamara & Rickard, 1989), lesbians/gays (Cass, 1979), and disabled individuals (Olkin, 1999) have similar processes may indicate experiential validity for such models as they relate to various oppressed groups.

Black Identity Development Models

Early attempts to define a process of minority identity transformation came primarily through the works of Black social scientists and educators (W. E. Cross, 1971; B. Jackson, 1975; C. W. Thomas, 1971). While there are several Black identity development models, the Cross model of psychological nigrescence (the process of becoming Black) is perhaps the most influential and well documented (W. E. Cross, 1971, 1991, 1995; W. S. Hall et al., 1972). The original Cross model was developed during the civil rights movement and delineates a five-stage process in which Blacks in the United States move from a White frame of reference to a positive Black frame of reference: *pre-encounter, encounter, immersion-emersion, internalization, and internalization-commitment*. The *pre-encounter* stage is characterized by individuals (African Americans) who consciously or unconsciously devalue their own Blackness and concurrently value White values and ways. There is a strong desire to assimilate and acculturate into White society. Blacks at this stage evidence self-hate, low self-esteem, and poor mental health (Vandiver, 2001). In the encounter stage, a two-step process begins to occur. First, the individual encounters a profound crisis or event that challenges his or her previous mode of thinking and behaving; second, the Black person begins to reinterpret the world, resulting in a shift in worldviews. Cross points out how the slaying of Martin Luther King, Jr. was such a significant experience for many African Americans. The person experiences both guilt and anger over being brainwashed by White society. In the third stage, immersion-emersion, the person withdraws from the dominant culture and becomes immersed in African American culture. Black pride begins to develop, but internalization of positive attitudes toward one's own Blackness is minimal. In the emersion phase, feelings of guilt and anger begin to dissipate with an increasing sense of pride. The next stage, internalization, is characterized by inner security as conflicts between the old and new identities are resolved. Global anti-White feelings subside as the person becomes more flexible, more tolerant, and more bicultural/multicultural. The last stage, internalization-commitment, speaks to the commitment that such individuals have toward social change, social justice, and civil rights. It is expressed not only in words, but also in actions that reflect the essence of their lives. It is important to note, however, that Cross's original model makes a major assumption: The evolution from the pre-encounter to the internalization stage reflects a movement from psychological dysfunction to psychological health (Vandiver, 2001).

Confronted with evidence that these stages may mask multiple racial identities, questioning his original assumption that all Blacks at the pre-encounter stage possess self-hatred and low self-esteem, and aware of the complex issues related to race salience, in his book *Shades of Black* W. E. Cross (1991) revised his theory of nigrescence. His changes, which are based on a critical review of the literature on Black racial identity, have increased the model's explanatory powers and promise high predictive validity (Vandiver et al., 2001; Worrell, Cross, & Vandiver, 2001). In essence, the revised model contains nearly all the features from the earlier formulation, but it differs in several significant ways. First, Cross introduces the concept of race salience, the degree to which race is an important and integral part of a person's approach to life. The Black person may either function with "race" consciousness playing a large role in his or her identity or a minimal one. In addition, salience for Blackness can possess positive (pro-Black) or negative (anti-Black) valence. Instead of using the term "pro-White" in the earlier pre-encounter stage, Cross now uses the term *race salience*. Originally, Cross believed that the rejection of Blackness and the acceptance of an American perspective were indicative of only one identity, characterized by self-hate and low self-esteem. His current model now describes two identities: (1) pre-encounter assimilation and (2) pre-encounter anti-Black. The former has low salience for race and a neutral valence toward Blackness, while the latter describes individuals who hate Blacks and hate being Black (high negative salience). In other words, it is possible for a Black person at the pre-encounter stage who experiences the salience of race as very minor and whose identity is oriented toward an "American" perspective not to be filled with self-hate or low self-esteem.

The sense of low self-esteem, however, is linked to the pre-encounter anti-Black orientation. According to Cross, such a psychological perspective is the result of miseducation and self-hatred. The miseducation is the result of the negative images about Blacks portrayed in the mass media, among neighbors, friends, and relatives, and in the educational literature (Blacks are unintelligent, criminal, lazy, and prone to violence). The result is an incorporation of such negative images into the personal identity of the Black person. Interestingly, the female Nisei student described earlier in this chapter, though Japanese American, would seem to possess many of the features of Cross' pre-encounter anti-Black identity.

Several other changes were made by Cross in his later stages. First, the immersion-emersion stage once described one fused identity (anti-White/ pro-Black) but is now divided into two additional ones: anti-White alone and anti-Black alone. While Cross speaks about two separate identities, it appears that there are three possible combinations: anti-White, pro-Black, and an anti-White/pro-Black combination. Second, Cross has collapsed the fourth and fifth stages (internalization and internalization-commitment) into one: internalization. He observed that minimal differences existed between the two stages except one of "sustained interest and commitment." This last stage is characterized by Black self-acceptance and can be manifested in three types of identities: Black nationalist (high Black positive race salience), biculturalist (Blackness and fused sense of Americanness), and multiculturalist (multiple identity formation, including race, gender, sexual orientation, etc.).

While Cross' model has been revised significantly and the newer version is more sophisticated, his original 1971 nigrescense theory continues to dominate the racial identity landscape. Unfortunately, this has created much confusion among researchers and practitioners. We encourage readers to familiarize themselves with his most recent formulation (W. E. Cross, 1991, 1995).

Asian American Identity Development Models

Asian American identity development models have not advanced as far as those relating to Black identity. One of the earliest heuristic, "type" models was developed by S. Sue and D. W. Sue (1971b) to explain what they saw as clinical differences among Chinese American students treated at the University of California Counseling Center: (1) *traditionalist*—a person who internalizes conventional Chinese customs and values, resists acculturation forces, and believes in the "old ways"; (2) *marginal person*—a person who attempts to assimilate and acculturate into White society, rejects traditional Chinese ways, internalizes society's negativism toward minority groups, and may develop racial self-hatred (à la the Nisei student); and (3) *Asian American*—a person who is in the process of forming a positive identity, who is ethnically and politically aware, and who becomes increasingly bicultural.

Kitano (1982) also proposed a type model to account for Japanese American role behaviors with respect to Japanese and American cultures: (1) positive-positive, in which the person identifies with both Japanese and White cultures without role conflicts; (2) negative-positive, in which there is a rejection of White culture and acceptance of Japanese American culture, with accompanying role conflicts; (3) positive-negative, in which the person accepts White culture and rejects Japanese culture, with concomitant role conflict; and (4) negative-negative, in which one rejects both.

These early type models suffered from several shortcomings (F. Y. Lee, 1991). First, they failed to provide a clear rationale for why an individual develops one ethnic identity type over another. While they were useful in describing characteristics of the type, they represented static entities rather than a dynamic process of identity development. Second, the early proposals seem too simplistic to account for the complexity of racial identity development. Third, these models were too population specific in that they described only one Asian American ethnic group (Chinese American or Japanese American), and one wonders whether they are equally applicable to Korean Americans, Filipino Americans, Vietnamese Americans, and so on. Last, with the exception of a few empirical studies (F. Y. Lee, 1991; D. W. Sue & Frank, 1973), testing of these typologies is seriously lacking.

In response to these criticisms, theorists have begun to move toward the development of stage/process models of Asian American identity development (J. Kim, 1981; F. Y. Lee, 1991; Sodowski, Kwan, & Pannu, 1995). Such models view identity formation as occurring in stages, from less healthy to more healthy evolutions. With each stage there exists a constellation of traits and characteristics associated with racial/ethnic identity. They also attempt to explain the conditions or situations that might retard, enhance, or impel the individual forward.

After a thorough review of the literature, J. Kim (1981) used a qualitative narrative approach with third-generation Japanese American women to posit a progressive and sequential stage model of Asian American identity development: ethnic awareness, White identification, awakening to social political consciousness, redirection to Asian American consciousness, and incorporation. Her model integrates the influence of acculturation, exposure to cultural differences, environmental negativism to racial differences, personal methods of handling race-related conflicts, and the effects of group or social movements on the Asian American individual.

1. The *ethnic awareness* stage begins around the ages of 3 to 4, when the child's family members serve as the significant ethnic group model. Positive or neutral attitudes toward one's own ethnic origin are formed depending on the amount of ethnic exposure conveyed by the caretakers.

2. The *White identification* stage begins when children enter school, where peers and the surroundings become powerful forces in conveying racial prejudice that negatively impacts their self-esteem and identity. The realization of "differentness" from such interactions leads to self-blame and a desire to escape racial heritage by identifying with White society.

3. The *awakening to social political consciousness* stage means the adoption of a new perspective, often correlated with increased political awareness. J. Kim (1981) believed that the civil rights and women's movements and other significant political events often precipitate this new awakening. The primary result is an abandoning of identification with White society and a consequent understanding of oppression and oppressed groups.

4. The *redirection* stage means a reconnection or renewed connection with one's Asian American heritage and culture. This is often followed by the realization that White oppression is the culprit for the negative experiences of youth. Anger against White racism may become a defining theme with, concomitant increases of Asian American self-pride and group pride.

5. The *incorporation* stage represents the highest form of identity evolution. It encompasses the development of a positive and comfortable identity as Asian American and consequent respect for other cultural/racial heritages. Identification for or against White culture is no longer an important issue.

Latino/Hispanic American Identity Development Models

While a number of ethnic identity development models have been formulated to account for Hispanic identity (Bernal & Knight, 1993; Casas & Pytluk, 1995; Szapocznik et al., 1982), the one most similar to those of African Amer-

Ruiz

icans and Asian Americans was proposed by A. S. Ruiz (1990). His model was formulated from a clinical perspective via case studies of Chicano/Latino subjects. Ruiz made several underlying assumptions. First, he believed in a culture-specific explanation of identity for Chicano, Mexican American, and Latino clients. While models about other ethnic group development or the more general ones were helpful, they lacked the specificity of Hispanic cultures. Second, the marginal status of Latinos is highly correlated with maladjustment. Third, negative experiences of forced assimilation are considered destructive to an individual. Fourth, having pride in one's cultural heritage and ethnic identity is positively correlated with mental health. Last, pride in one's ethnicity affords the Hispanic greater freedom to choose freely. These beliefs underlie the five-stage model.

1. *Causal stage.* During this period messages or injunctions from the environment or significant others either affirm, ignore, negate, or denigrate the ethnic heritage of the person. Affirmation about one's ethnic identity is lacking, and the person may experience traumatic or humiliating experiences related to ethnicity. There is a failure to identify with Latino culture.

2. *Cognitive stage.* As a result of negative/distorted messages, three erroneous belief systems about Chicano/Latino heritage become incorporated into mental sets: (1) Ethnic group membership is associated with poverty and prejudice; (2) assimilation to White society is the only means of escape; and (3) assimilation is the only possible road to success.

3. *Consequence stage.* Fragmentation of ethnic identity becomes very noticeable and evident. The person feels ashamed and is embarrassed by ethnic markers such as name, accent, skin color, cultural customs, and so on. The unwanted self-image leads to estrangement and rejection of one's Chicano/Latino heritage.

4. *Working-through stage.* Two major dynamics distinguish this stage. First, the person becomes increasingly unable to cope with the psychological distress of ethnic identity conflict. Second, the person can no longer be a "pretender" by identifying with an alien ethnic identity. The person is propelled to reclaim and reintegrate disowned ethnic identity fragments. Ethnic consciousness increases.

5. *Successful resolution stage.* This last stage is exemplified by greater acceptance of one's culture and ethnicity. There is an improvement in self-esteem and a sense that ethnic identity represents a positive and success-promoting resource.

The Ruiz model has a subjective reality that is missing in many of the empirically based models. This is expected, since it was formulated through a clinical population. It has the added advantage of suggesting intervention focus and direction for each of the stages. For example, the focus of counseling in the causal stage is disaffirming and restructuring of the injunctions; for the cognitive stage it is the use of cognitive strategies attacking faulty beliefs; for the consequence stage it is reintegration of ethnic identity fragments in a positive manner; for the working-through stage, ethnocultural identification issues are important; and for the successful resolution stage, the promotion of a positive identity becomes important.

A Racial/Cultural Identity Development Model

Earlier writers (Berry, 1965; Stonequist, 1937) have observed that minority groups share similar patterns of adjustment to cultural oppression. In the past several decades, Asian Americans, Hispanics, and American Indians have experienced sociopolitical identity transformations so that a *Third World consciousness* has emerged, with cultural oppression as the common unifying force. As a result of studying these models and integrating them with their own clinical observations, Atkinson, Morten, and Sue (1979, 1989, 1998) proposed a five-stage Minority Identity Development model (MID) in an attempt to pull out common features that cut across the population-specific proposals. D. W. Sue and D. Sue (1990, 1999) later elaborated on the MID, renaming it the Racial/Cultural Identity Development model (R/CID) to encompass a broader population. As discussed shortly, this model may be applied to White identity development as well.

The R/CID model proposed here is not a comprehensive theory of personality, but rather a conceptual framework to aid therapists in understanding their culturally different clients' attitudes and behaviors. The model defines five stages of development that oppressed people experience as they struggle to understand themselves in terms of their own culture, the dominant culture, and the oppressive relationship between the two cultures: *conformity, dissonance, resistance and immersion, introspection,* and *integrative awareness.* At each level of identity, four corresponding beliefs and attitudes that may help therapists better understand their minority clients are discussed. These attitudes/beliefs are an integral part of the minority person's identity and are manifest in how he or she views (a) the self, (b) others of the same minority, (c) others of another minority, and (d) majority individuals. Table 10.1 outlines the R/CID model and the interaction of stages with the attitudes and beliefs.

Conformity Stage

Similar to individuals in the pre-encounter stage (W. E. Cross, 1991), minority individuals are distinguished by their unequivocal preference for domi-

Table 10.1 **The Racial/Cultural Identity Development Model**

Stages of Minority Development Model	Attitude toward Self	Attitude toward Others of the Same Minority	Attitude toward Others of a Different Minority	Attitude toward Dominant Group
Stage 1— Conformity	Self-depreciating or neutral due to low race salience	Group-depreciating or neutral due to low race salience	Discriminatory or neutral	Group-appreciating
Stage 2— Dissonance and appreciating	Conflict between self-depreciating and group-appreciating	Conflict between group-depreciating views of minority hierarchy and feelings of shared experience	Conflict between dominant-held and group depreciating	Conflict between group-appreciating
Stage 3— Resistance and immersion	Self-appreciating	Group-appreciating experiences and feelings of culturocentrism	Conflict between feelings of empathy for other minority	Group-depreciating
Stage 4— Introspection	Concern with basis of self-appreciation	Concern with nature of unequivocal appreciation	Concern with ethnocentric basis for judging others	Concern with the basis of group-depreciation
Stage 5— Integrative awareness	Self-appreciating	Group-appreciating	Group-appreciating	Selective appreciation

Source: From Donald R. Atkinson, George Morten, and Derald Wing Sue, *Counseling American Minorities: A Cross Cultural Perspective*, 5th ed. Copyright © 1998 Wm. C. Brown Publishers, Dubuque, IA. All rights reserved. Reprinted by permission.

nant cultural values over their own. White Americans in the United States represent their reference group, and the identification set is quite strong. Lifestyles, value systems, and cultural/physical characteristics that most resemble White society are highly valued, while those most like their own minority group may be viewed with disdain or may hold low salience for the person. We agree with Cross that minority people at this stage can be oriented toward a pro-American identity without subsequent disdain or negativism toward their own group. Thus, it is possible for a Chinese American to feel positive about U.S. culture, values, and traditions without evidencing disdain for Chinese culture or feeling negatively about oneself (absence of self-hate). Nevertheless, we believe that they represent a small proportion of persons of color at this stage. Research on their numbers, on how they have handled the social-psychological dynamics of majority-minority relations, on how they have dealt with their minority status, and on how they fit into the stage models (progression issues) needs to be conducted.

We believe that the conformity stage continues to be most characterized by individuals who have bought into societal definitions about their minority status in society. Because the conformity stage represents, perhaps, the most damning indictment of White racism, and because it has such a profound negative impact on persons of color, understanding its sociopolitical dynamics is of utmost importance for the helping professional. Those in the conformity state are really victims of larger social-psychological forces operating in our society. The key issue here is the dominant-subordinate relationship between two different cultures (Atkinson, Morten, et al., 1998; Freire, 1970; B. Jackson, 1975). It is reasonable to believe that members of one cultural group tend to adjust themselves to the group possessing the greater prestige and power in order to avoid feelings of inferiority. Yet it is exactly this act that creates ambivalence in the minority individual. The pressures for assimilation and acculturation (melting-pot theory) are strong, creating possible culture conflicts. These individuals are victims of ethnocentric monoculturalism (D. W. Sue, 2004): (1) belief in the superiority of one group's cultural heritage—its language, traditions, arts-crafts, and ways of behaving (White) over all others; (2) belief in the inferiority of all other lifestyles (non-White); and (3) the power to impose such standards onto the less powerful group.

The psychological costs of racism on persons of color are immense. Constantly bombarded on all sides by reminders that Whites and their way of life are superior and that all other lifestyles are inferior, many minorities begin to wonder whether they themselves are not somehow inadequate, whether members of their own group are not to blame, and whether subordination and segregation are not justified. K. B. Clark and Clark (1947) first brought this to the attention of social scientists by stating that racism may contribute to a sense of confused self-identity among Black children. In a study of racial awareness and preference among Black and White children, they found that (a) Black children preferred playing with a White doll over a Black one, (b) the Black doll was perceived as being "bad," and (c) approximately one third, when asked to pick the doll that looked like them, picked the White one.

It is unfortunate that the inferior status of minorities is constantly reinforced and perpetuated by the mass media through television, movies, newspapers, radio, books, and magazines. This contributes to widespread stereotypes that tend to trap minority individuals: Blacks are superstitious, childlike, ignorant, fun loving, dangerous, and criminal; Hispanics are dirty, sneaky, and criminal; Asian Americans are sneaky, sly, cunning, and passive; Indians are primitive savages. Such portrayals cause widespread harm to the self-esteem of minorities who may incorporate them (D. W. Sue, 2003). The incorporation of the larger society's standards may lead minority group members to react negatively toward their own racial and cultural heritage. They may become ashamed of who they are, reject their own group identification, and attempt to identify with the desirable "good" White minority. In the *Autobiography of Malcolm X* (A. Haley, 1966), Malcolm X relates how he tried desperately to appear as White as possible. He went to painful lengths to straighten and dye his hair so that he would appear more like White males. It is evident that many minorities do come to accept White standards as a means of measuring physical attractiveness, attractiveness of personality, and social relationships. Such an orientation may lead to the phenomenon of racial self-hatred, in which people dislike themselves for being Asian, Black, Hispanic, or Native American. People at the conformity stage seem to possess the following characteristics.

1. *Attitudes and beliefs toward the self (self-depreciating attitudes and beliefs).* Physical and cultural characteristics identified with one's own racial/cultural group are perceived negatively, as something to be avoided, denied, or changed. Physical characteristics (black skin color, "slant-shaped eyes" of Asians), traditional modes of dress and appearance, and behavioral characteristics associated with the minority group are a source of shame. There may be attempts to mimic what is perceived as White mannerisms, speech patterns, dress, and goals. Low internal self-esteem is characteristic of the person.

2. *Attitudes and beliefs toward members of the same minority (group-depreciating attitudes and beliefs).* Majority cultural beliefs and attitudes about the minority group are also held by the person in this stage. These individuals may have internalized the majority of White stereotypes about their group. In the case of Hispanics, for example, the person may believe that members of his or her own group have high rates of unemployment because "they are lazy, uneducated, and unintelligent." Little thought or validity is given to other viewpoints, such as unemployment's being a function of job discrimination, prejudice, racism, unequal opportunities, and inferior education. Because persons in the conformity stage find it psychologically painful to identify with these negative traits, they divorce themselves from their own group. The denial mechanism most commonly used is, "I'm not like them; I've made it on my own; I'm the exception."

3. *Attitudes and beliefs toward members of different minorities (discriminatory).* Because the conformity-stage person most likely strives for identification with White society, the individual shares similar dominant attitudes and beliefs not only toward his or her own minority group, but

toward other minorities as well. Minority groups most similar to White cultural groups are viewed more favorably, while those most different are viewed less favorably. For example, Asian Americans may be viewed more favorably than African Americans or Latino/Hispanic Americans in some situations. While a stratification probably exists, we caution readers that such a ranking is fraught with hazards and potential political consequences. Such distinctions often manifest themselves in debates over which group is more oppressed and which group has done better than the others. Such debates are counterproductive when used to (1) negate another group's experience of oppression, (2) foster an erroneous belief that hard work alone will result in success in a democratic society, (3) shortchange a minority group (i.e., Asian Americans) from receiving the necessary resources in our society, and (4) pit one minority against another (divide and conquer) by holding one group up as an example to others.

4. *Attitudes and beliefs toward members of the dominant group (group-appreciating attitude and beliefs).* This stage is characterized by a belief that White cultural, social, and institutional standards are superior. Members of the dominant group are admired, respected, and emulated. White people are believed to possess superior intelligence. Some individuals may go to great lengths to appear White. Consider again the example from the *Autobiography of Malcolm X*, in which the main character would straighten his hair and primarily date White women. Reports that Asian women have undergone surgery to reshape their eyes to conform to White female standards of beauty may (but not in all cases) typify this dynamic.

Dissonance Stage

No matter how much one attempts to deny his or her own racial/cultural heritage, an individual will encounter information or experiences that are inconsistent with culturally held beliefs, attitudes, and values. An Asian American who believes that Asians are inhibited, passive, inarticulate, and poor in people relationships may encounter an Asian leader who seems to break all these stereotypes (e.g., the Nisei student). A Latino who feels ashamed of his or her cultural upbringing may encounter another Latino who seems proud of his or her cultural heritage. An African American who believes that race problems are due to laziness, untrustworthiness, or personal inadequacies of his or her own group may suddenly encounter racism on a personal level. Denial begins to break down, which leads to a questioning and challenging of the attitudes/beliefs of the conformity stage. This was clearly what happened when the Nisei student encountered discrimination at the restaurant.

In all probability, movement into the dissonance stage is a gradual process. Its very definition indicates that the individual is in conflict between disparate pieces of information or experiences that challenge his or her current self-concept. People generally move into this stage slowly, but a traumatic event may propel some individuals to move into dissonance at a much more rapid pace. W. E. Cross (1971) stated that a monumental event such as the assassination of a major leader like Martin Luther King, Jr. can often push people quickly into the ensuing stage.

1. *Attitudes and beliefs toward the self (conflict between self-depreciating and self-appreciating attitudes and beliefs).* There is now a growing sense of personal awareness that racism does exist, that not all aspects of the minority or majority culture are good or bad, and that one cannot escape one's cultural heritage. For the first time the person begins to entertain the possibility of positive attributes in the minority culture and, with it, a sense of pride in self. Feelings of shame and pride are mixed in the individual, and a sense of conflict develops. This conflict is most likely to be brought to the forefront quickly when other members of the minority group may express positive feelings toward the person: "We like you because you are Asian, Black, American Indian, or Latino." At this stage, an important personal question is being asked: "Why should I feel ashamed of who and what I am?"

2. *Attitudes and beliefs toward members of the same minority (conflict between group-depreciating and group-appreciating attitudes and beliefs).* Dominant-held views of minority strengths and weaknesses begin to be questioned as new, contradictory information is received. Certain aspects of the minority culture begin to have appeal. For example, a Latino/Hispanic male who values individualism may marry, have children, and then suddenly realize how Latino cultural values that hold the family as the psychosocial unit possess positive features. Or the minority person may find certain members of his group to be very attractive as friends, colleagues, lovers, and so forth.

3. *Attitudes and beliefs toward members of a different minority (conflict between dominant-held views of minority hierarchy and feelings of shared experience).* Stereotypes associated with other minority groups are questioned, and a growing sense of comradeship with other oppressed groups is felt. It is important to keep in mind however, that little psychic energy is associated with resolving conflicts with other minority groups. Almost all energies are expended toward resolving conflicts toward the self, the same minority, and the dominant group.

4. *Attitudes and beliefs toward members of the dominant group (conflict between group-appreciating and group-depreciating attitudes).* The person experiences

a growing awareness that not all cultural values of the dominant group are beneficial. This is especially true when the minority person experiences personal discrimination. Growing suspicion and some distrust of certain members of the dominant group develops.

Resistance and Immersion Stage

The minority person tends to endorse minority-held views completely and to reject the dominant values of society and culture. The person seems dedicated to reacting against White society and rejects White social, cultural, and institutional standards as having no personal validity. Desire to eliminate oppression of the individual's minority group becomes an important motivation of the individual's behavior. During the resistance and immersion stage, the three most active types of affective feelings are *guilt, shame,* and *anger.* There are considerable feelings of guilt and shame that in the past the minority individual has sold out his or her own racial and cultural group. The feelings of guilt and shame extend to the perception that during this past "sellout" the minority person has been a contributor and participant in the oppression of his or her own group and other minority groups. This is coupled with a strong sense of anger at the oppression and feelings of having been brainwashed by forces in White society. Anger is directed outwardly in a very strong way toward oppression and racism. Movement into this stage seems to occur for two reasons. First, a resolution of the conflicts and confusions of the previous stage allows greater understanding of social forces (racism, oppression, and discrimination) and his or her role as a victim. Second, a personal questioning of why people should feel ashamed of themselves develops. The answer to this question evokes feelings of guilt, shame, and anger.

1. *Attitudes and beliefs toward the self (self-appreciating attitudes and beliefs).* The minority individual at this stage is oriented toward self-discovery of one's own history and culture. There is an active seeking out of information and artifacts that enhance that person's sense of identity and worth. Cultural and racial characteristics that once elicited feelings of shame and disgust become symbols of pride and honor. The individual moves into this stage primarily because he or she asks the question, "Why should I be ashamed of who and what I am?" The original low self-esteem engendered by widespread prejudice and racism that was most characteristic of the conformity stage is now actively challenged in order to raise self-esteem. Phrases such as "Black is beautiful" represent a symbolic relabeling of identity for many Blacks. Racial self-hatred begins to be actively rejected in favor of the other extreme: unbridled racial pride.

2. *Attitudes and beliefs toward members of the same minority (group-appreciating attitudes and beliefs).* The individual experiences a strong sense of identi-

fication with and commitment to his or her minority group as enhancing information about the group is acquired. There is a feeling of connectedness with other members of the racial and cultural group, and a strengthening of new identity begins to occur. Members of one's group are admired, respected, and often viewed now as the new reference group or ideal. Cultural values of the minority group are accepted without question. As indicated, the pendulum swings drastically from original identification with White ways to identification in an unquestioning manner with the minority group's ways. Persons in this stage are likely to restrict their interactions as much as possible to members of their own group.

3. *Attitudes and beliefs toward members of a different minority (conflict between feelings of empathy for other minority group experiences and feelings of culturocentrism).* While members at this stage experience a growing sense of comradeship with persons from other minority groups, a strong culturocentrism develops as well. Alliances with other groups tend to be transitory and based on short-term goals or some global shared view of oppression. There is less an attempt to reach out and understand other racial-cultural minority groups and their values and ways, and more a superficial surface feeling of political need. Alliances generally are based on convenience factors or are formed for political reasons, such as combining together as a large group to confront an enemy perceived to be larger.

4. *Attitudes and beliefs toward members of the dominant group (group depreciating attitudes and beliefs).* The minority individual is likely to perceive the dominant society and culture as an oppressor and as the group most responsible for the current plight of minorities in the United States. Characterized by both withdrawal from the dominant culture and immersion in one's cultural heritage, there is also considerable anger and hostility directed toward White society. There is a feeling of distrust and dislike for all members of the dominant group in an almost global anti-White demonstration and feeling. White people, for example, are not to be trusted because they are the oppressors or enemies. In extreme form, members may advocate complete destruction of the institutions and structures that have been characteristic of White society.

Introspection Stage

Several factors seem to work in unison to move the individual from the resistance and immersion stage into the introspection stage. First, the individual begins to discover that this level of intensity of feelings (anger directed toward White society) is psychologically draining and does not permit one to really devote more crucial energies to understanding themselves or to their own racial-cultural group. The resistance and immersion stage tends to be a reaction against the dominant culture and is not proactive in allowing the individual to use all energies to discover who or what he or she is. Self-definition in the previous stage tends to be reactive (against White racism), and a need for positive self-definition in a proactive sense emerges.

Second, the minority individual experiences feelings of discontent and discomfort with group views that may be quite rigid in the resistance and immersion stage. Often, in order to please the group, the individual is asked to submerge individual autonomy and individual thought in favor of the group good. Many group views may now be seen as conflicting with individual ones. A Latino individual who may form a deep relationship with a White person may experience considerable pressure from his or her culturally similar peers to break off the relationship because that White person is the "enemy." However, the personal experiences of the individual may, in fact, not support this group view.

It is important to note that some clinicians often confuse certain characteristics of the introspective stage with parts of the conformity stage. A minority person from the former stage who speaks against the decisions of his or her group may often appear similar to the conformity person. The dynamics are quite different, however. While the conformity person is motivated by global racial self-hatred, the introspective person has no such global negativism directed at his or her own group.

1. *Attitudes and beliefs toward the self (concern with basis of self-appreciating attitudes and beliefs).* While the person originally in the conformity stage held predominantly to majority group views and notions to the detriment of his or her own minority group, the person now feels that he or she has too rigidly held onto minority group views and notions in order to submerge personal autonomy. The conflict now becomes quite great in terms of responsibility and allegiance to one's own minority group versus notions of personal independence and autonomy. The person begins to spend more and more time and energy trying to sort out these aspects of self-identity and begins increasingly to demand individual autonomy.

2. *Attitudes and beliefs toward members of the same minority (concern with the unequivocal nature of group appreciation).* While attitudes of identification are continued from the preceding resistance and immersion stage, concern begins to build up regarding the issue of group-usurped individuality. Increasingly, the individual may see his or her own group taking positions that might be considered quite extreme. In addition, there is now increasing resentment over how one's group may attempt to pressure or influence the individual into making decisions that may be inconsistent

with the person's values, beliefs, and outlooks. Indeed, it is not unusual for members of a minority group to make it clear to the member that if they do not agree with the group, they are against it. A common ploy used to hold members in line is exemplified in questions such as "How Asian are you?" and "How Black are you?"

3. *Attitudes and beliefs toward members of a different minority (concern with the ethnocentric basis for judging others).* There is now greater uneasiness with culturocentrism, and an attempt is made to reach out to other groups in finding out what types of oppression they experience and how this has been handled. While similarities are important, there is now a move-ment toward understanding potential differences in oppression that other groups might have experienced.

4. *Attitudes and beliefs toward members of the dominant group (concern with the basis of group depreciation).* The individual experiences conflict between attitudes of complete trust for the dominant society and culture and at-titudes of selective trust and distrust according to the dominant individ-ual's demonstrated behaviors and attitudes. Conflict is most likely to oc-cur here because the person begins to recognize that there are many elements in U.S. American culture that are highly functional and desir-able, yet there is confusion as to how to incorporate these elements into the minority culture. Would the person's acceptance of certain White cultural values make the person a sellout to his or her own race? There is a lowering of intense feelings of anger and distrust toward the domi-nant group but a continued attempt to discern elements that are ac-ceptable.

Integrative Awareness Stage

Minority persons in this stage have developed an inner sense of security and now can own and appreciate unique aspects of their culture as well as those in U.S. culture. Minority culture is not necessarily in conflict with White dominant cultural ways. Conflicts and discomforts experienced in the previ-ous stage become resolved, allowing greater individual control and flexibility. There is now the belief there are acceptable and unacceptable aspects in all cultures, and that it is very important for the person to be able to examine and accept or reject those aspects of a culture that are not seen as desirable. At the integrative awareness stage, the minority person has a strong commitment and desire to eliminate all forms of oppression.

1. *Attitudes and beliefs toward the self (self-appreciating attitudes and beliefs).* The culturally diverse individual develops a positive self-image and experi-ences a strong sense of self-worth and confidence. Not only is there an

integrated self-concept that involves racial pride in identity and culture, but the person develops a high sense of autonomy. Indeed, the client becomes bicultural or multicultural without a sense of having "sold out one's integrity." In other words, the person begins to perceive his or her self as an autonomous individual who is unique (individual level of identity), a member of one's own racial-cultural group (group level of identity), a member of a larger society, and a member of the human race (universal level of identity).

2. *Attitudes and beliefs toward members of same minority (group-appreciating attitudes and beliefs).* The individual experiences a strong sense of pride in the group without having to accept group values unequivocally. There is no longer the conflict over disagreeing with group goals and values. Strong feelings of empathy with the group experience are coupled with awareness that each member of the group is also an individual. In addition, tolerant and empathic attitudes are likely to be expressed toward members of one's own group who may be functioning at a less adaptive manner to racism and oppression.

3. *Attitudes and beliefs toward members of a different minority (group-appreciating attitudes).* There is now literally a reaching-out toward different minority groups in order to understand their cultural values and ways of life. There is a strong belief that the more one understands other cultural values and beliefs, the greater is the likelihood of understanding among the various ethnic groups. Support for all oppressed people, regardless of similarity to the individual's minority group, tends to be emphasized.

4. *Attitudes and beliefs toward members of the dominant group (attitudes and beliefs of selective appreciation).* The individual experiences selective trust and liking from members of the dominant group who seek to eliminate oppressive activities of the group. The individual also experiences openness to the constructive elements of the dominant culture. The emphasis here tends to be on the fact that White racism is a sickness in society and that White people are also victims who are also in need of help.

Therapeutic Implications of the R/CID Model

Let us first point out some broad general clinical implications of the R/CID model before discussing specific meanings within each of the stages. First, an understanding of cultural identity development should sensitize therapists and counselors to the role that oppression plays in a minority individual's development. In many respects, it should make us aware that our role as helping professionals should extend beyond the office and should deal with the many manifestations of racism. While individual therapy is needed, combating the forces of racism means a proactive approach for both the therapist and the client. For the therapist, systems intervention is often the answer. For culturally diverse clients, it means the need to understand, control, and direct those forces in society that negate the process of positive identity. Thus, a wider sociocultural approach to therapy is mandatory.

Second, the model will aid therapists in recognizing differences between members of the same minority group with respect to their cultural identity. It serves as a useful assessment and diagnostic tool for therapists to gain a greater understanding of their culturally different client. In many cases, an accurate delineation of the dynamics and characteristics of the stages may result in better prescriptive treatment. Therapists who are familiar with the sequence of stages are better able to plan intervention strategies that are most effective for culturally different clients. For example, a client experiencing feelings of isolation and alienation in the conformity stage may require a different approach than he or she would in the introspection stage.

Third, the model allows helping professionals to realize the potentially changing and developmental nature of cultural identity among clients. If the goal of multicultural counseling/therapy is intended to move a client toward the integrative awareness stage, then the therapist is able to anticipate the sequence of feelings, beliefs, attitudes, and behaviors likely to arise. Acting as a guide and providing an understandable end point will allow the client to understand more quickly and work through issues related to his or her own identity. We now turn our attention to the R/CID model and its implications for the therapeutic process.

Conformity Stage: Therapeutic Implications

For the vast majority of those in the conformity stage (belief in the superiority of White ways and the inferiority of minority ways), several therapeutic implications can be derived. First, persons of color are most likely to prefer a White therapist over a minority therapist. This flows logically from the belief that Whites are more competent and capable than are members of one's own race. Such a racial preference can be manifested in the client's reaction to a minority therapist via negativism, resistance, or open hostility. In some instances, the client may even request a change in therapist (preferably someone White). On the other hand, the conformity individual who is seen by a White therapist may be quite pleased about it. In many cases, the minority client, in identifying with White culture, may be overly dependent on the White therapist. Attempts to please, appease, and seek approval from the helping professional may be quite prevalent.

Second, most conformity individuals will find that attempts to explore cultural identity or to focus in upon feelings are very threatening. Clients in this stage generally prefer a task-oriented, problem-solving approach, because an exploration of identity may eventually touch upon feelings of low self-esteem, dissatisfaction with personal appearance, vague anxieties, and racial self-hatred, and may challenge the client's self-deception that he or she is not like the other members of his or her own race.

Whether you are a White or minority counselor working with a conformity individual, the general goal may be the same. There is an obligation to help the client sort out conflicts related to racial/cultural identity through some process of re-education. Somewhere in the course of counseling or therapy, issues of cultural racism, majority-minority group relations, racial self-hatred, and racial cultural identity need to be dealt with in an integrated fashion. We are not suggesting a lecture or solely a cognitive approach, to which clients at this stage may be quite intellectually receptive, but exercising good clinical skills that take into account the client's socioemotional state and readiness to deal with feelings. Only in this manner will the client be able to distinguish the difference between positive attempts to adopt certain values of the dominant society and a negative rejection of one's own cultural value (a characteristic of the integrative awareness stage).

While the goals for the White and minority therapist are the same, the way a therapist works toward them may be different. For example, a minority therapist will likely have to deal with hostility from the racially and culturally similar client. The therapist may symbolize all that the client is trying to reject. Because therapy stresses the building of a coalition, establishment of rapport, and to some degree a mutual identification, the process may be especially threatening. The opposite may be true of work with a White therapist. The culturally different client may be overeager to identify with the White professional in order to seek approval. However, rather than being detrimental to multicultural counseling/therapy, these two processes can be used quite effectively and productively. If the minority therapist can aid the client in working through his or her feelings of antagonism, and if the majority therapist can aid the client in working through his or her need to over-identify, then the client will be moved closer to awareness than to self-deception. In the former case, the therapist can take a nonjudgmental stance toward the client and provide a positive minority role model. In the latter, the White therapist needs to model positive attitudes toward cultural diversity. Both need to guard against unknowingly reinforcing the client's self-denial and rejection.

Dissonance Stage: Therapeutic Implications

As individuals become more aware of inconsistencies between dominant-held views and those of their own group, a sense of dissonance develops. Preoccupation and questions concerning self, identity, and self-esteem are most likely brought in for therapy. More culturally aware than their conformity counterparts, dissonance clients may prefer a counselor or therapist who possesses good knowledge of the client's cultural group, although there may still be a preference for a White helper. However, the fact that minority helping professionals are generally more knowledgeable of the client's cultural group may serve to heighten the conflicting beliefs and feelings of this stage. Since the client is so receptive toward self-exploration, the therapist can capitalize on this orientation in helping the client come to grips with his or her identity conflicts.

Resistance and Immersion Stage: Therapeutic Implications

Minority clients at this stage are likely to view their psychological problems as products of oppression and racism. They may believe that only issues of racism are legitimate areas to explore in therapy. Furthermore, openness or self-disclosure to therapists not of one's own group is dangerous because White therapists are "enemies" and members of the oppressing group.

Clients in the resistance and immersion stage believe that society is to blame for their present dilemma and actively challenge the establishment. They are openly suspicious of institutions such as mental health services because they view them as agents of the establishment. Very few of the more ethnically conscious and militant minorities will use mental health services, because of its identification with the status quo. When they do, they are usually suspicious and hostile toward the helping professional. A therapist working with a client at this stage of development needs to realize several important things.

First, he or she will be viewed by the culturally different client as a symbol of the oppressive society. If you become defensive and personalize the attacks, you will lose your effectiveness in working with the client. It is important not to be intimidated or afraid of the anger that is likely to be expressed; often, it is not personal and is quite legitimate. White guilt and defensiveness can only serve to hinder effective multicultural counseling/therapy. It is not unusual for clients at this stage to make sweeping negative generalizations about White Americans. The White therapist who takes a nondefensive posture will be better able to help the client explore the basis of his or her racial tirades. In general, clients at this stage prefer a therapist of their own race. However, the fact that you share the same race or culture as your client will not insulate you from the attacks. For example, an African American client may perceive the Black counselor as a sellout of his or her own race, or as an Uncle Tom. Indeed, the anger and hostility directed at the minority therapist may be even more intense than that directed at a White one.

Second, realize that clients in this stage will constantly test you. In earlier chapters we described how minority clients will pose challenges to therapists in order to test their sincerity, openness, nondefensiveness, and competencies.

Because of the active nature of client challenges, therapy sessions may become quite dynamic. Many therapists find this stage is frequently the most difficult to deal with because counselor self-disclosure is often necessary for establishing credibility.

Third, individuals at this stage are especially receptive to approaches that are more action oriented and aimed at external change (challenging racism). Also, group approaches with persons experiencing similar racial/cultural issues are well received. It is important that the therapist be willing to help the culturally different client explore new ways of relating to both minority and White persons.

Introspection Stage: Therapeutic Implications

Clients at the introspection stage may continue to prefer a therapist of their own race, but they are also receptive to help from therapists of other cultures as long as the therapists understand their worldview. Ironically, clients at this stage may, on the surface, appear similar to conformity persons. Introspection clients are in conflict between their need to identify with their minority group and their need to exercise greater personal freedom. Exercising personal autonomy may occasionally mean going against the wishes or desires of the minority group. This is often perceived by minority persons and their group as a rejection of their own cultural heritage. This is not unlike conformity persons, who also reject their racial/cultural heritage. The dynamics between the two groups, however, are quite dissimilar. It is very important for therapists to distinguish the differences. The conformity person moves away from his or her own group because of perceived negative qualities associated with it. The introspection person wants to move away on certain issues but perceives the group positively. Again, self-exploration approaches aimed at helping the client integrate and incorporate a new sense of identity are important. Believing in the functional values of White American society does not necessarily mean that a person is selling out or going against his or her own group.

Integrative Awareness Stage: Therapeutic Implications

Clients at this stage have acquired an inner sense of security as to self-identity. They have pride in their racial/cultural heritage but can exercise a desired level of personal freedom and autonomy. Other cultures and races are appreciated, and there is a development toward becoming more multicultural in perspective. While discrimination and oppression remain a powerful part of their existence, integrative awareness persons possess greater psychological resources to deal with these problems. Being action or systems oriented, clients respond positively to the designing and implementation of strategies aimed at community and societal change. Preferences for therapists are not based on race, but on those who can share, understand, and accept their worldviews. In other words, attitudinal similarity between therapist and client is a more important dimension than membership-group similarity.

Implications for Clinical Practice

We have already given considerable space to outlining specific therapeutic suggestions, so a repeat of these would be redundant. Rather, in proposing the R/CID model, we have been very aware of some major cautions and possible limitations that readers should take into account in working with minority clients.

1. Be aware that the R/CID model should not be viewed as a global personality theory with specific identifiable stages that serve as fixed categories. The process of cultural identity development is dynamic, not static. One of the major dangers is to use these stages as fixed entities. In actuality, the model should serve as a conceptual framework to help us understand development.

2. Do not fall victim to stereotyping in using these models. Most minority clients may evidence a dominant characteristic, but there are mixtures from other stages as well. Furthermore, situations and the types of presenting problems may make some characteristics more manifest than others. It is possible that minority clients may evidence conformity characteristics in some situations but resistance and immersion characteristics in others.

3. Know that minority development models are conceptual aids and that human development is much more complex. A question often raised in the formulation of cultural identity development models is whether identity is a linear process. Do individuals always start at the beginning of these stages? Is it possible to skip stages? Can people regress? In general, our clinical experience has been that minority and majority individuals in this society do tend to move at some gross level through each of the identifiable stages. Some tend to move faster than others, some tend to stay predominately at only one stage, and some may regress.

4. Know that identity development models begin at a point that involves interaction with an oppressive society. Most of these are weak in formulating a stage prior to conformity characteristics. Recent Asian immigrants to the United States are a prime example of the inadequacy of cultural identity development models. Many of the Asian immigrants tend to hold very positive and favorable views of their own culture and possess an intact racial/cultural identity already. What happens when

they encounter a society that views cultural differences as being deviant? Will they or their offspring move through the conformity stage as presented in this model?

5. Be careful of the implied value judgments given in almost all development models. They assume that some cultural resolutions are healthier than others. For example, the R/CID model obviously does hold the integrative awareness stage as a higher form of healthy functioning.

6. Be aware that racial/cultural identity development models seriously lack an adequate integration of gender, class, sexual orientation, and other sociodemographic group identities. William Cross has made some beginning attempts to do so.

7. Know that racial/cultural identity is not a simple, global concept. A great deal of evidence is mounting that while identity may sequentially move through identifiable stages, affective, attitudinal, cognitive, and behavioral components of identity may not move in a uniform manner. For example, it is entirely possible that the emotions and affective elements associated with certain stages do not have a corresponding one-to-one behavioral impact.

8. Begin to look more closely at the possible therapist and client stage combinations. As mentioned earlier, therapeutic processes and outcomes are often the function of the identity stage of both therapist and client. White identity development of the therapist can either enhance or retard effective therapy.

White Racial Identity Development: Therapeutic Implications

What Does It Mean to Be White?

42-year-old White businessman

> Q: *What does it mean to be White?*
> A: *Frankly, I don't know what you're talking about!*
> Q: *Aren't you White?*
> A: *Yes, but I come from Italian heritage. I'm Italian, not White.*
> Q: *Well then, what does it mean to be Italian?*
> A: *Pasta, good food, love of wine [obviously agitated]. This is getting ridiculous!*

OBSERVATIONS: *Denial and/or conflicted about being White. Claims Italian heritage, but unable to indicate more than superficial understanding of ethnic meaning. Expresses annoyance at the question.*

26-year-old White female college student

> Q: *What does it mean to be White?*
> A: *Is this a trick question? [pause] I've never thought about it. Well, I know that lots of Black people see us as being prejudiced and all that stuff. I wish people would just forget about race differences and see one another as human beings. People are people and we should all be proud to be Americans.*

OBSERVATIONS: *Seldom thinks about being White. Defensive about prejudicial associations with Whiteness. Desires to eliminate or dilute race differences.*

65-year-old White male retired construction worker

> Q: *What does it mean to be White?*
> A: *That's a stupid question [sounds irritated]!*
> Q: *Why?*

> A: *Look, what are you . . . Oriental? You people are always blaming us for stereo-typing, and here you are doing the same to us.*
>
> Q: *When you say "us," to whom are you referring?*
>
> A: *I'm referring to Americans who aren't colored. We are all different from one another. I'm Irish, but there are Germans, Italians, and those Jews. I get angry at the colored people for always blaming us. When my grandparents came over to this country, they worked 24 hours a day to provide a good living for their kids. My wife and I raised five kids, and I worked every day of my life to provide for them. No one gave me nothing! I get angry at the Black people for always whining. They just have to get off their butts and work rather than going on welfare. At least you people [reference to Asian Americans] work hard. The Black ones could learn from your people.*

OBSERVATIONS: *Believes question stereotypes Whites and expresses resentment with being categorized. Views White people as ethnic group. Expresses belief that anyone can be successful if they work hard. Believes African Americans are lazy and that Asian Americans are successful. Strong anger directed toward minority groups.*

34-year-old White female stockbroker

> Q: *What does it mean to be White?*
>
> A: *I don't know [laughing]. I've never thought about it.*
>
> Q: *Are you White?*
>
> A: *Yes, I suppose so [seems very amused].*
>
> Q: *Why haven't you thought about it?*
>
> A: *Because it's not important to me.*
>
> Q: *Why not?*
>
> A: *It doesn't enter into my mind because it doesn't affect my life. Besides, we are all unique. Color isn't important.*

OBSERVATIONS: *Never thought about being White because it's unimportant. People are individuals, and color isn't important.*

These are not atypical responses given by White Euro-Americans when asked this question. When people of color are asked the same question, their answers tended to be more specific:

29-year-old Latina administrative assistant

> Q: *What does it mean to be White?*
>
> A: *I'm not White; I'm Latina!*
>
> Q: *Are you upset with me?*
>
> A: *No. . . . Its just that I'm light, so people always think I'm White. Its only when I speak that they realize I'm Hispanic.*

Q: *Well, what does it mean to be White?*

A: *Do you really want to know? . . . Okay, it means you're always right. It means you never have to explain yourself or apologize. . . . You know that movie [Love Story, which features the line, "Love means never having to say you're sorry]? Well, being White is never having to say you're sorry. It means they think they're better than us.*

OBSERVATIONS: *Strong reaction to being mistaken for being White. Claims that being White makes people feel superior and is reflected in their disinclination to admit being wrong.*

39-year-old Black male salesman

Q: *What does it mean to be White?*

A: *Is this a school exercise or something? Never expected someone to ask me that question in the middle of the city. Do you want the politically correct answer or what I really think?*

Q: *Can you tell me what you really think?*

A: *You won't quit, will you [laughing]? If you're White, you're right. If you're Black, step back.*

Q: *What does that mean?*

A: *White folks are always thinking they know all the answers. A Black man's word is worth less than a White man's. When White customers come into our dealership and see me standing next to the cars, I become invisible to them. Actually, they may see me as a well-dressed janitor [laughs], or actively avoid me. They will search out a White salesman. Or when I explain something to a customer, they always check out the information with my White colleagues. They don't trust me. When I mention this to our manager, who is White, he tells me I'm oversensitive and being paranoid. That's what being White means. It means having the authority or power to tell me what's really happening even though I know it's not. Being White means you can fool yourself into thinking that you're not prejudiced, when you are. That's what it means to be White.*

OBSERVATIONS: *Being White means you view minorities as less competent and capable. You have the power to define reality. You can deceive yourself into believing you're not prejudiced.*

21-year-old Chinese American male college student (majoring in ethnic studies)

Q: *What does it mean to be White?*

A: *My cultural heritage class was just discussing that question this week.*

Q: *What was your conclusion?*

A: Well, it has to do with White privilege. I read an article by a professor at Wellesley. It made a lot of sense to me. Being White in this society automatically guarantees you better treatment and unearned benefits and privileges than minorities. Having white skin means you have the freedom to choose the neighborhood you live in. You won't be discriminated against. When you enter a store, security guards won't assume you will steal something. You can flag down a cab without the thought they won't pick you up because you're a minority. You can study in school and be assured your group will be portrayed positively. You don't have to deal with race or think about it.
Q: Are White folks aware of their White privilege?
A: Hell no! They're oblivious to it.

OBSERVATIONS: Being White means having unearned privileges in our society. It means you are oblivious to the advantages of being White. (D. W. Sue, 2003, pp. 115–120)

The Invisible Whiteness of Being

The responses given by White Euro-Americans and persons of color are radically different from one another. Yet the answers given by both groups are quite common and representative of the range of responses students give in our diversity and multicultural classes. White respondents would rather not think about their Whiteness, are uncomfortable or react negatively to being labeled White, deny its importance in affecting their lives, and seem to believe that they are unjustifiably accused of being bigoted simply because they are White.

Strangely enough, Whiteness is most visible to people of color when it is denied, evokes puzzlement or negative reactions, and is equated with normalcy. Few people of color react negatively when asked what it means to be Black, Asian American, Latino, or a member of their race. Most could readily inform the questioner about what it means to be a person of color. There seldom is a day, for example, in which we (the authors) are not reminded of being racially and culturally different from those around us. Yet Whites often find the question about Whiteness quite disconcerting and perplexing.

It appears that the denial and mystification of Whiteness for White Euro-Americans are related to two underlying factors. First, most people seldom think about the air that surrounds them and about how it provides an essential life-giving ingredient, oxygen. We take it for granted because it appears plentiful; only when we are deprived of it does it suddenly become frighteningly apparent. Whiteness is transparent precisely because of its everyday occurrence—its institutionalized normative features in our culture—and because Whites are taught to think of their lives as morally neutral, average, and ideal (D. W. Sue, 2004). To people of color, however, Whiteness is not invisible because it may not fit their normative qualities (values, lifestyles, experiential reality, etc.). Persons of color find White culture quite visible because even though it is nurturing to White Euro-Americans, it may invalidate the lifestyles of multicultural populations.

Second, Euro-Americans often deny that they are White, seem angered by being labeled as such, and often become very defensive (i.e., "I'm not White, I'm Irish." "You're stereotyping, because we're all different." "There isn't anything like a White race."). In many respects, these statements have validity. Nonetheless, many White Americans would be hard pressed to describe their Irish, Italian, German, or Norwegian heritage in any but the most superficial manner. One of the reasons is related to the processes of assimilation and acculturation. While there are many ethnic groups, being White allows for assimilation. While persons of color are told to assimilate and acculturate, the assumption is that there exists a receptive society. Racial minorities are told in no uncertain terms that they are allowed only limited access to the fruits of our society. Thus, the accuracy of whether Whiteness defines a race is largely irrelevant. What is more relevant is that Whiteness is associated with unearned privilege—advantages conferred on White Americans but not on persons of color. It is our contention that much of the denial associated with being White is related to the denial of White privilege, an issue we explore in a moment.

Understanding the Dynamics of Whiteness

Our analysis of the responses from both Whites and persons of color leads us to the inevitable conclusion that part of the problem of race relations (and by inference multicultural counseling and therapy) lies in the different world-views of both groups. It goes without saying that the racial reality of Whites is radically different from people of color (D. W. Sue, 2005). Which group, however, has the more accurate assessment related to this topic? The answer seems to be contained in the following series of questions: If you want to understand oppression, should you ask the oppressor or the oppressed? If you want to learn about sexism, do you ask men or women? If you want to understand homophobia, do you ask straights or gays? If you want to learn about racism, do you ask Whites or persons of color? It appears that the most accurate assessment of bias comes not from those who enjoy the privilege of power, but from those who are most disempowered (Hanna, Talley, & Guindon, 2000; Neville et al., 2001). Taking this position, the following assumptions are made about the dynamics of Whiteness.

First, it is clear that most White folks perceive themselves as unbiased individuals who do not harbor racist thoughts and feelings; they see themselves as working toward social justice and possess a conscious desire to better the life circumstances of those less fortunate than they. While admirable qualities, this self-image serves as a major barrier to recognizing and taking responsibility for admitting and dealing with one's own prejudices and biases. To admit to being racist, sexist, or homophobic requires people to recognize that the self-images that they hold so dear are based on false notions of the self.

Second, being a White person in this society means chronic exposure to ethnocentric monoculturalism as manifested in White supremacy (Constantine, 2006). It is difficult, if not impossible, for anyone to avoid inheriting the racial biases, prejudices, misinformation, deficit portrayals, and stereotypes of their forebears (Cokley, 2006). To believe that one is somehow immune from inheriting such aspects of White supremacy is to be naive or to engage in self-deception. Such a statement is not intended to assail the integrity of Whites, but to suggest that they also have been victimized. It is clear to us that no one was born wanting to be racist, sexist, or homophobic. Misinformation is not acquired by free choice, but is imposed upon White people through a painful process of cultural conditioning. In general, lacking awareness of their biases and preconceived notions, counselors may function in a therapeutically ineffective manner.

Third, if White helping professionals are ever able to become effective multicultural counselors or therapists, they must free themselves from the cultural conditioning of their past and move toward the development of a nonracist White identity. Unfortunately, many White Euro-Americans seldom consider what it means to be White in our society. Such a question is vexing to them because they seldom think of race as belonging to them—nor of the privileges that come their way by virtue of their white skin. Katz (1985, pp. 616–617) points out a major barrier blocking the process of White Euro-Americans investigating their own cultural identity and worldview:

> *Because White culture is the dominant cultural norm in the United States, it acts as an invisible veil that limits many people from seeing it as a cultural system. . . . Often, it is easier for many Whites to identify and acknowledge the different cultures of minorities than accept their own racial identity. . . . The difficulty of accepting such a view is that White culture is omnipresent. It is so interwoven in the fabric of everyday living that Whites cannot step outside and see their beliefs, values, and behaviors as creating a distinct cultural group.*

Ridley (1995, p. 38) asserts that this invisible veil can be unintentionally manifested in therapy with harmful consequences to minority clients:

> *Unintentional behavior is perhaps the most insidious form of racism. Unintentional racists are unaware of the harmful consequences of their behavior. They may be well-intentioned, and on the surface, their behavior may appear to be re-*

sponsible. Because individuals, groups, or institutions that engage in unintentional racism do not wish to do harm, it is difficult to get them to see themselves as racists. They are more likely to deny their racism.

The conclusion drawn from this understanding is that White counselors and therapists may be unintentional racists: (1) They are unaware of their biases, prejudices, and discriminatory behaviors; (2) they often perceive themselves as moral, good, and decent human beings and find it difficult to see themselves as racist; (3) they do not have a sense of what their Whiteness means to them; and (4) their therapeutic approaches to multicultural populations are likely to be more harmful (unintentionally) than helpful. These conclusions are often difficult for White helping professionals to accept because of the defensiveness and feelings of blame they are likely to engender. Nonetheless, we ask that White therapists and students not be turned off by the message and lessons of this chapter. We ask you to continue your multicultural journey in this chapter as we explore the question, "What does it mean to be White?"

Models of White Racial Identity Development

A number of multicultural experts in the field have begun to emphasize the need for White therapists to deal with their concepts of Whiteness and to examine their own racism (Corvin & Wiggins, 1989; Helms, 1984, 1990; Ponterotto, 1988; D. W. Sue et al., 1998). These specialists point out that while racial/cultural identity development for minority groups proves beneficial in our work as therapists, more attention should be devoted toward the White therapist's racial identity. Since the majority of therapists and trainees are White middle-class individuals, it would appear that White identity development and its implication for multicultural counseling/therapy would be important aspects to consider, both in the actual practice of clinical work and in professional training.

For example, research has found that the level of White racial identity awareness is predictive of racism (Pope-Davis & Ottavi, 1994; Wang, Davidson, Yakushko, Savoy, Tan, & Bleier, 2003): (1) The less aware subjects were of their White identity, the more likely they were to exhibit increased levels of racism; and (2) women were less likely to be racist (Spanierman, Poteat, Beer & Armstrong, 2006). It was suggested that this last finding was correlated with women's greater experiences with discrimination and prejudice. Evidence also exists that multicultural counseling/therapy competence is correlated with White racial identity attitudes (Neville et al. 2001). Other research suggests that a relationship exists between a White Euro-American therapist's racial identity and his or her readiness for training in multicultural awareness, knowledge, and skills (Carney & Kahn, 1984; Helms, 1990; Sabnani, Ponterotto, & Borodovsky, 1991; Utsey, Gernat, & Hammar, 2005). Since developing multicultural sensitivity is a long-term developmental task, the work of many researchers has gradually converged toward a conceptualization of the stages/levels/statuses of consciousness of racial/ethnic identity development for White Euro-Americans. A number of these models describe the salience of identity for establishing relationships between the White therapist and the culturally different client, and some have now linked stages of identity with stages for appropriate training (Bennett, 1986; Carney & Kahn, 1984; Sabnani et al., 1991).

The Hardiman White Racial Identity Development Model

One of the earliest integrative attempts at formulating a White racial identity development model is that of Rita Hardiman (1982). Intrigued with why certain White individuals exhibit a much more nonracist identity than do other White Americans, Hardiman studied the autobiographies of individuals who had attained a high level of racial consciousness. This led her to identify five White developmental stages: (1) naïveté—lack of social consciousness, (2) acceptance, (3) resistance, (4) redefinition, and (5) internalization.

1. The *naïveté stage* (lack of social consciousness) is characteristic of early childhood, when we are born into this world innocent, open, and unaware of racism and the importance of race. Curiosity and spontaneity in relating to race and racial differences tend to be the norm. A young White child who has almost no personal contact with African Americans, for example, may see a Black man in a supermarket and loudly comment on the darkness of his skin. Other than the embarrassment and apprehensions of adults around the child, there is little discomfort associated with this behavior for the youngster. In general, awareness and the meaning of race, racial differences, bias, and prejudice are either absent or minimal. Such an orientation becomes less characteristic of the child as the socialization process progresses. The negative reactions of parents, relatives, friends, and peers toward issues of race, however, begin to convey mixed signals to the child. This is reinforced by the educational system and mass media, which instill racial biases in the child and propel him or her into the acceptance stage.

2. The *acceptance stage* is marked by a conscious belief in the democratic ideal—that everyone has an equal opportunity to succeed in a free society and that those who fail must bear the responsibility for their failure. White Euro-Americans become the social reference group, and the socialization process consistently instills messages of White superiority and

minority inferiority into the child. The underemployment, unemployment, and undereducation of marginalized groups in our society are seen as support that non-White groups are lesser than Whites. Because everyone has an equal opportunity to succeed, the lack of success of minority groups is seen as evidence of some negative personal or group characteristic (low intelligence, inadequate motivation, or biological/cultural deficits). Victim blaming is strong as the existence of oppression, discrimination, and racism is denied. Hardiman believes that while the naïveté stage is brief in duration, the acceptance stage can last a lifetime.

3. Over time, the individual begins to challenge assumptions of White superiority and the denial of racism and discrimination. Moving from the acceptance stage to the *resistance stage* can prove to be a painful, conflicting, and uncomfortable transition. The White person's denial system begins to crumble because of a monumental event or a series of events that not only challenge but also shatter the individual's denial system. A White person may, for example, make friends with a minority coworker and discover that the images he or she has of "these people" are untrue. They may have witnessed clear incidents of unfair discrimination toward persons of color and may now begin to question assumptions regarding racial inferiority. In any case, the racial realities of life in the United States can no longer be denied. The change from one stage to another might take considerable time, but once completed, the person becomes conscious of being White, is aware that he or she harbors racist attitudes, and begins to see the pervasiveness of oppression in our society. Feelings of anger, pain, hurt, rage, and frustration are present. In many cases, the White person may develop a negative reaction toward his or her own group or culture. While they may romanticize people of color, they cannot interact confidently with them because they fear that they will make racist mistakes. This discomfort is best exemplified in a passage by Sara Winter (1977, p. 1):

   We avoid Black people because their presence brings painful questions to mind. Is it OK to talk about watermelons or mention "black coffee"? Should we use Black slang and tell racial jokes? How about talking about our experiences in Harlem, or mentioning our Black lovers? Should we conceal the fact that our mother still employs a Black cleaning lady?... We're embarrassedly aware of trying to do our best but to "act natural" at the same time. No wonder we're more comfortable in all-White situations where these dilemmas don't arise.

   According to Hardiman (1982), the discomfort in realizing that one is White and that one's group has engaged in oppression of racial/ethnic minorities may propel the person into the next stage.

4. Asking the painful question of who one is in relation to one's racial heritage, honestly confronting one's biases and prejudices, and accepting responsibility for one's Whiteness are the culminating marks of the *redefinition stage*. New ways of defining one's social group and one's membership in that group become important. The intense soul searching is most evident in Winter's personal journey as she writes,

> *In this sense we Whites are the victims of racism. Our victimization is different from that of Blacks, but it is real. We have been programmed into the oppressor roles we play, without our informed consent in the process. Our unawareness is part of the programming: None of us could tolerate the oppressor position, if we lived with a day-to-day emotional awareness of the pain inflicted on other humans through the instrument of our behavior. . . . We Whites benefit in concrete ways, year in and year out, from the present racial arrangements. All my life in White neighborhoods, White schools, White jobs and dealing with White police (to name only a few), I have experienced advantages that are systematically not available to Black people. It does not make sense for me to blame myself for the advantages that have come my way by virtue of my Whiteness. But absolving myself from guilt does not imply forgetting about racial injustice or taking it lightly (as my guilt pushes me to do). (Winter, 1977, p. 2)*

There is realization that Whiteness has been defined in opposition to people of color—namely, by standards of White supremacy. By being able to step out of this racist paradigm and redefine what her Whiteness meant to her, Winter is able to add meaning to developing a nonracist identity. The extremes of good/bad or positive/negative attachments to "White" and "people of color" begin to become more realistic. The person no longer denies being White, honestly confronts one's racism, understands the concept of White privilege, and feels increased comfort in relating to persons of color.

5. The *internalization stage* is the result of forming a new social and personal identity. With the greater comfort in understanding oneself and the development of a nonracist White identity comes a commitment to social action as well. The individual accepts responsibility for effecting personal and social change without always relying on persons of color to lead the way. As Winter explains,

> *To end racism, Whites have to pay attention to it and continue to pay attention. Since avoidance is such a basic dynamic of racism, paying attention will not happen naturally. We Whites must learn how to hold racism realities in our attention. We must learn to take responsibility for this process ourselves, without waiting for Blacks' actions to remind us that the problem exists, and without depending on Black people to reassure us and forgive us for our racist sins. In my*

experience, the process is painful but it is a relief to shed the fears, stereotypes, immobilizing guilt we didn't want in the first place. (1977, p. 2)

The racist-free identity, however, must be nurtured, validated, and supported in order to be sustained in a hostile environment. Such an individual is constantly bombarded by attempts to be resocialized into the oppressive society.

There are several potential limitations to the Hardiman (1982) model: (1) The select and limited sample that she uses to derive the stages and enumerate the characteristics makes potential generalization suspect; (2) the autobiographies of White Americans are not truly representative, and their experiences with racism may be bound by the era of the times; (3) the stages are tied to existing social identity development theories, and the model proposes a naïveté stage that for all practical purposes exists only in children ages 3 to 4 years (it appears tangential in her model and might better be conceptualized as part of the acceptance stage of socialization); and (4) there have been no direct empirical or other postmodern methods of exploration concerning the model to date. Despite these cautions and potential limitations, Hardiman has contributed greatly to our understanding of White identity development by focusing attention on racism as a central force in the socialization of White Americans.

The Helms White Racial Identity Development Model

Working independently of Hardiman, Janet Helms (1984, 1990, 1994, 1995) created perhaps the most elaborate and sophisticated White racial identity model yet proposed. Helms is arguably the most influential White identity development theorist. Not only has her model led to the development of an assessment instrument to measure White racial identity, but it also has been scrutinized empirically (Carter, 1990; Helms & Carter, 1990) and has generated much research and debate in the psychological literature. Like Hardiman (1982), Helms assumes that racism is an intimate and central part of being a White American. To her, developing a healthy White identity requires movement through two phases: (1) abandonment of racism and (2) defining a nonracist White identity. Six specific racial identity statuses are distributed equally in the two phases: contact, disintegration, reintegration, pseudoindependence, immersion/emersion, and autonomy. Originally, Helms used the term *stages* to refer to the six, but because of certain conceptual ambiguities and the controversy that ensued, she has abandoned its usage.

1. *Contact status.* People in this status are oblivious to and unaware of racism, believe that everyone has an equal chance for success, lack an understanding of prejudice and discrimination, have minimal experiences

with persons of color, and may profess to be color-blind. Such statements as "People are people," "I don't notice a person's race at all," and "You don't act Black" are examples. While there is an attempt to minimize the importance or influence of race, there is a definite dichotomy of Blacks and Whites on both a conscious and unconscious level regarding stereotypes and the superior/inferior dimensions of the races. Because of obliviousness and compartmentalization, it is possible for two diametrically opposed belief systems to coexist: (1) Uncritical acceptance of White supremacist notions relegates minorities into the inferior category with all the racial stereotypes, and (2) there is a belief that racial and cultural differences are considered unimportant. This allows Whites to avoid perceiving themselves as dominant group members, or of having biases and prejudices. Such an orientation is aptly stated by Peggy McIntosh in her own White racial awakening:

My schooling gave me no training in seeing myself as an oppressor, as an unfairly advantaged person, or as a participant in a damaged culture. I was taught to see myself as an individual whose moral state depended on her individual moral will. . . . Whites are taught to think of their lives as morally neutral, normative, and average, and also ideal, so that when we work to benefit others, this is seen as work which will allow "them" to be more like "us." (1989, p. 8)

2. *Disintegration status.* While in the previous status the individual does not recognize the polarities of democratic principles of equality and the unequal treatment of minority groups, such obliviousness may eventually break down. The White person becomes conflicted over irresolvable racial moral dilemmas that are frequently perceived as polar opposites: believing one is nonracist, yet not wanting one's son or daughter to marry a minority group member; believing that all men are created equal, even though society treats Blacks as second-class citizens; and not acknowledging that oppression exists, and then witnessing it (e.g., the beating of Rodney King). Conflicts between loyalty to one's group and humanistic ideals may manifest themselves in various ways. The person becomes increasingly conscious of his or her Whiteness and may experience dissonance and conflict, resulting in feelings of guilt, depression, helplessness, or anxiety. Statements such as, "My grandfather is really prejudiced, but I try not to be" and "I'm personally not against interracial marriages, but I worry about the children," are representative of personal struggles occurring in the White person.

    While a healthy resolution might be to confront the myth of meritocracy realistically, the breakdown of the denial system is painful and anxiety provoking. Attempts at resolution, according to Helms, may involve (1) avoiding contact with persons of color, (2) not thinking about race, and (3) seeking reassurance from others that racism is not the fault of Whites.

3. *Reintegration status.* This status can best be characterized as a regression in which the pendulum swings back to the most basic beliefs of White superiority and minority inferiority. In their attempts to resolve the dissonance created from the previous process, there is a retreat to the dominant ideology associated with race and one's own socioracial group identity. This ego status results in idealizing the White Euro-American group and the positives of White culture and society; there is a consequent negation and intolerance of other minority groups. In general, a firmer and more conscious belief in White racial superiority is present. Racial/ethnic minorities are blamed for their own problems.

I'm an Italian grandmother. No one gave us welfare or a helping hand when we came over [immigrated]. My father worked day and night to provide us with a decent living and to put all of us through school. These Negroes are always complaining about prejudice and hardships. Big deal! Why don't they stop whining and find a job? They're not the only ones who were discriminated against, you know. You don't think our family wasn't? We never let that stop us. In America everyone can make it if they are willing to work hard. I see these Black welfare mothers waiting in line for food stamps and free handouts. You can't convince me they're starving. Look at how overweight most of them are.... Laziness— that's what I see. (quoted from a workshop participant)

4. *Pseudoindependence status.* This status represents the second phase of Helms's model, which involves defining a nonracist White identity. As in the Hardiman model, a person is likely to be propelled into this phase because of a painful or insightful encounter or event that jars the person from the reintegration status. The awareness of other visible racial/ethnic minorities, the unfairness of their treatment, and a discomfort with their racist White identity may lead a person to identify with the plight of persons of color. There is an attempt to understand racial, cultural, and sexual orientation differences and a purposeful and conscious decision to interact with minority group members. However, the well-intentioned White person at this status may suffer from several problematic dynamics: (1) While intending to be socially conscious and helpful to minority groups, the White individual may unknowingly perpetuate racism by helping minorities adjust to the prevailing White standards; and (2) choice of minority individuals is based on how similar they are to him or her, and the primary mechanism used to understand racial issues is intellectual and conceptual. As a result, understanding has not reached the experiential and affective domains. In

other words, understanding Euro-American White privilege, socio-political aspects of race, and issues of bias, prejudice, and discrimination tend to be more an intellectual exercise.

5. *Immersion/emersion status.* If the person is reinforced to continue a personal exploration of him- or herself as a racial being, questions become focused on what it means to be White. Helms states that the person searches for an understanding of the personal meaning of racism and the ways in which one benefits from White privilege. There is an increasing willingness to confront one's own biases, to redefine White-ness, and to become more activistic in directly combating racism and oppression. This status is different from the previous one in two major ways: It is marked by (1) a shift in focus from trying to change Blacks to changing the self and other Whites and (2) increasing experiential and affective understanding that was lacking in the previous status. This later process is extremely important. Indeed, Helms believes that a successful resolution of this status requires an emotional catharsis or release that forces the person to relive or re-experience previous emotions that were denied or distorted. The ability to achieve this affective/experiential upheaval leads to a euphoria, or even a feeling of rebirth, and is a necessary condition to developing a new, nonracist White identity. As Winter states,

Let me explain this healing process in more detail. We must unearth all the words and memories we generally try not to think about, but which are inside us all the time: "nigger," "Uncle Tom," "jungle bunny," "Oreo," lynching, cattle prods, castrations, rapists, "black pussy," and black men with their huge penises, and hundreds more. (I shudder as I write.) We need to review three different kinds of material: (1) All our personal memories connected with blackness and black people including everything we can recall hearing or reading; (2) all the racist images and stereotypes we've ever heard, particularly the grossest and most hurtful ones; (3) any race-related things we ourselves said, did or omitted doing which we feel bad about today. . . . Most whites begin with a good deal of amnesia. Eventually the memories crowd in, especially when several people pool recollections. Emotional release is a vital part of the process. Experiencing feelings seems to allow further recollections to come. I need persistent encouragement from my companions to continue. (1977, p. 3)

6. *Autonomy status.* Increasing awareness of one's own Whiteness, reduced feelings of guilt, acceptance of one's role in perpetuating racism, and renewed determination to abandon White entitlement lead to an autonomy status. The person is knowledgeable about racial, ethnic, and cultural differences; values the diversity; and is no longer fearful, in-

timidated, or uncomfortable with the experiential reality of race. Development of a nonracist White identity becomes increasingly strong. Indeed, the person feels comfortable with his or her nonracist White identity, does not personalize attacks on White supremacy, and can explore the issues of racism and personal responsibility without defensiveness. A person in this status "walks the talk" and actively values and seeks out interracial experiences. Characteristics of the autonomy status can be found in the personal journey of Kiselica:

> *I was deeply troubled as I witnessed on a daily basis the detrimental effects of institutional racism and oppression on ethnic-minority groups in this country. The latter encounters forced me to recognize my privileged position in our society because of my status as a so-called Anglo. It was upsetting to know that I, a member of White society, benefited from the hardships of others that were caused by a racist system. I was also disturbed by the painful realization that I was, in some ways, a racist. I had to come to grips with the fact that I had told and laughed at racist jokes and, through such behavior, had supported White racist attitudes. If I really wanted to become an effective, multicultural psychologist, extended and profound self-reckoning was in order. At times, I wanted to flee from this unpleasant process by merely participating superficially with the remaining tasks . . . while avoiding any substantive self-examination. (1998, pp. 10–11)*

Helm's model is by far the most widely cited, researched, and applied of all the White racial identity formulations. Part of its attractiveness and value is the derivation of "defenses," "protective strategies," or what Helms (1995) formally labels *information-processing strategies* (IPSs), which White people use to avoid or assuage anxiety and discomfort around the issue of race. Each status has a dominant IPS associated with it: *contact* = obliviousness or denial; *disintegration* = suppression and ambivalence; *reintegration* = selective perception and negative out-group distortion; *pseudoindependence* = reshaping reality and selective perception; *immersion/emersion* = hypervigilance and reshaping: and *autonomy* = flexibility and complexity. Table 11.1 lists examples of IPS statements likely to be made by White people in each of the six ego statuses. Understanding these strategic reactions is important for White American identity development, for understanding the barriers that must be overcome in order to move to another status, and for potentially developing effective training or clinical strategies.

The Helms model, however, is not without its detractors. In an article critical of the Helms model and of most "stage" models of White racial identity development, Rowe, Bennett, and Atkinson (1994) raised some serious objections. First, they claim that Helms's model is erroneously based on racial/ethnic minority identity development models (discussed in the previous chapter). Because minority identity development occurs in the face of

Table 11.1 **White Racial Identity Ego Statuses and Information-Processing Strategies**

1. *Contact status:* satisfaction with racial status quo, obliviousness to racism and one's participation in it. If racial factors influence life decisions, they do so in a simplistic fashion. Information-processing strategy (IPS): Obliviousness.

Example: "I'm a White woman. When my grandfather came to this country, he was discriminated against, too. But he didn't blame Black people for his misfortunes. He educated himself and got a job: That's what Blacks ought to do. If White callers [to a radio station] spent as much time complaining about racial discrimination as your Black callers do, we'd never have accomplished what we have. You all should just ignore it" (quoted from a workshop participant).

2. *Disintegration status:* disorientation and anxiety provoked by irresolvable racial moral dilemmas that force one to choose between own-group loyalty and humanism. May be stymied by life situations that arouse racial dilemmas. IPS: Suppression and ambivalence.

Example: "I myself tried to set a nonracist example [for other Whites] by speaking up when someone said something blatantly prejudiced—how to do this without alienating people so that they would no longer take me seriously was always tricky—and by my friendships with Mexicans and Blacks who were actually the people with whom I felt most comfortable" (Blauner, 1993, p. 8).

3. *Reintegration status:* idealization of one's socioracial group, denigration, and intolerance for other groups. Racial factors may strongly influence life decisions. IPS: Selective perception and negative out-group distortion.

Example: "So what if my great-grandfather owned slaves. He didn't mistreat them and besides, I wasn't even here then. I never owned slaves. So, I don't know why Blacks expect me to feel guilty for something that happened before I was born. Nowadays, reverse racism hurts Whites more than slavery hurts Blacks. At least they got three square [meals] a day. But my brother can't even get a job with the police department because they have to hire less-qualified Blacks. That [expletive] happens to Whites all the time" (quoted from a workshop participant).

4. *Pseudoindependence status:* intellectualized commitment to one's own socioracial group and deceptive tolerance of other groups. May make life decisions to "help other racial groups." IPS: Reshaping reality and selective perception.

Example: "Was I the only person left in American who believed that the sexual mingling of the races was a good thing, that it would erase cultural barriers and leave us all a lovely shade of tan? . . . Racial blending is inevitable. At the very least, it may be the only solution to our dilemmas of race" (Allen, 1994, p. C4).

5. *Immersion/emersion status:* search for an understanding of the personal meaning of racism and the ways by which one benefits and a redefinition of Whiteness. Life choices may incorporate racial activism. IPS: Hypervigilance and reshaping.

Example: "It's true that I personally did not participate in the horror of slavery, and I don't even know whether my ancestors owned slaves. But I know that because I am White, I continue to benefit from a racist system that stems from the slavery era. I believe that if White people are ever going to understand our role in perpetuating racism, then we must begin to ask ourselves some hard questions and be willing to consider our role in maintaining a hurtful system. Then, we must try to do something to change it" (quoted from a workshop participant).

Table 11.1 **continued**

6. *Autonomy status:* informed positive socioracial group commitment, use of internal standards for self-definition, capacity to relinquish the privileges of racism. May avoid life options that require participation in racial oppression. IPS: Flexibility and complexity.

Example: "I live in an integrated [Black-White] neighborhood and I read Black literature and popular magazines. So, I understand that the media presents a very stereotypic view of Black culture. I believe that if more of us White people made more than a superficial effort to obtain accurate information about racial groups other than our own, then we could help make this country a better place for all peoples" (quoted from a workshop participant).

Source: Helms (1995, p. 185).

stereotyping and oppression, it may not apply to White identity, which does not occur under the same conditions. Second, they believe that too much emphasis is placed on the development of White attitudes toward minorities, and that not enough is placed on the development of White attitudes toward themselves and their own identity. Third, they claim that there is a conceptual inaccuracy in putting forth the model as developmental via stages (linear) and that the progression from less to more healthy seems to be based on the author's ethics. Last, Rowe (2006) attacks the Helms model of white racial identity development because it is based upon the White Racial Identity Attitude Scale (Helms & Carter, 1990) which he labels a "pseudoscience" because he asserts that the psychometric properties are not supported by the empirical literature. It is important to note that the critique of the Helms (1984) model has not been left unanswered. In subsequent writings, Helms (1994, 1995) has disclaimed the Rowe et al. (1994) characterization of her model and has attempted to clarify her position.

The continuing debate has proven beneficial for two reasons. First, the Helms model has evolved and changed (whether because of these criticisms or not) so that it has become even more intricate and clear. For example, Helms denies ever being a stage theorist, but to prevent continuing future confusion, she now prefers the term *status* and describes her thinking on this issue in detail (Helms, 1995). Second, in responding to the Helms model, Rowe et al. (1994) offered an alternative means of conceptualizing White identity that has contributed to the increasing understanding of White identity development.

Briefly, Rowe et al. (1994) prefer to conceptualize White racial identity as one of *types* or *statuses* rather than *stages*. They take care in explaining that these types are not fixed entities but are subject to experiential modification. They propose two major groupings, with seven types of racial consciousness: unachieved (avoidant, dependent, and dissonant) and achieved (dominative, conflictive, reactive, and integrative). Movement from type to type is dependent on the creation of dissonance, personal attributes, and the subsequent

Table 11.2 **Rowe, Bennett, and Atkinson's Model of White Racial Consciousness Types and Their Characteristics**

I. Unachieved

  A. Avoidant types ignore, avoid, deny, or minimize racial issues. They do not consider their own racial identity, nor are they seemingly aware of minority issues.

  B. Dependent types have minimal racial attitudes developed through person experience or consideration. They most often follow the lead of significant others in the life, such as would a child with his or her parent.

  C. Dissonant types often feel conflict between their belief systems and contradictory experiences. This type may break away from these attitudes depending on the degree of support or the intensity of the conflict. As such, it is a transitory status for the person.

II. Achieved

  A. Dominative types are very ethnocentric and believe in White superiority and minority inferiority. They may act out their biases passively or actively.

  B. Conflictive types oppose direct and obvious discrimination but would be unwilling to change the status quo. Most feel that discrimination has been eliminated and that further efforts constitute reverse racism.

  C. Reactive types have good awareness that racism exists but seem unaware of their personal responsibility in perpetuating it. They may overidentify with or be paternalistic toward minorities.

  D. Integrative types "have integrated their sense of Whiteness with a regard for racial/ethnic minorities . . . [and] integrate rational analysis, on the one hand, and moral principles, on the other, as they relate to a variety of racial/ethnic issues" (Rowe, Bennett, & Atkinson, 1994, p. 141).

environmental conditions encountered by the person. As a result, the primary gateway for change involves the dissonant type. Persons can move between all types except two unachieved ones, *avoidant* and *dependent*. These latter two are characterized by a lack of internalized attitudes. Space does not permit an extended discussion of the model; we have chosen to summarize these types and their characteristics in Table 11.2.

The Process of White Racial Identity Development: A Descriptive Model

Analysis of the models just discussed reveals some important differences. First, the identity development models seem to focus on a more definite and sequential movement through stages or statuses. They differ, however, in where they place the particular stages or statuses in the developmental process. Given that almost all models now entertain the possibility that development can vary (looping and recycling), the consciousness development model allows greater latitude conceptually for movement to various types. Rowe et al. (1994) seem to offer a more fluid process of racial experience by White people. Consequently, the model is also less bound by the context or era of the times (identity formed during the civil rights movement versus current times). The addition of nonachieved statuses is missing in the development theories and may capture more closely the "passive" feel that Whites experience in their racial identity development.

However, the essential concept of developing a positive White identity is conspicuously absent from the consciousness model. It lacks richness in allowing White people to view their developmental history better and to gain a sense of their past, present, and future. Struggling with racial identity and issues of race requires a historical perspective, which development theories offer. It is with this in mind that we have attempted to take aspects of White racial identity/consciousness development into consideration when formulating a descriptive model with practical implications.

In our work with White trainees and clinicians, we have observed some very important changes through which they seem to move as they work toward multicultural competence. We have been impressed with how Whites seem to go through parallel racial/cultural identity transformations. This is especially true if we accept the fact that Whites are as much victims of societal forces (i.e., they are socialized into racist attitudes and beliefs) as are their minority counterparts. No child is born wanting to be a racist! Yet White people do benefit from the dominant-subordinate relationship in our society. It is this factor that Whites need to confront in an open and honest manner.

Using the formulation of D. W. Sue and D. Sue (1990) and D. W. Sue et al. (1998), we propose a seven step process that integrates many characteristics from the other formulations. Furthermore, we make some basic assumptions with respect to those models: (1) Racism is an integral part of U.S. life, and it permeates all aspects of our culture and institutions (ethnocentric monoculturalism); (2) Whites are socialized into the society and therefore inherit all the biases, stereotypes, and racist attitudes, beliefs, and behaviors of the larger society; (3) how Whites perceive themselves as racial beings follows an identifiable sequence that can occur in a linear or nonlinear fashion; (4) the status of White racial identity development in any multicultural encounter affects the process and outcome of interracial relationships; and (5) the most desirable outcome is one in which the White person not only accepts his or her Whiteness but also defines it in a nondefensive and nonracist manner.

1. *Naïveté phase.* This phase is relatively neutral with respect to racial/cultural differences. It lasts during the first 3 years of life and is marked by a naïve curiosity about race. As mentioned previously, racial awareness and burgeoning social meanings are absent or minimal and the young child is generally innocent, open, and spontaneous regarding racial

differences. Between the ages of 3to 5, however, the young White child begins to associate positive ethnocentric meanings to his or her own group and negative ones to others. Bombarded by misinformation through the educational channels, mass media, and significant others in his or her life, a sense of superiority is instilled in the concept of whiteness and the inferiority of all other groups and their heritage. The following passage describes one of the insidious processes of socialization that leads to propelling the child into the conformity phase.

It was a late summer afternoon. A group of white neighborhood mothers, obviously friends, had brought their 4- and 5-year-olds to the local McDonald's for a snack and to play on the swings and slides provided by the restaurant. They were all seated at a table watching their sons and daughters run about the play area. In one corner of the yard sat a small black child pushing a red truck along the grass. One of the white girls from the group approached the black boy and they started a conversation. During that instant, the mother of the girl exchanged quick glances with the other mothers who nodded knowingly. She quickly rose from the table, walked over to the two, spoke to her daughter, and gently pulled her away to join her previous playmates. Within minutes, however, the girl again approached the black boy and both began to play with the truck. At that point, all the mothers rose from the table and loudly exclaimed to their children, "It's time to go now!" (Taken from D. W. Sue, 2003, pp. 89–90)

2. *Conformity phase.* The White person's attitudes and beliefs in this stage are very ethnocentric. There is minimal awareness of the self as a racial being and a strong belief in the universality of values and norms governing behavior. The White person possesses limited accurate knowledge of other ethnic groups, but he or she is likely to rely on social stereotypes as the main source of information. As we saw, Hardiman (1982) described this stage as an acceptance of White superiority and minority inferiority. Consciously or unconsciously, the White person believes that White culture is the most highly developed and that all others are primitive or inferior. The conformity stage is marked by contradictory and often compartmentalized attitudes, beliefs, and behaviors. A person may believe simultaneously that he or she is not racist but that minority inferiority justifies discriminatory and inferior treatment, and that minority persons are different and deviant but that "people are people" and differences are unimportant (Helms, 1984). As with their minority counterparts at this stage, the primary mechanism operating here is one of denial and compartmentalization. For example, many Whites deny that they belong to a race that allows them to avoid personal responsibility for perpetuating a racist system. Like a fish in water, White folks either have difficulty seeing or are unable to see the invis-

ible veil of cultural assumptions, biases, and prejudices that guide their perceptions and actions. They tend to believe that White Euro-American culture is superior and that other cultures are primitive, inferior, less developed, or lower on the scale of evolution. It is important to note that many Whites in this phase of development are unaware of these beliefs and operate as if they are universally shared by others. They believe that differences are unimportant and that "people are people," "we are all the same under the skin," "we should treat everyone the same," "problems wouldn't exist if minorities would only assimilate," and discrimination and prejudice are something that others do. The helping professional with this perspective professes color blindness, views counseling/therapy theories as universally applicable, and does not question their relevance to other culturally different groups. The primary mechanism used in encapsulation is denial—denial that people are different, denial that discrimination exists, and denial of one's own prejudices. Instead, the locus of the problem is seen to reside in the minority individual or group. Minorities would not encounter problems if they would only assimilate and acculturate (melting pot), value education, or work harder.

3. *Dissonance phase.* Movement into the dissonance stage occurs when the White person is forced to deal with the inconsistencies that have been compartmentalized or encounters information/experiences at odds with denial. In most cases, a person is forced to acknowledge Whiteness at some level, to examine their own cultural values, and to see the conflict between upholding humanistic nonracist values and their contradictory behavior. For example, a person who may consciously believe that all men are created equal and that he or she treats everyone the same suddenly experiences reservations about having African Americans move next door or having their son or daughter involved in an interracial relationship. These more personal experiences bring the individual face to face with his or her own prejudices and biases. In this situation, thoughts that "I am not prejudiced," "I treat everyone the same regardless or race, creed, or color," and "I do not discriminate" collide with the denial system. Additionally, some major event (the assassination of Martin Luther King, Jr., the Rodney King beating, etc.) may force the person to realize that racism is alive and well in the United States.

   The increasing realization that one is biased and that Euro-American society does play a part in oppressing minority groups is an unpleasant one. Dissonance may result in feelings of guilt, shame, anger, and depression. Rationalizations may be used to exonerate one's own inactivity in combating perceived injustice or personal feelings of prejudice; for example, "I'm only one person—what can I do?" or "Everyone is prejudiced, even minorities." As these conflicts ensue, the White person may retreat into the protective confines of White culture (encapsulation of the previous stage) or move progressively toward insight and revelation (resistance and immersion stage).

Whether a person regresses is related to the strength of positive forces pushing an individual forward (support for challenging racism) and negative forces pushing the person backward (fear of some loss). For example, challenging the prevailing beliefs of the times may mean risking ostracism from other White relatives, friends, neighbors, and colleagues. Regardless of the choice, there are many uncomfortable feelings of guilt, shame, anger, and depression related to the realization of inconsistencies in one's belief systems. Guilt and shame are most likely related to the recognition of the White person's role in perpetuating racism in the past. Guilt may also result from the person's being afraid to speak out on the issues or take responsibility for his or her part in a current situation. For example, the person may witness an act of racism, hear a racist comment, or be given preferential treatment over a minority person but decide not to say anything for fear of violating racist White norms. Many White people rationalize their behaviors by believing that they are powerless to make changes. Additionally, there is a tendency to retreat into White culture. If, however, others (which may include some family and friends) are more accepting, forward movement is more likely.

4.   *Resistance and immersion phase.* The White person who progresses to this stage will begin to question and challenge his or her own racism. For the first time, the person begins to realize what racism is all about, and his or her eyes are suddenly open. Racism is seen everywhere (advertising, television, educational materials, interpersonal interactions, etc.). This phase of development is marked by a major questioning of one's own racism and that of others in society. In addition, increasing awareness of how racism operates and its pervasiveness in U.S. culture and institutions are the major hallmark of this level. It is as if the person has awakened to the realities of oppression, sees how educational materials, the mass media, advertising, and other elements portray and perpetuate stereotypes, and recognizes how being White grants certain advantages denied to various minority groups.

There is likely to be considerable anger at family and friends, institutions, and larger societal values, which are seen as having sold him or her a false bill of goods (democratic ideals) that were never practiced. Guilt is also felt for having been a part of the oppressive system. Strangely enough, the person is likely to undergo a form of racial self-hatred at this stage. Negative feelings about being White are present, and the accompanying feelings of guilt, shame, and anger toward oneself and other Whites may develop. The *White liberal syndrome* may develop and be manifested in two complementary styles: the paternalistic protector role or the overidentification with another minority group (Helms, 1984; Ponterotto, 1988). In the former, the White person may devote his or her energies in an almost paternalistic attempt to protect minorities from abuse. In the latter, the person may actually want to identify with a particular minority group (Asian, Black, etc.) in order to escape his or her own Whiteness. The White person will soon discover, however, that these roles are not appreciated by minority groups and will experience rejection. Again, the person may resolve this dilemma by moving back into the protective confines of White culture (conformity stage), again experience conflict (dissonance), or move directly to the introspective stage.

5. *Introspective phase.* This phase is most likely a compromise of having swung from an extreme of unconditional acceptance of White identity to a rejection of Whiteness. It is a state of relative quiescence, introspection, and reformulation of what it means to be White. The person realizes and no longer denies that he or she has participated in oppression and benefited from White privilege, or that racism is an integral part of U.S. society. However, individuals at this stage become less motivated by guilt and defensiveness, accept their Whiteness, and seek to redefine their own identity and that of their social group. This acceptance, however, does not mean a less active role in combating oppression. The process may involve addressing the questions, "What does it mean to be White?" "Who am I in relation to my Whiteness?" and "Who am I as a racial/cultural being?"

    The feelings or affective elements may be existential in nature and involve feelings of disconnectedness, isolation, confusion, and loss. In other words, the person knows that he or she will never fully understand the minority experience, but feels disconnected from the Euro-American group as well. In some ways, the introspective phase is similar in dynamics to the dissonance phase in that both represent a transition from one perspective to another. The process used to answer the previous questions and to deal with the ensuing feelings may involve a searching, observing, and questioning attitude. Answers to these questions involve dialoging and observing one's own social group and actively creating and experiencing interactions with various minority group members as well.

6. *Integrative awareness phase.* Reaching this level of development is most characterized as (1) understanding the self as a racial/cultural being,

(2) being aware of sociopolitical influences regarding racism, (3) appreciating racial/cultural diversity, and (4) becoming more committed toward eradicating oppression. The formation of a nonracist White Euro-American identity emerges and becomes internalized. The person values multiculturalism, is comfortable around members of culturally different groups, and feels a strong connectedness with members of many groups. Most important, perhaps, is the inner sense of security and strength that needs to develop and that is needed to function in a society that is only marginally accepting of integrative, aware White persons.

7. *Commitment to antiracist action phase.* Someone once stated that the ultimate White privilege is the ability to acknowledge it but do nothing about it. This phase is most characterized by social action. There is likely to be a consequent change in behavior and an increased commitment toward eradicating oppression. Seeing "wrong" and actively working to "right" it requires moral fortitude and direct action. Objecting to racist jokes, trying to educate family, friends, neighbors, and coworkers about racial issues, taking direct action to eradicate racism in the schools, workplace, and in social policy (often in direct conflict with other Whites) are examples of individuals who achieve this status. Movement into this phase often can be a lonely journey for Whites because they are oftentimes isolated by family, friends, and colleagues who do not understand their changed worldview. Strong pressures in society to not rock the boat, threats by family members that they will be disowned, avoidance by colleagues, threats of being labeled a troublemaker, or not being promoted at work are all possible pressures for the White person to move back to an earlier phase of development. To maintain a nonracist identity requires Whites to become increasingly immunized to social pressures for conformance and to begin forming alliances with persons of color or other liberated Whites who become a second family to them. As can be seen, the struggle against individual, institutional, and societal racism is a monumental task in this society.

Implications for Clinical Practice

It is important to stress again the need for White Euro-American counselors to understand the assumptions of White racial identity development models. We ask readers to seriously consider the validity of these assumptions and engage one another in a dialogue about them. Ultimately, the effectiveness of White therapists is related to their ability to overcome sociocultural conditioning and make their Whiteness visible. To do so, the following guidelines and suggestions are given.

1. Accept the fact that racism is a basic and integral part of U.S. life and permeates all aspects of our culture and institutions. Know that as a White person you are socialized into U.S. society and, therefore, inherit the biases, stereotypes, and racist attitudes, beliefs, and behaviors of the society

2. Understand that the level of White racial identity development in a cross-cultural encounter (working with minorities, responding to multicultural training, etc.) affects the process and outcome of an interracial relationship (including counseling/therapy).

3. Work on accepting your own Whiteness, but define it in a nondefensive and nonracist manner. How you perceive yourself as a racial being seems to be correlated strongly with how you perceive and respond to racial stimuli.

4. Spend time with healthy and strong people from another culture or racial group. As a counselor, the only contact we usually have comes from working with only a narrow segment of the society. Thus, the knowledge we have about minority groups is usually developed from working with troubled individuals.

5. Know that becoming culturally aware and competent comes through lived experience and reality. Identify a cultural guide, someone from the culture who is willing to help you understand his or her group.

6. Attend cultural events, meetings, and activities led by minority communities. This allows you to hear from church leaders, attend community celebrations, and participate in open forums so that you may sense the strengths of the community, observe leadership in action, personalize your understanding, and develop new social relationships.

7. When around persons of color, pay attention to feelings, thoughts, and assumptions that you have when race-related situations present themselves. Where are your feelings of uneasiness, differentness, or outright fear coming from? Do not make excuses for these thoughts or feelings, dismiss them, or avoid attaching meaning to them. Only if you are willing to confront them directly can you unlearn the misinformation and nested emotional fears.

8. Dealing with racism means a personal commitment to action. It means interrupting other White Americans when they make racist remarks and jokes or engage in racist actions, even if it is embarrassing or frightening. It means noticing the possibility for direct action against bias and discrimination in your everyday life.

SOCIAL JUSTICE
DIMENSIONS IN
COUNSELING/THERAPY

Social Justice
Counseling/Therapy

12

Chapter

Multicultural counseling and therapy must be about social justice; providing equal access and opportunity to all groups; being inclusive; removing individual and systemic barriers to fair mental health treatment; and ensuring that counseling/therapy services are directed at the micro, meso, and macro levels of our society (D. W. Sue, 2001). As such, it is important for us to understand what we mean by social justice and why it is such an important foundation of multicultural counseling and therapy (Lee, 2007; Toporek, Gerstein, Fouad, Roysircar, & Israel, 2006; Warren & Constantine, 2007). Let us use a specific case study to illustrate how a social justice orientation represents a paradigm shift in how we view the locus of the problem and the need to develop organizational and systemic intervention skills.

Malachi Rolls (a pseudonym) is a 12-year-old African American student attending a predominantly White grade school in Santa Barbara, California. He has been referred for counseling by his teachers because of "constant fighting" with students on the school grounds. In addition, his teachers note that Malachi was doing poorly in class, inattentive, argumentative toward authority figures, and disrespectful. The most recent incident, an especially violent one, required the assistant principal to physically pull Malachi away to prevent him from seriously injuring a fellow student. He was suspended from school for 3 days and subsequently referred to the school psychologist. Malachi was diagnosed with a conduct disorder and the psychologist recommended immediate counseling to prevent the untreated disorder from leading to more serious antisocial behaviors. The recommended course of treatment consisted of medication and therapy aimed at eliminating Malachi's aggressive behaviors and "controlling his underlying hostility and anger."

Malachi's parents, however, objected strenuously to the school psychologist's diagnosis and treatment recommendations. They described their son as feeling isolated, having few friends, being rejected by classmates, feeling invalidated by teachers, and feeling "removed" from the content of his classes. They noted that all of the "fights" were generally instigated through "baiting" and "name calling" by his White classmates, that the school climate was hostile toward their son, that the curriculum was very Eurocentric and failed to include African Americans, and that school personnel and teachers seemed naive about racial or multicultural issues. They hinted strongly that racism was at work in the school district and enlisted the aid of the only Black counselor in the school, Ms. Jones. Although Ms. Jones seemed to be understanding and empathic toward Malachi's plight, she seemed reluctant to intercede on behalf of the parents. Being a recent graduate from the local college, Ms. Jones feared being ostracized by other school personnel.

The concerns of Malachi's parents were quickly dismissed by school officials as having little validity. These officials contended that Malachi needed to be more accommodating, to reach out and make friends rather than isolating himself, to take a more active interest in his schoolwork, and to become a good citizen. Further, they asserted it was not the school climate that was hostile, but that Malachi needed to "learn to fit in." "We treat everyone the same, regardless of race. This school doesn't discriminate," stated the school officials. (D. W. Sue & Constantine, 2003, pp. 214–215)

If you were a counselor or social worker, how would you address this case? Where would you focus your energies? Traditional clinical approaches would direct their attention to what they perceive as the locus of the problem—Malachi and his fighting with classmates. This approach makes several assumptions: (1) the locus of the problem resides in the person; (2) behaviors that violate socially accepted norms are considered maladaptive or disordered; (3) remediation or elimination of problem behaviors is the goal; (4) the social context or status quo guides the determination of normal versus abnormal and healthy versus unhealthy behaviors; and (5) the appropriate role for the counselor is to help the client "fit in" and become "a good citizen." Taking a social justice approach, however, might mean challenging these assumptions and even reversing them in the following way:

1. The locus of the problem may reside in the social system (other students, hostile campus environment, alienating curriculum, lack of minority teachers/staff/students, etc.) rather than the individual.

2. Behaviors that violate social norms may not be disordered or unhealthy.

3. While remediation is important, the more effective long-term solution is prevention.

4. The social norms, prevailing beliefs, and institutional polices and practices that maintain the status quo should be challenged and changed.

5. Organizational change requires a macrosystems approach involving other roles and skills beyond the traditional clinical one.

Principles of Social Justice counseling

These five perspectives illustrate several basic principles of social justice counseling, which is the topic of this chapter. Let us briefly describe some of them, using the case of Malachi to illustrate our points.

Principle One: A failure to develop a balanced perspective between person and system focus can result in false attribution of the problem. It is apparent that school officials have attributed the locus of the problem to reside in Malachi; that he is impulsive, angry, inattentive, unmotivated, disrespectful, and a poor student. He is labeled as possessing a conduct disorder with potential antisocial traits. Diagnosis of the problem is internal—that is, it resides in Malachi. When the focus of therapy is primarily on the individual, there is a strong tendency to see the locus of the problem as residing solely in the person (Cosgrove, 2006) rather than in the school system, curriculum, or wider campus community. As a result, well-intentioned counselors may mistakenly blame the victim (e.g., the problem is a deficiency of the person) when, in actuality, it may reside in the environment. We would submit that it is highly probable that Malachi is the victim of a monocultural educational environment that alienates and denigrates him (Davidson, Waldo, & Adams, 2006); curricula that does not deal with the contributions of African Americans or portrays them in a demeaning fashion; teaching styles that may be culturally biased; grading practices that emphasize individual competition; a campus climate that is hostile to minority students (perceived as less qualified); support services (counseling, study skills, etc.) that fail to understand the minority student experience; and the lack of role models (presence of only one Black teacher in the school). For example, would it change your analysis and focus of intervention if Malachi gets into fights because he is teased mercilessly by fellow students who use racial slurs (nigger, jungle bunny, burr head, etc.)? Suppose he is the only Black student on the campus and feels isolated. Suppose the curriculum doesn't deal with the contributions of African Americans and presents Black Americans in demeaning portrayals. In other words, suppose there is good reason for why this 12-year-old feels isolated, rejected, devalued, and misunderstood.

Principle Two: A failure to develop a balanced perspective between person and system focus can result in an ineffective and inaccurate treatment plan potentially harmful toward the client. A basic premise of the ecological model in social justice practice is the assumption that person-environment interactions are crucial to diagnosing and treating problems (Goodman, Liang, Helms, Latta, Sparks, & Weintraub, 2004). Clients, for example, are not viewed as isolated units, but as embedded in their families, social groups, communities, institutions, cultures, and in major systems of our society (Vera & Speight, 2003). Behavior is always a function of the interactions or transactions that occur between and among the many systems that comprise the life of the person. For example, a micro level of analysis may lead to one treatment plan while a macro analysis would lead to another. In other words, how a helping professional defines the problem affects the treatment focus and plan. If Malachi's problems are due to internal and intrapsychic dynamics, then it makes sense that the therapy be directed toward changing the person. The fighting behavior is perceived as dysfunctional and should be eliminated through Malachi learning to control his anger, or through medication that may correct his internal biological dysfunction. But, what if the problem is external? Will having Malachi stop his fighting behavior result in the elimination of teasing from White classmates? Will it make him more connected to the campus? Will it make him feel more valued and accepted? Will he relate more to the content of courses that denigrate the contributions of African Americans? Treating the symptoms or eliminating fighting behavior may actually make Malachi more vulnerable to racism.

Principle Three: When the client is the organization or a larger system and not an individual, it requires a major paradigm shift to attain a true understanding of problem and solution identification. Let us assume that Malachi is getting into fights because of the hostile school climate and the invalidating nature of his educational experience. Given this assumption, we ask the question "Who is the client?" Is it Malachi or the school? In his analysis of schizophrenia, R. D. Laing, an existential psychiatrist, once asked the following question: "Is schizophrenia a sick response to a healthy situation, or is it a healthy response to a sick situation?" In other words, if it is the school system that is dysfunctional (sick) and not the individual client, do we or should we adjust that person to a sick situation? In this case, do we focus on stopping the fighting behavior ? Or, if we view the fighting behavior as a healthy response to a sick situation, then eliminating the unhealthy situation (teasing, insensitive administrators and teachers, monocultural curriculum, etc.) should receive top priority for change (Lee, 2007).

Principle Four: Organizations are microcosms of the wider society from which they originate. As a result, they are likely to be reflections of the monocultural values and practices of the larger culture. In this case, it is not far-fetched to assume that White students, helping professionals, and educators may have inherited the racial biases of their forebears. Further, multicultural education specialists have decried the biased nature of the traditional curriculum. While education is supposed to liberate and convey truth and knowledge, it has oftentimes been the culprit in perpetuating false stereotypes and misinformation about various groups in our society. It has done this, perhaps not intentionally, but through omission, fabrication, distortion, or selective emphasis of information designed to enhance the contributions of certain groups over others. The result is that institutions of learning become sites that perpetuate myths and inaccuracies about certain groups in society, with devastating consequences to students of color. Further, policies and practices that "treat everyone the same" may themselves be culturally biased. If this is the institutional context from which Malachi is receiving his education, little wonder that he exhibits so-called problem behaviors. Again, the focus of change must be directed at the institutional level.

Principle Five: Organizations are powerful entities that inevitably resist change and possess many ways to force compliance among workers. To go against the policies, practices, and procedures of the institution, for example, can bring about major punitive actions. Let us look at the situation of the Black teacher, Ms. Jones. There are indications in this case that she understands that Malachi may be the victim of racism and a monocultural education that invalidates him. If she is aware of this factor, why is she so reluctant to act on behalf of Malachi and his parents? First, it is highly probable that, even if she is aware of the true problem, she lacks the knowledge, expertise, and skill to intervene on a systemic level. Second, there are many avenues open to institutions that can be used to force compliance on the part of employees. Voicing an alternative opinion against prevailing beliefs can result in ostracism by fellow workers, a poor job performance rating, denial of a promotion, or even an eventual firing. This creates a very strong ethical dilemma for mental health workers or educators when the needs of their clients differ from those of the organization or employer. The fact that counselors' livelihoods depend on the employing agency (school district) creates additional pressures to conform. How do counselors handle such conflicts? Organizational knowledge and skills become a necessity if the therapist is to be truly effective. So, even the most enlightened educator and counselor may find their good intentions thwarted by their lack of systems intervention skills and fears of punitive actions.

Principle Six: When multicultural organizational development is required, alternative helping roles that emphasize systems intervention must be part of the role repertoire of the mental health professional. Because the traditional counseling/therapy roles focus on one-to-one or small group relationships, they may not be productive when dealing with larger ecological and systemic issues. Competence in changing organizational policies, practices, procedures, and structures within institutions requires a different set of knowledge and skills that are more action oriented. Among them, consultation and advocacy become crucial in helping institutions move from a monocultural to a multicultural institution (Davidson, Waldo, & Adams, 2006). Malachi's school and the school district need a thorough cultural audit, institutional change in the campus climate, sensitivity training for all school personnel, increased racial/ethnic personnel at all levels of the school, revamping of the curriculum to be more multicultural, and so on. This is a major task that requires multicultural awareness, knowledge, and skills on the part of the consultant.

Principle Seven: Although remediation will always be needed, prevention is better. Conventional practice at the micro level continues to be oriented toward remediation rather than prevention. While no one would deny the important effects of biological and internal psychological factors on personal problems, more research now acknowledges the importance of sociocultural factors (inadequate or biased education, poor socialization practices, biased values, and discriminatory institutional policies) in creating many of the difficulties encountered by individuals. As therapists, we are frequently placed in a position of treating clients who represent the aftermath of failed and oppressive policies and practices. We have been trapped in the role of remediation (attempting to help clients once they have been damaged by sociocultural biases). While treating troubled clients (remediation) is a necessity, our task would be an endless and losing venture unless the true sources of the problem (stereotypes, prejudice, discrimination, and oppression) are changed. Would it not make more sense to take a proactive and preventative approach by attacking the cultural and institutional bases of the problem?

Social Justice Counseling

The case of Malachi demonstrates strongly the need for a social justice orientation to counseling and therapy. Indeed, multicultural counseling/therapy competence is intimately linked to the values of social justice (Hage, 2005; Sue, 2001; Warren & Constantine, 2007). If mental health practice is concerned with bettering the life circumstances of individuals, families, groups, and communities in our society, then social justice is the overarching umbrella that guides our profession. The welfare of a democratic society very much depends on equal access and opportunity, fair distribution of power and resources, and empowering individuals and groups with a right to determine their own lives. Smith (2003) defines a socially just world as having access to:

> *Adequate food, sleep, wages, education, safety, opportunity, institutional support, health care, child care, and loving relationships. "Adequate" means enough to allow [participation]in the world . . . without starving, or feeling economically trapped or uncompensated, continually exploited, terrorized, devalued, battered, chonically exhausted, or virtually enslaved (and for some reason, still, actually enslaved). (p. 167).*

Bell (1997) states that the goal of social justice is:

> *Full and equal participation of all groups in a society that is mutually shaped to meet their needs. Social justice includes a vision of society in which the distribution of resources is equitable and all members are physically and psychologically safe and secure. (p. 3)*

Given these broad descriptions, we propose a working definition of social justice counseling/therapy:

Social justice counseling/therapy is an active philosophy and approach aimed at producing conditions that allow for equal access and opportunity; reducing or eliminating disparities in education, health care, employment, and other areas that lower the quality of life for affected populations; encouraging mental health professionals to consider micro, meso, and macro levels in the assessment, diagnosis, and treatment of client and client systems; and broadening the role of the helping professional to include not only counselor/therapist but advocate, consultant, psychoeducator, change agent, community worker, etc.

It is clear that systems forces can be powerful and oppressive; Malachi Rolls is a prime example of how a failure to understand systemic dynamics may derail productive change. Becoming culturally competent requires not only changes at an individual practice level, but also changes associated with how we define our helping role. Unfortunately, an overwhelming majority of mental health practitioners desire to enter direct clinical service, especially counseling and psychotherapy (Shullman, Celeste, & Strickland, 2006). The mental health profession has implicitly or explicitly glamorized and defined the clinician as one who conducts his or her trade—working with individuals—in an office environment. While the development of individual intervention skills has been the main focus in many graduate training programs, little emphasis is given to other roles, activities, or settings (Toporek & McNally, 2006). Thus, not only might therapists be lacking in systems-intervention knowledge and skills, but they may also become unaccustomed to, and uncomfortable about, leaving their offices. Yet work with racial/ethnic minority groups and immigrant populations suggests that out-of-office sites/activities (client homes, churches, volunteer organizations, etc.) and alternative helping roles (ombudsman, advocates, consultants, organizational change agents, facilitators of indigenous healing systems, etc.) may prove more therapeutic and effective (Atkinson et al., 1993; Warren & Constantine, 2007). Social justice counseling with marginalized groups in our society is most enhanced when mental health professionals (1) can understand how individual and systemic worldviews shape clinical practice and (2) when they are equipped with organizational and systemic knowledge, expertise, and skills. Let us now turn our attention to both.

Understanding Individual and Systemic Worldviews

It has become increasingly clear that many diverse groups hold worldviews that differ from members of the dominant culture and their practicing therapists. In a broader sense, worldviews determine how people perceive their relationship to the world (nature, institutions, other people, etc.). Worldviews are highly correlated with a person's cultural upbringing and life experiences (Katz, 1985). Koltko-Rivera (2004) states "A wordview (or 'world view') is a set of assumptions about physical and social reality that may have powerful effects on cognition and behavior." Put in a much more practical way, not only are worldviews composed of our attitudes, values, opinions, and concepts, but they also affect how we think, define events, make decisions, and behave.

For marginalized groups in America, a strong determinant of world-views is very much related to the subordinate position assigned to them in society. Helping professionals who hold a worldview different from that of their clients, and who are unaware of the basis for this difference, are most likely to impute negative traits to clients. In most cases, for example, clients of color are more likely to have worldviews that differ from those of therapists. Yet many therapists are so culturally unaware that they respond according to their own conditioned values, assumptions, and perspectives of reality without regard for other views. Without this awareness, counselors who work with culturally diverse groups may be engaging in cultural oppression. Social justice counseling makes it a necessity to understand how race and culture-specific factors may interact in such a way as to produce people with different worldviews. Two different psychological orientations are important in the formation of worldviews: (1) locus of control and (2) locus of responsibility. The manner in which they interact results in the formation of four different psychological outlooks in life and their consequent characteristics, dynamics, and implications for social justice counseling.

Locus of Control

Rotter's (1966) historic work in the formulation of the concepts of internal-external control and the internal-external (I-E) dimension has contributed greatly to our understanding of human behavior. *Internal control* (IC) refers to people's beliefs that reinforcements are contingent on their own actions and that they can shape their own fate. *External control* (EC) refers to people's beliefs that reinforcing events occur independently of their actions and that the future is determined more by chance and luck. Early researchers (Lefcourt, 1966; Rotter, 1966, 1975) have summarized the research findings that correlated high internality with (1) greater attempts at mastering the environment, (2) superior coping strategies, (3) better cognitive processing of information, (4) lower predisposition to anxiety, (5) higher achievement motivation, (6) greater social action involvement, and (7) greater value on skill-determined rewards. As can be seen, these attributes are highly valued by U.S. society and constitute the core features of mental health.

Ethnic group members, people from low socioeconomic classes, and women score significantly higher on the external end of the locus-of-control continuum (see reviews by Sue, 1978 and Koltko-Rivera, 2004). Using the

I-E dimension as a criterion of mental health would mean that minority, poor, and female clients would be viewed as possessing less desirable attributes. Thus, a clinician who encounters a minority client with a high external orientation ("It's no use trying," "There's nothing I can do about it," and "You shouldn't rock the boat") may interpret the client as being inherently apathetic, procrastinating, lazy, depressed, or anxious about trying. The problem with an unqualified application of the I-E dimension is that it fails to take into consideration the different cultural and social experiences of the individual. This failure may lead to highly inappropriate and destructive applications in therapy. It seems plausible that different cultural groups, women, and people from a lower socioeconomic status (SES) have learned that control operates differently in their lives than how it operates for society at large (Ridley, 2005). For example, externality related to impersonal forces (chance and luck) is different from that ascribed to cultural forces, and from that ascribed to powerful others. Chance and luck operate equally across situations for everyone. However, the forces that determine locus of control from a cultural perspective may be viewed by the particular ethnic group as acceptable and benevolent. In this case, externality is viewed positively. American culture, for example, values the uniqueness, independence, and self-reliance of each individual. It places a high premium on self-reliance, individualism, and status achieved through one's own efforts. In contrast, the situation-centered Chinese culture places importance on the group (an individual is not defined apart from the family), on tradition, social roles-expectations, and harmony with the universe (Root, 1998). Thus, the cultural orientation of the more traditional Chinese tends to elevate the external scores. Note, however, that the external orientation of the Chinese is highly valued and accepted.

Likewise, high externality may constitute a realistic sociopolitical presence of influence from powerful others. For example, a major force in the literature dealing with locus of control is that of powerlessness. *Powerlessness* may be defined as the expectancy that a person's behavior cannot determine the outcomes or reinforcements that he or she seeks. There is a strong possibility that externality may be a function of a person's opinions about prevailing social institutions. For example, low SES individuals and Blacks are not given an equal opportunity to obtain the material rewards of Western culture. Because of racism, African Americans may be perceiving, in a realistic fashion, a discrepancy between their ability and attainment. In this case, externality may be seen as a malevolent force to be distinguished from the benevolent cultural ones just discussed. It can be concluded that while highly external people are less effectively motivated, perform poorly in achievement situations, and evidence greater psychological problems, this does not necessarily hold for minorities and low-income persons. Focusing on external forces may be motivationally healthy if it results from assessing one's chances for success against systematic and real external obstacles rather than unpredictable fate. Three factors of importance for our discussion can be identified.

The first factor, called *control ideology,* is a measure of general belief about the role of external forces in determining success and failure in the larger society. It represents a cultural belief in the Protestant ethic: Success is the result of hard work, effort, skill, and ability. The second factor, *personal control,* reflects a person's belief about his or her own sense of personal efficacy or competence. While control ideology represents an ideological belief, personal control is more related to actual control. Apparently, African Americans can be equally internal to Whites on control ideology, but when a personal reference (personal control) is used, they are much more external. This indicates that African Americans may have adopted the general cultural beliefs about internal control, but find that these cannot always be applied to their own life situations (because of racism and discrimination). It is interesting to note that Whites endorse control ideology statements at the same rate as they endorse personal control ones. Thus, the disparity between the two forms of control does not seem to be operative for White Americans. A third interesting finding is that personal control, as opposed to ideological control, is more related to motivational and performance indicators. A student high on personal control (internality) tends to have greater self-confidence, higher test scores, higher grades, and so on. Individuals who are high on the ideological measure are not noticeably different from their externally oriented counterparts.

The I-E continuum is useful for therapists only if they make clear distinctions about the meaning of the external control dimension. High externality may be due to (1) chance/luck, (2) cultural dictates that are viewed as benevolent, and (3) a political force (racism and discrimination) that represents malevolent but realistic obstacles. In each case, it is a mistake to assume that the former is operative for culturally diverse clients.

Locus of Responsibility

Another important dimension in world outlooks was formulated from attribution theory (E. E. Jones et al., 1972; J. M. Jones, 1997) and can be legitimately referred to as *locus of responsibility.* In essence, this dimension measures the degree of responsibility or blame placed on the individual or system. In the case of African Americans, their lower standard of living may be attributed to their personal inadequacies and shortcomings, or the responsibility for their plight may be attributed to racial discrimination and lack of opportunities. The former orientation blames the individual, while the latter explanation blames the system.

The degree of emphasis placed on the individual as opposed to the system in affecting a person's behavior is important in the formation of life orientations. Those who hold a person-centered orientation (1) emphasize the understanding of a person's motivations, values, feelings, and goals; (2) believe that success or failure is attributable to the individual's skills or personal inadequacies; and (3) believe that there is a strong relationship between ability, effort, and success in society. In essence, these people adhere strongly to the Protestant ethic that idealizes rugged individualism. On the other hand, situation-centered or system-blame people view the sociocultural environment as more potent than the individual. Social, economic, and political forces are powerful; success or failure is generally dependent on the socioeconomic system and not necessarily on personal attributes.

The causes of social problems in Western society are seen as residing in individuals who are thus responsible for them. Such an approach has the effect of labeling that segment of the population (racial and ethnic minorities) that differs in thought and behavior from the larger society as deviant. Defining the problem as residing in the person enables society to ignore situationally relevant factors and to protect and preserve social institutions and belief systems. Thus, the individual system-blame continuum may need to be viewed differentially for minority groups. An internal response (acceptance of blame for one's failure) might be considered normal for the White middle class, but for minorities it may be extreme and intrapunitive.

For example, an African American male client who has been unable to find a job because of prejudice and discrimination may blame himself ("What's wrong with me?" "Why can't I find a job?" "Am I worthless?"). Thus, an external response may be more realistic and appropriate ("Institutional racism prevented my getting the job"). Early research indicates that African Americans who scored external (blame system) on this dimension (1) more often aspired to nontraditional occupations, (2) were more in favor of group rather than individual action for dealing with discrimination, (3) engaged in more civil rights activities, and (4) exhibited more innovative coping behavior (Gurin, Gurin, Lao, & Beattie, 1969). It is important to note that the personal control dimension discussed in the previous section was correlated with traditional measures of motivation and achievement (grades), while individual systemblame was a better predictor of innovative social action behavior.

Formation of Worldviews

The two psychological orientations, locus of control (personal control) and locus of responsibility, are independent of one another. As shown in Figure 12.1, both may be placed on the continuum in such a manner that they intersect, forming four quadrants: internal locus of control–internal locus of responsibility (IC-IR), external locus of control–internal locus of responsibility

Figure 12.1

Graphic Representation of Worldviews

Source: From "Eliminating Cultural Oppression in Counseling: Toward a General Theory," by D. W. Sue, 1978, *Journal of Counseling Psychology, 25,* p. 422. Copyright 1978 by the *Journal of Counseling Psychology.* Reprinted by permission.

Locus of Control

Internal

Locus of responsibility

Internal person		External system
I **IC-IR**	**IV** **IC-ER**	
II **EC-IR**	**III** **EC-ER**	

External

(EC-IR), internal locus of control–external locus of responsibility (IC-ER), and external locus of control–external locus of responsibility (EC-ER). Each quadrant represents a different worldview or orientation to life. Theoretically, then, if we know the individual's degree of internality or externality on the two loci, we can plot them on the figure. We would speculate that various ethnic and racial groups are not randomly distributed throughout the four quadrants. The previous discussion concerning cultural and societal influences on these two dimensions would seem to support this speculation. Because our discussion focuses on the political ramifications of the two dimensions, there is an evaluative "desirable-undesirable" quality to each worldview.

Internal Locus of Control (IC)–Internal Locus of Responsibility (IR)

As mentioned earlier, high internal personal control (IC) individuals believe that they are masters of their fate and that their actions do affect the outcomes. Likewise, people high in internal locus of responsibility (IR) attribute their current status and life conditions to their own unique attributes; success is due to one's own efforts, and lack of success is attributed to one's shortcomings or inadequacies. Perhaps the greatest exemplification of the IC-IR philosophy is U.S. society. American culture can be described as the epitome of the individual-centered approach that emphasizes uniqueness, independence, and self-reliance. A high value is placed on personal resources for solving all problems, self-reliance, pragmatism, individualism, status achievement through one's own effort, and power or control over others, things, animals, and forces of nature. Democratic ideals such as "equal access to opportunity," "liberty and justice for all," "God helps those who help themselves," and "fulfillment of personal destiny" all reflect this worldview. The individual is held accountable for all that transpires. Constant and prolonged failure or the inability to attain goals leads to symptoms of self-blame (depression, guilt, and feelings of inadequacy). Most members of the White middle class would fall within this quadrant.

Five American patterns of cultural assumptions and values can be identified (E. C. Stewart, 1971; Pedersen, 1988; Wehrly, 1995). These are the building blocks of the IC-IR worldview and typically guide our thinking about mental health services in Western society. As we have seen in the Kluckhohn and Strodtbeck model (1961), these values are manifested in the generic characteristics of counseling. The five systems of assumptions may be described as follows.

1. *Definition of activity.* Western culture stresses an activity modality of doing, and the desirable pace of life is fast, busy, and driving. A being orientation that stresses a more passive, experimental, and contemplative role is in marked contrast to American values (external achievement, activity, goals, and solutions). Existence is in acting, not being. Activism is seen most clearly in the mode of problem solving and decision making. Learning is active, not passive. American emphasis is on planning behavior that anticipates consequences.

2. *Definition of social relations.* Americans value equality and informality in relating to others. Friendships tend to be many, of short commitment, nonbinding, and shared. In addition, the person's rights and duties in a group are influenced by one's own goals. Obligation to groups is limited, and value is placed on one's ability to influence the group actively. In contrast, many cultures stress hierarchical rank, formality, and status in interpersonal relations. Friendships are intense, of long term, and exclusive. Acceptance of the constraints on the group and the authority of the leader dictate behavior in a group.

3. *Motivation.* Achievement and competition are seen as motivationally healthy. The worth of an individual is measured by objective, visible, and material possessions. Personal accomplishments are more important than place of birth, family background, heritage, or traditional status. Achieved status is valued over ascribed status.

4. *Perception of the world.* The world is viewed as distinctly separate from humankind and is physical, mechanical, and follows rational laws. Thus, the world is viewed as an object to be exploited, controlled, and developed for the material benefit of people. It is assumed that control and exploitation are necessary for the progress of civilized nations.

5. *Perception of the self and individual.* The self is seen as separate from the physical world and others. Decision making and responsibility rest with the individual and not the group. Indeed, the group is not a unit but an aggregate of individuals. The importance of a person's identity is re-

inforced in socialization and education. Autonomy is encouraged, and emphasis is placed on solving one's own problems, acquiring one's own possessions, and standing up for one's own rights (see Table 12.1)

Therapeutic Implications

It becomes obvious that Western approaches to clinical practice occupy the quadrant represented by IC-IR characteristics. Most therapists are of the opinion that people must take major responsibility for their own actions and that they can improve their lot in life by their own efforts. The epitome of this line of thought is represented by the numerous self-help approaches currently in vogue in our field. Clients who occupy this quadrant tend to be White middle-class clients, and for these clients such approaches might be entirely appropriate. In working with clients from different cultures, however, such an approach might be inappropriate. Cultural oppression in therapy becomes an ever present danger.

External Locus of Control (EC)–Internal Locus of Responsibility (IR)

Individuals who fall into this quadrant are most likely to accept the dominant culture's definition for self-responsibility but to have very little real control over how they are defined by others. The term *marginal man* (person) was first coined by Stonequist (1937) to describe a person living on the margins of two cultures and not fully accommodated to either. Although there is nothing inherently pathological about bicultural membership, J. M. Jones (1997) feels that Western society has practiced a form of cultural racism by imposing its standards, beliefs, and ways of behaving onto minority groups. Marginal individuals deny the existence of racism; believe that the plight of their own people is due to laziness, stupidity, and a clinging to outdated traditions; reject their own cultural heritage and believe that their ethnicity represents a handicap in Western society; evidence racial self-hatred; accept White social, cultural, and institutional standards; perceive physical features of White men and women as an exemplification of beauty; and are powerless to control their sense of self-worth, because approval must come from an external source. As a result, they are high in person-focus and external control.

It is quite clear that marginal persons are oppressed, have little choice, and are powerless in the face of the dominant-subordinate relationship between the middle-class Euro-American culture and their own minority culture. According to Freire (1970), if this dominant-subordinate relationship in society were eliminated, the phenomenon of marginality would also disappear. For if two cultures exist on the basis of total equality (an ideal for biculturalism), then the conflicts of marginality simply do not occur in the person.

Table 12.1 The Components of White Culture: Values and Beliefs

Rugged Individualism
Individual is primary unit
Individual has primary responsibility
Independence and autonomy highly valued and
    rewarded
Individual can control environment

Competition
Winning is everything
Win/lose dichotomy

Action Orientation
Must master and control nature
Must always do something about a situation
Pragmatic/utilitarian view of life

Communication
Standard English
Written tradition
Direct eye contact
Limited physical contact
Control of emotions

Time
Adherence to rigid time
Time is viewed as a commodity

Holidays
Based on Christian religion
Based on White history and male leaders

History
Based on European immigrants' experience in the
    United States
Romanticize war

Protestant Work Ethic
Working hard brings success

Progress & Future Orientation
Plan for future
Delayed gratification
Value continual improvement and progress

Emphasis on Scientific Method
Objective, rational, linear thinking
Cause and effect relationships
Quantitative emphasis

Status and Power
Measured by economic possessions
Credentials, titles, and positions
Believe "own" system
Believe better than other systems
Owning goods, space, property

Family Structure
Nuclear family is the ideal social unit
Male is breadwinner and the head of the household
Female is homemaker and subordinate to the
    husband
Patriarchal structure

Esthetics
Music and art based on European cultures
Women's beauty based on blonde, blue-eyed, thin,
    young
Men's attractiveness based on athletic ability, power,
    economic status

Religion
Belief in Christianity
No tolerance for deviation from single god concept

Source: From *The Counseling Psychologist* (p. 618) by Katz, 1985, Beverly Hills, CA: Sage. Copyright 1985 by Sage Publications, Inc. Reprinted by permission.

Therapeutic Implications
The psychological dynamics for the EC-IR minority client are likely to reflect his or her marginal and self-hate status. For example, White therapists might be perceived as more competent and preferred than are therapists of the client's own race. To EC-IR minority clients, focusing on feelings may be very

threatening because it ultimately may reveal the presence of self-hate and the realization that clients cannot escape from their own racial and cultural heritage. A culturally encapsulated White counselor or therapist who does not understand the sociopolitical dynamics of the client's concerns may unwittingly perpetuate the conflict. For example, the client's preference for a White therapist, coupled with the therapist's implicit belief in the values of U.S. culture, becomes a barrier to effective counseling. A culturally sensitive helping professional needs to help the client (1) understand the particular dominant-subordinate political forces that have created this dilemma and (2) distinguish between positive attempts to acculturate and a negative rejection of one's own cultural values.

External Locus of Control (EC)–External Locus of Responsibility (ER)

The inequities and injustices of racism seen in the standard of living tend to be highly damaging to minorities. Discrimination may be seen in the areas of housing, employment, income, and education. A person high in system-blame and external control feels that there is very little one can do in the face of such severe external obstacles as prejudice and discrimination. In essence, the EC response might be a manifestation of (1) having given up or (2) attempting to placate those in power. In the former, individuals internalize their impotence even though they are aware of the external basis of their plight. In its extreme form, oppression may result in a form of "learned helplessness" (Seligman, 1982). When minorities learn that their responses have minimal effects on the environment, the resulting phenomenon can best be described as an expectation of helplessness. People's susceptibility to helplessness depends on their experience with controlling the environment. In the face of continued racism, many may simply give up in their attempts to achieve personal goals.

The dynamics of the placater, however, are not related to the giving up response. Rather, social forces in the form of prejudice and discrimination are seen as too powerful to combat at that particular time. The best one can hope to do is to suffer the inequities in silence for fear of retaliation. "Don't rock the boat," "keep a low profile," and "survival at all costs" are the phrases that describe this mode of adjustment. Life is viewed as relatively fixed, and there is little that the individual can do. Passivity in the face of oppression is the primary reaction of the placater. Slavery was one of the most important factors shaping the sociopsychological functioning of African Americans. Interpersonal relations between Whites and Blacks were highly structured and placed African Americans in a subservient and inferior role. Those Blacks who broke the rules or did not show proper deferential behavior were severely punished. The spirits of most African Americans, however, were not broken.

Conformance to White Euro-American rules and regulations was dictated by the need to survive in an oppressive environment. Direct expressions of anger and resentment were dangerous, but indirect expressions were frequent.

Therapeutic Implications

EC-ER African Americans are very likely to see the White therapist as symbolic of any other Black-White relations. They are likely to show "proper" deferential behavior and not to take seriously admonitions by the therapist that they are the masters of their own fate. As a result, an IC-IR therapist may perceive the culturally different client as lacking in courage and ego strength, and as being passive. A culturally effective therapist, however, would realize the basis of these adaptations. Unlike EC-IR clients, EC-ER individuals do understand the political forces that have subjugated their existence. The most helpful approach on the part of the therapist would be (1) to teach the clients new coping strategies, (2) to have them experience successes, and (3) to validate who and what they represent.

Internal Locus of Control (IC)–External Locus of Responsibility (ER)

Individuals who score high in internal control and system-focus believe that they are able to shape events in their own life if given a chance. They do not accept the fact that their present state is due to their own inherent weakness. However, they also realistically perceive that external barriers of discrimination, prejudice, and exploitation block their paths to the successful attainment of goals. There is a considerable body of evidence to support this contention. Recall that the IC dimension was correlated with greater feelings of personal efficacy, higher aspirations, and so forth, and that ER was related to collective action in the social arena. If so, we would expect that IC-ER people would be more likely to participate in civil rights activities and to stress racial identity and militancy.

Pride in one's racial and cultural identity is most likely to be accepted by an IC-ER person. The low self-esteem engendered by widespread prejudice and racism is actively challenged by these people. There is an attempt to redefine a group's existence by stressing consciousness and pride in their own racial and cultural heritage. Such phrases as "Black is beautiful" represent a symbolic relabeling of identity from Negro and colored to Black or African American. To many African Americans, *Negro* and *colored* are White labels symbolic of a warped and degrading identity given them by a racist society. As a means of throwing off these burdensome shackles, the Black individual and African Americans as a group are redefined in a positive light. Many racial minorities have begun the process in some form and have banded together into what was historically called the *Third World Movement* (Asian Americans, African Americans, Hispanic/Latino Americans, American Indians, and others). Studies on the Black social activists of the 1960s found they were generally better educated, more integrated into the social and political workings of their communities, and held more positive attitudes toward Black history and culture (racial pride). Finally, evidence tends to indicate they were more healthy along several traditional criteria for measuring mental health (Caplan, 1970).

Therapeutic Implications

There is much evidence to indicate that minority groups are becoming increasingly conscious of their own racial and cultural identities as they relate to oppression in U.S. society. If the evidence is correct, it is also probable that more and more minorities are most likely to hold an IC-ER worldview. Thus, therapists who work with the culturally different will increasingly be exposed to clients with an IC-ER worldview. In many respects, these clients pose the most difficult problems for the White IC-IR therapist. These clients are likely to raise challenges to the therapist's credibility and trustworthiness. The helping professional is likely to be seen as a part of the Establishment that has oppressed minorities. Self-disclosure on the part of the client is not likely to come quickly and, more than any other worldview, an IC-ER orientation means that clients are likely to play a much more active part in the therapy process and to demand action from the therapist.

An interesting transactional analysis of the mindsets of all four quadrants can be found in Figure 12.2.

Figure 12.2

Transactional Analysis of Cultural Identity Quadrants

Source: From *Counseling and Development in a Multicultural Society* (p. 399), by J. A. Axelson. Copyright © 1993 by Wadsworth, Inc. Reprinted by permission of Brooks/Cole Publishing Company, Pacific Grove, California 93950, a division of Wadsworth, Inc.

IC-IR	IC-ER
I. (Assertive/Passive) I'm O.K. and have control over myself. Society is O.K., and I can make it in the system.	*IV. (Assertive/Assertive)* I'm O.K. and have control, but need a chance. Society is not O.K., and I know what's wrong and seek to change it.
EC-IR	**EC-ER**
II. (Marginal/Passive) I'm O.K. but my control comes best when I define myself according to the definition of the dominant culture. Society is O.K.the way it is; it's up to me.	*III. (Passive/Aggresive)* I'm not O.K. and don't have much control; might as well give up or please everyone. Society is not O.K. and is the reason for my plight; the bad system is all to blame.

Social Justice Counseling: Organizational and Systemic Change
In Chapter 2, a Multidimensional Model of Cultural Competence was presented, where the foci for change could be aimed at the individual, professional, organizational, or societal levels (see Figure 2.3). These roughly correspond to the terms used in social justice work to describe the micro (individuals, families, and groups), meso (communities and organizations) and macro levels (social structures, ideologies, and policies) of intervention. The remainder of this chapter will concentrate on social justice work directed at organizations and systems.

Multicultural Organizational Development (Meso Level)

All helping professionals need to understand two things about institutions: (1) they work within organizations that are oftentimes monocultural in policies and practices and (2) the problems encountered by clients are often due to organizational or systemic factors. This is a key component of the ecological or person-in-environment perspective (Fouad, Gerstein, & Toporek, 2006)). In the former case, the policies and practices of an institution may thwart the ability of counselors to conduct culturally appropriate helping for their diverse clientele. In the latter case, the structures and operations of an organization may unfairly deny equal access and opportunity (access to health care, employment, and education) for certain groups in our society. It is possible that many problems of mental health are truly systemic problems caused by racism, sexism, and homophobia. Thus, to understand organizational dynamics and to possess multicultural institutional intervention skills are part of the social justice framework. Making organizations responsive to a diverse population ultimately means being able to help them become more multicultural in outlook, philosophy, and practice.

Multicultural organizational development (MOD) is a relatively new area of specialty that (1) takes a social justice perspective (ending of oppression and discrimination in organizations); (2) believes that inequities that arise within organizations may not primarily be due to poor communication, lack of knowledge, poor management, person-organization/fit problems, and so on, but to monopolies of power; and (3) assumes that conflict is inevitable and not necessarily unhealthy. Diversity trainers, consultants, and many I/O psychologists increasingly ascribe to MOD, which is based on the premise that organizations vary in their awareness of how racial, cultural, ethnic, sexual orientation, and gender issues impact their clients or workers.

Institutions that recognize and value diversity in a pluralistic society will provide healthy sites for workers and the consumers of their services. They will also be in a better position to offer culturally relevant services to their diverse populations and allow mental health agencies to engage in organizationally sanctioned roles and activities without the threat of punishment. Moving from a monocultural to a multicultural organization requires the counselor or change agent to understand the characteristics of that organization. Ascertaining what the organizational culture is like, what policies or practices either facilitate or impede cultural diversity, and how to implement change are crucial to healthy development. Perhaps the easiest way to understand what we mean by healthy organizations that are inclusive is to address what a culturally competent system of mental health care would look like.

Culturally Competent Mental Health Agencies

Social justice provides the rationale for mental health organizations to become multicultural, and the unmet needs of marginalized groups are foremost among them. To meet those needs, not only must an organization employ individuals with cultural competence, but the agency itself will need to have a *multicultural culture*, if you will. T. L. Cross et al. (1989) describe a detailed, six-stage developmental continuum of cultural competence for mental health agencies. These have been given the names (1) cultural destructiveness, (2) cultural incapacity, (3) cultural blindness, (4) cultural precompetence, (5) cultural competence, and (6) advocacy.

1. *Cultural destructiveness.* Cross et al. acknowledged the checkered history of organizations and research ostensibly designed to "help" certain racial/ethnic groups by identifying the first stage of (in)competence as cultural destructiveness. Programs that have participated in culture/race-based oppression, forced assimilation, or even genocide represent this stratum. Historically, many federal government programs aimed at American Indians fit this description, as do the infamous Tuskegee experiments, in which Black men with syphilis were deliberately left untreated, or the Nazi-sponsored medical experiments that singled out Jews, Gypsies, gays/lesbians, and the disabled, among other groups, for systematic torture and death under the guise of medical research.

2. *Cultural incapacity.* At this stage, organizations may not be intentionally culturally destructive, but they may lack the capacity to help minority clients or communities because the system remains extremely biased toward the racial/cultural superiority of the dominant group. The characteristics of cultural incapacity include discriminatory hiring and other staffing practices, subtle messages to people of color that they are not valued or welcome, especially as manifested by environmental cues (building location, decoration, publicity that uses only Whites as models, etc.), and generally lower expectations of minority clients, based on unchallenged stereotypical beliefs.

3. *Cultural blindness.* The third stage is one in which agencies provide services with the express philosophy that all people are the same, and the belief that helping methods used by the dominant culture are universally applicable. Despite the agency's good intentions, services are so ethnocentric as to make them inapplicable for all but the most assimilated minority group members. "Such services ignore cultural strengths, encourage assimilation, and blame the victim for their problems.... Outcome is usually measured by how closely a client approximates a middleclass, nonminority existence. Institutional racism restricts minority access to professional training, staff positions, and services" (T. L. Cross et al., 1989, p. 15). Organizations at this stage may have more of a fixation on "getting the numbers right" and eliminating any apparent signs of hostility toward new groups. While there may be a sincere desire to eliminate a majority group's unfair advantages, the focus may end up on limited and legalistic attempts to comply with equal employment or affirmative action regulations. It is difficult for organizations to move past this stage if Whites or other cultural majority members are not willing to confront the ways they have benefited from institutional racism, and risk trying new ways of sharing power.

4. *Cultural precompetence.* Agencies at this stage have at least looked at the artifacts and values of their organization to recognize their weaknesses in serving diverse groups and developing a multicultural staff (Schein, 1990). They may experiment with hiring more minority staff beyond the minimal numbers required to comply with Equal Employment Opportunity (EEO) goals, may recruit minorities for boards of directors or advisory committees, may work cooperatively to perform needs assessments with minority groups in their service area, and may institute cultural sensitivity training for staff, including management. They may propose new programs specifically for a particular ethnic/cultural group, but if planning is not done carefully, this program may end up marginalized within the agency. "One danger at this level is a false sense of accomplishment or of failure that prevents the agency from moving forward along the continuum.... Another danger is tokenism" (T. L. Cross et al., 1989, p. 16), when minority professionals are expected to raise the agency's level of cross-cultural efficacy by simply being present in slightly greater numbers. However, minority staff may lack training in many of the skills or knowledge areas that would allow them to translate their personal experience into effective counseling, not to mention training of coworkers.

   If the task of developing cultural awareness has been given to minority staff (or motivated majority staff) who do not have the clout to involve all elements of the agency, then "this pattern of program development allows for the phony embracing of multiculturalism because the dominant group can remain on the sidelines judging programs and helping the institution to continue on its merry way" (Barr & Strong, 1987, p. 21). These staff members may sacrifice job performance in other areas and then be criticized. Or they may work doubly hard because they are taking on the extra burden of cultural awareness activities, and then may not receive any acknowledgment, in patterns that continue the oppression of minorities (Gallegos, 1982).

5. *Cultural competence.* Agencies at this stage show "continuing selfassessment regarding culture, careful attention to the dynamics of difference, continuous expansion of cultural knowledge and resources, and a variety of adaptations to service models in order to better meet the needs of culturally diverse populations" (T. L. Cross et al., 1989, p. 17). They have a diverse staff at all levels, and most individuals will have reached the higher stages of individual racial/cultural identity awareness. That is, they are aware of and able to articulate their cultural identity, values, and attitudes toward cultural diversity issues. This will be true for both majority and minority culture members. Staff will regularly be offered or seek out opportunities to increase their multicultural skills and knowledge. There is recognition that minority group members have to be at least bicultural in U.S. society and that this creates mental health issues concerning identity, assimilation, values conflicts, and so on, for staff as well as clients. There will be enough multilingual staff available to offer clients choices in relating to service providers. If the agency has culture-specific programs under its umbrella, agency staff and clients perceive these programs as integral to the agency, and not just as junior partners.

6. *Cultural proficiency.* This stage encompasses the highest goals of multicultural development. These organizations are very uncommon, given that both the organizational culture and individuals within it are operating at high levels of multicultural competence, having overcome many layers of racism, prejudice, discrimination, and ignorance. Organizations at this stage seek to add to the knowledge base of culturally competent practices by "conducting research, developing new therapeutic approaches based on culture, and disseminating the results of demonstration projects" (T. L. Cross et al., 1989, p. 17), and follow through on their "broader social responsibility to fight social discrimination and advocate social diversity" in all forums (Foster, Jackson, Cross, Jackson, & Hardiman, 1988, p. 3).

Staff members are hired who are specialists in culturally competent practices, or are trained and supervised systematically to reach competency. Every level of an agency (board members, administrators, counselors, and consumers) regularly participates in evaluations of the agency's multicultural practices and environment and is able to articulate the agency's values and strategies concerning cultural diversity. If the agency runs culture-specific programs, these programs are utilized as resources for everyone in the agency and community, and not perceived as belonging just to that ethnic community (Muñoz & Sanchez, 1996).

Just as we have described a culturally competent system of mental health care for all groups, we encourage counselors and therapists to work toward addressing social justice issues (equity) that involve employment, educational, legal, and governmental institutions and agencies. For example, what would a fair and equitable educational system look like? How could business and industry move toward equal access and opportunity in the hiring, retention, and promotion of all employees? And, what role can counselors play to help achieve these social justice goals? As we have repeatedly emphasized, providing a healthy organizational climate will do much to improve mental health and the quality of living for all groups in our society.

Systemic Change (Macro Level)

Increasingly, leaders in the field of counseling psychology have indicated that the profession should promote the general welfare of society; be concerned with the development of people, their communities, and their environment; and should promote social, economic, and political equity consistent with the goals of social justice (Toporek, Gerstein, et al., 2006). Thus, social justice counseling includes social and political action that seeks to ensure all people have equal access to the resources, employment, services, and opportunities they require to meet their basic human needs and to develop fully (Goodman et al., 2004). If mental health professionals are concerned with the welfare of society, and if society's purpose is to enhance the quality of life for all persons, then they must ultimately be concerned with the injustices and obstacles that oppress, denigrate, and harm those in our society (Warren & Constantine, 2007). They must be concerned with issues of classicism, racism, sexism, homophobia, and all the other "isms" that deny equal rights to everyone. As mentioned previously, counselors/therapists practice at three levels: micro—where the focus is on individuals, families, and small groups; meso—where the focus communities and organizations; and macro—where the focus is on the larger society (statutes and social policies).

Conventional clinical work operates primarily from the micro level, is aimed primarily at helping individuals, and is not adequate in dealing with these wider social issues. It is too time consuming, is aimed at remediation, and does not recognize the fact that many problems clients encounter may actually reside in the social system. Let us use the example of racism to illustrate some of the basic tenets of antiracism work that are consistent with a social justice approach. We use racism as an example, but social justice work extends to all forms of cultural oppression (poverty, inadequate health care, immigrant rights, educational inequities, etc.) that deny equal access and opportunity.

Antiracism as a Social Justice Agenda

It is not enough for psychologists to simply work with those victimized by stereotyping, prejudice, and discrimination at the micro levels. It is not enough for psychologists, on an individual basis, to become bias free and culturally sensitive when the very institutions that educate, employ, and govern are themselves biased in policy, practice, assumption, and structure. In using race and racism as an example of the need to combat social justice issues on a systemic level, psychologists need to realize that racial attitudes and beliefs are formed from three main sources: schooling and education, mass media, and peers and social groups (Sue, 2003). Just as these channels can present a biased social construction of knowledge regarding race and race relations, they also offer hope as vehicles to overcome intergroup hostility, misunderstanding, and the development of norms associated with equity and social justice.

In essence, psychologists can be helpful in working for a multicultural curriculum in society that stresses social justice (equity and antiracism). It must be done in the schools, all media outlets, and in the many groups and organizations that touch the lives of our citizens. Yet, to use these tools of socialization to combat racism and to reconstruct a nonbiased racial reality mean psychologists must impact social policy. Work at the local, state, and federal levels involve psychologists in political advocacy and social change.

Gordon Allport, a social psychologist well known for his classic book, *The Nature of Prejudice* (1954), proposed conditions that offer a guide to antiracism work. Since its publication, others have conducted revealing and important work on reducing prejudice through creating conditions found to lower intergroup hostility. It has been found that racism is most likely to diminish under the following conditions: (1) having intimate contact with people of color, (2) experiencing a cooperative rather than competing environment, (3) working toward mutually shared goals as opposed to individual ones, (4) exchanging accurate information rather than stereotypes or misinformation, (5) interacting on equal footing with others rather than an unequal or imbalanced one, (6) viewing leadership or authority as supportive of intergroup harmony, and (7) feeling a sense of unity or interconnectedness with all humanity (Jones, 1997; Sue, 2003). Further, it appears that no one single condition alone is sufficient to overcome bigotry. To be successful in combating racism, all conditions must coexist in varying degrees to reduce prejudice.

Social Justice Requires Counseling Advocacy Roles

To achieve these conditions in our society is truly an uphill battle. But, just as the history of the United States is the history of racism, it is also the history of antiracism as well. There have always been people and movements directed toward the eradication of racism, including abolitionists, civil rights workers, private organizations (Southern Poverty Law Center, NAACP, and B'nai Brith), political leaders, and especially people of color. Racism, like sexism, homophobia, and all forms of oppression, must be on the forefront of social justice work. Efforts must be directed at social change in order to eradicate bigotry and prejudice. In this respect, psychologists must use their knowledge and skills to (1) impact the channels of socialization (education, media, groups/organizations) to spread a curriculum of multiculturalism, and (2) aid in the passage of legislation and social policy (affirmative action, civil rights voting protections, sexual harassment laws, etc.). To accomplish these goals, we need to openly embrace systems intervention roles identified by Atkinson et al., (1993): advocate, change agent, consultant, adviser, facilitator of indigenous support systems, and facilitator of indigenous healing methods. In closing, we include the words of Toporek (2006, p. 496) about the social justice agenda and its implications for psychologists:

> *The vastness of social challenges facing humanity requires large-scale intervention. Although the expertise of counseling psychologists is well suited to individual empowerment and local community involvement, likewise, much of this expertise can, and should, be applied on a broad scale. Public policy decisions such as welfare reform, gender equity, same-sex marriage and adoption, and homelessness must be informed by knowledge that comes from the communities most affected. Counseling psychologists, with expertise in consulting, communicating, researching, and direct service, are in a unique position to serve as that bridge.*

MULTICULTURAL COUNSELING AND SPECIFIC POPULATIONS

COUNSELING AND THERAPY INVOLVING MINORITY GROUP COUNSELORS/THERAPISTS

Minority Group Therapists: Working with Majority and Other Minority Clients

13

Chapter

Kavita, a clinician of South Asian descent, is unsure of her ethnic identity and has trouble balancing being American with being South Asian. Seeing South Asian clients only makes this conflict more important to her. Will this affect her attitudes toward treating minority clients? (Gurung & Mehta, 2001, p. 139)

My challenge has been in my work with men. I have always felt somewhat constrained with my male clients and did not like the impact it had on our therapy. I had talked to other women therapists about my difficulties and found that they had similar experiences. My problems became most evident to me when issues related to privilege, gender, and power needed to be discussed. I found myself caught between being too adversarial and challenging on one hand and the "all-giving" protector trained to soothe pain on the other. (Kort, 1997, p. 97)

As a Black counselor, I sometimes have difficulties working with clients of Asian background, especially when they claim to be victims of prejudice. How can they claim to be oppressed when they are so successful? At most college campuses, they are everywhere, taking slots away from us. Sometimes I think they are whiter than Whites. (workshop participant)

These three vignettes illustrate some of the complex counseling issues when minority group therapists work with members of their own group, work with majority culture clients, and work with different minority clients. Although our discussion has focused primarily on the need of White therapists to acknowledge their assumptions, values, and biases when working with clients of color, the same applies to therapists of color as well. Multicultural counseling/therapy is more than White-Black, White-Latino, White-Asian, and so forth. It also includes Asian American-African American, Latino American-African American, Native American-Asian American, and a multitude of combinations where the counselor is from a marginalized group (GLBT, women, a counselor with a disability, etc.)

There are two reasons why dealing with these counseling relationships is important, especially interracial/interethnic counseling. First, demographers predict that within several short decades, people of color will become a numerical majority. The increase in populations of color has meant that contact between the groups has also become more frequent, oftentimes resulting in strains and conflicts between Blacks and Asians, Asians and Latinos, and Latinos and Blacks. Second, the number of therapists from diverse groups is also increasing and as indicated throughout, therapists of color are not immune from their own cultural socialization or inheriting the biases of the society as well. For example, one of us found it difficult in clinical work to be nonjudgmental or empathetic to oppositional children during family sessions. Instead of patience and understanding, feelings of disapproval when children would speak disrespectfully to a parent would emerge. During self-reflection, the therapist was able to identify the source of these reactions. As a child, he was exposed to a cultural background in which obedience to parents was of paramount importance. Hierarchical communication patterns were the norm, and he was unaware that he used this standard when working with families. It is clear that everyone, regardless of race, gender, sexual orientation, and so on, needs to examine the impact of their own value system or experiences as members of marginalized groups when providing therapy to those of the majority culture or a member of a different ethnic minority group. As with White therapists, the values and assumptions are often invisible to therapists of color as well, and may influence the provision of therapy.

The Politics of Interethnic and Interracial Bias and Discrimination

People of color generally become very wary about discussing interethnic and interracial misunderstandings and conflicts between various groups for fear that such problems may be used by those in power to (1) assuage their own guilt feelings and excuse their own racism—"People of color are equally racist, and why should I change when they can't even get along with one another," (2) divide and conquer—"as long as people of color fight among themselves, they can't form alliances to confront the establishment," and (3) divert attention away from the injustices of society by defining problems as residing between various racial groups. Further, as discussed previously, readers have to understand that minority prejudice toward other groups (i.e., people of color or Whites) occurs under an umbrella of White racial superiority; while minority groups may discriminate they do not have the systemic power to oppress on a large-scale basis. In other words, while they may be able to hurt one another on an individual basis and to individually discriminate against White Americans, they possess little power to cause systemic harm, especially to White Americans. Some people of color have even taken the stand that interethnic prejudice among minorities only serves to benefit those in power.

As a result, people of color are sometimes cautioned not to "air dirty laundry" in public. These concerns are certainly legitimate and we would be remiss in not alerting readers to how society has historically used conflicts between racial groups as a justification for continued oppression and avoidance in dealing with White racism. But the admonition "don't air dirty laundry in public" speaks realistically to the existence of miscommunications, disagreements, misunderstandings, and potential conflicts between and among ethnic/racial minority groups. When people of color constituted a small percentage of the population, it was to their advantage to become allies in a united front to challenge the sources of injustice. Avoiding or minimizing interethnic group differences and conflicts served a functional purpose: to allow them to form coalitions of political, economic, and social power to effect changes in society. While historically beneficial on a political and systemic level, the downside has been a neglect in dealing with interracial differences that have proved to become problematic.

We believe that the time has long passed when not openly addressing these issues continues to hold unquestioned merit. People of color have always known that they, too, harbor prejudices and detrimental beliefs about other groups. Feminists have acknowledged difficulty in relating to men who hold traditional beliefs about appropriate female gender roles. GLBT groups describe negative reactions to straights who voice beliefs that gay sex is immoral, marriage should be between a man and a woman, or that their religion condemns such a "lifestyle." If we look at the relationship between groups of color, for example, misunderstandings and mistrust become very obvious. In the early 1990s, the racial discourse in urban America was dominated by African American boycotts of Korean mom and pop grocery stores that was followed by the looting, firebombing, and mayhem that engulfed Los Angeles (Chang, 2001). Many in the Black community felt that the Koreans were exploiting their communities as had White businesses. Reports of Hispanic and Black conflicts in the inner cities have also been reported throughout the country. As Latinos have surpassed Blacks in numbers, they have increasingly demanded a greater voice in communities and the political process. Since Latinos and Blacks tend to gravitate toward the same inner-city areas and compete for the same jobs, great resentment has grown between the groups (Wood, 2006). The immigration issue has also sparked fierce debate within the Latino and Black communities, as some Blacks believe jobs are being lost to the huge influx of Latinos (Gonzales, 1997). In essence, the discourse of race that once was confined to Black-White relations has become increasingly multiethnic and multiracial. These differences are reflected in the perceptions groups of color have toward one another. In one major national survey (National Conference of Christians and Jews, 1994), it was found:

1. More than 40 percent of African Americans and Hispanics, and one of every four Whites believe that Asian Americans are "unscrupulous, crafty and devious in business."

2. Nearly half the Hispanic Americans surveyed and 40 percent of African Americans and Whites believe Muslims "belong to a religion that condones or supports terrorism."

3. Blacks think they are treated far worse than Whites and worse than other minority groups when it comes to getting equal treatment in applying for mortgages, in the media, and in job promotions.

4. Only 10 percent of African Americans—a staggeringly low number— believe the police treat them as fairly as other groups.

5. African Americans believe that everyone else is treated with more equality, and especially that Asian Americans are doing better.

6. There is tremendous resentment of Whites by all minority groups.

7. Two-thirds of minorities think Whites "believe they are superior and can boss people around," "are insensitive to other people," "control power and wealth in America," and "do not want to share it with non-Whites."

Two primary conclusions are noteworthy here: First, racial/ethnic groups also experience considerable mistrust, envy, and misunderstandings toward one another as well. Surprisingly, African Americans and Latinos held stronger negative beliefs about Asian Americans than did White Americans (40 percent versus 25 percent)! Second, and not surprisingly, people of color continue to hold beliefs and attitudes toward Whites that are very negative and filled with resentments, anger, and strong mistrust. If these conclusions are true, then we might ask the following questions. What effect does interethnic bias on the part of therapists of color have upon their culturally diverse clients? If an African American therapist works with an Asian American client or vice versa, what therapeutic issues are likely to arise? Likewise, in light of the strong negative feelings expressed by all groups of color against Whites, how might a therapist of color react intentionally and unintentionally toward their White clients? Some might argue, however, that a therapist of color working with a White client may be different than a therapist of color working with a client of color because power differentials still exist on a systemic level for White clients. Little in the way of research or conceptual scholarly contributions has addressed these issues or questions. It may not be far-fetched, however, to surmise that these racial combinations may share some similar dynamics and clinical issues to White therapist-client of color dyads.

Multicultural Counseling in Minority-Majority and Minority-Minority Relationships

Not only do we need to engage in self-examination, but it is also clear that we are a stimulus to clients through appearance, speech, or other factors that reflect differences. These perceived differences may influence the development of a therapeutic relationship. We've had clients make statements such as "I like Chinese food" and "the Chinese are very smart and family oriented," or exhibit some discomfort when meeting us for the first time. In one study (Fuertes & Gelso, 2000), male Hispanic counselors who spoke with a Spanish accent were rated lower in expertise by Euro-American students than those counselors without an accent. This phenomenon may also exist for therapists with other accents and may need to be discussed in therapy to allay anxiety in both the therapist and the client. One graduate student from Bosnia would discuss her accent and would let clients know that English was her second language. Although her command of English was good, this explanation helped establish a more collaborative relationship. Acknowledging differences, or investigating the reasons for client reactions, are important since they may affect the therapeutic process. In one instance, an African American psychology intern working with a man in his 70s noticed that the client persisted in telling stories about the "Negro fellas" that he served with in the army. He made positive comments about his Black comrades and talked about their contributions to the unit. The intern responded by saying *"I guess you noticed I'm Black"* (Hinrichsen, 2006, p. 31). This response led to a discussion of client concerns that he would say something that might be considered offensive. He also worried about whether the intern could understand the experience of an older White man. White therapists facing an ethnic minority client often struggle with whether to ask, *"How do you feel working with a White therapist?"* This situation is also faced by minority therapists working with White clients. When differences between therapist and client are apparent (e.g., ethnicity, gender, ability, age) or revealed (e.g., religion, sexual orientation), acknowledging them is important. Both African American and Caucasian American students revealed a stronger preference for openness and self-disclosure when asked to imagine a counselor of a different ethnicity (Cashwell, Shcherbakova & Cashwell, 2003). Self-disclosure, or the acknowledgment of differences, may increase feelings of similarity between therapist and client and reduce concerns about differences. In this respect, the same might apply when both the therapist and client are persons of color but are from a different racial/ethnic group.

As we have mentioned earlier, cultural differences can impact the way we perceive events. This was clearly seen in a study involving Chinese American and Caucasian American psychiatrists (Li-Repac, 1980). Both groups of therapists viewed and rated videotaped interviews with Chinese and Caucasian patients. When rating White patients, Caucasian therapists were more likely to use terms such as "affectionate," "adventurous," and "capable," whereas Chinese therapists used terms such as "active," "aggressive," and "rebellious" to describe the same patients. Similarly, White psychiatrists described Chinese patients as "anxious," "awkward," "nervous," and "quiet," while Chinese psychiatrists were more likely to use the terms "adaptable," "alert," "dependable," and "friendly." It is clear that both majority and minority therapists are influenced by their ethnocentric beliefs and values.

Problematic relationship issues involving other areas of diversity may also impact the therapist-client relationship. Kort (quoted at the beginning of the chapter) talked about her difficulties in maintaining an objective perspective in working with men, especially regarding issues of gender and privilege. Similarly, therapists who are gay or lesbian, have a disability, are older, or are of a different religion need to be aware of their own value orientation and the impact it may have with a more mainstream client. How would you deal with clients who have a very different perspective than your own or who may harbor negative feelings toward member of your group? In the research literature there have been few studies examining the influence of culturally diverse or different therapists working with White, majority culture clients or with different minority group members. We believe this area needs more attention, particularly in view of the continuing growth of practitioners in the field who are members of ethnic minorities or other diverse groups.

Therapist-Client Matching

It is often believed that matching the therapist and client on ethnicity, gender, or other dimensions will result in a more positive therapeutic outcome due to similarities in experience, language, or values. However, the findings regarding this are mixed and difficult to interpret since: (1) some involve analogue studies (hypothetical situations) where student or clients indicate their preference regarding the ethnicity of a therapist, (2) comparisons usually involve only a few ethnic groups, (3) most involve very small samples, (4) samples tend to be regional and may not be representative of the population at large, and (5) the outcome measures differ from study to study. It is important to keep these limitations in mind when evaluating existing research, especially when contradictory findings occur. In a meta-analytic review of therapist and client racial-ethnic matching with African American and Caucasian American clients focused on the variables of overall functioning, drop-out rate, and total number of sessions attended, no significant differences were found between ethnically matched and nonethnically matched dyads (Shin et al., 2005). Similar results were found in a large-scale study that involved 4,483 college students and 376 therapists from 42 university counseling centers. There was little evidence that therapist-client ethnicity match was associated with either working alliance or outcome. However, the percentage of ethnic minority participants in the study was relatively small (African American, 3.0 percent, Asian American, 4.2 percent, Hispanic American, 7.7 percent, and Alaskan/Native American, 0.3 percent; Erdur, Rude, Baron, Draper, & Shankar et al., 2000). The results are in contrast to research that indicates that African American clients state a preference for an African American therapist (Karlsson, 2005). However, an initial expressed preference may change in actual therapy, where similar attitudes and beliefs may be more important than ethnic match. In a review of research on therapist-client match that includes both analogue and actual sessions, Flaherty and Adams (1998) reached the following conclusions:

- Among White, middle-class clients, gender matching was beneficial only for women and may be detrimental to men. That is, both male and female clients prefer women therapists, showing more symptom improvement and satisfaction with treatment than with male therapists.

- White clients are about equally satisfied with white and nonwhite therapists.

- African Americans prefer to be treated by individuals of their ethnic group.

- African American clients are more likely to drop out of treatment with a therapist of a different race and more likely to drop out with a same-sex therapist.

- Ethnic matching correlated consistently with increased treatment duration and decreased dropout among Asian ethnic groups

The age of the client as well as the specific problem involved may also be important in the outcome of therapist-client ethnic matching. In a study of 600 adolescents with substance abuse issues, Wintersteen, Mensinger, and Diamond (2005) investigated the impact of gender and racial match on alliance and treatment dropout. The researchers found that gender matching produced higher alliance ratings and was more likely to lead to completed treatment. Racial matching also produced greater retention in therapy but did not lead to high patient ratings regarding the therapeutic alliance. Racial mismatching did have a negative impact on retention in this study, especially when ethnic minority boys were treated by Caucasian therapists. In contrast to the results reported by Flaherty and Adams (1998), boys rated their alliance with female therapists low and were more likely to terminate. This difference may be a result of the developmental stage of adolescents and/or because the issue involved was substance abuse.

Certain therapist-client ethnic mismatches may be more problematic than others. In examining the outcome of actual therapy sessions, matching has been found to be important for Asian clients. Ethnic matching resulted in significantly more sessions, attended with lower dropout rates (Flaskerud, 1991). These results may reflect the importance of linguistic ability, since ethnic match was also found to be a positive predictor of outcome among Mexican Americans for whom English was not their primary language (Sue et al., 1991). There are also some preliminary findings involving ethnic matching between African American therapists and Asian American clients and white clients in therapy with Asian therapists (Erdur et al., 2000). Asian American clients seen by African American therapists rated the working alliance lower than those working with other ethnic group or White therapists. Similarly, White clients rated their alliance with Asian therapists lower than White clients seen by other therapists. These findings should be regarded with caution because of the very small number of Asian American clients who worked with African American therapists ($n = 10$) or White clients who had an Asian therapist ($n = 14$); however, it does bring forth the possibility that certain ethnic combinations of therapist and client may be more problematic than others.

The impact of ethnic matching may also depend on client characteristics such as the degree of adherence to cultural values. Kim and Atkinson (2002) found that Asian American clients with strong traditional values rated Asian American therapists as more empathetic and credible than more Westernized clients. Conversely, Western-oriented clients judged European American counselors to be more empathetic than did clients with high adherence to Asian cultural values. Thus, in ethnically similar therapist-client matches, potential matches or mismatches in cultural identity may need to be explored.

Communication Style Differences

Communication style differences (see Chapter 7), which may be displayed by ethnic minorities or therapists, can also impact the expectations or responsiveness of clients from different backgrounds. American Indians, for example, are more likely to speak softly, use an indirect gaze, and interject less frequently, whereas Caucasian Americans are more likely to speak loudly, have direct eye contact, and show a direct approach. These same characteristics may be displayed by therapists in interacting with clients. Ethnic minority therapists need to be aware of their nonverbal style and determine whether it is affecting the therapeutic relationship. In a study of nonverbal communication (Kim, Liang, & Li, 2003), five Asian American and five European American female therapists were observed conducting one session of career counseling with three Asian American volunteer clients. During the session, Euro-American therapists smiled more frequently and had more postural shifts than did Asian American therapists. In terms of client ratings, frequency of smiles was correlated with positive feelings about the session. Although the numbers of therapists and clients were few and the study involved an analogue setting, it lends some support to the view that cultural differences in verbal and nonverbal style of communicating feelings may affect the therapist-client relationship.

Issues Regarding Stage of Ethnic Identity

The stage of identity of ethnic minority therapists may also affect their work with clients. Kavita, in the example cited at the beginning of the chapter, reveals a struggle in identity between being either South Asian or American. This conflict may be unconscious but is displayed by minority therapists during therapy, especially with clients of the same ethnicity. In a study of 150 students of Indian descent, those who were more "Westernized" expressed less interest in serving minority clients. Some individuals may reject their own ethnic group, preferring to have the majority culture as their standard. In this case, ethnic minority therapists may have to acknowledge and resolve identity issues, since it may affect their reactions to a client from the same ethnicity or in dealing with clients from the majority culture.

> *Mikki, a 27-year-old social worker who immigrated to Israel from Ethiopia at the age of 10, worked in a municipal unit for adolescents in distress.... Recognizing the huge gap between his family's traditional lifestyle and the modernity of the Israelis, he soon became to feel ashamed of his parents ... he rejected the boys who represented his traditional Ethiopian self and favored those who represented the Israeli part of him. (Yedidia, 2005, pp. 165–166)*

During supervision, Mikki came to realize that his hostility to Ethiopian boys was a result of countertransference and that it reflected the inner conflict he was having between his identification as an Ethiopian versus that of an Israeli. Mikki's reaction was not unusual: Yedidia found this same type of identity conflict among other immigrant therapists from Ethiopia and Russia. Immigrant and ethnic minority therapists need to consider possible identity conflicts in their work with culturally or ethnically similar clients. It is highly possible that ethnic minority therapists at the conformity stage of identity development (see Chapter 10) may either respond defensively or negatively to an ethnically similar client who is struggling with identity issues.

Ethnic Minority and Majority Therapist Perspectives

Davis and Gelsomino (1994) examined the cross-racial practice experiences of White and minority social work practitioners (33 White, 17 Black, and 3 American Indian). They were asked their perceptions of effectiveness in working with culturally different clients and the source of the clients' problems. Both White and Black therapists believed they worked equally well with White clients. However, the ethnic minority therapists reported being the recipient of greater hostility in cross-racial practice, and White therapists regarded themselves as less effective with minority clients. Interestingly, both groups of therapists had similar views regarding the clients' problems—difficulties among minority clients were attributed to external sources while internal factors were seen as more important for White clients. While the attribution of causes may have some justification, we believe that this response may shortchange both White and minority clients. Environmental and individual contributions to problems should be assessed for all clients.

In a study of 12 therapists (5 African American and 7 Euro-Americans) and their responses to clients who were racially different from themselves, some differences and similarities were found (Knox, Burkard, Johnson, Suzuki, & Ponterotto, 2003): African American therapists were more likely to routinely address race with ethnic minority clients or when race seemed to be part of the presenting problem. They were also more likely to bring up race if they observed discomfort from their Euro-American clients. Euro-American therapists addressed race less frequently with clients and reported feeling discomfort when doing so. Both groups of therapists did not bring up the issue of race if it was not deemed to be important or if they sensed the client was uncomfortable with the topic. African American therapists reported being more direct in addressing race through either questions or confrontation; one participant asked a client directly what it was like to talk to an African American therapist. Euro-American therapists would also ask but did so less frequently and somewhat less directly: *"You know, I'm a White woman. How do you see that as affecting our relationship here?"* (Knox et al., p. 467). Most therapists believed that addressing race had a positive effect on the therapeutic alliance and in the outcome of therapy. They felt that therapists who are responsive to cultural issues would be perceived by clients, especially those from ethnic minorities, as more credible and culturally competent. We believe that all therapists should be willing to discuss differences with clients but also be aware of situations where this might not be beneficial.

In summary, it is clear that cultural competence goals do not apply only to White helping professionals. All therapists and counselors, regardless of race, culture, gender, and sexual orientation need to (1) become aware of their own worldviews, their biases, values, and assumptions about human behavior, (2) understand the worldviews of their culturally diverse clients, and (3) develop culturally appropriate intervention strategies in working with culturally diverse clients. Race, culture, ethnicity, gender, and sexual orientation are functions of everyone.

Implications for Clinical Practice

1. As with majority culture therapists, ethnic minority and therapists from other diverse groups need to identify cultural issues, values, beliefs, and experiences that may interfere with the provision of therapy to their clients.

2. The therapist's outward appearance, nonverbal behavior, and characteristics—such as accents—may influence the client's perception of credibility and the therapeutic relationship.

3. The use of self-disclosure in acknowledging differences may increase feelings of similarity between the client and therapist.

4. Awareness of communication style differences between the therapist and the client is important. A therapist may inform the client that he or she tends to be more cognitive (or other style) and ask if this is workable with the client.

5. Therapists must evaluate their stage of identity and determine how it might impact work with clients of the same or different ethnicity.

6. Addressing ethnic or other differences between the therapist and client can be helpful. In terms of therapists of color, clients are aware of the ethnic difference, and bringing it up in a routine manner deals with the "elephant in the room." However, therapists need to use their clinical judgment to determine when it might be contraindicated.

COUNSELING AND
THERAPY WITH
RACIAL/ETHNIC
MINORITY GROUP
POPULATIONS

Counseling African Americans

14

Chapter

During Hurricane Katrina, Blacks felt abandoned by the government and were so distrustful that they believed the poor neighborhoods were allowed to be flooded so that wealthy areas such as the French Quarter in New Orleans would remain dry. They pointed out a photo depicting a Black man and White woman who were shown carrying bread from a grocery store. The caption for the Black man was "looting" while that for the White woman was "finding" her goods. (J. Washington, 2005)

The fact that several school personnel made derogatory remarks about [Black] parents in front of researchers made us wonder what they would say in our absence. At the end of two consecutive meetings, one of which lasted only 5 minutes, the teacher commented that the brevity of the conference did not matter because the parent "wouldn't have understood it anyway." (Harry, Klingner, & Hart, 2005)

Through the media and even in school, I could see that in many people's eyes, Blacks and Whites were not equal. I sometimes felt that I was under attack, but this did nothing but build my strength, character and resilience. (Murphy, 2005, p. 315)

In 2005, the African American population numbered 34,361,740, or about 12.2 percent of the U.S. population. In addition, 1.9 million people reported being Black and one or more other races (U.S. Census Bureau, 2005c). Of the increase since 1980, 16 percent was due to immigration. The poverty rate for African Americans remains over two times higher than that of White Americans (25 versus 12 percent), and the unemployment rate is twice as high (11 versus 5 percent). Their disadvantaged status, as well as racism and poverty, contribute to the following statistics. In the 25 to 29 age group, nearly 12 percent of Black men were in prison or jail as compared to 1.7 percent of White males (Associated Press, 2006, May 21). Over 20 percent of Black males are temporarily or permanently banned from voting in Texas, Florida, and

Virginia because of felony convictions (Cose et al., 2000). The lifespan of African Americans is 5 to 7 years shorter than that of White Americans (N. B. Anderson, 1995; Felton, Parson, Misener, & Oldaker, 1997).

Although these statistics are grim, much of the literature is based on individuals of the lower social class who are on welfare or unemployed, and not enough is based on other segments of the African American population (Ford, 1997; Holmes & Morin, 2006). This focus on one segment masks the great diversity that exists among African Americans, who may vary greatly from one another on factors such as socioeconomic status, educational level, cultural identity, family structure, and reaction to racism. Many middle- and upper-class African Americans are receptive to the values of the dominant society, believe that advances can be made through hard work, feel that race has a relative rather than a pervasive influence in their lives, and embrace their heritage. As Hugh Price, former president of the National Urban League observed, *"This country is filled with highly successful black men who are leading balanced, stable, productive lives working all over the labor market"* (Holmes & Morin, 2006, p. 1). However, even among this group of successful Black men earning $75,000 a year or more, 6 in 10 reported being victims of racism, and that someone close to them was murdered or had been in jail.

The African American population is becoming increasingly heterogeneous in terms of social class, educational level, and political orientation. In this chapter we discuss value differences exhibited by many African Americans, issues of racism and discrimination, research findings, and their implications for treatment.

African American Values, Research, and Implications for Counseling and Therapy

Family Characteristics

Increasingly larger percentages of African American families are headed by single parents. In 2000, 32 percent of all African American families involved married couples, as compared to 53 percent for all households (U.S. Census Bureau, 2005c). The African American family has been generally described as matriarchal; among lower-class African American families, over 70 percent are headed by women. Black females who are unmarried account for nearly 60 percent of births, and of these mothers the majority are teenagers.

However, these statistics lack an acknowledgment of the strengths in the African American family structure. For many, there exists an extended family network that provides emotional and economic support. Among families headed by females, the rearing of children is often undertaken by a large number of relatives, older children, and close friends. Within the Black family exists adaptability of family roles, strong kinship bonds, a strong work and achievement ethic, and strong religious orientation (Hildebrand, Phenice, Gray, & Hines, 1996; McCollum, 1997). African American men and women value behaviors such as assertiveness; within a family, males are more accepting of women's work roles and are more willing to share in the responsibilities traditionally assigned to women, such as picking up children from school. Despite the challenges of racism and prejudice, many African American families have been able to instill positive self-esteem in their children.

Implications. Our reaction to African American families is due to our Eurocentric, nuclear family orientation. Many assessment forms and evaluation processes are still based on the middle-class Euro-American perspective of what constitutes a family. The different family structures indicate the need to consider various alternative treatment modes and approaches in working with Black Americans. In working with African American families, the counselor often has to assume various roles, such as advocate, case manager, problem solver, and facilitating mentor (Ahai, 1997). In many cases the counselor not only has to intervene in the family but also has to deal with community interventions. A number of African American families who go into counseling are required to do so by the schools, courts, or police. Issues that may need to be dealt with include feelings about differences in ethnicity between the client and counselor, and clarification of the counselor's relationship to the referring agency.

For family therapy to be successful, counselors must first identify their own set of beliefs and values regarding appropriate roles and communication patterns within a family. One must be careful not to impose these beliefs on a family. For example, African American parents, especially those of the working class, are more likely than White parents to use physical punishment to discipline their children (E. E. Pinderhughes, Dodge, Bates, Pettit, & Zelli, 2000). However, while some types of physical discipline have been related to more acting out behavior in White children, this was not found in African American children (Deater-Deckard, Dodge, Bates, & Pettit, 1996). Physical discipline should not necessarily be seen as indicative of a lack of parental warmth, or negativity. Similarly, although critical comments by family members have been found to contribute to relapse for certain mental disorders in White clients, this effect was not found with Black clients. It is possible that seemingly "critical" behavior by Black family members is, in fact, perceived as a sign of caring and concern (Rosenfarb, Bellack, & Aziz, 2006).

Parent education approaches based on White, intact, nuclear families are often inappropriate for African American families. In fact, they may perpetuate the view that minorities have deficient child-rearing skills. Attempts are being made to develop culturally sensitive parent education programs for

African Americans that focus on responses to racism by the family, culture conflicts, single parenting, drug abuse, and different types of discipline. Differences in family functioning should not be automatically seen as deficits (Gorman & Balter, 1997).

Kinship Bonds and Extended Family and Friends

A mother, Mrs. J., brought in her 13-year-old son, Johnny, who she said was having behavioral problems at home and in school. During the interview, the therapist found out that Johnny had five brothers and sisters living in the home. In addition, his stepfather, Mr. W., also lived in the house. The mother's sister, Mary, and three children had recently moved in with the family until their apartment was repaired. The question "Who is living in the home?" caught this. The mother was also asked about other children not living at home. She had a daughter living with an aunt in another state. The aunt was helping the daughter raise her child. When asked, "Who helps you out?" the mother responded that a neighbor watches her children when she has to work and that both groups of children had been raised together. Mrs. J.'s mother also assisted with her children.

Further questioning revealed that Johnny's problem developed soon after his aunt and her children moved in. Before this, Johnny had been the mother's primary helper and took charge of the children until the stepfather returned home from work. The changes in the family structure that occurred when the sister and her children moved in produced additional stress on Johnny. Treatment included Mrs. J. and her children, Mr. W., Mary and her children, and Mrs. J.'s mother. Pressures on Johnny were discussed, and alternatives were considered. Mrs. J.'s mother agreed to take in Mary and her children temporarily. To deal with the disruption in the family, follow-up meetings were conducted to help clarify roles in the family system. Within a period of months, behavioral problems in the home and school had stopped for Johnny. He once again assumed a parental role to help out his mother and stepfather.

Implications. Montague (1996) pointed out several important considerations to make when working with Black families. Because of the possibility of an extended or nontraditional family arrangement, questions should be directed toward finding out who is living in the home and who helps out. It is also important to work to strengthen the original family structure and try to make it more functional rather than change it. One of the strengths of the African American family is that men, women, and children are allowed to adopt multiple roles within the family. An older child like Johnny could adopt a parental role while the mother might take on the role of the father. The grandmother may be a very important family member who also helps raise the children. Her influence and help should not be eliminated, but the goal should be to make the working alliance with the other caregivers more efficient.

Educational Orientation

African American parents encourage their children to develop career and educational goals at an early age in spite of the obstacles produced by racism and economic conditions. The gap in educational attainment between Black and White children is gradually narrowing. The high school graduation rate for African Americans has increased to 74.2 percent versus 80 percent for White Americans, although African Americans still are behind in receiving their bachelor's degree (14.3 versus 24.3 percent) as compared to White Americans (U.S. Census Bureau, 2005c). However, problems are still found in academic performance. Especially at risk are African American boys, who show a tendency toward disidentification (the disengagement of academic performance from self-esteem), subsequently losing interest in academics during middle and high school. Behavior problems in school may also be related to parental acknowledgment of racism; African American parents who denied racism had preschool children with higher rates of behavior problems compared to parents who actively took steps to confront experiences with racism (Caughy, O'Campo, & Muntaner, 2004).

The educational environment is often negative for African American children. They are two to five times more likely to be suspended from school and receive harsher consequences than their White peers (Monroe, 2005). School personnel often hold stereotypes of African American parents as being neglectful or incompetent and blame the child's problem on a lack of support for schooling by the families. As one teacher stated, *"The parents are the problem! They [the African American children] have absolutely no social skills, such as not knowing how to walk, sit in a chair . . . it's cultural"* (Harry & Klinger, 2005, p. 105). These negative views were not at all confirmed by observations made by the researchers after visiting the homes of parents who were criticized; they often observed good parenting skills, support for education, and love for their children.

Implications. Factors associated with school failure, especially in African American males, must be identified, and intervention strategies must be applied. This may involve systems, family, and individual interventions. Many school systems have predominantly White teaching staffs, but the student population has changed from being predominantly White to predominantly minority. Because of this, teaching skills that were effective in the past may no longer work. For example, many African American youths display an animated, persuasive, and confrontational communication style, while schools have norms of conformity, quietness, teacher-focused activities, and individualized, competitive activities. Indeed, mainstream teachers may see communication patterns, nonstandard movements, and walking style as aggression or misbehavior (Duhaney, 2000; Monroe, 2005). It is important for educators to recognize culturally based behaviors that are not intended to be disruptive. Many teachers are not sensitive to these cultural differences and may respond inappropriately to minority group members. Students often learn best when curricula and classroom styles are modified, taking cultural factors into consideration.

Spirituality

> *D is a 42-year-old African American woman who was married for 20 years and recently divorced. She presented with depressive-like symptoms—feelings of loneliness, lack of energy, lack of appetite, and crying spells. She was raising two children with very little support from her ex-husband.... Although part of the treatment focused on traditional psychological interventions such as cognitive restructuring, expression of feelings, and changing behaviors, D's treatment also consisted of participating in two church-related programs. D's treatment involved participating in the women's ministry of her church to decrease her emotional and social isolation and to develop a support network. Treatment also involved participation in "The Mother to Son Program." The purpose of this program is to provide support to single mothers parenting African American boys. The program provides support for parents and rites of passage programs and mentors for Black boys. (Queener & Martin, 2001, p. 120)*

Spirituality and religion play an important role in many African American families and provide comfort in the face of oppression and economic support. Participation in religious activities allows for opportunities for self-expression, leadership, and community involvement. Among a sample of low-income African American children, those whose parents regularly attended church had fewer problems (Christian & Barbarin, 2001).

Implications. If the family is heavily involved in church activities or has strong religious beliefs, the counselor could enlist resources (e.g., the pastor or minister) to deal with problems involving conflicts within the family, school, or community. For many African American families spiritual beliefs play an important role and may have developed as part of a coping strategy to deal with stressors. Churches should be considered as much a potential source of information as are clinics, schools, hospitals, or other mental health professionals. Church personnel may have an understanding of the family dynamics and living conditions of the parishioners. A pastor or minister can help create sources of social support for family members and help them with social and economic issues. In addition, programs for the enrichment of family life may be developed jointly with the church.

Ethnic or Racial Identity

Many believe that minorities go through a sequential process of racial identity or consciousness. For African Americans, the process involves a transformation from a non-Afrocentric identity to one that is Afrocentric (although some African Americans already have a Black identity through early socialization). The W. E. Cross (1991, 1995) model, which was described in detail in Chapter 10, identifies several of these stages: pre-encounter, encounter, immersion-emersion, and internalization.

Implications. Those who are at the pre-encounter level are less likely to report racial discrimination, while those in the immersion stage tend to be younger and least satisfied with societal conditions (Hyers, 2001). African Americans with the greatest internalization of racial identity report the highest self-esteem (Pierre & Mahalik, 2005). Additionally, African American preferences for counselor ethnicity are related to the stage of racial identity (Atkinson & Lowe, 1995). Parham and Helms (1981) found that African Americans at the pre-encounter stage preferred a White counselor, while those in the other stages preferred a Black counselor. Often, however, the most important counselor characteristic for African American students is the cultural sensitivity of the counselor. A culturally sensitive counselor (one who acknowledges the possibility that race or culture might play a role in the client's problem) is seen as more competent than is a culture-blind counselor (one who focuses on factors other than culture and race when dealing with the presenting problem; Pomales, Claiborn, & LaFromboise, 1986; Want, Parham, Baker, & Sherman, 2004). Among a group of working class African American clients, the degree of therapeutic alliance with the European American counselor was affected not only by the stage of racial identity of the client, but also by similarities in gender, age, attitudes, and beliefs. Additionally, clients who had parenting, drug use, or anxiety problems looked for therapists' understanding regarding these specific issues (Ward, 2005).

African American Youth

For many urban Black adolescents, life is complicated by problems of poverty, illiteracy, and racism. The homicide rate for African American youth between the ages of 15 and 24 was nearly 10 times that of White youth in 1989; their suicide rate increased to over twice that of other teenagers between 1980 and 1992; and they are more likely to contract sexually transmitted diseases than other groups of teenagers (Harvey & Rauch, 1997). Unemployment can range from 37 percent to nearly 50 percent among Black teenagers. Most African American youth feel strongly that race is still a factor in how people are judged (Gannett News Service, 1998). African American children are well aware of occupational status. In one study, they identified service jobs as those performed by *"only Black people"* and high-status jobs as those performed by White Americans (Bigler & Averhard, 2003).

Issues presented in counseling may differ to some extent between males and females. African American adolescent females, like other females, are burdened by living in a male-dominated society, face issues with racial identity and negative stereotypes, and strive to succeed in relationships and careers. They often undertake adult responsibilities such as the care of younger siblings and household duties at an early age. As a group, although they encounter both racism and sexism, they display higher self-confidence, lower levels of substance use, and more positive body images than do White female adolescents (Belgrave, Chase-Vaughn, Gray, Addison, & Cherry, 2000). Their awareness of racial and gender issues is reflected in the following comments:

> *Well, in this time I think it's really hard to be an African American woman . . . we are what you call a double negative; we are Black and we are a woman and it's really hard. . . .*
> *I'd rather say I'm African-American than I'm Black because of the connection with the land, knowing that I come from somewhere. . . .*
> *[Racial identity] is important to me because society sees African American females as always getting pregnant and all that kind of thing and being on welfare. (Shorter-Gooden & Washington, 1996, p. 469)*

In this sample of young African American females, Shorter-Gooden and Washington (1996) found that the struggle over racial identity was a more salient factor than was gender identity in establishing self-definition. These adolescents believed that they had to be strong and determined to overcome the obstacles in society's perception of Blackness. About half had been raised by their mother, and most indicated the importance of the mother-daughter relationship. Careers were also important to two-thirds of the females; most felt that the motivation to succeed academically was instilled by their parents. In counseling young African American women, issues involving racial identity and conflict should be explored, and their sense of internal strength should be increased, because it appears to serve as a buffer to racism and sexism. African American females often have to deal with the double issue of being both Black and female. They have to fight against negative images to prevent those images being incorporated into their own belief systems; simultaneously, they must develop pride and dignity in Black womanhood (Jordan, 1997).

Black youth often do not come to counseling willingly. Often they come because they have been referred or brought in by their parents. Because of this, cooperation may be difficult:

Michael is a 19-year-old African American male who was brought to counseling by his aunt, Gloria, with whom he has lived for the past 2 years. Gloria is concerned about Michael's future as a result of his being present during a recent drug raid at the home of some friends.... Although Michael graduated from high school and is employed part-time at a fast food restaurant, he is frustrated with this work and confused about his future. He believes that Black men "don't get a fair shake" in life, and therefore is discouraged about his prospects about getting ahead.... Michael's aunt... is concerned that Michael's peers are involved in gangs and illegal activities. She thinks the rap music he listens to is beginning to fill his head with hate and anger.... Michael's major issues center around developing a positive identity as an African American man and discovering his place in the world. (Frame & Williams, 1996, p. 22)

Implications. The type of socialization that African American children and teenagers receive from their parents has been found to be related to social anxiety. Facing racism, African American parents may (1) address racism and prejudice directly and help their children identify with their own race; (2) discuss race only when the issue is brought up by their children and consider it to be of minor importance; (3) focus on human values and ignore the role of race. Neal-Barnett and Crowther (2000) found that the third approach was related to higher levels of social anxiety, particularly with African American peers. Ignoring racial issues in socialization left children vulnerable to anxiety when Black peers accused them of "acting White." They had not had the opportunity to develop coping strategies. Racial socialization of children by African American families helped to buffer the negative effects of racist discrimination (Fischer & Shaw, 1999). Protective factors have included increasing positive feelings about self and enhancing the sense of culture for African American youth (Belgrave et al., 2000).

In the case of Michael, Frame and Williams (1996) suggested several strategies for working with Black youth. The first involves the use of metaphors and is based on the African tradition of storytelling. Instead of just responding to "Black men don't get a fair shake," the counselor could get Michael to help identify family phrases or Biblical stories that instill hope. Additional metaphors could be generated from the writings of contemporary African American figures. The second strategy could be support for Michael's struggle with societal barriers. He could envision himself as a crusader for human rights and learn how to direct his anger in appropriate ways. Third, Michael could be asked to bring in his rap music and discuss what is appealing about it. Issues addressed in the lyrics could be explored, and the counselor could help with decisions regarding healthy outlets for his feelings of anger or despair. Fourth, family and community support systems could be generated. Members of the extended family, the pastor, teachers, and other important individuals in Michael's life could be asked to meet together in Aunt Gloria's home. All the members could share information about their struggles and search for identity. Use of these techniques, derived from African American experiences, can lead to personal empowerment.

Racism and Discrimination

The existence of racism has produced a variety of defensive and survival mechanisms among Black Americans. Sixty-one percent of African Americans believe that the federal response to the disaster caused by Katrina would have been faster if White populations had been involved (Washington, 2005). This cultural mistrust, or "healthy cultural paranoia," acts as a coping strategy (Phelps, Taylor, & Gerard, 2001). A lack of trust and feelings of discrimination exist for social services and medical support, especially among the youth (Miller, Seib, & Dennie, 2001). Only 9 percent of African Americans believe that they are treated the same as White Americans (Tilove, 2001). The experience of perceived racial discrimination leads to lower levels of mastery and higher levels of psychological distress (Broman, Mavaddat, & Hsu, 2000).

Discriminatory practices may also account for the fact that African Americans are less likely than their White counterparts to receive an antidepressant for depression and less likely to receive the newer selective serotonin reuptake inhibitor (SSRI) medications (Blazer, Hybels, Somonsick, & Hanlon, 2000; Melfi, Croghan, Hanna, & Robinson, 2000). Even when receiving medication, African Americans are less likely to use it for themselves or their children because of beliefs about possible side effects and effectiveness (Schnittker, 2003).

Implications. Since the mental health environment is a microcosm of the larger society, the mental health professional should be willing to address and anticipate possible mistrust from African American clients (Whaley, 2001). If the problem is due to discriminatory practices by an institution, the therapist may have to operate at the institutional level by making certain that clinics evaluate their procedures to ensure prescribing appropriate medications for African American clients. In other cases, the therapist may have to examine the African American client's response to the problem situation. The client may have only a limited or reflexive problem-solving capability. When counseling a client about dealing with situations in which racism plays a part, the counselor must assist the client in developing a wider range of options and encourage the development of a more conscious, problem-solving mode. The

Figure 14.1

The Interaction of Four Sets of Factors in the Jones Model

Source: From "Psychological Functioning in Black Americans: A Conceptual Guide for Use in Psychotherapy," by A. C. Jones, 1985, *Psychotherapy, 22,* p. 367. Copyright 1982 by *Psychotherapy.* Reprinted by permission of the Editor, *Psychotherapy.*

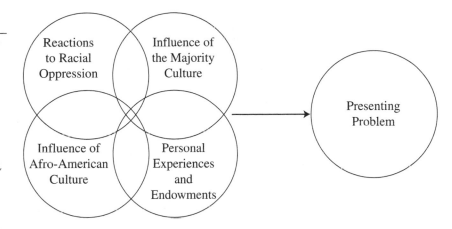

client must consider the way he or she usually deals with racism and consider other options that might be more productive.

A. C. Jones (1985) feels that four sets of interactive factors must be considered in working with an African American client (see Figure 14.1). The first factor involves the reaction to racial oppression. Most African Americans have faced racism, and the possibility that this factor might play a role in the present problem should be examined. Vontress and Epp (1997) described this factor as "historical hostility," a reaction in response to current and past suffering endured by the group. Because of this, problems are often perceived through this filter. The second factor is the influence of African American culture on the client's behavior. Clients may vary greatly in their identification with African American traditions. The third factor involves the degree of adoption of majority culture values. The task of the therapist is to help the client understand his or her motivation and make conscious, growth-producing choices. The fourth factor involves the personal experiences of the individual. African Americans differ significantly in their family and individual experiences. For some, this last category may be much more significant than racial identity.

Implications for Clinical Practice

In working with African American youth and adults in counseling situations, certain suggestions can be made about the elements necessary during the vital first few sessions. The first sessions are crucial in determining whether the client will return. The following steps may help by explaining what counseling is and enlisting the assistance of the client. Prior experiences may render issues of trust very important. The counselor can deal with these issues by discussing them directly and by being open, authentic, and empathetic. The African American client will often make a decision based on his or her interpersonal evaluation of the counselor. As one client stated, *"I am assessing to see if that person [counselor] is willing to go that extra mile and speak my language and talk about my Blackness..."* (Ward, 2005, p. 475). The role of the counselor may have to be much broader for the African American client than for the White client. He or she may have to be more directive, serve in an educative function, and help the client deal with agencies or with issues involving employment and health. Although the order of these elements can be modified and some can be omitted, these steps may be helpful to the counselor and client:

1. During the first session, it may be beneficial to bring up the reaction of the client to a counselor of a different ethnic background. (Although African Americans show a same-race preference, being culturally competent has been shown to be even more important.) A statement such as, "Sometimes clients feel uncomfortable working with a counselor of a different race. Would this be a problem for you?" or a variant can be used.

2. If the clients are referred, determine their feelings about counseling and how it can be made useful for them. Explain your relationship with the referring agency and the limits of confidentiality.

3. Identify the expectations and worldviews of African American clients, find out what they believe counseling is, and explore their feelings about counseling. Determine how they view the problem and the possible solutions.

4. Establish an egalitarian relationship. In contrast to other ethnic groups, most African Americans tend to establish a personal commonality with the counselor. This may be accomplished by self-disclosure. If the client appears hostile or aloof, discussing some noncounseling topics may be useful.

5. Determine whether and how the client has responded to discrimination and racism, both in unhealthy and healthy ways. Also, examine issues around racial identity (many clients at the pre-encounter stage will not believe that race is an important factor). For some, the identification with Afrocentricity may be important in establishing a positive self-identity. In these cases, elements of African/African American culture should be incorporated in counseling. This can be achieved through readings, movies, music, and discussions of African American mentors.

6. Assess the positive assets of the client, such as family (including relatives and nonrelated friends), community resources, and church.

7. Determine the external factors that might be related to the presenting problem. This may involve contact with outside agencies for financial

and housing assistance. Do not dismiss issues of racism as "just an excuse;" instead, help the client identify alternative means of dealing with the problems.

8. Help the client define goals and appropriate means of attaining them. Assess ways in which the client, family members, and friends have handled similar problems successfully.

9. After the therapeutic alliance has been formed, collaboratively determine the interventions. Usually problem-solving and time-limited approaches are more acceptable.

Counseling American Indians and Alaskan Natives

Some American Indians want to abolish Columbus day and instead have a holiday that honors indigenous people . . . It bothers these young Indians that people still believe Christopher Columbus discovered America when there already were indigenous people living here. (Hanson, 2006, p. 1)

The U.S. Government had judged that Indians were incapable of managing their own land, so they placed the property in a trust in 1887 and promised that the Indians would receive the income from their land. They never did. On December 1999, a Federal judge ruled that the government had breached its sacred trust duties. (Maas, 2001)

Of the 175 Indian languages spoken in the United States, only about 20 are passed on from mothers to babies. James Jackson, Jr., remembered his experience in a boarding school when a teacher grabbed him when he was speaking his native language and threatened to wash out his mouth with soap: "That's where we lost it [our language]." (Brooke, 1998)

15

Chapter

In North America, wars and diseases that resulted from contact with Europeans decimated the American Indian population. It is estimated that the population of American Indians had decreased to only 10 percent of its original number by the end of the eighteenth century. The experience of American Indians in America is not comparable to that of any other ethnic group. In contrast to immigrants, who arrived with few resources and struggled to gain equality, American Indians had resources. They had land and status that were gradually eroded by imperial, colonial, and then federal and state policies (K. W. Johnson et al., 1995). Extermination and seizure of lands seemed to be the primary policy toward the North Americans. Experience with this type of contact prompted this observation from a Delaware warrior: "I admit that there are good White men, but they bear no proportion to the bad; the bad must be the strongest, for they rule." Indians suffered massive losses of their land.

During the 1830s, over 125,000 Indians from different tribes were forced from their homes in many different states to a reservation in Oklahoma. The move was traumatic for Indian families and, in many cases, disrupted their cultural traditions. Assaults against the Indian culture occurred in attempts to "civilize" the Indians. Many Indian children were forced to be educated in English-speaking boarding schools. They were not allowed to speak their own language and had to spend 8 continuous years away from their families and tribes. Children were also removed from their homes and placed with non-Indian families until the Indian Child Welfare Act of 1978 (Blanchard, 1983; Choney et al., 1995; K. W. Johnson et al., 1995). These practices had a great negative impact on family and tribal cohesion and prevented the transmission of cultural values from parents to children. The following case study illustrates some of the disruptions caused by a boarding school experience.

> *Mary was born on the reservation. She was sent away to school when she was 12 and did not return to the reservation until she was 20. By the time she returned, her mother had died from pneumonia. She didn't remember her father, who was the medicine man of the tribe, very well. Shortly after she returned, she became pregnant by a non-Indian man she met at a bar.*
>
> *Mary's father . . . looked forward to teaching and leaving to his grandson John the ways of the medicine man. . . . John felt his grandfather was out of step with the 20th century. . . . Mary . . . could not validate the grandfather's way of life . . . she remembered having difficulty fitting in when she returned to the reservation. . . . In response to the growing distance between the two men, she became more and more depressed and began to drink heavily. (Sage, 1997, p. 48)*

In the past, the tribe, through the extended family, was responsible for the education and training of the children. The sense of identity developed through this tradition has been undermined. In addition, even recent history is full of broken treaties, the seizure or misuse of Indian land, and battles (often led by the U.S. government) to remove or severely limit fishing and hunting rights. These acts have made the American Indians very suspicious of the motives of the majority culture, and most of them do not expect to be treated fairly by non-Indian agencies (K. W. Johnson et al., 1995).

> *One of the most serious failings of the present system is that Indian children are often removed from the custody of their natural parents by nontribal government authorities who have no basis for intelligently evaluating the cultural and social premises underlying Indian home life and childrearing. Many of the individuals who decide the fate of our children are at best ignorant of our cultural values, and at worst contemptuous of the Indian way and convinced that removal, usually to a non-Indian household or institution, can only benefit an Indian child. (Congressional Record, 1997)*

Chief Calvin Isaac of the Mississippi Band of Choctaw Indians spoke these words during the house hearings of 1978 in support of the Indian Child Welfare Act. Statistics were cited that indicated over 90 percent of American Indian children were being placed by state courts and child welfare workers into non-Indian homes (Congressional Record, 1997). Such placements weakened the cultural identity of the children and weakened the tribes as well since values could not be passed on to the children. The passage of the act dramatically reduced this type of placement, although amendments to strengthen or weaken it continue to be brought up.

Implications. When working with American Indian children and families, the mental health professional should be aware of the political relationship as it exists between American Indians, the different states, and the U.S. government. The Indian Child Welfare Act has important implications for child protective services, runaways, and adoption procedures. In general, decisions regarding the placement of American Indian children are to be held in tribal courts. If they are to be removed from their parents, the first placements to be considered should be with extended family members, other tribal members, or other Indian families. Testimony from expert witnesses who are familiar with the specific Indian cultural group must be obtained before children can be removed from their homes. The counselor should understand the history of oppression that has existed and understand local issues and specific tribal history (Dana, 2000).

The American Indian and the Alaskan Native

American Indians/Alaskan Natives form a highly heterogeneous group composed of 561 distinct tribes, some of which consist of only four or five members (Bureau of Indian Affairs, 2005). The American Indian, Eskimo, and Aleut population grew rapidly to 2,500,000 by the year 2005. An additional 1.81 million claim to have Indian roots (U.S. Census Bureau , 2006a). Female householders with no husband present represented 27 percent of families versus 17 percent of the U.S. average. Fewer American Indians are high school graduates than the general U.S. population (71 percent versus 80 percent). Their income level is only 62 percent of the U.S. average, and the poverty rate is twice as high (U.S. Bureau of the Census, 2006a). Health statistics also paint a dismal picture. The alcoholism mortality rate is six times higher than that for the U.S. population as a whole (Frank, Moore, & Ames, 2000). Injury related deaths (motor vehicle crashes, suicides, homicides, drownings) are much higher than that of the overall U.S. rate (CDC, 2003). Among Native American women at a private care facility in New Mexico, mood disorders were reported by 21 percent, 47 percent had an anxiety disorder, and 14 percent had alcohol dependence or abuse. These rates are two to two and one half times higher than found in the general population (Duran et al., 2004). Rates of obesity and diabetes are much higher in this group than in the U.S. population (Balderas, 2000).

Over 60 percent of American Indians are of mixed heritage, having Black, White, and Hispanic backgrounds. In addition, American Indians differ in their degree of acculturation (Trimble, Fleming, Beauvais, & Jumper-Thurman, 1996). The majority of American Indians do not live on reservations, in part because of the lack of economic opportunities (K. W. Johnson et al., 1995), although many are returning because of casino jobs or a more nurturing environment. One man who returned described his need for a more "friendly place, friendly face, and friendly greetings" (Shukovsky, 2001, p. A1).

What constitutes an Indian is often an area of controversy. The U.S. Census depends on self-report of racial identity; some tribes have developed their own criteria and specify either tribal enrollment or blood quantum levels. Ken Hansen, chairman of the Samish tribe, stated, "It is a fundamental right of any nation, including tribal nations, to define their own membership. If a person meets the criteria for membership in a tribe, they are Indian" (Shukovsky, 2001, p. A13). Congress has formulated a legal definition. An individual must have an Indian blood quantum of at least 25 percent to be considered an Indian. This definition has caused problems both within and outside the Indian community. Some believe that belonging to a tribe should be the most important criterion and that those who do not have a tribal affiliation are "wanna-bes."

Tribe and Reservation

For the many Indians living on reservations and for those living in urban areas, the tribe is of fundamental importance. The relationship that Indians have with their tribes is different from that between non-Indians and their societies. Indians see themselves as an extension of their tribe.

Implications. The tribe and reservation provide American Indians with a sense of belonging and security, forming an interdependent system. Status and rewards are obtained by adherence to tribal structure. Indians judge themselves in terms of whether their behaviors are of benefit to the tribe. Personal accomplishments are honored and supported if they serve to benefit the tribe. Interventions with American Indian families and individuals should include an assessment of the importance of tribal relationships in any decision-making process. The reservation itself is very important for many American Indians, even among those who do not reside there. Many use the word "here" to describe the reservation and the word "there" to describe everything that is outside. The reservation is a place to conduct ceremonies and social events and to maintain cultural identity. Indians who leave the reservation to seek greater opportunities often may lose their sense of personal identity (M. J. Anderson & Ellis, 1995; Lone-Knapp, 2000).

American Indian/Alaskan Native Characteristics, Values, and Implications on Behavior

Family Structure

It is difficult to describe "the Indian family." It varies from matriarchal structures seen in the Navajo, where women govern the family, to patriarchal structures, in which men are the primary authority figures. Some generalizations can be made, however. American Indians are characterized by a high fertility rate, a large percentage of out-of-wedlock births, and strong roles for women. For most tribes, the extended family is the basic unit. Children are often raised by relatives such as aunts, uncles, and grandparents who live in separate households (Garrett, 2006; Hildebrand et al., 1996).

Implications. The concept of the extended family is often misunderstood by those in the majority culture, who operate under the concept of the nuclear family. The extended family often includes distant relatives and even non-blood friends. It is not unusual to have youngsters stay in a variety of different households. Misinterpretations can be made if one thinks that only the parents should raise and be responsible for the children. In working with American Indian children, the counselor should determine the roles of other family members so that interventions can include appropriate individuals. If the other family members play important roles, they should be invited to attend the sessions. The emphasis on collectivism is strong. If the goals or techniques of therapy lead to discord with the family or tribe, they will not be utilized. Interventions may have to be developed with the help of the family, relatives, friends, elders, or tribal leaders.

American Indian Values

Because of the great diversity and variation among American Indians/Alaskan Natives, it is difficult to describe a set of values that encompasses all groups. However, certain generalizations can be made regarding Indian values (Garrett, 2006; Garwick & Auger, 2000; Swinomish Tribal Mental Health Project, 1991).

1. *Sharing.* Among Indians, honor and respect are gained by sharing and giving, while in the dominant culture, status is gained by the accumulation of material goods.

Implications. Once enough money is earned, Indians may stop working and spend time and energy in ceremonial activities. The accumulation of wealth is not a high priority, but is a means to enjoy the present with others. Strategies to deal with alcohol and drug use may have to take into consideration the value of sharing.

2. *Cooperation.* Indians believe that the tribe and family take precedence over the individual. Indian children tend to display sensitivity to the opinions and attitudes of their peers. They will actively avoid disagreements or contradictions. Most do not like to be singled out and made to perform in school unless the whole group would benefit.

Implications. Indian children may be seen as unmotivated in school because of their reluctance to compete with peers in the classroom. Instead of going to an appointment, they may assist a family member needing help. Indians work hard to prevent discord and disharmony.

3. *Noninterference.* Indians are taught not to interfere with others and to observe rather than react impulsively. Rights of others are respected. This value influences parenting style.

Implications. It is important to be aware of how cultural influences have shaped our perception of what is right or wrong in parent-child relationships. American Indians are more indulgent and less punitive to their children than are parents from other ethnic groups (MacPhee, Fritz, & Miller-Heyl, 1996). Euro-American parenting styles may conflict with American Indian values. A culturally sensitive parent education program has been developed for American Indians that involves (1) use of the oral tradition by storytelling to teach lessons to children; (2) understanding of the spiritual nature of child rearing and the spiritual value of children; and (3) use of the extended family in child rearing. The eight-session program involves a half-hour social time for parents and children before each session. Storytelling and a potluck meal are included. The focus is the application of traditional teaching methods (nurturing, use of nature to teach lessons, and use of harmony as a guiding principle for family life; Gorman & Balter, 1997).

4. *Time orientation.* Indians are very much involved in the present rather than the future. Ideas of punctuality or planning for the future may be unimportant. Life is to be lived in the here and now.

Implications. Things get done according to a rational order and not according to deadlines. In the majority culture, delay of gratification and planning for future goals are seen as important qualities. In working with these issues, the counselor should acknowledge the value differences and their potential conflict and help the individual or family develop possible strategies to deal with these.

5. *Spirituality.* The spirit, mind, and body are all interconnected. Illness is a disharmony between these elements.

Implications. Traditional curative approaches attempt to restore the harmony of these systems. The sweat lodge and vision quest are often used to reestablish the connections between the mind, body, and spirit. To treat a problem successfully, all of these elements have to be considered and addressed. Positive emotions can be curative. Medicine is in each event, memory, place, or person, such as talking to an old friend on the phone or watching children play (M. T. Garrett & Wilbur, 1999). The counselor should help the client identify the factors involved in disharmony; determine curative events, behaviors, and feelings; and utilize client-generated solutions so that a balance is obtained.

6. *Nonverbal communication.* Learning occurs by listening rather than talking. Direct eye contact with an elder is seen as a sign of disrespect. Indian families tend to ask few direct questions.

Implications. Differences in nonverbal communication can lead to misunderstandings. Several families reported misunderstandings with teachers. An American Indian child who did not look directly at the teacher talking to her was accused of being disrespectful (Garwick & Auger, 2000). This interpretation was premature, since the teacher was not aware that among many Indian groups, eye contact between a child and an elder indicates a lack of respect. The mother explained that this was the way her child was brought up. There have been reported cases in which the lack of eye contact has been regarded as a deficit. For example, a behavior modification procedure was employed to shape eye contact in a Navaho girl (Everett, Proctor, & Cortmell, 1989). It is important to determine whether specific behaviors are due to cultural values or are actual problems.

Specific Problem Areas for American Indians/Alaskan Natives

Education

American Indian children appear to do well during the first few years of school. However, by the fourth grade, a pattern of decline and dropping out develops. Due to a variety of factors, a significant drop in achievement motivation occurs around the seventh grade. Few American Indians who pursue higher education graduate (Juntunen et al., 2001). Although some have argued that American Indian cultural values and beliefs are incompatible with those of the educational system, there is increasing support for the view that perceived barriers to mobility are the culprit for the reduced academic performance. In other words, academic success does not lead to the rewards obtained by White Americans. Once American Indian children realize their "Indianness," achievement motivation drops (Wood & Clay, 1996). In addition, many youth can find jobs on the reservation, so they do not see the necessity for "White man's education." The inability to complete an education perpetuates the cycle of poverty and lack of opportunities and may contribute to the high suicide rate among American Indian adolescents (Keane, Dick, Bechtold, & Manson, 1996).

Implications. Fewer American Indians and Alaskan Natives than White Americans finish high school, and 11 percent have a bachelor's degree versus 24 percent of the U.S. population (U.S. Census Bureau, 2006a). The blame for dropout rates has generally been placed on the individual rather than the school environment. Youths who left school often reported feeling "pushed out," and mistrusted teachers who represented the White community that exerted control over their economic, social, and religious lives (Deyhle & Swisher, 1999). At a systems level, changes need to be made in public schools and higher education to accommodate some of the social and cultural differences of American Indian and Alaskan Native students and the hostile environment they face. Teachers should understand the sociocultural history regarding education with American Indian students and utilize curriculum that reflect the students' cultural background (Reyhner, 2002). Schools must address the perceived lack of reward for academic achievement among these groups. The reasons for these statistics must be remedied. Some tribes have given up on the public school system and have developed their own learning centers and community colleges. Schools must help students bridge the two worlds of Native American and White cultures.

Acculturation Conflicts

Not only do Indian children and adolescents face the same developmental problems that all young people do, but they are also in a state of conflict over exposure to two very different cultures. They are caught between expectations of their parents to maintain traditional values and the necessity to adapt to the majority culture (Rieckmann, Wadsworth, & Deyhle, 2004). In one study of American Indian adolescents, the most serious problems identified involved family relationships, grades, and concerns about the future. In addition, boys frequently cited their Indianness or being Indian as a problem. Surprisingly, one-third of the girls reported feeling that they did not want to live (Bee-Gates, Howard-Pitney, LaFramboise, & Rowe, 1996).

Although some of the value differences between Indians and non-Indians have been presented, many Indians are acculturated and hold the values of the larger society. The degree of Indian identity versus acculturation and assimilation should always be considered, since it influences receptivity in counseling. Five cultural orientation types were formulated by M. T. Garrett and Pichette (2000):

1. *Traditional.* The individual may speak little English, thinks in the native language, and practices traditional tribal customs and methods of worship.
2. *Marginal.* The individual may speak both languages but has lost touch with his or her cultural heritage and is not fully accepted in mainstream society.
3. *Bicultural.* The person is conversant with both sets of values and can communicate in a variety of contexts.
4. *Assimilated.* The individual embraces only the mainstream culture's values, behaviors, and expectations.
5. *Pantraditional.* Although the individual has only been exposed to or adopted mainstream values, he or she has made a conscious effort to return to the "old ways."

Implications. It is clear that within-group differences have to be considered in working with American Indians. Because of differences in acculturation, approaches that might be appropriate for a given individual might not be appropriate for all Indians. For example, the types of problems and the therapeutic process and goals appropriate for an American Indian living on a rural reservation may be very different from those appropriate for an urbanized Indian who retains few of the traditional beliefs. An American Indian with a traditional orientation may be unfamiliar with the expectations of the dominant culture. In contrast, assimilated or marginal American Indians may face issues such as (1) the denial and lack of pride in being a Native American; (2) pressure to adopt the majority cultural values; (3) guilty feelings over not knowing or participating in his or her culture; (4) negative views of Native Americans; and (5) a lack of a support and belief system. The mental health professional should assess for tribal affiliation if any, languages spoken, self-identity, where the individual grew up, and if there is a current relationship to a tribe or tribal culture (M. T. Garrett & Pichette, 2000). Different strategies will have to be developed according to the degree of cultural identity. Those who are traditionally oriented may need to develop the skills and resources to deal with mainstream society. Acculturated individuals may need to examine value and self-identity conflicts.

Domestic Violence

Domestic violence, along with physical and sexual assault, is quite high in many native communities. American Indian women suffer a higher rate of violence (3.5 times higher) than the national average (Bhungalia, 2001). This may be an underestimate. Many do not report assaults because of the tension that exists between law enforcement and women. This level of domestic violence may be a result of the loss of traditional status and roles for both men and women, as well as social and economic marginalization.

Implications. During counseling, it may be difficult to determine whether domestic violence is occurring in a family or couple. American Indian women who are abused may remain silent because of cultural barriers, a high level of distrust with White-dominated agencies, fear of familial alienation, and a history of the inadequacy of state and tribal agencies to prosecute domestic crimes (Bhungalia, 2001). Jurisdictional struggles between state and tribal authorities may result in a lack of help for women. Many tribes acknowledge the problem of family violence and have developed community-based domestic violence interventions. Strategies need to be developed from the American Indian perspective; using material or resources from the majority culture can raise issues of domination (Hamby, 2000). When working with a domestic violence issue with an American Indian woman, tribal issues, tribal programs, and family support should be identified.

Suicide

> *Robert Jaycob Jensen was first. The lanky 17-year-old Sioux Indian, who'd been drinking heavily and having run-ins with police all summer, slipped into his family's dank basement last Aug. 30. Over toward the corner, past the rusted-out furnace and broken sewer line, he threaded a braided leather belt over a board nailed between floor beams, buckled it around his neck and hanged himself.*
>
> *On Nov. 16, in the same basement with the same type of belt, Robert's 16-year-old cousin and best friend, Charles Gerry, hanged himself. Three other Indian youths have since taken their lives.... In the 5 months since Robert's death, 43 reservation boys and girls have attempted suicide. ("Rash of Indian Suicides," 1998)*

The suicide epidemic is thought to be the result of alcohol abuse, poverty, boredom, and family breakdown. American Indian youth have twice the rate of attempted and completed suicide as other youth. Adolescence to adulthood is the time of greatest risk for suicide, especially among young males (EchoHawk, 1997; Middlebrook, LeMaster, Beals, Novins, & Manson, 2001). Among a sample of 122 American Indian middle school children living on a North Plains reservation, 20 percent had made a nonfatal suicide attempt and of this group, nearly half had made attempts two or more times (LaFromboise, Medoff, Lee, & Harris, in press).

Implications. It is difficult to address many of the societal and economic issues that face American Indians. For those who live on a reservation or identify with a tribe, community involvement or programs may exist or may need to be developed. However, there appears to be only a weak association between participation in traditional activities and suicidal ideation (LaFromboise et al., in press). Any program developed should be culturally consistent. A promising culturally tailored suicide intervention program was implemented by LaFromboise and Howard-Pitney (1995) at the request of the Zuni Tribal High School. The participants were involved in either an intervention or a no-intervention condition. Scores on a suicide probability measure indicated that 81 percent of the students were in the moderate to severe risk ranges. Of the participants, 18 percent reported having attempted suicide, and 40 percent reported knowing of a relative or friend who had committed suicide. The program involved the development of suicide intervention skills through role-playing. Other components included self-esteem building, identifying emotions and stress, recognizing and eliminating negative thoughts or emotions, receiving information on suicide and intervention strategies, and setting personal and community goals. The program was effective in reducing feelings of hopelessness and suicidal probability ratings. Although the long-term effects of the program are not known, the approach seems promising in the prevention of suicide. Intervention programs may have to be developed and targeted for specific tribes. Suicide ideation among the Pueblo was associated with a friend's suicidal behavior, while it was associated with lower self-esteem and depression among the Northern plain adolescents (LaFromboise, 2006).

Alcohol and Substance Abuse

Substance abuse is one of the greatest problems faced by American Indians. They are six times more likely to die of alcohol-related causes than the general U.S. population (Frank, Moore, & Ames, 2000). In Indian Health Service hospitals approximately 21 percent of hospitalizations are for alcohol-related problems (*Morbidity and Mortality Weekly Report,* 1994). In Alaska, 32 percent of American Indians/Alaskan Natives of childbearing age reported heavy drinking, which is responsible for the disproportionately high percentage of cases of fetal alcohol syndrome reported in this population (Centers for

Disease Control, 1994). In addition, drug abuse and dependence are very high among young Indian clients. However, it must be remembered that many American Indians/Alaskan Natives do not drink or only drink moderately. Abstinence is high among certain tribes, such as the Navajo (Myers, Kagawa-Singer, Kumanyika, Lex, & Markides, 1995).

A variety of explanations have been put forth to indicate possible reasons for the rise in alcohol abuse (see Figure 12.1). Substance abuse is often related to low self-esteem, cultural identity conflicts, lack of positive role models, abuse history, social pressure to use substances, hopelessness about life, and a breakdown in the family (Swinomish Tribal Mental Health Project, 1991; Yee et al., 1995). The use of illicit substances is related to the 50 percent dropout rate from school by American Indian youth (Beauvais, Chavez, Oetting, Deffenbacher, & Cornell, 1996). Heavy alcohol use is associated with both low general self-efficacy and feelings of powerlessness in life (Taylor, 2000). Drinking alcoholic beverages may initially have been incorporated into cultural practices as an activity of sharing, giving, and togetherness (Swinomish Tribal Mental Health Project, 1991).

Implications. Successful residential drug treatment programs have incorporated appropriate cultural elements. If alcohol use has been incorporated into tribal or family customs or traditions, the problem would have to be addressed at both the systems and the individual level. Community-oriented programs engage the entire community rather than specific individuals. It had the advantage of directly involving community leaders (Hawkins, Cummins & Marlatt, 2004). Because of the history of conflicts between tribal, state, and federal agencies, one must be careful not to be seen as imposing "White solutions" to problems on the reservation. One tribal community reduced their alcoholism rate from 95 percent to 5 percent in 10 years by creating a community culture in which alcoholism was not tolerated, while revitalizing traditional culture (Thomason, 2000). Work within the resources of the tribes. Many have developed programs to deal with alcohol and substance abuse issues.

Implications for Clinical Practice

1. Before working with American Indians, explore ethnic differences and values. It is important to be aware of our own cultural biases and how they might hinder the counseling relationship and the development of appropriate goals.
2. Determine the cultural identity of the client and family members and their association with a tribe or a reservation. Many American Indians

adhere completely to mainstream values; others, especially those on or near reservations, are more likely to hold to traditional values.

3. Understand the history of oppression, and be aware of or inquire about local issues associated with the tribe or reservation for traditionally oriented American Indians. Many may be distrustful of agencies.

4. Evaluate using a client-centered listening style initially, and determine when to use more structure and questions. Try not to hurry the individual. Allow him or her time to finish statements and thoughts.

5. Assess the problem from the perspective of the individual, family, extended family, and, if appropriate, the tribal community. Try to determine the cultural experiential aspects.

6. If necessary, address basic needs first, such as problems involving food, shelter, child care, and employment. Identify possible resources, such as Indian Health Services or tribal programs.

7. Be careful not to overgeneralize, but evaluate for problems such as domestic violence, substance abuse, depression, and suicidality during assessment. In addition, determine the appropriateness of a mind-body-spirit emphasis.

8. Identify possible environmental contributors to problems such as racism, discrimination, poverty, and acculturation conflicts.

9. Help children and adolescents determine whether cultural values or an unreceptive environment contribute to their problem. Strategize different ways of dealing with the conflicts.

10. Help determine concrete goals that incorporate cultural, family, extended family, and community perspectives.

11. Determine whether child-rearing practices are consistent with traditional Indian methods and how they may conflict with mainstream methods.

12. In family interventions, identify extended family members, determine their roles, and request their assistance.

13. Generate possible solutions with the clients and consider their consequences from the individual, family, and community perspectives. Include strategies that may involve cultural elements and that focus on holistic factors (mind, body, spirit).

Counseling Asian Americans and Pacific Islanders

16

Chapter

Among traditionally oriented Chinese Americans, depression is described with terms such as boredom, discomfort, pain, dizziness, or other physical symptoms, rather than as feelings of sadness. Many feel that a diagnosis of depression is "morally unacceptable" or "experientially meaningless." (Kleinman, 2004)

Eric Liu, the son of immigrants from Taiwan, who graduated from Yale and has written speeches for President Clinton, doesn't feel like an "Asian American." He believes the identity is contrived and unnecessary. (Chang, 1998)

Approximately 25 percent of Americans hold very strong negative stereotypes of Chinese Americans. Henry S. Tang, whose organization sponsored the poll, responded to the findings by stating, "What these numbers do is force us into a realization that we're always having to earn our recognition over and over again." (Richardson & MacGregor, 2001, p. E1)

The Asian American population is growing rapidly and, as of 2007, is currently over 10 million. It includes people from the Far East, Southeast Asia, or the Indian subcontinent. An additional 1,700,000 census respondents checked Asian and one other ethnic group. Because of immigration over two-thirds of Asians are overseas-born, with 79 percent speaking a language other than English at home, and about 40 percent speaking English less than "very well." In fact, with the exception of Japanese Americans, Asian American populations are now principally composed of internationally born individuals. Native Hawaiian and Pacific Islanders totaled 378,782 and numbered 860,965 when combined with those of more than one race (U.S. Census Bureau, 2005e).

Between-group differences within the Asian American population may be quite large, since the population is composed of at least 40 distinct subgroups that differ in language, religion, and values (Sandhu,

1997). They include the larger Asian groups in the United States (Chinese, Filipinos, Koreans, Asian Indians, and Japanese), refugees and immigrants from Southeast Asia (Vietnamese, Laotians, Cambodians, and Hmongs), and Pacific Islanders (Hawaiians, Guamanians, and Samoans). Compounding the difficulty in making any generalization about the Asian American population are within-group differences. Individuals diverge on variables such as migration or relocation experiences, degree of assimilation or acculturation, identification with the home country, facility in their native languages and in English, family composition and intactness, amount of education, and degree of adherence to religious beliefs.

Asian Americans: A Success Story?

In contrast to many Third World groups, the contemporary image of Asian Americans is that of a highly successful minority that has "made it" in society (Yin, 2000). Indeed, a close analysis of census figures (U.S. Census Bureau, 2004c) seems to support this contention. Of those over the age of 25, 44 percent of Asian/Pacific Islanders had at least a bachelor's degree, versus 24 percent of their White counterparts. Approximately 10 percent of all students at Harvard, 40 percent of those at Berkeley, and 19 percent of those at MIT are Asian Americans (Sandhu, 1997). Words such as "intelligent," "hardworking," "enterprising," and "disciplined" are frequently applied to this population (Morrissey, 1997). The median income of Asian American families was $59,300, versus $50,000 for the U.S. population as a whole (U.S. Census Bureau, 2004c).

A closer analysis of the status of Asian Americans reveals disturbing truths that contrast with popular views of their success story. First, in terms of economics, references to the higher median income of Asian Americans do not take into account (1) the higher percentage of Asian American families having more than one wage earner, (2) a higher prevalence of poverty despite the higher median income (14 versus 8 percent for the U.S. population), and (3) the discrepancy between education and income. For example, high rates of poverty exist among Hmong, Guamanian, Indonesian, and Cambodian populations in the United States (Iwasaki, 2006a).

Second, in the area of education, Asian Americans show a disparate picture of extraordinarily high educational attainment and a large, undereducated mass. Among the Hmong, only 40 percent have completed high school, and fewer than 14 percent of Tongans, Cambodians, Laotians, and Hmongs 25 years and older have a bachelor's degree (U.S. Census Bureau, 2005e). When averaged out, this bimodal distribution indicates how misleading statistics can be.

Third, there is now widespread recognition that, apart from being tourist attractions, Chinatowns, Manilatowns, and Japantowns in San Francisco and New York represent ghetto areas with prevalent unemployment, poverty, health problems, and juvenile delinquency. People outside these communities seldom see the deplorable social conditions that exist behind the bright neon lights, restaurants, and quaint shops. Over one-third of the residents in these areas complain of depression and emotional tension (S. Sue, D. W. Sue, L. Sue, & Takeuchi, 1995). Mass murders committed over the years have been traced to Chinese juvenile gangs operating in Chinatowns, and recent news reports show this trend to be on the increase.

Fourth, although Asian Americans underutilize mental health services, it is not clear if this is due to low rates of socioemotional adjustment difficulties, discriminatory mental health practices, or cultural values inhibiting self-referral (Asai & Kameoka, 2005). It is possible that much of the mental illness, the adjustment problems, and the juvenile delinquency among Asians are hidden. The discrepancy between official and real rates of adjustment difficulties may be due to cultural factors such as the shame and disgrace associated with admitting to emotional problems, the handling of problems within the family rather than relying on outside resources, and the manner of symptom formation, such as a low prevalence of acting-out disorders.

Fifth, Asian Americans have been exposed to discrimination and racism throughout history and continue to face anti-Asian sentiments. In 1995, the number of hate crimes against Asian Americans rose, with assaults increasing by 11 percent and aggravated assaults by 14 percent (Matthee, 1997). Although some are fourth- and fifth-generation Americans, many are still identified as "foreign" and are regarded with suspicion. In a survey of a representative sample of 1,216 adults to determine their attitudes toward Asian Americans, several disturbing findings were reported (Committee of 100, 2001). Nearly one-third indicated that Chinese Americans would be more loyal to China than the United States, and nearly half of all the people surveyed believed that Chinese Americans would pass secret information to China. About a quarter of the sample would disapprove if someone in their family married an Asian American, and 17 percent would be upset if a "substantial" number of Asian Americans moved into their neighborhoods.

It is important for counselors, academic advisors, and educators who work with Asian Americans to look behind the success myth and to understand the historical and current experiences of Asians in America. The matter is even more pressing for counselors when we realize that Asian Americans underutilize counseling and other mental health facilities and are more likely to seek help at a counseling service rather than at a psychiatric facility. The approach of this chapter is twofold. First, we attempt to indicate how the interplay of social and cultural forces have served to shape and define the lifestyle of recent immigrants/refugees and American-born Asians. Second, we explore how an understanding of Asian American values and social experiences necessitate the need for modifications in counseling and psychotherapeutic practices when working with this population.

Traditional Asian Cultural Values, Behavior Patterns, and Implications for Therapy

In the following section, we present some of the cultural values, behavioral characteristics, and expectations about therapy of Asian Americans, as well as their implications for counseling. Much of the following consists of group generalizations whose accuracy must be determined for each individual client or family, and are not to be applied in a stereotypic manner. Although cultural knowledge is important in helping the counselor identify potential conflict areas, one must be careful not to apply cultural information rigidly. It must be remembered that within- and between-group differences are quite large—some individuals and families are quite acculturated, and others retain a more traditional cultural orientation (Kim, 2007). Cultural differences, such as the degree of assimilation, socioeconomic background, family experiences, and educational level, impact each individual in a unique manner. Knowledge of cultural values can help generate hypotheses about the way an Asian might view a disorder and his or her expectations of treatment. It must also be remembered that values and behavior patterns evolve and change over time. The therapist's task is to help the clients identify or develop a variety of ways of dealing with problems within cultural constraints and to develop the skills to negotiate cultural differences with the larger society.

Collectivistic Orientation

> *I was born and raised in Korea and came to the United States in 1968. . . . I must move back to Seoul to take care of my aging mother. I am a man of Asian values (filial piety), and they (his children) are young college graduates of American values (career advancement and development). (Choi, 1999, p. 7)*

Instead of promoting individual needs and personal identity, Asian families tend to have a family and group orientation. Children are expected to strive for family goals and not to engage in behaviors that would bring dishonor to the family. Asian American parents tend to show little interest in a child's viewpoint regarding family matters. Instead, the emphasis is on family harmony, adapting to the needs of others, and adherence to "correct" values (Rothbaum, Morelli, Pott, & Liu-Constant, 2000). Asian American adolescents appear to retain the expectation to assist, support, and respect their family even when exposed to a society that emphasizes adolescent autonomy and independence (Fuligni et al., 1999). While Euro-American parents rated being "self-directed" as the most important attribute in children's social competence, Japanese American parents chose "behaves well" (O'Reilly, Tokuno, & Ebata, 1986). Chinese American parents also believed that politeness and calmness were more important to inculcate in their children than did Euro-American parents (Jose, Huntsinger, & Liaw, 2000). Asian American families differ in the degree in which they place individual needs over family needs. In the case just given, Choi (1999) has accepted the fact that his adult children will not stay with his wife (their mother) while he is in Korea to take care of his mother. He decries American society, in which individualism prevails over collectivism. However, he acknowledges that his children have honored the family by being successful. He understands that they define family obligations in a different manner.

Implications. Because of a possible collectivistic orientation, it is important to consider the family and community context during assessment and problem definition. It is important to be open to different family orientations and not automatically consider interdependence as a sign of enmeshment. After doing an individual analysis, you might also ask questions such as, "How does your family see the problem?" For traditionally oriented Asian Americans, a focus on individual client needs and wishes may run counter to the values of collectivism. Determining whether the client is aware of conflicting expectations is also important. Goals and treatment approaches may have to include a family focus (e.g., "How important are considerations of your family in deciding how to deal with the problem?" and "How would achieving the different goals affect you, your family, friends, and social community?"). Questions such as these allow the therapist to assess the degree of collectivism in the client. Acculturated Asian Americans with an individualistic orientation can often benefit from traditional counseling approaches, but the family should still be assessed, since conflicts due to acculturation differences are common.

Hierarchical Relationships

Traditional Asian American families tend to be hierarchical and patriarchal in structure, with males and older individuals occupying a higher status. Communication flows down from the parent to the child, who is expected to defer to the adults. The sons are expected to carry on the family name and tradition. Even when they are married, their primary allegiance is to the parents. In general, the mother serves to mediate communication within the family. Second-generation Chinese American high school students place a higher priority on filial piety and obedience to their parents and authorities than do their Euro-

American counterparts (Feldman & Rosenthal, 1990). Third-generation Japanese Americans still feel the pressure of parental obligations (Ina, 1997). Between-group differences do exist. Among Asian American groups, Japanese Americans are the most acculturated. The majority are third- to fourth-generation Americans. Filipino American families tend to be more egalitarian, while Korean, Southeast Asian, and Chinese American families tend to be more patriarchal and traditional in orientation (Blair & Qian, 1998).

Implications. In family therapy it is important to determine the family structure and communication pattern. Does it appear to be egalitarian or hierarchical? If the structure is not clear, addressing the father first and then the mother may be most productive. If English is a problem, use an interpreter with the parents. Having children interpret for the parents can be counterproductive because it upsets the hierarchical structure. For very traditionally oriented families, having communication from members directed to the therapist is more congruent with cultural values than having the family members address one another. It is also important to assess for status change within the family. It is not uncommon among Asian immigrants for women to retain their occupational status while men are either underemployed or unemployed. A loss of male status may result in family conflict. The father may become even more authoritarian to maintain his status. In such cases, it is helpful to cast societal factors as the identified patient.

Parenting Styles

> *When she does something wrong, I think, something like misbehavior, something not good, I will sit down first, think about how to solve this problem. If I have difficulty, I will consult an expert on how to solve this problem. (Kass, 1998, p. 3)*

Hou-Lin Li and his wife, Luying Deng, had completed a parent education course after being accused of slapping their 8-year-old daughter for lying and forging their signature on a disciplinary note from a teacher. For this, the state prosecutor, Richard Devine, charged the parents with child abuse and threatened them with deportation back to China. In one sample of undergraduates, Asian American students reported a somewhat higher level of physical and emotional punishment from their parents than did their Euro-American counterparts (Meston, Heiman, Trapnell, & Carlin, 1999). Asian American parenting styles tend to be more authoritarian and directive than in Euro-American families, although a relaxed style is used with children younger than the age of 6 or 7 (Jose et al., 2000; Meston et al., 1999). Problem behavior in children is thought to be due to a lack of discipline. However, differences in parenting style between Asian American groups have been found. Japanese and Filipino American families tend to have the most egalitarian relationships, while Korean, Chinese, and Southeast Asian Americans are more authoritarian (Blair & Qian, 1998).

Implications. Egalitarian or Western-style parent effectiveness training strategies may run counter to traditional rearing patterns. Traditional Asian American families may feel that their parenting skills are being criticized when exposed to Western techniques or styles. Instead of attempting to establish egalitarian relationships, there can be a focus on identifying different aspects of parenting. Rather than just punishment, Asian parenting styles typically include caretaking, teaching, modeling, and playing. The therapist can help refocus parenting to utilize the more positive aspects of Asian child-rearing strategies. These would be couched in terms of helping the children with problems rather than altering poor parenting. It is also important to commiserate with parents in terms of raising children in a society with different cultural standards.

Emotionality

Strong emotional displays, especially in public, are considered to be signs of immaturity or a lack of control. In many Asian families, there is generally less open display of emotions, especially to older children (Rothbaum, et al., 2000). Care and concern are shown by attending to the physical needs of family members. The father maintains an authoritative and distant role and is generally not emotionally demonstrative or involved with his children. His role is to provide for the economic and physical needs of the family. Shame and guilt are used to control and train the children. Mothers are more responsive to the children but use less nurturance and more verbal and physical punishments than do Euro-American mothers (Kelly & Tseng, 1992). However, mothers are expected to meet the emotional needs of the children and often serve as the intermediary between the father and the children. When the children are exposed to more open displays of emotions from Western society, they may begin to question the comparative lack of emotion displayed by their parents. Chang-Rae Lee (1995, p. 58), in a novel, describes his father as *"unencumbered by the needling questions of existence and self-consciousness. . . . I wasn't sure he had the capacity to love."*

Implications. Counseling microskills that focus directly on emotions may be uncomfortable and produce shame for traditional Asian Americans. Emotional behavior can be recognized in a more indirect manner. For example, if an individual shows discomfort, the therapist could respond by saying either *"You look uncomfortable"* or *"This situation would make someone uncomfortable."* In both cases the discomfort would be recognized, but we have found that Asian American students are more responsive to the second, more indirect acknowledgment of emotions. C.-R. Lee's (1995) reaction to his father's lack of emotional responsiveness could lead to a discussion of value conflicts and how to deal with them instead of blame. It is also helpful to focus on behaviors more than emotions and identify how family members are meeting each other's needs. In one study (Juang & Tucker, 1991), care and concern between an Asian couple were shown more by taking care of the physical needs of the partner than by verbally expressing care. Western marital therapy, which emphasizes verbal and emotional expressiveness as the main goal, may not be adequate in dealing with some Asian couples or families.

Holistic View on Mind and Body

A female client complained about all kinds of physical problems such as dizziness, loss of appetite, an inability to complete household chores, and insomnia. She asked the therapist if her problem could be due to "nerves." The therapist suspected depression since these are some of the physical manifestations of the disorder and asked the client if she felt depressed and sad. At this point, the client paused and looked confused. She finally stated that she feels very ill and that these physical problems are making her sad. Her perspective is that it was natural for her to feel sad when sick. As the therapist followed up by attempting to determine if there was a family history of depression, the client displayed even more discomfort and defensiveness. Although the client never directly contradicted the therapist, she did not return for the following session. (Tsui & Schultz, 1985)

Because the mind and body are considered inseparable, Asian Americans may present emotional difficulties through somatic complaints. Physical complaints are a common and culturally accepted means of expressing psychological and emotional stress. It is believed that physical problems cause emotional disturbances and that these will disappear as soon as there is appropriate treatment of the physical illness. Instead of talking about anxiety and depression, the mental health professional will often hear complaints involving headaches, fatigue, restlessness, and disturbances in sleep and appetite (Yeung, Chang, Gresham, Nierenberg, & Fava, 2004). Even psychotic patients typically made somatic complaints and sought treatment for those physical ailments (Nguyen, 1985).

Implications. Treat somatic complaints as real problems. Inquire about medications or other physical treatments they may use. To determine if psychological factors are also involved, inquire in the following manner: "Dealing with headaches and dizziness can be quite troublesome; how are these affecting your mood, relationships, etc.?" This approach legitimizes the physical complaints but allows an indirect way to assess psychosocial factors. Develop an approach that would deal both with somatic complaints and with the consequences of being "ill."

Academic and Occupational Goals

I want to write. I have to write. . . . This is not the choice my parents would make, and surely not the choice they would wish me to make. . . . I must not let it deter my progress or shut down my dreams, my purpose. (Ying, Coombs, & Lee, 1999, p. 357)

There is great pressure for children to succeed academically and to have a successful career, since both would be indicative of a good family upbringing. As a group, Asian Americans perform better academically than do their Euro-American counterparts. Although Asian American students have high levels of academic achievement, they also have more fear of academic failure compared to their Euro-American peers. They spend twice as much time each week on academics as their non-Asian counterparts (Eaton & Dembo, 1997). However, this is often accompanied with a price. Asian American adolescents report feeling isolated, depressed, and anxious, and reported little praise for their accomplishments from their parents (Lorenzo, Pakiz, Reinherz, & Frost, 1995). Asian American parents often have specific career goals in mind for their children (generally in technical fields or the hard sciences). Because choice of vocation may reflect parental expectations rather than personal talent, Asian college students appear more uncertain and lacking in information regarding careers (Lucas & Berkel, 2005). Deviations from either academic excellence or "appropriate" career choices can produce conflict between family members.

Implications. Have parents recognize other positive behaviors and contributions made by their children, not just academic performance. Some may not do well academically. Indicate that there are many ways that parents can feel proud of their children. Asian American students often have a lack of clarity regarding vocational interests and may need information about occupations (Lucas & Berkel, 2005). For career or occupational conflicts, acknowledge that the parents are seeking success for their children but that there are many new career options. Give them information about areas other than technical fields. For individual clients, discuss the conflict between academic goals defined by the parents and individual desires. Present this as a culture conflict issue and identify the best way of presenting the child's side to the parents.

Racism and Prejudice

Asian Americans continue to face issues of racism and discrimination. Very negative stereotypes of this group are still held by a large number of American adults. Asian Americans report significantly more workplace discrimination than do their Caucasian counterparts (M. P. Bell, Harrison, & McLaughlin, 1997). Southeast Asian refugees who experienced racial discrimination reported high rates of depression (Noh, Beiser, Kaspar, Hou, & Rummens, 1999).

Implications. A therapist must assess the effects of possible environmental factors such as racism on mental health issues in Asian Americans. A client should not internalize an issue that is based on discriminatory practices. Instead, the focus should be on how to deal with racism and on possible efforts to change the environment. If a problem occurs in school, the therapist should determine the receptivity of the Asian American's peers and the school's academic and social environment to this ethnic group. The same would be done with the place of employment. Intervention may have to occur at a systems level, and the therapist may have to be an advocate for the client.

Acculturation Conflicts between Parents and Children

Children of Asian descent who are exposed to different cultural standards often attribute psychological distress to their parent's backgrounds and different values. The issue of not quite fitting in with their peers and being considered "too Americanized" by their parents is common. The acculturation gap is perceived by Chinese immigrant mothers to be higher with their sons than daughters (Buki, Ma, Strom & Strom, 2003). The inability to resolve differences in acculturation results in misunderstandings, miscommunication, and conflict (R. M. Lee, Choe, Kim, & Ngo, 2000). Parents may feel at a loss in terms of how to deal with their children. Some respond by becoming more rigid. One Asian Indian daughter described her parents as displaying a "museumization of practices." On a trip to India, she discovered that there was a wide difference between the parents' version of "Indian" and what Indians in India actually did. Her parents' version was much more restrictive (Das Gupta, 1997). Parent-child conflicts are among the most common presenting problems for Asian American college students seeking counseling (Lee, Su, & Yoshida, 2005).

Implications. To prevent interpersonal exchanges between parents and their children, the problem should be reframed or conceptualized as acculturation conflicts. In this way both the parents and their children can discuss cultural standards and the expectations from larger society.

Identity Issues

As Asians become progressively more exposed to the standards, norms, and values of the wider U.S. society, increasing assimilation and acculturation are frequently the result. Bombarded on all sides by peers, schools, and the mass media, which uphold Western standards as better than their own, Asian Americans are frequently placed in situations of extreme culture conflict that may lead to much pain and agony regarding behavioral and physical differences. Asian American college women report lower self-esteem and less satisfaction with their racially defined features than do their Caucasian counterparts (Mintz & Kashubeck, 1999). C.-R. Lee (1995) described his experiences as "straddling two worlds and at home in neither." He felt alienated from both American and Korean cultures. As with other adolescents, those of Asian American descent also struggle with the question of "Who am I?" Individuals undergoing acculturation conflicts may respond in the following manner (Huang, 1994):

1. *Assimilation.* Seeks to become part of the dominant society to the exclusion of his or her own cultural group.
2. *Separation.* Identifies exclusively with the Asian culture.
3. *Integration/biculturalism.* Retains many Asian values but adapts to the dominant culture by learning necessary skills and values.
4. *Marginalization.* Perceives one's own culture as negative, but is unable to adapt to majority culture.

Implications. Identity issues are a problem for some Asian Americans and not for others. Some believe that ethnic identity is not salient or important. Assessing the ethnic self-identity of clients is important because it can impact problem definition and the choice of techniques used in therapy. Assimilated Asian clients are generally receptive to Western styles of counseling and may not want reminders of their ethnicity. Traditionally identified Asians are more likely to be recent immigrants or refugees, and they tend to retain strong cultural values and be more responsive to a culturally adapted counseling approach. Bicultural Asian Americans adhere to some traditional values, while also incorporating many Western values. Ethnic self-identity can also influence conceptualization of presenting problems. Acculturated Asian American college students have beliefs similar to those of counselors, while less acculturated students who hold traditional views do not (Mallinckrodt, Shigeoka, & Suzuki, 2005).

Psychotherapy Is a Foreign Concept to Many Asian Americans

Explain the nature of the counseling and therapy process and the necessity of obtaining information.

Implications. Describe the client's role. Indicate that the problems may be individual, relational, environmental, or a combination of these, and that you will perform an assessment of each of these areas. Introduce the concept of *coconstruction*—that the problem and solutions are developed with the help of the client and the counselor. Coconstruction reduces the chance that the therapist will impose his or her theoretical framework on the client. For example, the therapist might explain, "In counseling we try to understand the problem as it affects you, your family, friends, and community, so I will ask you questions about these different areas. With your help we will also consider possible solutions that you can try out."

Expectations of Counseling

Counselors often believe that they should adopt an authoritarian or highly directive stance with Asian American clients. What is actually expected by Asian clients is an active role by the counselor in structuring the session and guidelines on the types of responses that they will be expected to make. It can be helpful for the therapist to accept the role of being the expert regarding therapy, while the client is given the role of expert regarding his or her life. Thus, clients assist the therapist by facilitating understanding of the problem and possible means of approaching the problem (Chen & Davenport, 2005).

Implications. The counselor should be directive but ensure the full participation from clients in developing goals and intervention strategies. Suggestions can be given and different options presented for consideration by the client. The client can select the option that he or she believes will be the most useful in dealing with the problem. Also, encourage the client to develop his or her own solutions. The consequences for any action should be considered, not only for the individual clients, but for the possible impact on the family and community. Even among acculturated Asian American college students, the preference for a helper role involves advice, consultation, and the facilitation of family and community support systems (Atkinson, Kim, & Caldwell, 1998). The opportunity for Asian American clients to try interventions on their own promotes the cultural value of self-sufficiency.

Counseling Interventions

Asian American clients expect concrete goals and strategies focused on solutions. Mental health professionals must be careful not to impose techniques or strategies.

Implications. Focus on the specific problem brought in by the client, and help the client develop his or her goals for therapy. This allows the client to present his or her concerns and reduces the chance that the therapist's worldview will be imposed on the client. Determine what needs to be done if cultural or family issues are involved. Therapy should be time limited, focus on concrete resolution of problems, and deal with the present or immediate future. Cognitive-behavioral and other solution-focused strategies are useful in working with Asian Americans (Chen & Davenport, 2005). However, as with other Eurocentric approaches, these approaches need to be altered because the focus is on the individual, whereas the unit of treatment for Asian Americans may actually be the family, community, or society. Modify cognitive-behavioral approaches to incorporate a collectivistic rather than an individualistic perspective. For example, assertiveness training can be altered for Asian clients who have difficulty in asserting themselves. First, consider possible cultural and social factors that may affect assertiveness (values placed on modesty, minority status, etc.). Then identify situations where assertiveness might be functional, such as in class or when seeking employment, and situations where a traditional cultural style might be more appropriate (with elders or parents). Next, determine anxiety-producing cognitions and possible cultural or societal influences. Finally, substitute appropriate thoughts and employ role-playing to increase assertiveness in specific situations. This alteration of a cognitive-behavioral approach considers cultural factors and is concrete, allowing clients to establish self-control.

Family Therapy

Although family therapy would seem to be the ideal medium in which to deal with problems for Asian Americans, certain difficulties exist. Most therapy models are based on Euro-American perspectives of egalitarian relationships and require verbal and emotional expressiveness. Some models assume that a problem in a family member is reflective of dysfunction between family members. In addition, the use of direct communication from child to parents, confrontational strategies, and nonverbal techniques such as "sculpting" may be an affront to the parents.

Implications. Assess the structure of the Asian American family. Is it hierarchical or more egalitarian? What is their perception of healthy family functioning? How are decisions made in the family? How are family members showing respect and contributing to the family? Focus on the positive aspects of the family and reframe conflicts to reduce confrontation. Expand systems theory to include societal factors such as prejudice, discrimination, poverty, and conflicting cultural values. Issues revolving around the pressures of being an Asian American family in this society need to be investigated. Describe the session as a solution-oriented one and explain that family problems are not uncommon. Have communication from family members come through the therapist. Function as a culture-broker in helping the family negotiate conflicts with the larger society.

Implications for Clinical Practice

Although Asian culture dictates general principles and values, there is a range of acceptable responses in dealing with situations. Helping Asian American clients formulate different culturally acceptable practices for specific problems can improve their problem-solving abilities. In addition, Asian Americans also must develop skills to interact with the larger society and to achieve a balance when conflicting values are involved. The following guidelines are based on Asian American cultural values, but the therapist or counselor must be aware of the large differences in degree of acculturation in this population. Many of the counseling skills learned in current mental health programs will be effective with modifications.

1. Be aware of cultural differences between the therapist and the client as regarding counseling, appropriate goals, and process. How would they affect work with Asian Americans who have a collectivistic, hierarchical, and patriarchal orientation?

2. Build rapport by discussing confidentiality and explaining the client role and the need to coconstruct the problem definition and solutions.

3. Assess not just from an individual perspective but include family, community, and societal influences on the problem. Obtain the worldview and ethnic identity of the Asian American client.

4. Conduct a positive assets search. What strengths, skills, problem-solving abilities, and social supports are available to the individual or family?

5. Consider or reframe the problem, when possible, as one in which issues of culture conflict or acculturation are involved.

6. Determine whether somatic complaints are involved and assess their influence on mood and relationships.

7. Take an active role, but allow Asian Americans to choose and evaluate suggested interventions.

8. Use problem-focused, time-limited approaches that have been modified to incorporate possible cultural factors.

9. With family therapy, the therapist should be aware that Western-based theories and techniques may not be appropriate for Asian families. Determine the structure and communication pattern among the members. It may be helpful to address the father first and to initially have statements by family members directed to the therapist. Focus on positive aspects of parenting such as modeling and teaching. Use a solution-focused model.

10. In couples counseling, assess for societal or acculturation conflicts. Determine the way that caring, support, or affection is shown. Among traditional Asians, providing for the needs of the other is as or more important than verbalizations of affection. Obtain their perspective on the goals for better functioning.

11. With Asian children and adolescents, common problems involve acculturation conflicts with parents, feeling guilty or stressful over academic performance, negative self-image or identity issues, and struggle between interdependence and independence.

12. Among recent immigrants or refugees, assess for living situation, culture conflict, and social or financial condition. Case management skills may be needed to secure help obtaining food and other community resources.

13. Consider the need to act as an advocate or engage in systems-level intervention in cases of institutional racism or discrimination.

Counseling Hispanic/Latino Americans

17

Chapter

I can remember having to hide when I was a kid.... I would come home and my parents would be maybe 20 or 30 minutes late, and I would cry until they got home because I was afraid they had been deported. (Modie, 2001, p. A6)

It was sometimes hard to adjust. When I went outside, I was in America, but inside my house, it was Mexico. My father was the leader of the house. It wasn't that way for some of my American friends. (Middleton, Arrendondo, & D'Andrea, 2000, p. 24)

Jennifer Cortes received the panicked call just after 11 A.M. Immigration officers were at Bellingham's Northwest Health Care Linen where her husband, Ezequiel Rosas-Cortes, worked sorting laundry.... Agents turned Jennifer away as they arrested her husband, an illegal immigrant who, for the first time, had felt confident enough to attend the local fair without fearing arrest. (Gambrell, 2006, p. A1)

A thick scar below his right elbow reminds him of his first days in the fields, when he slipped and fell on some sharp farming tools.... Like many farmworker children, Gonzales went to work to help his family pay the bills. He was a good student until he dropped out at age 15. He hasn't given up hope ... but his family comes first. (Kramer, 1998, p. A6)

In this chapter, the terms *Latino* and *Hispanic* encompass individuals living in the United States with ancestry from Mexico, Puerto Rico, Cuba, El Salvador, the Dominican Republic, and other Latin American countries. However, the terms are not accepted by all groups; some individuals prefer to be referred to as Latinos or *La Raza* (the race). Even within specific subgroups, there are different opinions on the appropriate terms of identification. Some Hispanics from Mexico may refer to themselves as *Mexicano, Mexican American, Chicano,* or *Spanish American* (Comas-Diaz, 2001; G. M. Gonzalez, 1997). The term Hispanic (official

U.S. Government designation) will be employed in this chapter to indicate the common background of Spanish language and customs. Although Hispanics share many characteristics, it is important to be aware that distinct differences exist both within and between the different groups.

In physical characteristics, the appearance of Hispanics varies greatly and may include resemblance to North American Indians, Blacks, Asians, or fair-skinned Europeans. The U.S. Census recognizes the term as an ethnic designator and not a racial one. Thus, Hispanics can be members of any racial grouping. Mexican Americans are mostly of *mestizo* ancestry (mixed Spanish and native Aztec-Indian blood). Throughout Latin America, the immigration of European, African, and Asian populations has resulted in a wide range of physical characteristics.

According to the U.S. Census (U.S. Census Bureau, 2004d), Hispanic Americans comprise a population of over 35 million, of whom nearly 67 percent are of Mexican descent, 8.6 percent are from Puerto Rico (Puerto Rico became a commonwealth on July 25, 1952, and its residents are U.S. citizens who can move between the island and the mainland without any restrictions), 3.7 percent are Cuban, and the remaining 22 percent are primarily from Central and South America. Because of their high birthrate and ongoing immigration patterns, Hispanics are currently the largest minority group in the United States. Hispanic Americans are a highly heterogeneous population with large between-group and within-group differences. Some individuals are oriented toward their ethnic group, while others are quite acculturated to mainstream values. Some have lived for generations within the United States, while a large proportion are recent immigrants. There are an estimated 11 million illegal immigrants from Latin American countries (Moore, 2001). Those who are undocumented occupy the lowest rung of the labor pool and are often taken advantage of because they have no legal status. It is estimated that almost half of all migrant farm workers are here illegally, many of whom rarely seek health care because of cost and the fear of discovery (*New York Times* News Service, 2001).

The majority of Hispanic Americans is situated in metropolitan areas of the United States, but Hispanic Americans populate every state, including Alaska and Hawaii. In certain states and cities they make up a substantial percentage of the population. Mexican Americans reside primarily in the Western states (they account for 40 percent of the population of New Mexico and 34 percent of the residents of California and Texas), but have increasingly migrated to the Southeastern states. Most Puerto Ricans reside in the Northeastern states and most Cubans live in Florida (U.S. Census, 2004d).

Hispanics are overrepresented among the poor, have high unemployment, and often live in substandard housing. Most are blue collar workers and hold semiskilled or unskilled occupations. There is a significant discrepancy between the annual incomes of Hispanics and Caucasians. Hispanics are much more likely than Whites to be unemployed (8.1 versus 5.1 percent). In 2002, 21.4 percent of Hispanics lived in poverty as compared to 7.8 percent of Whites. Over 30 percent of Hispanic children were living in poverty versus 17.7 percent of all children in the United States. Puerto Ricans appear to have the highest rate of poverty, while Cubans have the highest incomes (U.S. Census Bureau, 2003).

Traditional Hispanic Values, Characteristics, Behavior Patterns, and Implications for Therapy

In the following sections we consider the values, characteristics, and issues faced by Hispanic families and individuals and consider their implications in treatment. Remember that these are generalizations and their applicability needs to be assessed for particular Hispanic clients and families.

Family Values

Family tradition is an important aspect of life for Hispanic Americans. Family unity (*familismo*) is seen as very important, as are respect for and loyalty to the family. Cooperation rather than competition among family members is stressed. Interpersonal relationships are maintained and nurtured within a large network of family and friends. The development and maintenance of interpersonal relationships are very central to Hispanic families (Dingfelder, 2005a, 2005b). There is deep respect and affection among friends and family. Hispanic American students are more likely to endorse the following items than are White students: loyalty to the family, strictness of child rearing, religiosity, and respect for adults (Negy, 1993). For many Hispanic Americans, the extended family includes not only relatives but often nonblood "relatives" such as the best man, maid of honor, and godparents. Each member of the family has a role: grandparents (wisdom), mother (abnegation), father (responsibility), children (obedience), and godparents (resourcefulness; Lopez-Baez, 2006; Ruiz, 1995).

Implications. Because of these familial and social relationships, outside help is generally not sought until resources from the extended family and close friends are exhausted. Even in cases of severe mental illness, many Hispanic families waited two or more months before seeking treatment (Urdaneta, Saldana, & Winkler, 1995). Although there are many positive features of the extended family, emotional involvement and obligations with a large number of family and friends may function as additional sources of stress. Since family relationships are so important, decisions may be made that impact the individual negatively. Allegiance to the family is of primary importance, taking precedence over any outside concerns, such as school attendance or work (Avila & Avila, 1995; Franklin & Soto, 2002). For example, older children may be kept at home in order to help care for ill siblings or parents, to attend family functions (Hildebrand et al., 1996) or to meet a family financial obligation (Headden, 1997). Under these circumstances, problematic behaviors (i.e., absenteeism) may need to be addressed, but are best understood as a conflict between cultural and societal expectations. Possible solutions are then sought that acknowledge cultural expectations but at the same time meet the demands of societal requirements such as school attendance. Problem definition and solution may need to incorporate the perspectives of both the nuclear and extended family members.

Family Structure

Hispanics live in family households that are larger than those of non-Hispanics with 26.5 percent having five or more members (U.S. Census Bureau, 2003). Traditional Hispanic families are hierarchical in form, with special authority given to the elderly, the parents, and males. Within the family, the father assumes the role of the primary authority figure. Sex roles are clearly delineated (Avila & Avila, 1995; Lopez-Baez, 2006; Mejia, 1983). The sexual behaviors of adolescent females are severely restricted, while male children are afforded greater freedom to come and go as they please. Children are expected to be obedient, are usually not consulted on family decisions, and are expected to contribute financially to the family when possible. Parents reciprocate by providing for them through young adulthood and even during marriage. This type of reciprocal relationship is a lifelong expectation. Older children are expected to take care of and protect their younger siblings when away from home, and the older sister may function as a surrogate mother. Even during adolescence, many think of themselves and function as young adults. Marriage and parenthood often occur early in life and are seen as stabilizing influences.

Implications. When conducting individual or family sessions with Hispanic clients, assess the structure of the family, looking particularly for the family hierarchy. Paniagua (1994) recommends interviewing the father for a few minutes during the beginning of the first session, showing recognition of the father's authority, and sensitivity to cultural factors in counseling. In a more acculturated family, the father could still be addressed first, followed by the mother and the children. The pattern of mothers talking and children listening may be comfortable and expected in the traditional culture (Lefkowitz, Romo, Corona, Au, & Sigman, 2000). Also, in traditionally oriented Hispanic American families, less importance may be placed on shared interests and joint activities between husband and wife, with more emphasis on social events involving families and friends (Negy & Woods, 1992). Deviations from the traditional cultural pattern may produce conflict in family functioning. Determine how decisions are made within the family. If conflicts arise over cultural roles and expectations for family members, assess and treat the problem as a clash between cultural values and mainstream societal expectations. Often, conflicts among family members involve differences in acculturation. In less acculturated families, Szapocznik and Kurtines (1993) recommend that acculturation play the role of the identified patient, and the counselor use reframing and negotiation of the conflicting cultural norms and values. Determining different ways in which family members can both demonstrate their allegiance to the family structure and resolve conflicts can be beneficial. One such approach is demonstrated in the following case:

> *During family therapy, a Puerto Rican mother indicated to her son, "You don't care for me anymore. You used to come by every Sunday and bring the children. You used to respect me and teach your children respect. Now you go out and work, you say, always doing this or that. I don't know what spirit [que diablo] has taken over you." (Inclan, 1985, p. 332)*

In response, the son indicated that he was working hard and sacrificing for the children—that he wanted to be a success in the world and an individual of whom his children could be proud. In examining the case, it is clear that the mother is expressing disappointment. She defines love as being with her, having the family gather together, and subordinating individual desires for the family. The son has adopted a middle-class set of values stressing individual achievement, doing, and the future. The clash in value differences was at the root of the problem. In working with this family, the therapist provided an alternative way of viewing the conflict instead of using terms such as "right" or "wrong." He explained that our views are shaped by the values that we hold. He asked about the socialization process that the mother had undergone. She emphasized the "good old days" and the socialization and values of her childhood. The son indicated the pain he felt in losing the understanding of his parents, but he felt he had to change in order to succeed in the United States. The therapist pointed out that different adaptive styles may be necessary for different situations and that what is right is dependent on the social context. Both of them began to acknowledge that they still loved one another but might have to show it in different ways. As a result of the sessions, the mother and son accepted one another and understood the nature of the original conflict.

Sex Role Expectations

In working with Hispanic Americans, the counselor will often face problems dealing with conflicts over sex roles. In the traditional culture, men are expected to be strong, dominant, and the provider for the family (*machismo*), whereas women are expected to be nurturant, submissive to the male, and self-sacrificing (*marianismo*). As head of the family, the male expects the members to be obedient to him. Those with higher levels of ethnic identity are more likely to subscribe to traditional male and female roles (Abreu, Goodyear, Campos, & Newcomb, 2000). Areas in which males may have sex-role conflicts include the following (Avila & Avila, 1995; Constantine, Gloria, & Baron, 2006; Hildebrand et al., 1996):

1. *Submissiveness or assertion in the area of authority.* The Hispanic male may have difficulty interacting with agencies and individuals outside of the family and may feel that he is not fulfilling his role. In addition, changes involving greater responsibility of the wife and children may produce problems related to his authority.

2. *Feelings of isolation and depression because of the need to be strong.* Talking about or sharing views of problems with others may be seen as a sign of weakness. With the additional stress of living in a very different culture, the inability to discuss feelings of frustration and anxiety can produce isolation.

3. *Conflicts over the need to be consistent in his role.* As ambiguity and stress increase, there may be more rigid adherence to traditional roles.

4. *Anxiety over questions of sexual potency.*

For females, conflicts may involve (1) expectations to meet the requirements of the traditional role, (2) anxiety or depression over not being able to live up to these standards, and (3) inability to express feelings of anger (Avila & Avila, 1995; Lopez-Baez, 2006; Zanipatin, Welch, Yi, & Bardina, 2005). Many Hispanic women are socialized to feel that they are inferior and that suffering and being a martyr are characteristics of a good woman. With greater exposure to the dominant culture, such views may be questioned. Certain roles may change more than others. Some women may be very modern in their views of education and employment, but remain traditional in the area of sexual behavior and personal relationships. Others remain very traditional in all areas. Some writers (G. M. Gonzalez, 1997; A. Ruiz, 1981) caution that Hispanic sex roles may be misunderstood and are not as negative, inflexible, or rigid as they are sometimes described. For example, the concept of masculinity or machismo includes being a good provider. Egalitarian decision making appears to be increasing with later generations of Mexican Americans. Also, many Hispanic women assert their influence indirectly and "behind the scenes," thus preserving the appearance of male control (L. L. Hayes, 1997).

Implications. Adherence to traditional roles among Hispanics is decreasing rapidly in the urban class. Part of the reason for the change is that many women are required to act independently in the work setting and to deal with schools and other agencies. In some cases, the woman may become the wage earner, a role that traditionally belongs to the male. As women become more independent, men may feel anxiety. Both may feel that the man is no longer fulfilling his role. Counselors must be able to help the family deal with the anxiety and suspiciousness associated with role change. For both males and females, role conflict is likely to occur if the male is unemployed, if the female is employed, or both. Since both feel that the male should be the provider for the family, an additional source of stress can occur. Acculturation has impacted relationships between husbands and wives. In one study of Mexican Americans, less avoidance of conflicts and more expression of feeling during arguments were found in families where both husband and wife were acculturated. Husbands who were acculturated or bicultural reported more conflicts concerning sex and more verbal aggression from their wives as compared to nonacculturated husbands (Flores, Tschann, Marin, & Pantoja, 2004). The findings indicate the need to consider the potential impact of acculturation on marital relationships.

In dealing with sex-role conflicts, the counselor faces a dilemma and a potential value conflict. If the counselor believes in equal relationships, should he or she move the clients in this direction? Therapists working with cultural values different from their own must be particularly careful not to impose their views on their clients. Instead, they must try not only to help the client achieve their goals of greater independence, but to accomplish this within a cultural framework as well. The consequences of change also must be considered. Any counselor who works to help a female client achieve more independence without apprising her of potential problems within her family and community is not fulfilling his or her obligations. Again, the conflicts in sex roles in both men and women can be cast as involving differing expectations from their ethnic group and mainstream values. Reframing the problem as an external issue that the couple or family can face jointly can reduce intrafamily conflicts and result in problem-solving approaches to deal with the different sets of expectations.

Spirituality and Religiosity

> Mrs. Lopez, age 70, and her 30-year-old daughter sought counseling because they had a very conflictual relationship.... The mother was not accustomed to a counseling format.... At a pivotal point in one session, she found talking about emotional themes overwhelming and embarrassing.... In order to reengage her, the counselor asked what resources she used when she and her daughter quarreled. She ... prayed to Our Lady of Guadalupe. (Zuniga, 1997, p. 149)

The therapist employed a culturally adapted strategy of having Mrs. Lopez use prayer to understand her daughter and to find solutions for the counseling sessions. This format allowed Mrs. Lopez to discuss spiritual guidance and possible solutions to the problem. The use of a cultural perspective allowed the sessions to continue. The Catholic religion has a major influence in Hispanic groups and is a source of comfort in times of stress. There is strong belief in the importance of prayer and religious views that include: (1) sacrifice in this world is helpful to salvation, (2) being charitable to others is a virtue, and (3) you should endure wrongs done against you (Yamamoto & Acosta, 1982). The consequences of these beliefs are that many Hispanics have difficulty behaving assertively. Life's misfortunes are seen as inevitable, and Hispanics often feel resigned to their fate (*fatalismo*). In addition to the Catholic perspective, some Hispanics believe that evil spirits cause mental health problems.

Implications. During assessment, it is important to determine the possible influence of religious or spiritual beliefs. If there is a strong belief in fatalism, instead of attempting to change it, the therapist might acknowledge this attitude and help the individual or family determine the most adaptive response to the situation. A therapist might say, "Given that the situation is unchangeable, how can you and your family deal with this?" You are still attempting to have the client develop problem-solving skills within certain parameters. The strong reliance on religion can be a resource. The use of prayer may be used to reinforce problem-solving behaviors since God's support is evoked. Fatalism may be countered by stressing "Ayudate, que Dios te ayudara" which is the equivalent of "God helps those who help themselves" (Organista, 2000).

Acculturation Conflicts

As with many ethnic minority groups, Hispanic Americans are faced with a society that has a set of values distinctly different from their own. Some maintain their traditional orientation, whereas others assimilate and exchange their native cultural practices and values for those of the host culture. A bicultural orientation allows individuals to maintain some components of the native culture and to incorporate some practices and beliefs of the host culture. Miranda and Umhoefer (1998a, 1998b) believed that a bicultural orientation may be the "healthiest" resolution to acculturation conflicts. In their study, they found that both high- and low-acculturated Mexican Americans scored high on social dysfunction, alcohol consumption, and acculturative stress. Bicultural individuals appeared to fare much better because of an ability to accept and negotiate aspects of both cultures. Perhaps additional stressors are involved with either the complete rejection or acceptance of the values of the host culture (Miville, Koonce, Darlington, & Whitlock, 2000; Miranda & Umhoefer, 1998a, 1998b). Some of the issues involved in culture conflict are evident in the following:

An Hispanic teenager, Mike, was having difficulty knowing "who he was" or what group he belonged with. His parents had given him an Anglo name to ensure his success in American society. They only spoke to him in English because they were fearful that he might have an accent. During his childhood, he felt estranged from his relatives. His grandparents, aunts, and uncles could speak only Spanish, so they were able to communicate only through nonverbal means. At school, he did not fit in with his African American peers, and he also felt different from the Mexican American students who would ask him why he was unable to speak Spanish. The confusion over his ethnic identity was troublesome for him. He attempted to learn Spanish in college but was unable to do so. (Avila & Avila, 1995)

During middle school Hispanic children begin to have questions about their identity. Should they adhere to mainstream values? Few role models exist for Hispanic Americans. The representation of Hispanic Americans on television has actually decreased over the last 30 years. They currently account for only 2 percent of characters in 139 prime-time series. In depictions, they are more likely to behave criminally or to be violent (Espinosa, 1997). The mixed heritage of many Hispanic Americans raises additional identity questions. If they are of Mexican/Indian heritage, should they call themselves "Mexican American," "Chicano," "Latino," or "Spanish American"? What about mixtures involving other racial backgrounds? An ethnic identity provides a sense of belonging and group membership. Many Hispanic youngsters undergo this process of searching for an identity. This struggle may be responsible for such problems as the following: (1) Mexican American adolescents report more depressive symptoms and conduct disorders than White youth; (2) small-town Mexican American youth have more severe and elevated rates of alcohol and drug abuse; and (3) suicidal behaviors are high in Hispanic female adolescents and Puerto Rican males (Roberts & Sobhan, 1992; Tortolero & Roberts, 2001).

Implications. Ethnic identity issues should be recognized and incorporated within the school curriculum with modules on ethnicity, focusing on what it means to be Hispanic, Chicano, or Spanish speaking. Case studies of contributions made by different ethnic group members can be presented. Conflicts between mainstream values and ethnic group values can be discussed, and students can engage in brainstorming for methods to bridge their differences. Teaching styles can be altered to accommodate different cultural learning styles. It should be stressed that ethnic identity is part of the normal development process. In many cases, a bicultural perspective may be the most functional, since such a perspective does not involve the wholesale rejection of either culture. In psychotherapy, the degree of acculturation should be assessed because it has implications for treatment. Hispanic Americans with minimal acculturation rarely present mental health issues to counselors and may believe that counseling will take only one session (Dittman, 2005; G. M. Gonzalez, 1997). Second-generation Hispanic Americans are usually bilingual, but frequently with only functional use of either language. They are often exposed to Spanish at home and exposed to English in the school and on television. Second-generation Hispanic Americans are often marginal in both native and majority cultures. Acculturation also may influence perceptions of counseling and responses to counseling. Mexican Americans with a strong traditional orientation may have more difficulty being open and self-disclosing than are those with a strong orientation toward the dominant culture (G. M. Gonzalez, 1997).

Because knowledge of the acculturation level is important, it should be assessed by inquiring about the specific Hispanic group that the individual is from, generational status, primary language, religious orientation and strength of religious beliefs, where they live, the reason for immigration (if immigrants), the extent of extended family support, and other information related to acculturation. The therapist needs to determine both the degree of adherence to traditional values and to that of the larger society (Dingfelder, 2005b).

Educational Characteristics

Peer pressure to drop out can be nearly overwhelming in the Hispanic community, as DeAnza Montoya, a pretty Santa Fe teen, can attest. In her neighborhood, it was considered "anglo" and "nerdy" to do well in school.... "In school they make you feel like a dumb Mexican," she says, adding that such slights only bring Hispanics closer together. (Headden, 1997, p. 64)

Educationally, Hispanic Americans have not been faring well in the public schools. Hispanic students have a very high dropout rate. More than two of five Hispanics aged 25 or older have not completed high school, and more than a quarter have less than a 9th-grade level education (U.S. Census, 2003). Over one-third drop out before completing high school. This is nearly double the rate for Blacks and nearly four times higher than the rate for White students (Moore, 2001). The high pregnancy rate for Hispanic girls also contributes to school dropout rates. In California, Hispanic adolescents are four times more likely than White adolescents to become parents (Russell & Lee, 2004). A number of problems contribute to the high dropout rate of Hispanic students. As mentioned earlier, many of the educational difficulties faced by Hispanics relate to their varied proficiency with English. Spanish is the primary language spoken in the homes of over half of Hispanic Americans, and a much larger percentage regularly listen to or speak Spanish on a more limited basis. Second-generation Hispanics are often bilingual. However, their command of both English and Spanish is often limited. Many are exposed first to Spanish in the home and then to English in the school. However, there is some optimism regarding education. Between 1993 and 2003, the college enrollment of Hispanic students rose nearly 70 percent (Hayes, 2006).

Implications. In general, schools have been poorly equipped to deal with large numbers of Spanish-speaking students. The move against bilingual education and the rapid immersion of Spanish-speaking students in English may increase their already excessive numbers in special education classrooms. This would be a disservice to students who are placed there merely because of poor English skills, the use of tests not standardized for Spanish-speaking populations, or the improper administration of tests (Middleton et al., 2000). Teachers who do not have proficiency in Spanish may have a difficult time preparing understandable lessons for students with limited English skills and may have no means of effectively evaluating their performance. The inability to communicate with Hispanic parents compounds the problem and hampers information passed through parent-teacher conferences. Many low-income Hispanic parents feel that they have no right to question the teacher or school decisions. Some are unable to attend conferences because of work requirements, and this may be interpreted as a lack of caring about the child's education. To engage parents, conferences should be scheduled at flexible hours. Child care should be made available, as well as interpreters if the teacher is not bilingual. Face-to-face communication or other personal contact is more successful than written material (even if written in Spanish) since many parents have limited Spanish literacy skills. Trust develops slowly, and it is important to identify and support the family's strengths rather than focusing on its shortcomings (Espinosa, 1997). Altering instructional strategies to fit cultural values is important. Instead of saying to a child, "Good work, you should be proud of yourself," the teacher could respond, "Good work, your family will be proud of you" and have the child take the work home to show the parents (J. A. Vasquez, 1998).

Immigration, Racism, Discrimination, and Other Societal Factors

Complex interaction of stressors such as racism, acculturation conflicts, and fatalism can lead to a number of mental disorders (Gee, Ryan, Laflamme, & Holt, 2006). The high level of acculturative stress found among adult Mexican immigrants results in depressive symptoms and suicidal ideation. The severing of ties to family and friends in Mexico, the loss of coping and financial resources, language inadequacy, unemployment, and culture conflict all function as stressors for recent immigrants (Hovey, 2000). Acculturation conflicts with the family and perceived societal racism also impact Hispanic adolescents. In a national poll, 16 percent of Hispanic Americans indicated that prejudice was the most important issue facing them (Krupin, 2001). Possibly because of issues such as these, Hispanic students (11 percent) are at a greater risk for depression and are more likely than are Euro-American students (6 percent) to attempt suicide (Tortolero & Roberts, 2001). Many youths attempt to deal with family distress, discrimination in the school and community, feelings of hopelessness, and a lack of family support by involvement in gang activities (Baca & Koss-Chioino, 1997). Additionally, Hispanics underutilize resources for their children. While most young children under six are citizens, one or both parents may be noncitizens. Because of this they may be reluctant to seek assistance (Capp et al., 2005).

Implications. A clinician must assess not only for intrapsychic issues but also for the degree that external conditions are involved with mental health issues. Because many suffer from poverty, stressors attributable to inadequate food and shelter or from dealing with bureaucracies and unemployment have to be dealt with (De La Cancela, 1985; J. M. Vazquez, 1997). Careful assessment of the source of emotional disturbance is necessary before appropriate action can be taken, and this should be done very early in the counseling session. One case involved a married migrant worker in his mid-50s who came into therapy complaining that he heard threatening voices. He was afraid to leave his home. In working with him, A. Ruiz (1981) recommended an analysis of external causes first. In this case, it is suggested that the worker undergo a complete physical examination, with special attention to exposure to pesticides and other agricultural chemicals that might result in mental symptoms. It is also possible that the feelings of fear displayed by the individual stem from factors such as suspiciousness of outside authorities, family fears of deportation, or recent encounters with creditors. External factors that are specific to the experience of Hispanic Americans must be examined along with intrapsychic mental health issues.

Assessment and Linguistic Issues

Assessments should always be interpreted within a sociocultural context and in the primary language of the client. As a result, use of appropriate assessment instruments and consequent interpretations must be done in the cultural and linguistic context of the client. Considerable evidence suggests that differences obtained in assessment are often the result of linguistic differences, not pathology.

Implications. Traditional assessments do not place much emphasis on language differences, validity of tests for ethnic minorities, or the influence of cultural or social factors. Acculturation issues accompany many disorders in Hispanic Americans and can be used as a modifier or specifier to mental disorders. It is important to attend to all the Axes in the *Diagnostic and Statistical Manual of Mental Disorders,* 4th ed. (*DSM-IV-TR*). Axis 4 can help identify psychosocial and environmental issues such as language barriers, discrimination, immigration stress, and poverty (Gonzalez et al., 1997).

Because of the lack of bilingual counselors, problems in diagnosis can occur with Hispanic clients who are not conversant in English. For example, Marcos (1973) found that Mexican American patients were seen as suffering from greater psychopathology when interviewed in English than when interviewed in Spanish. However, interpreters themselves may present difficulties in the counseling process, such as distortions in communication. Personal relationships may also develop between the interpreter and the client. In one case, a client offered to care for the translator's child (Cooper & Costas, 1994). Marcos (1979) found that distortions may result from (1) the interpreter's language competence and translation skills, (2) the interpreter's lack of psychiatric knowledge, and (3) the attitudes of the counselor.

Implications for Clinical Practice

Several writers (Bean, Perry, & Bedell, 2001; Paniagua, 1994; Ruiz, 1995; Velasquez et al., 1997) have made suggestions regarding how to conduct the initial session with Hispanic Americans.

1. It is important to engage in a respectful, warm, and mutual introduction with the client. Less acculturated Hispanic Americans expect a more formal relationship. The counselor will be seen as an authority figure and should be formally dressed.

2. Give a brief description of what counseling is and the role of each participant. Less acculturated Hispanic Americans often expect medication and to meet for only one or two sessions.

3. Explain the notion of confidentiality. Even immigrants with legal status have inquired about whether the information shared during counseling would "end up in the hands of the Border Patrol or other immigration authorities" (Velasquez et al., 1997, p. 112). Immigrant families may also be uncertain about the limits of confidentiality, especially as it applies to child abuse or neglect issues. Physical discipline is used more often in Hispanic families (this is also the case for lower-class Whites) than in middle-class White families. They may be fearful about how their child-rearing practices will be perceived.

4. Have the client state in his or her own words the problem or problems as he or she sees them. Determine the possible influence of religious or

spiritual beliefs. Use paraphrasing to summarize the problem as you understand it and make sure that the client knows you understand it.

5. Assess the acculturation level.

6. Consider whether there are cultural or societal aspects to the problem. What are the impacts of racism, poverty, and acculturative stress on the problem?

7. Determine whether a translator is needed. Be careful not to interpret slow speech or long silences as indicators of depression or cognitive dysfunction. The individual may just be struggling with English communication skills.

8. Determine the positive assets and resources available to the client and his or her family. Have they, other family members, or friends dealt with similar problems?

9. Help the clients prioritize the problems and determine what they perceive as the important goals. What are their expectations? How will they know when the goals have been achieved?

10. Discuss possible consequences of achieving indicated goals for the individual, family, and community.

11. Discuss the possible participation of family members and consider family therapy. Within the family, determine the hierarchical structure as well as the degree of acculturation of the different members. Focus on the problems produced by conflicting values.

12. Assess possible problems from external sources, such as the need for food, shelter, or employment, or stressful interactions with agencies. Provide necessary assistance in developing and maintaining environmental supports.

13. Explain the treatment to be used, why it was selected, and how it will help achieve the goals.

14. With the client's input, determine a mutually agreeable length of treatment. It is better to offer time-limited, solution-based therapies.

15. Remember that *personalismo* is a basic cultural value of Hispanic Americans. Although the first meetings may be quite formal, once trust has developed, the clients may develop a close personal bond with the counselor. He or she may be perceived as a family member or friend and may be invited to family functions and given gifts. These behaviors are cultural and not evidence of dependency or a lack of boundaries.

16. Consistently evaluate the client's or family's response to the therapeutic approach you have chosen.

Counseling Individuals of Multiracial Descent

18

Chapter

Hector was a 16-year-old boy whose mother was European American and whose father immigrated to the United States from Mexico. Hector was referred for counseling because he was acting out in school and making frequent racist remarks. He appeared to be White and openly claimed only his White identity. . . . He frequently joked about "Mexicans." Hector admitted that although he knew he made racist remarks, he did not like strangers to make derogatory comments about Mexicans or Mexican Americans (McDowell et al., 2005, p. 408).

Pro golfer Tiger Woods stood on the fairway green surrounded by reporters and fans. As he was peppered with questions after another outstanding tournament, one reporter asked how he felt to be the first Black superstar golfer. Tiger, however, preferred to refer to himself as "Cablinasian" because he was a racial mixture of Caucasian, Black, Indian, and Asian ancestry. Despite this constant correction to the press, Woods is nearly always referred to as an African American. (Eddings, 1997)

An adult male of Latino/Middle Eastern descent tried to pull together a university acknowledgment of the celebration El Dia de los Muertos (Day of the Dead), a holiday during which Mexican families remember the dead and the continuity of life. In doing so, he received responses such as "'. . . why are you doing that?' I'm like, because it comes from my culture. And they just look at me and they're like, 'What exactly are you? . . .'" (Miville, Constantine, Baysden, & So-Lloyd, 2005, p. 511). Multiracial individuals are often faced with the "What are you?" question.

For years, many multiracial individuals have fought for the right to identify themselves as belonging to more than one racial group. Our society, however, is one that tends to force people to choose one racial identity over another or imposes a singular racial identity upon them. In the case of Hector, described previously, counseling helped him understand why he was embarrassed regarding his Mexican heritage.

He admitted making jokes before someone else could do so at his expense. People of mixed race heritage are often ignored, neglected, and considered nonexistent in our educational materials, media portrayals, and psychological literature (Root, 1992a, 1996; Torres, 1998). Such dynamics may lead to major psychological and social stressors for multiracial individuals in identity formation, lowered self-esteem, and an existence between the margins of two or more cultures (Root, 2001). Further, mental health professionals receive little training in working with multiracial clients victimized by having monoracial categories imposed upon them (Gillem, Lincoln, & English, 2007). Indeed, many counselors have conscious and unconscious attitudes, biases, and stereotypes similar to the layperson regarding race mixing (miscegenation) and racial contamination (hypodescent).

In more ways than one, the 2000 census set in motion a complex psychological and political debate for the first time because it allowed people to check more than one box for their racial identities, and to be counted as multiracial (allowing students to choose more than one race box on college applications has also been approved by the U.S. Department of Education (Asquith, 2006). Proponents have argued that it is unfair to force one identity on multiracial people; that it creates alienation and identity confusions, denies racial realities, that there should be pride in being multiracial, and that there are strong medical reasons for knowing one's racial heritage. Custom, history, and prejudices, however, continue to affect perceptions regarding a singular racial identity. Further, many civil rights organizations, including the National Association for the Advancement of Colored People (NAACP), believe that such counts will dilute the strength of their constituencies because census numbers on race and ethnicity figure into many calculations involving antidiscrimination laws, voting, and dispersal of funds for minority programs. Caught in the struggle—and often victimized—are persons of mixed racial heritage.

Facts and Figures Related to Biracial/Multiracial Populations

Mental health professionals would benefit from awareness and knowledge related to the following facts (taken from J. J. Johnson, 1992; Root, 1992b; Rosenblatt, Karis, & Powell, 1995; U.S. Census Bureau, 2005d; Wehrly, Kenney, & Kenney, 1999).

- The biracial baby boom in the United States started in 1967 when the last laws against race mixing (anti-miscegenation) were repealed. As a result, there has been a rapid increase in interracial marriage and a subsequent rise in the number of biracial children in the United States. The number of children living in families where one parent is White and the other is Black, Asian, or American Indian has tripled from 1970 to 1990. This does not include children of single parents or children whose parents are divorced.

- 7.3 million individuals reported more than one race. Because Hispanic or Latino may be of any race, data for racial combinations overlap with the data for Hispanics. Among those reporting two or more races, 31 percent reported being Hispanic. Other combinations included (1) White and some other race: 2.3 million; (2) White and American Indian, Alaska native: 1.3 million; (3) White and Asian: 862,000; and (4) White and African American: 792,000 (U.S. Census Bureau, 2005d). This may be an underestimate of the multiracial population since many multiracial individuals may choose to self-identify with only one race.

- Compounding accurate counting is the fact that 30 to 70 percent of African Americans are multiracial by multigenerational history; virtually all Latinos and Filipinos are multiracial, as are the majority of American Indians and Native Hawaiians.

- When gender is taken into consideration, Latinas and Asian American and Native American women are more likely than their male counterparts to marry interracially, although Black and White men have a higher interracial marriage rate than males of other races. The highest rate of interracial marriage is between White men and Asian women, and the lowest is between White men and Black women.

Implications. These statistics raise major questions regarding the monoracial and multiracial climate of our society. For example, why are the offspring of a Black-White union considered Black by our society? Why not White? Why is it easier for us to accept the notion that children of certain mixed couples (Asian/White, Native American/White, etc.) are multiracial, while other combinations that involve African Americans are not? Why do some people of mixed-race heritage perceive or choose to identity themselves with only one race? Are certain interracial relationships more acceptable than others? Why? What accounts for the fact that Asian American women and Latinas are more likely than their male counterparts to marry out?

Mental health professionals who work with multiracial clients need to understand the implications to these questions if they are to be effective with their racially mixed clients. They need to examine their own attitude regarding interracial couples and multiracial children (Gillem et al., 2007; Kenney, 2002). In our journey to understand the implications of the issues confronting multiracial individuals, we concentrate on several themes that have been identified as important in working with this population.

Hypodescent: The "One Drop of Blood" Rule

Alvin Poussaint, an African American Harvard psychiatrist, stood before a packed audience and posed a pointed question to them: "Do you know how powerful Black blood is?" After an awkward silence, he answered, "It is so powerful that one tiny drop will contaminate the entire bloodstream of a White person!" What Poussaint was referring to is called hypodescent, or the "One Drop Rule," a social system that maintains the myth of monoracialism by assigning the person of mixed racial heritage to the least desirable racial status (Root, 1996). In essence, hypodescent has even more insidious and devious motives.

First, it was an attempt by White European immigrants to maintain racial purity and superiority by passing laws against interracial marriages (antimiscegenation), primarily directed at Blacks and Native Americans. As early as the 1660s, laws were passed making it a crime for "Negro slaves" to marry "freeborn English women" (Wehrly et al., 1999). Interestingly, such laws were clear evidence of gender bias because they were based on property rights (women perceived as property) and (1) men of color could not have access to valued property while (2) White men could have sexual access to Black women as property (Pascoe, 1991). If White women were caught in a sexual liaison with a Black man, she also could be considered the property of the master. Second, not only could racial purity be maintained, but hypodescent thinking and laws also generated additional property for slave owners. Africans were brought over as slave laborers; the more slaves an owner possessed, the greater his or her wealth (free labor). Thus, economically, it was beneficial to classify offspring of a Black-White union as "Negro" because it increased property. Third, the prevalent beliefs of the time were that "Negroes and Indians" were subhuman creatures, uncivilized, lower in intellect, and impulsively childlike. One drop of Black blood in a person would make him or her contaminated and Black. Indeed, in 1894 in the case of *Plessy v. Ferguson* the Supreme Court ruled that a person who was seven-eighths White and one-eighth Black and "maintained that he did not look Negro" was nonetheless to be classified as Negro (Davis, 1994).

The rule of hypodescent applies to other racial/ethnic minority groups as well, but it appears to fluctuate more widely than for African Americans. While groups of color are often averse to discussing a social desirability ranking among them, conventional wisdom and some data suggest that African Americans are often considered less desirable than are their Asian American counterparts (Jackson et al., 1996), although the latter is still considered significantly less desirable than Whites. It also appears that whether one is a man or a woman of a minority group affects how he or she is perceived by society. For example, images of Asian American women are much more favorable (domestic, petite, exotic, and sexually pleasing) than are their male counterparts (passive, emasculated, inhibited, and unattractive; D. W. Sue & D. Sue, 1999). These findings offer an explanation for why interracial marriages between Asian Americans and European Americans occur more frequently than between Blacks and Whites; why mixed-race children of a former union are more likely to be considered multiracial while unions of the latter are still more likely to be considered Black; and why Asian American women are more likely than their male counterparts to marry out (Lewandowski & Jackson, 2001; Jackman, Wagner, & Johnson, 2001). This not only has often been the basis of hard feelings and resentments between African Americans and Asian Americans, but also has created friction among men and women within the Asian American population as well as other racial minority groups. It is important to understand that the issue of antagonisms between racial/ethnic minority groups and between the sexes of a group is the result of a biased sociopolitical process and is not inherent in race or gender. The true cause is society's differential acceptance and stereotyping of minority groups, and the role that men and women play in the process.

Implications. Many multiracial individuals face forces that impose a racial identity upon them, and that identity is likely to be among the lowest statuses defined by the society. Even if their mixed racial heritage is acknowledged, it is generally considered lesser than that of a White person. As indicated by W. E. Cross (1991), multiracial children, when asked their heritage, may answer one way internally and another way to the questioner. The external answer may be an attempt to fit in, to not violate the expectations of the interrogator, or to take the path of least resistance. For example, answering that one is biracial may not be satisfactory to the questioner and will result in further probing. The child or adolescent is often unable to identify his or her conflicts and feelings about being multiracial and settles for the answer most likely to end the questions: a monoracial answer that may result in internal disharmony, a false sense of self, social marginality, and guilt (McDowell et al., 2005; Winn & Priest, 1993).

Racial/Ethnic Ambiguity, or "What Are You?"

Racial/ethnic ambiguity refers to the inability of people to distinguish the monoracial category of the multiracial individual from phenotypic characteristics. These traits play a major role in how people perceive the person. If African American traits are dominant, the One Drop Rule will automatically classify the person as Black, despite the answer of the multiracial individual: "She says she's mixed, but she is really Black." For those multiracial individuals with ambiguous features, the "What are you?" question becomes a constant dilemma. Possessing a volume of racial components, the multiracial person may not possess the language or sophistication to answer properly. Our society, for example, places a continuing negative association with the process and dynamics that produce a multiracial child (interracial marriages and relationships) and the language associated with offspring is often unfamiliar and undesirable in usage. Such terms as "Mulatta(o)" (African/European), "Afroasian" (African/Asian), "Mestiza(o)" (Indian/Spanish), and so on are confusing to most people, including the multiracial child (Root 1992a, 1996). Second, the "What are you?" question almost asks a biracial child to justify his or her existence in a world rigidly built on the concepts of racial purity and monoracialism. This is reinforced by a multiracial person's attempt to answer such a question by discerning the motives of the interrogator: "Why is the person asking?" "Does it really matter?" "Are they really interested in the answer, or am I going to violate their expectations?" "Do they see me as an oddity?" If the person answers "American," this will only lead to further inquiry (Ramirez, 1996). If the answer is "mixed," the interrogator will query further: "What ethnicity are you?" If the answer is "part White and Black," other questions follow: "Who are your parents?" "Which is Black?" "Why did they marry?" The multiracial person begins to feel picked apart and fragmented when questioned about the components of his or her race (Root, 1990). The problem with giving an answer is that it is never "good enough." The communication from our society is quite clear: "You do not belong in this world, and there is something wrong with you." We cannot stress enough how often multiracial persons face a barrage of questions about their racial identities, from childhood to adulthood (Houston, 1997; Wehrly et al., 1999). The inquisition can result in invalidation, conflicting feelings of loyalties to the racial/ethnic identities of parents, internal trauma, and confused identity development.

Implications. Multiracial children often feel quite isolated and find little support, even from their parents. This is especially true for monoracial parents who themselves are not multiracial. How, for example, does a White mother married to a Black husband raise her child? White? Black? Mixed? Other? Parents of interracial marriages may fail to understand the challenges encountered by their children, gloss over differences, or raise the child as if he or she were monoracial. The child may therefore lack a role model and feel even greater loneliness. Even being a multiracial parent may not result in greater empathy or understanding of the unique challenges faced by their multiracial children, especially if the parents (themselves victims of a monoracial system) have not adequately resolved their own sense of identity conflicts. Therapists can help interracial couples understand each other's worldview, especially if the value differences between them are large, and to prepare their children for questions regarding racial heritage (Kenney, 2002). The problem is compounded by the gender of the parents and the multiracial child. One clinical study of ten families found that when the mother is White and the father Black, daughters are more likely to identify with the mother's racial background; and when the mother is Black and the father White, boys and girls will likely identify with being Black (Bowles, 1993). In almost all of these cases, the children expressed shame in not being able to include their father's heritage as part of their identity and experienced anxiety, depression, and difficulty in coping. Interestingly, it was found that the one child raised as biracial seemed to be the healthiest of the entire group.

The Marginal Syndrome, or Existing between the Margins

Root (1990) asserted that mixed-race people begin life as "marginal individuals" because society refuses to view the races as equal and because their ethnic identities are ambiguous. They are often viewed as fractionated people—composed of fractions of a race, culture, or ethnicity. A person who is Asian, White European, and African may not be acceptable to any group. None of these groups may view the multiracial person as being truly Asian, White, or Black. They will encounter prejudice and discrimination not only from the dominant group, but from secondary ethnic groups as well (Brown, 1997). One study of Black and Japanese biracials found that half felt that not belonging to one racial group was the true negative aspect of their identity struggles (C. C. I. Hall, 1980). Stonequist (1937) first coined the term *identity purgatory* to describe the existence of a person of mixed race who lives on the margins of one or several worlds, not fully included in any.

In Chapter 10 we spent considerable time discussing racial/cultural identity development among minority groups. Several major criticisms have been leveled at these theories: (1) they were developed from a monoracial perspective (African Americans, Asian Americans, etc.) rather than a multiracial one; (2) they falsely assume that multiracial individuals will be accepted by their parent culture or cultures; and (3) their linear nature is inadequate to describe the complexity of the many possible multiracial resolutions (Root, 1990, 1992a, 1996; Kerwin & Ponterotto, 1995; Poston, 1990). In an early biracial identity development model, Poston (1990) described five stages.

At the *personal identity* stage, biracial children's sense of self is largely independent of ethnic heritage; at the *choice of group categorization* stage, the youngster feels pressures to identify with one racial orientation by either parents, peers or societal forces. At the *enmeshment/denial* stage, there are likely to be considerable negative feelings, whether conscious or unconscious, regarding the denial of one of the racial heritages. At the *appreciation* stage, the person begins to value the racial roots of both parents; and at the *integration* stage, wholeness and integration of both identities occur. Multiracial individuals confront the process of resolving marginality and developing a healthy identity throughout their entire lives (Gillem et al., 2007). Perhaps the most sophisticated of the multiracial identity development models is the one proposed by Root (1990, 1998). We focus here on Root's descriptions of the four possible healthy resolutions of marginality.

1.   The multiracial individual may accept the identity assigned by society. Thus, a product of a Black-Japanese union may be considered Black by his or her friends, peers, and family. Root believes that this can be a positive choice if the person is satisfied with the identity, receives family support, and is active rather than passive in evidencing the identity. Of all the identities, however, this is the most likely to be fluid and to change radically in different situations. If the person, for example, moves to another community or part of the country, the assigned racial identity may become Japanese or even mixed.

2.   The person may choose to resolve marginality through the ability to identify with both groups. "I think a lot of us are chameleons. We can sit in a group of White people and feel different, but still fit in. . . . But we can turn around and sit in a group of Black people, even though we are not Black in the same way" (Miville et al., 2005, p. 512). In this case, the person is very much like the "protean person," able to shift from one identity (White American) when with one group and another identity (African American) when with a different group. The method of adaptation is healthy as long as the person does not lose his or her sense of self-integrity, views the ability to move in two worlds as positive, and can relate well to positive aspects of both identities and cultures.

3.   The person may decide to choose a single racial identity in an active manner. While it may appear similar to the first option, it differs in two ways: (1) the person makes the choice of racial group identity (not society), and (2) the identity is less prone to shifting when the situational context changes. However, as indicated in the case of the Latino/Middle Eastern individual at the beginning of the chapter, self-identity may not be accepted by other groups. Again, this is a healthy identity when the group with whom the individual chooses to identify does not marginalize the person and if the individual does not deny his or her other racial heritage.

4.   Identification with a new "mixed-race heritage" or multiracial identity is another option. "I think it [being multiracial] has made me expertly cued to cultural cues. Kind of as an observer I'm always trying to learn, 'ok, what's going on here, how does one act here and what are the cultural norms'" (Suyemoto, 2004, p. 216). In fact, there appears to be a movement toward a bicultural/biracial or multicultural/multiracial identity rather than identifying with only one race (Brunsma, 2005; Suzuki-Crumly & Hyers, 2004). This identity allows equal valuing of all aspects of one's racial/cultural heritage, good ability to relate to both groups, and feelings of being well integrated. While not directly addressed, it appears that this identification has

many options and alternatives. For example, individuals who choose this route may appear quite different from one another. In other words, there are many ways to be of mixed race.

Implications. While not unlike monoracial identity development models, several important distinctions are made. First, resolutions occur not only between dominant-subordinate group relations (culture-conflicts), but often within racial identities as well (White-Asian, Native American-Black, etc.). Second, resolutions can involve more than a conflict between two racial groups (Black, White, and Asian). Third, the complexity of multiple resolutions may be different depending on the type of multiracial combination, gender, and other group identity factors, such as socioeconomic status, age, and sexual orientation. Fourth, identities may shift and are fluid depending on the situational context. Last, multiracial identity development models entertain the notion that there is more than one resolution that can lead to a healthy adjustment.

In therapy, issues regarding identity sometimes come to the surface in work with multiracial individuals (although it should not be assumed that this is the source of their problem). While marginality may be considered unhealthy, positive resolution can occur with any of the choices discussed. Therapists should be aware of the growing number of multiracial individuals who are choosing "multiracial" as their ethnic identity. This choice should not be considered pathological and interpreted as confusion or an inability to commit to an integrated identity (Suyemoto, 2004). However, racial identity is often influenced by environmental factors. Where the child grows up (i.e., in an integrated neighborhood and school versus in an ethnic community) can have a great impact on identity. Physical appearance also influences the sense of group belonging and racial self-identification among multiracial individuals (AhnAllen, Suyemoto, & Carter, 2006). These are issues that may need to be addressed with multiracial children and adolescents. Being multiracial by itself does not lead to emotional problems. Instead, it is societal reaction to race that can introduce difficulties. Issues of racial identity and racial discrimination among multiracial adolescents have been found to be related to substance abuse and other problem behaviors (Choi, Harachi, Gillmore, & Catalano, 2006).

Stereotypes and Myths of Multiracial Individuals and Interracial Couples

There is considerable evidence that the myths and stereotypes associated with multiracial individuals and interracial couples are attempts to prevent the mixing of races through stigmatizing them (Wehrly et al., 1999). Unfortunately, it appears that sociopsychological research on this topic has often perpetuated and reinforced these beliefs and has carried over into our everyday beliefs about race mixing and mixed-race people. It is not unusual, for example, to discern beliefs suggesting that multiracial children are inferior to monoracial ones and that they are more prone to major social and psychological problems (Jackman et al., 2001). Further, interracial unions are filled with images of unhappy and unstable couples, or deficiencies in partners who choose to marry out of their race.

Early research and writings on the characteristics and dynamics of interracial relationships and marriages focused primarily on negative attributes. Most prevalent were beliefs that individuals who chose to marry out were possessed of low self-esteem, filled with self-loathing, and harbored feelings of inferiority (Beigel, 1966); rebelling against parental authority (Saxton, 1968); and evidencing mental problems (Brayboy, 1966). Stereotypes fluctuate depending on the race and the gender of the person marrying out. A White person who violated social norms against interracial marriages would be seen as experimenting with the "exotic," attempting to express a liberal view, possessing very low self-esteem, or being a social/occupational failure unable to attract a member of his or her own race (Rosenblatt et al., 1995). Members of a minority group would often be seen as trying to elevate themselves socially, economically, and psychologically.

Sexual stereotypes also play a major role in the perception of men and women who are involved in interracial relationships/marriages. Asian American women are often perceived by the wider society as exotic and erotic creatures, eager to please men, domestically oriented, and likely to be submissive; their male counterparts, however, are seen as sexually emasculated, passive and unassertive, inhibited, and lacking in social confidence (S. Sue & D. W. Sue, 1971a). These are quite pervasive beliefs, whether conscious or unconscious. Some suggest that the higher rate of marrying out for Asian American women may be due to these myths. Regardless, there does seem to be greater positive associations with Asian American women, and they are more socially acceptable than are their male counterparts. On the other hand, Black men and women are often described as possessing "primitive sexuality," being "animalistic," passionate, potent, and sexually virile (Frankenberg, 1993). While Asian American men may not be seen as a competitive threat, African American men with their "aggressive and promiscuous sexual behaviors" are seen as a danger to White women. History is replete with incidents of the wider society's hostility and antagonisms toward Black men.

Stereotypes of multiracial individuals are also largely negative. Due to legal (until as recently as 1967) and social prohibitions against interracial relationships, it is not difficult to see why multiracial children may also be subjected to negative perceptions. Products of an "unholy and immoral union," multiracial individuals are seen as being doomed to an immoral or troubled existence, likely to suffer identity problems and low self-esteem, and to be marginal persons who are socially isolated. On the other hand, multiracial individuals are also described as inordinately beautiful and handsome in a physical sense, but even then it is associated with promiscuity and the sexual myths of this population.

Implications. In general, the myths about mixed marriages and multiracial people imply that these unions are the result of unhealthy motives by the partners, and that offspring are doomed to suffer many deficiencies and pathologies. The early studies cited and the assumptions they made suffer from several problems. First, if partners in mixed marriages and multiracial individuals suffer from greater identity issues, conflicts, and psychological problems, then they are more often the result of an intolerant and hostile society. They are caused from the bias, discrimination, and racism of people rather than anything inherent in the marriage or the "unhealthy" qualities of those involved. Second, we already know that to a large extent research is influenced by and reflects societal views. It seems likely, therefore, that early researchers most likely asked questions and designed studies that attributed a problem-oriented definition of multiracial people. The focus then becomes identifying pathology, rather than the healthy and functional traits of a group. Third, in the case of interracial relationships/marriages, current research now suggests that these marriages are based on the same ingredients as are intraracial marriages: love, companionship, and compatible interests and values (Lewandowski & Jackson, 2001; Porterfield, 1982; Rosenblatt et al., 1995). Last, the image of multiracial individuals is an unbalanced one. Increasingly, research reveals that beneficial sociopsychological traits may be the outcome of a multiracial heritage, including: increased sense of uniqueness, better ability to relate to more diverse groups, greater tolerance and understanding of people, ability to deal with racism, enjoying what many groups have to offer, greater variety in one's life, and better ability to build alliances with many diverse people and groups (Root, 1996; Rosenblatt et al., 1995; Wehrly et al., 1999).

A Multiracial Bill of Rights

> *Countless numbers of times I have fragmented and fractionalized myself in order to make the other more comfortable in deciphering my behavior, my words, my loyalties, my choice of friends, my appearance, my parents, and so on. And given my multiethnic history, it was hard to keep track of all the fractions, to make them add up to one whole. It took me over 30 years to realize that fragmenting myself seldom served a purpose other than to preserve the delusions this country has created around race.*

> *Reciting the fractions to the other was the ultimate act of buying into the mechanics of racism in this country. Once I realized this, I could ask myself other questions. How exactly does a person be one-fourth, one-eighth, or one-half something? To fragment myself and others, "she is one-half Chinese and one-half white," or "he is one-quarter Native, one-quarter African American, and one-half Spanish" was to unquestioningly be deployed to operate the machinery that disenfranchised myself, my family, my friends, and others I was yet to meet. (Root, 1996, pp. 4–5)*

These words were written by Maria Root, a leading psychologist in the field of multiracial identity and development. She believes that our society has relegated multiracial persons to deviant status, minimized their contributions to society, and ignored their existence because they do not fit into our monoracial classification. In her personal and professional journey, Root (1996) has developed a *Bill of Rights for Racially Mixed People* that is composed of three major affirmations: resistance, revolution, and change.

1. Resistance refers to the multiracial individual's right to resist the belief system imposed by society, the data on which they are based, and the rationalizations used to justify the status quo regarding race relations. It means refusing to fragment, marginalize, or disconnect from others and the self. The following four assertions embody resistance.
    I have the right not to:

    -   Justify my existence in this world.
    -   Keep the races separate within me.
    -   Be responsible for people's discomfort with my physical ambiguity.
    -   Justify my ethnic legitimacy.

2. *Revolution* refers to multiracial people, or anyone who enters into an interracial relationship, who chooses to "cross the boundaries" of race relations. According to Root, these individuals are often seen as "race traitors" who can create an emotional/psychic earthquake that challenges the reality of our oppressive racial system. The following four assertions embody revolution.
    I have the right to:

    -   Identify myself differently than strangers expect me to.
    -   Identify myself differently from how my parents identify me.
    -   Identify myself differently than my brothers and sisters.
    -   Identify myself differently in different situations.

3.   *Change* refers to the active attempt to build connections, wholeness, and a sense of belonging to one another. While the two other sets of assertions are attempts to free one from the racialized existence of a monoracial system, connections acknowledge that our social fates are intertwined and dependent on one another. According to Root, this sense of belonging serves as a force against perpetrating atrocities against fellow human beings. The following four assertions embody change:

I have the right to:

- Create a vocabulary to communicate about being multiracial.
- Change my identity over my lifetime—and more than once.
- Have loyalties and identify with more than one group of people.
- Choose freely whom I befriend and love.

Implications.   Root's Bill of Rights is much more complex and meaningful than is described here. It has major implications for the mental health provider because it challenges our notions of a monoracial classification system, reorients our thoughts about the many myths of multiracial persons, makes us aware of the systemic construction and rationalizations of race, warns us about the dangers of fractionating identities, and advocates freedom of choice for the multiracial individual. For the mental health provider, much of importance can be derived from the 12 assertions contained in the Bill of Rights.

Implications for Clinical Practice

While monoracial minority groups have many similarities with multiracial ones, the latter are likely to experience unique stressors related to their multiple racial/ethnic identities, in addition to dealing with racism. For example, most monoracial minorities find their own groups receptive and supportive of them. Multiracial individuals may be placed in an awkward situation where none of their groups of origin accept them. Likewise, an African American youngster can expect psychological and emotional support from his or her parents. The parents share common experiences with their sons and daughters, can act as mentors, and relate to the experiences their children encounter with respect to minority status. However, multiracial children may be the products of monoracial parents. In any case, some helpful guidelines include the following:

1.   Become aware of your own stereotypes and preconceptions regarding interracial relationships and marriages. When you see a racially mixed couple, do you pay extra attention to them? What thoughts and images

do you have? Only when you are able to become aware of your biases will you be able to avoid imposing them upon your clients.

2. When working with multiracial clients, avoid stereotyping. Like interracial relationships, all of us have been culturally conditioned to believe certain things about racially mixed people. In general, these images are based on mistaken beliefs that deny the mixed-race heritage of the person, and his or her uniqueness.

3. See multiracial people in a holistic fashion rather than as fractions of a person. This means being careful when dealing with the "What are you?" question. In most cases, it is important to emphasize the positive qualities of the total person rather than seeing the person as parts.

4. Remember that being a multiracial person often means coping with marginality, isolation, and loneliness. These feelings are not the result of internal problems but are generally brought about by external factors related to prejudice. Nevertheless, mixed-race persons often experience strong feelings of loneliness, rejection, forced choice situations, guilt/ shame from not fully integrating all aspects of their racial heritage, differentness, and anger. These feelings have often been submerged and hidden because there is no one to share them with who understands. As mentioned earlier, mixed-race children often come from homes with monoracial parents.

5. With mixed-race clients, emphasize the freedom to choose one's identity. Root's Bill of Rights is helpful here. There is no one identity suitable for everyone. The racial identity models discussed in this chapter all have limitations, and it is important to note that identities are both changing and fluid rather than fixed.

6. Take an active psychoeducational approach. Multiracial individuals are often subjected to a rigid monoracial system that stereotypes and fits them into rigid categories. Oftentimes, children may learn to internalize the stereotypes and accept an identity imposed upon them. Somewhere in the counseling process, clients can be helped to understand the forces of oppression, and the counselor can empower them to take an active part in formulating their identities.

7. Since mixed race people are constantly portrayed as possessing deficiencies, stress their positive attributes and the advantages of being multiracial and multicultural.

8. Recognize that family counseling may be especially valuable in working with mixed-race clients, especially if they are children. Frequently, parents (themselves often monoracial) are unaware of the unique conflicts related to their child's multiracial journey. Parents can be taught to empower their children, convey positive aspects of being multiracial,

and help them integrate a healthy identity. Root (1998), for example, suggested things like giving mixed-race children a first and/or middle name that connects them to their heritage, developing answers to the "What are you?" question, being positive about one's multiple heritage, attending community events of the family's heritage, and avoiding negative remarks about people of color.

9. When working with multiracial clients, ensure that you possess basic knowledge of the history and issues related to hypodescent (the One Drop Rule), ambiguity (the "What are you?" question, marginality, and racial/cultural identity. The knowledge cannot be superficial but must entail a historical, political, social, and psychological understanding of the treatment of race, racism, and monoracialism in this society. In essence, these four dynamics form the context that the multiracial individual deals with on a continuing basis.

COUNSELING AND SPECIAL CIRCUMSTANCES INVOLVING RACIAL/ETHNIC POPULATIONS

Counseling Arab Americans

1,264 teenagers were asked to identify what role in a movie or on television a person from different ethnic backgrounds would be most likely to play. For Arab Americans, the roles were that of a terrorist or a convenience store clerk. This result was obtained even though the study predated the September 11, 2001, terrorist attacks. (Zogby, 2001a)

Just days after the September 11 attacks, Frank Silva Roque shot and killed Balbir Singh Sodhi, a Sikh American, who was merely standing in front of a gas station. Roque shot him while driving by in a pickup.

Elkugia, who was born in Libya, plays center at Eastlake High School in Washington State. While playing basketball for the team, she wears a headscarf and a long jersey and athletic pants instead of shorts. Her clothing reflects her Muslim faith and is a "form of modesty." She was voted homecoming queen for her high school. (Iwasaki, 2006a)

Arabs are individuals who originate from countries located in the Middle East and North Africa and whose primary language is Arabic. The vast majority are adherents of the religion Islam. Large numbers of Arab immigrants have arrived in the United States since 1875, but not until recently has much attention been paid to this cultural group. Although Arab Americans have been always been exposed to prejudice and discrimination, negative behavior directed toward this group has been exacerbated by the conflicts in the Middle East and the September 11, 2001, attacks on the United States. "Arab-appearing" individuals or those who are Muslims (followers of Islam) have been subject to discrimination and attacks. In a letter to his constituents, Representative Virgil Goode wrote "I fear that in the next century we will have many more Muslims in the United States if we do not adopt the strict immigration policies that I believe are necessary to preserve the values and beliefs traditional to the United States of America" (Frommer, 2006, pp. 1). Goode wrote this letter in response to the request of an elected Muslim representative to use the Quran during his ceremonial swearing in. Hate crimes again Muslims are second only to those perpetrated against Jewish Americans (Uniform Crime Report, 2005). In this chapter, we will present some of the characteristics, values, family life, and struggles over racism of Arabs in American society.

Characteristics of the Arab American Population

Arab Americans are a diverse group, comprised of individuals from about 20 different countries. Because of the categorizations used in the U.S. Census, it is difficult to come up with the precise number of Arab Americans. It is estimated that the total number of U.S. residents of Arab ancestry alone is 850,027. In combination with another ancestry, the total rises to 1,189,731. (U.S. Census Bureau, 2005f). Arab Americans are heterogeneous in terms of race, religion, and political ideology. Approximately 56 percent are from Lebanon, 14 percent from Syria, 11 percent from Egypt, 9 percent from Palestine, 4 percent from Jordan, 2 percent from Iraq, and 4 percent from other countries (El-Badry, 2006). Arabic is the official language of Arab countries.

The majority of Arab Americans arrived in two major waves (Suleiman, 1999). The first lasted from 1875 to World War II and primarily involved Arab Christians from Lebanon and Syria who immigrated for economic reasons. The second wave occurred from World War II to the present. It includes Palestinians, Iraqis, and Syrians who left in order to escape the Arab-Israeli conflicts and civil war. This latter group included larger numbers of Muslims. The aftermath of the September 11 attacks initially reduced Arab immigration. However, it has once again increased, and more than 40,000 immigrants from Muslim countries such as Egypt, Pakistan, and Morocco were admitted to the United States in 2005 (Elliott, 2006). In comparison with the U.S. population as a whole, Arab Americans are more likely to be married (61 versus 54 percent), male (57 versus 49 percent), young, and more educated (41 percent have bachelor's degree, versus 24 percent of national populace). Sixty-nine percent indicate they speak a language other than English at home, but 65 percent speak English "very well." The majority work as executives, professionals, and office and sales staff. Forty-two percent work in management positions, and Arab American income is higher than the national median income ($41,000 versus $37,000). However, the poverty rate is also higher (17 percent versus 12 percent; U.S. Census Bureau, 2005f).

Facts Regarding Arab Americans and Islam

The following are some facts about Arab Americans and Islam (Detroit Free Press, 2001; Jackson & Nassar-McMillan, 2006)

- Muslims are followers of the religion Islam.

- Islam is practiced worldwide. In fact, there are more Muslims in Indonesia than in all of the Arab countries combined.

- The Quran is the Muslim holy book. It teaches nonviolence.

- Most Arab Americans are Christians, although there are also large Muslim groups within the United States. Most Arab countries are Muslim.

- The majority of Arab Americans are U.S. citizens, born in the United States.

- Most Arab Americans do not wear traditional clothing as portrayed in the mass media. However, some Arab American women do wear traditional clothing and do so because of the Islamic teachings of modesty and belief that it is liberating to dress in traditional clothing.

- Arabs may have dark or light skin, blue or brown eyes. Arabs have been classified, at different times, as African, Asian, White, or European.

- Some Arab Americans of prominence include Ralph Nader (political activist), George Mitchell (former senator), actors Tony Shalhoub (Monk), and Marlo Thomas (That Girl), Helen Thomas (White House Press Corps), Doug Flutie (former NFL quarterback), and Christa McAuliffe (teacher who died aboard the space shuttle Challenger).

Stereotypes, Racism, and Prejudice

Arabs and Arab Americans have been stereotyped in movies as sheiks, barbarians, or terrorists. As was mentioned in the poll of teenagers at the beginning of the chapter, the expected roles for Arabs in movies and television were those of a terrorist or convenience store clerk. Islam has also been portrayed as a violent religion. In fact, in 2006, Pope Benedict XVI created a storm of protests from the Muslim world when he read a quote from a 14th century emperor: "Show me just what Muhammad brought that was new, and there you will find only evil and inhuman, such as his command to spread by the sword the faith he preached." The pope later professed "total and profound respect for all Muslims" and said he was trying to make the point that religion and violence do not go together. Nonetheless, the reaction of the Muslim world shows the sensitivity involved when religious issues are brought up. These situations also impact the way Arab Americans are viewed in the United States.

The terrorist attacks on September 11, 2001, had a profound impact on how Arab Americans were viewed in the United States. After September 11, hate crimes increased, with thousands of Arab American males subjected to deportation hearings, airline passenger profiling, vandalism of mosques, physical violence, and increased discrimination (Moradi & Hasan, 2004). Many Arab Americans have felt cautious regarding qualities that might draw attention to them, such as their dress or their names. Some women who previously wore headscarves discontinued the practice or stayed inside their homes. Arab Americans were angered, upset, and dismayed by the terrorist attacks, as were all Americans. At the same time, they were aware of the increased negative response by the public to those of Arab descent. A national opinion poll of Arab Americans conducted right after the September 11 attacks (Zogby, 2001b) revealed that, of those surveyed:

- 69 percent would support all-out war against countries that harbor or aid terrorists who attacked the United States.

- 65 percent were embarrassed because the attacks were committed by people from Arab countries.

- 61 percent worried about the long-term effects of discrimination against Arab Americans.

- 20 percent had "personally experienced discrimination because of their ethnicity," and 45 percent said they knew of someone who has experienced such discrimination since the September 11 attacks.

- 54 percent believed there was justification for law enforcement to engage in extra questioning and inspections of people with Middle Eastern accents or features.

The poll results indicate that Arab Americans reacted as did other Americans to the attack, and even supported retaliation against countries supporting the terrorist attacks. They even supported profiling in the aftermath of September 11. Certainly, reactions to certain questions such as racial profiling may have changed since the time of that survey. Some of the fears regarding discrimination have been realized. In a report covering incidents involving Arab Americans occurring between September 11, 2001, and October 11, 2002 (American-Arab Anti Discrimination Committee [ADC], 2003), the following were reported:

- Over 700 violent incidents were directed at Arab Americans or those perceived to be Arab Americans or Muslims during the first 9 weeks after the September 11 attacks.

- Over 800 cases of employment discrimination against Arab Americans occurred.

- Over 80 cases of illegal or discriminatory removal from aircrafts after boarding occurred (removal based on perceived ethnicity).

- Thousands of Arab men were required to submit to a "voluntary interview" by government officials.

- Numerous instances of denial of services and housing discrimination occurred.

Even 6 years after September 11, Arab Americans are wary. For example, a Muslim woman has stopped giving to Muslim charities, assuming that her donation would be monitored by authorities. An Imam (leader of prayer at a mosque) in Sacramento shaved part of his beard. Nearly everyone who attends a mosque has reported being called a profane name in public, being profiled at airports, or having been visited by authorities. Because of the harassment and resulting fear, some have stopped attending prayer at a mosque (Sahagun, 2006).

Implications. Because many Americans have negative views of Muslims and Arab Americans, mental health professionals should examine their own attitudes toward Islam and Arab Americans in general.

- Have you been influenced by the negative stereotypes regarding individuals of this group and their religion? Would you feel less safe if your plane had Arab-looking passengers, or if you noticed a fellow passenger carrying a Quran? What do you think when you see an Arab American wearing traditional clothing? What would be your reaction if an Arab American woman came in wearing a headscarf?

- It is important to realize that Arab Americans, especially those who appear to be from an Arab country or are Muslims, have had to endure negative stereotypes and have faced increasing prejudice and discrimination.

- Therapists should be informed regarding antidiscrimination policies, provide clients with information about discriminatory policies, and support client efforts to challenge discrimination. If clients are encountering job or housing discrimination, the therapist can make them aware of their legal rights and assist them in taking appropriate actions. Hate crimes should be reported to the police. Employment discrimination can be reported to the Equal Employment Opportunities Commission.

- The web site for the American-Arab Anti-Discrimination Committee (ADC) offers legal resources and information on addressing discrimination in these and other areas. Mental health professionals may find it helpful to assess for the possibility of discriminatory actions directed toward clients and be willing to explore these experiences.

Religious and Cultural Background

Muslims or the followers of Islam believe in one God and individual accountability for their actions. The name of their religion, Islam, means submission to God. Islam does not support violence or terror. Quran is the equivalent of the Bible in Christianity and is considered to be the literal word of God. Islam is one of the fastest growing religions in the United States. Between 17 to 30 percent of the U.S. Muslims are converts to the faith (U.S. Department of State, 2002). Within Islam, there are two major sects—Sunni and Shiite. The Sunnis are the largest group, accounting for about 90 percent of Muslims worldwide. The remaining 10 percent are Shiites. The difference between the two groups is similar to that between Protestantism and Roman Catholicism in the United States. It is estimated that about four to six million Muslims are living in the United States. The ethnic composition of this group include: 33 percent South-Central Asian (Pakistani, Indian, Bangladeshi, Afghani); 30 percent African American; and 25 percent Arab (J. I. Smith, 2006). Most Muslims in America and throughout the world are Sunni, while those in Iraq, Bahrain, Lebanon and Iran are mainly Shi'a. The lives of Muslims are governed by laws derived from the Quran, which deals with social issues, family life, economics and business, sexuality, and other aspects of life. Adherence to Islam is demonstrated by a declaration of faith ("There is no god but God and Muhammad is his messenger"). Muslims engage in the ritual of prayer five times a day. There is also a yearly fast during the period of Ramadam, during which time individuals focus on inner reflection, devotion to God, and spiritual renewal. Almsgiving and a pilgrimage to Mecca are additional signs of devotion (Nobles & Sciarra, 2000).

Family Structure and Values

Family structure and values differ widely, depending on the specific country of origin or acculturation level of the Arab American. An Arab American engineer living in San Francisco made the following observation: "American values are, by and large, very consistent with Islamic values, with a focus on family, faith, hard work, and an obligation to better self and society" (U.S Department of State, 2002, p. 1). Some generalizations can be made. Family obligations and interdependence among members are very important. Because of the group orientation, there is pressure for conformity, and children are expected to behave in a socially acceptable manner. Parents expect to and do remain part of their child's life for as long as possible. In traditionally oriented families, the oldest son is trained to become the head of the extended family. Family roles are complementary, with men serving as providers and head of the family and women maintaining the home and rearing children. The role of the mother is one of affection to the children, while the father tends to be aloof, generating both fear and respect. In traditional Arab American families, there is a strong sense of a community and an identity that revolves around culture and God. Hospitality is considered to be very important. They will ask a guest if they prefer to have coffee or tea rather than the style of most Americans, which is to ask guests if they want something to drink (Hodge, 2002; Nobles & Sciarra, 2000). Treatment for personal problems may be considered shameful, and outside help may be sought only as a last resort. Problems are often disclosed only to family or community members. In general, boys are advised by older males, while girls are advised by older females. Opposite-sex discussions with other than a family member may be problematic (Jackson & Nassar-McMillan, 2006).

Acculturation Conflicts

As with many groups that face discrimination and prejudice, some members do not acknowledge their ethnic background and have changed their names to be more "American sounding." Some try to hide their religious and ethnic identities by wearing American style clothing. Many have assimilated. This is more characteristic of the first wave of Arab American immigrants, who were primarily Christian. The second wave of Arab immigrants tend to maintain their traditional identity, choosing to live in ethnic Arab communities. In some respects, they withdraw from certain aspects of American society. They are more likely to be Muslim and practice their religion in an open fashion. Some women in this group may wear the *hijab,* or head scarf, as a sign of modesty. Traditionally oriented Arab Americans often maintain contact with people from their country of origin. Some Arab Americans are bicultural and accept both their Arab and American identities (Nobles & Sciarra, 2000). The September 11th attack also appeared to strengthen the identity of being an Arab American. In the Zogby (2001b) poll, 88 percent responded that they were proud of their heritage and 84 percent said their ethnic heritage is important in defining their identity. Identification with other Arabs is also important, and 83 percent said that securing Palestinian rights is personally important to them.

Implications. Because the culture, values, and religion differ from one Arab individual or family to the other, the therapist needs to determine the way a specific family is operating, rather than responding in a stereotypical manner. Acculturation and/or assimilation may have occurred for some individuals. Others may adhere strongly to traditional cultural and religious standards. This is probably more common among Arab American Muslims. Generational acculturation conflicts are common, with children acculturating more quickly than parents. This may be especially problematic for traditionally oriented Arab Americans who adhere to a hierarchical family structure in which the children are expected to "behave appropriately."

Implications for Clinical Practice

Arab Americans are a very diverse group in terms of religion, culture, country of origin, and degree of acculturation. In general, non-Arab Americans have little knowledge about this group and have been exposed to misinformation. Because of this, many individuals view the action of extremist Islamic groups to represent the view of Muslims. As mental health workers, we need to understand Arab culture and Muslim beliefs. The following are recommendations for working with Arab American clients (Hodge, 2002; Jackson & Nassar-McMillan, 2006):

1. Identify your attitudes about Arab Americans and Muslims.

2. Recognize that many face discrimination and violence because of their Arab background or their religious beliefs.

3. Be ready to help those who have been discriminated against in seeking legal recourse.

4. Recognize that Arab Americans are very diverse, and that you must not stereotype. Collaborate with them to gain an understanding of their lifestyle and beliefs.

5. Inquire about importance of religion in their lives.

6. Determine the structure of the family through questions and observation. With traditional families, try addressing the husband or male first. Traditional families may appear to be enmeshed.

7. Be careful of self-disclosures that may be interpreted as a weakness. This will reduce the therapist's status among some Arab Americans. Positive self-disclosures are fine.

8. Acculturation conflicts may occur in families.

9. In traditionally oriented Arab Americans families, there may be reluctance to share family issues or to express negative feelings with a therapist.

10. There may be greater acceptance to holistic approaches that incorporate family members and the religious or social community.

11. Be open to exploring spiritual beliefs and the use of prayer or fasting to reduce distress.

12. Cognitive-Behavioral strategies may be productive for Muslims if distressing thoughts are modified with beliefs from the Quran.

Counseling Jewish Americans

On July 28, 2006, Naveed Haq, a Muslim, went to the Jewish Federated Office in Seattle, shot one woman to death and wounded five others. His motive for the shooting was based on his belief that Jews are responsible for the conflict in the Middle East.

Of the 1,314 hate crimes motivated by religious bias, the overwhelming number have been anti-Jewish (68.5 percent). The second highest, 11.1 percent, were anti-Islamic. (Uniform Crime Statistics, 2005)

David Duke spoke to a group of Holocaust deniers at a conference on the Holocaust convened by Iran's president in 2006. During his speech, the former Imperial Wizard of the Ku Klux Klan and Louisiana State Representative claimed that the Holocaust was a hoax perpetrated by European Jews to justify the occupation of Palestine and the creation of Israel. (Fathi, 2006)

20

Chapter

J ewish Americans have long been targets of discrimination and prejudice. That such prejudice continues to this day is revealed in the astonishing statistics that of all religious hate crimes reported in 2004, over 68 percent were directed against individuals who are Jewish. Prejudicial reactions against Jews are not only overt day-to-day events such as vandalism, assaults, or direct displays of anti-Semitism, but may also come to the surface during worldwide events that involve Israel, the Middle East, or even in regard to the celebration of religious holidays. Prejudice may also be revealed by individuals during periods of personal difficulties, such as in 2006 when actor and director Mel Gibson said, "Jews are responsible for all the wars in the world" (Gibson has apologized for his statement), or in the termination of Judith Regan, an editor, from HarperCollins Publishers. During a contentious discussion with the publisher's attorney, Ms. Regan purportedly made a statement complaining that a "Jewish cabal," referring to members of the publishing firm, was against her (Hall, 2006). The publishers had decided not to sell a controversial book by O. J. Simpson that Ms. Regan had produced. Although Jewish Americans have experienced discrimination both within the United States and throughout the world, they have received little attention from the multicultural literature.

In this chapter, we cover Jewish Americans and issues related to their demographic characteristics and their experiences with prejudice and discrimination, identity, and religious beliefs. We will begin by considering the characteristics of Jewish Americans. Jews are currently defined in several ways, including (1) people who practice Judaism and have a Jewish ethnic background, (2) people who have converted to Judaism but who do not have Jewish parents, and (3) individuals with a Jewish ethnic background who do not practice Judaism, but still maintain cultural identification and connection to their Jewish descent. The Jewish population in the United States is estimated to be 5.2 million (Berkofsky, 2006) It is the largest Jewish community in the world, although there are also large populations in Canada and Argentina. The earliest Jews to arrive in the United States were from Spain and Portugal. The second group of Jewish immigrants was from Germany and Eastern Europe. The German Jews left because of persecution and/or for economic reasons. By World War I, 250,000 German-speaking Jews had arrived in America. Eastern European Jews came to America as a result of overpopulation, poverty, and persecution. Between 1880 and 1942, over two million Jews from Russia, Austria-Hungary, and Romania entered the United States, and constituted the largest group of Jews in the United States. Because of their historical and political background, they tended to embrace socialism, leading to support of liberal policies in America (Singer, 2002; Zollman, 2006).

Approximately 85 percent of adult Jews were born in the United States and almost all are native English-speakers. Some American Jews speak Hebrew, Yiddish, and Spanish (those who emigrated from Latin America). Of Jews born outside the United States, most are from the former Soviet Union. Jews are a highly educated group, with 55 percent of those 18 and older receiving at least a bachelor's degree. Most consider themselves to be a minority group and feel that the heritage is "very" or "somewhat" important to them, and 50 percent report "strong emotional ties" to Israel. In general, Jews describe themselves as politically "liberal" or "very liberal." About 60 percent have reported being discriminated against, a rate similar to that reported by African Americans (Berkofsky, 2006; Goldberg, 2000).

Of concern to many Jews is that the size of their population in the United States is declining. According to the findings of the 2000–2001 National Jewish Survey, their population is diminishing in size because of aging, falling birth rate, intermarriage, and assimilation. The following are specific findings of the 2000–2001 National Jewish Survey (Berkofsky, 2006): Since 1990, the Jewish population in the United States has decreased from 5.5 million to 5.2 million; the Jewish population is older than the general population, with larger percentages of Jews in the 65 and older group than in the total U.S. population; intermarriage rates are about 50 percent, and only 33 percent of these couples raise their children as Jews, whereas 96 percent of Jewish couples raise their children as Jews; about 52 percent of Jewish women between the ages of 30 to 34 have not had any children, compared to 27 percent of all American women; the fertility rate of Jewish women is below that needed to maintain the population. These findings indicate a continued reduction in the number of Jews in America.

Most Jews do not follow all religious traditions, but retain strong Jewish connections by celebrating Yom Kippur, Hanukah, and Passover, keeping kosher homes, and attending synagogue services. Jews are well represented in all aspects of American society in terms of business, education, politics, entertainment, and the arts. Some well-known Jews include politicians Barney Franks, Eliot Spitzer, Joe Lieberman, Barbara Boxer, and editor William Kristol; mental health professionals Albert Ellis, Aaron Beck, and Sigmund Freud; and actors Scarlett Johansson and Natalie Portman.

Experiences with Prejudice and Discrimination

Although Jewish individuals have achieved great success, it is evident that they remain targets of prejudice, discrimination, and even violence.

- According to FBI statistics for 2005 (Uniform Crime Report, 2005), the number of anti-Jewish hate crimes was the largest against any religion, over six times higher than the second highest targeted group, Muslims.

- The Anti-Defamation League (ADL, 2006) reported that in 2005, there were a total of 1,757 anti-Semitic incidents including harassment, threats, assaults, and vandalism such as property damage and swastikas scratched into walls.

- In a national poll of American voters (Council for the National Interest, 2006), 39 percent of Americans believe that the "Israeli lobby" was a key factor responsible for the United States going to war in Iraq and confronting Iran. Forty percent of those polled disagreed, and 20 percent were uncertain. Among Jewish Americans, 77 percent disagreed with this view.

- In a survey of Americans (ADL, 2005), it was found that that 14 percent of the adults surveyed hold "hard core" anti-Semitic beliefs. Many believe that Jews have too much power in the United States. One third believe that Jews are more loyal to Israel than to America, and 30 percent believe that Jews were responsible for the death of Christ. Anti-Jewish sentiments were also found among ethnic minorities. Thirty-five percent of foreign-born Hispanics and 36 percent of African Americans hold anti-Semitic beliefs and are likely to endorse the statement "Jews don't care what happens to anyone but their own kind." Many of the respondents also believed that Jews have had too much influence on Middle East policies.

It is evident that Jewish Americans continue to face a great deal of prejudice, even with the successes they have had in American society. Anti-Semitic attitudes within ethnic minority populations are especially troubling to Jews because of a shared experience with prejudice and discrimination. Jews were in the forefront of the civil rights movement in the 1960s. Half of the White Freedom Riders and civil rights attorneys were Jews. Several reasons may exist regarding the anti-Semitic attitudes of one-third of foreign-born Hispanic immigrants and African Americans toward Jewish Americans. First, many do not perceive Jews as a disadvantaged minority and second, Jews have not been supportive of affirmative action because they have been negatively impacted by affirmative actions quotas since they are not considered to be a minority. Instead of quotas, they favor advancement based on merit (Shapiro, 2006).

Jewish Identity and Religion

An older Jewish woman asked her therapist "Have you heard of the Holocaust?" (Hinrichsen, 2006, p. 30). The Holocaust represents an incredibly traumatic period in Jewish history. During this period, the Nazi Germans murdered approximately six million Jewish men, women, and children. There were many more who survived inhumane treatment after being imprisoned in forced labor and concentration camps, but whose lives have been affected forever. What constitutes Jewish identity is complex and highly personal. An important aspect is a sense of shared cultural and historical experiences. *Holocaust deniers,* individuals who do not acknowledge or who question the existence of the genocide that occurred during the Holocaust not only invalidate the loss and suffering of Holocaust victims and their families, but also strike at an important part of Jewish identity.

In a Jewish Identity Survey (2001), individuals were considered to be Jewish: (1) if they regarded themselves as Jewish by religion, (2) if they are of Jewish parentage or upbringing but had no religion, or (3) if they are Jewish by choice. About half who identify as Jewish adhere to Judaism. However, the other Jews are secular (believe in science rather than faith). They do not belong to a synagogue and may celebrate some Jewish holidays, but do not consider them religious activities. These individuals still consider themselves

Jews because of the commonality of history, culture, and experiences. Friedman, Friedlander, and Blustein (2005) conducted interviews of 10 Jewish adults to understand their perspective regarding identity. All participants indicated a fluidity of identity over the years. One stated, "As I have said, when I was a kid, it made me feel a little bit different in certain situations, but now I would sound very proud to be associated with Jewish people and to be Jewish. I would say it has gotten stronger." Another commented on their Jewish identity by responding "...it's the dips and valleys in my life... it is pretty much a constant, but it does go up and down" (p. 79). Among the participants, identity was influenced by childhood experiences such as attending Jewish holidays with family members, eating in a Kosher dining room, and encouragement by parents toward Judaism. As adults, some expressed feelings of guilt for not practicing religious customs. Some had a deep Jewish identity, but did not engage in Jewish rituals. However, most expressed pride about being Jewish. From this phenomenological study, Jewish identity appears to be defined differently by those who practice Judaism versus individuals who are secular and do not engage in Jewish religious practices. For many, Jewish identity revolves around common experiences and history, rather than religion.

Judaism, with its belief in one omnipotent God who created humankind, was one of the earliest monotheistic religions. According to Judaism, God established a covenant with the Jewish people and revealed his commandments to them in the Torah, the holy book. The most important commandments are the Ten Commandments. Judaism also celebrates certain holidays. One of the most important is Yom Kippur, the Day of Atonement. It is a time set aside to atone for sins during the past year. Even Jews who are not religious will fast, contemplate, or attend service at a synagogue. Within Judaism, the degree of adherence to religious tradition varies. Those who are Orthodox or Traditional follow all traditions and aspects of the religious belief. In the Conservative movement, the followers believe that religious laws and traditions can change to suit the times, and the Reform or Progressive movement advocates the freedom of individuals to make choices about which traditions to follow (Rich, 2004). Individuals are allowed to convert to Judaism, although the requirements may vary according to the specific sect. Most require three processes to be successfully achieved: (1) studies on Judaism and the observance of the commandments, (2) immersion in a ritual bath, and for males, (3) circumcision (symbolic circumcision may be allowed by some sects).

Implications. A well-known mental health practitioner and educator, Stephen Weinrach, was proud of his Jewish identity and was an outspoken critic of the mental health organization to which he belonged for being blind to the plight of Jewish Americans. He wrote:

Issues that have concerned Jews have failed to resonate with the counseling profession, including, for the most part, many of the most outspoken advocates for multicultural counseling.... The near universal failure of those committed to multicultural counseling to rail against anti-Semitism and embrace the notion of Jews as a culturally distinct group, represents the most painful wound of all. (Weinrach, 2002, p. 310)

In his article, Weinrach made the following observations regarding the mental health profession:

- Counseling associations ignore requests from Jewish members to re-schedule meetings when the meetings conflict with Jewish holidays.
- Texts on multicultural counseling do not address Jews as a diverse group.
- The National Board for Certified Counselors scheduled the National Counseling Exam on Yom Kippur, a day when work is not permitted.
- Few articles in counseling journals have involved Jewish Americans, and, in some texts, Jews have been portrayed in a stereotypic manner.

In our opinion, Weinrach has made some valid points. In writing this chapter, we found very few articles on counseling or therapy with Jewish Americans, although numerous articles were easily located for the other diverse groups covered in this text. We must recognize the degree of prejudice and discrimination faced by Jewish Americans and re-examine policies that may be insensitive to their concerns.

Counseling and Therapy with Jewish Clients

In *Jewish Issues in Multiculturalism: A Handbook for Educators and Clinicians*, Langman (1999) indicates the difficulty of using culturally appropriate interventions because of the diversity of Jewish cultures. He does offer some guiding principles of importance for mental health providers. First, it is very important to be respectful of and knowledgeable about Jewish culture. Because most clinicians are from a Christian background, the Jewish traditions, values, and religious rituals of importance that define a Jew's identity are often overlooked, are invisible, or are dismissed. As seen in Chapter 5, therapists might be guilty of microaggressions in the session. For example, Langman provides the example of a Jewish client who requests that an appointment not be scheduled during Yom Kippur. The therapist's response was: "What, do you need to pray or something?" The client felt humiliated, devalued, ashamed, and unsupported.

Second, Jewish identity is an intimate aspect for many Jews, and a therapist should strive to be aware of the full spectrum of Jewish identities within religious as well as nonreligious Jews. As our prior section indicates, knowledge of the history of anti-Semitism, its effects on identity, and possible internalized anti-Semitism in clients should be recognized. Langman (1999) discusses the latter as a result of an insidious social conditioning process that makes some Jews ashamed of their ethnic and religious heritage. In this respect, he views the sociopolitical process that equates Jewish differences as deviance to be the culprit and encourages counselors not to "blame the victim."

Third, Langman (1999) makes it clear that therapists need to be aware of their own values, assumptions and biases that may be detrimental to their Jewish clients. He cites research that indicates: Jews are viewed as being "cold," "hostile," and "obstructive," while White non-Jews are seen as being more "warm," "friendly," and "helpful." He encourages counselors to explore any feelings of negativism toward Jews and Jewish culture. The therapist needs to explore his or her feelings toward Jews, Judaism, Jewishness, and/or Israel.

Last, when dealing with an Orthodox Jew, it may be desirable to consult with a rabbi. Since almost half of Jews are not associated with a synagogue or only have slight connections with a congregation, it is not a constant requirement. Rather, Langman believes the therapist must be open to and willing to work with rabbis on behalf of their clients. Religious doubts, religiously prohibited behaviors, and those behaviors associated with guilt or shame may require clarification before full therapy can continue. Consultation is easier if the counselor has spent time cultivating relationships with the Jewish community.

Implications for Clinical Practice

1. As members of mental health professions, we must be aware of policies or expectations that do not take Jewish American concerns into consideration. Do we schedule meeting or appointments that conflict with Jewish holidays?

2. We need to examine our attitudes and beliefs regarding Jewish Americans. Are their problems invisible to us? Is our failure to acknowledge the discrimination experienced by those of the Jewish faith a reflection of anti-Semitism?

3. Jewish Americans are the most targeted religious group for hate crimes and discrimination. A 78-year-old woman who was depressed and mildly cognitive impaired, asked an intern, "Are you Jewish?" (Hinrich-

sen, 2006, p. 30). When the intern inquired about the question, the client stated that she had experienced discrimination from non-Jews and was uncertain whether or not the intern would understand her difficulties. Because many Jewish Americans are well educated and economically secure, we often do not understand that they may suffer from discrimination or hate.

4. Jewish American mental health professionals should also feel free to bring up their concerns when they are subjected to insensitivity or discrimination.

5. Jewish counselors should be careful when working with Jewish clients. Assumptions regarding client identity and issues should not be based on the counselor's own sense of identity and beliefs regarding Judaism (Friedman, Friedlander, & Blustein, 2005).

Counseling Immigrants

In a recent election, voters who had a Hispanic surname and were registered as democrats in Orange County, California, received the following notice in the mail "You are advised that if your residence in this country is illegal or you are an immigrant, voting in a federal election is a crime that could result in jail time." (Prengaman, 2006)

The sign outside of one of Philadelphia's famous cheesesteak joints reads "This is AMERICA: WHEN ORDERING 'PLEASE SPEAK ENGLISH.'" The owner put up the sign because of the number of people who could not order in English, primarily immigrants from Latin America and Asia. This sign has been challenged by the City's Commission on Human Relations who argue that the sign discourages customers of "certain backgrounds" from eating there. (Associated Press, 2006a)

In our society, immigrants have received a mixed reception from both the government and the public. The strong backlash against the Bush administration's (2004) proposal to pass a guest worker program for undocumented immigrants, calls for building a border fence between Mexico and the United States, and the formation of a citizen's vigilante group (Minute Men) to patrol the borders makes it clear that many resent the presence of immigrants. The letter mentioned earlier was written in Spanish and sent to 14,000 Hispanic voters who were registered as democrats in Orange County, California. The letter implied that immigrant status precludes the right to vote, despite the fact that immigrants who are naturalized citizens do have voting privileges. Interestingly, it is believed the letter originated from a republican candidate, Tan D. Nguyen, who, himself, is a Vietnamese immigrant. This is not the only time intimidation tactics have been used in Orange County. In 1998, a Republican candidate posted uniformed guards outside 20 voting places in Hispanic neighborhoods to prevent "noncitizens" from voting. In this case, a civil lawsuit alleging intimidation of Hispanic voters was filed against both the candidate and the county GOP. It resulted in a $400,000 settlement (Prengaman, 2006). Not only are immigrants and refugees faced with the stress of moving to and living in another country, but they are exposed to an increasingly hostile environment for a number of different reasons.

Population Characteristics of Immigrants

The U.S. Census Bureau (2004a) estimates there are over 33 million immigrants living in the United States, which is about 12 percent of the population. About half have arrived since 1990. Of these immigrants, it is estimated that 36 percent are legally documented or legally admitted as permanent residents. These individuals hold a *green card* (a card which is actually yellow and white) indicating that they have permission to reside and work in the United States. They must carry a copy of the card with them and can only vote when U.S. citizenship is not required. Thirty-two percent of immigrants are *naturalized citizens*. Naturalized citizens are foreign nationals who have become citizens of the United States. Approximately 28 percent of immigrants are undocumented. This primarily includes individuals who entered the United States without permission and those who have violated their temporary admission status. Over half of the immigrant population originates from Latin America, with Mexico being the largest contributor. Other countries providing the most recent legal immigrants include India, the Philippines, China, El Salvador, the Dominican Republic, Vietnam, Columbia, Guatemala, and Russia. Immigrants, particularly those from Latin America, tend to earn lower wages and have a higher incidence of poverty. About one-third have not completed high school as compared to 12.5 percent of the total adult population. However, the percentage of immigrants with a bachelor's degree or advanced degree is slightly higher compared to those born in the United States.

Immigration Policy and Factors Influencing Receptivity to Immigrants

Historically, some U.S. immigration policies and laws have been unfair and exclusionary (Chung & Bemak, 2007). Until 1952, only White persons were allowed to become naturalized citizens. With the Immigration Act of 1965, people from any nation were finally allowed to become naturalized citizens. In part, this change was due to the impact of the civil rights movement in the United States. However, there are still attempts to exclude immigrant rights. In 2006, the Ohio legislature passed a law that allowed election officials at polling places to make the following inquiries of immigrants or individuals who appear that they might be immigrants:

- Are you a native or naturalized citizen?
- Where were you born?
- What official documentation do you possess to prove your citizenship? Please provide that documentation.

In addition, the individual was required to declare, under oath, that he or she was the person named in the documentation. U.S. District Court Judge Boyko overturned this voting code as being unconstitutional on October 4, 2006.

Many citizens are opposed to the number of immigrants entering the United States and the idea of providing a path to citizenship for illegal immigrants. In the latter case, the argument is often made that illegal immigrants violated the law by not following immigration policy and procedures, and that they are a drain on the social system. Those on the other side of the debate counter that business has benefited from and continues to rely on the work provided by undocumented workers, many of whom have lived in the United States for decades, paying taxes and contributing to their communities. In fact, the vast majority of migrant workers pay taxes, yet only minimally uses health care, welfare, or other social services (Massey, Durand, & Malone, 2002).

Recently, many states and communities have passed, or are in the process of passing, laws against the provision of social and other services to undocumented immigrants. In 1994, California passed Proposition 187, which denied undocumented immigrants a public school education, medical assistance, and other government services. This proposition was later ruled to be unconstitutional. In the latter half of 2005, House Bill 4437 was passed in the House of Representatives, combining border protection, illegal immigration control, and antiterrorism efforts. Under the law, faith-based groups or "good Samaritans" could be prosecuted for assisting undocumented immigrants. Had this bill also passed in the Senate, undocumented immigrants would be classified as aggravated felons, and local law enforcement could enforce the immigration laws. This would certainly reduce reports of crimes and/or potentially increase abuse toward and feelings of fear within the population of undocumented immigrants.

Implications. It is clear that societal and governmental reactions to immigrants are influenced by social conditions. They become negative when economic conditions result in a loss of jobs or limited housing.

- In areas experiencing economic stress, negative feelings toward immigrants increase if immigrants are viewed as taking jobs from those born in the United States. Conflicts are sometimes seen between immigrants and U.S.-born members of ethnic minorities.

- In cities such as Dallas, Miami, Chicago, New York, and Los Angeles, some of the confrontations have been violent. Most have involved issues regarding jobs, schools, and housing, particularly when there is a perception that immigrants are taking jobs and other resources away from U.S.-born citizens.

- As Ada Edwards, a radio director, noted, "In some communities there is a . . . shortage in low-income housing. So, when you have low-income groups and they're all [competing] for the same house, they start working against each other instead of looking at the problem of availability of low-income housing" (American Friends Service Committee, 2006a, p. 2).

- The September 11, 2001, terrorist attacks had a dramatic impact on attitudes toward immigrants. Not only were Arab Americans viewed with suspicion (see Chapter 23) but anyone appearing to be foreign was also considered suspect. Immigrants became regarded as possible terrorists. Since the trauma of September 11, the movement toward legalization of undocumented immigrants has slowed and there has been a dramatic decline in admission of refugees (Patrick, 2004).

- The *nativism* movement, promoting the position that only U.S. "natives" (understood to be people of European descent) belong here is receiving greater support (American Friends Service Committee, 2006b, 2006c).

- Similarly, the English-only movement, viewed by many immigrants and others as being exclusionary, is strengthening. The majority of Americans, including immigrants, support the recognition of English as the national language of the United States. Paradoxically, Hispanics feel more strongly that English should be taught to children of immigrant families than do non-Hispanic Whites or Blacks (92 percent, 87 percent, and 83 percent, respectively; Pew Hispanic Center, 2006). The English-only stance taken by businesses or services may cause many more immigrants to feel excluded due to language.

- The debate over a path to citizenship for undocumented immigrants has also gained prominence in recent years and has led to a number of large pro-immigration demonstrations. Unfortunately, it has also fueled anti-immigrant feeling in some quarters. Over half of Hispanics polled in a national survey reported they have seen an increase in discrimination because of the debate over immigration policy (Suro & Escobar, 2006).

The Impact of September 11, 2001, on Immigrants

The impact of September 11th, with its resulting emphasis on preventing the entry of and identifying terrorists, has increased feelings of nationalism throughout the United States. The climate of fear has led to an even further decrease in the utilization of medical or government services by immigrants. Immigrants already use less than half of health care resources compared to the average U.S. citizen (National Immigration Law Center, 2006). Among immigrants, even those who are permanent legal residents, there is a fear of deportation or of not being granted citizenship. Applicants are afraid that seeking assistance might show that they are unable to live here independently. There is also concern among undocumented immigrants that agencies might contact authorities if services are sought. Mental health professionals should be aware of concerns that might affect help-seeking and discuss them with immigrant clients. Immigrant clients may see the therapist as an arm of government. Children of immigrants born in the United States are citizens, but may harbor great fear and anxiety regarding the immigration status of their parents, siblings, or other close family members.

Implications. Until these issues are discussed, trust is difficult to obtain. The therapist should also be aware of certain rights or exclusions associated with immigrants (Bernstein, 2006):

- Hospitals are required to provide emergency care to anyone, including undocumented immigrants. Other treatments depend on local laws. Information regarding other immigrant issues can be obtained from the National Immigration Law Center at http://www.nilc.org/immspbs/index.htm.
- Free community clinics exist that will treat individuals regardless of immigration status. A list of these clinics can be found at http://www.uniteforsight.org/sitemap.
- Immigrants can ask for interpreter services from health care providers.
- Most documented immigrants are not eligible to receive Medicaid, food stamps or social security benefits during their first five years in the United States or longer, regardless of how much they have paid in taxes.

Cultural and Community Adjustments

One of the most difficult challenges faced by immigrants is their adjustment and adaptation to a completely different society, cultural customs, and the mixed reception by U.S. citizens. Placed in unfamiliar settings, adjusting to climactic differences, and lacking familiar community and social support, many may experience severe culture shock (Chung & Bemak, 2007). Feelings of isolation, loneliness, disorientation, helplessness, anxiety, and depression may characterize the immigration experience. The only sources of comfort and support are the small circle of relatives or friends, who are also finding it difficult to adjust psychologically to a different way of life. Left to fend for themselves, they must learn how to negotiate the educational system, acquire language proficiency, and seek employment. All three of these major challenges require immigrants to attain knowledge and understanding of the workings of U.S. society, sometimes an overwhelming task.

Implications. In additional to traditional mental health services, psychoeducational approaches are required to aid immigrants in acquiring (1) education and training for themselves and their children; (2) knowledge of employment opportunities, job searching, and the ability to manage financial demands; and (3) language proficiency to insure success in this society.

- The counselor will often have to play a number of roles such as an educator (providing information on services to immigrants and educating them about their rights and responsibilities), and advocate (helping them negotiate the institutional policies and structures of the health care, education, and employment systems).

- Play roles that actively intervene in the life and community of immigrants. To do that effectively, however, means having the ability to understand the life circumstance of immigrant groups, to have developed liaisons with the community, and to be familiar with community resources aimed at helping migrants adjust to a new world.

Barriers to Seeking Treatment

Multiple barriers exist for immigrants in their utilization of social and mental health services. As mentioned earlier, immigrants utilize health care services much less than U.S. citizens. Mental health providers need to understand how cultural, linguistic, and informational deficits affect immigrants.

Implications. In a survey of health care providers, several barriers to accessing services were identified:

- Communication difficulties due to language differences: More than 50 percent of the providers identified language barriers as the major source of difficulty regarding service delivery. This affects critical areas such as obtaining accurate results during assessment and testing. The providers also mentioned that it is sometimes difficult to obtain interpreter services, especially when there are many diverse dialects within a specific ethnic language. This barrier has the greatest impact with Latino and Asian immigrants since they are the least likely of the immigrant groups to have learned English (Weisman et al., 2005).

- Lack of knowledge of mainstream service delivery: Many immigrants lack knowledge about the health care system in the United States when compared to their native country. Extra time is required when providers try to explain clinic practices and paperwork. Oftentimes, apparent noncompliance in following through with recommendations is due to poor understanding of services.

- Cultural factors: Important information may be difficult to obtain. Many immigrant groups are hesitant to reveal family issues or matters of personal concern because of the cultural importance of privacy (Chung & Bemak, 2007). Women who were abused by their husbands or have been sexual assaulted may not talk about these issues because of cultural norms regarding family issues and shame, as well as fear of deportation. A stigma exists for many immigrants in seeking help for mental health problems. Emotional dysfunctions may be identified as being "crazy," or there is fear that the difficulties will be blamed on the family.

- Lack of resources: Many immigrant families are poor and lack the means of transportation to go to the service location. In addition, there may be a lack of time to attend sessions, due to the economic necessity to work as many hours as possible or limited flexibility in work schedules.

Implications for Clinical Practice

As mentioned in Chapters 6, 16, and 17, many immigrants who come from Asian and Latino backgrounds hold cultural belief systems that are collectivistic and consider interpersonal relationships and social networks to be of paramount importance. The Western worldview, however, is individualistic and stresses the importance of autonomy, mastery, and control of the environment. Mental health systems that value independence over interdependence, separate mental functioning from physical functioning, attribute causation as internally located, and seek to explain events from a Western empiricist approach can be at odds with the cultural belief systems of immigrants. For example, certain Asian groups believe in animism and the influence of spirits in the causes of emotional problems. An unenlightened counselor or therapist may inadvertently impose their belief systems on immigrant populations and communicate a disrespect or invalidation of their worldview.

1. It is important for counselors and therapists to consider the belief systems, values, and healing practices of various immigrants in their assessment, diagnosis, and treatment activities. Understanding and

validating the client's conceptualization within their cultural matrix is important in providing culturally relevant services.

2. Mental health providers should consider offering services within the community rather than outside of it. These services should be made culturally relevant, and staffed partially by members of the community who share in and understand the population being served.

3. Consider having on staff indigenous healers or elders in the community that can validate and legitimize the services offered. For example, the Asian American Community Mental Health Services in Oakland, California has an Asian Monk on staff who works hand-in-hand with mental health providers. Belief systems and Eastern and Western practices need not be at odds with one another, but can have a positive additive effect.

4. Keep current regarding what is happening at the local, state, and federal level related to immigration issues, particularly the tone of the debate. As our review indicates, sociopolitical conditions and public policy can have either positive or detrimental impact on the life experience of immigrants.

5. Remember that immigrants face multiple stressors, including the stress of moving to and living in another country, learning another language, and negotiating new social, economic, political, educational, and social systems. It is often a confusing and frightening experience. Mental health providers who understand the complexities of this situation can do much to reassure clients by demystifying the process.

6. In the course of assessment and diagnosis of mental disorders, take into account environmental factors, language barriers, and potential exposure to discrimination and hostility.

7. Do not assume that the client has an understanding of mental health services or counseling. Give a description of what counseling is and the role of the therapist and client.

8. Use skilled and knowledgeable interpreters when providing services.

Counseling Refugees

Deng fled the civil war in Sudan and has been in the United States for the past 2 years. He is 28 years old and spent 4 years in a refugee camp before coming to the United States. He describes fleeing burning villages outside of Darfur and seeing many people from his own family and community slaughtered, raped, and beaten. He remembers running and hiding, being near starvation, drinking muddy water, avoiding crocodiles and once a lion, and being alarmed when bombs dropped nearby. . . . He wonders what happened to his family and friends and feels guilty for having escaped. He arrived in the United States without parents or family and with no possessions. (Chung & Bemak, 2007, p. 133)

Deng's escape from Sudan, the trauma he experienced, and his status in the United States are not uncommon for refugees. In many respects, his arrival in this country is similar to that of immigrants discussed in the previous chapter. What characterizes the life experience of many refugees, however, is their premigration trauma, often life threatening in nature. Posttraumatic Stress (PTSD) and Anxiety Disorders occur with high frequency in this population. Further, the impact of trauma is likely to be exacerbated by the challenges of adjustment to a new world. In this chapter, we choose to focus on a few of the major hurdles encountered by refugees—effects of severe trauma, cultural differences, and linguistic problems.

Between 1987 and the year 2000, the United States admitted about 460,000 refugees. As opposed to immigrants who voluntary left their country of origin, refugees fled their country because of persecution (Chung & Bemak, 2007). An annual ceiling and a predetermined allotment for specific geographical locations limit the number of refugees accepted by the U.S. government; both of these limits sometimes change from year to year (Rytina, 2005). The admission ceiling for refugees has declined steadily in the past 26 years. During 2005, over 53,813 refugees from Somalia, Laos, Cuba, Russia, Liberia, Ukraine, Sudan, Vietnam, Iran, and Ethiopia were admitted to the United States. In addition, over 25,000 individuals (including their immediate family members) were granted *asylum* to the United States in 2005. Asylees are individuals who meet the criteria for refugee status and who are physically present in the United States or at a point of entry when granted permission to reside in the United States. The countries recently contributing the greatest number to this group are China, Columbia, Haiti, and Venezuela (Batalova, 2006). Similar to many refugees, asylum seekers have been uprooted from their countries of origin, often after suffering years of persecution or torture directed toward themselves and toward family, friends, or even their entire community.

Special Problems Involving Refugees

Refugees are individuals who flee their country of origin in order to escape persecution due to race, religion, nationality, political opinion, or membership in a particular social group (Chung & Bemak, 2007). Some of the problems faced by refugees are similar to those found with other immigrants. However, differences exist. In general, refugees are under more stress than immigrants are. As Bemak, Chung, and Bornemann (1996) point out, immigrants are individuals who have had time to prepare for their move to the United States. With refugees, the escape is often sudden and traumatic. Disruptions in families often occur, with some family members left behind. Refugees often spend years in resettlement camps and may be resettled in any country willing to accept them. Refugees have been exposed to more traumas, although undocumented immigrants are also subject to robbery, beating, and sexual assaults.

For example, Central American refugees from El Salvador, Guatemala, Nicaragua, and Honduras related violent experiences such as witnessing beatings and killings, fearing for their own lives or that of family members, being injured, or being a victim of sexual assault. These Central American refugees tended to show high levels of mistrust to service providers and reported feelings of isolation (Asner-Self & Marotta, 2005). Similarly, Bosnia refugees suffer from Anxiety Disorders such as PTSD and depression related to the destruction of their family and social networks due to genocide. Most report that memories of the war intrude into their daily lives. Being displaced from their country of origin, Bosnian family members express concern about adapting to a new culture and country.

Losing their cultural identity is also a worry. Refugees want their children to learn their native language and to maintain family and cultural traditions, even simple ones such as the ritual of drinking coffee together. The Americanization of children is of special concern to Bosnian parents, given the U.S. societal emphasis on openness and individuality. Bosnian parents may worry about the academic and social adjustment of their children and what they perceive to be a lack of discipline in American society. Lacking a support or community group, many Bosnians feel estranged and isolated. Because of the need to work, many have low-wage jobs that prevent them from monitoring their children (Weine et al., 2006). In order to have a strong therapeutic relationship with traumatized refugees, it is especially important to establish trust and to recognize that the disclosure of traumatic experiences may take time.

Some 1.5 million refugees from Southeast Asia have arrived in the United States since 1975. The majority are Vietnamese, Cambodian, Khmer, and Laotian (Chung et al., 1997). The vast majority of Vietnamese, who left just before the fall of Saigon in 1975, had only a few days to decide whether to leave their country. Southeast Asian refugees often have had to wait in camps for years before immigrating to countries such as the United States, Australia, and France. Many Cambodians have experiences with death by starvation in their immediate family or conflict with the Vietcong (L.-R. L. Cheung, 1987). Refugees often face culture shock when exposed to Western society. Many report feelings of homesickness and concerns over the breakup of family and community ties. There are often worries about the future, difficulties communicating in English, and unemployment. Refugees and their family members have high rates of PTSD and depression (Chun, Eastman, Wang, & Sue, 1998).

Considerations in Work with Refugees

Trauma, loss, and feelings of displacement are very great among refugees. Before proceeding with our analysis, however, it is important to note that the vast majority of refugees are able to make a healthy transition to life in the United States. Burnett and Thompson (2005) developed an outline of important considerations when working with refugees that we believe can also be helpful for all immigrants. This section deals with adjustment problems and issues for those seeking therapy and treatment.

Effects of Past Persecution, Torture, or Trauma

The premigration experiences of many refugees are often filled with the atrocities of war, torture and killings, sexual assaults, incarcerations, and a continuing threat of death. To see loved ones raped, beaten, and killed may have lasting, long-term consequences. Studies reveal that refugees are more at risk for mental health problems that involve Posttraumatic Stress Disorders (PTSD), depression, and anxiety (Bemak & Chung, 2002). Refugees often report PTSD symptoms such as nightmares, dissociation, intrusive thoughts, and hyper vigilance (Chung & Bemak, 2007). Because of this, it may be difficult to relate these experiences to a therapist. Women may be even more affected if they have been sexually abused or assaulted. In some countries, sexually assaulted women are shunned and considered unfit to marry.

Implications. Because there may be a lack of understanding regarding PTSD symptoms, therapists should help victims understand why they occur. In doing so, the symptoms can be normalized as reactions to trauma that anyone in their situation would develop.

- Therapists can give reassurance that the symptoms can be treated and they are not signs that they are "going crazy."
- There may be a hesitation to relay experiences of torture because of fear or feelings of shame and humiliation.
- Clients should be allowed to go at their own pace in bringing up these experiences.
- Questions related to exposure to weapons, violence, or other stressful incidents might allow for greater comfort in revealing traumatic experiences (Asner-Self and Marotta, 2005).

Culture and Health

It is important to consider the culture perspective of immigrants and refugees regarding mental and physical disorders to determine how their views might be different from the dominant culture. Many immigrants take a somatic view of psychological disorders, that is, that mental disorders are the result of physical problems. If this belief is expressed, the therapist should first work with the somatic complaints.

Implications. Intake assessments should include questions that identify the impact of cultural beliefs on both the cause of problems and appropriate treatment.

The following questions are suggested by Dowdy (2000):

- *"What do you think is causing your problem?"* This helps to understand the client's perception of the factors involved.
- *"Why is this happening to you?"* This question taps into the issue of causality and possible spiritual or cultural explanations of the problem. If this does not elicit a direct answer, you can then inquire, *"What does your mother (husband, family members, or friends) believe is happening to you?"*
- *"What have you done to treat this condition?"* *"Where else have you sought treatment?"* These questions explore previous interventions and the possible use of home remedies.

- *"How has this condition affected your life?"* This question helps identify health and social issues related to the concern.
- *"How can I help you?"* This addresses the reason for the visit and expectations of therapy from the client.

Safety Issues and Coping with Loss

Refugees often come from politically unstable situations. In these cases, issues of safety are salient and must be addressed. Some clients may have faced the adversarial experience of having to prove that they were persecuted before being allowed into the United States. Because of this, there may be problems relating experiences for fear of being disbelieved. The loss of friends, family, and status is very troubling to immigrants and refugees. Refugees often feel guilty about leaving other family members behind and may go through a bereavement process. Many will not be able to resume their previous level of occupational and social functioning. It is important to identify their perception about what is lost.

Implications. Refugees and immigrants may be suspicious about revealing personal information and whether or not the information will be given to the government.

- Confidentiality and the reason for the assessments should be carefully discussed. Since problem behaviors or mental difficulties may be seen as a source of shame for the individual and their entire family, knowing that the information obtained will be confidential will offer some relief.
- Acknowledge the difficulty involved in sharing private information but indicate that it is necessary in order to develop the best solutions. To determine the possibility that cultural constraints exist, the counselor might also state something like the following: "Sometimes people in counseling believe that family issues should stay in the family. How do you feel about this belief?"
- Through their experience with governmental powers in the homelands, refugees may also be concerned about providing information, or may be very wary of how information will be used. Reassurance needs to be given.
- To understand the loss experienced by refugees, it may be beneficial to obtain a migration narrative as part of the assessment. This provides an understanding of the individual's social and occupational life prior to leaving their country of origin.
- Obtain information regarding their family life, friends, and activities by asking questions such as: "How would you describe your daily life in

your country of origin? What did you like and dislike about your country? What was family life like? What kind of job, or family roles did you have? What was your community like? How did you decide to immigrate or to flee your country?" With Hispanics, inquire about their transit from Mexico, Central America, or the Caribbean, and any traumas associated with this process. "What happened before, during, and after the immigration or refugee experience? What differences do you see between living in your country and living in America? What do you see as advantages and disadvantages of living in either country?"

- Inquire about their experience with resettlement camps. If family members were separated, find out who left first and who was left behind. Also, inquire about their experiences with prejudice and discrimination. This process gives a clearer picture of the perceived losses and experiences of refugees (Weisman et al., 2005).

Gender Issues and Domestic Violence

Male immigrants often face the loss of status and develop a sense of powerlessness. They have lost their assigned roles within the family and society as a whole and are often unemployed or underemployed. Because women may find it easier to gain employment, the resulting change in the balance of power increases the risk of domestic violence as men attempt to reestablish their authority and power. Domestic violence is also a characteristic of PTSD. Among many refugee groups, women are socialized to sacrifice their own personal needs for the good of their husbands and children. Such training leads to ignoring or denying their own pains or symptoms so that their family needs are taken care of (Ro, 2002). Fear of reporting partner abuse is made more difficult because of economic dependence or fear of retaliation(Quiroga & Flores-Ortiz, 2000).

Implications. As with other cases involving family violence, the following steps are recommended (Lum, 1999).

- Assess the lethality of the situation. If there is a high degree of danger, develop a safety plan. The woman should know where she and her children can stay if she needs to leave home. The therapist should help identify shelters or other resources available for the particular immigrant group to which the woman belongs.
- If the degree of violence is nonlethal and the woman does not want to leave the home, provide psychoeducational information on abusive relationships, the cycle of violence, and legal recourse. Give crisis numbers or other contact information to use if the violence escalates.

- Convey an understanding of the both the cultural and situational obstacles the client faces. Forming a strong therapeutic relationship is especially important if no support is available from other family members or friends. In congruence with cultural perspectives, the woman's role may be defined as the one who protects and cares for everyone's welfare.

- Attempt to expand support systems for the client, especially within the client's community. Support groups and services are now available for a number of different immigrant groups.

Linguistic and Communication Issues

The use of interpreters is often necessary in order to adequately assess client needs, explain clinic policy, and establish rapport with refugees who are not conversant in English. However, many therapists and interpreters are not aware of the dynamics involved or the impact on the traditional dyadic therapeutic relationship when adding another individual. Mental health professionals need to know some of these issues when using interpreters. Most interpreters receive little or no training in working with traumatized refugees, and they often experience uncontrollable feelings of emotional distress when hearing traumatic stories because they came from backgrounds similar to those of the clients (Miller, 2005).

In other words, the revelations sometimes produced a "re-experiencing of their own trauma," resulting in a tendency to disengage emotionally. For example, one interpreter, herself a refugee from Bosnia, discovered that in order to protect herself from distressing feelings as she was interpreting for Bosnian refugee clients, she became dismissive and casual when describing the violent events brought up by the clients. In another case, a therapist observed, "I had one interpreter start shaking. It was too much for her. The client had been raped, and it was a woman interpreter and a woman client . . . she just became incredibly upset and angry" (Miller et al., 2005, p. 34). Talking with the therapist after a difficult session, learning to tolerate distress, engaging in other activities, and reaching out to family and friends mitigated their feelings of distress.

Therapists also reported that they developed reactions to the interpreters. Some initially thought of the interpreters as a "black box" or a "translation machine" or an "unfortunate necessity" whose interpersonal qualities were unimportant. As time went on, however, therapists realized that interpreters form part of a three-person alliance. Often clients initially developed a stronger attachment to the interpreter than to the therapist. Because of this, the therapists needed to deal with feelings of "being left out" and to accept that their relationships with clients might develop in a slower fashion. Therapists also began to use the interpreters as additional resources by obtaining the interpreter's thoughts regarding issues discussed in sessions and responding to them as cultural consultants. In general, therapists were highly appreciative of interpreters and did not perceive any long-term negative impact on the therapy process or progress. Some even mentioned that the presence of an interpreter mitigated the intensity of the emotional impact of hearing such traumatic stories. Several infrequent problems did exist, however. In some cases, therapists believed interpreters were interjecting their own opinions or intervening directly with client. In other situations, interpreters questioned the interventions of the therapist— apparently because they did not understand the therapeutic approach.

Implications. These results indicate the necessity of specific training in the best practices for both therapists and interpreters.

- Interpreters should receive brief training regarding specific mental disorders and the interventions employed in therapy, specifically regarding the treatment of trauma, grief, and loss.
- Because interpreters are affected emotionally by refugee experiences, therapists should discuss self-care strategies for the interpreters, as well as ways of dealing with exposure to traumatic reports.
- The refugees clearly did not regard the interpreter merely as a translation machine. Because of this, interpreters should be selected or trained in the relationship skills that are needed in therapy. In the triadic relationship, interpersonal skills such as empathy and congruence are necessary.
- Therapists should also receive training on how to work effectively with interpreters and become conversant with different models of interpreting. Some prefer simultaneous translation, while others prefer delayed translation.

Therapists should also be aware that, in many cases, the therapeutic alliance may form first with the interpreter. Many therapists who have worked with interpreters understand that, for non-English speaking clients, interpreters are the bridge between the therapist and client and are critical in assessment and the provision of therapy.

Implications for Clinical Practice

1. Be aware that the client may have day-to-day stressors such as limited resources, a need for permanent shelter, lack of employment, or frus-

trating interactions with agencies. Allow time to understand and provide support related to these immediate needs, or help the client locate resources related to specific needs.

2. Be knowledgeable and conversant with the refugee groups you work with, their premigration traumas, and psychological strategies used to cope with stress.

3. Understand symptom manifestations likely to indicate posttraumatic stress, and other mental disorders that may arise from experiences of war, imprisonment, persecution, rape, and torture.

4. Allow time for clients to share their backgrounds, their premigration stories, and changes in their lives since immigrating.

5. Inquire about client beliefs regarding the cause of their difficulties, listening for sociopolitical, cultural, religious, or spiritual interpretations.

6. Carefully explain the therapeutic approach that will be used, why that approach was selected, and how it will help the client make desired changes.

Counseling and Therapy with Other Multicultural Populations

Counseling Sexual Minorities

23

Chapter

Pentagon guidelines that classify homosexuality as a mental disorder have been changed because of concerns expressed by mental health professionals. Pentagon officials removed it from this category and placed it with conditions such as bed-wetting, stammering or stuttering, sleepwalking, and insect venom allergies. (Baldor, 2006)

Jacob Williams, a preschool student, was playing when a little girl who had been observing him asked where his dad was. Jacob responded by saying he didn't have a father but had two moms. The little girl was confused but later walked up to one of the two mothers and said she had "figured it out." She had two granddads, so Jacob could have two moms. (Wingert & Kantrowitz, 2000)

"Transgendered people are the second-class citizens, and bisexuals are below even them. We're the white trash of the gay world, a group whom it is socially acceptable not to accept. Feeling awkward among straights is what it feels like to be bi. Being distrusted among gays is what it feels like too." (Pajor, 2005, p. 575)

Homosexuality involves the affectional and/or sexual orientation to a person of the same sex. In self-definitions, most males prefer the term *gay men* to homosexual, and most females prefer the term *lesbian*. It is difficult to get an accurate estimate on the number of gay, lesbian, and bisexual individuals in the United States. It is estimated that approximately 4 to 10 percent of the U.S. population is homosexual (J. L. Norton, 1995). The Williams Institute (2006) took data from U.S. Census Bureau (2001) and other government statistics to estimate that the percentage of individuals identifying themselves as gay men, lesbian, or bisexual were the highest in the following cities: San Francisco (15.4 percent), Seattle (12.9 percent), Atlanta (12.8 percent), Minneapolis (12.5 percent), Boston (12.3 percent), Oakland (12.1 percent), Sacramento (9.8 percent), Portland, Ore (8.8 percent), Denver, (8.2

percent), and Long Beach (8.l percent). Approximately 7 percent of a national sample of 6,254 boys and 5,686 girls reported having a same-sex attraction or relationship (Russell & Joyner, 2001). Transgender individuals include transsexuals and others who cross-dress for a variety of reasons.

The mood of the country seems to exhibit contradictory attitudes and actions toward sexual minorities. In some cases, there appears to be a greater acceptance of gay, lesbian, bisexual, or transgendered (GLBT) individuals and their lifestyles. Younger Americans appear to be more accepting: 41 percent of those between the ages of 18 and 29 support same sex marriage, as opposed to 28 percent of Americans overall (Rosenberg, 2004). Even with progress occurring on these fronts, however, discrimination and violence against these populations remain high.

Positive developments include the following:

- In a survey of the U.S. public (American Enterprise Institute, 2004), a large majority supported job protection, antidiscrimination in housing, and health benefits for gays and lesbians.

- The Washington Supreme Court held that gays may be entitled to the estates of partners who have died, even without a will. The unanimous decision overturned a lower court that had ruled the claim invalid because same-sex marriage is illegal in Washington (Skolnik, 2001).

- New York City is making it easier for transgendered individuals to switch the gender listed on their birth certificates, even without undergoing sex-change operations (Caruso, 2006)

- The city of San Francisco decided in February, 2001, to expand health care benefits to include psychotherapy, medical treatment, and surgery for sex-conversion operations for transgendered city employees.

Examples of continuing prejudice include the following:

- Currently, only six states are without a same-sex marriage ban; however, with the exception of Massachusetts, officials of these states do not issue licenses to same-sex couples (Peterson, 2006).

- Efforts to ban gay men and lesbians from adopting children have emerged as part of the culture war that began during the 2004 elections and the rejection of same-sex marriage. In at least 16 states there are attempts to pass laws against adoption by gay men and lesbians (Stone, 2006).

- According to the Department of Justice (2006), there were 1,197 incidents of crimes committed against individuals of different sexual orientations in 2004. The vast majority were directed against gay men.

Same-Sex Relationships Are Not Signs of Mental Disorders

Although the American Psychiatric Association and the American Psychological Association no longer consider homosexuality to be a mental disorder, some individuals still harbor this belief. Trent Lott, the Senate Republican whip, described homosexuality as a disorder akin to alcoholism, kleptomania, and sexual addiction—a condition that should be treated. The American Psychiatric Association first voted in 1973 to remove homosexuality from the *Diagnostic and Statistical Manual of Mental Disorders (DSM)*. However, it did create a new category, ego-dystonic homosexuality, in the third edition of the *DSM* (American Psychiatric Association, 1980) for individuals with (1) "a lack of heterosexual arousal that interferes with heterosexual relationships" and (2) "persistent distress from unwanted homosexual arousal." This category was eliminated in the face of argument that it is societal pressure and prejudice that create the distress.

The American Psychological Association took an even stronger stand and adopted a official policy statement that "homosexuality per se implies no impairment in judgment, stability, reliability, or general social or vocational capabilities" and indicated that mental health professionals should take the lead in removing the stigma of mental illness that has long been associated with homosexual orientations (Conger, 1975). A number of studies (Berube, 1990; Gonsiorek, 1982; Hooker, 1957; Reiss, 1980) have demonstrated few adjustment differences between individuals with a homosexual or heterosexual orientation. As one researcher concluded, "Homosexuality in and of itself is unrelated to psychological disturbance or maladjustment. Homosexuals, as a group, are not more psychologically disturbed on account of their homosexuality" (Gonsiorek, 1982, p. 74). However, exposure to societal discrimination may be responsible for the recent findings that lesbian and gay youth report elevated rates of Major Depression, Generalized Anxiety Disorder, and substance abuse (Rienzo, Button, Sheu & Li, 2006). Gay men also reported high rates of major depression. Lesbians appear to fare better and reported mental health equal to that of their heterosexual counterparts (DeAngelis, 2002). Individuals who are gay, lesbian, bisexual or transgendered are at higher risk for substance- and alcohol-related problems (Cochran, Keenan, Schober, & Mays, 2000; Kennedy, 2005). Compared to heterosexuals, GLBT individuals are more likely to have been abused as children and adults. Sexual assaults in adulthood were reported by 11.6 percent of gay men, 13.2 percent of bisexual men, and 1.6 percent of heterosexual men. Among women, the rates of sexual assault were 15.5 percent of lesbians, 16.9 percent of bisexual women, and 7.5 percent of heterosexual women (Balsam, Rothblum & Beauchaine, 2005). Gender identity issues and cross-dressing can be characterized as mental disorders according to the mental health organizations. However, transgender individuals are hoping that they can follow the success and path taken by the gay liberation movement and eliminate the classification as a mental disorder.

A number of research studies reveal that bias continues to exist among mental health professionals. In one study, 97 counselors read a fictitious intake report about a bisexual woman seeking counseling with no indication that the problem involved her sexual orientation. The problems involved career choice, issues with parents over independence, ending a two-year relationship with another woman, and problems with her boyfriend. Thus, issues involved were boundaries with parents, career choice, and romantic relationships. Counselors with the most negative attitude regarding bisexuality believed that the problems stemmed from her sexual orientation and rated her lower in psychosocial functioning (Mohr, Israel, & Sedlacek, 2001).

Garnets, Hancock, Cochran, Goodchilds, and Peplau (1998) conducted a survey of biased or beneficial responses that therapists heard of or knew of from other therapists or clients in counseling. The following biased or inappropriate practices were reported:

1. Believing that homosexuality is a form of mental illness. Some therapists continue to believe that homosexuality represents a personality disorder or other mental disturbance and is not just a different lifestyle.

2. Failing to understand that a client's problem, such as depression or low self-esteem, can be a result of the internalization of society's view of homosexuality.

3. Assuming that the client is heterosexual, thereby making it harder to bring up issues regarding sexual orientation.

4. Focusing on sexual orientation when it is not relevant. Problems may be completely unrelated to sexual orientation, but some therapists continue to focus on it as the major contributor to all presented problems.

5. Attempting to have clients renounce or change their sexual orientation. For example, a lesbian was asked by the therapist to date men.

6. Trivializing or demeaning homosexuality. A therapist responded to a lesbian who brought up that she was "into women" that he didn't care, since he had a client who was "into dogs."

7. Lacking an understanding of identity development in lesbian women and gay men, or viewing homosexuality solely as sexual activity.

8. Not understanding the impact of possible internalized negative societal pressures or homophobia on identity development.

9. Underestimating the consequences of "coming out" for the client. Such suggestion should be provided only after a careful discussion of the pros and cons of this disclosure.

10. Misunderstanding or underestimating the importance of intimate relationships for gay men and lesbians. One therapist reportedly advised a

lesbian couple who were having problems in their relationship to not consider it a permanent relationship and consider going to a gay bar to meet others.

11. Using the heterosexual framework inappropriately when working with lesbian and gay male relationships. One couple was given a book to read dealing with heterosexual relationships.

12. Presuming that clients with a different sexual orientation cannot be good parents and automatically assuming that their children's problems are a result of the orientation.

Implications. Although mental health organizations have acknowledged that homosexuality is not a mental disorder, it is recognized that a "need for better education and training of mental health practitioners" exists (Division 44/Committee on Lesbian, Gay, and Bisexual Concerns Joint Task Force, 2000). Heterosexist bias in therapy needs to be acknowledged and changed. Curriculum changes and the infusion of information about gay and lesbian concerns and lifestyles are receiving more emphasis in mental health programs. Some of these changes may be having an effect. In a recent survey of psychologists, 92.4 percent viewed the GLBT lifestyle and identity as "acceptable" and 58 percent had a gay-affirmatic approach to therapy (Kilgore, Sideman, Amin, Baca, & Bohanske, 2005). Research on GLBT populations has focused on a "sickness" model and can be characterized as victim blaming (Martin & Knox, 2000). We also need to address the positive characteristics and relationships found in these groups.

Many still consider the departure from heterosexual norms as repugnant or a sign of psychological maladjustment. We have to examine possible stereotypes that we have of GLBT clients. Certain changes in the provision of mental health services have been found to be helpful. GLBT perceived counselors more positively, indicated a greater willingness to disclose personal information, and reported greater comfort in disclosing sexual orientation when a counseling interview was free of heterosexist language (e.g., using the term partner or spouse instead of boyfriend or girlfriend, husband and wife; Dorland & Fischer, 2001). Workshops and training in the use of nondiscriminatory intake forms and identifying psychological and health issues faced by many GLBT clients are helpful means of increasing the effectiveness of health care providers (Blake, Ledsky, Lehman, & Goodenow, 2001).

GLBT Couples and Families

About 1.2 million people are part of gay and lesbian couples in the United States, representing a 300 percent increase since 1990. There are about as many lesbian as gay male couples (Cohn, 2001). Many face the frustration of not being able to get married, although the public supports other rights for them. Denise Penn, a bisexual, feels this contradiction. While her neighbors are quite accepting of her partners or friends of either sex, she felt shaken over the battle on Proposition 22, which banned gay marriage. Her "accepting" neighbors displayed signs reading "PROTECT MARRIAGE" (Leland, 2000).

The intimate relationships of gay and lesbian couples appear to be similar to those of heterosexual individuals. However, among lesbian couples there is a more egalitarian relationship. Household chores and decision making are equally shared. Also, many GLBT couples and individuals are showing increasing interest in becoming parents. However, the ability of gays and lesbians to adopt children is being challenged in many states (Stone, 2006). In fact, Catholic services has decided to stop providing adoption services in Massachusets because the state allows gay men and lesbian women to adopt children (LeBlanc, 2006). Children of GLBT couples show healthy cognitive and behavioral functioning. It has been concluded that heterosexual family structures are not necessary for healthy child development. Children raised by gay men and lesbian women are as mentally healthy as children with heterosexual parents. They do not display problems with sexual identity, school or social adjustment, nor are they any more likely to display a same-sex sexual orientation (Dingfelder, 2005a).

Implications. Along with problems that are faced by heterosexual couples and families, GLBT individuals also face prejudice and discrimination from society. In relationships, each may differ in internalized homophobia or the extent to which they are "out" to others in their social, work, or family networks. They may be uncomfortable showing public displays of affection or feel the need to hide their sexual orientation (Blando, 2001). In evaluating GLBT parents or determining their suitability as adoptive parents, mental health professionals should determine their attitudes and beliefs regarding GLBT individuals. The empirical data indicates that GLBT parenting styles and child-rearing practices do not differ from that of their heterosexual counterparts. One concern commonly expressed has been the impact of GLBT parenting on the sexual orientation of the children. Research shows that children raised by gay and lesbian parents do not have problems with gender identity, gender role behavior, sexual orientation, or sexual adjustment (Crawford, McLeod, Zamboni, & Jordan, 1999). Problems faced by gay and lesbian couples may include legal issues with adoption, medical benefits for same-sex couples, and prejudice. In addition to normal developmental issues, children of GLBT parents may face having to explain to peers or classmates their nontraditional family with two dads, two moms, or dads dressed as women. Family and parenting resources available for both therapists and gay and lesbian parents include *Social Services for Gay and Lesbian Couples* by Kurdek (1994), *Lesbians and Gays in Couples and Families* by Laird and Green

(1996), *Lesbian Step Families* by Wright (1998), and *Out of the Ordinary: Essays on Growing Up with Gay, Lesbian, and Transgender Parents* (Howey & Samuels, 2000).

GLBT Youth

As compared to heterosexual adolescents, GLBT youth report more substance use, high-risk sexual behaviors, suicidal thoughts or attempts, and personal safety issues (Blake et al., 2001; R. Lee, 2000; Rienzo et al., 2006). They are more likely to have been involved in a fight that needed medical attention (Russell, Franz, & Driscoll, 2001). Gay and lesbian youths face discrimination and harassment in schools. In a study of Massachusetts high school students, gay, lesbian, and bisexual students were more likely than their peers to be confronted with a weapon at school (32.7 vs. 7.1 percent) or not attend school because of safety concerns (25.1 vs. 5.1 percent). In addition, they were more likely to have attempted suicide during the past year than were their heterosexual-identified counterparts. The suicide rate does not appear to be because of their sexual orientation but because their school, home, and social environments have been compromised (Russell & Joyner, 2001). However, recent studies show little difference in suicide rates between GLBT and heterosexual youth (DeAngelis, 2002). The murder of Brandon Teena, who was the inspiration for the movie *Boys Don't Cry*, illustrates the problems faced by transgender youth.

Implications. Mental health professionals need to address the problems of GLBT youth at both the systems and individual levels. To improve the school environment, inclusion of gay and transgender issues in the curriculum, addressing self-management and social skills relevant to GLBT youth, provision of adequate social services, and a nondiscriminatory school environment can be advocated. Although most schools have policies which prohibit antigay discrimination or harassment, only 30 percent offer any education regarding sexual orientation and less than 30 percent of school districts provide training for teachers and staff regarding sexual orientation issues (Rienzo et al., 2006). It is important to have policies that protect GLBT youth from harassment and violence. School staff should be trained on sexual orientation issues. Support groups for GLBT and heterosexual students to discuss GLBT issues in a safe and confidential environment are also important. Counseling services should be provided for GLBT students and family members (Blake et al., 2001). GLBT youth need safe places to meet others and to socialize. Community-based supports involving hotlines and youth clubs can be helpful. Such organizations defuse possible harassment and violence in school and allow gay students to gain support and create openly gay lives (Peyser & Lorch, 2000). A useful resource for both the counselor and GLBT youth is

Queer Kids: The Challenge and Promise for Lesbian, Gay, and Bisexual Youth by Owens (1998). The book discusses how children and adolescents cope with emerging sexual orientation. In individual counseling sessions, assess for substance use, suicidality, social support, and self-esteem issues. Appropriate coping skills and support groups can be identified and strengthened.

Identity Issues

The slow discovery of being different is agonizing. As one individual observed, *"Imagine learning about love and sexuality in a heterosexual world when your preference is for people of the same gender"* (Parker & Thompson, 1990). Awareness of sexual orientation for gay males and lesbians tends to occur in the early teens, with sexual self-identification during the mid-teens, same-sex experience in the mid-teens, and same-sex relationships in the late teens (Blake et al., 2001). In a study of 156 gay, lesbian, and bisexual youth, 57 percent consistently self-identified as gay/lesbian, 18 percent of bisexuals transitioned to gay/lesbian, and 15 percent consistently identified as bisexual. Female youth were more consistent with their identity than males. Bisexual youth displayed more cognitive dissonance related to sexual orientation than did consistently gay and lesbian youth (Rosario, Schrimshaw, Hunter, & Braun, 2006). The struggle for identity involves one's internal perceptions, in contrast to the external perceptions or assumptions of others about one's sexual orientation. The individual must learn to accept his or her internal identity, often struggling with the society's definition of what is healthy. To come to an appropriate resolution, the individual ceases struggling to be "straight" and begins to establish a new identity, self-concept, and understanding of what constitutes a good life. Often during this period, individuals must deal with issues of grief over letting go of the old identity (Browning, Reynolds, & Dworkin, 1998; Parker & Thompson, 1990). Individuals with gender identity issues also report feeling "different" at an early age. One activist described gender dysphoria as "one of the greatest agonies ... when your anatomy doesn't match who you are inside" (Wright, 2001). Cross-sex behaviors and appearance are highly stigmatized in school and society.

Implications. Adolescence is a time of exploration and experimentation. Heterosexual activity does not mean one is a heterosexual, nor does same sex activity indicate homosexuality. Many GLBT youth describe feeling "different" from early childhood. When their sexual identity is acknowledged, they must deal with a stigmatized identity. Many feel alone and isolated, having no one to talk to. They feel emotionally disconnected to others since the discovery of their secret may lead to rejection. Accurate information about homosexuality is lacking (Ryan & Futterman, 2001b). Many pretend to be straight or avoid discussing sexuality. Because of this they lack the ability to obtain support and nurturance from parents, families, or peer groups. The mental health professional must help GLBT youth develop coping and survival skills and to expand environmental supports. Several online resources exist: American Psychological Association (APA), http://www.apa.org; Gay, Lesbian, and Straight Education Network (GLSEN), http://www.glsen.org; Parents, Family, and Friends of Lesbians and Gays (PFLAG), http://www.pflag.org; and Youth Resource, http://www.youthresource.com. These provide accurate information and resources for GLBT youth. If you work in schools, indicate availability by displaying posters supporting diversity, including sexual orientation.

Coming Out

The decision to *come out* is extremely difficult and is often influenced by the overwhelming sense of isolation the individual feels. In maintaining the secret, relationships with friends and family may be seriously affected. Coming out to parents and friends can lead to rejection, anger, and grief. This is especially difficult for adolescents who are emotionally and financially dependent on their family. About two-thirds of youth come out to their mothers, about one-third to their fathers, and 42 percent come out to both parents (Savin-Williams, 2001). Parents may feel a loss for their children in terms of the picture that society has painted of appropriate relationships. They may worry that their parenting was the cause of the sexual orientation (Shannon & Woods, 1998). Coming out may be even more difficult for ethnic minorities. Lindsey (2005), who is an African American, was asked to write a chapter on sexual diversity for the 2005 edition of *Our Bodies, Ourselves*. She notes, "In the mainsteam media, both gay and straight, coming out is portrayed in an extremely idealized and simplistic way. The gay person, always white and middle class, decides he or she is gay, tells familes and friends, might experience a little homophobia . . . and ends up marching proudly down the main thoroughfare of a progressive major metropolitan area . . ." (p. 186). The experience for people of color is often different when individuals coming out must face both rejection from their communities and racism from the majority culture. Among the working poor, it also means the possibility of losing their jobs. Black and Latino gay and lesbian youth are more reluctant to disclose their sexual orientation than are their White counterparts (Rosario, Schrimshaw & Hunter, 2004).

Implications. The decision of when to come out should be carefully considered. To whom does the individual want to reveal the information? What are the possible effects and consequences of the self-disclosure for the individual and the recipient of the information? What new sources of support among family, friends, or community are available for them? If the individual is already in a relationship, how will the disclosure affect his or her partner? Have they also considered the consequences? In many cases, it may be best not to tell. If the individual has considered the implications of coming out and still desires to do so, the counselor should offer specific help and preparation in determining how this should be accomplished. Role-plays and the discussion of possible reactions should be practiced. If parents were open, counseling sessions would be helpful for them to obtain accurate information. Many parents will also have to deal with grief (past goals for their children, weddings, and grandchildren) and guilt issues (whether their parenting was responsible). They will have to deal with the societal stigma of having a homosexual family member and may benefit from receiving information and education regarding myths and stereotypes of homosexuality. If the parents are rejecting, the individual must strengthen other sources of social support. Also, the mental health professional should help the client identify the external sources for their issues over identity, rather than allow self-blame to occur. Issues for ethnic minorities may be more complex since they may also involve cultural and class variables.

Aging

> *The two older women often sit next to each other in identical recliners. . . . Evenings they hold hands under a blanket on the sofa watching TV. . . . They've been partners for 18 years. More than anything, they want to stay together in old age. (King, 2001, p. B1)*

The two women—Selma Kannel, 75, and Nancy King, 67—are worried about their remaining years. If one needs to go to a nursing home, will the partner be allowed to make health care decisions for the other, and will people respond to their relationship negatively? It is estimated that up to 3 million GLBT individuals in the United States are over the age of 65 (King, 2001). The elderly gay are less likely to have revealed their sexual orientations to others when compared to the younger generations (Donahue & McDonald, 2005). If still in the closet, the individual may be hesitant to reveal his or her sexual orientation and attempt to hide it when dealing with health or government agencies. One man accompanied his partner, who was dying of cancer, to see the surgeon. Initially the physician was surprised to see the male patient accompanied by a man and became hostile, but he later talked to him as if he were the next of kin (King, 2001). In addition, as with other segments of U.S. society, ageism exists in gay and lesbian communities. All of these can produce a great deal of concern among the GLBT elderly in obtaining health care and responding to a diminishing social support system.

Implications. With GLBT elderly, issues of coming out may have to be addressed as need for health care or social services increases. The mental health counselor can assist them in developing additional coping skills, expand their social support system, and advocate or help locate services for the elderly gay. Advocacy groups exist for older gay men and lesbians, and their number is increasing. One organization, Senior Action in a Gay Environment (SAGE), provides counseling, educational and recreational activities, and discussion groups for older GLBT individuals. The Gay and Lesbian Association of Retiring Persons (GLARP) develops and operates retirement communities for GLBT individuals and provides them with support and education on aging (Donahue & McDonald, 2005). In addition, teleconferences exist for homebound seniors. For example, the Friend and Visitor's Program that connects volunteers with elderly GLBT individuals. In Seattle, the Rainbow Train gives caregivers and medical practitioners the skills they need for working with older GLBT patients. Communities geared toward retired gay and lesbian residents have been developed. Many organizations have added the transgender community to their mission statements. The mental health professional needs to be aware of these resources and advocate changes in laws regarding GLBT partners' rights to participate in health care decision.

Implications for Clinical Practice

1. Examine your own views regarding heterosexuality and determine their impact on work with GLBT clients. A way to personalize this perspective is to assume that some of your family, friends, or coworkers may be GLBT.

2. Read the "Guidelines for Psychotherapy with Lesbian, Gay, and Bisexual Clients" (Division 44/Committee on Lesbian, Gay, and Bisexual Concerns, 2000).

3. Develop partnerships, consultation, or collaborative efforts with local and national GLBT organizations.

4. Assure that your intake forms, interview procedures, and language are free of heterosexist bias, and include a question on sexual behavior, attraction, or orientation.

5. Do not assume that the presenting problems are necessarily the result of sexual orientation, but be willing to address possible societal issues and their role in the problems faced by GLBT clients.

6. Remember that common mental health issues may include stress due to prejudice and discrimination; internalized homophobia; the coming out process; a lack of family, peer, school, and community supports; being a victim of assault; suicidal ideation or attempts; and substance abuse.

7. Realize that GLBT couples may have problems similar to those of their heterosexual counterparts, but may also display unique concerns such differences in the degree of comfort with public demonstrations of their relationship or reactions from their family of origin.

8. Assess spiritual and religious needs. Many GLBT individuals have a strong faith in religion but encounter exclusion. Religious support is available. The Fellowship United Methodist Church accepts all types of diversity and is open to a gay congregation.

9. Because many GLBT clients have internalized the societal belief that they cannot have long-lasting relationships, have materials available that portray healthy and satisfying GLBT relationships.

10. Recognize that a large number of GLBT clients have been subject to hate crimes. Depression, anger, Posttraumatic Stress, and self-blame may result. They may believe the attack was deserved and exhibit a low sense of mastery (Herek, Gillis, & Cogan, 1999). These conditions need to be assessed and treated.

11. For clients still dealing with internalized homosexuality, help them establish a new affirming identity. Some deal with possible discrimination by assuming a heterosexual identity and avoiding the issue of sexuality with others, while some are able to reveal their true identity. The consequences of each of these reactions need to be considered both from the individual and environmental perspective.

12. Remember that in group therapy, a GLBT individual may have specific concerns over confidentiality and different life stressors as compared with their heterosexual counterparts. In these situations, a decision has to be made to determine if the group can be restructured to be helpful to GLBT clients.

13. A number of therapeutic strategies can be useful with internalized homophobia, prejudice, and discrimination. They can include identifying and correcting cognitive distortions, coping skills training, assertiveness training, and utilizing social supports.

14. If necessary, take systems-level intervention to schools, employment, and religious organizations. Diversity workshops can help organizations acquire accurate information regarding sexual diversity.

15. Conduct research on the mental health needs of the GLBT communities and the effectiveness of current programs.

Counseling Older Adult Clients

"Are we ready for our bath?" "You want to take your medicine now, don't you?" (Williams, Kemper, & Hummert, 2005, p. 15). Elderspeak such as this refers to the use of patronizing speech similar to baby talk with exaggerated intonation, elevated pitch, and use of childish names such as "honey" and "good girl." Many older adults consider elderspeak demeaning and patronizing. It is important to avoid the use of such communication; simplification of speech or repetition should be employed only in cases indicated by the person's communication level.

For Mrs. B., things got worse before they got better. . . . For a time, she was taking multiple psychoactive medications and her cognitive function deteriorated at a rapid rate. Medication washout was instituted, and her orientation and memory rebounded. A year later, after an intervening small stroke, her memory function is slightly worse, but her mood is brighter, she communicates well. (La Rue & Watson, 1998)

The population of older individuals in the United States is growing. The increase in the number of those aged 65 and over has exceeded the growth rate of the population as a whole. During the past decade the 85-year-old and older group has increased by 38 percent, while those between ages 75 and 84 increased by 23 percent. There are about 35 million people living in the United States who are over 65, and the population is expected to number 70 million by the year 2030 and constitute 20 percent of the population (U.S. Census Bureau, 2006b). Those 85 years and above are the fastest growing segment of the older population, and this trend is expected to continue for many years. Because females live longer than males, at age 65 there are only 39 men for every 100 women.

Older individuals are subject to negative stereotypes and discrimination. Ageism has been defined as negative attitudes toward the process of aging or toward older individuals. Women who are older are even more likely to be viewed negatively by society as a whole and many internalize ageist norms (Hatch, 2005). Our visual entertainment, news, and advertising media are dominated by youth, with few exceptions. Information about older people often comes from youthful interviewers who do not have the appropriate perspective for the experiences of the older generation. One exception is Donald M. Murray, at the age of 81, is a Boston columnist that covers issues of age and emphasizes some of the positive aspects of aging. In a column written in 1998, he extols the virtues of old age:

> *I am not elderly, I am old and proud of it. I am aged, like a good cheese. I am a walking history book, an elder of the tribe, tested, tempered, wise.... I can leave parties early.... I enjoy melancholy, even revel in it. (Cited in Frankel, 1998, p. 16)*

Implications. Ageism influences how both the general public and mental health professionals perceive older persons. In a review of attitudes towards older individuals, Palmore (2005) found that older adults were thought to be rigid and inadaptable in their thought processes, lacking in health, intelligence, and alertness, and as having either no sexual interest or, if they were sexually active, as engaging in an activity inappropriate for their age. Jokes about old age abound and are primarily negative in nature. These negative stereotypes lead to feelings of being less valued members of society. As a result of ageism, older individuals may come to accept these views and suffer a loss of self-esteem. In fact, they also believe that they will suffer mental decline. When a group of older individuals was asked if they felt there was a strong possibility that they would become senile, 90 percent responded affirmatively (Grant, 1996).

Unfortunately, studies have found that mental health professionals also display age bias (Weiss, 2005). As a group they expressed reluctance to work with older adults, perceived them as less interesting, having a poorer prognosis, more set in their ways, and less likely to benefit from mental health services. Mental health problems in older adults are attributed to aging. The view appears to be that mental illness is normal for older clients but abnormal for younger ones (Danzinger & Welfel, 2000). Stereotyping and ageism have limited the access of older adults to needed services. We are an aging society, yet we are poorly prepared to handle our currently aged population and certainly not equipped for the coming baby boomer generation (Palmore, 2005). The elderly population is underserved and little understood. A. U. Kim and Atkinson (1998) noted that few training programs in counseling deal with older populations. Information is lacking on therapies and medications for older individuals. As a group, they are less likely to receive new treatments for heart attacks or other illnesses, and older women are less likely to receive radiation and chemotherapy after breast cancer surgery. This is surprising, since a healthy 70-year-old individual can be expected to live at least 10 years more (People's Medical Society Newsletter, 1998).

There is an increasing need for mental health professionals to work with older Americans. It is important that the necessary education and skills development be obtained from resources such as graduate courses, self-guided study, or continuing education. It is important to be aware of the changes (biological, psychological, and social) that generally accompany aging, as well as the types of psychopathology that are experienced by older adults (Qualls, 1998a).

Problems of Older Adults

Physical and Economic Health

Older adults are more likely than younger populations to suffer from physical impairments such as some degree of hearing or vision loss and cardiovascular diseases. About one-fourth of adults between the ages of 65 and 74 suffer from some hearing impairment, and this is increased to about two out of five for those over the age of 75 (Desselle & Proctor, 2000). Half of older adults have difficulties falling asleep or insomnia (APA, 2001c). The majority of older individuals, however, are quite healthy and able to live independent lives requiring only minimal assistance. Only 5 percent of people 65 and over live in nursing homes; and this total increases to only 22 percent by age 85 (Heller, 1998). Approximately 9 percent of those between the ages of 65 and 69 require personal assistance for daily activities; at the age of 85 and over, about 50 percent require assistance. In all age categories, women are more likely to need assistance than are men (U.S. Census Bureau, 2005a).

Implications. When providing mental health services for older adults, the possibility that physical limitations exist should be considered. Make sure that the environment is receptive for the older client. The room should be adequately lighted and any limiting physical condition identified. Determine the mode of communication that is most comfortable for the individual. If older clients have or have used eyeglasses or hearing aids, make sure they are present in the session. Because co-morbid physical conditions often exist such as cardiovascular disease and hypertension, rule out the possibility that the mental health problem may be a result of multiple medications or their interactions. Side effects are particularly troublesome for the older adults, especially since they have decreased lean muscle mass and total body water, along with a decrease in liver mass. Because of these changes, patients should be on lower dosages of certain drugs such as phenothiazines and bezodiazepines (Masand, 2000). A physician or psychiatrist should have evaluated the individual to determine if the mental symptoms may have physical causes. Also, many of the mental health problems of the older poor and minority adults are due to poverty, unemployment, poor living conditions, discrimination, and the lack of receptivity of health care providers. Case management or advocacy skills may be needed to address these issues.

Mental Health

There is a perception that rates of mental illness are high among older persons. This may be due to observation of mentally ill adults living in nursing homes. In actuality, older individuals have rates of affective disorders lower than that of younger adults, although their rates for anxiety disorders approximate that of the general population (APA Working Group, 1999). Although rates of mental illness appear to be lower among older adults, the rates are higher among those in nursing homes and other kinds of senior housing. Only about 6 percent of older adults are in the community mental health system, which is far below the proportion predicted according to their percentage in the population (Heller, 1998). Part of the problem may be that both the health providers and older individuals conceptualize mental health issues or symptoms as due to physical health or aging, rather than psychological factors (Heller, 1998). The consequences are that older adults are not very likely to be referred for treatment by physicians to mental health professionals.

Mental Deterioration or Incompetence

> *After 49 years of teaching in Whatcom County schools, including the last 26 as a substitute, Mitch Evich has come across all kinds of students. "Recently I've worked in classes that were lovely, you can't beat them," Evich said. "Of course, other classes, I wish I could," he said with a laugh. Evich, now 81, has no immediate plans on ending his substitute teaching career. (Lane, 1998, p. A1)*

A common view of older persons is that they are mentally incompetent. Words such as "senile" reflect this perspective. However, only a minority of older persons have dementia. Most are still mentally sharp and benefit from the store of knowledge that they have acquired over a lifetime. Some 5 to 10 percent of individuals over the age of 65 have mild to moderate dementia; this increases to l5 to 20 percent for those over 75 years of age, and 25 to 50 percent of those over 85 (American Psychiatric Association, 1997; Saunders, 1998). By the year 2040, it is estimated that 7 million people in the United States will have Alzheimer's disease (Freeborne, 2000). Even with cognitive problems, Saunders found that patients with dementia attempt to maintain a sense of competence and dignity. They would blame their confusion on external events, such as being pressured too much. Older persons with dementia can still show varied aspects of themselves. One woman responded to an inability to recall her husband's name humorously, by using a metaphor, stating that her brain was "off key." Another responded to memory problems by joking that "my brain is gone on strike, I think" (Saunders, 1998, p. 67). Despite their memory impairment, older individuals often use humor and demonstrate their competence and verbal sophistication through their use of metaphors.

Implications. Most older adults will show some decline in certain cognitive abilities, which is considered to be part of the normal developmental process. A substantial minority of the very old will show declines that are greater than would be expected, to the point of taking away their ability to communicate or even to recognize loved ones. Alzheimer's disease is the leading cause of progressive dementia. Some older adults show an intermediate cognitive decline beyond those typically associated with normal aging and dementia. This decline may or may not be progressive (APA, Presidential Task Force, 1998). The mental status exam can give some indication of problem areas, but the most frequently used assessment is the Mini-Mental State Examination (MMSE). This test takes about 5 to 10 minutes to administer and has normative and validity data. It is comprised of eleven items and assesses orientation, registration, attention and calculation, recall, language, and visual motor integrity. Early detection allows for treatment and advance planning (wills, estate and other legal matters, and dealing with potential problems such as driving).

Steps in evaluating dementia and other cognitive changes (APA, Presidential Task Force, 1998) include the following:

- Obtain a self-report from the client regarding possible changes in memory or cognitive functions.
- Be aware that reported memory problems, or lack thereof, may be due to lack of awareness or denial.
- Obtain reports from family members and friends on estimations of cognitive performance. Be especially alert to discrepancies.
- Take a careful history of the onset and progression of the cognitive changes.
- Remember to assess for possible side effects of medication or other physical conditions that may be related to cognitive declines.
- Assess for depression since it can also result in dementia-like performance or the over-reporting of cognitive problems. Remember that depression and dementia can also occur together.

Family Intervention

Although dementia has a gradual progression, the effects of this disorder impact both the afflicted individual and family members. Family members often do not understand that patients with dementia may not retain what they are told. They may attempt to offer corrected statements and become frustrated when the individual with the disorder has forgotten it again. Some may believe the behavior is willful or may try to assume responsibility over all behaviors, even when the older person can perform effectively in some areas. Guilt is often expressed through statements such as, "Am I doing the right thing?" (LaRue & Watson, 1998). Another frequent problem is that adult children may infantilize or dominate a parent with a cognitive decline. They assume that their actions are in the best interest of their parent, but fail to take the parent's own preferences or values into consideration. Adult children tend to overemphasize values related to physical or mental health, whereas parents expressed preference for values related to self-identity and autonomy. In general, the focus is on the family's point of view of disability, rather than parent's (Orel, 1998).

Caregiving responsibility differs between the different ethnic groups. Forty-two percent of Asian Americans provide care for their aging parents or other older relatives versus 34 percent of Hispanic Americans, 28 percent of African Americans, and 19 percent of White Americans. Guilt from not doing enough for the extended family is reported by 72 percent of Asian Americans, 65 percent of Hispanic Americans, 54 percent of African Americans, and 44 percent of White Americans. Caregiving demands are especially high for women. Caregiving may be stressful and increase conflict among family members. When working with family members who care for a relative with dementia, a mental health professional should address the following issues (American Psychiatric Association, 1997):

1. The need for patience and understanding when working with individuals with dementia.

2. The potential stresses on family members and the need to develop more coping strategies.

3. Education of family members regarding the neurological problems, how they are manifested in behavior, and available treatments. In the early stages, memory problems are primary symptoms. Language and spatial dysfunction tend to occur later. Delusions and hallucinations may also occur in the late stage.

4. Practical solutions for problems such as how to deal with agitation, wandering, and other safety issues. Exercise is helpful but should be supervised. Identification on clothing and medical alert bracelets is helpful if unsupervised departures do occur. In the beginning stages of dementia, the individual should be advised not to drive.

5. The family dynamics as they relate to the caregiving situation and how responsibilities should be allocated.

6. Improving communication of the family members.

7. Cultural factors involving caregiving responsibilities and guilt need to be addressed.

8. Community resources such as the Alzheimer's Association and other support groups.

9. Financial and legal matters involving the patient, such as a power of attorney.

10. Decisions that may need to be made, such as under what circumstance the afflicted person would need to be cared for in a nursing home or other outside agency.

Elder Abuse and Neglect

Agnes, 85 years old, lost her husband last year. Because of her own problems with arthritis and congestive heart failure, Agnes moved in with her 55-year-old daughter, Emily. The situation is difficult for all of them. Sometimes Emily feels as if she's at the end of her rope, caring for her mother, worrying about her college-age son and her husband, who is about to be forced into early retirement. Emily has caught herself calling her mother names and accusing her mother of ruining her life. (APA, 2001b, p. 1)

Over two million older Americans are victims of psychological or physical abuse and neglect. This statistic is probably only about 20 percent of actual cases because underreporting of abuse or neglect generally occurs in the family home, although a minority is reported in nursing homes. The family circumstances that are associated with abuse and neglect are (1) a pattern and history of violence in family, (2) stress and life adjustment in accommodating an older parent or relative, (3) financial burdens, (4) overcrowded quarters, and (5) marital stress due to changes in living arrangements (U.S. Department of Health and Human Services, 1998). In addition, caregiver stress has been directly related to the time spent providing assistance (Bookwala & Schulz, 2000).

Implications. To reduce the prevalence of elder abuse and neglect, several steps can be taken with the general public and those caring for older adults (APA, 2001b). First, continued public education can bring the problem out in the open and increase awareness of the risk factors involved in abuse. Second, respite care or having someone else such as family members, friends, or hired workers take over can be quite helpful. Even a few hours per week away or a vacation from the responsibility can reduce stress. Third, increasing social contact and support is also likely to help keep stress manageable. Assistance may also be possible from religious or community organizations.

Specific disease organization and support groups can furnish both needed information and support.

Substance Abuse

"I wouldn't get up in the morning," she said. "I realized I was using alcohol to raise my spirits. It raises your spirits for a little while, and then you become depressed.... With people dying around you, you feel more lonely and isolated." (Wren, 1998, p. 12)

Alcohol abuse can begin after a loss. Genevieve May, a psychiatrist, started abusing alcohol after the death of her husband. Finding that this was not the solution, Dr. May entered the Betty Ford Center and was successfully treated at age 83. It is estimated that 17 percent of adults aged 60 and older abuse alcohol or prescription drugs; some of the misuse of prescription drugs may involve confusion over or misunderstanding of the directions. Because older adults take an average of five different prescription drugs a day, the chance of negative drug interactions or reactions with alcohol increases dramatically (Guerra, 1998). Often these reactions resemble psychological or organic conditions. Older problem drinkers are more likely to be unmarried, report more stress, have more financial problems, report persistent interpersonal conflicts with others, and have fewer social resources (Brennan & Moos, 1996). About 30 percent started drinking after the age of 60 because of depression and negative life changes (Guerra, 1998).

Implications. Older adults rarely seek treatment for substance abuse problems because of shame and perhaps because they feel uncomfortable in programs that also deal with drugs such as heroin or crack cocaine. One 74-year-old woman who was in group therapy with younger drug abusers asked, "What is crack?" She was successfully treated only after entering a program for older adults (Wren, 1998). As compared to younger substance abusers, older patients responded better to more structured program policies, more flexible rules regarding discharge, more comprehensive assessment, and more outpatient mental health aftercare (Moos, Mertens, & Brennan, 1995). Late-onset alcohol and drug abuse problems seem to be related to stressors such as the death of family members, spouses, or friends; retirement issues; family conflicts; physical health problems; or financial concerns. Some of these stressors are developmental issues of later life and need to be identified and treated (APA Working Group on the Older Adult Brochure, 1998).

Depression and Suicide

The rate for depression increases for males with age, while the higher rate of depression in women decreases after the age of 60. In men, depression is associated with vascular disease, erectile dysfunction, and decreased testosterone. Depression needs to be identified and treated since it is also seen as an independent risk factor for cardiovascular and cerebrovascular disease. Suicide rates are also high among older adults (Miller, 2005). Especially at risk are white men 85 and older, a demographic whose suicide rate is about six times the national rate. Suicides in individuals 65 and older accounted for 19 percent of all suicides in 1997. Among the older adults, men are seven times more likely to commit suicide than women (Roose, 2001). Factors associated with suicide included being separated, divorced, or alone; suffering depression; having an anxiety disorder; having physical or medical problems; and dealing with family conflict or loss of a relationship. Caucasian men were at greater risk for suicide than were non-Caucasian men or women (Florio, Hendryx, Jensen, & Rockwood, 1997). Although rates of depression are lower among older individuals than in the population as a whole, depression still plays a role in many suicides. In women, depression is related to financial loss; for men, the loss of health is the greatest stressor (Ponzo, 1992). Healthy, normally functioning older adults do not appear to be at greater risk for depression than younger adults. What seems to be age-related depression is often depression over physical health problems and the related disability. Aging, independent of declining health problems, does not increase the risk of depression (Roberts, Kaplan, Shema, & Strawbridge, 1997).

Implications. It is very important to assess for depression and suicidality in older adults. The best instrument for depression is the Geriatric Depression Scale, which was specifically developed for older adults. It has age-related norms and omits somatic symptoms that may be associated with physical problems and not depression. Major depression tends to be unrecognized in older adults and is a significant predictor of suicide. Because depression often co-occurs with physical illnesses such as cardiovascular disease, stroke, diabetes, and cancer, health providers and patients often believe that the mood disturbance is a normal consequence of problems, so it goes untreated. Many who commit suicide visited a primary care physician very close to the time of suicide (20 percent on the same day, 40 percent within 1 week, and 70 percent within 1 month; National Institute of Mental Health, 2000). There is an urgent need to detect and adequately treat depression in order to reduce suicide among older individuals. A number of biological and psychological treatments have been effective in treating depression in older adults. Newer antidepressants such as the selective serotonin reuptake inhibitors (SSRIs) have fewer side effects, making them more likely to be adhered to by older adults (important since rates of noncompliance with medication are high among older adults; Cooper et al., 2005). Cognitive-behavioral therapy and interpersonal therapy are also useful in reducing depression with this population (Gorenstein et al., 2005). Approximately 80 percent of older adults with depression overcome it if they are given appropriate treatment. Especially effective is the combination of drug and psychotherapy.

Sexuality in Old Age

The topic of sexuality and the aging process appears to be given even less consideration now than it was 10 years ago. Underlying this neglect is the belief that sexuality should not be considered in the aged. One physician notes,

> *I recently worked in an infectious disease clinic where I met a patient in her late 60s who was infected with the human immunodeficiency virus (HIV). My surprise at seeing an older woman with an infection associated with unprotected sex or injecting drug use, made me realize I had preconceptions about aging and the elderly.... My attitudes could be construed as sexist in nature. (McCray, 1998, pp. 1035–1036)*

Over 10 percent of all new cases of AIDS occur in individuals older than 50 (Center for AIDS Prevention Studies, UCSF, 2006). In our youth-oriented society, sexual activity among older persons is thought rare and even considered to be inappropriate. Older adults are not expected to be interested in sex. However, sexual interest and activity continue well into the 80s and 90s for many individuals (Diokno, Brown, & Herzog, 1990; Kun & Schwartz, 1998). In a study of 1,216 older people with a mean age of 77.3, nearly 30 percent had participated in sexual activity during the past month, and 67 percent were satisfied with their current level of sexual activity. Men were more sexually active than women, but less satisfied with their level of sexual activity. Age did not appear to be related to sexual satisfaction (Matthias, Lubben, Atchison, & Schweitzer, 1997). Most respondents voiced positive reactions to their sexual experiences such as, "Physical satisfaction is not the only aim of sex.... It is the nearness of someone throughout the lonely nights of people in their 70s and 80s" and "I believe sex is a wonderful outlet for love and physical health and worth trying to keep alive in advancing age.... It makes one feel youthful and close to one's mate and pleased to 'still work'" (B. Johnson, 1995, p. A23). Of the more than 600 older women surveyed, 35 percent said that their present level of sexual interest had decreased. However, Johnson found that two-thirds said that they were very interested in sexual intercourse and that most believed they had liberal sexual attitudes.

Changes do occur in sexual functioning in both older men and women. In men, erections occur more slowly and need more continuous stimulation, but they can be maintained for longer periods of time without the need for ejaculation. The refractory period increases so that it may take a day or two for the man to become sexually responsive again. Antihypertensive drugs, vascular diseases of the penile arteries, and diabetes are common causes of impotence in men. For women, aging is associated with a decline of estrogens, and vaginal lubrication decreases. However, sexual responsiveness of the clitoris is similar to that of younger women. Sexual activities remain important for older men and women. Medical and psychological methods have been successful in treating sexual dysfunctions in older adults.

Implications. As with younger adults, sexual concerns and functioning should be assessed in older adults because it is considered an important activity. One psychology intern remarked, "You just never think the same about your older clients [or your grandparents] after you have an 80-year-old woman telling you how much she enjoys oral sex" (Zeiss, 2001, p. 1). Treatments and medications such as Viagra are now available to improve sexual functioning in older adults. Knowledge of these advances is important when counseling older adults. Emotional stressors (retirement, caregiving, and lifestyle changes) as well as physical changes can produce problems in sexual functioning and should also be assessed. The mental health professional should determine the reason for the difficulties and employ or suggest appropriate interventions. Mental health professionals can obtain a number of journal articles dealing with sexuality in older adults and successful forms of treatment from the APA *Aging and Human Sexuality Resource Guide* (APA, 2001a). Client information on sexuality can also be obtained from the National Institute on Aging and *Love and Life: A Healthy Approach to Sex for Older Adults* (a kit that contains brochures, training materials, and videotapes for use by older adult organizations) from the National Council on Aging.

Multiple Discrimination

Minority status in combination with older age can produce a double burden. For example, older lesbian women may still encounter discrimination on the basis of their sexual orientation. Some remain distressed over their lack of acceptance from the heterosexual community and even family members. They observe that neighbors interact with them but do not invite them over. In addition, they may feel isolated from the lesbian community:

> *I was shocked and hurt when one of them [a young lesbian] who considers herself quite liberated didn't want to dance with me at a local lesbian bar, but she did dance with others. (Jacobson & Samdahl, 1998, p. 242)*

The woman attributed this rejection to her being older than the other women. She points out that in lesbian newsletters or activities, there was seldom anything about older women. Unfortunately, even minority members who have experienced discrimination themselves can display ageism.

Implications. The therapist should assess for potential problems of multiple discrimination when working with older adults who have disabilities or are from different cultural groups, social classes, or sexual minorities. An individual can come to terms with factors associated with ageism and find different sources of social support, or actively work to change the negative societal attitudes.

Implications for Clinical Practice

Older adults have to deal with issues such as the loss of friends and other significant individuals, the cultural devaluation of their group, health and physical problems, forced isolation, and having more limited financial resources (Myers & Harper, 2004). However, many develop alternative support systems in the community and have contact with extended family members. Social contacts are important, and engaging in either paid or volunteer work enhances the self-esteem and life satisfaction of older individuals (Acquino, Russell, Cutrona, & Altmaier, 1996). Issues that older adults face may include chronic illness and disability, loss of loved ones, caregiving for a loved one, and change of roles (Knight & McCallum, 1998).

The following are suggestions in offering mental health services to older adults (APA, 2004; Knight & McCallum, 1998; Qualls, 1998a):

1. Obtain specific knowledge and skills in counseling older adults. Critically evaluate your own attitudes about aging and quality of life.

2. Be knowledgeable about legal and ethical issues that arise when working with older adults (e.g., competency issues).

3. Determine the reason for evaluation and the social aspects related to the problem, such as recent losses, financial stressors, and family issues.

4. Show older adults respect and give them as much autonomy as possible, regardless of the issues involved or mental status. When communicating with older adults (Pennington, 2004):

    - Give attention and listen to the individual.
    - Talk to rather than about the person.
    - Use respectful language (not elderspeak) and don't be overly sweet.
    - Treat the person as an adult.
    - Take his or her concerns seriously.

5. Identify medical conditions and medications, because mental conditions are often a result of physical problems, or drug interactions or side effects.

6. Presume competence in older adult clients unless the contrary is obvious.

7. If necessary, slow the pace of therapy to accommodate cognitive slowing.

8. Provide information in a manner that approximates the client's level of reading and comprehension, using alternative methods such as simplified visuals or videotapes if necessary.

9. Involve older adults in decisions as much as possible. If there are cognitive limitations, it may be necessary to use legally recognized individuals.

10. Use multiple assessments and include relevant sources (client, family members, significant others, and health care providers).

11. Determine the role of family caregivers, educate them about the disorder, and help them develop strategies to reduce burnout.

12. When working with an older couple, help negotiate issues regarding time spent alone and together (especially after retirement). Arguments over recreation are common. There is too much "couple time" and no "legitimate" reason for separateness.

13. Recognize that it is important to help individuals who are alone establish support systems in the community.

14. Help the older adult develop a sense of fulfillment in life by discussing the positive aspects of their experiences. Success can be defined as having done one's best or having met and survived challenges. A life review is often helpful.

15. Determine the older adult's views of the problem, belief system, stage-of-life issues, educational background, and social and ethnic influences.

16. Assist in interpreting the impact of cultural issues such as ethnic group membership, gender, and sexual orientation on their lives.

17. For adults very close to the end of their lives, help them deal with a sense of attachment to familiar objects by having them decide how heirlooms, keepsakes, and photo albums will be distributed and cared for. Counseling can improve the quality of life for older adults or help them resolve late-life issues.

Counseling Women

You never see someone that looks like me as a scientist. No matter how long I stay here. When I walk through the campus, no one's ever gonna look at me and just think that I'm a physicist ... I guess the things that made other people find it hard to see me as a scientist are making it hard for me to see myself as a scientist, too. (Soffa Caldo, Chicana college senior; Ong, 2005, p. 593)

A study in the Journal of the American Medical Association *reports that girls in their teens are almost as likely as adult women to experience abuse in relationships. One in five girls reported physical or sexual abuse in a relationship. These girls were also more likely to report eating disorders, drug use, suicidal thoughts and risky sexual behavior." (K. S. Palmer, 2001, p. A17)*

In *Beyond bias and barriers: Fulfilling the potential of women in academic science and engineering,* the National Academies (2006) report that women face barriers in many fields of science and engineering that are not accounted for by biological differences in ability, hormonal influences, ambition, or childrearing demands. Although women make up 51 percent of the United States population, they are underrepresented in positions of power and are victimized by stereotyping and discrimination. Some progress has been made in promoting gender equality, but inequities continue. The National Coalition for Women and Girls in Education (1998, 2002) reports that (1) girls and women continue to be underrepresented in areas such as math and sciences; (2) women continue to predominate in low-wage, traditional female tracks; (3) women comprise 73 percent of elementary and secondary school teachers but only 35 percent of principals; (4) pay disparities between male and female educators persist at all levels; (5) female students continue to receive less attention, encouragement, and praise than male students; and (6) sexual harassment of females continues to be pervasive (81 percent of 8th- through 11th-graders, 30 percent of undergraduates, and 40 percent of graduate students have been sexually harassed). Teachers are often unaware that they may be promoting sexism by providing differential responses to male and female students (Frawley, 2005). In one study of third-grade teachers who believed they had a gender-free style, the following were observed: (1) accommodations were made for boys to stop disagreements rather than confronting them; (2) boys were allowed to speak out of turn while girls were not; and (3) when girls spoke out of turn, they were reminded to raise their hands (Garrahy, 2001).

Implications. In the educational areas, mental health professionals need to be involved in advocating for changes at the system levels involving curriculum and staffing. Coursework for future teachers should include demonstrations and discussion of responses that may inadvertently convey gender-restrictive messages. Attitudes do affect performance. In a series of studies, R. P. Brown and Josephs (1999) found that gender-specific performance concerns affect performance. Women who believed a math test would indicate they were especially weak in math performed worse than women who believed it would indicate whether they were exceptionally strong in this area. Thus, the stereotype that women are bad at math affected their performance. Attitudes and expectations regarding stereotyped personality characteristics and appropriate career choices need to be addressed in educational programs.

Problems Faced by Women

Economic Status

Although single mothers make up less than 20 percent of all families, they constitute nearly half of the families in poverty in 2002 (U.S Census Bureau, 2002) In terms of income, females make less than their male counterparts across all racial groups. This disparity is most pronounced between White women and White men, with women earning less than three-fourths of the salaries earned by men (U.S. Census Bureau, 2002). Nontraditional career fields are often not hospitable to women, resulting in the larger percentage of women who remain in "feminine" careers. Females are overrepresented in occupations such as secretary (96.7 percent), cashier (75 percent), nurse's aide (88.3 percent), elementary school teacher (80.3 percent), and receptionist (93.9 percent), and they are underrepresented in administrative positions (U.S. Department of Labor, 2005). Even in occupations where women represent the numerical majority, they earn less than men in the same field (Atkinson & Hackett, 1998).

Implications. Women in poverty often need assistance with economic issues, housing, and food. Mental health professionals may need to use case management skills to obtain needed resources for the client. Due to financial considerations, mental health services should be provided in convenient locations such as family planning clinics, primary health care provider offices, and government assistance offices. Child care and other onsite programs for family members as the mother receives counseling can increase participation in the mental health system.

Barriers to Career Choices

College women perceive more obstacles to their career choices than do males. They believe that they will have a more difficult time getting hired, experience discrimination, be treated differently, and experience negative sexual comments from superiors or coworkers. Minority college women perceived even higher career barriers because of both gender and ethnic background issues (Luzzo & McWhirter, 2001; Ong, 2005). The underrepresentation of women in certain fields is due in part to gender role stereotypes. Some jobs require characteristics not generally associated with females. When a woman behaves in a manner that is not considered to be feminine, negative consequences may result. If a woman displays a task-oriented style of leadership that violates the gender norm of modesty, she is rated as competent but incurs cost in low social attraction and likability ratings. Men displaying the same leadership style are rated high in competence and are better liked (Rudman, 1998).

Even successful businesswomen report barriers to advancement on the corporate ladder (Lyness & Thompson, 2000). These were manifested in the following manner:

1. Women were made to feel that they are tokens, not a good fit at senior management levels, and that they need to change in some way. They perceived discomfort from the men working with them, did not have the same gender role models, and felt they had to perform at a higher level than men.

2. Men heightened cultural boundaries by emphasizing camaraderie and differences from women, thus excluding them from the information necessary for job performance. This was exemplified in the male use of the "good old boys network." Informal networking was more useful to male managers than to female managers for getting promoted.

3. Women received less and less effective mentoring than male executives. Some of the problems were limited access to potential mentors, mentors unwilling to work with them, and the misinterpretation of a mentorship request as a sexual invitation.

The influences on career are somewhat different with African American women, who face the issues of both racism and sexism. Among these women, the most important variables related to a successful career included the promotion of education by the family, positive relationships with family members, family gender socialization (androgynous sex roles), and positive values toward work. One African American woman attributed her success to her extended family. She stated,

> *Learning and academics were very important to my grandmother. She taught us: if you can't learn you can't change things. That has carried over to my work life in the corporate world, because there it is all about change. And people who can't learn or aren't academically gifted either fail or become dated and useless. (Pearson & Bieschke, 2001, p. 305)*

Implications. Mental health professionals should help expand the career choices available to women. In doing so, a comprehensive approach must be involved. One program (Sullivan & Mahalik, 2000) increased the career self-efficacy of college women by having them:

- Identify successful performance accomplishments.

- Participate in vicarious or observational learning. This was accomplished by interviewing women outside the groups about their career decision-making processes, discussing observations about their career decision-making insights, and reading material on women's unique career development.

- Attend to emotional arousal and learn to manage anxiety through relaxation and adaptive self-talk. The women learned to identify and challenge self-defeating thoughts.

- Career self-efficacy was increased in this group of women by developing self-evaluation skills, identifying career paths by successful women, promoting skills to deal with anxiety, and helping them understand the impact of gender socialization issues in their careers.

Discrimination and Victimization

Approximately 20 percent of female students report being physically or sexually abused by their dating partner. The abuse is associated with increased use of drugs, binge drinking, considering and attempting suicide, unhealthy or disordered eating patterns, and intercourse before the age of 15 (Silverman, Raj, Mucci, & Hathaway, 2001). It is clear that victims of abuse often suffer from depression and other emotional difficulties. The majority of women who are in treatment for childhood sexual abuse suffer from PTSD (Rodriguez, Ryan, Vande Kemp, & Foy, 1997). Sexual harassment is also quite prevalent in the work environment.

> *One woman who suffered 6 years of harassment from her male colleagues that included lewd behavior and suggestive comments finally threatened to report them. They responded by saying, "Fine. We know where your car is, and we know where you live." (Lewis et al., 1998, p. D5)*

As with many women in the same circumstances, the woman decided not to fight back. Over 70 percent of women office workers have reported harassment at their place of employment (Piotrkowski, 1998). Women respond to the harassment by attempting to ignore it, taking a leave of absence, or using alcohol to cope. Lower job satisfaction, poorer physical health, and higher levels of depression and anxiety can be the result of harassment (Fitzgerald, Drasgow, Hulin, Gelfand, & Magley, 1997).

Implications. Violence and sexual harassment against girls and women are highly prevalent and can lead to a number of mental health problems. Even among adolescents, screening should be performed for dating abuse, especially in cases where suicidal thought, use of drugs, or disordered eating patterns exist. Prevention strategies should be developed that are appropriate to school settings. The APA Policy Office (2001) recommends support for policy initiatives, including legal and legislative reform addressing the issue of violence against women; improved training for mental health workers to recognize and treat victims; the dissemination of information on violence against women to churches, community groups and educational institutions, and the general public; and the exploration of psychoeducational and sociocultural intervention to change male objectification of women.

Gender Issues

The stereotyped standards of beauty expressed through advertisements and the mass media have had an impact on the health and self-esteem of girls and women. Societal pressure for females to be thin has led to the internalization of an unrealistic body shape as the ideal and has resulted in body dissatisfaction and disordered eating patterns and dieting (Sinclair, 2006). It is estimated that 35 percent of women engage in disordered eating, and many attempt to control their weight through self-induced vomiting and the use of laxatives (Kendler et al., 1991). Bulimia nervosa is 10 times more common in females than in males and affects up to 3 percent of women between the ages of 13 and 20 (McGilley & Pryor, 1998). The need to meet societal standards for thinness or beauty becomes more intense when girls at the ages of 12 and 13 begin to date and to experience the physical changes associated with puberty. They become more concerned about their physical appearance and are more likely to start dieting (Heatherton, Mahamedi, Striepe, Field, & Keel, 1997).

Implications. Programs need to address the influence of societal emphasis on thinness as the standard by which girls and women should judge themselves. In one program, marketing students from different high schools approached several large department stores requesting that the displays show a more diverse range of body types. The students pointed out to store managers that half of the teens and adult women in the United States wear a size 14 or larger and that the mannequins and models were size 8 or less. In support of their position, they cited a survey done at their schools that indicated that 93 percent of the students wanted to see more diverse body types in advertisements and in magazines. Only one department store, Union Bay, advertised using a range of body types or "healthy looking" models (Cronin, 1998). Programs directed at changing the unrealistically thin female image promoted by advertisers, magazines, and other mass media may be effective ways of reducing body dissatisfaction in females.

In individual counseling, Sands (1998) suggested the following when working with females with disordered eating patterns. First, encourage them to identify the cultural and social context for the behavior so that they do not engage in self-blame. A gender role analysis identifies messages that they receive from society (girls must be thin, pretty, and sexy). Second, determine the consequences of the gender-related messages and the self-statements associated with them. Third, choose an appropriate message (e.g., "Being healthy is important, so I will eat and exercise appropriately") and develop a plan to implement the change.

Affective Disorders

Up to seven million women currently have depression, which is twice the rate found in men (Schwartzman & Glaus, 2000). Factors contributing to depression in women include poor socioeconomic status, unhealthy societal gender standards, and Posttraumatic Stress (Culbertson, 1997). Women feel the pressure to fulfill stereotyped feminine social roles in which they are evaluated according to physical beauty, modesty, and marriageability. Deviating from these standards can lead to self-doubt, poor self-image, and depression (Sands, 1998). Poor body image and eating disturbances predict increases in depressive symptoms in adolescent girls. Depression stems from body dissatisfaction, failure to obtain a superslim body by exercising or dieting, and guilt from the use of vomiting or laxatives to control weight (Stice & Bearman, 2001). E. P. Cook (1990) believed also that women devalue their relationship capabilities. Depression may result from their socialization to try to maintain relationships at the cost of their own needs and wishes. Failures in relationships are often seen as personal failures, compounding stress and affecting mood.

Minority women have multiple characteristics that are subject to discrimination and prejudice and see additional obstacles to achieving their life goals. African American teenagers who were interviewed concerning their multiple minority status were quite aware of the discrimination that they face.

> *I'm a black female and black females are the lowest. The black female has a hard time, for one, because she's black, two, because she's a female, and I think it would take more for me to strive to get what I want.... (Olsen, 1996, p. 113)*

African American teenagers in this study were aware of the negative messages regarding their ethnicity and also the disparagement of the female gender role. Although they acknowledged the disadvantages of their gender, not one of them wanted to be a boy.

Implications. Assess for environmental factors such as poverty, racism, economic conditions, and poor or abusive relationships. Identify the possible impact of sexism or gender messages on the individual's well-being. Some believe that depression is an extreme version of society's prescribed female role (passivity, low self-esteem, dependence on others; Sands, 1998). During adolescence, gender intensification becomes stronger, and there is increased societal pressure to be pretty, popular, and feminine. Deviations from this standard result in isolation from others and rejection from the peer group. In therapy it is important to address the stressors faced by females and identify the societal and cultural factors, as well as individual influences. Women may need to understand the power differential in society, the expectations for their gender, and the impact those expectations may have on their mood states. Identifying cognitions based on stereotypes and developing more realistic coping self-statements can reduce depression. Learning to act assertively can counteract the patterns of helplessness and low self-esteem (Sands, 1998).

Depression in women is associated with an increased risk of cardiovascular disease, which is the leading cause of death in women. Consequently, mental health professionals should also educate women about the risk and likelihood of developing coronary heart disease (CHD). Other health risk factors such as smoking, a high fat diet, sedentary lifestyle, and obesity should be addressed, and psychological intervention should be used to modify these behaviors. A woman should also know the symptoms of CHD (e.g., fatigue, dizziness, and fainting, in addition to the more classic signs involving pain or pressure in the chest, sweating, or pain radiating to the neck, jaw, arm, or back; Schwartzman & Glaus, 2000).

Aging

With the emphasis on youth and the sexism that exists in our society, older women are viewed more negatively than older men. Some women believed that age discrimination was evidenced by younger people not relating to them socially; by preference given to younger females in stores, restaurants, and other public establishments; by reduced dating opportunities; and by being "invisible" to men (Committee on Women in Psychology, 1999). Women increasingly outnumber men as they age, and there are five women for every two men over the age of 75. There are relatively few positive images of older women. In addition, older women are thought to face additional stressors such as the "empty nest" syndrome and menopause (Lippert, 1997). About 53 million women are over the age of 45 and are experiencing or have experienced menopause. Responses to it may be impacted by ageism and sexism, depending on the meaning that is ascribed to it. Some may believe that sexual attractiveness and youth are lost at menopause. Younger women have more negative attitudes toward menopause than do menopausal and post-menopausal women (Huffman & Myers, 1999).

However, many of these midlife stressors do not appear to be difficult transitions for most women. Of a group of women between the ages of 40 and 59 asked about how they felt about "this time in life," nearly three-fourths felt "very happy" or "happy," and nearly two-thirds found it "not very confusing" or "not confusing at all." Only 13.7 percent felt "unhappy" or "very unhappy." Most were enjoying midlife because of increased independence, freedom from worrying about what others think, freedom from parenting, and the ability to define their own identity based on their own interests (McQuaide, 1998). Similar findings were reported for several groups of well-educated women. Instead of being concerned about a midlife crisis, aging, the empty nest syndrome, or menopause, the middle-aged women were involved in a midlife review, had a strong sense of identity, were confident, and felt a sense of power over their lives (A. J. Stewart & Ostrove, 1998). These findings indicate that transitions through midlife for older women are easier than were previously assumed—at least among well-educated women. Differences in transition may be found with women of other generations, minority women, or those from other social classes.

Implications. Mental health professionals must be careful not to make assumptions about the so-called midlife crisis in women and how such transitions are affecting clients. Some women are grandmothers in graduate school, others are new mothers at 40, and some have multiple careers (Lippert, 1997). Women may need to become aware of contradictory feelings that may be associated with various midlife transitions such as a simultaneous sense of loss and sense of freedom when children leave home. The personal meaning and reaction to these events should be understood. Support loss of roles by affirming new commitments in life. Assist in developing personal meaning through self-exploration. Help them understand that some anxiety is to be expected when going through transitions, and that it is an opportunity to achieve greater personal development. For women who are depressed after menopause, discuss the impact of sociocultural attitudes toward women and aging. Determine what their fears and expectations of the process are. Provide information on the process and the availability of support groups. An excellent resource is http://www.menopause.org.

Feminist Identity Theory

An identity development model comparable to that for ethnic minority members has been developed for women. Feminist therapists believe that the patriarchal aspect of U.S. society is responsible for many of the problems faced by women. They believe that women show a variety of reactions to their subordinate status in society. The following stages represent an evolution of consciousness of societal subjugation of women and the development of the feminist identity (McNamara & Rickard, 1998).

1. *Passive acceptance.* During this stage, the female accepts traditional gender roles, sees them as advantageous to her, and considers men to be superior to women. She is unaware of or denies prejudice or discrimination. Male contributions to the arts, business, and theater are valued more than those of women.

2. *Revelation.* Events involving sexism occur in a way that cannot be denied or ignored. The individual becomes personally awakened to prejudice, becomes angry, and feels guilty at being previously unaware. There is intense self-examination and dichotomous thinking. All men are seen as oppressive and all women as positive.

3. *Embeddedness-emanation.* The woman begins to form close emotional relationships with other women. With their help she is able to express her emotions in a supportive environment. Her feminist identity is becoming solidified, and she engages in more relativistic rather than dualistic thinking regarding males.

4. *Synthesis.* During this stage, a positive feminist identity is fully developed. Sexism is no longer considered the cause of all social and personal problems, and other causal factors are considered. The woman can take a stance different from that of other feminists and still maintain her feminist identity.

5. *Active commitment.* The woman is now interested in turning her attention toward making societal changes.

Although some women go through these stages, it is not clear how applicable this model is to most women. This theory is based on W. E. Cross's

1971 view of the development of African American identity. Cross has since revised his model (W. E. Cross, 1995), particularly as it applies to the passive-acceptance stage (pre-encounter). Individuals at this stage may feel that characteristics of race (gender) are of low salience or are not more important than other things such as religion, lifestyle, or social status. They may see progress as due to personal effort and motivation. Many individuals at this stage who have this attitude are mentally healthy. Feminist identity theory is of fairly recent origin, and there is need for further research to determine whether it is applicable to most women.

Therapy for Women

Feminist therapists have been instrumental in pointing out the sexist nature of our society, even in the counseling process. It is important for counselors to be aware of possible biases when working with female clients. For example, what are the attributes believed to be aspects of a healthy female? In past research, qualities such as being more submissive, emotional, and relationship-oriented were seen as positive qualities in women (Atkinson & Hackett, 1998). If counselors adhere to these standards, consciously or unconsciously, these attitudes may be conveyed to clients in the counseling session. One study of family therapy sessions revealed that counselors interrupted women more often than they interrupted men (Werner-Wilson, Price, Zimmerman, & Murphy, 1997). Even though the therapists were not aware of this behavior, they were subtly conveying gender role expectations to the family. Gender role expectations are difficult to eliminate.

Biases can also exist for certain diagnostic categories. Some of the personality disorders may be based on exaggerated gender characteristics. Self-dramatization and exaggerated emotional expressions; intense fluctuations in mood, self-image, and interpersonal relationships; and reliance on others and the inability to assume responsibilities are aspects of Histrionic, Borderline, and Dependent Personality Disorders, respectively. Not surprisingly, women are more likely to be diagnosed with these disorders. Another problematic category is Premenstrual Dysphoric Disorder, which is included in the *DSM-IV-TR* as a diagnosis that requires further study. The essential features include marked change in mood, anger, and depression or anxiety accompanied by complaints of breast tenderness and bodily aches that interfere with work or social activities. The symptoms occur one week before menses and remit a few days afterwards. Critics of this category acknowledge that many women have some of these symptoms, but argue that the symptoms should be accepted as a physical reaction.

Many of our theories are male-oriented. Granello and Beamish (1998) argued that the concept of codependency needs to reconceptualized since many women would receive this label. Codependency in women may reflect a sense of connectedness, nurturance, the role of placing the needs of the family over themselves, and devoting their energies to the home and relationships. Three problems exist with this concept in the family systems model. First, there is no acknowledgement of the unequal distribution of power within families. Codependent behavior may be a result of a power imbalance between men and women. Second, several key concepts such as differentiation of self and anxiety due to emotional fusion are reflective of male stereotypic characteristics. Third, disturbances are always interpreted on the system rather than individual members. Under this scenario, women who are abused can be seen as contributors to the problem. Fourth, the problematic relationship can be interpreted not as one from the woman, but rather the inability or unwillingness of the male to relate in a mutually empathetic manner. Thus, in many cases, a woman's desire for connectedness is not pathological, but a strength that may be an important part of her self-concept.

Implications for Clinical Practice

Both male and female counselors must be careful not to foster traditional sex roles and must be aware of sexist assumptions. Presenting problems need to be understood within a societal context in which devaluation of women is a common occurrence; gender conceptualizations need to be considered integral aspects of counseling and mental health. Both traditional and nontraditional gender roles can be confining. Each female client must choose what is best for her, despite gender conceptions or political correctness.

Fitzgerald and Nutt (1998) identified some guidelines for counselors who counsel women. These guidelines indicate the importance of incorporating features of feminist and nonsexist components in all our counseling programs:

1. Possess up-to-date information regarding the biological, psychological, and sociological issues that impact women. For example, knowledge about menstruation, pregnancy, birth, infertility and miscarriage, gender roles and health, and discrimination, as well as their impact on women, is important.
2. Recognize that most counseling theories are male-centered and require modification when working with women. For example, cognitive approaches can focus on societal messages.
3. Attend workshops to explore gender-related factors in mental health and be knowledgeable about issues related to women.

4. Maintain awareness of all forms of oppression and understand how they interact with sexism.

5. Employ skills that may be particularly appropriate for the needs of women, such as assertiveness training, gender role analysis, and consciousness-raising groups.

6. Assess sociocultural factors to determine their role in the presenting problem.

7. Help clients realize the impact of gender expectations and societal definitions of attractiveness on the mental health of women so that they do not engage in self-blame.

8. Be ready to take an advocacy role in initiating systems-level changes as they relate to sexism in education, business, and other endeavors.

9. Assess for the possible impact of abuse or violence in all women.

Counseling Individuals with Disabilities

26
Chapter

Currently, over 2.6 million veterans are receiving disability benefits. The number of veterans who are disabled will continue to increase as the war in Iraq continues. Survivors often suffer from head, spinal injuries, and other injuries. (Information Clearing House, 2006)

A 77-year-old woman has been on hemodialysis for 10 years and also has seizures, arthritis, and strokes. Communication with the social worker is not going well since the patient has impaired hearing. The daughter explains that her mother has hearing aids but does not wear them, complaining that they hurt her ears. The social worker directs all her questions to the daughter, leaving the mother wondering what is being discussed. (Desselle & Proctor, 2000)

In 1988 I became obviously disabled. I walk with crutches and a stiff leg. Since that time I no longer fulfill our cultural standard of physical attractiveness. But worse, there are times when people who know me don't acknowledge me. When I call their name and say, "Hello," they often reply, "Oh, I didn't see you." I have also been mistaken for people who do not resemble me. For example, I was recently asked, "Are you a leader in the disability movement?" While I hope to be that someday, I asked her, "Who do you believe I am?" She had mistaken me for a taller person with a different hair color, who limps but does not use a walking aid. The only common element was our disability. My disability had become my persona. This person saw it and failed to see me. (Buckman, 1998, p. 19)

Danielle Buckman, the woman in the last vignette, is a psychotherapist who teaches university courses on counseling people with disabilities and, due to her own struggle with multiple sclerosis, has firsthand experiences with discriminatory reactions from the general public. Since Ms. Buckman is in midlife, she also expresses concern about the triple whammy involving gender, disability, and aging issues.

Attitudes toward individuals with disabilities run the gamut from ignorance to a lack of understanding to being overprotective or overly sympathetic. People without handicaps often do not know how to respond to people with disabilities. In the second vignette, the social worker was talking to the daughter as if the mother were not present. The daughter felt frustrated and responded,

> *You are not even trying to communicate with my mother. . . . She can understand you if you look at her and speak slowly and clearly. . . . Imagine how you would feel if you and your spouse went to the doctor to consult about a major surgery you were scheduled for and the doctor directed the conversation only to your spouse as if you were not intelligent enough to know what was being discussed. (Desselle & Proctor, 2000, p. 277)*

Of the 72.3 million families in the United States, about 21 million have at least one member with a disability (U.S. Census Bureau, 2005b). The stress associated with disabilities increases the risk for psychiatric or substance abuse (Turner, Lloyd, & Taylor, 2006). Mental health professionals need to understand the nature of disabilities and treat individuals with dignity. For example, most people without hearing loss do not understand that hearing aids can amplify all sounds, resulting in jumbled hearing, which is why many do not wear them. The public often has low expectations for individuals with disabilities. Kerry Clifford, who has a physical disability, believes that the public's reaction is similar to that of Samuel Johnson's to a dog walking on two legs. He is reported to have said, "It is not done well, but you are surprised to see it done at all" (Vacc & Clifford, 1995). Most people without disabilities assume that disability in one area also affects others. One example is responding to an individual who is mute by speaking more loudly or making exaggerated facial and hand gestures (Taggart, 2001).

Implications. Mental health professionals need to address their discomfort with disabilities in clients and to recognize that they are also subject to disability prejudice. Several suggestions from APA (2001a) are helpful:

1. Instead of thinking about a "disabled woman," change the emphasis by using the phrase "a woman with a disability." This emphasizes the individual rather than the limitation.

2. Do not sensationalize disability by referring to the achievements by some as "superhuman" or "extraordinary." It creates unfair expectations. Most have the same range of skills as do nondisabled individuals. Avoid the use of phrases such as "afflicted with" or "a victim of." They evoke pity and conjure up a nonfunctional status.

3. Respond to an individual with a disability according to their skills, personality, and other personal attributes rather than his or her disability. It is also important to get specific information about disabilities, either by reading the literature or consulting with mental health professionals with disabilities. See Table 26.1 for additional suggestions when working with individuals with physical disabilities.

The most common forms of disabling conditions are arthritis and rheumatism, back and spine problems, and cardiovascular disease (*Journal of the American Medical Association,* 2000). A national survey (National Organization on Disability, 1998) reported dismal statistics on the well-being of Americans with disabilities. Of adults with disabilities, only 29 percent have any type of employment, compared to 79 percent of the general public. This 50 point difference is not due to a lack of interest in working; in fact, 72 percent of individuals with disabilities want to work. Over one-third of adults with disabilities have incomes of $15,000 or less, compared to 12 percent of those without disabilities. Only about one third of adults with disabilities are very satisfied with life, compared to 61 percent of the non-disabled public. Worse, 20 percent of adults with disabilities have not finished high school, compared to 9 percent of those without disabilities—a ratio of more than two to one. Individuals with disabilities earn only two-thirds the income of coworkers without disabilities; minorities with disabilities have an even lower income than Whites with disabilities (Atkinson & Hackett, 1998). It was in part due to dismal statistics like these that Congress passed the Americans with Disabilities Act.

Implications. Mental health professionals need to be in the forefront of assisting individuals with disabilities to obtain employment and to complete education to their potential. Some of the work might involve educating employers about specific disabilities. Greatest prejudice is displayed to hidden disabilities such as HIV or psychiatric conditions. As a person with schizophrenia stated, "I don't want to tell anybody, because people who aren't ill, they do have a tendency sometimes to treat you different... we've got to disguise ourselves a lot..." (Goldberg, Killeen, & O'Day, 2005). Education to staff about these conditions can work to allay fears (A. Thomas, 2001). About 6 percent of students enrolled in postsecondary educational institutions have disabilities. Most involve visual, hearing, or orthopedic problems (Palmer & Roessler, 2000). Mental health professionals can prepare them for success at the college level by teaching them to be self-advocates, for example, by identifying and requesting accommodations when applying to and attending college. Communication and negotiation skills can be developed through role-play. Independence can be encouraged by managing money, doing laundry, eating appropriately, or performing other daily living skills (Ericksen-Radtke & Beale, 2001).

Table 26.1   **Things to Remember when Interacting with Individuals with Disabilities**

1. People with physical disabilities (arthritis, mobility problems, wheelchair users, limited or no use of limbs).

   ■ Do not use or move items such as wheelchairs, crutches, and canes without permission. They are considered part of the individual's "personal space."

   ■ Ask if assistance is required before providing it; if your offer is accepted, ask for instructions and follow them.

   ■ Address the individual directly rather than a person who accompanies the client.

   ■ Sit at eye level to facilitate comfort in communication.

   ■ Make certain access from parking to your office is possible.

2. People with vision loss.

   ■ Identify yourself and anyone else who is present when greeting them. If the individual does not extend a hand, offer a verbal welcome.

   ■ Offer the use of your arm and guide—rather than steer or push—the individual. Give verbal instructions.

   ■ If a service dog is present, do not pet or play with it.

   ■ Determine the best way of presenting information. Some are able to read large text, while others may use Braille or audiotapes. Ask about preference at the beginning.

   ■ Let the individual know if you are moving about or if the conversation is to end.

   ■ Give verbal cues when offering a seat. Place the individual's hand on the back of the chair, and they will not need further help.

3. People who are deaf or hard of hearing.

   ■ Ask about the individual's preferred communication (some use American Sign Language and identify culturally with the deaf community, while others may prefer to communicate orally, read lips, or rely on residual hearing).

   ■ Address the individual directly rather than a person accompanying the client.

   ■ Realize that talking very loud does not enhance communication.

   ■ To get attention, call the person by name. If there is no response, lightly touch the individual on the arm or shoulder.

   ■ Do not pretend to understand if you do not.

   ■ Do not include interpreters in the conversation. They are to relay information.

   ■ Make direct eye contact and keep your face and mouth visible.

   ■ If there is extreme difficulty communicating orally, ask if writing is acceptable.

Table 26.1   continued

4. People with speech impediments

- Allow the individual to finish speaking before you speak.

- Realize that communication may take longer and plan accordingly. Do not rush through.

- Face the individual and give full eye contact.

- Address the individual directly.

- Do not pretend to understand if you do not.

- When appropriate, use yes or no questions.

- Repeat to demonstrate or check for understanding, but remember that speech impediments do not indicate limited intelligence.

Source: Adapted from United Cerebral Palsy (2001).

The Americans with Disabilities Act

The Americans with Disabilities Act (ADA) was signed into law in 1990, extending the federal mandate of nondiscrimination toward individuals with disabilities to state and local governments and the private sector. Congress defined disability as "a physical or mental impairment that substantially limits one or more of the major life activities of such individual." It includes individuals with mental retardation, hearing impairment or deafness, orthopedic impairments, learning disabilities, speech impairment, and other health or physical impairments. Psychiatric disorders covered include Major Depression, Bipolar Disorder, Panic and Obsessive-Compulsive Disorders, Personality Disorders, Schizophrenia, and rehabilitation from drug use or addiction. Conditions not covered include sexual behavior disorders, compulsive gambling, Kleptomania, Pyromania, and current substance abuse (Sleek, 1998). Under this definition, there are 49 million to 54 million Americans with disabilities, of whom 24 million have a severe form. While more than 60 percent of people 65 and over have a disability, the largest number of this population are of working age (Wellner, 2001). The prevalence of disability ranges from 5.8 percent for children under 18 to 53.9 percent for those 65 and over (U.S. Census Bureau, 1995). The number recognized by the ADA is in fact now higher, since HIV has recently been added as a disability.

The ADA has had an impact on many businesses with employees with disabilities. Unfortunately, the law has been whittled away and the courts have supported businesses rather than people with disabilities more than 90 percent of the time. The National Council on Disability has promoted a bill to "restore the original intent" of the Americans with Disabilities Act (AAPD News, 2006). A large number have made adjustments and accommodations:

> *Mike Johnson wasn't asking for special treatment at work, but his bosses thought they'd better provide it anyway. Two months after being hospitalized for bipolar disorder, Johnson, an accomplished, 35-year-old sales executive, told his boss that he was feeling "stressed out." The boss also noticed that Johnson overbooked his schedule during his manic phases and would wake up late and miss appointments during depressive periods. (Sleek, 1998, p. 15)*

Mike Johnson's employer was able to retain a valuable executive with Bipolar Disorder by developing a flexible work schedule that allowed him to have time off for therapy.

Implications. Mental health professionals working with individuals with disabilities should know the federal and state laws applicable to these individuals. They should know the rights of individuals with disabilities in school and work settings. Under the ADA, employers cannot discriminate against an individual with a disability during employment or promotion if they are otherwise qualified, cannot inquire about a disability but only about the ability to perform the job, are required to make "reasonable" accommodation for people with disabilities, and cannot use tests that will cause individuals to be screened out due to disabilities (Vacc & Clifford, 1995). The counselor should also be aware of problems in using standardized assessment tools with individuals who have disabilities. Finally, it is important for counselors to understand that individuals with the same disability may show a wide range of functional difficulties and accomplishments.

Congress passed the ADA in 1990 to address the following issues:

1. Historically, society has tended to isolate and segregate individuals with disabilities, and despite some improvements, such forms of discrimination against individuals with disabilities continue to be a serious and pervasive social problem.

2. Unlike individuals who have experienced discrimination on the basis of race, color, sex, national origin, religion, or age, individuals who have experienced discrimination on the basis of disability have often had no legal recourse to redress such discrimination.

3. Individuals with disabilities continually encounter various forms of discrimination, including intentional exclusion; the discriminatory effects of architectural, transportation, and communication barriers; overprotective rules and policies; failure to make modifications to existing facilities and practices; exclusionary qualification standards and criteria;

segregation; and relegation to lesser services, programs, activities, benefits, jobs, or other opportunities.

4. Census data, national polls, and other studies have documented that people with disabilities, as a group, occupy an inferior status in our society and are severely disadvantaged socially, vocationally, economically, and educationally.

5. The nation's goals regarding individuals with disabilities are to ensure equality of opportunity, full participation, independent living, and economic self-sufficiency. The act prohibits discrimination in employment, telecommunications, transportation, and public services and accommodations (Atkinson & Hackett, 1998).

Implications. Mental health professionals need to ensure that the services they provide address these legal and ethical standards (APA, 1998). Do not separate out or give unequal service to clients with disabilities unless you must do so to provide a service that is as effective as that provided to those without disabilities.

- Do not deny your services to a client with a disability. You may refer him or her if that individual requires treatment outside your area of specialization.

- Watch for criteria that screen out clients with disabilities. For instance, do not require a driver's license for payment by check. Use policies, practices, and procedures in your office that can be modified for those with disabilities, such as making sure service guide animals are permitted in your office.

- You may need to provide auxiliary aids and services, such as readers, sign-language interpreters, Braille materials, large-print materials, videotapes and audiotapes, and computers when necessary to communicate with your clients with disabilities. You may have to use alternative forms of communication, such as notepads and pencils, when these forms are appropriate.

- Evaluate your office for structural and architectural barriers that prevent individuals with disabilities from getting the services they need from you. In one study, a large majority of individuals with disabilities reported difficulties obtaining care because of environmental barriers or office layout (CDC, 2006). Change these barriers when they can be readily changed (without much difficulty or expense). Look at ramps, parking spaces, curbs, shelving, elevator control buttons, widths of doorways, and heights of toilet seats.

- When remodeling or building new offices, hire an architect or contractor familiar with ADA requirements.

Myths about People with Disabilities

There are many myths associated with people with disabilities (American Friends Service Committee, 1998):

1. *Most are in wheelchairs.* Of the 49 million individuals with disabilities, only about 10 percent use wheelchairs, crutches, or walkers. Most have disabilities related to cardiovascular problems, blindness, developmental disabilities, or invisible disabilities such as asthma, learning disabilities, or epilepsy.

2. *People with disabilities are a drain on the economy.* It is true that 71 percent of working-age persons with disabilities are not working. However, 72 percent of those want to work. Discrimination has kept them out of the workforce.

3. *The greatest barriers to people with disabilities are physical ones.* In actuality, negative attitudes and stereotypes are the greatest impediments and the most difficult to change.

4. *Businesses dislike the ADA.* Actually, 82 percent of executives surveyed believe that it is worth implementing and note that implementation expenses are minimal.

5. *Government health insurance covers people with disabilities.* Of the 29.5 million disabled individuals between the ages of 15 and 64, 18.4 million have private insurance, Medicaid covers 4.4 million, and 5.1 million have no health insurance.

Programs for Individuals with Disabilities

In the past, programs for persons with disabilities focused on rehabilitation rather than assistance to allow them to develop independent living skills. There has been gradual recognition that deficiencies in experiences and opportunities limit the individual's development. The services received by individuals with disabilities are most effective when they enable independence, self-determination, and productive participation in society (Humes, Szymanski, & Hohenshil, 1989). However, the statistics on the outcome of educational programs have not been very positive. One survey found that only 27 percent of individuals with disabilities go to college, compared to 68 percent of those without disabilities, and 30 percent drop out of high school. Three to five years after graduation from high school, only 57 percent are employed, compared to 69 percent of youth without disabilities (Wagner & Blackorby, 1996). Clearly, new approaches are needed. Several programs have obtained promising results.

Ted Stabelfeldt is a 19-year-old male, paralyzed from the shoulders down, who discovered the DO-IT program at the University of Washington. This program links high school students with disabilities who are interested in science and math with computer technology that is designed to work from their areas of strength. Todd is able to operate his computer with a hollow mouth wand. He types by pointing the wand to letters on the screen and blowing into the wand to make it operate like a computer mouse. One puff represents a single click and two puffs represent a double-click. Todd has learned to operate the computer efficiently, but admits that the most difficult part was not learning the new technology, but getting over his own negative attitudes toward disability: "When I attended DO-IT, that all changed. I met 40 other gimps—that's what I call them. I realized, hey, man, they're cool. They're real people too" (H. T. George, 1998, p. B2).

Todd's computer skills helped him obtain a job writing medical software. Of the 136 students who participated in the program, over 50 percent are going into technical schools or colleges, and over 25 percent have found employment. There has been a shift in the orientation of programs for people with disabilities from remediation or "making them as normal as possible" to identifying and strengthening skills that they possess.

The Bridges from School to Work program, which involved 2,258 students, was also successful. The disabilities included learning disabilities (52 percent), mental retardation (22 percent), emotional disability (14 percent), and other disabilities (12 percent). The last category included epilepsy, sensory impairments, head injuries, and orthopedic and mobility impairments. Participants had moderate to severe disabilities. The program involved prevocational orientation for both the family and the student. Information on job preparation, job expectations, and skills training was followed by internship placement in local businesses. The 12-week internship involved job skills training and monitoring of performance by the employers. Of the participants who completed their internships, 71 percent were offered jobs by the same or a different employer. In a 6-month follow-up, 84 percent of the participants were employed or had enrolled in college. The program was successful both through helping youths with disabilities make the transition to employment or further education and by opening doors in the business community (Fabian, Lent, & Willis, 1998).

Implications. Mental health professionals working with individuals with disabilities should be aware of the number of different programs offering employment and educational assistance. The National Library Service for the Blind and Physically Handicapped produces talking books and magazines on cassette for readers who are legally blind or cannot read printed material. Books and magazines are available free of charge to patrons, and most titles are offered on loan by postage-free mail to library patrons (Lazzaro, 2001).

The American Printing House for the Blind offers a database for audio-books, large print, computer disk, and Braille. Books can also be downloaded into talking handheld readers. The National Association of the Deaf operates the captioned media program, and the National Braille Press offers a selection of Braille books and magazines. Software programs can turn text into Braille through the use of a Braille printer, and scanners can convert print from books into speech. It is important for mental health professions to be aware of the ways current technology is enhancing the quality of life and employment opportunities for people with disabilities. Vocational and support group information can also be obtained over the Internet.

Counseling Issues with Individuals with Disabilities

Many counselors and other mental health professionals do not know how to deal with clients who have disabilities.

> *A 33-year-old client with hearing difficulties has problems at work. Her employer claims that she does not follow orders and inquires about attention or memory problems. The psychologist administers the Wechsler Adult Intelligence Scale–Revised (WAIS-R), the Wechsler Memory Scale–Revised, and the Minnesota Multiphasic Personality Inventory (MMPI) and finds no evidence of memory or attentional deficits. The MMPI results suggest mild paranoid and depressive tendencies. (Leigh, Corbett, Gutman, & Morere, 1996)*

In this case the psychologist concluded that the problems at work were a result of the woman's depression and paranoid tendencies. There is no mention in his report of the possible impact of her hearing loss on either the results of the assessments or her ability to adapt to the work environment. In fact, it is likely that the woman's hearing impairment accounted for the majority of the presenting symptoms.

Implications. Helping professionals often display the same attitude as the general public toward individuals with disabilities and may feel uncomfortable or experience guilt or pity when working with them. As when working with other oppressed groups, the counselor must examine his or her view of clients with disabilities and identify and question prejudicial assumptions. A client's disability should not be the sole focus for counseling. Environmental contributions to problems should also be identified. Issues involving frustrations with architectural barriers or with negative stereotypes or prejudices need to be addressed in counseling (Vacc & Clifford, 1995).

Kemp and Mallinckrodt (1996) pointed out some of the errors that can occur in counseling relationships with individuals with disabilities. First, errors involving omission may be made. The counselor may fail to ask questions about critical aspects of the client's life because the assumption is made that the issue is unimportant due to the presence of the disability. For example, sexuality and relationship issues may be ignored because of the belief that the individual lacks the ability or interest in pursuing these intimacies. Affective issues may also be avoided, since the counselor may be uncomfortable addressing the impact of the disability on the client. The counselor may display a lowered expectation of the client's capabilities. Second, errors of commission may be made. In this case, the counselor assumes without justification that certain issues should be important because of the disability, when they are not. Personal problems faced by the client are all assumed to be a result of the disability. Career and academic counseling may become a focus even when it is not the client's interest. Other errors identified by Kemp and Mallinckrodt that may be made when working with clients with disabilities are not addressing the disability at all, encouraging dependency and the "sick" role, countertransference in wanting to "rescue" the client, and having a lowered expectation of the client's capabilities.

First, it is generally appropriate to ask a client about a disability and its nature. In doing so, it is important not to succumb to the "spread" phenomenon that often exists with disabilities. This refers to believing that the disability encompasses unrelated aspects of the individual. For example, a person in a wheelchair may also be thought to have a cognitive problem. Second, you might ask if there are ways that the disability is part of the presenting problem (Olkin, 1999). Such an approach allows the therapist to address the disability directly. If the disability is of recent origin, assess factors such as coping style, whether they blame themselves or others for the injury, and the amount of social support available (Rabasca, 1999).

Models of Disability

Olkin (1999) believed that there are three models of disability affecting the way the condition is perceived. First, the *moral model* focuses on the "defect" as representing some form of sin or moral lapse. Feelings of shame occur for both the individuals with the disability and family members who feel responsible. The disability is perceived as a test of faith. Second, the *medical model* is paternalistic in nature. Disability represents a defect or loss of function that resides in the individual. Action is taken to cure or rehabilitate the conditions. Its advantage over the moral model is that it removes the notion of sin for the disability. In addition, the medical model has been responsible for many technological advances. Third, the *minority model* is a relatively new model in which disability is seen as an external problem involving an environment that fails to accommodate the needs of individuals with disabilities and is filled with negative societal attitudes. As such, there are many similarities between the experiences of individuals who are disabled and those of other minority groups.

Implications.   The mental health professional needs to identify the way the disability is viewed by the particular individual involved and by family members, since this will likely influence problem definition and intervention strategies. Much of the research indicates that empowering individuals and caregivers increases life satisfactions. This may need to be done within the model adhered to by the family. If the moral model is involved, the source for the interpretation of the disability as due to sin or a test of faith must be identified. Religious support may offer meaningful relief. Within this context, different alternative strategies can be generated. The goal is to reduce guilt, give meaning to the experience, generate support from the religious community, and develop problem-solving approaches. With the medical model, the focus is on a physical condition that lies within the disabled individual. The rehabilitation approach attempts to use technology and training to "normalize" the individual and to have him or her fit into the existing environment. The patient is passive and receives treatment. Lately, there has been increasing emphasis on independent functioning within this model. Mental health professionals can help clients and family members not only to obtain technological resources but also to develop more strongly independent living skills and to advocate for appropriate accommodations in the school and work environments. The minority model is useful in that societal attitudes are seen as a large part of the problem faced by individuals with disabilities. The focus is to change the environment to facilitate the potential of individuals who have disabilities. Inoculating them to societal prejudices and discrimination protects their self-esteem. The emphasis is on self-empowerment and self-advocacy.

Life Satisfaction and Depression

> *I should have picked up the pieces and made the adjustment, and not dwell on it . . . the problem is the rest of the world is dwelling on it. Every time you go out there, you're reacting to all this ridiculous attitude problem, the architectural barriers, the financial discrimination, and this place won't hire you and this company won't insure you and that potential lover won't look at you. . . . So that reopens the wound maybe twenty times a day and yet you're supposed to have made the adjustment . . . (Noonan et al., 2004, p. 72)*

As was indicated earlier, ratings of life satisfaction among individuals with disabilities tended to be lower than those for people without disabilities. However, these ratings depend on the type of disability and when the ratings were given. Some individuals adjust well, while others remain chronically distressed. In one study of the life satisfaction of people with traumatic spinal cord injuries, 37 percent indicated they were "very satisfied" and 31 percent "somewhat satisfied." This compares to 50 percent "very satisfied" and 40 percent "somewhat satisfied" among the general population. An interesting aspect of the study was that those who perceived themselves as in control were the most satisfied (Chase, Cornille, & English, 2000). Individuals with disabilities often rate satisfactions such as communication, thinking, and relating socially as more important than being able to walk or to dress oneself. Unfortunately, many mental health professionals display a negative attitude toward disability. In one study, only 18 percent of physicians and nurses imagined that they would be glad to be alive if they had a high-level spinal cord injury. Of 128 persons with this condition, 92 percent were glad to be alive.

Implications. Mental health and health care providers often underestimate the quality of life for individuals with disabilities and attempt to have them become content with their condition. Signs of depression or suicidal thoughts among individuals with disabilities might be accepted as normal because of a low quality of life. Interventions may be considered useless. The research seems to show that many individuals with disabilities feel quite satisfied with their lives, and that increasing their sense of control is important. Individuals with disabilities can develop self-efficacy by learning or being encouraged to direct their own personal assistance services and to make decisions over important aspects of their lives. As with other conditions, suicidal thoughts or wishes may surface and should be treated. Some support the right of individuals with disabilities to assisted suicide. However, disability organizations argue that individuals with disabilities are an oppressed group and could be coerced to end their lives (Batavia, 2000).

Sexuality and Reproduction

Men and women with disabilities often express concerns over sexual functioning and reproduction. They worry about their sexual attractiveness and how to relate to or find a partner. Some may not know if it is still possible to have children. Mental health professionals who are uncomfortable with these topics may overlook these areas, especially as it may apply to individuals with disabilities.

Implications. Clearly, both clients and therapists need to be educated on these subjects as they relate to the specific disabilities. Many individuals who have a disability receive the societal message that they should not be sexual or that they are sexually unattractive. This concern should be addressed and assessed both individually and to the couple, if applicable. Sexual relationships are based on communication and emotional responsiveness to one another. The mental health professional can help individuals or couples develop new ways of achieving sexual satisfaction. Old messages regarding sexuality may have to be replaced with new ones. Sexual pleasure is possible even with a loss of sensation in the genitals (e.g., with spinal cord injuries). Many women with spinal cord injuries are still capable of orgasms and sexual pleasure from stimulation of the genitals or other parts of the body. The injury also does not preclude the ability to become pregnant or deliver a child. Problems with lubrication may occur, but they can be treated with water-based lubricants such as K-Y jelly. Many women with spinal cord injuries are even able to have a vaginal delivery. Among men with spinal cord injuries, many are able to attain an erection and ejaculate, although they may have to learn new forms of stimulation. Sensate focus exercises can help individuals increase awareness of the areas of the body that may be open to sexual stimulation (Tepper, 2001). Online resources for sexual information include the following:

- *PeopleNet DisAbility DateNet (http://www.members.aol.com/bobezwriter/pnet .htm)*. This site provides information and the opportunity to participate in discussions on dating, sexuality, and relationships.
- *Through the Looking Glass (http://www.lookingglass.org)*. This site provides resources for adults and parents with disabilities and parents of children with disabilities.
- *DisAbled Women's Network (DAWN; http://www. serv1.thot.net/~dawn/who .html)*. This site also provides information on parenting from a feminist perspective.

Spirituality and Religiosity

Spirituality and religious beliefs can be a source of inner strength and support. One woman with a disability wrote, "It sort of helps me to identify myself, thinking I am a woman created by God and I am so precious and I am so loved and I have so much beauty inside of me" (Nosek & Hughes, 2001, p. 23).

Implications. The mental health professional should determine the role, if any, that religious beliefs or spirituality play in the life of a client with a disability. The woman in the previous example was able to have a positive sense of self partly through her spirituality. The vast majority of Americans believe in God and indicate that their approach to life is grounded in faith (Elliot, Kilpatrick, & McCullough, 1999). Such beliefs could be a source of support for both the caregivers and the patients. In other cases, individuals may believe that their disability is a punishment from God or may blame God for not preventing the injury. These issues should also be addressed and resolved. In any event, the importance of religious beliefs to the clients should be determined.

Family Counseling

Family caregivers now operate as integral parts of the health care system and provide services that were once performed by professional health care providers. They will probably assume even greater caregiving roles in the future. It is therefore important to help reduce the impact of stressors both on the caregivers and on the family member with the disability. With family members, emotional issues such as distress, guilt, self-punishment, or anger may need to be dealt with. Family members may feel responsible for the condition and have a primarily negative focus.

Implications. Individuals with the disability and their family members can decide to withdraw from others or to make positive changes. Hulnick and Hulnick (1989) suggested focusing on choices that can be made. For example, the counselor can ask questions such as "What are you doing that perpetuates the situation?" and "Are you aware of other choices that would have a different result?" These questions are empowering, since clients realize that they have the ability to make choices. Instead of viewing disability as a problem, reframing can be used to identify opportunities through questions such as "In what ways could you use this situation to your advancement?" or "What can you learn from this experience?" Among family caregivers, several attributes led to greater satisfaction both in them and in the individuals with the disability (Elliot, Shewchuk, & Richards, 1999). The first involved employing problem-solving strategies by defining the problem, generating alternatives, evaluating alternatives, implementing solutions, and evaluating outcomes. This helped increase the self-efficacy of the family members and increased their ability to develop coping strategies. The second consisted of developing a more positive orientation toward their ability to meet the demands of the situation. These approaches can improve the emotional health of both the caregivers and family members with disabilities. Reframing can also be useful. One psychologist who is blind believes that he may be less threatening to clients who are self-conscious or that they might respect the fact that he has faced and overcome difficult issues (Clay, 1999). Albert Ellis, the founder of rational-emotive therapy, has experienced the disabilities of diabetes, tired eyes, deficient hearing, and other physical handicaps but has successfully utilized cognitive approaches, such as reframing, to deal with his disabilities. For example, because he cannot keep his eyes open for any length of time, he focuses on the positive aspects of conducting therapy sessions with his eyes closed. He tells himself that with his eyes shut he can (1) focus "unusually well" on his clients' verbalizations (tone of voice, hesitations, etc.), (2) identify more easily their irrational thoughts, (3) help clients feel more relaxed, and (4) serve as a healthy model of an individual with a disability (Ellis, 1997). Ellis has thus been able to redefine his disability as a useful feature in conducting therapy.

Implications for Clinical Practice

1. Identify your beliefs, assumptions, and attitudes about individuals with disabilities.

2. Understand the prejudice, discrimination, inconveniences, and barriers faced by individuals with disabilities.

3. Redirect internalized self-blame for the disability to societal attitudes.

4. Employ the appropriate communication format and address the client directly rather than an accompanying individual.

5. Determine if the disability is related to the presenting problem or if it will impact treatment strategies. If it is not an issue, continue with your usual assessments.

6. If the disability is related to the problem, identify whether the client adheres to the moral model (disability is a result of moral lapse or a sin), medical model (disability is a physical limitation), or minority model (disability is the result of a lack of accommodation by the environment).

7. If formal tests are employed, provide appropriate accommodations. Interpret the results with care since most are not standardized with members of this population.

8. Recognize that family members and other social supports are important. Include them in your assessment, goal formation, and selection of techniques. It is also important to determine their model of disability.

9. Identify environmental changes or accommodations that are associated with the problem and assist the family to change them.

10. Help family members reframe the problem so that positives can be identified. Strengthen positive attributes.

11. Develop self-advocacy skills for both the individual with the disability and the family members.

12. Note that counseling strategies that focus on problem identification, developing and implementing changes, and evaluating effectiveness are useful.

13. Realize that mental health professionals may have to serve as advocates or consultants to initiate changes in academic and work settings.

References

Abraham, M. (1999). Sexual abuse in South Asian immigrant marriages. *Violence Against Women, 5,* 591–618.

Abreu, J. M., Goodyear, R. K., Campos, A., & Newcomb, M. D. (2000). Ethnic belonging and traditional masculinity ideology among African Americans, European Americans and Latinos. *Psychology of Men and Masculinity, 1,* 75–86.

Acquino, J. A., Russell, D. W., Cutrona, C. E., & Altmaier, E. M. (1996). Employment status, social support, and life satisfaction among the elderly. *Journal of Counseling Psychology, 43,* 480–489.

Ahai, C. E. (1997). A cultural framework for counseling African Americans. In C. C. Lee (Ed.), *Multicultural issues in counseling* (2nd ed., pp. 73–80). Alexandria, VA: American Counseling Association.

AhnAllen, J. M., Suyemoto, K. L. & Carter, A. S. (2006). Relationship between physical appearance, sense of belonging and exclusion, and racial/ethnic self-identification among multiracial Japanese European Americans. *Cultural Diversity and Ethnic Minority Psychology, 12,* 673–686.

Ahuvia, A. (2001). Well-being in cultures of choice: A cross-cultural perspective. *American Psychologist, 56*(1), 77.

Alexander, C., Langer, E., Newman, R., Chandler, H., & Davies, J. (1989). Transcendental meditation, mindfulness and longevity: An experimental study with the elderly. *Journal of Personality and Social Psychology, 57,* 950–964.

Alexander, C., Rainforth, M., & Gelderloos, P. (1991). Transcendental meditation, self actualization and psychological health: A conceptual overview and statistical meta-analysis. *Journal of Social Behavior and Personality, 6,* 189–247.

Allison, K. W., Crawford, I., Echemendia, R., Robinson, L., & Knepp, D. (1994). Human diversity and professional competence: Training in clinical and counseling psychology revisited. *American Psychologist, 49,* 792–796.

Allport, G. W. (1961). *Pattern and growth in personality.* New York: Holt, Rinehart & Winston.

Alter, J. (2005, Sept. 19). The other America. *Newsweek,* p. 40–48.

Alter, J. (2006, Sept. 4). Still blind to the poverty. *Newsweek,* p. 38.

American-Arab Anti-Discrimination Committee (ADC). (2003). Report on hate crimes and discrimination against Arab Americans. Retrieved 12/16/2006 from http://www.adc.org/hate_crimes.htm

American Association of People with Disabilities (AAPD) News (2006). Bipartisan legislation introduced to restore ADA protections. *AAPD News,* pp. 1, 3.

American Counseling Association. (1995). Summit results in formation of spiritual competencies. *Counseling Today,* p. 30.

American Friends Service Committee. (1998). *People with disabilities.* Philadelphia: Affirmative Action Office.

American Friends Service Committee (2006a). Immigrants and racial/ethnic tensions. Retrieved 12/11/2006 from http://www.afsc.org/immigrants-rights/learn/racial-ethnic.htm

American Friends Service Committee (2006b). Immigration law and policy. Retrieved 12/11/2006 from http://www.afsc.org/immigrants-rights/learn/law-policy.htm

American Friends Service Committee (2006c). Understanding anti-immigrant movements. Retrieved 12/11/2006 from http//www.afsc.org/immigrants-rights/learn/anti-immigrant.htm

American Enterprise Institute. (2004). AEI study on homosexuality and gay marriage. Retrieved 12/10/2006 from http://www.aei.org/include/pub_print.asp?pubID=20867

American Psychiatric Association. (1997). Practice

guidelines for the treatment of patients with Alzheimer's disease and other dementias of late life. *American Journal of Psychiatry, 154,* 1–39.

American Psychiatric Association. (2000). *Diagnostic and Statistical Manual of Mental Disorders–Fourth Edition, Text Revision (DSM-IV-TR).* Washington, DC: Author.

American Psychological Association (APA). (2001a). *Aging and human sexuality resource guide.* Washington, DC: Author.

American Psychological Association (APA). (2001b). *Elder abuse and neglect: In search of solutions.* Washington, DC: Author.

American Psychological Association (APA). (2001c). *Older adults and Insomnia Resource Guide.* Washington, DC: Author.

American Psychological Association (APA). (2004). Guidelines for psychological practice with older adults. *American Psychologist, 59,* 236–260.

American Psychological Association (APA). (2006). APA's Response to international and national disasters and crises: Addressing diverse needs. *American Psychologist, 61,* 513–521.

American Psychological Association Division 44/ Committee on Lesbian, Gay, and Bisexual Concerns Joint Task Force On Guidelines for Psychotherapy with Lesbian, Gay, and Bisexual Clients (2000). Guidelines for psychotherapy with lesbian, gay, and bisexual clients. *American Psychologist, 55,* 1440–451.

American Psychological Association, Presidential Task Force on the Assessment of Age Consistent Memory Decline and Dementia. (1998). *Guidelines for the evaluation of dementia and age-related cognitive decline.* Washington, DC: Author.

American Psychological Association Task Force on Socioeconomic Status (SES). (April 2006). *Draft report of the APA Task Force on socioeconomic status.*

American Psychological Association Working Group on the Older Adult Brochure. (1998). *What practitioners should know about working with older adults.* Washington, DC: American Psychological Association.

Anderson, M. J., & Ellis, R. (1995). On the reservation. In N. A. Vacc, S. B. DeVaney, & J. Wittmer (Eds.), *Experiencing and counseling multicultural and diverse populations* (3rd ed., pp. 179–198). Bristol, PA: Accelerated Development.

Anderson, N. B. (1995). Behavioral and sociocultural perspectives on ethnicity and health: Introduction to the special issue. *Health Psychology, 14,* 589–591.

Anti-Defamation League. (2006). Annual ADL Audit: Anti-Semitic incidents decline in 2005 but levels still of concern in U.S. Retrieved 12/7/06 from http://www.adl.org/PresRele/ASUS12/audit_2005.htm

Anti-Defamation League. (2005). ADL Survey: Anti-Semitism declines slightly in America: 14 Percent of Americans hold 'strong' anti-Semitic beliefs. Retrieved 12/7/06 from http://www.adl.org/PresRele/ASUS_12/4680_12.htm

Asai, M. O., & Kameoka, V. A. (2005). The influence of Sekentei on family caregiving and underutilization of social services among Japanese caregivers. *Social Work, 50,* 111–118.

Asner-Self, K. K., & Marotta, S. A. (2005). Developmental indices among Central American immigrants exposed to war-related trauma: Clinical implications for counselors. *Journal of Counseling and Development, 83,* 163–172.

Asquith, C. (2006). College applications to include new multi-racial box. *Diverse Issues in Higher Education, 23,* p. 21.

Associated Press. (2006, June 12). Philly eatery's English-only sign under fire. Retrieved 12/12/2006 from http://www.msnbc.msn.com/id/13272368/

Associated Press. (2006, May 21). U.S. report: 2.2 million now in prison, jails. Retrieved from http://www.msnbc.msn.com/id/12901873/

Atkinson, D. R. (1983). Ethnic similarity in counseling psychology: A review of research. *The Counseling Psychologist, 11,* 79–92.

Atkinson, D. R. (1985). Research on cross-cultural counseling and psychotherapy: A review and update of reviews. In P. B. Pederson (Ed.), *Handbook of cross-cultural counseling and therapy* (pp. 191–197). Westport, CT: Greenwood Press.

Atkinson, D. R., Bui, U., & Mori, S. (2001). Multiculturally sensitive empirically supported treatments—an oxymoron? In J. G. Ponterotto,

J. M. Casas, L. A. Suzuki, & C. M. Alexander (Eds.), *Handbook of multicultural counseling* (pp. 542–574). Thousand Oaks, CA: Sage.

Atkinson, D. R., & Hackett, G. (1998). *Counseling diverse populations* (2nd ed.). Boston: McGraw-Hill.

Atkinson, D. R., Kim, B. S. K., & Caldwell, R. (1998). Ratings of helper roles by multicultural psychologists and Asian American students: Initial support for the three-dimensional model of multicultural counseling. *Journal of Counseling Psychology, 45,* 414–423.

Atkinson, D. R., & Lowe, S. M. (1995). The role of ethnicity, cultural knowledge, and conventional techniques in counseling and psychotherapy. In J. G. Ponterotto, J. M. Casas, L. A. Suzuki, & C. M. Alexander (Eds.), *Handbook of multicultural counseling* (pp. 387–414). Thousand Oaks, CA: Sage.

Atkinson, D. R., Maruyama, M., & Matsui, S. (1978). The effects of counselor race and counseling approach on Asian Americans' perceptions of counselor credibility and utility. *Journal of Counseling Psychology, 25,* 76–83.

Atkinson, D. R., Morten, G., & Sue, D. W. (1979). *Counseling American minorities: A cross-cultural perspective.* Dubuque, IA: Brown.

Atkinson, D. R., Morten, G., & Sue, D. W. (1989). A minority identity development model. In D. R. Atkinson, G. Morten, & D. W. Sue (Eds.), *Counseling American minorities* (pp. 35–52). Dubuque, IA: W. C. Brown.

Atkinson, D. R., Morten, G., & Sue, D. W. (Eds.). (1998). *Counseling American minorities* (5th ed.) Boston: McGraw-Hill.

Atkinson, D. R., & Schein, S. (1986). Similarity in counseling. *The Counseling Psychologist, 14,* 319–354.

Atkinson, D. R., Thompson, C. E., & Grant, S. K. (1993). A three-dimensional model for counseling racial/ethnic minorities. *The Counseling Psychologist, 21,* 257–277.

Avila, D. L. & Avila, A. L. (1995). Mexican Americans. In N. A. Vacc, S. B. DeVaney, & J. Wittmer (Eds.), *Experiencing and counseling multicultural and diverse populations* (3rd ed., pp. 119–146). Bristol, PA: Accelerated Development.

Baca, L. M., & Koss-Chioino, J. D. (1997). Development of a culturally responsive group counseling model for Mexican American adolescents. *Journal of Multicultural Counseling and Development, 25,* 130–141.

Balderas, J. B. (2001, August 12). American Indians' enemy: Diabetes, lifestyle, diets blamed as 50% of Native Americans over 45 are affected. *The Washington Post,* p. A2.

Baldor, L. C. (2006, Nov. 16). Pentagon alters homosexuality guidelines. Yahoo News, http://news.yahoo.com/s/ap/20061116/ap_on_go_cas_st_pe/military_gays

Balsam, K. F., Rothblum, E. D., & Beauchaine, T. P. (2005). Victimization over the life span: A comparison of lesbian, gay, bisexual, and heterosexual siblings. *Journal of Consulting and Clinical Psychology, 73,* 477–487.

Banaji, M. R., & Greenwald, A. G. (1995). Implicit gender stereotyping in judgments of fame. *Journal of Personality and Social Psychology, 68*(2), 181–198.

Bankart, C. P. (1997). *Talking cures: A history of Western and Eastern psycho therapies.* Pacific Grove, CA: Brooks/Cole.

Banks, J. A., & Banks, C. A. (1993). *Multicultural education.* Boston: Allyn & Bacon.

Barker, A. (2006, March 3). Suit: W. Va. police chief denied gay man CPR. *Charleston Daily Mail,* p. 6a.

Barongan, C., Bernal, G., Comas-Diaz, L., Iijima Hall, C. C., Nagayama Hall, G. C., LaDue, R. A., Parham, T. A., Pedersen, P. B., Porche-Burke, L. M., Rollock, D., & Root, M. P. P. (1997). Misunderstandings of multiculturalism: Shouting fire in crowded theaters. *American Psychologist, 52,* 654–655.

Barr, D. J., & Strong, L. J. (1987, May). Embracing multiculturalism: The existing contradictions. *ACU-I Bulletin,* pp. 20–23.

Batalova, J. (2006). Spotlight on refugees and asylees in the United States. Retrieved 12/10/06 from http://www.migrationinformation.org/USFocus/print.ctf?ID=415

Batavia, A. I. (2000). The relevance of data on physician and disability on the right of assisted suicide. *Psychology, Public Policy, and Law, 6,* 546–558.

Bauer, H. M., Rodriguez, M. A., Quiroga, S. S., & Flores-Ortiz, Y. G. (2000). Barriers to health care for abuse Latina and Asian immigrant women. *Journal of Health Care for the Poor and Underserved, 11*, 33–44.

Bean, R. A., Perry, B. J., & Bedell, T. M. (2001). Developing culturally competent marriage and family therapists: Guidelines for working with Hispanic families. *Journal of Marital and Family Therapy, 27*, 43–54.

Beauvais, E., Chavez, E. L., Oetting, E. R., Deffenbacher, J. L., & Cornell, G. R. (1996). Drug use, violence, and victimization among white American, Mexican American, and American Indian dropouts, students with academic problems, and students in good academic standing. *Journal of Counseling Psychology, 43*, 292–299.

Becvar, D. S., & Becvar, R. J. (2003). *Family therapy: A systemic integration* (5th ed.). Needham Heights, MA: Allyn & Bacon.

Bee-Gates, D., Howard-Pitney, B., LaFromboise, T., & Rowe, W. (1996). Help-seeking behavior of Native American Indian high school students. *Professional Psychology: Research and Practice, 27*, 495–499.

Beigel, H. G. (1966). Problems and motives in interracial relationships. *Journal of Sex Research, 2*, 185–205.

Belgrave, F. Z., Chase-Vaughn, G., Gray, F., Addison, J. D., & Cherry, V. R. (2000). The effectiveness of a culture- and gender-specific intervention for increasing resiliency among African American preadolescent females. *Journal of Black Psychology, 26*, 133–147.

Bell, D. (1993). *Faces at the bottom of the well: The permanence of racism.* New York: Basic Books.

Bell, L. A. (1997). Theoretical foundations for social justice education. In M. Adams, L. A. Bell, & P. Griffin (Eds.), *Teaching for diversity and social justice: A sourcebook* (pp. 3–15). New York: Routledge.

Bell, M. P., Harrison, D. A., & McLaughlin, M. E. (1997). Asian American attitudes towards affirmative action in employment: Implications for the model minority myth. *Journal of Applied Behavioral Science, 33*, 356–377.

Bemak, F., Chung, R. C.-Y., & Bornemann, T. (1996). Counseling and psychotherapy with refugees. In P. Pedersen, J. Draguns, W. Lonner, & J. Trimble (Eds.), *Counseling across cultures* (4th ed., pp. 243–265). Thousand Oaks, CA: Sage.

Bennett, M. J. (1986). A developmental approach to training for intercultural sensitivity. *International Journal of Intercultural Relations, 10*, 179–196.

Benokraitis, N.V. (1997). *Subtle sexism: Current practice and prospects for change.* Thousand Oaks, CA: Sage.

Berg, S. H. (2006). Everyday sexism and posttraumatic stress disorder in women. *Violence Against Women, 12*(10), 970–88.

Berkofsky, J. (2006). A snapshot of American Jewry. Retrieved 12/15/2006 from http://www.myjewishlearning.com/history_community/Jewish_Wor

Berman, J. (1979). Counseling skills used by Black and White male and female counselors. *Journal of Counseling Psychology, 26*, 81–84.

Bernal, M. E., & Castro, F. G. (1994). Are clinical psychologists prepared for service and research with ethnic minorities? A report of a decade of progress. *American Psychologist, 49*, 797–805.

Bernal, M. E., & Knight, G. P. (1993). *Ethnic identity: Formation and transmission among Hispanics and other minorities.* Albany: State University of New York Press.

Bernstein, B. (1964). Elaborated and restricted codes: Their social origins and some consequences. In J. J. Gumperz & D. Hymes (Eds.), The ethnography of communication. *American Anthropologist, 66*, 55–69.

Bernstein, N. (2006, March 3). Recourse grows slim for immigrants who fall ill. *New York Times*, p. A.14

Berry, B. (1965). *Ethnic and race relations.* Boston: Houghton Mifflin.

Berube, A. (1990). *Coming out under fire: The history of gay men and women in World War II.* New York: Free Press.

Bhungalia, L. (2001). Native American women and violence. *National NOW Times, 33*, 5, 13.

Bienvenu, C., & Ramsey, C. J. (2006). The culture of socioeconomic disadvantage: Practical approaches to counseling. In C. C. Lee (Ed.),

Multicultural issues in counseling (3rd ed., pp. 345–353). Alexandria, VA: American Counseling Association.

Bigler, R. S., & Averhart, C. J. (2003). Race and the workforce: Occupational status, aspirations, and stereotyping among African American children. *Developmental Psychology, 39,* 572–580.

Black, L. (1996). Families of African origin: An overview. In M. McGoldrick, J. Giordano, & J. K. Pearce (Eds.), *Ethnicity and family therapy* (pp. 57–65). New York: Guilford.

Blair, S. L., & Qian, Z. (1998). Family and Asian students' educational performance. *Journal of Family Issues, 19,* 355–374.

Blake, S. M., Ledsky, R., Lehman, T., & Goodenow, C. (2001). Preventing sexual risk behaviors among gay, lesbian, and bisexual adolescents: The benefits of gay-sensitive HIV instruction in schools. *American Journal of Public Health, 91,* 940–946.

Blanchard, E. L. (1983). The growth and development of American Indians and Alaskan Native children. In G. J. Powell, J. Yamamoto, A. Romero, & A. Morales (Eds.), *The psychosocial development of minority group children* (pp. 96–103). New York: Brunner/Mazel.

Blando, J. A. (2001). Twice hidden: Older gay and lesbian couples, friends, intimacy. *Generations, 25,* 87–89.

Blazer, D. G., Hybels, C. F., Somonsick, E. M., & Hanlon, J. T. (2000). Marked differences in antidepressant use by race in an elderly community sample: 1986–1996. *American Journal of Psychiatry, 157,* 1089–1094.

Bloom, S. (1997). *Creating sanctuary.* New York: Routledge.

Bookwala, J., & Schulz, R. (2000). A comparison of primary stressors, secondary stressors, and depressive symptoms between elderly caregiving husbands and wives. *Psychology and Aging, 15,* 607–616.

Bourne, D., Watts, S., Gordon, T., & Figueroa-Garcia, A. (2006). Analysis: One year after hurricane Katrina—Issues of social disadvantage and political process. In *Communiqué,* August issue, 3–9. Washington, DC: Office of Ethnic Minority Affairs, American Psychological Association.

Bowles, D. D. (1993). Bi-racial identity: Children born to African-American and White couples. *Clinical Social Work Journal, 21,* 417–427.

Boyd-Franklin, N. (2003). *Black families in therapy.* New York: Guilford.

Brammer, R. (2004). *Diversity in counseling.* Belmont, CA: Brooks Cole.

Brayboy, T. L. (1966). Interracial sexuality as an expression of neurotic conflict. *Journal of Sex Research, 2,* 179–184.

Brecher, R., & Brecher, E. (1961). The happiest creatures on earth? *Harpers, 222,* 85–90.

Brennan, P. L., & Moos, R. H. (1996). Late-life drinking behavior. *Alcohol Health and Research World, 20,* 197–204.

Breytspraak, L., Kendall, L., & Halpert, B. (2006). What do you know about aging? A quiz. Retrieved from http://cas.umkc.edu/cas/Aging FactsQuiz.htm

Brinkley, D. (1994). *Saved by the light.* New York: Villard Books.

Broman, C. L., Mavaddat, R., & Hsu, S.-Y. (2000). The experience and consequences of perceived racial discrimination: A study of African Americans. *Journal of Black Psychology, 26,* 165–180.

Brooke, J. (1998, April 9). Indians strive to save their languages. *The New York Times,* p. 1.

Brown, R. P., & Josephs, R. A. (1999). A burden of proof: Stereotype relevance and gender differences in math performance. *Journal of Personality and Social Psychology, 76,* 246–257.

Browning, C., Reynolds, A. L., & Dworkin, S. H. (1998). Affirmative psychotherapy for lesbian women. In D. R. Atkinson & G. Hackett (Eds.), *Counseling diverse populations* (2nd ed., pp. 317–334). Boston: McGraw-Hill.

Brunsma, D. L. (2005). Interracial families and racial identity of mixed-race children: Evidence from the early childhood longitudinal study. *Social Forces, 84,* 1131–1157.

Buckman, D. F. (1998). The see-through syndrome. *Inside MS, 16,* p. 19.

Buki, L. P., Ma, T-C., Strom, R. D., & Strom, S. K. (2003). Chinese immigrant mothers of adolescents: Self-perceptions of acculturation effects on parenting. *Cultural Diversity and Ethnic Minority Psychology, 9,* 127–140.

Bureau of Indian Affairs. (2005). Indian entities recognized and eligible to receive services from the United States Bureau of Indian Affairs. *Federal Register, 70,* 71194.

Burke, G. (2005, Oct. 24). Translating isn't kid stuff. *San Jose Mercury News,* p. 5B.

Burn, S. M. (2000). Heterosexuals' use of "fag" and "queer" to deride one another: A contributor to heterosexism and stigma. *Journal of Homosexuality, 40,* 1–11.

Burn, S. M., Kadlee, K., & Rexer, B. S. (2005). Effects of subtle heterosexism on gays, lesbians, and bisexuals. *Journal of Homosexuality, 49,* 23–38.

Burnett, A., & Thompson, K. (2005). Enhancing the psychosocial well-being of asylum seekers and refugees. In K. H. Barrett & W. H. George (Eds.), *Race, culture, psychology, and law* (pp. 205–224). Thousand Oaks, CA.: Sage.

Burris, J. (2005). Aging persons. In K. L. Guadalupe & D. Lum (Eds.), *Multidimensional contextual practice* (pp. 270–286). Belmont, CA: Brooks Cole.

Butler D., & Geis, F. L. (1990). Nonverbal affect responses to male and female leaders: Implications for leadership evaluations. *Journal of Personality and Social Psychology, 58,* 48–59.

Canino, G., & Roberts, R. E. (2001). Suicidal behavior among Latino youth. *Suicide and Life-Threatening Behavior, 31,* 122–131.

Capps, R., Fix, M., Ost, J., Reardon-Anderson, J., & Passel, J. S. (2005). The health and and well-being of young children of immigrants. *Immigrant families and workers: Facts and perspectives.* Washington, DC: Urban Institute.

Carney, C. G., & Kahn, K. B. (1984). Building competencies for effective cross-cultural counseling: A developmental view. *The Counseling Psychologist, 12,* 111–119.

Carter, R. T. (1990). The relationship between racism and racial identity among White Americans: An exploratory investigation. *Journal of Counseling and Development, 69,* 46–50.

Carter, R. T. (1995). *The influence of race and racial identity in psychotherapy.* New York: Wiley.

Carter, R. T. (Ed.). (2005). *Handbook of racial-cultural psychology and counseling.* Hoboken, NJ: Wiley.

Caruso, D. B. (2006, Nov. 8). New York City seeks to redefine the rules on gender identity. *Seattle Post-Intelligencer,* p. A14.

Casas, J. M., & Pytluk, S. D. (1995). Hispanic identity development. In J. G. Ponterotto, J. M. Casas, L. A. Suzuki, & C. M. Alexander (Eds.), *Handbook of multicultural counseling* (pp. 155–180). Thousand Oaks, CA: Sage.

Cashwell, C. S., Shcherbakova, J. & Cashwell, T. H. (2003). Effect of client and counselor ethnicity on preference for counselor disclosure. *Journal of Counseling and Development, 81,* 196–201.

Cass, V. C. (1979). Homosexual identity formation: A theoretical model. *Journal of Homosexuality, 4,* 219–235.

Caughy, M. O., O'Campo, P. J., & Muntaner (2004). Experiences of racism among African American parents and the mental health of their preschool-aged children. *American Journal of Public Health, 94,* 2118–2124.

Centers for AIDS Prevention Studies, UCSF. (2006, May 11). What are the HIV prevention needs of adults over 50? Retrieved from http://www.caps.ucsf.edu/over50.html

Centers for Disease Control (CDC). (1992). Alcohol-related hospitalizations–Indian Health Service and Tribal Hospitals, United States. *Morbidity and Mortality Weekly Report, 41,* 757–760.

Centers for Disease Control (CDC). (1994). Prevalence and characteristic of alcohol consumption and fetal alcohol awareness—Alaska, 1991 and 1993. *Morbidity and Mortality Weekly Report, 43,* 3–6.

Centers for Disease Control (CDC). (2003). Injury mortality among American Indian and Alaska Native children and youth—United States, 1989–1998. *Morbidity and Mortality Weekly Report, 52,* 697–701.

Centers for Disease Control (CDC). (2006). Environmental barriers to health care among persons with disabilities—Los Angeles County, California, 2002–2003. *Morbidity and Mortality Weekly Report, 55,* 48.

Chang, E. T. (2001). Bitter fruit: The politics of Black-Korean conflict in New York City (Review). *Journal of Asian American Studies, 4*(3), 295–298.

Chang, J., & Sue, S. (2005). Culturally sensitive

research: Where have we gone wrong and what do we need to do now. In M. G. Constantine & D. W. Sue (Eds.), *Strategies for building multicultural competence in mental health and educational settings* (pp. 229–246). Hoboken, NJ: Wiley.

Chang, Y. (1998, June 22). Asian identity crisis. *Newsweek*, p. 68.

Chase, B. W., Cornille, T. A., & English, R. W. (2000). Life satisfaction among persons with spinal cord injuries. *Journal of Rehabilitation, 66*, 14–20.

Chavez, L. G. (2005). Latin American healers and healing: Healing as a redefinition process. In R. Moodley & W. West (Eds.), *Integrating traditional healing practices into counseling and psychotherapy* (pp. 85–99). Thousand Oaks, CA: Sage.

Cheatham, H., Ivey, A. E., Ivey, M. B., Pedersen, P., Rigazio-DiGilio, S., Simek-Morgan, L., & Sue, D. W. (1997). Multicultural counseling and therapy I: Metatheory—Taking theory into practice. In A. E. Ivey, M. B. Ivey, & L. Simek-Morgan (Eds.), *Counseling and psychotherapy: A multicultural perspective* (pp. 133–169). Boston: Allyn & Bacon.

Cheek, D. (1987). *Assertive White... puzzled White.* San Luis Obispo, CA: Impact.

Chen, C. P. (2005). Morita therapy: A philosophy of Yin/Yang coexistence. In R. Moodley & W. West (Eds.), *Integrating traditional healing practices into counseling and psychotherapy* (pp. 221–232). Thousand Oaks, CA: Sage.

Chen, E., Matthews, K. A., & Boyce, W. T. (2002). Socioeconomic differences in children's health: How and why do these relationships change with age? *Psychological Bulletin, 128*, 295–329.

Chen, S. W-H., & Davenport, D. S. (2005). Cognitive-behavioral therapy with Chinese American clients: Cautions and modifications. *Psychotherapy: Theory, Research, Practice, Training, 42*, 101–110.

Chen, Z. (2001). Chinese American children's ethnic identity: Measurement and implications. *Communication Studies, 51*, 74–95.

Cheung, F. K., & Snowden, L. R. (1990). Community mental health and ethnic minority populations. *Community Mental Health Journal, 26*, 277–291.

Choi, K-H., & Wynne, M. E. (2000). Providing services to Asian Americans with developmental disabilities and their families: Mainstream service providers' perspective. *Community Mental Health Journal, 36*, 589–595.

Choi, Y. H. (1999, September 7). Commentary: Asian values meet western realities. *The Los Angeles Times*, p. 7.

Choi, Y. H., Harachi, T. W., Gilmore, M. R. & Catalano, R. F. (2006). Are multiracial adolescents at greater risk? Comparisons of rates, patterns, and correlates of substance use and violence between monoracial and multiracial adolescents. *American Journal of Orthopsychiatry, 76*, 86–97.

Choney, S. K., Berryhill-Paapke, E., & Robbins, R. R. (1995). The acculturation of American Indians: Developing frameworks for research and practice. In J. G. Ponterotto, J. M. Casas, L. A. Suzuki, & C. M. Alexander (Eds.), *Handbook of multicultural counseling* (pp. 73–92). Thousand Oaks, CA: Sage.

Christian, M. D., & Barbarin, O. A. (2001). Cultural resources and psychological adjustment of African American children: Effects of spirituality and racial attribution. *Journal of Black Psychology, 27*, 43–63.

Chung, R. C. Y., & Bemak, F. (2007). In M. G. Constantine (Ed.), *Clinical practice with people of color* (pp. 125–142). New York: Teachers College Press.

Clark, K. B., & Clark, M. K. (1947). Racial identification and preference in Negro children. In T. M. Newcomb & E. L. Hartley (Eds.), *Readings in social psychology* (pp. 169–178). New York: Holt, Reinhart & Winston.

Clay, R. A. (1999). Four psychologists help others to see. *APA Monitor, 30*, 1–4.

Cochran, S. D., Keenan, C., Schober, C., & Mays, V. M. (2000). Estimates of alcohol use and clinical treatment needs among homosexually active men and women in the U.S. population. *Journal of Consulting and Clinical Psychology, 68*, 1062–1071.

Cohn, D. (2001, August 23). Count of gay couples up 300 percent. *The Washington Post*, pp. 1–3.

Cokley, K. (2006). The use of race and ethnicity in

psychological practice: A review. In R. T. Carter (Ed.), *Handbook of racial-cultural psychology and counseling* (pp. 249–261). Hoboken, NJ: Wiley.

Colarossi, L. (2005). A response to Danis & Lockhart: What guides social work knowledge about violence against women? *Journal of Social Work Education, 41,* 147–159.

Coleman, J. (2003, April 2). Bill would ban using children as interpreters. *San Jose Mercury News,* p. A 01.

Comas-Diaz, L. (2001). Hispanics, Latinos, or Americanos: The evolution of identity. *Cultural Diversity and Ethnic Minority Psychology, 7,* 115–120.

Comas-Diaz, L., & Greene, B. (1994). Women of color with professional status. In L. Comas-Diaz & B. Greene (Eds.), *Women of color: Integrating ethnic and gender identities in psychotherapy* (p. 347–388). New York: Guilford.

Committee of 100. (2001). *American attitudes toward Chinese Americans and Asian Americans.* New York: Author.

Committee on Women in Psychology. (1999). *Older psychologists survey.* Washington, DC: American Psychological Association.

Condon, J. C., & Yousef, F. (1975). *An introduction to intercultural communication.* New York: Bobbs-Merrill.

Conger, J. (1975). Proceedings of the American Psychological Association, Incorporated, for the year 1974: Minutes of the annual meeting of Council of Representatives. *American Psychologist, 30,* 620–651.

Congressional Record. (1997). *Indian Child Welfare Act Amendments of 1997—Hon. George Miller.* Washington, DC: Author.

Constantine, M. G. (2006). Institutional racism against African Americans. In M. G. Constantine & D. W. Sue (Eds.), *Addressing racism* (pp. 33–41). Hoboken, NJ: Wiley.

Constantine, M. G. (2007). Racial microaggressions against African American clients in a cross-racial counseling relationship. *Journal of Counseling Psychology, 54,* 1–16.

Constantine, M. G., Gloria, A. M. & Baron, A. (2006). Counseling Mexican American college students. In C. C. Lee (Ed.), *Multicultural issues in counseling* (3rd ed., pp. 207–222). Alexandria, VA: American Counseling Association.

Constantine, M. G., Myers, L. J., Kindaichi, M., & Moore, J. L. (2004). Exploring indigenous mental health practices: The roles of healers and helpers in promoting well-being in people of color. *Counseling and Values, 48,* 110–125.

Constantine, M. G., & Sue, D. W. (2005). *Strategies for building multicultural competence in mental health and educational settings.* Hoboken, NJ: Wiley.

Constantine, M. G., & Sue, D. W. (2006). *Addressing racism.* Hoboken, NJ: Wiley.

Cook, E. P. (1990). Gender and psychological distress. *Journal of Counseling and Development, 68,* 371–375.

Cooper, C., Carpenter, I., Katona, C., Scholl, M., Wagner, C., Fialova, D., et al. (2005). The Ad-HOC study of older adults' adherence to medication in 11 countries. *American Journal of Geriatric Psychiatry, 13,* 1067–1076.

Cooper, C., & Costas, L. (1994). Ethical challenges when working with Hispanic/Latino families: Personalismo. *The Family Psychologist, 10,* 32–34.

Corey, G. (2005). *Theory and practice of counseling and psychotherapy* (7th ed.). Belmont, CA: Brooks Cole.

Corvin, S., & Wiggins, F. (1989). An antiracism training model for White professionals. *Journal of Multicultural Counseling and Development, 17,* 105–114.

Cose, E., Smith, V. E., Figueroa, A., Stefanakos, V. S., & Contreras, J. (2000, November 13). American's prison generation. *Newsweek,* 42–49.

Cosgrove, L. (2006). The unwarranted pathologizing of homeless mothers: Implications for research and social policy. In R. L. Toporek, L. H. Gerstein, N. A. Fouad, G. Roysircar, & T. Israel (Eds.), *Handbook for social justice in counseling psychology* (pp. 200–214). Thousand Oaks, CA: Sage.

Council for the National Interest. (2006). Poll: Forty percent of American voters believe the Israel Lobby has been a key factor in going to war in Iraq and now confronting Iran. Retrieved 12/7/06 from http://www.cnionline.org/learn/polls/czandlobby/index2.htm

Crawford, I., McLeod, A., Zamboni, B. D., & Jordan, M. B. (1999). Psychologists' attitudes toward gay and lesbian parenting. *Professional Psychology: Research and Practice, 30,* 394–401.

Cronin, M. E. (1998, June 11). Body type–body hype—local high-school students challenge marketing of super-thin image. *Seattle Times,* p. E1.

Cross, T. L., Bazron, B. J., Dennis, K. W., & Isaacs, M. R. (1989). *Towards a culturally competent system of care.* Washington, DC: Child and Adolescent Service System Program Technical Assistance Center.

Cross, W. E. (1971). The Negro-to-Black conversion experience: Towards a psychology of Black liberation. *Black World, 20,* 13–27.

Cross, W. E. (1991). *Shades of Black: Diversity in African American identity.* Philadelphia: Temple University Press.

Cross, W. E. (1995). The psychology of Nigrescence: Revising the Cross model. In J. G. Ponterotto, J. M. Casas, L. A. Suzuki, & C. M. Alexander (Eds.), *Handbook of multicultural counseling* (pp. 93–122). Thousand Oaks, CA: Sage.

Cross, W. E., Smith, L., & Payne, Y. (2002). Black identity. In P. B. Pedersen, J. G. Draguns, W. J. Lonner, & J. E. Trimble (Eds.), *Counseling across cultures* (pp. 93–108). Thousand Oaks, CA: Sage.

Croteau, J. M., Lark, J. S., Lidderdale, M. A., & Chung, Y. B. (2005). *Deconstructing heterosexism in the counseling professions.* Thousand Oaks, CA: Sage.

Culbertson, F. M. (1997). Depression and gender. *American Psychologist, 52,* 25–31.

Dana, R. H. (1993). *Multicultural assessment perspectives for professional psychology.* Needham Heights, MA: Allyn & Bacon.

Dana, R. H. (2000). The cultural self as a locus for assessment and intervention with American Indian/Alaska Natives. *Journal of Multicultural Counseling and Development, 28,* 66–82.

Danzinger, P. R., & Welfel, E. R. (2000). Age, gender and health bias in counselors: An empirical analysis. *Journal of Mental Health Counseling, 22,* 135–149.

Darwin, C. (1859). *On the origin of species by natural selection.* London: Murray.

Das Gupta, M. (1997). "What is Indian about you?": A gendered, transnational approach to ethnicity. *Gender and Society, 11,* 572–596.

D'Augelli, A. R. (1989). Lesbians' and gay men's experiences of discrimination and harassment in a university community. *American Journal of Community Psychology, 17,* 317–321.

Davidson, M. M., Waldo, M., & Adams, E. M. (2006). Promoting social justice through preventive interventions in schools. In R. L. Toporek, L. H. Gerstein, N. A. Fouad, G. Roysircar, & T. Israel (Eds.), *Handbook for social justice in counseling psychology* (pp. 117–129). Thousand Oaks, CA: Sage.

Davis, L. E., & Gelsomino (1994). As assessment of practitioner cross-racial treatment experiences. *Social Work, 39,* 116–123.

Day, S. X. (2004). *Theory and design in counseling and psychotherapy.* Boston: Houghton Mifflin.

Daya, R. (2005). Buddhist moments in psychotherapy. In R. Moodley & W. West (Eds.), *Integrating traditional healing practices into counseling and psychotherapy* (pp. 182–193). Thousand Oaks, CA: Sage.

Deater-Deckard, K., Dodge, K. A., Bates, J. E., & Pettit, G. S. (1996). Physical discipline among African American and European American mothers: Links to children's externalizing behaviors. *Developmental Psychology, 32,* 1065–1072.

de Gobineau, A. (1915). *The inequality of human races.* New York: Putnam.

De La Cancela, V. (1985). Toward a sociocultural psychotherapy for low-income ethnic minorities. *Psychotherapy, 22,* 427–435.

De La Cancela, V. (1991). Working affirmatively with Puerto Rican men: Professional and personal reflections. In M. Bograd (Ed.), *Feminist approaches for men and women in family therapy* (pp. 195–211). New York: Harrington Park Press.

Department of Justice. (2006). *Uniform Crime Report: Hate crime statistics, 2005.* Washington, DC: Author.

DePaulo, B. M. (1992). Nonverbal behavior and self-presentation. *Psychological Bulletin, 111,* 203–243.

Desselle, D. C., & Proctor, T. K. (2000). Advocating for the elderly hard-of-hearing population: The deaf people we ignore. *Social Work, 45*, 277–281.

Detroit Free Press. (2001). 100 questions and answers about Arab Americans: A journalist's guide. Retrieved 12/15/2006 from http://www.freep.com/legacy/jobspage/arabs/arab1.html

DeVos, T., & Banaji, M. R. (2005). American = White? *Journal of Personality and Social Psychology, 88*, 447–466.

Deyhle, D., & Swisher, K. (1999). Research in American Indian and Alaska Native Education: From assimilation to self-determination. *Review of Research in Education, 22*, 113–194.

Dingfelder, S. F. (2005a). Close the gap for Latino patients. *Monitor on Psychology, 36*, 58–61.

Dingfelder, S. F. (2005b). The kids are all right. *Monitor on Psychology, 36*, p. 66–68.

Diokno, A. C., Brown, M. B., & Herzog, A. R. (1990). Sexual functioning in the elderly. *Archives of Internal Medicine, 150*, 197–200.

Dittmann, M. (2005). Homing in on Mexican Americans' mental health access. *Monitor on Psychology, 36*, 70–72.

Dixon, D. (2006). Characteristics of Asia born in the United States. Retrieved 12/10/06 from http://www.migrationinformation.org/USFocus/print.ctf?ID=415.

Dolliver, R. H., Williams, E. L., & Gold, D. C. (1980). The art of Gestalt therapy or: What are you doing with your feet now? *Psychotherapy: Theory, Research & Practice, 17*, 136–142.

Donahue, P., & McDonald, L. (2005). Gay and Lesbian aging: Current perspectives and future directions for social work practice and research. *Families in Society, 86*, 359–366.

Dorland, J. M., & Fischer, A. R. (2001). Gay, lesbian, and bisexual individuals' perceptions: An analogue study. *Counseling Psychologist, 29*, 532–547.

Douglas, E. M. (2006). Familial violence socialization in childhood and later life approval of corporal punishment: A cross-cultural perspective. *American Journal of Orthopsychiatry, 76*, 23–30.

Douglis, R. (1987). The beat goes on. *Psychology Today*, (Nov.), 37–42.

Dovidio, J. F., & Gaertner, S. L. (2000). Aversive racism and selective decisions: 1989–1999. *Psychological Science, 11*, 315–319.

Dovidio, J. F., Gaertner, S. L., Kawakami, K., & Hodson, G. (2002). Why can't we all just get along? Interpersonal biases and interracial distrust. *Cultural diversity and Ethnic Minority Psychology, 8*, 88–102.

Dowdy, K. G. (2000). The culturally sensitive medical interview. *JAAPA, 13*, 91–104.

Downing, N. E., & Roush, K. L. (1985). From passive acceptance to active commitment: A model of feminist identity development for women. *Counseling Psychologist, 13*, 695–709.

Draguns, J. G. (1976). Counseling across cultures. Common themes and distinct approaches. In P. B. Pedersen, W. J. Lonner, & J. G. Draguns (Eds.), *Counseling across cultures* (pp. 1–16). Honolulu: University of Hawaii Press.

Draguns, J. G. (2002). Universal and cultural aspects of counseling and psychotherapy. In P. B. Pedersen, J. G. Draguns, W. J. Lonner, & J. E. Trimble (Eds.), *Counseling across cultures* (pp. 29–50). Thousand Oaks, CA: Sage.

Duhaney, L. M. G. (2000). Culturally sensitive strategies for violence prevention. *Multicultural Education, 7*, 10–19.

Duran, B., Sanders, M., Skipper, B., Waitzkin, H., et al. (2004). Prevalence and correlates of mental disorders among Native American women in primary care. *American Journal of Public Health, 94*, 71–77.

Duran, E. (2006). *Healing the soul wound.* New York: Teachers College Press.

Dworkin, S. H. (2000). Individual therapy with lesbian, gay, and bisexual clients. In R. M. Perez, K. A. DeBord, & K. J. Bieschke (Eds.), *Handbook of counseling and psychotherapy with lesbian, gay, and bisexual clients* (pp. 157–181). Washington, DC: American Psychological Association.

Eadie, B. J. (1992). *Embraced by the light.* Carson City, NV: Gold Leaf Press.

Eakins, B. W., & Eakins, R. G. (1985). Sex differences in nonverbal communication. In L. A. Samovar & R. E. Porter (Eds.), *Intercultural communication: A reader* (pp. 290–307). Belmont, CA: Wadsworth.

Eaton, M. J., & Dembo, M. H. (1997). Differences in

the motivational beliefs of Asian Americans. *Journal of Educational Psychology, 89*, 433–440.

EchoHawk, M. (1997). Suicide: The scourge of Native American people. *Suicide and Life Threatening Behavior, 27*, 60–67.

Economic Policy Institute. (2006). *Minimum wage: Facts at a glance.* Retrieved from http://www.epi.org/content.cfm/issueguides_minwage_min wagefacts

Eddings, J. (1997). Counting a "new" type of American. *U.S. News & World Report, 123*, 22–23.

Eliade, M. (1972). *Shamanism: Archaic techniques of ecstasy.* New York: Pantheon.

El-Badry, S. (2006). Arab American demographics. Retrieved 12/15/2006 from http://www.allied-media-com/Arab-American/Arab %20american%

Elliott, A. (2006, Sep 10). Muslim immigration has bounced back. *Seattle Times*, p. A18.

Elliott, T. R., Kilpatrick, S. D., & McCullough, M. E. (1999). Religion and spirituality in rehabilitation psychology. *Rehabilitation Psychology, 44*, 388–402.

Elliott, T. R., Shewchuk, R. M., & Richards, J. S. (1999). Caregiver social problem-solving abilities and family member adjustment to recent-onset physical disability. *Rehabilitation Psychology, 44*, 104–123.

Ellis, A. (1997). Using rational emotive behavior therapy techniques to cope with disability. *Professional Psychology: Research and Practice, 28*, 17–22.

Erdur, O., Rude, S., Baron, A., Draper, M. & Shankar, L. (2000). Working alliance and treatment outcome in ethnically similar and dissimilar client–therapist pairings. *Research Reports of the Research Consortium of Counseling and Psychological Services in Higher Education, 1*, 1–20.

Ericksen-Radtke, M. M., & Beale, A. V. (2001). Preparing students with learning disabilities for college: Pointers for parents–part 2. *Exceptional Parent, 31*, 56–57.

Espinosa, P. (1997). School involvement and His-panic parents. *The Prevention Researcher, 5*, 5–6.

Everett, F., Proctor, N., & Cortmell, B. (1989). Providing psychological services to American Indian children and families. In D. R. Atkinson, G. Morten, & D. W. Sue (Eds.), *Counseling American minorities* (3rd ed., pp. 53–71). Dubuque, IA: W. C. Brown.

Fabian, E. S., Lent, R. W., & Willis, S. P. (1998). Predicting work transition outcome for students with disabilities: Implications for counselors. *Journal of Counseling and Development, 76*, 311–316.

Fadiman, A. (1997). *The spirit catches you and you fall down.* New York: Farrar, Straus & Giroux.

Faiver, C., Ingersoll, R. E., O'Brien, E., & McNally, C. (2001). *Explorations in counseling and spirituality.* Belmont, CA: Brooks Cole.

Falicov, C. J. (2005). Mexican families. In M. McGoldrick, J. Giordano, & N. Garcia-Preto (Eds.), *Ethnicity and family therapy* (pp. 229–241). New York: Guilford.

Fang, C. Y., & Meyers, H. F. (2001). The effects of racial stressors and hostility on cardiovascular reactivity in African American and Caucasian men. *Health Psychology, 20*, 64–70.

Farley, O. W., Smith, L. L., & Boyle, S. W. (2003). *Introduction to social work.* Boston: Allyn & Bacon.

Fathi, N. (2006, Dec. 12). Iran opens conference on Holocaust. *New York Times.* Retrieved 12/11/2006 from http://www.nytimes.com/12/12/world/middleeast/12holocaust

Feagin, J. R. (1989). *Racial and ethnic relations.* Englewood Cliffs, NJ: Prentice Hall.

Feldman, S. S., & Rosenthal, D. A. (1990). The acculturation of autonomy expectations in Chinese high schoolers residing in two western nations. *International Journal of Psychology, 25*, 259–281.

Felton, G. M., Parson, M. A., Misener, T. R., & Oldaker, S. (1997). Health promoting behavior of black and white college women. *Western Journal of Nursing Research, 19*, 654–664.

Festinger, L. (1957). *A theory of cognitive dissonance.* Evanston, IL: Row & Peterson.

Fischer, A. R., & Shaw, C. M. (1999). African Americans' mental health and perceptions of racist discrimination: The moderating effects of racial socialization experiences and self-esteem. *Journal of Counseling Psychology, 46*, 395–407.

Fitzgerald, L. F., Drasgow, F., Hulin, C. L., Gelfand, M. J., & Magley, V. J. (1997). Antecedents and consequences of sexual harassment in organizations: A test of an integrated model. *Journal of Applied Psychology, 82,* 578–589.

Fitzgerald, L. F., & Nutt, R. (1998). The Division 17 principles concerning the counseling/psychotherapy of women: Rationale and implementation. In D. R. Atkinson & G. Hackett (Eds.), *Counseling diverse populations* (2nd ed., pp. 239–270). Boston: McGraw-Hill.

Flaherty, J. A. & Adams, S. (1998). Therapist-Patient race and sex matching: Predictors of treatment duration. *Psychiatric Times, 15,* 1–4.

Flaskerud, J. H. (1991). Effects of an Asian client-therapist language, ethnicity and gender match on utilization and outcome in therapy. *Community Mental Health Journal, 27,* 31–42.

Flores, E., Tschann, J. M., Marin, B. V., & Pantoja, P. (2004). Marital conflict and acculturation among Mexican American husbands and wives. *Cultural Diversity and Ethnic Minority Psychology, 10,* 39–52.

Florio, E. R., Hendryx, M. S., Jensen, J. E., & Rockwood, T. H. (1997). A comparison of suicidal and nonsuicidal elders referred to a community mental health center program. *Suicide and Life, 27,* 182–193.

Ford, D. Y. (1997). Counseling middle-class African Americans. In C. C. Lee (Ed.), *Multicultural issues in counseling* (2nd ed., pp. 81–108). Alexandria, VA: American Counseling Association.

Foster, B. G., Jackson, G., Cross, W. E., Jackson, B., & Hardiman, R. (1988). Workforce diversity and business. Alexandria, VA: American Society for Training and Development. (Reprinted from *Training and Development Journal,* April 1988).

Fouad, N. A., Gerstein, L. H., & Toporek, R. L. (2006). Social justice and counseling psychology in context. In R. L. Toporek, L. H. Gerstein, N. A. Fouad, G. Roysircar, & T. Israel (Eds.), *Handbook for social justice in counseling psychology* (pp. 1–16). Thousand Oaks, CA: Sage.

Fraga, E. D., Atkinson, D. R., & Wampold, B. E. (2002). Ethnic group preferences for multicultural counseling competencies. *Cultural Diversity and Ethnic Minority Psychology, 10,* 53–65.

Frame, M. W., & Williams, C. B. (1996). Counseling African Americans: Integrating spirituality in therapy. *Counseling and Values, 41,* 16–28.

Frank, J. W., Moore, R. S., & Ames, G. M. (2000). Historical and cultural roots of drinking problems among American Indians. *American Journal of Public Health, 90,* 344–351.

Frankel, M. (1998, May 24). The oldest bias. *New York Times Magazine,* pp. 16–17.

Frankenberg, R. (1993). *Euro-American women: Race matters.* Minneapolis: University of Minnesota Press.

Franklin, A. J. (2004). *From brotherhood to manhood: How Black men rescue their relationships and dreams from the invisibility syndrome.* Hoboken, NJ: Wiley.

Franklin, C. G., & Soto, I. (2002). Editorial: Keeping Hispanic youth in school. *Children and Schools, 24,* 139–143.

Franklin, J. H. (1988). A historical note on black families. In H. P. McAdoo (Ed.), *Black families* (pp. 3–14). Newbury Park, CA: Sage.

Frawley, T. (2005). Gender bias in the classroom: Current controversies and implications for teachers. *Childhood Education, 81,* 221–227.

Freeborne, N. (2000). Alzheimer's disease: The possibility of prevention and early treatment. *Journal of the American Academy of Physician Assistants, 13,* 32–38.

Freire, P. (1970). *Cultural action for freedom.* Cambridge: Harvard Educational Review Press.

Freud, S. (1960). Psychopathology of everyday life. In J. Strachey (Ed. and Trans.), *The standard edition of the complete psychological works of Sigmund Freud* (6th ed.). London: Hogarth Press.

Friedman, M. L., Friedlander, M. L. & Blustein, D. L. (2005). Toward an understanding of Jewish identity: A phenomenological study. *Journal of Counseling Psychology, 52,* 77–83.

Frommer, F. J. (2006, Dec. 20). Congressman criticized for Muslim letter. Retrieved 12/20/2006 from http://seattlepi.newsource.com/national/1133AP_Ellison_Quran.html

Fuertes, J. N. (1999). Asian-Americans' and African Americans' initial perceptions of Hispanic counselor. *Journal of Multicultural Counseling and Development, 27,* 122–135.

Fuertes, J. N., & Gelso, C. J. (2000). Hispanic counselors' race and accent and Euro Americans' universal-diverse orientation: A study of initial perceptions. *Cultural Diversity and Ethnic Minority Psychology, 6,* 211–219.

Fuertes, J. N., Mueller, L. N., Chauhan, R. V., Walker, J. A., & Ladany, N. (2002). An investigation of European American therapists' approach to counseling African American clients. *Counseling Psychologist, 30,* 763–788.

Fukuyama, M. A. (2003). Integrating spirituality in multicultural counseling: "A Worldview." In F. D. Harper & J. McFadden (Eds.), *Culture and counseling: New approaches* (pp. 184–195). Boston: Allyn & Bacon

Fukuyama, M. A., & Sevig, T. D. (1999). *Integrating spirituality into multicultural counseling.* Thousand Oaks, CA: Sage.

Fuligni, A. J., Burton, L., Marshall, S., Perez-Febles, A., Yarrington, J., Kirsh, L. B., & Merriwether-DeVries, C. (1999). Attitudes toward family obligations among American adolescents with Asian, Latin American, and European backgrounds. *Child Development, 70,* 1030–1044.

Gaertner, S. L. (1973). Helping behavior and racial discrimination among liberals and conservatives. *Journal of Personality and Social Psychology, 25,* 335–341.

Gaertner, S. L., & Dovidio, J. F. (2006). Understanding and addressing contemporary racism: From aversive racism to the common ingroup. *Journal of Social Issues, 61*(3), 615–639

Gallegos, J. S. (1982). Planning and administering services for minority groups. In M. J. Austin & W. E. Hershey (Eds.), *Handbook on mental health administration* (pp. 87–105). San Francisco: Jossey-Bass.

Gallo, L. C., & Matthews, K. A. (2003). Understanding the association between socioeconomic status and physical health: Do negative emotions play a role? *Psychological Bulletin, 129,* 10–51.

Gallup, G. (1995). *The Gallup poll: Public opinion 1995.* Wilmington, DE: Scholarly Resources.

Galton, F. (1869). *Hereditary genius: An inquiry into its laws and consequences.* London: Macmillan.

Gambrell, J. (2006, Oct. 13). Local wife says raided workers harmed no one. *Bellingham Herald,* pp. A.1,8.

Gannett News Service. (1998, May 26). Young Americans optimistic, but face deep racial divisions. *The Bellingham Herald,* p. A7.

Garcia-Preto, N. (1996). Puerto Rican families. In M. McGoldrick, J. Giordano, & J. K. Pearce (Eds.), *Ethnicity and family therapy* (pp. 183–199). New York: Guilford.

Garcia-Preto, N. (2005). Puerto Rican families. In M. McGoldrick, J. Giordano, & N. Garcia-Preto (Eds.), *Ethnicity and family therapy* (2nd ed., pp. 242–255). New York: Guilford.

Garfield, J. C., Weiss, S. L., & Pollock, E. A. (1973). Effects of a child's social class on school counselors' decision making. *Journal of Counseling Psychology, 20,* 166–168.

Garnets, L., Hancock, K. A., Cochran, S. D., Goodchilds, J., & Peplau, L. A. (1998). Issues in psychotherapy with lesbians and gay men: A survey of psychologists. In D. R. Atkinson & G. Hackett (Eds.), *Counseling diverse populations* (2nd ed., pp. 297–316). Boston: McGraw-Hill.

Garrahy, D. A. (2001). Three third-grade teachers' gender-related beliefs and behavior. *Elementary School Journal, 102,* 81–94.

Garrett, J. T., & Garrett, M. W. (1994). The path of good medicine: Understanding and counseling Native American Indians. *Journal of Multicultural Counseling and Development, 22,* 134–144.

Garrett, M. T. (2006). When Eagle speaks: Counseling Native Americans. In C. C. Lee (Ed.), *Multicultural issues in counseling: New approaches to diversity* (pp. 25–53). Alexandria, VA: American Counseling Association

Garrett, M. T., & Carroll, J. J. (2000). Mending the broken circle: Treatment of substance dependence among Native Americans. *Journal of Counseling and Development, 78,* 379–388.

Garrett, M. T., & Pichette, E. F. (2000). Red as an apple: Native American acculturation and counseling with or without reservation. *Journal of Counseling and Development, 78,* 3–13.

Garwick, A. G., & Auger, S. (2000). What do providers need to know about American Indian culture? Recommendations from urban Indian family caregivers. *Families, Systems & Health, 18,* 177–190.

Gee, G. C., Ryan, A., Laflamme, D. J. & Holt, J.

(2006). Self-reported discrimination among African descendants, Mexican Americans, and other Latinos in the New Hampshire REACH initiative: The added dimension of immigration. *American Journal of Public Health, 96,* 1821–1828.

George, H. T. (1998, July 14). Young quadriplegic has a dream. *Seattle Post-Intelligencer,* p. B2.

Gheytanchi, A., Joseph, L., Gierlach, E., Kimpara, S., Housley, J., Franco, Z. E., & Beutler, L. E. (2007). The dirty dozen: Twelve failures of the hurricane Katrina response and how psychology can help. *American Psychologist, 62,* 118–130.

Gillem, A. R., Lincoln, S. K., & English, K. (2007). Biracial populations. In M. G. Constantine (Ed.), *Clinical practice with people of color* (pp. 104–124). New York: Teachers College Press.

Goldberg, J. J. (2000, May 5). A portrait of American Jews. *The Jewish Journal,* pp. 1–2.

Goldberg, S. G., Killeen, M. B., & O'Day, B. (2005). The disclosure conundrum: How people with psychiatric disabilities navigate employment. *Psychology, Public Policy, and Law, 11,* 463–500.

Gonsiorek, J. C. (1982). Results of psychological testing on homosexual populations. *American Behavioral Scientist, 25,* 385–396.

Gonzalez, G. M. (1997). The emergence of Chicanos in the twenty-first century: Implications for counseling, research, and policy. *Journal of Multicultural Counseling and Development, 25,* 94–106.

Gonzalez, G. M., Castillo-Canez, I., Tarke, H., Soriano, F., Garcia, P., & Velasquez, R. J. (1997). Promoting the culturally sensitive diagnosis of Mexican Americans: Some personal insights. *Journal of Multicultural Counseling and Development, 25,* 156–161.

Goodman, L. A., Liang, B., Helms, J. E., Latta, R. E., Sparks, E., & Weintraub, S. R. (2004). Training counseling psychologists as social justice agents. *The Counseling Psychologist, 32,* 793–837.

Gorenstein, E. E., Kieber, M. S., Mohiman, J., De-Jesus, M., et al. (2005). Cognitive-behavioral therapy for management of anxiety and medication taper in older adults. *American Journal of Geriatric Psychiatry, 13,* 901–909.

Gorman, J. C., & Balter, L. (1997). Culturally sensitive parent education: A critical review of quantitative research. *Review of Educational Research, 67,* 339–369.

Gossett, T. F. (1963). *Race: The history of an idea in America.* Dallas, TX: Southern Methodist University Press.

Gottesfeld, H. (1995). Community context and the underutilization of mental health services by minority patients. *Psychological Reports, 76,* 207–210.

Graham, M. (2005). Maat: An African-centered paradigm for psychological and spiritual healing. In R. Moodley & W. West (Eds.), *Integrating traditional healing practices into counseling and psychotherapy* (pp. 210–220). Thousand Oaks, CA: Sage.

Granello, D. H., & Beamish, P. M. (1998). Reconceptualizing codependency in women: A sense of connectedness, not pathology. *Journal of Mental Health Counseling, 20,* 344–358.

Grant, L. D. (1996). Effects of ageism on individual and health care providers' responses to healthy aging. *Health and Social Work, 21,* 9–14.

Grayson, D. (1987) Gender/ethnic expectations and student expectations. A summary of the areas of disparity. Unpulished manuscript, Earlham, IA: GrayMill Foundation.

Grieger, I., & Toliver, S. (2001). Multiculturalism on predominantly White campuses: Multiple roles and functions for the counselor. In J. G. Ponterotto, J. M. Casas, L. A. Suzuki, & C. M. Alexander (Eds.), *Handbook of multicultural counseling* (pp. 825–848). Thousand Oaks, CA: Sage.

Grier, W., & Cobbs, P. (1968). *Black rage.* New York: Basic Books.

Grier, W., & Cobbs, P. (1971). *The Jesus bag.* San Francisco: McGraw-Hill.

Guadalupe, K. L., & Lum, D. (2005). *Multidimensional contextual practice.* Belmont, CA: Brooks Cole.

Guerra, P. (1998, July). Older adults and substance abuse: Looking at the "invisible epidemic." *Counseling Today,* pp. 38,43.

Gurin, P., Gurin, G., Lao, R., & Beattie, M. (1969). Internal-external control in the motivational dynamics of negro youth. *Journal of Social Issues, 25,* 29–54.

Gurung, R. A. R., & Mehta, V. (2001). Relating ethnic identity, acculturation, and attitudes toward treating minority clients. *Cultural Diversity and Ethnic Minority Psychology, 7*, 139–151.

Gushue, G. V., & Sciarra, D. T. (1995). Culture and families: A multidimensional approach. In J. G. Ponterotto, J. M. Casas, L. A. Suzuki, & C. M. Alexander (Eds.), *Handbook of multicultural counseling* (pp. 586–606). Thousand Oaks, CA: Sage.

Guthrie, R. V. (1997). *Even the rat was White: A historical view of psychology* (2nd ed.). New York: Harper and Row.

Habemann, L., & Thiry, S. (1970). The effect of socioeconomic status variables on counselor perception and behavior. Unpublished master's thesis, University of Wisconsin, Madison.

Hage, S. M. (2004). A closer look at the role of spirituality in psychology training programs. *Professional Psychology: Research and Practice, 37*, 303–310.

Hage, S. M. (2005). Future considerations for fostering multicultural competence in mental health and educational settings: Social justice implications. In M. G. Constantine & D. W. Sue (Eds.), *Strategies for building multicultural competence in mental health and educational settings* (pp. 285–302). Hoboken, NJ: Wiley.

Haley, A. (1966). *The autobiography of Malcolm X.* New York: Grove Press.

Haley, J. (1967). Marriage therapy. In H. Greenwald (Ed.), *Active psychotherapy* (pp. 189–223). Chicago: Aldine.

Hall, C. C. I. (1980). *The ethnic identity of racially mixed people: A study of Black Japanese.* Unpublished doctoral dissertation, University of California, Los Angeles.

Hall, E. T. (1959). *The silent language.* Greenwich, CT: Premier Books.

Hall, E. T. (1969). *The hidden dimension.* Garden City, New York: Doubleday.

Hall, E. T. (1974). *Handbook for proxemic research.* Washington, DC: Society for the Ontology of Visual Communications.

Hall, E. T. (1976). *Beyond culture.* New York: Anchor Press.

Hall, G. C. N. (2001). Psychotherapy research with ethnic minorities: Empirical, ethical, and conceptual issues. *Journal of Counseling and Clinical Psychology, 69*, 502–510.

Hall, S. (2006). Judith Regan goes down fighting. Retrieved 12/19/2006 from http://www.eonline.com/print/index.jsp?uuid=14864409-90ae-45e6

Hall, W. S., Cross, W. E., & Freedle, R. (1972). Stages in the development of Black awareness: An exploratory investigation. In R. L. Jones (Ed.), *Black psychology* (pp. 156–165). New York: Harper & Row.

Halleck, S. L. (1971, April). Therapy is the handmaiden of the status quo. *Psychology Today, 4*, 30–34, 98–100.

Hamby, S. L. (2000). The importance of community in a feminist analysis of domestic violence among American Indians. *American Journal of Community Psychology, 28*, 649–669.

Hanna, F. J., Talley, W. B., & Guindon, M. H. (2000). The power of perception: Toward a model of cultural oppression and liberation. *Journal of Counseling and Development, 78*, 430–446.

Hansen, J. C., Stevic, R. R., & Warner, R. W. (1982). *Counseling: Theory and process.* Toronto: Allyn & Bacon.

Hanson, L. (2006, Oct. 9). Indian youths' march challenges Columbus 'myth.' *Knight Ridder Tribune Business News,* p. 1.

Hardiman, R. (1982). White identity development: A process oriented model for describing the racial consciousness of White Americans. *Dissertation Abstracts International, 43*, 104A. (University Microfilms No. 82-10330).

Harner, M. (1990). *The way of the shaman.* San Francisco: Harper and Row.

Harper, F. D., & McFadden, J. (Eds.). (2003). *Culture and counseling: New approaches.* Boston: Allyn & Bacon.

Harrell, J. P., Hall, S., & Taliaferro, J. (2003). Physiological responses to racism and discrimination: An assessment of the evidence. *American Journal of Public Health, 93*, 243–248.

Harry, B., Klingner, J. K. & Hart, J. (2005). African American families under fire: Ethnographic views of family strengths. *Remedial and Special Education, 26*, 101–112.

Hastings, D. (2005, August 9). No way out: Many poor stuck in Houston. Retrieved from http://www.comcast.net/includes/article/print.jsp

Hastings, D. (2005, March 27). Teens struggle to survive on reservation. *Bellingham Herald,* p. A.7.

Hatch, L. R. (2005). Gender and ageism. *Generations, 29,* 19–25.

Hawkins, E. H., Cummins, L. H. & Marlatt, G. A. (2004). Preventing substance abuse in American Indian and Alaska Native youth: Promising strategies for healthier communities. *Psychological Bulletin, 130,* 304–323.

Hayes, D. (2006). ACE report cites enrollment gains, retention problems. *Diverse Issues in Higher Education, 23,* 21.

Hayes, L. L. (1997, August). The unique counseling needs of Latino clients. *Counseling Today,* pp. 1, 10.

Hayes, P. A. (2001). *Addressing cultural complexities in practice: A framework for clinicians and counselors.* Washington, DC: American Psychological Association.

Headden, S. (1997). The Hispanic dropout mystery. *US. News & World Report, 123,* 64–65.

Heatherton, T. F., Mahamedi, F., Striepe, M., Field, A. E., & Keel, P. (1997). A 10-year longitudinal study of body weight, dieting, and eating disorders. *Journal of Abnormal Psychology, 106,* 117–125.

Heesacker, M., & Carroll, T. A. (1997). Identifying and solving impediments to the social and counseling psychology interface. *The Counseling Psychologist, 25,* 171–179.

Heesacker, M., Conner, K., & Pritchard, S. (1995). Individual counseling and psychotherapy: Allocations from the social psychology of attitude change. *The Counseling Psychologist, 23,* 611–632.

Heinrich, R. K., Corbin, J. L., & Thomas, K. R. (1990). Counseling Native Americans. *Journal of Counseling & Development, 69,* 128–133.

Heller, K. (1998). Prevention activities for older adults: Social structures and personal competencies that maintain useful social roles. In D. R. Atkinson & G. Hackett (Eds.), *Counseling diverse populations* (2nd ed., pp. 183–198). Boston: McGraw-Hill.

Helms, J. E. (1984). Toward a theoretical explanation of the effects of race on counseling: A Black and White model. *The Counseling Psychologist, 12,* 153–165.

Helms, J. E. (1990). *Black and White racial identity: Theory, research, and practice.* New York: Greenwood.

Helms, J. E. (1994). How multiculturalism obscures racial factors in the therapy process: Comment on Ridley et al. (1994), Sodowsky et al. (1994), Ottavi et al. (1994), and Thompson et al. (1994). *Journal of Counseling Psychology, 41,* 162–165.

Helms, J. E. (1995). An update of Helms's White and people of color racial identity models. In J. G. Ponterotto, J. M. Casas, L. A. Suzuki, & C. M. Alexander (Eds.), *Handbook of multicultural counseling* (pp. 181–191). Thousand Oaks, CA: Sage.

Helms, J. E., & Carter, R. T. (1990). Development of the White racial identity attitude inventory. In J. E. Helms (Ed.), *Black and White racial identity: Theory, research and practice* (pp. 67–80). Westport, CT: Greenwood.

Helms, J. E., & Richardson, T. Q. (1997). How multiculturalism obscures race and culture as different aspects of counseling competency. In D. B. Pope-Davis & H. L. K. Coleman (Eds.), *Multicultural counseling competencies* (pp. 60–79). Thousand Oaks, CA: Sage.

Henkin, W. A. (1985). Toward counseling the Japanese in America: A cross-cultural primer. *Journal of Counseling & Development, 63,* 500–503.

Herek, G. M., Cogan, S. C., & Gillis, J. R. (2002). Victim experiences of hate crimes based on sexual orientation. *Journal of Social Issues, 58,* 319–399.

Herek, G. M., Gillis, J. R., & Cogan, J. C. (1999). Psychological sequelae of hate-crime victimization among lesbian, gay, and bisexual adults. *Journal of Consulting and Clinical Psychology, 67,* 945–951.

Herring, R. D. (1997). *Counseling diverse ethnic youth.* Fort Worth, TX: Harcourt Brace.

Herring, R. D. (1999). *Counseling with Native American Indians and Alaskan Natives.* Thousand Oaks, CA: Sage.

Herrnstein, R., & Murray, C. (1994). *The bell curve: Intelligence and class structure in American life.* New York: Free Press.

Hershberger, S. L. & D'Augelli, A. R. (2000). Issues in counseling lesbian, gay, and bisexual adolescents. In R. M. Perez, K. A. DeBord, & K. J. Bieschke (Eds.), *Handbook of counseling and psychotherapy with lesbian, gay, and bisexual clients* (pp. 225–247). Washington, DC: American Psychological Association.

Highlen, P. S. (1994). Racial/ethnic diversity in doctoral programs of psychology: Challenges for the twenty-first century. *Applied and Preventive Psychology, 3,* 91–108.

Highlen, P. S. (1996). MCT theory and implications for organizations/systems. In D. W. Sue, A. E. Ivey, & P. B. Pedersen (Eds.), *A theory of multicultural counseling and therapy* (pp. 65–85). Pacific Grove, CA: Brooks/Cole.

Hildebrand, V., Phenice, L. A., Gray, M. M., & Hines, R. P. (1996). *Knowing and serving diverse families.* Englewood Cliffs, NJ: Prentice Hall.

Hills, H. I., & Strozier, A. A. (1992). Multicultural training in APA approved counseling psychology programs: A survey. *Professional Psychology: Research and Practice, 23,* 43–51.

Hines, P. M., & Boyd-Franklin, N. (1996). African American families. In M. McGoldrick, J. Giordano, & J. K. Pearce (Eds.), *Ethnicity and family therapy* (pp. 66–84). New York: Guilford.

Hines, P. M., & Boyd-Franklin, N. (2005). African American families. In M. McGoldrick, J. Giordano, & N. Garcia-Preto (Eds.), *Ethnicity and family therapy* (2nd ed., pp. 87–100). New York: Guilford.

Hinrichsen, G. A. (2006). Why multicultural issues matter for practitioners working with older adults. *Professional Psychology: Research and Practice, 37,* 29–35.

Ho, M. K. (1987). *Family therapy with ethnic minorities.* Newbury Park, CA: Sage.

Ho, M. K. (1997). *Family therapy with ethnic minorities* (2nd ed.). Thousand Oaks, CA: Sage.

Hodge, D. R. (2002). Working with Muslim youth: Understanding the values and beliefs of Islamic discourse. *Children and Schools, 24,* 6–20.

Hodge, D. R. (2003). Value differences between so-cial workers and members of the working and middle classes. *Social Work, 48,* 107–119.

Hodge, D. R. (2005). Social work and the house of Islam: Orienting practitioners to the beliefs and values of Muslims in the United States. *Social Work, 50,* 162–173.

Holmes, S. A., & Morin, R. (2006, June 3). Black men torn between promise and doubt. Retrieved 6/3/2006 from http://www.msnbc.nsn.com/id/print/1/displaymode/1098

Hong, G. K., & Domokos-Cheng Ham, M. (2001). *Psychotherapy and counseling with Asian American clients.* Thousand Oaks, CA: Sage.

Hooker, E. (1957). The adjustment of the male overt homosexual. *Journal of Projective Techniques, 21,* 18–31.

Hoshmand, L. T. (2006). *Culture, psychotherapy and counseling.* Thousand Oaks, CA: Sage.

Houston, H. R. (1997). "Between two cultures": A testimony. *Amerasia Journal, 23,* 149–154.

Hovey, J. D. (2000). Acculturative stress, depression, and suicidal ideation in Mexican immigrants. *Cultural Diversity and Ethnic Minority Psychology, 6,* 134–151.

Howard, R. (1992). Folie á deux involving a dog. *American Journal of Psychiatry, 149,* 414.

Howey, N., & Samuels, E. (Eds.). (2000). *Out of the ordinary: Essays on growing up with gay, lesbian, and transgender parents.* New York: St. Martin.

Huang, L. N. (1994). An integrative approach to clinical assessment and intervention with Asian-American adolescents. *Journal of Clinical Child Psychology, 23,* 21–31.

Hudson, C. G. (2005). Socioeconomic status and mental illness: Tests of the social causation and selection hypotheses. *American Journal of Orthopsychiatry, 75,* 3–18.

Huffman, S. B., & Myers, J. E. (1999). Counseling women in midlife: An integrative approach to menopause. *Journal of Counseling and Development, 77,* 258–266.

Hulnick, M. R., & Hulnick, H. R. (1989). "Life's challenges: Curse or opportunity?" Counseling families of persons with disabilities. *Journal of Counseling and Development, 68,* 166–170.

Humes, C. W., Szymanski, E. M., & Hohenshil, T. H. (1989). Roles of counseling in enabling persons with disabilities. *Journal of Counseling and Development, 68,* 145–150.

Huuhtanen, P. (1994). Improving the working conditions of older people: An analysis of attitudes toward early retirement. In G. P. Keita & J. J. Hurrel, Jr. (Eds.), *Job stress in a changing workforce* (pp. 197–206). Washington, DC: American Psychological Association.

Huygen, C. (2006). Understanding the needs of lesbian, gay, bisexual, and transgender people living with mental illness. *Medscape General Medicine, 8,* 29–34.

Hutchison, S. (2006, Feb. 15). Women turn insult into aptitude adjustment. *Knight Ridder Tribune Business News,* p. 1.

Hyers, L. L. (2001). A secondary survey analysis study of African American ethnic identity orientation in two national samples. *Journal of Black Psychology, 27,* 139–171.

Hylton, M. E. (2005). Heteronormalitivity and the experiences of lesbian and bisexual women as social work students. *Journal of Social Work Education, 41,* 67–82.

Ina, S. (1997). Counseling Japanese Americans. In C. C. Lee (Ed.), *Multicultural issues in counseling* (2nd ed., pp. 189–206). Alexandria, VA: American Counseling Association.

Inclan, J. (1985). Variations in value orientations in mental health work with Puerto Ricans. *Psychotherapy, 22,* 324–334.

Information Clearing House. (2006, Nov. 3). Iraq war will cost more-than-$2-trillion. Retrieved 12/11/2006 from http://www.information clearinghouse.info/article15499.htm

Irvine, J. J., & York, D. E. (1995). Learning styles and culturally diverse students: A literature review. In J. A. Banks & C. A. McGee Banks (Eds.), *Handbook of research on multicultural education* (pp. 484–497). New York: McMillan.

Ivey, A. E. (1981). Counseling and psychotherapy: Toward a new perspective. In A. J. Marsella & P. B. Pedersen (Eds.), *Cross-cultural counseling and psychotherapy.* New York: Pergamon.

Ivey, A. E. (1986). *Developmental therapy.* San Francisco: Jossey-Bass.

Ivey, A. E., D'Andrea, M., Ivey, M. B., & Simek-Morgan, L. (2002). *Theories of counseling and psychotherapy: A multicultural perspective.* Boston: Allyn & Bacon.

Ivey, A. E., D'Andrea, M., Ivey, M. B., & Simek-Morgan, L. (2007). *Theories of counseling and psychotherapy: A multicultural perspective* (2nd ed.). Boston: Allyn & Bacon.

Ivey, A. E., & Ivey, M. B. (2003). *Intentional interviewing and counseling.* Pacific Grove, CA: Brooks Cole.

Ivey, A. E., Ivey, M., Myers, J., & Sweeney, T. (2005). *Developmental counseling and therapy.* Boston: Lahaska.

Iwamasa, G. (Chair). (1993). *Can multicultural sensitivity be taught to therapists in training?* Symposium conducted at the Annual Convention of the American Psychological Association, New York, NY.

Iwasaki, J. (2006a, Dec. 19). The best of both worlds. Retrieved 12/19/2006 from http://seattlepi.nwsource.com/printer2/index.asp?ploc=t&ref

Iwasaki, J. (2006b, April 28). Struggles of Asian Pacific Americans described in report. *Seattle Post-Intelligencer,* p. B1–B2.

Jackman, C. F., Wagner, W. G., & Johnson, J. T. (2001). The attitudes toward multiracial children scale. *Journal of Black Studies, 27,* 86–99.

Jackson, B. (1975). Black identity development. *Journal of Educational Diversity, 2,* 19–25.

Jackson, L. A., Hodge, C. N., Gerard, D. A., Ingram, J. M., Ervin, K. S., & Sheppard, L. A. (1996). Cognition, affect and behavior in the prediction of group attitudes. *Personality and Social Psychology Bulletin, 22,* 306–316.

Jackson, L. C. (1999). Ethnocultural resistance to multicultural training: Students and faculty. *Cultural Diversity and Ethnic Minority Psychology, 5,* 27–36.

Jackson, M. L., & Nassar-McMillan, S. (2006). Counseling Arab Americans. In C. C. Lee (Ed.), *Multicultural issues in counseling: New approaches to diversity* (3rd ed., pp. 235–247). Alexandria, VA: American Counseling Association.

Jacobson, S., & Samdahl, D. M. (1998). Leisure in the lives of old lesbians: Experiences with and responses to discrimination. *Journal of Leisure Research, 30,* 233–255.

Jenkins, A. H. (1982). *The psychology of the Afro-American*. New York: Pergamon.

Jensen, J. V. (1985). Perspective on nonverbal intercultural communication. In L. A. Samovar & R. E. Porter (Eds.), *Intercultural communication: A reader* (pp. 256–272). Belmont, CA: Wadsworth.

Johnson, B. (1995, January 19). Elderly women need not abandon sexuality. *Seattle Post-Intelligencer*.

Johnson, J. J. (1992). Developmental pathways: Toward an ecological theoretical formulation of race identity in Black-White biracial children. In M. P. P. Root (Ed.), *Racially mixed people in America* (pp. 37–49). Newbury Park, CA: Sage.

Johnson, K. W., Anderson, N. B., Bastida, E., Kramer, B. J., Williams, D., & Wong, M. (1995). Macrosocial and environmental influences on minority health. *Health Psychology, 14*, 601–612.

Jones, A. C. (1985). Psychological functioning in Black Americans: A conceptual guide for use in psychotherapy. *Psychotherapy, 22*, 363–369.

Jones, C., & Shorter-Gooden, K. (2003). *Shifting: The double lives of Black women in America*. New York: HarperCollins.

Jones, E. E., Kanouse, D., Kelley, H. H., Nisbett, R. E., Valins, S., & Weiner, B. (Eds.). (1972). *Attribution: Perceiving the causes of behavior*. Morristown, NJ: General Learning Press.

Jones, J. M. (1972). *Prejudice and racism*. Reading, MA: Addison Wesley.

Jones, J. M. (1997). *Prejudice and racism* (2nd ed.). New York: McGraw-Hill.

Jordan, J. M. (1997). Counseling African American women from a cultural sensitivity perspective. In C. C. Lee (Ed.), *Multicultural issues in counseling* (2nd ed., pp. 109–122). Alexandria, VA: American Counseling Association.

Jordan, K. (1998). The cultural experiences and identified needs of the ethnic minority supervisee in the context of Caucasian supervision. *Family Therapy, 25*, 181–187.

Jose, P. E., Huntsinger, C. S., Huntsinger, P. R., & Liaw, L. (2000). Parental values and practices relevant to young children's social development in Taiwan and the United States. *Journal of Cross-Cultural Psychology, 31*, 677–702.

Jourard, S. M. (1964). *The transparent self*. Princeton, NJ: D. Van Nostrand.

Juang, S.-H., & Tucker, C. M. (1991). Factors in marital adjustment and their interrelationships: A comparison of Taiwanese couples in America and Caucasian American couples. *Journal of Multicultural Counseling and Development, 19*, 22–31.

Jung, C. G. (1960). The structure and dynamics of the psyche. In *Collected Works, 8*. Princeton, NJ: Princeton University Press.

Juntunen, C. L., Barraclough, D. J., Broneck, C. L., Seibel, G. A., Winrow, S. A., & Morin, P. M. (2001). American Indian perspectives on the career journey. *Journal of Counseling Psychology, 48*, 274–285.

Kabat-Zinn, J. (1990). *Full catastrophe living*. New York: Delacorte.

Kamarck, T., & Jennings, J. R. (1991). Biobehavioral factors in sudden cardiac death. *Psychological Bulletin, 109*, 42–75.

Karlsson, R. (2005). Ethnic matching between therapist and patient in psychotherapy: An overview of findings, together with methodological and conceptual issues. *Cultural Diversity and Ethnic Minority Psychology, 11*, 113–129.

Kass, J. (1998, May 11). State's attorney needs some sense knocked into him. *Chicago Tribune*, p. 3.

Katz, J. H. (1985). The sociopolitical nature of counseling. *The Counseling Psychologist, 13*, 615–624.

Keane, E. M., Dick, R. W., Bechtold, D. W., & Manson, S. M. (1996). Predictive and concurrent validity of the Suicide Ideation Questionnaire among American Indian Adolescents. *Journal of Abnormal Child Psychology, 24*, 735–747.

Kearney, L. K., Draper, M., & Baron, A. (2005). Counseling utilization of ethnic minority college students. *Cultural Diversity and Ethnic Minority Psychology, 11*, 272–285.

Keita, G. P., & Hurrell, J. J., Jr. (1994). *Job stress in a changing workforce*. Washington, DC: American Psychological Association.

Kelly, M., & Tseng, H. (1992). Cultural differences in childrearing: A comparison of immigrant Chinese and Caucasian American mothers. *Journal of Cross-Cultural Psychology, 23*, 444–455.

Kemp, N. T., & Mallinckrodt, B. (1996). Impact of

professional training on case conceptualization of clients with a disability. *Professional Psychology: Research and Practice, 27,* 378–385.

Kendler, K. S., MacLean, C., Neal, M., Kessler, R., Heath, A., & Eaves, L. (1991). The genetic epidemiology of bulimia nervosa. *American Journal of Psychiatry, 148,* 1627–1637.

Kennedy, A. (2005, April). Rainbow recovery: Counseling GLBT substance abusers. *Counseling Today,* pp. 29–30.

Kennedy, J. L. (1996). *Job interviews for dummies.* Foster City, CA: IDG Books Worldwide.

Kenney, K. R. (2002). Counseling interracial couples and multiracial individuals: Applying a multicultural counseling competency framework. *Counseling and Human Development, 35,* 1–11.

Kerwin, C., & Ponterotto, J. G. (1995). Biracial identity development: Theory and research. In J. Ponterotto, J. M. Casas, L. A. Suzuki, & C. M. Alexander (Eds.), *Handbook of multicultural counseling* (pp. 199–217). Newbury Park, CA: Sage.

Khamphakdy-Brown, S., Jones, L. N., Nilsson, J. E., Russell, E. B. & Klevens, C. L. (2006). The empowerment program: An application of an outreach program for refugee and immigrant women. *Journal of Mental Health Counseling, 28,* 38–47.

Kilgore, H., Sideman, L., Amin, K., Baca, L. & Bohanske, B. (2005). Psychologists' attitudes and therapeutic approaches towards gay, lesbian, and bisexual issues continue to improve: An update. *Psychotherapy: Theory, Research, Practice, Training, 42,* 395–400.

Kim, A. U., & Atkinson, D. R. (1998). What counselors need to know about aging and sexuality. In D. R. Atkinson & G. Hackett (Eds.), *Counseling diverse populations* (2nd ed., pp. 217–233). Boston: McGraw-Hill.

Kim, B. S. K., & Atkinson, D. R. (2002). Asian American client adherence to Asian cultural values, counselor expression of cultural values, counselor ethnicity, and career counseling process. *Journal of Counseling Psychology, 49,* 3–13.

Kim, B. S. K., Liang, C. T. H., & Li, L. C. (2003). Counselor ethnicity, counselor nonverbal behavior, and session outcome with Asian American clients: Initial findings. *Journal of Counseling and Development, 81,* 202–209.

Kim, J. (1981). The process of Asian American identity development: A study of Japanese-American women's perceptions of their struggle to achieve personal identities as Americans of Asian ancestry. *Dissertation Abstracts International, 42,* 155 1A. (University Microfilms No. 81-18080)

Kim, J. G. S. (2002). Racial perceptions and psychological well being in Asian and Hispanic Americans. *Dissertation Abstracts International, 63(2-B),* 1033B.

Kim, S. C. (1985). Family therapy for Asian Americans: A strategic structural framework. *Psychotherapy, 22,* 342–356.

Kimmel, S. B., & Mahalik, J. R. (2005). Body image concerns of gay men: The role of minority stress and conformity to masculine norms. *Journal of Consulting and Clinical Psychology, 73,* 1185–1190.

King, M. (2001, October 7). Concerns of elder gays. *Seattle Times,* pp. B1, 9.

Kiselica, M. S. (1998). Preparing anglos for the challenges and joys of multiculturalism. *The Counseling Psychologist, 26,* 5–21.

Kitano, H. H. L. (1982). Mental health in the Japanese American community. In E. E. Jones & S. J. Korchin (Eds.), *Minority mental health* (pp. 149–164). New York: Praeger.

Kleinman, A. (2004). Culture and depression. *New England Journal of Medicine, 351,* 951–953.

Kluckhohn, F. R., & Strodtbeck, F. L. (1961). *Variations in value orientations.* Evanston, IL: Row, Patterson, & Co.

Knight, B. G., & McCallum, T. J. (1998). Adapting psychotherapeutic practice for older clients: Implications of the contextual, cohort-based, maturity, specific challenge model. *Professional Psychology: Research and Practice, 29,* 15–22.

Knox, S., Burkard, A. W., Johnson, A. J., Suzuki, L. A., & Ponterotto, J. G. (2003). African American and European American therapists' experiences of addressing race in cross-racial psychotherapy dyads. *Journal of Counseling Psychology, 50,* 466–481.

Kochman, T. (1981). *Black and White styles in conflict.* Chicago: University of Chicago Press.

Kochman, T. (1994). Black and White cultural styles in pluralistic perspective. In G. R. Weaver (Ed.), *Culture, communication, and conflict: Readings in intercultural relations* (pp. 293–308). Needham Heights, MA: Ginn Press.

Koltko-Rivera, M. E. (2004). The psychology of worldviews. *Review of General Psychology, 8,* 3–58.

Kort, B. (1997). Female therapist, male client: Challenging beliefs—a personal journey. *Women and Therapy, 20,* 97–100.

Kramer, F. (1998, May 24). On nation's farms, some workers give up childhood—"I just want to go back to school," a youngster tells child-labor forum. *Seattle Times,* p. A6.

Krieger, N., & Sidney, S. (1996). Racial discrimination and blood pressure: The CARDIA study of young Black and White adults. *American Journal of Public Health, 86,* 1370–1378.

Krupin, S. (2001, July 25). Prejudice, schools key concerns of Hispanics. *Seattle Post Intelligencer,* p. A7.

Kun, K. E., & Schwartz, R. W. (1998). Older Americans with HIV/AIDS. *SIECUS Report, 26,* 12–14.

Kurdek, L. A. (Ed.). (1994). *Social services for gay and lesbian couples.* Binghampton, NY: Hayworth Press.

Kwee, M. (1990). *Psychotherapy, meditation and health.* London: East-West.

LaBarre, W. (1985). Paralinguistics, kinesics and cultural anthropology. In L. A. Samovar & R. E. Porter (Eds.), *Intercultural communication: A reader* (pp. 272–279). Belmont, CA: Wadsworth.

LaFromboise, T. D. (1998). American Indian mental health policy. In D. A. Atkinson, G. Morten, & D. W. Sue (Eds.), *Counseling American minorities: A cross-cultural perspective* (pp. 137–158). Boston: McGraw-Hill.

LaFromboise, T. D. (2006). American Indian youth suicide prevention. *Prevention Researcher, 13,* 16–18.

LaFromboise, T. D., & Howard-Pitney, B. (1995). The Zuni Life Skills Development Curriculum. *Journal of Counseling Psychology, 42,* 479–486.

LaFromboise, T. D., Medoff, L., Lee, C. C., & Harris,

A. (in press). Psychosocial and cultural correlates of suicidal ideation among American Indians: Early adolescents on a Northern Plains reservation. *Research on Human Development.*

Laing, R. D. (1967). *The divided self.* New York: Pantheon.

Laing, R. D. (1969). *The politics of experience.* New York: Pantheon.

Laird, J., & Green, R. (1996). *Lesbians and gays in couples and families.* San Francisco: Jossey-Bass.

Lane, M. (1988, June 22). At age 81, teacher's lessons are timeless. *Bellingham Herald,* p. A1.

Langman, P. F. (1999). *Jewish issues in multiculturalism: A handbook for educators and clinicians.* Northvale, NJ: Jason Aronson.

La Rue, A., & Watson, J. (1998). Psychological assessment of older adults. *Professional Psychology: Research and Practice, 29,* 5–14.

Lass, N. J., Mertz, P. J., & Kimmel, K. (1978). The effect of temporal speech alterations on speaker race and sex identification. *Language and Speech, 21,* 279–290.

LaVeist, T. A., Chamberlain, D., & Jarrett, N. C. (2000). Social status and perceived discrimination in the national health care system: How and why. In C. J. Hogue, M. A. Hargraves, and K. S. Collins (Eds.), *Minority health in America* (pp. 194–208). Baltimore: John Hopkins University Press.

Lazzaro, J. (2000). Electric books: SF publishers embrace alternative formats such as audio, large print, braille, e-books, and descriptive and captioned video. *Science Fiction Chronicle, 22,* 24–25.

LeBlanc, S. (2006, March 11). Catholic group ends adoption role: Massachusetts law on gay parents is cited. *Chicago Tribune,* p. 4.

Lee, C. C. (1996). MCT Theory and implications for indigenous healing. In D. W. Sue, A. E. Ivey, & P. B. Pedersen (Eds.), *A theory of multicultural counseling and therapy* (pp. 86–98). Pacific Grove, CA: Brooks/Cole.

Lee, C. C. (2007*). Counseling for social justice.* Alexandria, VA: ACA.

Lee, C. C., & Armstrong, K. L. (1995). Indigenous models of mental health intervention: Lessons from traditional healers. In J. G. Ponterotto, J. M. Casas, L. A. Suzuki, & C. M. Alexander

(Eds.), *Handbook of multicultural counseling* (pp. 441–456). Thousand Oaks, CA: Sage.

Lee, C. C., Oh, M. Y., & Mountcastle, A. R. (1992). Indigenous models of helping in nonwestern countries: Implications for multicultural counseling. *Journal of Multicultural Counseling and Development, 20,* 1–10.

Lee, C.-R. (1995). *Native speaker.* New York: Berkley Publishing Group.

Lee, E. (1996). Chinese families. In M. McGoldrick, J. Geordano, & J. K. Pearce (Eds.), *Ethnicity and family therapy* (pp. 249–267). New York: Guilford.

Lee, F. Y. (1991). *The relationship of ethnic identity to social support, self-esteem, psychological distress, and help-seeking behavior among Asian American college students.* Unpublished doctoral dissertation, University of Illinois, Urbana-Champaign.

Lee, R. (2000). Health care problems of lesbian, gay, bisexual, and transgender patients. *Western Journal of Medicine, 172,* 403–408.

Lee, R. M., Choe, J., Kim, G., & Ngo, V. (2000). Construction of the Asian American Family Conflicts Scale. *Journal of Counseling Psychology, 47,* 211–222.

Lee, R. M., Su, J., & Yoshida, E. (2005). Coping with intergenerational family conflict among Asian American college students. *Journal of Counseling Psychology, 52,* 389–399.

Lee, Y. T. (1993). Psychology needs no prejudice but the diversity of cultures. *American Psychologist, 48,* 1090–1091.

Lefcourt, H. (1966). Internal versus control of reinforcement: A review. *Psychological Bulletin, 65,* 206–220.

Lefkowitz, E. S., Romo, L. F. L., Corona, R., Au, T. K.-F., & Sigman, M. (2000). How Latino American and European American adolescents discuss conflicts, sexuality, and AIDS with their mothers. *Developmental Psychology, 36,* 315–325.

Leigh, I. W., Corbett, C. A., Gutman, V., & Morere, D. A. (1996). Providing psychological services to deaf individuals: A response to new perceptions of diversity. *Professional Psychology: Research and Practice, 27,* 364–371.

Leland, J. (2000, March 20). Shades of gray. *Newsweek,* 46–49.

Leong, F. T. L. (1986). Counseling and psychotherapy with Asian-Americans: Review of literature. *Journal of Counseling Psychology, 33,* 196–206.

Leong, F. T. L., Wagner, N. S., & Kim, H. H. (1995). Group counseling expectations among Asian American students: The role of culture-specific factors. *Journal of Counseling Psychology, 42,* 217–222.

Leong, F. T. L., Wagner, N. S., & Tata, S. P. (1995). Racial and ethnic variations in help-seeking attitudes. In J. G. Ponterotto, J. M. Casas, L. A. Suzuki, & C. M. Alexander (Eds.), *Handbook of multicultural counseling* (pp. 415–438). Thousand Oaks, CA: Sage.

Lewandowski, D. A., & Jackson, L. A. (2001). Perceptions of interracial couples: Prejudice at the dyadic level. *Journal of Black Psychology, 27,* 288–303.

Lewis, J. A., Lewis, M. D., Daniels, J. A., & D'Andrea, M. J. (1998). *Community Counseling.* Pacific Grove, CA: Brooks/Cole.

Lin, Y. (2001). The effects of counseling styles and stages on perceived counselor effectiveness from Taiwanese female University clients. *Asian Journal of Counselling, 8,* 35–60.

Lindsey, E. S. (2005). Reexamining gender and sexual orientation: Revisioning the representation of queer and trans people in the 2005 edition of *Our Bodies, Ourselves. NWSA Journal, 17,* 184–189.

Lippert, L. (1997). Women at midlife: Implications for theories of women's adult development. *Journal of Counseling and Development, 76,* 16–22.

Li-Repac, D. (1980). Cultural influences on clinical perception: A comparison between Caucasian and Chinese-American therapists. *Journal of Cross-Cultural Psychology, 11,* 327–342.

Liu, W. M., Ali, S. R., Soleck, G., Hopps, J., Dunston, K., & Pickett, T. (2004). Using social class in counseling psychology research. *Journal of Counseling Psychology, 51,* 3–18.

Liu, W. M., Hernandez, J., Mahmood, A., & Stinson, R. (2006). Linking poverty, classism, and racism in mental health: Overcoming barriers to multicultural competency. In M. G. Constantine & D. W. Sue (Eds.), *Addressing racism* (pp. 65–86). Hoboken, NJ: Wiley.

Liu, W. M., & Pope-Davis, D. B. (2005). The working alliance, therapy ruptures and impasses, and counseling competence: Implications for counselor training and education. In R. T. Carter (Ed.), *Handbook of racial-cultural psychology and counseling* (pp. 148–167). Hoboken, NJ: Wiley.

Liu, W. M., Soleck, G., Hopps, J., Dunston, D., & Pickett, T. (2004). A new framework to understand social class in counseling: The social class worldview model and modern classism theory. *Journal of Multicultural Counseling and Development, 32,* 95–116.

Livneh, H., Wilson, L. M. & Pullo, R. E. (2004). Group counseling for people with physical disabilities. *Focus on Exceptional Children, 36,* 1–18.

Locke, D. C. (1998). *Increasing multicultural understanding.* Thousand Oaks, CA: Sage.

Lone-Knapp, F. (2000). Rez talk: How reservation residents describe themselves. *American Indian Quarterly, 24,* 635–640.

Lopez-Baez, S. I. (2006). Counseling Latinas: Culturally responsive interventions. In C. C. Lee (Ed.), *Multicultural issues in counseling* (3rd ed., pp. 187–194). Alexandria, VA: American Counseling Association.

Lorant, V., Deliege, D., Eaton, W., Robert, A., Philippot, P., & Ansseau, M. (2003). Socioeconomic inequalities in depression: A meta-analysis. *American Journal of Epidemiology, 157,* 98–112.

Lorenzo, M. K., Pakiz, B., Reinherz, H. Z., & Frost, A. (1995). Emotional and behavioral problems of Asian American adolescents: A comparative study. *Child and Adolescent Social Work Journal, 12,* 197–212.

Lorion, R. P. (1973). Socioeconomic status and treatment approaches reconsidered. *Psychological Bulletin, 79,* 263–280.

Lorion, R. P. (1974). Patient and therapist variables in the treatment of low-income patients. *Psychological Bulletin, 81,* 344–354.

Lucas, M. S., & Berkel, L. A. (2005). Counseling needs of students who seek help at a university counseling center: A closer look at gender and multicultural issues. *Journal of College Student Development, 46,* 251–266.

Lum, D. (2004). *Social work practice and people of color* (5th ed.). Belmont, CA: Brooks Cole.

Lum, J. L. (1999). Family violence. In L. C. Lee & N. W. S. Zane (Eds.), *Handbook of Asian American psychology* (pp. 505–526). Thousand Oaks, CA: Sage.

Lum, R. G. (1982). Mental health attitudes and opinions of Chinese. In E. E. Jones & S. J. Korchin (Eds.), *Minority mental health.* New York: Praeger.

Luzzo, D. A., & McWhirter, E. H. (2001). Sex and ethnic differences in the perception of educational and career-related barriers and levels of coping efficacy. *Journal of Counseling and Development, 79,* 61–67.

Lyness, K. S., & Thompson, D. E. (2000). Climbing the corporate ladder: Do female and male executives follow the same route? *Journal of Applied Psychology, 85,* 86–101.

Maas, P. (2001, September 9). The broken promise. *Parade Magazine,* 4–6.

MacPhee, D., Fritz, J., & Miller-Heyl, J. (1996). Ethnic variations in personal social networks and parenting. *Child Development, 67,* 3278–3295.

Mallinckrodt, B., Shigeoka, S., & Suzuki, L. A. (2005). Asian and Pacific Island American students' acculturation and etiology beliefs about typical counseling presenting problems. *Cultural Diversity and Ethnic Minority Psychology, 11,* 227–238.

Malone, H. (1999, Sept. 25). Asian task force encouraged by drop in domestic abuse deaths. *Boston Globe,* p. B3.

Manoleas, P., Organista, K., Negron-Valasquez, G., & McCormick, K. (2000). Characteristics of Latino mental health clinicians: A preliminary examination. *Community Mental Health Journal, 36,* 383–394.

Marcos, L. R. (1973). The language barrier in evaluating Spanish-American patients. *Archives of General Psychiatry, 29,* 655–659.

Martin, J. I., & Knox, J. (2000). Methodological and ethical issues in research on lesbians and gay men. *Social Work Research, 24,* 51–59.

Martinez, C. R. & Eddy, J. M. (2005). Effects of culturally adapted parent management training on Latino youth: Behavioral health outcomes.

Journal of Consulting and Clinical Psychology, 73, 841–851.

Masand, P. S. (2000). Side effects of antipsychotics in the elderly. *Journal of Clinical Psychiatry, 61,* 43–51.

Maslow, A. H. (1968). *Toward a psychology of being.* Princeton, NJ: Van Nostrand.

Massey, D. S., Durand, J., & Malone, N. (2002). *Beyond smoke and mirrors: Mexican immigration in an era of economic integration.* New York: Russell Sage Foundation.

Matthee, I. (1997, Sept. 9). Anti-Asian hate crimes on rise in U.S. but state sees decline in such offenses. *Seattle Post-Intelligencer,* p. A3.

Matthias, R. E., Lubben, J. E., Atchison, K. A., & Schweitzer, S. O. (1997). Sexual satisfaction among very old adults: Results from a community-dwelling Medicare population survey. *The Gerontologist, 37,* 6–14.

Mau, W. C., & Jepson, D. A. (1988). Attitudes toward counselors and counseling processes: A comparison of Chinese and American graduate students. *Journal of Counseling and Development, 67,* 189–192.

Maykovich, M. H. (1973). Political activation of Japanese American youth. *Journal of Social Issues, 29,* 167–185.

McCormick, R. (2005). The healing path: What can counselors learn from aboriginal people about how to heal? In R. Moodley & W. West (Eds.), *Integrating traditional healing practices into counseling and psychotherapy* (pp. 293–304). Thousand Oaks, CA: Sage.

McCray, C. C. (1998). Ageism in the preclinical years. *Journal of the American Medical Association, 279,* 1035. Copyright 1998. American Medical Association.

McDowell, T., Ingoglia, L., Serizawa, T., Holland, C., et al. (2005). Raising multicultural awareness in family therapy through critical conversations. *Journal of Marital and Family Therapy, 31,* 399–412.

McGilley, B. M., & Pryor, T. L. (1998). Assessment and treatment of bulimia nervosa. *American Family Physician, 57,* 2743–2750.

McGoldrick, M., Giordano, J., & Garcia-Preto, N. (2005). *Ethnicity and family therapy.* New York: Guilford.

McIntosh, P. (1989, July/August). White privilege: Unpacking the invisible knapsack. *Peace and Freedom,* pp. 8–10.

McNamara, K., & Rickard, K. M. (1989). Feminist identity development: Implications for feminist therapy with women. *Journal of Counseling and Development, 68,* 184–193.

McNamara, K., & Rickard, K. M. (1998). Feminist identity development: Implications for feminist therapy with women. In D. R. Atkinson & G. Hackett (Eds.), *Counseling diverse populations* (2nd ed., pp. 271–282). Boston: McGraw-Hill.

McQuaide, S. (1998). Women at midlife. *Social Work, 43,* 21–31.

Mehrabian, A. (1972). *Nonverbal communication.* Chicago: Aldene-Atherton.

Mejia, D. (1983). The development of Mexican-American children. In G. J. Powell, J. Yamamoto, A. Romero, & A. Morales (Eds.), *The psychosocial development of minority group children* (pp. 77–114). New York: Brunner/Mazel.

Melfi, C. A., Croghan, T. W., Hanna, M. P., & Robinson, R. L. (2000). Racial variation in antidepressant treatment in a Medicaid population. *Journal of Clinical Psychiatry, 61,* 16–21.

Meston, C. M., Heiman, J. R., Trapnell, P. D., & Carlin, A. S. (1999). Ethnicity, desirable responding, and self-reports of abuse: A comparison of European- and Asian-ancestry undergraduates. *Journal of Counseling and Clinical Psychology, 67,* 139–144.

Middlebrook, D. L., LeMaster, P. L., Beals, J., Novins, D. K., & Manson, S. M. (2001). Suicide prevention in American Indian and Alaska Native communties: A critical review of programs. *Suicide and Life-Threatening Behavior, 31,* 132–149.

Middleton, R., Arrendondo, P., & D'Andrea, M. (2000, December). The impact of Spanish-speaking newcomers in Alabama towns. *Counseling Today,* 24.

Mikulas, W. L. (2006). Integrating the world's psychologies. In L. T. Hoshmand (Ed.), *Culture, psychotherapy and counseling* (pp. 91–111). Thousand Oaks, CA: Sage.

Miller, K. E. (2005). Association between illness and suicide risk in older adults. *American Family Physician, 71,* 1404–1405.

Miller, K. E., Zoe, L. M., Pazdirek, L., Caruth, M. & Lopez, D. (2005). The role of interpreters in psychotherapy with refugees: An exploratory study. *American Journal of Orthopsychiatry, 75,* 27–39.

Miller, M. D., & Silberman, R. L. (1996). Using interpersonal psychotherapy with depressed elders. In H. S. Zarit & B. G. Knight (Eds.), *A guide to psychotherapy and aging: Effective clinical interventions in a life-stage context* (pp. 83–99). Washington, DC: American Psychological Association.

Miller, S. T., Seib, H. M., & Dennie, S. P. (2001). African American perspectives on health care: The voice of the community. *Journal of Ambulatory Care Management, 24,* 37–42.

Mindess, A. (1999). *Reading between the signs.* Yarmouth, ME: Intercultural Press.

Mintz, L. B., Bartels, K. M., & Rideout, C. A. (1995). Training in counseling ethnic minorities and race-based availability of graduate school resources. *Professional Psychology: Research and Practice, 26,* 316–321.

Mintz, L. B., & Kashubeck, S. (1999). Body image and disordered eating among Asian American and Caucasian college students: An examination of race and gender differences. *Psychology of Women Quarterly, 23,* 781–796.

Minuchin, S. (1974). *Families and family therapy.* Cambridge, MA: Harvard University Press.

Mio, J. S. (2005). Academic mental health training settings and the multicultural guidelines. In M. G. Constantine & D. W. Sue (Eds.), *Strategies for building multicultural competence in mental health and educational settings* (pp. 129–144). Hoboken, NJ: Wiley.

Mio, J. S., & Morris, D. R. (1990). Cross-cultural issues in psychology training programs: An invitation for discussion. *Professional Psychology: Theory and Practice, 21,* 434–441.

Miranda, A. O., & Umhoefer, D. L. (1998a). Acculturation, language use, and demographic variables as predictors of the career self-efficacy of Latino career counseling clients. *Journal of Multicultural Counseling and Development, 26,* 39–51.

Miranda, A. O., & Umhoefer, D. L. (1998b). Depression and social interest differences between Latinos in dissimilar acculturation stages. *Journal of Mental Health Counseling, 20,* 159–171.

Miranda, J., Green, B. L., Krepnick, J. L., Chung, J., Siddique, J., Belin, T. & Revicki, D. (2006). One-year outcomes of a randomized clinical trial treating depression in low-income minority women. *Journal of Counseling and Clinical Psychology, 74,* 99–111.

Miville, M. L., Constantine, M. G., Baysden, M. F., & So-Lloyd, G. (2005). Chameleon changes: An exploration of racial identity themes of multiracial people. *Journal of Counseling Psychology, 52,* 507–516.

Miville, M. L., Koonce, D., Darlington, P., & Whitlock, B. (2000). Exploring the relationship between racial/cultural identity and ego identity among African Americans and Mexican Americans. *Journal of Multicultural Counseling and Development, 28,* 208–224.

Modie, N. (2001, July 25). New hope for the immigrants in limbo. *Seattle Post-Intelligencer,* pp. A1, A6.

Mohr, J. J., Israel, T., & Sedlacek, W. E. (2001). Counselors' attitudes regarding bisexuality as predictors of counselors' clinical responses: An analogue study of a female bisexual client. *Journal of Counseling Psychology, 48,* 212–222.

Mollica, R. F., Wyshak, G., & Lavelle, J. (1987). The psychosocial impact of war trauma and torture on Southeast Asian refugees. *American Journal of Psychiatry, 144,* 1567–1572.

Monroe, C. R. (2005). Why are "Bad Boys" always Black? Causes of disproportionality in school discipline and recommendations for change. *The Clearing House, 79,* 45–50.

Montague, J. (1996). Counseling families from diverse cultures. A nondeficit approach. *Journal of Multicultural Counseling and Development, 24,* 37–41.

Moodley, R. (2005). Shamanic performances: Healing through magic and the supernatural. In R. Moodley & W. West (Eds.), *Integrating traditional healing practices into counseling and psychotherapy* (pp. 2–14). Thousand Oaks, CA: Sage.

Moodley, R., & West, W. (Eds.). (2005). *Integrating traditional healing practices into counseling and psychotherapy.* Thousand Oaks, CA: Sage.

Moore, K. A. (2001). Time to take a closer look at Hispanic children and families. *Policy & Public Human Services, 59,* 8–9.

Moos, R. H., Mertens, J. R., & Brennan, P. L. (1995). Program characteristics and readmission among older substance abuse patients: Comparisons with middle-aged and younger patients. *Journal of Mental Health Administration, 22,* 332–346.

Moradi, B., & Hasan, N. T. (2004). Arab American persons' reported experiences of discrimination and mental health: The mediating role of personal control. *Journal of Counseling Psychology, 51,* 418–428.

Moradi, B. & Subich, L. M. (2004). Examining the moderating role of self-esteem in the link between experiences of perceived sexist events and psychological distress. *Journal of Counseling Psychology, 51,* 50–56.

Morales, A. T., & Sheafor, B. W. (2004). *Social work* (10th ed.). Boston: Allyn & Bacon.

Morrison, M. A., & Morrison, T. G. (2002). Development and validation of a scale measuring prejudice toward gay men and lesbian women. *Journal of Homosexuality, 43,* 15–37.

Morrison, T. G., Kenny, P., & Harrington, A. (2005). Modern prejudice toward gay men and lesbian women: Assessing the viability of a measure of modern homonegative attitudes within an Irish context. *Genetic, Social, and General Psychology Monographs, 131,* 219–250.

Morrissey, M. (1997, October). The invisible minority: Counseling Asian Americans. *Counseling Today, 1,* 21–22.

Moynihan, D. P. (1965). Employment, income and the ordeal of the Negro family. *Daedalus,* pp. 745–770.

Mullavey-O'Byrne, C. (1994). Intercultural communication for health care professionals. In R. W. Brislin & T. Yoshida (Eds.), *Improving intercultural interactions* (pp. 171–196). Thousand Oaks, CA: Sage.

Muñoz, R. H., & Sanchez, A. M. (1996). *Developing culturally competent systems of care for state mental health services.* Boulder, CO: Western Interstate Commission for Higher Education.

Murphy, A. J. (2005). Life stories of black male and female professionals: An inquiry into the salience of race and sports. *Journal of Men's Studies, 13,* 313–319.

Myers, H. F., Kagawa-Singer, M., Kumanyika, S. K., Lex, B. W., & Markides, K. S. (1995). Panel III: Behavioral risk factors related to chronic diseases in ethnic minorities. *Health Psychology, 14,* 613–621.

Myers, J. E., & Harper, M. C. (2004). Evidence-based effective practices with older adults. *Journal of Counseling and Development, 82,* 207–218.

Nassar-McMillan, S. C. (2007). Arab American populations. In M. G. Constantine (Ed.), *Clinical practice with people of color* (pp. 85–103). New York: Teachers College Press.

National Academies. (2006). *Beyond bias and barriers: Fulfilling the potential of women in academic science and engineering.* Washington, DC: National Academies Press.

National Association of Social Workers. (2000). *Code of ethics.* Retrieved 12/08/06 from http://www.naswdc.org/Code/ethics.htm.

National Coalition for Women and Girls in Education. (2002). *Title IV at 30: Report card on gender equality.* Washington, DC: Author.

National Conference of Christians and Jews. (1994). *Taking America's pulse: A summary report of the national survey report of intergroup relations.* New York: Author.

National Council on Interpreting in Health Care. (2005). *National standards of practice for interpreters in health care.* Santa Rosa, CA: Author.

National Immigration Law Center. (2006). Fact about immigrants' low use of health services and public benefits. Retrieved 12/14/2006 from http://www.nilc.org

National Organization on Disability/Louis Harris Survey. (1998). Americans with disabilities still face sharp gaps in securing jobs, education, transportation, and in many areas of daily life. New York: Louis Harris and Associates.

Neal-Barnett, A. M., & Crowther, J. H. (2000). To be female, middle class, anxious, and Black. *Psychology of Women Quarterly, 24,* 129–136.

Negy, C. (1993). Anglo- and Hispanic-Americans' performance on the Family Attitude Scale and its implications for improving measurements of acculturation. *Psychological Reports, 73,* 1211–1217.

Negy, C., & Woods, D. J. (1992). The importance of acculturation in understanding research with Hispanic-Americans. *Hispanic Journal of Behavioral Sciences, 14,* 224–247.

Nemoto et al. (2005). Promoting health for transgender women: Transgender resources and neighborhood space (TRANS) program in San Francisco. *American Journal of Public Health, 95,* 382–384.

Neville, H. A., Worthington, R. L., & Spanierman, L. B. (2001). Race, power, and multicultural counseling psychology: Understanding White privilege and color-blind racial attitudes. In J. Ponterotto, J. M. Casas, L. A. Suzuki, & C. M. Alexander (Eds.), *Handbook of multicultural counseling* (pp. 257–288). Thousand Oaks, CA: Sage.

New York Times News Service. (2001, May 13). Fear keeps migrant workers from doctors. *The Bellingham Herald,* p. A8.

Ngo-Metzger, Q., Massagli, M. P., Clarridge, B. R., Manocchia, M., Davis, R. B., Iezzoni, L. I. & Phillips, R. S. (2003). Linguistic and cultural barriers to care: Perspectives of Chinese and Vietnamese immigrants. *Journal of General Internal Medicine, 18,* 44–52.

Nguyen, S. D. (1985). Mental health services for refugees and immigrants in Canada. In T. C. Owen (Ed.), *Southeast Asian mental health: Treatment, prevention, services, training, and research* (pp. 261–282). Washington, DC: National Institute of Mental Health.

Nichols, M. P., & Schwartz, R. C. (2002). *The essentials of family therapy.* Boston: Allyn & Bacon.

Nishihara, D. P. (1978). Culture, counseling, and ho'oponopono: An ancient model in a modern context. *Personnel and Guidance Journal, 56,* 562–566.

Nobles, A. Y., & Sciarra, D. T. (2000). Cultural determinants in the treatment of Arab Americans: A primer for mainstream therapists. *American Journal of Orthopsychiatry, 70,* 182–191.

Noh, S., Beiser, M., Kaspar, V., Hou, F., & Rummens, J. (1999). Perceived racial discrimination, depression, and coping: A study of Southeast Asian refugees in Canada. *Journal of Health and Social Behavior, 40,* 193–207.

Noonan, B. M., Gallor, S. M., Hensler-McGinnis, N. F., Fassinger, R. E., Wang, S., & Goodman, J. (2004). Challenge and success: A qualitative study of the career development of highly achieving women with physical and sensory disabilities. *Journal of Counseling Psychology, 51,* 68–80.

Norton, J. L. (1995). The gay, lesbian, bisexual populations. In N. A. Vacc, S. B. DeVaney, & J. Wittmer (Eds.), *Experiencing and counseling multicultural and diverse populations* (3rd ed., pp. 147–177). Bristol, PA: Accelerated Development.

Nosek, M. A., & Hughes, R. B. (2001). Psychospiritual aspects of sense of self in women with physical disabilities. *Journal of Rehabilitation, 67,* 20–25.

Nwachuku, U., & Ivey, A. (1991). Culture specific counseling: An alternative approach. *Journal of Counseling and Development, 70,* 106–111.

Nydell, M. K. (1996). *Understanding Arabs: A guide for westerners.* Yarmouth, ME: Intercultural Press.

Oakland Tribune. (2006, August 8). A tale of two stories about anti-Semitism. *Oakland Tribune,* p. 1.

Olkin, R. (1999). *What psychotherapists should know about disability.* New York: Guilford.

Olsen, C. S. (1996). African-American adolescent women: Perceptions of gender, race, and class. *Marriage and Family Review, 24,* 105–121.

Ong, M. (2005). Body projects of young women of color in physics: Intersections of gender, race, and science. *Social Problems, 52,* 593–617.

O'Reilly, J. P., Tokuno, K. A., & Ebata, A. T. (1986). Cultural differences between Americans of Japanese and European ancestry in parental valuing of social competence. *Journal of Comparative Family Studies, 17,* 87–97.

Orel, N. A. (1998). Ethical considerations in assessing the competency of older adults: A provision of informed consent. *Journal of Mental Health Counseling, 20,* 189–201.

Organista, K. C. (2000). Latinos. In J. R. White & A. S. Freeman (Eds.), *Cognitive-behavioral group therapy: For specific problems and populations* (pp. 281–303). Washington, DC: American Psychological Association.

Ornstein, R. E. (1972). *The psychology of consciousness.* San Francisco: Freeman.

Oslin, D. W. (2006). The changing face of substance misuse in older adults. *Psychatric Times, 23,* 41–45.

Owens, R. E., Jr. (1998). *Queer kids: The challenges and promise for lesbian, gay, and bisexual youth.* New York: Harrington Park Press.

Pack-Brown, S. P., & Williams, C. B. (2003). *Ethics in a multicultural context.* Thousand Oaks, CA: Sage.

Pajor, C. (2005). White trash: Manifesting the bisexual. *Feminist Studies, 31,* 570–575.

Palmer, C., & Roessler, R. T. (2000). Requesting classroom accommodations: Self-advocacy and conflict resolution training for college students with disabilities. *Journal of Rehabilitation, 66,* 38–43.

Palmer, K. S. (2001, September 10). Younger women turn wrong way to escape abusive boyfriends. *USA Today,* p. A17.

Palmore, E. (2005). Three decades of research on ageism. *Generations, 29,* 87–90.

Paniagua, F. A. (1994). *Assessing and treating culturally diverse clients.* Thousand Oaks, CA: Sage.

Paniagua, F. A. (1998). *Assessing and treating culturally diverse clients* (2nd ed.). Thousand Oaks, CA: Sage.

Paniagua, F. A. (2001). *Diagnosis in a multicultural context.* Thousand Oaks, CA: Sage.

Pankhania, J. (2005). Yoga and its practice in psychological healing. In R. Moodley & W. West (Eds.), *Integrating traditional healing practices into counseling and psychotherapy* (pp. 246–256). Thousand Oaks, CA: Sage.

Parham, T. A. (1989). Cycles of psychological nigrescence. *The Counseling Psychologist, 17,* 187–226.

Parham, T. A. (1993). White researchers conducting multi-cultural counseling research: Can their efforts be "Mo Betta"? [Reaction]. *The Counseling Psychologist, 21,* 250–256.

Parham, T. A. (1997). An African-centered view of dual relationships. In B. Herlihy & G. Corey (Eds.), *Boundary issues in counseling* (pp. 109–112). Alexandria, VA: American Counseling Association.

Parham, T. A. (2002). *Counseling persons of African descent.* Thousand Oaks, CA: Sage.

Parham, T. A., & Helms, J. E. (1981). The influence of black students' racial attitudes on preferences for counselor's race. *Journal of Counseling Psychology, 28,* 250–257.

Parham, T. A., White, J. L., & Ajamu, A. (1999). *The psychology of Blacks: An African centered perspective* (3rd ed.). Englewood Cliffs, NJ: Prentice Hall.

Parker, S., & Thompson, T. (1990). Gay and bisexual men: Developing a healthy identity. In D. Moore & F. Leafgren (Eds.), *Men in conflict* (pp. 113–121). Alexandria, VA: American Counseling Association.

Parks, F. M. (2003). The role of African American folk beliefs in the modern therapeutic process. *Clinical Psychology: Science and Practice, 10,* 456–471.

Pascoe, P. (1991). Race, gender, and intercultural relations: The case of interracial marriage. *Frontiers: A Journal of Women Studies, 12,* 5–18.

Patrick, E. (2004). The U.S. refugee resettlement program. Retrieved from http://www .migrationinformation.org/USFocus/print .cfm?ID=229.

Pavkov, T. W., Lewis, D. A., & Lyons, J. S. (1989). Psychiatric diagnosis and racial bias: An empirical investigation. *Professional Psychology: Research & Practice, 20,* 364–368.

Paynter, S. (2006, Nov. 13). Pelosi has earned her way to the housetop. *Seattle Post Intelligencer,* pp. C1–C2.

Pearson, J. C. (1985). *Gender and communication.* Dubuque, IA: W. C. Brown.

Pearson, S. M., & Bieschke, K. J. (2001). Succeeding against the odds: An examination of familial influences on the career development of professional African women. *Journal of Counseling Psychology, 48,* 301–309.

Pedersen, P. B. (1988). *Handbook for developing multicultural awareness.* Alexandria, VA: American Association for Counseling and Development Press.

Pedersen, P. B. (2000). *A handbook for developing multicultural awareness.* Alexandria, VA: American Counseling Association.

Pennington, D. (2004, July). Until the 'sunset': Helping persons who are older and their caregivers to cope with Alzheimer's, other forms of dementia. *Counseling Today, 22–23.*

People's Medical Society Newsletter. (1998). Are seniors being shortchanged? *People's Medical Society Newsletter, 17,* p. 1, 6.

Peregoy, J. J., & Gloria, A. M. (2007). American Indians and Alaskan Native populations. In M. G. Constantine (Ed.), *Clinical practice with people of color* (pp. 61–84). New York: Teachers College Press.

Peterson, K. (2006, Nov. 8). Seven more states ban gay marriage but Ariz. bucks trend. Retrieved from http://www.stateline.org/live/ViewPage .action?site NoedId/

Pew Hispanic Center. (2006). Hispanic attitudes towards learning English. Retrieved 09/12/2006 from http://www.pewhispanic.org.

Peyser, M., & Lorch, D. (2000). High school controversial. *Newsweek,* 54–56.

Phan, L. T., Rivera, E. T. & Roberts-Wilbur, J. (2005). Understanding Vietnamese refugee women's identity development from a sociopolitical and historical perspective. *Journal of Counseling and Development, 83,* 305–312.

Phelps, R. E., Taylor, J. D., & Gerard, P. A. (2001). Cultural mistrust, ethnic identity, racial identity, and self-esteem among ethnically diverse Black university students. *Journal of Counseling and Development, 79,* 209–216.

Pierce, C. (1995). Stress analogs of racism and sexism: Terrorism, torture, and disaster. In C. Willie, P. Rieker, B. Kramer, & B. Brown (Eds.), *Mental heath, racism, and sexism* (pp. 277–293). Pittsburgh, PA: University of Pittsburgh Press.

Pierre, M. R., & Mahalik, J. R. (2005). Examining African self-consciousness and Black racial identity as predictors of Black men's psychological well-being. *Cultural Diversity and Ethnic Minority Psychology, 11,* 28–40.

Pinderhughes, C. A. (1973). Racism in psychotherapy. In C. Willie, B. Kramer, & B. Brown (Eds.), *Racism and mental health* (pp. 61–121). Pittsburgh, PA: University of Pittsburgh Press.

Pinderhughes, E. E., Dodge, K. A., Bates, J. E., Pettit, G. S., & Zelli, A. (2000). Discipline responses influences of parents' socioeconomic status, ethnicity, beliefs about parenting, stress, and cognitive-emotional processes. *Journal of Family Psychology, 14,* 380–400.

Piotrkowski, C. S. (1998). Gender harassment, job satisfaction, and distress among employed White and minority women. *Journal of Occupational Health Psychology, 3,* 33–43.

Plomin, R. (1989). Environment and genes: Determinants of behavior. *American Psychologist, 44,* 105–111.

Plummer, D. C. (2001). The quest for modern manhood: Masculine stereotypes, peer culture and the social significance of homophobia. *Journal of Adolescence, 24,* 15–23.

Poasa, K. H., Mallinckrodt, B. & Suzuki, L. (2000). Causal attributions for problematic interactions: A qualitative cultural comparison of Western Samoa, American Samoa, and U.S. *Counseling Psychologist, 28,* 32-60.

Pomales, J., Claiborn, C. D., & LaFromboise, T. D. (1986). Effects of Black students' racial identity on perceptions of White counselors varying in cultural sensitivity. *Journal of Counseling Psychology, 34,* 123–131.

Ponterotto, J. G. (1988). Racial consciousness development among white counselors' trainees: A stage model. *Journal of Multicultural Counseling and Development, 16,* 146–156.

Ponterotto, J. G., & Sabnani, H. B. (1989). "Classics" in multicultural counseling: A systematic 5-year content analysis. *Journal of Multicultural Counseling and Development, 17,* 23–37.

Ponterotto, J. G., Utsey, S. O. & Pedersen, P. B. (2006). *Preventing prejudice: A guide for counselors, educators, and parents.* Thousand Oaks, CA: Sage.

Ponzo, Z. (1992). Promoting successful aging: Problems, opportunities, and counseling guidelines. *Journal of Counseling and Development, 71,* 210–213.

Pope-Davis, D. B., & Ottavi, T. M. (1994). Examining the association between self-reported multicultural counseling competencies and demographic and educational variables among counselors. *Journal of Counseling and Development, 72,* 651–654.

Porterfield, E. (1982). *African American-American intermarriages in the United States.* New York: Haworth.

Poston, W. S. (1990). The biracial identity development model: A needed addition. *Journal of Counseling and Development, 69,* 152–155.

Prengaman, P. (2006, Oct. 19). Calif. Candidate to exit race. Retrieved from http://news.yahoo.com/s/ap/20061010/ap_on_re_us/immigration_voting_threat

President's Commission on Mental Health. (1978). *Report from the President's Commission on Mental Health.* Washington, DC: U.S. Government Printing Office.

PR Newswire. (2005, April 13). One in five U.S. workers report racial and gender discrimination exists in the workplace. *PR Newswire,* p. 1.

Pyke, K. (2000). "The normal American family" as an interpretive structure of family life among grown children of Korean and Vietnamese immigrants. *Journal of Marriage and the Family, 62,* 240–255.

Qualls, S. H. (1998a). Marital therapy with later life couples. In D. R. Atkinson & G. Hackett (Eds.), *Counseling diverse populations* (2nd ed., pp. 199–216). Boston: McGraw-Hill.

Qualls, S. H. (1998b). Training in geropsychology: Preparing to meet the demand. *Professional Psychology: Research and Practice, 29,* 23–28.

Queener, J. E., & Martin, J. K. (2001). Providing culturally relevant mental health services: Collaboration between psychology and the African American church. *Journal of Black Psychology, 27,* 112–122.

Quiroga, S. S., & Flores-Ortiz, Y. G. (2000). Barriers to health care for abused Latina and Asian immigrant women. *Journal of Health Care for the Poor and Underserved, 11,* 33–44.

Rabasca, L. (1999). Guidelines for spinal cord injuries don't go far enough. *APA Monitor, 30,* 1–2.

Ramirez, D. A. (1996). Multiracial identity in a color-conscious world. In M. P. P. Root (Ed.), *The multiracial experience: Racial borders as the new frontier* (pp. 49–62). Newbury Park, CA: Sage.

Ramos-McKay, J. M., Comas-Diaz, L., & Rivera, L. A. (1988). Puerto Ricans. In L. Comas-Diaz & E. E. H. Griffith (Eds.), *Clinical Guidelines in Cross-Cultural Mental Health* (pp. 204–232). New York: Wiley.

Ramsey, S., & Birk, J. (1983). Preparation of North Americans for interaction with Japanese: Considerations of language and communication style. In D. Landis & R. W. Brislin (Eds.), *Handbook of intercultural training: Volume III* (pp. 227–259). New York: Pergamon.

Red Horse, J. G. (1983). Indian family values and experiences. In G. J. Powell, J. Yamamoto, A. Romero, & A. Morales (Eds.), *The psychosocial development of minority group children* (pp. 258–272). New York: Brunner/Mazel.

Red Horse, J. G., Lewis, R., Feit, M., & Decker, J. (1981). Family structure and value orientation in American Indians. In R. H. Dana (Ed.), *Human services for cultural minorities.* Baltimore: University Park Press.

Reyhner, J. (2002). American Indian/Alaska Native education: An overview. Retrieved May 7, 2005, from http://jan.ucc.nau.edu/~jar/AIE/Ind_Ed.html

Rezentes, W. C. III. (2006). Hawaiian psychology. In L. T. Hoshmand (Ed.), *Culture, psychotherapy and counseling* (pp. 113–133). Thousand Oaks, CA: Sage.

Rich, T. R. (2004). Judaism 101. Retrieved 12/08/07 from http://www.jewfaq.org/

Richardson, L., & MacGregor, H. E. (2001, April 30). To be Chinese in America: A poll finds that Chinese Americans are still viewed in a "very negative" light. *The Los Angeles Times,* p. E1.

Ridley, C. R. (2005). *Overcoming unintentional racism in counseling and therapy* (2nd ed.). Thousand Oaks, CA: Sage.

Rieckmann, T. R., Wadsworth, M. E. & Deyhle, D. (2004). Cultural identity, explanatory style, and depression in Navajo adolescents. *Cultural Diversity and Ethnic Minority Psychology, 10,* 365–382.

Rienzo, B. A., Button, J. W., Sheu, J-J., & Li, Y. (2006). The politics of sexual orientation issues in American schools. *Journal of School Health, 76,* 93–97.

Reiss, B. F. (1980). Psychological tests in homosexuality. In J. Marmor (Ed.), *Homosexual behavior: A modern reappraisal* (pp. 296–311). New York: Basic Books.

Riessman, F. (1962). *The culturally deprived child.* New York: Harper & Row.

Rivera, A. N. (1984). *Toward a psychotherapy for Puerto Ricans.* Rio Piederis, PR: CEDEPP.

Ro, M. (2002). Moving forward: Addressing the health of Asian American and Pacific Islander women. *American Journal of Public Health, 92,* 516–519.

Roberts, R. E., Kaplan, G. A., Shema, S. J., & Strawbridge, W. J. (1997). Does growing old increase the risk for depression? *American Journal of Psychiatry, 154,* 1384–1390.

Roberts, R. E., & Sobhan, M. (1992). Symptoms of depression in adolescence: A comparison of Anglo, African, and Hispanic Americans. *Journal of Youth and Adolescents, 21,* 639–650.

Robinson, T. L., & Howard-Hamilton, M. F. (2000). *The convergence of race, ethnicity, and gender.* Columbus, OH: Merrill.

Rodriguez, N., Ryan, S. W., Vande Kemp, H., & Foy, D. W. (1997). Posttraumatic stress disorder in adult female survivors of child sexual abuse: A comparison study. *Journal of Consulting and Clinical Psychology, 65,* 53–59.

Rogan, R. G., & Hammer, M. R. (1998). An exploratory study of message affect and behavior: A comparison between African Americans and Euro-Americans. *Journal of Language and Social Psychology, 17,* 449–464.

Rogers, C. R. (1961). *On becoming a person.* Boston: Houghton Mifflin.

Romero, D. (1985). Cross-cultural counseling: Brief reactions for the practitioner. *The Counseling Psychologist, 13,* 665–671.

Roose, S. P. (2001). Men over 50: An endangered species. *Psychiatry Clinical Updates.* New York: Medscape.

Root, M. P. P. (1990). Resolving "other" status: Identity development of biracial individuals. In L. S. Borwn & M. P. P. Root (Eds.), *Diversity and complexity in feminist therapy* (pp. 185–205). New York: Haworth.

Root, M. P. P. (Ed.). (1992a). *Racially mixed people in America.* Thousand Oaks, CA: Sage.

Root, M. P. P. (1992b). Reconstructing the impact of trauma on personality. In M. Ballou & L. Brown (Eds.), *Theories of personality and psychopathology: Feminist reappraisal* (pp. 229–265). New York: Guilford.

Root, M. P. P. (Ed.). (1996). *The multiracial experience.* Thousand Oaks, CA: Sage.

Root, M. P. P. (1998). Facilitating psychotherapy with Asian American clients. In D. R. Atkinson, G. Morten, & D. W. Sue (Eds.), *Counseling American minorities: A cross-cultural perspective* (pp. 214–234). Boston: McGraw-Hill.

Root, M. P. P. (2001). Negotiating the margins. In J. G. Ponterotto, J. M. Casas, L. A. Suzuki, & C. M. Alexander (Eds.), *Handbook of multicultural counseling.* Thousand Oaks, CA: Sage.

Rosario, M., Schrimshaw, E. W., & Hunter, J. (2004). Ethnic/racial differences in the coming out process of lesbian, gay, and bisexual youths: A comparison of sexual identity development over time. *Cultural Diversity and Ethnic Minority Psychology, 10,* 215–228.

Rosario, M., Schrimshaw, E. W., Hunter, J., & Braun, L. (2006). Sexual identity development among lesbian, gay, and bisexual youths: Consistency and change over time. *Journal of Sex Research, 43,* 46–58.

Rosenberg, D. (2004, May 24). The 'Will & Grace.' *Newsweek,* 38–39.

Rosenblatt, P. C., Karis, T. A., & Powell, R. D. (1995). *Multiracial couples.* Thousand Oaks, CA: Sage.

Rosenfarb, I. S., Bellack, A. S., & Aziz, N. (2006). Family interactions and the course of schizophrenia in African American and White patients. *Journal of Abnormal Psychology, 115,* 112–120.

Rosenthal, R., & Jacobson, L. (1968). *Pygmalion in the classroom.* New York: Holt, Rinehart & Winston.

Rothbaum, F., Morelli, G., Pott, M., & Liu-Constant, Y. (2000). Immigrant-Chinese and Euro-American parents' physical closeness with young children: Themes of family relatedness. *Journal of Family Psychology, 14,* 334–348.

Rotter, J. (1966). Generalized expectancies for internal versus external control of reinforcement. *Psychological Monographs, 80,* 1–28.

Rotter, J. (1975). Some problems and misconceptions related to the construct of internal versus external control of reinforcement. *Journal of Consulting and Clinical Psychology, 43,* 56–67.

Rouse, B. A., Carter, J. H., & Rodriguez-Andrew, S. (1995). Race/ethnicity and other sociocultural influences on alcoholism treatment for women. *Recent Developments in Alcoholism, 12,* 343–367.

Rowe, W. (2006). White racial identity: Science, faith and pseudoscience. *Journal of Multicultural Counseling and Development. 34, 235–243.*

Rowe, W., Bennett, S., & Atkinson, D. R. (1994). White racial identity models: A critique and alternative proposal. *The Counseling Psychologist, 22,* 120–146.

Roysircar, G. (2004). Child survivor of war: A case study. *Journal of Multicultural Counseling and Development, 32,* 168–178.

Rudman, L. A. (1998). Self-promotion as a risk factor for women: The costs and benefits of counter-stereotypical impression management. *Journal of Personality and Social Psychology, 74,* 629–645.

Ruiz, A. (1981). Cultural and historical perspectives in counseling Hispanics. In D. W. Sue (Ed.), *Counseling the culturally different: Theory & practice* (pp. 186–215). New York: Wiley.

Ruiz, A. S. (1990). Ethnic identity: Crisis and resolution. *Journal of Multicultural Counseling and Development, 18,* 29–40.

Ruiz, P. (1995). Assessing, diagnosing and treating culturally diverse individuals: A Hispanic perspective. *Psychiatric Quarterly, 66,* 329–341.

Russell, S. (1988). *At home among strangers.* Washington, DC: Gallaudet University Press.

Russell, S. T., Franz, B. T., & Driscoll, A. K. (2001). Same-sex romantic attraction and experience of violence in adolescence. *American Journal of Public Health, 91,* 903–906.

Russell, S. T., & Joyner, K. (2001). Suicide attempts more likely among adolescents with same-sex sexual orientation. *American Journal of Public Health, 91,* 1276–1281.

Russell, S. T., & Lee, F. C. H. (2004). Practitioners' perspectives on effective practices for Hispanic teenage pregnancy prevention. *Perspectives on Sexual and Reproductive Health, 36,* 142–149.

Rutter, M. (1991). Nature, nurture, and psychopathology: A new look at an old topic. *Developmental Psychopathology, 3,* 125–136.

Ryan, C., & Futterman, D. (2001a). Experience, vulnerabilities and risks of lesbian and gay students. *The Prevention Researcher, 8,* 6–8.

Ryan, C., & Futterman, D. (2001b). Lesbian and gay adolescents: Identity development. *The Prevention Researcher, 8,* 1–5.

Ryan, W. (1971). *Blaming the victim.* New York: Pantheon.

Rytina, N. F. (2004). *Refugee applicants and admissions to the United States.* Washington, DC: Department of Homeland Security.

Sabnani, H. B., Ponterotto, J. G., & Borodovsky, L. G. (1991). White racial identity development and cross-cultural counselor training. *The Counselor Psychologist, 19,* 76–102.

Sahagun, L. (2006, Sept. 8). A post-9/11 identity shift. *Seattle Post-Intelligencer,* pp. A1, 22.

Samuda, R. J. (1998). *Psychological testing of American minorities.* Thousand Oaks, CA: Sage.

Sandhu, D. S. (1997). Psychocultural profiles of Asian and Pacific Islander Americans: Implications for counseling and psychotherapy. *Journal of Multicultural Counseling and Development, 25,* 7–22.

Sandhu, D. S., Leung, A. S., & Tang, M. (2003). Counseling approaches with Asian Americans and Pacific Islander Americans. In F. D. Harper & J. McFadden (Eds.), *Culture and counseling* (pp. 99–114). Boston: Allyn & Bacon.

Sands, T. (1998). Feminist counseling and female adolescents: Treatment strategies for depression. *Journal of Mental Health Counseling, 20,* 42–54.

Satir, V. (1967). *Conjoint family therapy.* Palo Alto, CA: Science & Behavior Books.

Satir, V. (1983). *Conjoint family therapy* (3rd ed.). Palo Alto, CA: Science and Behavior Books.

Saunders, P. A. (1998). "My brain's on strike." The construction of identity through memory accounts by dementia patients. *Research on Aging, 20,* 65–90.

Savin-Williams, R. C. (2001). *Mom, Dad. I'm gay.* Washington, DC: American Psychological Association.

Saxton, L. (1968). *The individual, marriage, and the family.* Belmont, CA: Wadsworth.

Schein, E. H. (1990). Organizational culture. *American Psychologist, 45(2)*, 109–119.

Schindler-Rainman, E. (1967). The poor and the PTA. *PTA Magazine, 61(8)*, 4–5.

Schnittker, J. (2003). Misgivings of medicine? African Americans' skepticism of psychiatric medication. *Journal of Health and Social Behavior, 44*, 506–514.

Schofield, W. (1964). *Psychotherapy: The purchase of friendship*. Englewood Cliffs, NJ: Prentice Hall.

Schwartzman, J. B., & Glaus, K. D. (2000). Depression and coronary heart disease in women: Implications for clinical practice and research. *Professional Psychology: Research and Practice, 31*, 48–57.

Seligman, M. E. P. (1982). *Helplessness: On depression, development and death*. San Francisco: Freeman.

Seligman, M. E. P., & Csikszentmihalyi, M. (2001). Reply to comments. *American Psychologist, 56*, 89–90.

Serrano, J. P., Latorre, J. M., Gatz, M., & Montanes, J. (2004). Life review therapy using autobiographical retrieval practice for older adults with depressive symptomatology. *Psychology and Aging, 19*, 272–277.

Shade, B. J., & New, C. A. (1993). Cultural influences on learning: Teaching implications. In J. A. Banks & C. A. McGee Banks (Eds.), *Multicultural education* (pp. 317–331). Boston: Allyn & Bacon.

Shannon, J. W., & Woods, W. J. (1998). Affirmative psychotherapy for gay men. In D. R. Atkinson & G. Hackett (Eds.), *Counseling diverse populations* (2nd ed., pp. 335–351). Boston: McGraw-Hill.

Shapiro, D. H. (1982). Overview: Clinical and physiological comparison of meditation with other self control strategies. *American Journal of Psychiatry, 139*, 267–274.

Shapiro, E. (2006). Civil rights and wrongs. Retrieved 12/15/2006 from http://www.myjewishlearning.com/history_community/Modern

Shin, S-M., Chow, C., Camacho-Gonsalves, T., Levy, R. J., Allen, I. E., & Leff, H. S. (2005). A meta-analytic review of racial-ethnic matching for African American and Caucasian American clients and clinicians. *Journal of Counseling Psychology, 52*, 45–56.

Shockley, W. (1972). Determination of human intelligence. *Journal of Criminal Law and Criminology, 7*, 530–543.

Shorter-Gooden, K., & Washington, N. C. (1996). Young, Black, and female: The challenge of weaving an identity. *Journal of Adolescence, 19*, 465–475.

Shostrom, E. L. (Producer). (1977). *Three approaches to psychotherapy: II* [Motion picture]. Corona Del Mar, CA: Psychological and Educational Films.

Shukovsky, P. (2001, March 29). "Urban Indians" are going home. *Seattle Post-Intelligencer*, pp. A1, A13.

Shullman, S. L., Celeste, B. L., & Strickland, T. (2006). Extending the Parsons Legacy: Applications of counseling psychology in pursuit of social justice. In R. L. Toporek, L. H. Gerstein, N. A. Fouad, G. Roysircar, & T. Israel (Eds.), *Handbook for social justice in counseling psychology* (pp. 499–513). Thousand Oaks, CA: Sage.

Silverman, J. G., Raj, A., Mucci, L. A., & Hathaway, J. E. (2001). Dating violence against adolescent girls and associated substance use, unhealthy weight control, sexual risk behavior, pregnancy, and suicidality. *Journal of the American Medical Association, 286*, 572–579.

Silverstein, L. B. (2006). Integrating feminism and multiculturalism: Scientific fact or science fiction? *Professional Psychology: Research and Practice, 37*, 21–28.

Sinclair, S. L. (2006). Object lessons: A theoretical and empirical study of objectified body consciousness in women. *Journal of Mental Health Counseling, 28*, 48–68.

Singelis, T. (1994). Nonverbal communication in intercultural interactions. In R. W. Brislin & T. Yoshida (Eds.), *Improving intercultural interactions* (pp. 268–294). Thousand Oaks, CA: Sage.

Singer, D. (2002). *American Jewish year book 2002*. New York: American Jewish Committee.

Skarupski, Mendes del Leon, Bienias, J. L., Barnes, L L., et al. (2005). Black-White differences in depressive symptoms among older adults over time. *Journal of Gerontology, 60B*, 136–142.

Skolnik, S. (2001, November 2). Same-sex estate rights backed. *Seattle Post-Intelligencer,* p. B1.

Sleek, S. (1998, July). Mental disabilities no barrier to smooth and efficient work. *Monitor,* p. 15.

Smith, D. P. (2005). The sweat lodge as psychotherapy. In R. Moodley & W. West (Eds.), *Integrating traditional healing practices into counseling and psychotherapy* (pp. 196–209). Thousand Oaks, CA: Sage.

Smith, E. J. (1981). Cultural and historical perspectives in counseling Blacks. In D. W. Sue (Ed.), *Counseling the culturally different: Theory and practice* (pp. 141–185). New York: Wiley.

Smith, J. I. (2006). Patterns of Muslim immigration. Retrieved 12/15/2006 from http://usinfo.state .gov/products/pubs/muslimlife/immigrat.htm

Smith, J. M. (2003). *A potent spell: Mother love and the power of fear.* Boston: Houghton Mifflin.

Smith, L. (2005). Psychotherapy, classism, and the poor: Conspicuous by their absence. *American Psychologist, 60,* 687–696.

Smith, L. (2006). Addressing classism, extending multicultural competence, and serving the poor. *American Psychologist, 61,* 338–339.

Smith, M. E. (1957). Progress in the use of English after twenty-two years by children of Chinese ancestry in Honolulu. *Journal of Genetic Psychology, 90,* 255–258.

Smith, M. E., & Kasdon, L. M. (1961). Progress in the use of English after twenty years by children of Filipino and Japanese ancestry in Hawaii. *Journal of Genetic Psychology, 99,* 129–138.

Smith, N. G., & Ingram, K. M. (2004). Workplace heterosexism and adjustment among lesbian, gay, and bisexual individuals: The role of unsupportive social interactions. *Journal of Counseling Psychology, 51,* 57–67.

Snowden, L. R., & Cheung, F. H. (1990). Use of inpatient mental health services by members of ethnic minority groups. *American Psychologist, 45,* 347–355.

So, J. K. (2005). Traditional and cultural healing among the Chinese. In R. Moodley & W. West (Eds.), *Integrating traditional healing practices into counseling and psychotherapy* (pp. 100–111). Thousand Oaks, CA: Sage.

Sodowsky, G. R., Kwan, K. K., & Pannu, R. (1995).

Ethnic identity of Asians in the United States. In J. G. Ponterotto, J. M. Casas, L. A. Suzuki, & C. M. Alexander (Eds.), *Handbook of multicultural counseling* (pp. 123–154). Thousand Oaks, CA: Sage.

Solomon, A., & Wane, J. N. (2005). Indigenous healers and healing in a modern world. In R. Moodley & W. West (Eds.), *Integrating traditional healing practices into counseling and psychotherapy* (pp. 52–60). Thousand Oaks, CA: Sage.

Solórzano, D., Ceja, M., & Yosso, T. (2000). Critical race theory, racial microaggressions, and campus racial climate: The experiences of African American college students. *The Journal of Negro Education, 69*(1/2), 60–73.

Spanierman, L. B., Armstrong, P. I., Poteat, V. V., & Beer, A. M. (2006). Psychosocial costs of racism to Whites: Exploring patterns through cluster analysis. *Journal of Counseling Psychology, 17,* 81–87.

Stanback, M. H., & Pearce, W. B. (1985). Talking to "the man": Some communication strategies used by members of "subordinate" social groups. In L. A. Samovar & R. E. Porter (Eds.), *Intercultural communication: A reader* (pp. 236–253). Belmont, CA: Wadsworth.

Steele, C. M., & Aronson, J. (1995). Stereotype threat and the intellectual test performance of African Americans. *Journal of Personality and Social Psychology, 69,* 797–811.

Stewart, A. J., & Ostrove, J. M. (1998). Women's personality in middle age: Gender, history, and midcourse corrections. *American Psychologist, 53,* 1185–1194.

Stewart, E. C. (1971). *American cultural patterns: A cross-cultural perspective.* Pittsburgh, PA: Regional Council for International Understanding.

Stice, E., & Bearman, S. K. (2001). Body-image and eating disturbances prospectively predict increases in depressive symptoms in adolescent girls: A growth curve analysis. *Developmental Psychology, 37,* 597–607.

Stone, A. (2006, Feb. 20). Drives to ban gay adoption heat up in 16 states. Retrieved from http://www.comcast.net/news/usatoday/index.jsp?fn=/2006/02/20/241702.html

Stonequist, E. V. (1937). *The marginal man*. New York: Charles Scribner's Sons.

Strawbridge, W. J., Cohen, R. D., Shema, S. J., & Kaplan, G. A. (1997). Frequent attendance at religious services and mortality over 28 years. *American Journal of Public Health, 87,* 957–961.

Strickland, B. R. (2000). Misassumptions, misadventures, and the misuse of psychology. *American Psychologist, 55,* 331–338.

Strong, S. R. (1969). Counseling: An interpersonal influence process. *Journal of Counseling Psychology, 15,* 215–224.

Study: 2020 begins age of the elderly. (1996, May 21). *USA Today*, p. 4a.

Sue, D. (1990). Culture in transition: Counseling Asian-American men. In D. Moore & F. Leafgren (Eds.), *Men in conflict* (pp. 53–165). Alexandria, VA: American Association for Counseling and Development.

Sue, D., Sue, D. W., & Sue, S. (2006). *Understanding abnormal behavior* (7th ed.). Boston: Houghton Mifflin.

Sue, D. W. (1978). Eliminating cultural oppression in counseling: Toward a general theory. *Journal of Counseling Psychology, 25,* 419–428.

Sue, D. W. (1980). *Counseling the culturally different: Theory and practice*. New York: Wiley.

Sue, D. W. (1990). Culture specific techniques in counseling: A conceptual framework. *Professional Psychology, 21,* 424–433.

Sue, D. W. (1993). Confronting ourselves: The White and racial/ethnic minority researcher. *The Counseling Psychologist, 21,* 244–249.

Sue, D. W. (1995). Multicultural organizational development: Implications for the counseling profession. In J. G. Ponterotto, J. M. Casas, L. A. Suzuki, & C. M. Alexander (Eds.), *Handbook of multicultural counseling* (pp. 474–492). Thousand Oaks, CA: Sage.

Sue, D. W. (2001). Multidimensional facets of cultural competence. *The Counseling Psychologist, 29,* 790–821.

Sue, D. W. (2003). *Overcoming our racism: The Journey to liberation*. San Francisco: Jossey Bass.

Sue, D. W. (2004). Whiteness and ethnocentric monoculturalism: Making the invisible, visible. *American Psychologist, 59,* 761–769.

Sue, D. W. (2005). Racism and the conspiracy of silence. *The Counseling Psychologist. 33,* 100–114.

Sue, D. W., Arredondo, P., & McDavis, R. J. (1992). Multicultural competencies/standards: A call to the profession. *Journal of Counseling and Development, 70*(4), 477–486.

Sue, D. W., Bernier, J. B., Durran, M., Feinberg, L., Pedersen, P., Smithe, E., et al. (1982). Position paper: Cross-cultural counseling competencies. *The Counseling Psychologist, 10,* 45–52.

Sue, D. W., Bingham, R., Porche-Burke, L., & Vasquez, M. (1999). The diversification of psychology: A multicultural revolution. *American Psychologist, 54,* 1061–1069.

Sue, D. W., Bucceri, J., Lin, A., Nadal, K., & Torino, G. (2007). Racial microaggressions and the Asian American experience. *Cultural Diversity and Ethnic Minority Psychology, 13,* 72–81.

Sue, D. W., Capodilupo, C. M., & Holder, A. H. (2007). Racial microaggressions in the life experience of African Americans. *Professional Psychology: Research and Practice.*

Sue, D. W., Capodilupo, C. M., Torino, G., Bucceri, J., Holder, A. H., Nadal, K., & Esquilin, M. E. (in press). Racial microaggressions in everyday life: Implications for clinical practice. *American Psychologist.*

Sue, D. W., Carter, R. T., Casas, J. M., Fouad, N. A., Ivey, A. E., Jensen, M., LaFromboise, T., et al. (1998). *Multicultural counseling competencies: Individual and organizational development*. Thousand Oaks, CA: Sage.

Sue, D. W., & Constantine, M. G. (2003). Optimal human functioning in people of color in the United States. In W. Bruce Walsh (Ed.), *Counseling psychology and optimal human functioning* (pp. 151–169). Mahwah, NJ: Erlbaum.

Sue, D. W., & Frank, A. C. (1973). A topological approach to the study of Chinese- and Japanese-American college males. *Journal of Social Issues, 29,* 129–148.

Sue, D. W., Ivey, A. E., & Pedersen, P. B. (1996). *A theory of multicultural counseling and therapy*. Pacific Grove, CA: Brooks Cole.

Sue, D. W., & Kirk, B. A. (1973). Differential characteristics of Japanese-American and Chinese-

American college students. *Journal of Counseling Psychology, 20,* 142–148.

Sue, D. W., Parham, T. A., & Santiago, G. B. (1998). The changing face of work in the United States: Implications for individual institutional and societal survival. *Cultural Diversity and Mental Health, 4,* 153–164.

Sue, D. W., & Sue, D. (1990): *Counseling the culturally different: Theory and practice.* New York: Wiley.

Sue, D. W., & Sue, D. (1999). *Counseling the culturally different: Theory and practice* (3rd ed.). New York: Wiley.

Sue, D. W., & Sue, S. (1972). Counseling Chinese-Americans. *Personnel & Guidance Journal, 50,* 637–644.

Sue, D. W., & Torino, G. C. (2005). Racial-cultural competence: Awareness, knowledge and skills. In R. T. Carter (Ed.), *Handbook of racial-cultural psychology and counseling* (pp. 3–18). Hoboken, NJ: Wiley.

Sue, J., Lee, R. M., & Vang, S. (2005). Intergenerational family conflict and coping among Hmong American college students. *Journal of Counseling Psychology, 52,* 482–489.

Sue, S. (1999). Science, ethnicity and bias: Where have we gone wrong? *American Psychologist, 54,* 1070–1077.

Sue, S., Allen, D., & Conaway, L. (1975). The responsiveness and equality of mental health care to Chicanos and Native Americans. *American Journal of Community Psychology, 45,* 111–118.

Sue, S., Fujino, D. C., Hu, L., Takeuchi, D. T., & Zane, N. W. S. (1991). Community mental health services for ethnic minority groups: A test of the cultural responsiveness hypothesis. *Journal of Consulting and Clinical Psychology, 59,* 533–540.

Sue, S., & McKinney, H. (1974). Delivery of community health services to black and white clients. *Journal of Consulting and Clinical Psychology, 42,* 794–801.

Sue, S., McKinney, H., Allen, D., & Hall, J. (1974). Delivery of community health services to Black & White clients. *Journal of Consulting Psychology, 42,* 794–801.

Sue, S., & Sue, D. W. (1971a). Chinese-American personality and mental health. *Amerasian Journal, 1,* 36–49.

Sue, S., & Sue, D. W. (1971b). *The reflection of culture conflicts in the psychological problems of Chinese and Japanese students.* Paper presented at the American Psychological Association Convention, Honolulu, HI.

Sue, S., Sue, D. W., Sue, L., & Takeuchi, D. T. (1995). Psychopathology among Asian Americans: A model minority? *Cultural Diversity and Mental Health, 1,* 39–51.

Suleiman, M. W. (1999). *The Arab immigrant experience.* Philadelphia: Temple University Press.

Sullivan, K. R., & Mahalik, J. R. (2000). Increasing career self-efficacy for women: Evaluating a group intervention. *Journal of Counseling and Development, 78,* 54–62.

Sundberg, N. D. (1981). Cross-cultural counseling and psychotherapy: A research overview. In A. J. Mansella & P. B. Pedersen (Eds.), *Cross-cultural counseling and psychotherapy* (pp. 29–38). New York: Pergamon.

Suro, R., & Escobar, G. (2006). 2006 National survey of Latinos: The immigration debate. Retrieved 09/12/2006 from http://pewhispanic.org/reports/report.php?

Susman, N. M., & Rosenfeld, H. M. (1982). Influence of culture, language and sex on conversation distance. *Journal of Personality and Social Psychology, 42,* 66–74.

Sutton, C. T., & Broken Nose, M. A. (2005). American Indian families: An overview. In M. McGoldrick, J. Giordano, & N. Garcia-Preto (Eds.), *Ethnicity and family therapy* (pp. 43–54). New York: Guilford.

Suyemoto, K. L. (2004). Racial/ethnic identities and related attributed experiences of multiracial Japanese European Americans. *Journal of Multicultural Counseling and Development, 32,* 206–221.

Suzuki, L. A., Kugler, J. F., & Aguiar, L. J. (2005). Assessment practices in racial-cultural psychology. In R. T. Carter (Ed.), *Handbook of racial-cultural psychology and counseling* (pp. 297–315). Hoboken, NJ: Wiley.

Suzuki-Crumly, J., & Hyers, L. L. (2004). The relationship among ethnic identity, psychological well-being, and intergroup competence: An investigation of two biracial groups. *Cultural Di-*

versity and Ethnic Minority Psychology, 10, 137–150.

Swim, J. K., & Cohen, L. L. (1997). Overt, covert, and subtle sexism. *Psychology of Women Quarterly, 21,* 103–118.

Swim, J. K., Hyers, L. L., Cohen, L. L., & Ferguson, M. J. (2001). Everyday sexism: Evidence for its incidence, nature, and psychological impact from three daily diary studies. *Journal of Social Issues, 57,* 31–53.

Swim, J. K., Mallett, R., & Stangor, C. (2004). Understanding subtle sexism: Detection and use of sexist language. *Sex Roles, 51,* 117–128.

Swinomish Tribal Mental Health Project. (1991). *A gathering of wisdoms.* LaConner, WA: Swinomish Tribal Community.

Szapocznik, J., & Kurtines, W. M. (1993). Family psychology and cultural diversity: Opportunities for theory, research, and application. *American Psychologist, 48,* 400–407.

Szapocznik, J., Santisteban, D., Kurtines, W. M., Hervis, O. E., & Spencer, F. (1982). Life enhancements counseling: A psychosocial model of services for Cuban elders. In E. E. Jones & S. J. Korchin (Eds.), *Minority mental health* (pp. 296–329). New York: Praeger.

Szasz, T. S. (1970). The crime of commitment. In *Readings in clinical psychology today* (pp. 167–169). Del Mar, CA: CRM Books.

Szasz, T. S. (1971). *The myth of mental illness.* New York: Hoeber.

Szasz, T. S. (1987). The case against suicide prevention. *American Psychologist, 41,* 806–812.

Szasz, T. S. (1999). *Fatal freedom: The ethics and politics of suicide.* Westport, CT: Praeger.

Tafoya, N., & Del Vecchio, A. (2005). Back to the future: An examination of the Native American holocaust experience. In M. McGoldrick, J. Giordano, & N. Garcia-Preto (Eds.), *Ethnicity and family therapy* (pp. 55–63). New York: Guilford.

Taggart, C. (2001, October 14). Disability for a day is enlightening. *Spokesman Review,* p. B1.

Talleyrand, R. M., Chung, R. C. Y., & Bemak, F. (2006). Incorporating social justice in counselor training programs: A case study example. In R. L. Toporek, L. H. Gerstein, N. A. Fouad, G. Roysircar, & T. Israel (Eds.), *Handbook for social justice in counseling psychology* (pp. 44–58). Thousand Oaks, CA: Sage.

Taylor, M. J. (2000). The influence of self-efficacy on alcohol use among American Indians. *Cultural Diversity and Ethnic Minority Psychology, 6,* 152–167.

Taylor, S., & Kennedy, R. (2003). Feminist framework. In J. Anderson & R. W. Carter (Eds.), *Diversity perspectives for social work practice* (pp. 171–197). Boston: Allyn & Bacon.

Tepper, M. S. (2001). *Sexual healing with a disability.* Sexual Health Network. Available at www.sexualhealth.com.

Terman, L. M. (1916). *The measurement of intelligence.* Boston: Houghton Mifflin.

Thigpen, C. H., & Cleckley, H. M. (1954). A case of multiple personality. *Journal of Abnormal Social Psychology, 49,* 135–151.

Thomas, C. W. (1970). Different strokes for different folks. *Psychology Today, 4,* 49–53, 80.

Thomas, C. W. (1971). *Boys no more.* Beverly Hills, CA: Glencoe Press.

Thomas, A., & Sillen, S. (1972). *Racism and psychiatry.* New York: Brunner/Mazel.

Thomas, M. B., & Dansby, P. G. (1985). Black clients: Family structures, therapeutic issues, and strengths. *Psychotherapy, 22,* 398–407.

Thompson, L. W., Powers, D. V., Coon, D. W., Takagi, K., McKibbin, C. & Gallagher-Thompson, D. (2000). Older adults. In J. R. White & A. S. Freeman (Eds.), *Cognitive-behavioral group therapy: For specific problems and populations* (pp. 235–261). Washington, DC: American Psychological Association.

Thoresen, C. E. (1998). Spirituality, health and science: The coming revival? In S. R. Roemer, S. R. Kurpius, & C. Carmin (Eds.), *The emerging role of counseling psychology in health care* (pp. 409–431). New York: Norton.

Thurlow, C. (2001). Naming the "outsider within": Homophobic perjoratives and the verbal abuse of lesbian, gay and bisexual high school pupils. *Journal of Adolescence, 24,* 25–38.

Thurow, L. (1995, November 19). Why their world might crumble. *New York Times Magazine.*

Tilove, J. (2001, July 11). Gap in Black-White views

growing, poll finds. *Seattle Post-Intelligencer,* p. A1.

Tobin, J. J., & Friedman, J. (1983). Spirits, shamans, and nightmare death: Survivor stress in a Hmong refugee. *American Journal of Orthopsychiatry, 53,* 439–448.

Toporek, R. L. (2006). Social action in policy and legislations: Individuals and alliances. In R. L. Toporek, L. H. Gerstein, N. A. Fouad, G. Roysircar, & T. Isracl (Eds.), *Handbook for social justice in counseling psychology* (pp. 489–498). Thousand Oaks, CA: Sage.

Toporek, R. L., Gerstein, L. H., Fouad, N. A., Roysircar, G., & Israel, T. (2006). Future directions for counseling psychology: Enhancing leadership, vision, and action in social justice. In R. L. Toporek, L. H. Gerstein, N. A. Fouad, G. Roysircar, & T. Israel (Eds.), *Handbook for social justice in counseling psychology* (pp. 533–552). Thousand Oaks, CA: Sage.

Toporek, R. L., & McNally, C. J. (2006). Social justice training in counseling psychology: Needs and innovations. In R. L. Toporek, L. H. Gerstein, N. A. Fouad, G. Roysircar, & T. Israel (Eds.), *Handbook for social justice in counseling psychology* (pp. 37–43). Thousand Oaks, CA: Sage.

Toporek, R. L., & Williams, R. A. (2006). Ethics and professional issues related to the practice of social justice in counseling psychology. In R. L. Toporek, L. H. Gerstein, N. A. Fouad, G. Roysircar, & T. Israel (Eds.), *Handbook for social justice in counseling psychology* (pp. 17–34). Thousand Oaks, CA: Sage.

Torres, M. M. (1998). *Understanding the multiracial experience through children's literature: A protocol.* Unpublished doctoral dissertation, California School of Professional Psychology, Alameda.

Tortolero, S. R., & Roberts, R. E. (2001). Differences in nonfatal suicide behavior among Mexican and European American middle school children. *Suicide and Life-Threatening Behavior, 31,* 214–223.

Triandis, H. C. (2000). Cultural syndromes and subjective well-being. In E. Diener & E. M. Suh (Eds.), *Culture and subjective well-being* (pp. 13–36). London: MIT Press.

Trimble, J. E., Fleming, C. M., Beauvais, F., &

Jumper-Thurman, P. (1996). Essential cultural and social strategies for counseling Native American Indians. In P. B. Pedersen, J. G. Draguns, W. J. Lonner, & J. E. Trimble (Eds.), *Counseling across cultures* (4th ed., pp. 177–209). Thousand Oaks, CA: Sage.

Tsui, P., & Schultz, G. L. (1985). Failure of rapport: When psychotherapeutic engagement fails in the treatment of Asian clients. *American Journal of Orthopsychiatry, 55,* 561–569.

Turner, R. J., Lloyd, D. A., & Taylor, J. (2006). Physical disability and mental health: An epidemiology of psychiatric and substance disorders. *Rehabilitation Psychology, 51,* 214–223.

Uba, L. (1994). *Asian Americans.* New York: Guilford.

Uniform Crime Report. (2005). Hate crime statistics: Incidents and offenses. Washington, DC: U.S. Department of Justice.

Urdaneta, M. L., Saldana, D. H., & Winkler, A. (1995). Mexican-American perceptions of severe mental illness. *Human Organization, 54,* 70–77.

U.S. Census Bureau. (1995). *Population profile of the United States.* Washington, DC: U.S. Government Printing Office.

U.S. Census Bureau. (2001). *Population profile of the United States.* Washington, DC: U.S. Government Printing Office.

U.S. Census Bureau. (2002). *Poverty in the United States.* Washington, DC: U.S. Government Printing Office.

U.S. Census Bureau (2003). *The Hispanic population in the United States: March 2002.* Washington, DC: U.S. Government Printing Office.

U.S. Census Bureau (2004a). *The foreign-born population in the United States: 2003.* Washington, DC: U.S. Government Printing Office.

U.S. Census Bureau (2004b). *We the people: Aging in the United States.* Washington, DC: U.S. Department of Commerce.

U.S. Census Bureau (2004c). *We the people: Asians in the United States.* Washington, DC: U.S. Government Printing Office.

U.S. Census Bureau (2004d). *We the people: Hispanics in the United States.* Washington, DC: U.S. Government Printing Office.

U.S. Census Bureau (2005a). *65+ in the United States:*

2005. Washington, DC: U.S. Government Printing Office.

U.S. Census Bureau (2005b). *Disability and American families: 2000*. Washington, DC: U.S. Government Printing Office.

U.S. Census Bureau (2005c). *We the people: Blacks in the United States*. Washington, DC: U.S. Government Printing Office.

U.S. Census Bureau (2005d). *We the people of more than one race in the United States*. Washington, DC: U.S. Government Printing Office.

U.S. Census Bureau (2005e). *We the people: Pacific Islanders in the United States*. Washington, DC: U.S. Government Printing Office.

U.S. Census Bureau (2005f). *We the people of Arab ancestry in the United States*. Washington, DC: U.S. Government Printing Office.

U.S. Census Bureau (2006a). *We the people: American Indians and Alaska Natives in the United States*. Washington, DC: U.S. Government Printing Office.

U.S. Census Bureau (2006b). *65+ in the United States: 2005*. Washington, DC: U.S. Government Printing Office.

U.S. Department of Health and Human Services. (1998). *The national elder abuse incidence study*. Washington, DC: Government Printing Office.

U.S. Department of Labor. (2005). *20 leading occupations of employed women, U.S.* Rockville, MD: U.S. Department of Labor.

U.S. Department of Labor, Women's Bureau. (1992). *Women workers outlook to 2005*. Washington, DC: Author.

U.S. Department of State (2002). Muslim life in America. Retrieved 12/15/2006 from http://usinfo.state.gov/products/pubs/muslimlife

U.S. Public Health Service. (2001). *A report of the surgeon general on minority mental health*. Rockville, MD: U.S. Department of Health and Human Services.

Utsey, S. O., Gernat, C. A., & Hammar, L. (2005). Examining white counselor trainees' reactions to racial issues in counseling and supervision dyads. *The Counseling Psychologist. 33*, 449–478.

Utsey, S. O., Grange, C., & Allyne, R. (2006). Guidelines for evaluating the racial and cultural environment of graduate training programs in professional psychology. In M. G. Constantine & D. W. Sue (Eds.), *Addressing racism* (pp. 213–232). Hoboken, NJ: Wiley.

Utsey, S. O., Walker, R. L., & Kwate, N. O. A. (2005). Conducting quantitative research in a cultural context. In M. G. Constantine & D. W. Sue (Eds.), *Strategies for building multicultural competence in mental health and educational settings* (pp. 247–268). Hoboken, NJ: Wiley.

Vacc, N. A., & Clifford, K. (1995). Individuals with a physical disability. In N. A. Vacc, S. B. DeVaney, & J. Wittmer (Eds.), *Experiencing and counseling multicultural and diverse populations* (3rd ed., pp. 231–272). Bristol, PA: Accelerated Development.

Vandiver, B. J. (2001). Psychological nigrescence revisited: Introduction and overview. *Journal of Multicultural Counseling and Development, 29,* 165–173.

Vandiver, B. J., Fhagen-Smith, P. E., Cokley, K. O., Cross, W. E., & Worrell, F. C. (2001). Cross's nigrescence model: From theory to scale to theory. *Journal of Multicultural Counseling and Development, 29,* 174–200.

Vasquez, J. A. (1998). Distinctive traits of Hispanic students. *The Prevention Researcher, 5,* 1–4.

Vazquez, L. A., & Garcia-Vazquez, E. (2003). Teaching multicultural competence in the counseling curriculum. In D. B. Pope-Davis, H. L. K. Coleman, W. M. Liu, & R. L. Toporek (Eds.), *Handbook of multicultural competencies in counseling and psychology* (pp. 546–561). Thousand Oaks, CA: Sage.

Vedantam, S. (2005, June 6). Patients' diversity is often discounted. *Washington Post*, p. A01.

Velasquez, R. J., Gonzales, M., Butcher, J. N., Castillo-Canez, I., Apodaca, J. X., & Chavira, D. (1997). Use of the MMPI-2 with Chicanos: Strategies for counselors. *Journal of Multicultural Counseling and Development, 25,* 107–120.

Vera, E. M., Buhin, L., & Shin, R. Q. (2006). The pursuit of social justice and the elimination of racism. In M. G. Constantine & D. W. Sue (Eds.), *Addressing racism* (pp. 271–287). Hoboken, NJ: Wiley.

Vera, E. M., & Speight, S. L. (2003). Multicultural

competence, social justice, and counseling psychology: Expanding our roles. *The Counseling Psychologist, 31,* 253–272.

Vontress, C. E. (1971). Racial differences: Impediments to rapport. *Journal of Counseling Psychology, 18,* 7–13.

Vontress, C. E., & Epp, L. R. (1997). Historical hostility in the African American client: Implications for counseling. *Journal of Multicultural Counseling and Development, 25,* 170–184.

Wagner, M. M., & Blackorby, J. (1996). Transition from high school to work or college: How special education students fare. *The Future of Students, 6,* 103–120.

Waldman, F. (1999). Violence or discipline? Working with multicultural court-ordered clients. *Journal of Marital and Family Therapy, 25,* 503–515.

Wallace, B. A., & Shapiro, S. L. (2006). Mental balance and well-being: Building bridges between Buddhism and western psychology. *American Psychologist, 61,* 690–701.

Walsh, R., & Shapiro, S. L. (2006). The meeting of meditative disciplines and Western psychology. *American Psychologist, 61,* 227–239.

Walsh, R., & Vaughan, F. (Eds.). (1993). *Paths beyond ego. The transpersonal vision* (pp. 387–398). Los Angeles: J. P. Tarcher.

Wang, Y., Davidson, M. M., Yakushko, O. F., Savoy, H. B., Tan, J. A., & Bleier, J. K. (2003). The Scale of Ethnocultural Empathy: Development, validation, and reliability. *Journal of Counseling Psychology, 50, 221–234.*

Want, V., Parham, T. A., Baker, R. C., & Sherman, M. (2004). African Americans students' ratings of Caucasian and African American counselors varying in racial consciousness. *Cultural Diversity and Ethnic Minority Psychology, 10,* 123–136.

Ward, E. C. (2005). Keeping it real: A grounded theory study of African American clients engaging in counseling at a community mental health agency. *Journal of Counseling Psychology, 52,* 471–481.

Warren, A. K., & Constantine, M. G. (2007). Social justice issues. In M. G. Constantine (Ed.), *Clinical practice with people of color* (pp. 231–242). New York: Teachers College Press.

Washington, A. T. (2005, Sept. 6). Timidity no answer to racism in Katrina debacle. *Washington Times,* p. B2.

Washington, J. (2005). Katrina riles, rallies black America. *Bellingham Herald,* p. A3.

Weber, S. N. (1985). The need to be: The sociocultural significance of Black language. In L. A. Samovar & R. E. Porter (Eds.), *Intercultural communication: A reader* (pp. 244–253). Belmont, CA: Wadsworth.

Wehrly, B. (1995). *Pathways to multicultural counseling competence.* Pacific Grove, CA: Brooks Cole.

Wehrly, B., Kenney, K. R., & Kenney, M. E. (1999). *Counseling multiracial families.* Thousand Oaks, CA: Sage.

Weine, S., Feetham, S., Kulauzovic, Y., Knafl, K., Besic, S., Klebic, A., Muzurovic, J., Spahovic, D., & Pavkovic, I. (2006). A family beliefs framework for socially and culturally specific preventive interventions with refugee youth and families. *American Journal of Orthopsychiatry, 76,* 1–9.

Weinrach, S. G. (1987). Ellis and Gloria: Positive or negative model? *Psychotherapy, 23,* 642–647.

Weinrach, S. G. (2002). The counseling profession's relationship to Jews and the issues that concern them: More than a case of selective awareness. *Journal of Counseling and Development, 80,* 300–314.

Weir, E. C. (2004). Identifying and preventing ageism among heath-care professionals. *International Journal of Therapy and Rehabilitation, 11,* 56–63.

Weiss, I. (2005). Interest in working with the elderly: A cross-national study of graduating social work students. *Journal of Social Work Education, 41,* 379–391.

Weisman, A., Feldman, G., Gruman, C., Rosenberg, R., Chamorro, R. & Belozersky, I. (2005). Improving mental health services for Latino and Asian immigrant elders. *Professional Psychology: Research and Practice, 36,* 642–648.

Werner-Wilson, R. J., Price, S. J., Zimmerman, T. S., & Murphy, M. J. (1997). Client gender as a process variable in marriage and family therapy: Are women clients interrupted more than men clients? *Journal of Family Psychology, 11,* 373–377.

Wester, S. R., Vogel, D. L., Wei, M. & McLain, R. (2006). African American men, gender role conflict, and psychological distress: The role of racial identity. *Journal of Counseling and Development, 84,* 419–429.

Whaley, A. L. (2001). Cultural mistrust and mental health services for African Americans: A review and meta-analysis. *The Counseling Psychologist, 29,* 513–521.

White, J. L., & Parham, T. A. (1990). *The psychology of Blacks.* Englewood Cliffs, NJ: Prentice Hall.

White, R. W. (1963). Ego and reality in psychoanalytic theory: A proposal regarding independent ego energies. *Psychological Issues, 3,* 1–210.

Whitman, J. S., Glosoff, H. L., Kocet, M. M. & Tarvydas, V. (2006, July). Exploring ethical issues related to conversion or reparative therapy. *Counseling Today,* pp. 14–15.

Wilkinson, D. (1993). Family ethnicity in American. In H. P McAdoo (Ed.), *Family ethnicity: Strength in diversity.* Newbury Park, CA: Sage.

Williams, K., Kemper, S., & Hummert, M. L. (2005). Enhancing communication with older adults: Overcoming elderspeak. *Journal of Psychosocial Nursing and Mental Health Services, 43,* 12–16.

Williams Institute. (2006) Cities with highest percentage of gays, lesbians, bisexuals. Retrieved 12/08/06 from http://www.law.ucla.edu/williamsinstitute/press/

Willie, C. V. (1981). *A new look at Black families.* Bayside, NY: General Hall.

Wilson, L. L., & Stith, S. M. (1991). Culturally sensitive therapy with Black clients. *Journal of Multicultural Counseling and Development, 19,* 32–43.

Winn, N. N., & Priest, R. (1993). Counseling biracial children: A forgotten component of multicultural counseling. *Family Therapy, 20,* 29–36.

Winter, S. (1977). Rooting out racism. *Issues in Radical Therapy, 17,* 24–30.

Wintersteen, M. B., Mensinger, J. L. & Diamond, G. S. (2005). Do gender and racial differences between patient and therapist affect therapeutic alliance and treatment retention in adolescents? *Professional Psychology: Research and Practice, 36,* 400–408.

Wolfgang, A. (1985). The function and importance of nonverbal behavior in intercultural counseling. In P. B. Pedersen (Ed.), *Handbook of cross-cultural counseling and therapy* (pp. 99–105). Westport, CT: Greenwood.

Wood, D. B. (2006, May 25). Rising black-Latino clash on jobs. *Christian Science Monitor.* Retrieved from http://www.csmonitor.com/2006/0525/p01s03-ussc.html

Wood, P. B., & Clay, W. C. (1996). Perceived structural barriers and academic performance among American Indian high school students. *Youth and Society, 28,* 40–46.

Wood, P. S., & Mallinckrodt, B. (1990). Culturally sensitive assertiveness training for ethnic minority clients. *Professional Psychology: Research & Practice, 21,* 5–11.

Worrell, F. C., Cross, W. E., & Vandiver, B. J. (2001). Nigrescence theory: Current status and challenges for the future. *Journal of Multicultural Counseling and Development, 29,* 201–211.

Wren, C. S. (1998, June 5). Many women 60 and older abuse alcohol and prescribed drugs, study says. *New York Times,* p. 12.

Wrenn, C. G. (1962). The culturally-encapsulated counselor. *Harvard Educational Review, 32,* 444–449.

Wrenn, C. G. (1985). Afterward: The culturally-encapsulated counselor revisited. In P. B. Pedersen (Ed.), *Handbook of cross-cultural counseling and therapy* (pp. 323–329). Westport, CT: Greenwood Press.

Wright, J. M. (1998). *Lesbian step families.* Binghamton, NY: Harrington Park Press.

Wright, K. (2001). To be poor and transgender. *The Progressive, 65,* 21–24.

Yakushko, O. & Chronister, K. M. (2005). Immigrant women and counseling: The invisible others. *Journal of Counseling and Development, 83,* 292–298.

Yamamoto, J., & Acosta, F. X. (1982). Treatment of Asian-Americans and Hispanic-Americans: Similarities and differences. *Journal of the Academy of Psychoanalysis, 10,* 585–607.

Yau, T. Y., Sue, D., & Hayden, D. (1992). Counseling style preference of international students. *Journal of Counseling Psychology, 39,* 100–104.

Yedidia, T. (2005). Immigrant therapists' unresolved identity problems and countertransference. *Clinical Social Work Journal, 33,* 159–171.

Yee, B. W. K., Castro, F. G., Hammond, W. R., John, R., Wyatt, G. E., & Yung, B. R. (1995). Risk-taking and abusive behavior among ethnic minorities. *Health Psychology, 14*, 622–631.

Yeh, C. J., Ma, P.-W., Madan-Babel, A., Hunter, C. D., Jung, S., Kim, A. B., Akitaya, K., & Sasaki, K. (2005). The cultural negotiations of Korean immigrant youth. *Journal of Counseling and Development, 83*, 172–182.

Yeung, A., Chang, D., Gresham, R. L., Nierenberg, A. A., & Fava, M. (2004). Illness beliefs of depressed Chinese American patients in primary care. *Journal of Nervous and Mental Disease, 192*, 324–327.

Yick, A. G., & Agbayani-Siewert, P. (1997). Perceptions of domestic violence in a Chinese American community. *Journal of Interpersonal Violence, 12*, 832–846.

Yin, X.-H. (2000, May 7). Asian Americans: The two sides of America's "model minority." *The Los Angeles Times*, p. M1.

Ying, Y.-W., Coombs, M., & Lee, P. A. (1999). Family intergenerational relationship of Asian American adolescents. *Cultural Diversity and Ethnic Minority Psychology, 5*, 350–363.

Zanipatin, J., Welch, S. S., Yi, J., & Bardina, P. (2005). Immigrant women and domestic violence. In K. H. Barrett & W. H. George (Eds.), *Race, culture, psychology, and law* (pp. 375–389). Thousand Oaks, CA: Sage.

Zastrow, C. (2004). *Introduction to social work and social welfare* (8th ed.). Belmont, CA: Brooks Cole.

Zeiss, A. M. (2001). *Aging and human sexuality resource guide.* Washington, DC: American Psychological Association.

Zogby, J. J. (2001a, March). National survey: American teen-agers and stereotyping. Retrieved 12/7/2006 from http://www.niaf.org/research/report_zogby.asp

Zogby, J. J. (2001b, Oct.). Arab American attitudes and the September 11 attacks. Retrieved 12/7/2006 from http://www.aaiusa.org/PDF/attitudes.pdf

Zollman, J. W. (2006). Three waves of immigration. Retrieved 12/15/2006 from http://www.myjewishlearning.com/history_community/Modern

Zuniga, M. E. (1997). Counseling Mexican American seniors: An overview. *Journal of Multicultural Counseling and Development, 25*, 142–155.

Author Index

Subject Index